Personal Epistemology: The Psychology of Beliefs About Knowledge and Knowing

Personal Epistemology: The Psychology of Beliefs About Knowledge and Knowing

Edited by

Barbara K. Hofer
Middlebury College

and

Paul R. Pintrich
The University of Michigan, Ann Arbor

LEA

LAWRENCE ERLBAUM ASSOCIATES, PUBLISHERS

2002   Mahwah, New Jersey   London

Lawrence Erlbaum Associates, Inc., Publishers
10 Industrial Avenue
Mahwah, New Jersey 07430

Cover design by Kathryn Houghtaling Lacey

Library of Congress Cataloging-in-Publication Data

Personal epistemology: the psychology of beliefs about knowledge and knowing/ edited by Barabara K. Hofer and Paul R. Pintrich.
   p. cm.
   Includes bibliographical references and index.
   ISBN 0-8058-3518-0 (alk. paper) — ISBN 0-8058-5235-2 (pbk. alk. paper)
   1. Educational psychology. 2. Knowledge, Theory of. I. Hofer, Barbara K. II. Pintrich, Paul R.

LB1051.P415 2001
370.15—dc21   0-068182

About the Editors

Barbara K. Hofer is an Assistant Professor of Psychology at Middlebury College in Middlebury, Vermont. She received an Ed.M. from the Harvard Graduate School of Education and a Ph.D. from the University of Michigan in Education and Psychology. She is the recipient of the American Psychological Association's McKeachie Early Teaching Award and the American Educational Research Association's Research Review Award (with co-editor, Paul Pintrich) for a review of the literature on epistemological thinking. She has published a dozen articles and book chapters on personal epistemology, self-regulated learning, and cross-cultural issues in education, and is a regular presenter at APA and AERA.

Paul R. Pintrich is Professor of Education and Psychology and Chair of the Combined Program in Education and Psychology at The University of Michigan, Ann Arbor. He also serves as the Associate Dean for Research for the School of Education at Michigan. His research focuses on the development of motivation, epistemological thinking, and self-regulated learning in adolescence. He has published over 100 articles, book chapters and books including co-authoring or co-editing 8 books. He is the past editor of the American Psychology Association journal for Division 15-Educational Psychology, *Educational Psychologist*.

His research has been funded by the National Science Foundation (NSF), the Office of Educational Research and Improvement (OERI) in the Department of Education, the Spencer Foundation, and the Kellogg Foundation. He is a Fellow of the American Psychological Association and has been a National Academy of Education Spencer Fellow. Along with his co-author Barbara Hofer, he won the 1999 Best Research Review Article Award from the American Educational Research Association for an article on epistemological thinking that appeared in *Review of Educational Research*. He is currently President-Elect of Division 5-Educational and Instructional Psychology for the International Association of Applied Psychology and President-Elect for Division 15-Educational Psychology for the American Psychological Association. He also has won the Class of 1923 Award from the College of Literature, Science, and Arts and the School of Education at The University of Michigan for excellence in undergraduate teaching.

Contents

Preface

The study of individual beliefs about knowledge and knowing has engaged researchers from a variety of fields, with differing terminology, research paradigms, and areas of interest. Few other topics that lie at the intersection of education and psychology are likely to span so wide a range of intellectual territory, or to excite the interest of individuals with such varied professional training. In addition, both theory building and empirical research in this field have grown dramatically in the past decade. The need to clarify and synthesize central issues in the field and the growing interest in the work provided the impetus for this volume. This book provides an overview of the theoretical and methodological approaches to the study of personal epistemology from a psychological and educational perspective. We hope this will be of interest to graduate and professional researchers, educational practitioners, teacher educators, science and math educators, and administrators who are interested in examining the current viewpoints of central theoreticians and researchers working in this area.

The current models of personal epistemology are rich and varied, developed through decades of meticulous research, but they have yet to be discussed within one book. Accordingly, each of the central researchers in this area was invited to contribute a chapter to the first section of the book, providing an overview and update of their respective models. We hope that this will provide, in one location, a clear picture of the current state of the art as viewed by those who laid the foundation for the current emerging research and who continue to shape the direction of the field for new researchers.

The second section of the book includes new perspectives on theoretical and conceptual approaches to personal epistemology. These chapters address several of the more challenging aspects of the underlying assumptions in the research on epistemology and offer provocative insights about areas that need the attention of researchers.

One of the central concerns in the field has been that of methodology. Early approaches favored open-ended interviews as a means of eliciting individuals' beliefs and this tradition has been continued by those adhering to a phenomenological approach. More recently, written instrumentation has been developed, and work in this area continues. Many questions remain about the underlying assumptions of each approach and there are a range of concerns inherent in measuring epistemological understanding, but the quality of research in this area is dependent on the development of reliable and valid measures of the construct. Several individuals engaged in designing new methodological approaches for the study of personal epistemology contributed chapters to the third section of this volume.

Although much of the work in this area presumes that epistemological beliefs and theories are domain general, there are a number of researchers interested in beliefs particular to domains. The most advanced of this work has been in mathematics and science. Understanding students' beliefs about and within a particular discipline has proven to be a fruitful line of inquiry for researchers and of value to those teaching in these disciplinary areas. The chapters in the fourth section of the book reflect some of the most recent research on discipline-specific epistemology.

The authors in each of the four sections have concluded their chapters with suggestions for future research. We hope that this will help shape an agenda for the field as a whole and will provide researchers with a coherent picture of the work that needs to be done in furthering our understanding of personal epistemology. We are indebted to each of the authors for their willingness to step back and examine their work in progress, to reflect on the state of the field, and to take the time to contribute to the learning and development of other researchers. We have learned from the chapters in this volume and hope that readers will benefit in similar ways. We also hope that readers will respond to the suggestions in these chapters and initiate a new era of epistemological research that will lead to a better understanding of development and learning as well as to instructional improvement.

Introduction

1

Personal Epistemology as a Psychological and Educational Construct: An Introduction

Barbara K. Hofer
Middlebury College

In our most mundane encounters with new information and in our most sophisticated pursuits of knowledge, we are influenced by the beliefs we hold about knowledge and knowing. What has been called personal epistemology, epistemological beliefs or theories, ways of knowing, or epistemic cognition, is activated as we engage in learning and knowing. For example, as we read the morning paper, we may make judgments about the credibility of the claims in a particular article or about the source of information. In our professional lives, we confront the learning of new skills and ideas and make determinations about their value and worth to us. As citizens, we are called on to judge competing claims from officials and politicians, to weigh evidence, and to make decisions about issues of importance to ourselves and our communities. And in the classroom, students regularly encounter new information and may approach the learning process quite differently depending on whether they view knowledge as a set of accumulated facts or an integrated set of constructs, or whether they view themselves as passive receptors or active constructors of knowledge. In each of these situations the adequacy of our epistemological theories will in some way determine what and how we make meaning of the information we encounter. As both the amount and the availability of information increase, and as the tools of access change rapidly, we need a better understanding of personal epistemology and its relation to learning. This book is dedicated to such a pursuit.

As a philosophical enterprise, epistemology is concerned with the origin, nature, limits, methods, and justification of human knowledge. The term "epistemic," by contrast, relates to knowledge more generally, and to the conditions for acquiring it. From a psychological and educational perspective, the focus of concern among those studying personal epistemology or epistemic cognition is how the individual develops conceptions of knowledge and knowing and utilizes them in developing understanding of the world. This includes beliefs about the definition of knowledge, how knowledge is constructed, how knowledge is evaluated, where knowledge resides, and how knowing occurs.

With a foundation that can be traced both to Piaget's attention to "genetic epistemology" and to Perry's original work on the epistemological development of college students, a body of research has developed that addresses issues related to beliefs about knowing and knowledge as experienced by the individual learner. This study of personal epistemology draws on diverse research traditions, paradigms, and disciplines, and has been conducted by educational, developmental, and instructional psychologists, as well as researchers in the areas of higher education, counseling, science and math education, reading and literacy studies, and teacher education. As a result, although both theory building and empirical research in this field have grown dramatically in the past decade, the results have appeared in disparate locations and the work has been labeled under different constructs. This volume is an attempt to address several needs: to bring together the work from differing areas, to provide researchers with an opportunity to communicate their current perspectives on personal epistemology, and to lay the foundation for continuing research by suggesting important questions and directions for future study. Contributors include both pioneering researchers who bring a long-term perspective to ongoing work as well as new researchers in the field.

In the chapters that follow, these researchers address several central issues that concern those working in this area. What is the current perspective on each of the prominent conceptual models of personal epistemology? What other conceptual and theoretical issues need attention? What are the methodological problems that we need to address and how might we best proceed to do so? What do the new disciplinary approaches to understanding epistemology offer? Each of the contributors to this volume was invited to choose to focus on one of these key areas and to conclude with suggestions for future research.

THEORETICAL MODELS OF PERSONAL EPISTEMOLOGY

A quick sketch of the history of the field suggests that several overlapping lines of study have provided a rich portrait of how epistemological understanding develops. (For a review of the literature, see Hofer & Pintrich, 1997.) When Perry began studying Harvard freshmen in the late 1950s to investigate why students responded in dramatically different ways to the plurality of the college experience, he expected that personality differences might offer a plausible explanation. Perhaps students high in obedience to authority, for example, were those who expected faculty members to deliver "truth" from the lecture pulpit and who were frustrated by classes where they were expected to consider and evaluate multiple perspectives. What his longitudinal study unveiled, however, was a road map to the development of epistemology during late adolescence, as influenced by a liberal arts education. Belief in a dualistic view of knowledge, often characteristic of the first-year college student, was typically challenged and transformed, in an advancement toward an evolving capacity for intellectual commitments in the face of relativism. This trajectory has been widely utilized as a heuristic for interpreting college student development, and Perry's book, *Forms of Intellectual and Ethical Development in the College Years: A Scheme* (Perry, 1970), reissued in paperback in 1998, has become a field guide for college professors striving to interpret the patterned diversity of responses to their instruction. In his chapter on Perry's work, William Moore reviews and reconsiders the Perry scheme, providing an update on extensions and refinements of the model and addressing the relevance of the scheme today.

Perry's work was the starting point for several other meticulous, longitudinal, qualitative studies that have furthered enhanced our knowledge of the role that personal epistemology plays in intellectual development. Interested in the experience of women as learners and aware of the absence of women in the theory-building stage of research in prior studies, Belenky, Clinchy, Goldberger and Tarule conducted interviews with women from diverse educational settings. Included in their extensive interview protocol were a set of questions based on Perry's work; ultimately, however, responses to these questions became central to their analysis and interpretation. Their landmark study of "women's ways of knowing" provided the first portrait of the epistemological perspectives of women and the developmental course of these views, elaborated in a five-position model that parallels and richly extends Perry's model. Among other contributions, the model offered in *Women's Ways of Knowing* (Belenky, Clinchy, Goldberger, & Tarule, 1986) addressed women's relation to knowledge and knowing, brought the terms "separate knowing" and "connected knowing" into educators' vocabulary, and heightened awareness of the role of gender in epistemological development. Blythe Clinchy provides a fresh look at the model and these aspects in particular.

In spite of the outcome of their research, neither Perry and his staff nor Belenky, et al. deliberately set out to conduct a study of epistemological development per se, nor were either team interested in exploring gender differences. By contrast, Marcia Baxter Magolda, drawing on Perry's work, directed her attention explicitly to what she has termed "epistemological reflection" and to the role of gender. Her longitudinal study of students at a small Midwestern liberal arts college suggests gender-related patterns in knowing within her four-point model

(Baxter Magolda, 1992). Baxter Magolda has continued to interview the students in her sample, and her chapter offers us the opportunity to view how such development continues into early adulthood.

One of the most comprehensive bodies of work in the study of intellectual development has been the work of Karen Kitchener and Patricia King, whose Reflective Judgment model encompasses both personal epistemology and skills of critical thinking (King & Kitchener, 1994). Kitchener also introduced the construct of epistemic cognition (Kitchener, 1983), a monitoring process that occurs in the solving of ill-structured problems. In their chapter, they explicate the relation between these constructs and review two decades of research on epistemic cognition and their seven-stage model of the development of reflective judgment. This model was empirically derived from individuals' responses to questions that elicit epistemological assumptions while reasoning about complex, open-ended problems.

A departure from the developmental approach was initiated by Marlene Schommer, who has conceptualized personal epistemology as a system of more-or-less independent beliefs, hypothesized as five distinct dimensions of epistemology that may or may not develop in synchrony (Schommer, 1994). The categorization of "beliefs" also distinguishes this approach from earlier work, as the developmental schemes address personal epistemology as a complex, integrated, structural scheme. Furthermore, Schommer's contribution has been the introduction of a written instrument for assessing these beliefs, by asking individuals to respond to a set of items, scored on a continuum (Schommer, 1990; Schommer, Crouse, & Rhodes, 1992). Schommer-Aikins describes the evolution of her framework, reflects on the value of this work, and explicates her thinking about several central assumptions of the model.

In providing updated looks at each of the five main models of personal epistemology, we hope that the reader will be able to gain perspective on both their commonalities and their differences, and to engage questions that have concerned those doing research in this field. First and foremost, are these researchers addressing the same construct? Is the difference in labels a reflection of meaningful distinctions that need preserving, or do the similarities in the developmental trajectories of each model suggest an underlying idea that could be represented in a single term? Is it worthwhile or possible to consolidate the theoretical work that has developed in this area? How might we achieve greater conceptual clarity?

Other questions are suggested by how the various models are conceptualized, and particularly by the difference in the developmental models and the work of Schommer and others who have utilized the epistemological beliefs model. Is this a cognitive process or a set of beliefs? How do these distinctions affect what we study and how we study it? Are the dimensions of personal epistemology structurally integrated or potentially independent of one another? Does epistemology encompass beliefs about learning as well as beliefs about knowledge? What work remains to be done in the development of the models?

Conceptual Issues

As the study of personal epistemology has grown, researchers have begun to take a look at both the larger view of development in which this construct is situated as well as some of the more vexing details. Moving beyond the distinct models, other conceptual questions concern researchers in this area. What exactly is it that is developing in these models? How does personal epistemology relate to cognitive development? How does it relate to skills of critical thinking? Does it develop in a linear fashion or is it recursive? What is the process by which beliefs change? How does our psychological understanding of personal epistemology map on to philosophical positions in epistemology? And how might we use such an understanding from philosophical traditions to better inform our own work? These are some of the questions that are currently under discussion and which several contributors to this volume were interested in addressing.

A review of the existing developmental models (Hofer & Pintrich, 1997) suggests that each of the primary models posit developmental trajectories that parallel one another. Regardless of the number of stages, positions, or perspectives, the sequence invariably suggests movement from a dualistic, objectivist view of knowledge to a more subjective, relativistic stance and ultimately to a contextual, constructivist perspective of knowing. In their chapter on epistemological thinking—and why it matters—Deanna Kuhn and Michael Weinstock identify the developmental tasks inherent in the growth of epistemological understanding. They suggest that it is this coordination of the subjective and objective dimensions of knowing that is the essence of epistemological development and describe their research in measuring the progression of this cognitive process from childhood to adulthood. Their work is an attempt to clarify and simplify our understanding of epistemological development and to situate it within our knowledge about cognitive development.

Not only has the trajectory of development appeared to be similar in the models outlined by the early researchers in this area, but the starting point for most of these schemes often appeared to coincide with the first year in college. As a review of the developmental models indicates, most of the early theory building was derived from empirical studies of college students, and rarely were younger individuals assessed for their epistemological awareness. Only recently have researchers begun to explore the epistemological assumptions operative earlier in life, and their findings suggest a progression that resembles the developmental path of older students, pointing perhaps to the recursiveness of this process. Michael Chandler, Darcy Hallett, and Bryan Sokol explore the perplexing issue of how to interpret conflicting findings about the timing of various epistemological shifts in thinking. Recent research that investigates the epistemology of younger individuals, as well as research that theoretically bridges epistemology and theory of mind, have lead these authors to examine the competing claims about the sequenced restructuring of beliefs, a premise that is fundamental to any of the models of epistemological development.

But just how does epistemological development occur? What explanatory mechanisms might help us better understand this process? Most developmental theorists presume a Piagetian explanation of equilibration, which posits that a mismatch between the individual's current beliefs and his or her environment lead to a reconsideration of the beliefs and to either an assimilation of the new ideas into the existing scheme or an accommodation of that scheme. This view has motivated a host of suggestions for the promotion of intellectual and epistemological development in the classroom. Newer work on conceptual change has provided another model for understanding belief change, suggesting that individuals must be dissatisfied with existing conceptions, and find new concepts intelligible, plausible, and fruitful. Furthermore, affective, motivational, and contextual factors play a role in activating the change process (Pintrich, Marx, & Boyle, 1993). Lisa Bendixen addresses the role that epistemic doubt plays in fostering epistemological development and reports on a phenomenological study of this issue. Her model of epistemic belief change offers both a mechanism for how such change is prompted and insight into a developmental process that is consistent with both Piagetian equilibration and conceptual change theory.

How we capture and describe the construct of interest—whether we tag an individual's epistemology as a set of "beliefs," for example—has ontological implications, which have often been ignored. We might consider such ideas to reside within the individual as a trait, or we could conceptualize that they are organized into a coherent, invariant developmental sequence that changes only gradually, or we might view epistemological conceptions as contextual and malleable. These diverse views of the construct direct our attention to differing methodological approaches, lead to differing understandings of the construct, and point to differing interventions in the classroom. David Hammer and Andrew Elby address the implications of our ontological views of personal epistemology and provide an alternative framework for consideration. Viewing personal epistemology as a framework of epistemological resources, they envision this as more fine-grained and context-specific than the beliefs and theories suggested in other models. They reject the idea that personal epistemology is relatively stable or traitlike, but hypothesize that it is more likely to be situated in educational contexts. Their chapter also outlines the implications for both instruction and research suggested by the framework they propose.

In the final chapter in this section by Jill Fitzgerald and James Cunningham, we come full circle to the philosophical origins of the field. Having been guided in the previous chapter to investigate ontological assumptions about epistemology, we are now assisted in exploring our own epistemological stances. Theoretical outlooks on knowledge guide our approaches and methodology and yet may be underexamined or ill-defined. Fitzgerald and Cunningham provide an epistemological framework that may be useful both in clarifying personal stances as well as in suggesting a guideline for interpreting the epistemological positions of individuals in our research studies. This framework is structured along a multivariate continuum of seven core epistemological issues, ranging from "Can we have knowledge of a single reality independent of the knower?" to "To what degree is knowledge discovered versus created?" Responses to these questions enable identification of the distinguishing characteristics of an epistemological stance, from empiricism to poststructuralism.

The authors in this section provide provocative challenges to researchers interested in personal epistemology and to the educators interested in interpreting student epistemology. Their guidance may be fruitful in the process of refining our own understanding of the core meaning of epistemology, how we can best model it, and the process by which it develops.

METHODOLOGICAL CONCERNS IN THE STUDY OF PERSONAL EPISTEMOLOGY

One of the most difficult aspects of the study of personal epistemology has been how to capture something as elusive as individual conceptions of knowledge and knowing. Perry (1970) approached this inquiry in two steps, and both of his approaches have been continued in some fashion by later researchers. He preselected participants based on their scores on the Checklist of Educational Values, a questionnaire he developed on the basis of personality research. Those selected were then invited at the end of each academic year to interviews that began with the seemingly simple question, "Would you like to say what has stood out for you during the year?" With this open-ended approach and an unwavering faith in the individual's ability to describe his or her own meaning-making process—especially with the caring support of a skillful interviewer—Perry was able to elicit detailed reports from students, which he and his staff then analyzed for structural similarities.

Items from Perry's original questionnaire live on in the most widely used paper-and-pencil measure of personal epistemology, Schommer's Epistemological Beliefs Questionnaire. Other written instruments have been designed to tap some aspects of Perry's scheme, e.g., the Learning Environment Preferences, or LEP (Moore, 1989). The phenomenological approach of his interviews and the resulting findings have been the basis of several lines of research. Both Belenky et al. (1986) and Baxter Magolda (1992), for example, used more refined interview protocols that drew on Perry's questions and methodology and that allowed individuals to freely interpret their own ways of knowing. Their schemes of development, like Perry's, emerged in the analysis of transcript data.

Another approach to assessing epistemological development has been to interview individuals about ill-structured problems, probe their reasoning, and score responses according to stages. King and Kitchener (1994) have asked participants in their studies to think about such problems as chemical additives in food or the building of the pyramids and then respond to a series of questions, each of which addresses one or more aspects of Reflective Judgment. A similar method was used by Kuhn (1991), who scored responses to sets of ill-structured problems (e.g., criminal recidivism) along a three-level scale based on Perry's scheme. These fairly structured interviews permit the probing of reasoning that questionnaires and other written instruments lack.

Interviews have been particularly useful at the theory-building stage, during the development of conceptual models and schemes. The early researchers in this area were interested in discovering how participants made meaning, not in checking participants' perceptions relative to a preconceived scheme. Now that these models are in place, however, can they be used as the basis for more efficient methods of data collection? Or when we surrender the ability to ask follow-up questions that interviews provide, do we lose more than we gain? Can we fully capture individual epistemology when we impose meaning through the questions we ask? Can epistemology be effectively measured through self-report continua, such as Likert-type scales? And as Hammer and Elby question in their chapter, what ontological assumptions do we make about epistemology when we expect that it can be captured out of context? These and other questions have occupied researchers in this field, whose work is sometimes hampered by the paucity of well-established measures for the constructs of interest.

Interest in paper-and-pencil measures of epistemology has been driven by the interest in larger-scale studies, particularly for pretest and posttest measures of programs designed to foster intellectual development and critical thinking, and for research on the relation between personal epistemology and other constructs, such as learning strategies, motivation, and academic performance. If we want to assess whether a particular program is affecting student development or to investigate whether epistemological beliefs affect academic outcomes, interviews are a costly and cumbersome approach. They are time-consuming to administer, require skilled interviewers, must be transcribed for analysis, and need to be scored by trained raters. Thus a number of individuals have developed paper-and-pencil measures of personal epistemology based on the developmental models created from interview studies (see Hofer & Pintrich, 1997, for an overview.) Under the leadership of Karen Kitchener and Patricia King, a team of researchers have been working on the development of a paper-and-pencil measure of reflective judgment or epistemic cognition. Phillip Wood, Karen Kitchener, and Laura Jensen provide a progress report on their work to date and the rationale for structuring an assessment around ill-structured problems.

The written instrumentation for measuring personal epistemology that currently has the most widespread use is Schommer's Epistemological Beliefs Questionnaire, which does not measure stages or positions of development, but utilizes a Likert-type scale to assess dimensions of epistemological beliefs. Among several recent attempts to refine this type of questionnaire for the assessment of epistemological beliefs, Gregory Schraw, Lisa Bendixen, and Michael Dunkle describe their development and validation of the Epistemic Belief Inventory, modeled on Schommer's questionnaire. Their report may be of particular use to those seeking to understand the construction of such instruments and who wish to compare existing instruments for research purposes.

Phillip Wood and CarolAnne Kardash provide a critique of the current research in personal epistemology, addressing both design issues and concerns about statistical analyses, areas of importance to those developing studies in this area. They also provide an example of their own research, an assessment of the dimensions of personal epistemology through a factor analysis of items used by both Schommer (1990) and Jehng, Johnson, and Anderson (1993).

Considerable questions remain in the area of methodology as researchers work to assess and interpret individual epistemology. Can we trust that what we are eliciting is a reasonable approximation of what we are trying to understand? How capable are we as individuals of describing our own beliefs about how we come to know, what we think knowing is, and how we perceive knowledge? Can we get at these ideas directly or do we need more subtle measures? Can beliefs be observed in action, or inferred from particular acts? Do we need a broad spectrum of methods?

Discipline-Specific Epistemological Beliefs

Much of the conceptual and empirical work on personal epistemology presumes that epistemological beliefs and theories are domain general. From the developmental perspective, this is congruent with the conception that each stage contains an integration and structured conception of ideas. Even in Schommer's scheme, with dimensions that are more or less independent, there has still been an assumption, supported moderately in one study (Schommer & Walker, 1995), that beliefs are likely to vary little depending on the subject matter. However, another approach has been to presume that in much the same way that disciplines are in part defined by the differing modes of knowing and thus have inherent differences epistemologically, that individuals are also likely to hold differing beliefs about disciplines (Hofer, 2000). In addition, a number of researchers have pursued research on beliefs particular to academic disciplines, most notably in mathematics and science. Understanding students' beliefs about and within a particular discipline has considerable implications for how students learn and understand an area of study, and may also reveal particular impediments to learning.

Those working in the tradition of a domain-general model of personal epistemology share a consensus on some aspects of what epistemological understanding encompasses and disagree on others. Beliefs about the nature of knowledge and knowing are presumed across the models, yet issues of whether beliefs about learning and intelligence should be included remain in dispute. But general agreement exists as to the core of the area of inquiry. Those interested in discipline-specific beliefs, however, narrow the focus to a particular belief while at the same time widening the beliefs under investigation, with little agreement among them. So, for example, those interested in scientific beliefs may include such questions as "What is a scientist?" and some of those working in mathematics have included motivational and self-efficacy constructs within their scope of study. More work may be needed to achieve clarity in these areas, as research on discipline-specific beliefs receives more attention.

In early studies of discipline-specific beliefs, Schoenfeld identified typical student beliefs about the nature of mathematics (Schoenfeld, 1992), which he and other researchers (Lampert, 1990; Hofer, 1999) view as having significant consequences for how students pursue mathematical study. Eric De Corte, Peter Op 't Eynde, and Liven Verschaffel review the work on mathematical beliefs with attention to the relation between belief and knowledge and offer a categorization of beliefs, disentangling three component sets: beliefs about mathematics education, beliefs about the self in relation to mathematics, and beliefs about the social context of learning mathematics. In the area of mathematics beliefs, researchers have particularly attended to those beliefs that may be faulty or counterproductive to learning mathematics, and the authors address both the issue of "misbeliefs" and how instruction can foster more appropriate and productive beliefs about mathematics.

The most expansive area of work on discipline-related beliefs has been in the area of science learning. Three chapters in this section report on recent research that explores how students view science and how instruction might shape this. Philip Bell and Marcia Linn suggest that students have a repertoire of ideas about science, and describe, in particular, the development of views of science inquiry that they have elicited from students in their longitudinal studies of science instruction. Their case studies of student inquiry into the same problems in the eighth, tenth, and twelfth grade illuminate how students develop an understanding of science through collaborative debate.

Beliefs about the disciplines are often developed in early exposure to instruction in the area, yet little work has addressed beliefs of children in elementary school. In the context of an inquiry-based science program, Anastasia Danos Elder examines fifth graders' beliefs about the nature of knowledge in science. Her study utilizes a written questionnaire with both open-ended and scaled items, designed to tap five constructs central to a conceptualization of science beliefs. These include the purpose of science, the changeability of science, the role of experiments, the coherence of science, and the source of science knowledge. Her findings provide the groundwork for future studies of this age group and indicate the importance of attending to student beliefs in the development of science instruction at the elementary level.

Pursuing both the issue of conceptual change learning in science and the crosscultural aspect of epistemology that has seldom been addressed, Gaoyin Qian and Julin Pan describe the relation between science beliefs, refutational text, and motivational goals in a comparison of American and Chinese high school students. Their work highlights the value of refutational text in fostering conceptual change and gives us a sense of the issues faced in assessing epistemological beliefs across cultures. As we expand this work beyond the original populations, more work may be needed in the identification of dimensions and refinement of instruments.

The work of these authors and others who have addressed discipline-specific beliefs raises important questions for researchers and educators. How do we integrate the disciplinary views with the more global approaches to epistemology? How do individuals coordinate these beliefs? Is there an underlying framework of epistemology that provides a mental platform for these disciplinary beliefs or are these unrelated?

SUMMARY

The study of personal epistemology as a psychological construct with educational implications is at a critical point. The work that has been done is substantial and it is time to coordinate the disparate research strands that are linked under this umbrella, to recognize it as a significant area of study, and to bring these issues into the mainstream of educational and developmental psychology. Beliefs about knowledge and knowing have a powerful influence on learning, and deepening our understanding of this process can enhance teaching effectiveness. In particular, we need considerably more effort addressed toward either unifying our language or clarifying our existing distinctions in terminology, improving methodological approaches so that comparable studies can be conducted, and in considering the relation between epistemological understanding and other key constructs. The contributors to this volume have taken up these charges and the field will surely benefit both from their work and from those who draw on their excellent and timely suggestions.

REFERENCES

Baxter Magolda, M. B. (1992). *Knowing and reasoning in college: Gender-related patterns in students' intellectual development*. San Francisco: Jossey Bass.

Belenky, M. F., Clinchy, B. McV., Goldberger, N., & Tarule, J. (1986). *Women's ways of knowing: The development of self, voice and mind*. New York: Basic Books.

Hofer, B. K. (1999). Instructional context in the college mathematics classroom: Epistemological beliefs and student motivation. *Journal of Staff, Program, and Organizational Development, 16(2)*, 73–82.

Hofer, B. K. (2000). Dimensionality and disciplinary differences in personal epistemology. *Contemporary Educational Psychology*.

Hofer, B. K., & Pintrich, P. R. (1997). The development of epistemological theories: Beliefs about knowledge and knowing and their relation to learning. *Review of Educational Research, 67(1)*, 88–140.

Jehng, J. C. J., Johnson, S. D., & Anderson, R. C. (1993). Schooling and students' epistemological beliefs about learning. *Contemporary Educational Psychology 18*, 23–25.

King, P. M., & Kitchener, K. S. (1994). *Developing reflective judgment: Understanding and promoting intellectual growth and critical thinking in adolescents and adults*. San Francisco: Jossey-Bass.

Kitchener, K. S. (1983). Cognition, metacognition, and epistemic cognition. *Human Development, 26*, 222–232.

Kuhn, D. (1991). *The skills of argument*. Cambridge: Cambridge University Press.

Lampert, M. (1990). When the problem is not the question and the solution is not the answer: Mathematical knowing and teaching. *American Educational Research Journal, 27*, 29–63.

Moore, W. S. (1989). The "Learning Environment Preferences": Exploring the construct validity of an objective measure of the Perry scheme of intellectual development. *Journal of College Student Development, 30*, 504–514.

Perry, W. G. (1970). *Forms of intellectual and ethical development in the college years: A scheme*. New York: Holt, Rinehart and Winston.

Pintrich, P. R., Marx, R. W., & Boyle, R. A. (1993). Beyond cold conceptual change: The role of motivational beliefs and classroom contextual factors in the process of conceptual change. *Review of Educational Research, 63*(2), 167–199.

Schoenfeld, A. (1992). Learning to think mathematically: Problem solving, metacognition, and sense making in mathematics. In D. A. Grouws (Ed.), *Handbook of research on mathematics teaching and learning*, pp. 334–370. New York: Macmillan.

Schommer, M. (1990). Effects of beliefs about the nature of knowledge on comprehension. *Journal of Educational Psychology, 82*, 498–504.

Schommer, M. (1994). An emerging conceptualization of epistemological beliefs and their role in learning. In R. Garner & P. A. Alexander (Eds.), *Beliefs about text and instruction with text*, pp. 25–40). Hillsdale, NJ: Erlbaum.

Schommer, M., Crouse, A., & Rhodes, N. (1992). Epistemological beliefs and mathematical text comprehension: Believing it is simple does not make it so. *Journal of Educational Psychology, 82*, 435–443.

Schommer, M., & Walker, K. (1995). Are epistemological beliefs similar across domains? *Journal of Educational Psychology, 87*(3), 424–432.

I

Conceptual Models
of Personal Epistemology

2

Understanding Learning in a Postmodern World: Reconsidering the Perry Scheme of Intellectual and Ethical Development

William S. Moore
Washington State Board for
Community & Technical Colleges

It has been almost thirty years now since the official publication of Bill Perry's book, *Forms of Intellectual and Ethical Development in the College Years: A Scheme* (1970), although at long last, the book has been reissued in paperback (1998, by Jossey-Bass) with a new introduction by Lee Knefelkamp, one of the first and most significant translators of Perry's work into educational practice. In the time since the original publication of Perry's book, scholarship across a wide range of domains, including educational research, has expanded and fractured in ways analogous to the process depicted in the Perry scheme. Issues of race, class, power, and elitism have been added to gender as the bases for various forms of cultural critique, and virtually all existing "truths" have been deconstructed and called into question. In academic scholarship, and increasingly in the popular press, there has been much talk of shifting paradigms, with modernism giving way to "postmodernism," and "deconstructionism" raising analytical critiques of existing theories and perspectives (Burbules & Rice, 1991). Gergen (1991) describes one form of this thinking:

> Postmodernism does not bring with it a new vocabulary for understanding ourselves, new traits or characteristics to be explored. Its impact is more

apocalyptic than that: the very concept of personal essences is thrown into
doubt . . . (1991, p.7)

In the view of Burbules and Rice, this extreme form of deconstruction and
postmodernism is really more of an "antimodernism," often functioning as a form
of "pure" relativism at a cultural scale:

Having deconstructed all metanarratives and radically relativized all possible values, antimodernism is left with no clear way of justifying any alternatives . . . In our view, this antimodernist position is unsustainable either
intellectually or practically. (1991, p. 398)

In contrast to this antimodern approach, Burbules and Rice argue for a true postmodern perspective that would extend and reconstruct modernist thinking, in effect moving beyond the underlying "either/or" dualism inherent in deconstruction to a new "both/and" synthesis.

Given these perspectives, certainly the Perry model, grounded as it is in the
white, privileged world of Harvard University of the 1950s and 1960s, has been
subject to this critique, and it is fair to ask: What is the continuing relevance of
such a model for today's postmodern world? I will argue in this chapter that the
Perry scheme represents the kind of reconstruction and synthesis described by
Burbules and Rice as necessary for a genuinely postmodern understanding of the
world. In fact, key elements of recent scholarship related to knowledge, learning,
and assessment confirm and reinforce perspectives defined or suggested by
Perry's work. Even after thirty years of extensive and varied scholarship, the
Perry scheme continues to reflect the most critical dimension to educators' understanding of learning and students' approaches to learning. As Van Hecke
(1990) notes:

Unique among cognitive theories, Perry traced connections between students' basic epistemological stances and their attitudes towards the educational environment in ways that dramatically illustrated the relevance of
epistemological thought to educational practice. (p. 6)

In its representations of both intellectual and epistemological perspectives
(and their interrelationships), the model continues to focus our attention on the
intimate connections between the individual learner, subject matter, and process of understanding, and remains a rich heuristic framework, particularly given
the current resurgence of attention to student learning and notions of learning-
centered institutions (Barr & Tagg, 1995; Cross, 1998; National Research Council, 1999).

After a brief review of the original scheme and subsequent refinements, I will
address several areas of new scholarship in an effort to clarify the core ideas reflected in Perry's work. In the process, I hope to show that the basic tenets of the

Perry scheme are robust enough to incorporate key aspects of this ensuing scholarship, and that a number of critiques of the model raised over the years misinterpret the model in ways that undercut the critique, not the Perry scheme. Finally, I will close with a few suggestions for future research in this area.

REVIEW OF MODEL

Based on a series of open-ended interviews conducted primarily with Harvard undergraduates during the late 1950s and through the 1960s, and since replicated with a wide variety of students and institutions, the Perry scheme emerged from exhaustive qualitative analyses of the ways in which the students described their experiences and transformations over their college years (Perry, 1970, 1981, 1998). Perry and his colleagues were looking for, and expecting to find, personality differences, in particular aspects of the authoritarian personality notions popular at the time (Adorno, Frenkel-Brunswick, Levinson, & Sanford, 1950). Instead of stable individual differences in personality, however, what Perry and his colleagues found was a consistent educational journey—what Perry characterized as "an intellectual Pilgrim's Progress"(1974, p. 3). In his original book describing the study, Perry (1998) compares the developmental progression seen in the model to "the fall" as depicted in the book of Genesis in the Bible, with this particular fall centered on students' understanding of knowledge and learning. As in Genesis, the fall consists not of goodness and evil per se, but of the knowledge of goodness and evil, or as Perry describes it, "the knowledge of values and therefore the potential of judgment . . . in a world devoid of Eden" (1970, p. 60–61). More precisely, this particular progression traces a fall from a world of Absolutes and Truth into a world of contexts and Commitments in which one must take stands and choose as a way of making meaning in one's life through identity choices.

The Perry model reflects the critical intertwining of cognitive and affective perspectives at the heart of a college education—a difficult journey toward more complex forms of thought about the world, one's discipline/area of study, and one's self. Perry's work underscores the notion that the most powerful learning, the learning most faculty really want to see students achieve as a result of their experiences with classes/curricula, involves significant qualitative changes in the way learners approach their learning and their subject matter. Nine distinct stages, or what Perry prefers to call "positions," as in positions from which to view the world, were discerned in the students' common paths, although two, the first and the last, were hypothetical extensions of the empirical work, constructed for the sake of elegance and completeness. In Perry's original conceptualization of the scheme, Positions 1 through 5 describe the primarily intellectual portion of the scheme: systematic, structural change toward increasing differentiation and complexity. In Positions 6 through 9, the primary focus of the journey shifts to what Perry calls ethical concerns in the classical Greek sense: issues of identity and commitments in a relativistic world. Following the conventions of some of the most significant refinements in the ongoing evolution of the model (Knefelkamp, 1974; Knefelkamp & Slepitza, 1978; Moore, 1991, 1994), the sequence of nine positions of the scheme can be grouped into four major categories: Dualism, Multiplicity, Contextual Relativism, and Commitment within Relativism.

Dualism: Positions 1–2

While Position 1 has rarely been found empirically, either in the initial work or in subsequent research (Moore, 1994), it represents the original "Garden of Eden" in terms of one's view of the nature of knowledge and truth. In the Position 1 perspective, there is a completely unquestioned view of truth as Absolute Truth in stark black-and-white terms. The identification with the Authority figure—parent, teacher, church—is absolute and unquestioned, with no tolerance for alternative points of view. In Position 2, different perspectives and beliefs are now acknowledged but are simply wrong. Thinking in this position is characterized by dichotomies and dualisms, i.e., We-Right-Good vs. They-Wrong-Bad or some variation. The world thus consists essentially of two boxes—rights and wrongs—and there is generally little trouble in distinguishing one from the other.

Multiplicity: Positions 3–4

Perry describes the entire progression across the first five positions as "successive modifications of right-wrong dualism in attempting to account for diversity in human opinion, experience, and 'truth'" (Perry, 1974, p.3). The modification in Position 3 represents the first acknowledgment of legitimate uncertainty in the world; instead of two boxes or categories, there are now three—right, wrong, and "not yet known." Thus, the knowledge that is not yet known is knowable, and will be determined at some point in the future. This acceptance of uncertainty as legitimate, albeit temporary, is a profound departure from the dualistic perspective, and for many students an exciting one. Positions 3 and 4, then, are characterized as Multiplicity—the confrontation and coping with diversity and "multiples" in virtually everything.

The initial solution to the problem of uncertainty is that "there are obviously right ways, or methods, to find the right answers," and learning becomes a focus on process and methodology. In Position 4, the "not yet known" notion of Position 3 often becomes a new certainty of "we'll never know for sure," and thus what is most important is one's own thinking. Self-processing and a sense of idea ownership increases, but frequently in Position 4 the stance taken is that there is no nonarbitrary basis for determining what's right (Benack, 1982); hence an attitude of "do your own thing" or "anything goes" tends to prevail in this position.

Contextual Relativism: Position 5 (and beyond)

The movement from Position 4 to Position 5 is arguably the most significant transition within the Perry scheme. This transition represents a fundamental transformation of one's perspective—from a vision of the world as essentially dualistic, with a growing number of exceptions to the rule in specific situations, to a vision of a world as essentially relativistic and context-bound with a few right/wrong exceptions. The most significant distinction between the pseudorelativism of Position 4 and the contextual relativism of Position 5 is the self-consciousness of being an active maker of meaning. As Perry makes clear even in the title of his book (1998), one's task in life is finally understood fully as intellectual and ethical—a question of judgments and meaning-making in both academic and personal contexts. Johnson (1981) clarifies this crucial distinction:

> In position five . . . we recognize that any act of knowing (thinking, talking, reading, writing) requires taking a point of view, and we are forced to acknowledge our own. From this point on, thinking becomes acting, [and] "knowing" will always represent a placing of oneself, for better or worse, in one or another of many possible positions in relation to persons or [ideas]." (p. 3)

Commitment Within Relativism: Positions 6–9

As defined by the model, the primary developmental emphasis shifts beginning in Position 6 from intellectual to ethical: namely, the anticipation, clarification, and ongoing refinement of Commitments. These "Commitments"—distinguished from commitments or what Perry referred to as "considered choices" by being chosen in the face of legitimate alternatives, after experiencing genuine doubt, and reflecting a clear affirmation of one's self or identity—define one's identity in a contextually relativistic world. Perry's original contention was that the changing perspective beyond Position 5 are not structural changes, at least not in the same way as in the earlier positions, and there is some substantial work (Slepitza, 1984) supporting that notion. Other researchers (e.g., King & Kitchener, 1994) dispute this contention, and Perry himself seemed to raise questions in later writings (e.g., 1985). Unfortunately, there has been little additional work done on these upper positions, partly due to the necessity of researching them through qualitative interviews, and partly because work with both the Perry scheme and other related models (e.g., Baxter Magolda, 1992; King & Kitchener, 1994) concentrates on undergraduate students, a population rarely reflecting post-contextual-relativistic thinking.

Space does not permit a more detailed description of the Perry model here; more thorough summaries are available elsewhere (Moore, 1994; Perry, 1998).

Overall, however, the Perry scheme reflects two central interwoven dynamics: 1) confronting and coping with diversity and uncertainty with respect to new learning, and 2) the attendant evolution of meaning-making about learning and self. As depicted in the nine qualitatively distinct positions (and transitions between them) of the Perry scheme, learners cycle through three increasingly complex encounters with diversity in the form of multiples:

- multiple opinions about a given subject or issue (Positions 1 through 3);
- multiple contexts/perspectives from which to understand or analyze issues or arguments (Positions 4 through 6);
- multiple Commitments through which one defines his or her values and identity (Positions 7 through 9).

As learners confront these levels of "multiplicity," their meaning-making shifts and evolves in predictable ways. Most significantly, knowledge is seen as increasingly conjectural and uncertain, open to (and requiring) interpretation. This central epistemology about knowledge and learning triggers parallel shifts in the learner's views about the role of the teacher—moving from an Authority as the source of "Truth" to an authority as a resource with specific expertise to share, as well as the role of the student—moving from a passive receptor of facts to an active agent in defining arguments and creating new knowledge.

SUBSEQUENT THEORETICAL EXTENSIONS/REFINEMENTS OF MODEL

As with any particularly powerful theory, the Perry scheme has been dynamic, not static. In the thirty years since the original publication of Perry's study there has been an evolution in perspectives related to the model in two broad areas:

- Clarifications/refinements of concepts/terms within the original theoretical framework, and
- Extensions of the original work.

Clarifications/Refinements

Understanding Relativism. As Lee Knefelkamp (1998) points out in her introduction to the new edition of Perry's book, over the years there has been considerable misunderstanding of Perry's use of the term "relativism," and a resulting criticism of the model as endorsing the kind of relativism that Allan Bloom (1987) and others have railed against over the years. In fact, from the beginning Perry was clear that there is a crucial distinction between the absolute relativism often seen in Position 4 and the contextual relativism of Position 5. The latter perspective understands and allows for the necessity of judgments based on evidence; the former does not. Unfortunately, studies over the years (Baxter Magolda, 1992; King & Kitchener, 1993; Mines & Kitchener, 1986; Moore, 1991, 1994; Thompson, 1990) indicate that few students graduating from college reason consistently from a contextually relativistic perspective (which is perhaps at least partially why Bloom and others are complaining!).

Direction and Shape of Development.   The original depiction of the scheme, built around the patterned progression noted in the student interviews, was distinctly linear and hierarchical. At the same time, Perry did describe three phenomena he termed "deflections from growth": **retreat** (from the diversity of relativism); **escape** (something akin to alienation); and **temporizing** (generally an unwillingness to acknowledge the need for Commitment as a way to define one's identity). Over the years, people working with the scheme, including Perry himself (1985), came to view the journey as more recursive and fluid (more like the notions of development in Kegan, 1983, 1994), and to see what were once considered "deflections" as often necessary and appropriate responses to particular contexts or circumstances. Temporizing, in particular, came to be seen as a respite from the challenges of development, and not undesirable at all. Moreover, as Knefelkamp (1998) notes, what was once a single model is now three "models": "general" Perry, or the original overall perspective; "contextual" Perry, the varying ways in which learners make sense of particular contexts (e.g., different disciplines); and "functional" Perry, or the way the model can be used to understand how people recycle through earlier perspectives in confronting new and unfamiliar learning situations.

Extensions

In the years since the publication of Perry's book and model, there has been a considerable amount of work exploring similar or related issues, both in this country as well as around the world, and much of that work will be highlighted later in this chapter. Three particular efforts are worth a special note, however, as they reflect the most direct ties to Perry's original theoretical framework, and indeed represent the most explicit extensions of the Perry model: 1) the work of Mary Belenky, Blythe Clinchy, Nancy Goldberger, and Jill Tarule (*Women's Ways of Knowing,* 1986); 2) Marcia Baxter Magolda's longitudinal efforts at the University of Miami at Ohio (1985, 1992); and 3) the work on "Reflective Judgment" (King & Kitchener, 1994). These lines of research are described in separate chapters in this volume. What is important to note here is that while these authors have generally claimed that their work represents theories separate from the Perry scheme, there is no compelling evidence that these frameworks in fact define distinct theories. All of these efforts represent important areas of scholarship with respect to intellectual development, but rather than being separate theoretical models they extend and expand descriptions of the same fundamental journey described by Perry's framework (see Van Hecke, 1990, for a lengthier discussion of this issue related to Reflective Judgment).

THE PERRY MODEL AND RECENT SCHOLARSHIP ON LEARNING

In the years since the original work on the Perry scheme, there has been a growing interest in and expanding scholarship related to three key arenas that underscore and reinforce the perspectives of the Perry scheme: knowledge, learning, and assessment.

Knowledge

Situated Cognition. Like other areas of scholarship, epistemology, the study of knowledge itself, has been influenced greatly by the various modes of postmodern thought and become quite varied and complex (see, for example, Banks, 1994; Collins, 1990; Damarin, 1996; Harding, 1991; Harding & Hintikka, 1983; Minnich, 1990). One strand of this work particularly germane to the present discussion centers on the notion of knowledge as "situated cognition" (Brown, Collins, & Duguid, 1989; Lave, 1988; Lave & Wenger, 1991). From this perspective, knowledge needs to be viewed contextually and as "fundamentally influenced by the activity, context, and culture in which it is used" (McLellan, 1996, p.6), gained through involvement in authentic activities related to a specific discipline or area of practice. Rather than viewing knowledge as a collection of inert facts—a "body of knowledge," in common parlance—this position holds that knowledge is more usefully viewed as similar to a conceptual tool, properly understood only through regular use-in-context.

Constructivism. In terms of a focus on knowledge, the other significant area of theoretical work in recent years is constructivism, an epistemology that

> rejects the notion that knowledge is fixed, independent of the knower and consists of accumulating 'truths.' Rather, knowledge is produced by the knower from existing beliefs and experiences. (Airasian & Walsh, 1997, p. 445)

The roots of this perspective are in philosophy (Rorty, 1991), and the bulk of the conceptual and empirical work has been in a K–12 educational context (see, for example, Bereiter, 1994; Brooks & Brooks, 1993; Driver, Asoko, Leach, Mortimer, & Scott, 1994; Fosnot, 1989; Sigel & Cocking, 1977; Steffe & Gale, 1995; Wilson, 1998). Both Airasian and Walsh (1997) and Driver et al. (1994) note that there have been two major strands of this work, one emphasizing individual cognitive development and meaning construction a la Piaget (1977), the other focusing on knowledge as socially constructed in discourse communities (O'Loughlin, 1992). While some authors (O'Loughlin, 1992) insist on dichotomizing these strands, Driver et al. (1994) argue, and I agree, that both approaches are necessary for a full understanding of learning. In any case, both strands support and reinforce the Perry scheme perspective in their emphasis on meaning-making, whatever its origin, as being central to the learning process. Moreover, what is particularly useful about this scholarship for the present argument is that constructivism, like the Perry scheme, addresses an epistemology focused not just on knowledge in some abstract sense but in the specific context of how people learn and approach learning.

Critical Perspective: Social Constructivism and Assumptions of Development. Over the years, particularly in the social constructivism literature, critics of models like Piaget's have tended to include the Perry scheme in their critique (Bruffee, 1993; O'Loughlin, 1992; Williams, 1989), arguing that such developmental perspectives emphasize individual cognition and universal forms of thought to the exclusion of sociocultural and contextual factors. More specifically, they question, among other things:

- the assumption of universality (the implied vision of "normal" development);
- the alleged "inevitability" of development as depicted by such models;
- the lack of specific attention to historical and sociocultural contexts, and
- the potential for "pigeonholing" learners with stage (position) labels.

Given that this critique rests in the assumption that Perry's work is Piagetian in nature, it is important to clarify the distinct differences between a model like Perry's and the strict Piagetian notions of stages and development. Kohlberg and Armon (1984) argue that while models like Perry's are considered essentially structural and in most cases do attempt to meet the Piagetian stage criteria, there is only a general fit between the models and the criteria. Thus it is more useful to draw a distinction between "hard" (Piagetian) and "soft" (e.g., Perry) structural models than to force models like Perry's into a strict Piagetian mold. For Kohlberg and Armon, the soft structural models represent a "new way of doing research in adult development, a way that has emerged from the Piagetian paradigm" (1984, p. 394). Their recommendation is that what needs to be abandoned in adult development research is not the notion of stages, but rather Piaget's strict criteria for stage construction. (For more details on these issues, see Commons, Sinnott, Richards, & Armon, 1989, 1990.)

More importantly, while all of the issues raised are legitimate concerns in the abstract, they either don't apply or are generally taken into consideration by Perry and those working with the Perry scheme. As Knefelkamp (1998) points out, neither Perry nor any of his major interpreters have made assumptions of universality or comprehensiveness for the model; the scheme has always been clearly grounded in Western higher education. Although there is an explicit sense that the more complex and inclusive positions—certainly through Position 5—encompass more adequate ways of viewing the world than do the earlier perspectives, there is no sense of "inevitability" about the developmental progression in the scheme. The scheme focuses on the individual's meaning-making about knowledge, but in no way discounts or excludes the role of peer groups or other sociocultural influences in shaping these perspectives. Finally, the potential for the misuse of labels and categories was an ongoing concern for Perry (1985) himself:

> Persons are too complex to 'fit into' any theory or category. Theories and categories only illuminate certain aspects of persons . . . How then, are our models to help us, and with what purpose? We want them to extend our efficacy as educators. But efficacy implies power, and here's the rub. If the power is to label students the better to develop them, we shall dehumanize them and ourselves . . . (p. 4)

Learning

Learning as Development. What do we mean by the terms "development" or "developmental" in the context of the Perry scheme, and how are those notions related to learning? The work of the educational and developmental theorist Nevitt Sanford (1969) provides a useful reference point. According to Sanford, development:

- refers to "the organization of increasing complexity" (p. 47), and thus is distinct from simple notions of "change" or "growth"
- involves the whole individual—in development, intellect, emotion, and action are all inseparable and in interaction
- is progressive in that there is an order to the succession of developmental changes that take place
- reflects an interaction between the person and the environment

For Sanford, and for Perry, true education, especially liberal arts education, was fundamentally about this kind of development—namely, the evolution of individuals' thinking structures and meaning-making toward greater and more adaptive complexity. Hanna Holborn Gray, then president of the University of Chicago, once defined an educated person as:

> [someone with a] respect for rationality and [an understanding of] some of the limits of rationality as well . . . [also] independent critical intelligence, and a sense not only for the complexity of the world and different points of view but of the standards he or she would thoughtfully want to be pursuing in making judgments.

> (*Time* magazine, 1982, p. 70)

Perry's framework closely mirrors this vision, and subsequent developmental theorizing and research simply elaborates on and refines the connection (e.g., Commons, Richards, & Armon, 1984; Fowler, 1983; Kegan, 1983, 1994; Kohlberg, 1969, 1981; Resnick, 1987). The parallels underscore the significance of a model like the Perry scheme for outcomes assessment and teaching/learning issues in higher education, particularly in a Western context.

Deep Learning.   An extensive and growing body of international research (principally Australia, Great Britain, the Netherlands, Scotland and Sweden) has explored the nature of student learning and approaches to learning in various context-specific settings (Biggs, 1987; Laurillard, 1979, 1993; Marton, Hounsell, & Entwistle, 1984; Ramsden, 1988, 1992; van Rossum, Diejkers, & Hamer, 1985). According to this literature, deep learning involves qualitative changes in the complexity of students' thinking about and conceptualizations of context-specific subject matter—in other words, **development,** to use Sanford's definition. While this work was conducted largely independent of the Perry scheme work underway in the United States, many of the researchers were familiar with and appreciative of Perry's contributions. As Ramsden (1988) notes:

> Perry discovered that the learning difficulties experienced by new college students were not rooted in their lack of motivation, their study skills, or their ability; they sprang from their view of knowledge itself . . . Perry's work helps us to realize that the educational process may actually create misconceptions of what learning is about. (p. 18)

In addition to identifying deep learning as a crucial educational outcome, this research also uses the terms **deep**—a focus on applications and underlying meanings, and **surface**—an emphasis on rote memorization of facts—to characterize the different approaches students took to their learning (Biggs, 1987; Entwistle & Ramsden, 1983; Marton & Saljo, 1976; Marton, Dall'Alba, & Beaty, 1993; Saljo, 1979; van Rossum & Diejkers, 1984; van Rossum, Diejkers, and Hamer, 1985). In the work done in the Netherlands (van Rossum, Diejkers, & Hamer, 1985), analyses of in-depth student interviews defined six different "learning conceptions"—three interpreted as "deep" approaches, three as "surface" approaches—with considerable parallels to the major positions of the Perry scheme:

> The learning conception gives us a clear picture of qualitatively different views on learning and moreover seems to be strongly connected with qualitatively different ways of thinking and acting, e.g., different study strategies . . . Learning conceptions . . . show the development of the student from novice to expert in learning . . . The development of the view on learning should, in our opinion, be seen as a parallel to the intellectual and ethical development of the adolescent (cf. Perry, 1970), in short as an aspect of the

growth to a personal philosophy." (van Rossum, Diejkers & Hamer, 1985,
p. 636–637)

Unlike some of the other research groups working in this area (e.g., Laurillard,
1979), van Rossum and his colleagues argued that there did seem to be a developmental process at work:

> ... [W]e are of the opinion that the found differences in learning concep-
> tions, study strategies, etc. not only reflect differences *between* people, but
> also different stages in the (identity) development of the individual ...
> especially with the epistemological development of students within a certain
> context, namely, the academic system. (van Rossum & Diejkers, 1984, p. 2)

Critical Perspective: Marton's Phenomenography.   Marton (1981) argues that
phenomenography—emphasizing a focus on people's conceptions of reality and
the world around them rather than a focus on the reality itself—is an essential
approach to understanding complex phenomena, including learning. For the most
part, Marton's work clearly reinforces the Perry scheme, arguing that meaning-
making needs to be considered the most central aspect of learning. At the same
time, however, Marton disagreed with the notion of structural stages in individual
meaning-making with respect to learning, believing that to the extent that structures existed they centered on the subject matter or concept in question, and not
the individual learner:

> We cannot gain knowledge about learning *as such,* nor about [operational]
> structures *as such,* and not even about a conception of [subject matter] *as
> such* ... [The] most obvious implication is that we can hardly categorize
> individuals unambiguously in terms of their possessing (or not possessing)
> structures or even conceptions ... [However], individual stability across
> contents and situations is neither denied nor assumed by us. In our view, it
> should be a target of empirical investigation rather than being taken for
> granted: it should be regarded as something to be described and analyzed.
> (Marton, 1981, p. 195)

Marton's argument for empirical work in this area is certainly persuasive, but his
critique of the Perry scheme presumes unnecessarily a false dichotomy, i.e., that relatively stable meaning-making structures exist either within individuals or around
topics/subject matters.

Assessment

In recent years the educational outcomes assessment literature has reflected more
than its share of overly simplistic and narrowly defined efforts. At the same time,
there has also been a consistent, and arguably growing, body of work emphasiz-

ing more in-depth, qualitative approaches to relatively complex student learning outcomes (Berlak et al., 1992; Wiggins, 1993, 1998). There are two aspects of this work worth noting in more detail: 1) efforts to develop and refine "authentic" assessments, which are designed around meaningful performances and specific, "real-world" contexts (Newmann, 1996; Wiggins, 1993, 1998; Wineburg, 1991, 1997), and a resulting emphasis on the centrality of interpretation and judgment; and 2) a serious attention to student self-assessment and an acknowledgment that student self-report data, rather than being inherently suspect, have a crucial role to play in our understanding of student learning.

Interpretive Framework.   A contextually relativistic sense of assessment is embodied in a growing explicit focus on issues of interpretation and judgment with respect to educational assessment and research. A succinct description of this perspective comes from Louis Sass (1990):

> . . . [T]he facts of social science are not facts at all but interpretations of interpretations . . . The interpretive position is not necessarily opposed to traditional empiricist research in the human sciences; [but] whatever their degree of statistical rigor, the knowledge they acquire is built on the sands of interpretation. (p. 52–53)

This understanding is gaining some favor in the realm of educational assessment (Berlak et al., 1992; Gifford & O'Connor, 1992; Musil, 1992; Wolf, Bixby, Glenn, & Gardner, 1991), even though it continues to be underappreciated and marginalized to an extent in this age of public accountability (Moore, 1999). Nevertheless, this interpretive perspective is very much in keeping with the fundamental tenets of the Perry scheme concerning the central role of meaning-making and interpretation in coming to judgment in a complex world. As Torosyan (1999) notes:

> [Perry] . . . was the first educational theorist to suggest that the postclassical science radical re-conception of how we judge truth or validity of our observations of reality would hold even more strongly for social sciences and educational/psychological practice. (p. 7)

Self-Assessment.   In addition to being firmly grounded in a more contextual understanding of the world, these new approaches to assessment often emphasize student self-assessment (MacGregor, 1994). This focus has much in common with the international literature on learning noted earlier, and to a considerable extent builds on the implications of Perry's work. If the most significant learning is developmental in nature and reflected in qualitative changes in the complexity of learners' thinking about a given concept or subject matter, then understanding students' meaning-making about those subject-related phenomena is essential to assessing that learning. Simply put, if we want to understand how students are thinking about any of these issues, we need to ask them. As Brown and Duguid (1996) assert:

> If you want to understand learning and what is learned in any interaction, you have to investigate from the point of view of that learner . . . The shade that events, circumstances, or interactions take on in the process of learning are determined through active appropriation . . . [which] is simultaneously an act of sense-making in terms of the learner's view of the world. (p.48–49)

Critical Perspective: Epistemology and Learning? Hofer and Pintrich (1997), while acknowledging that "in terms of the psychological reality of the network of individuals' beliefs, beliefs about learning, teaching and knowledge are probably intertwined" (p.116), argue that such links were not part of Perry's original work, and in any event should be ignored for assessment purposes.

> . . . Those who built on Perry's work and attempt to design written means of assessment of the Perry scheme often . . . seem to confound perceptions of educational experience with epistemology . . . Although these instruments were designed to measure aspects of Perry's model, a careful review of Perry's positions does not show these issues of classroom learning and teaching as part of the original scheme . . . In terms of conceptual clarity, it seems to us that the domain of epistemological beliefs should be limited to individuals' beliefs about knowledge as well as reasoning and justification processes regarding knowledge. (Hofer & Pintrich, p. 116)

From the perspective of work to date both on the Perry scheme and in areas like situated cognition and authentic assessment, pursuing the kind of "clarity" Hofer and Pintrich suggest would seem to come at the price of contextual authenticity. After all, the focus of the Perry scheme is on understanding epistemology in the situated context of learning, not studying epistemological beliefs per se. Thus understanding the individual's sense of learning (as well as sense of self-as-learner) and the broader framework of the sociocultural context of the learning are essential to the process. For the assessment of the model to ignore the critical connections to learning would miss crucial aspects of what makes the Perry scheme particularly relevant to a higher education context.

SUMMARY AND FUTURE
DIRECTIONS FOR RESEARCH

In this chapter, I have attempted to place the theoretical framework known as the Perry scheme into a wider context of subsequent scholarship and conceptualization around knowledge, learning, and assessment, work which both reinforces and can be incorporated into the perspectives of Perry's model. The scheme represents an effort to interpret differences in learners' understandings of and approaches to learning, especially in structured academic environments. These differences clearly exist; the central question is what models or frameworks we might use to help understand these differences and improve the processes of teaching and learning, recognizing that any models we use are themselves cultural constructions (or in Sass's words, "interpretations of interpretations").

When Perry and his colleagues found perspective differences not only between individuals but also over time with the same students, they were forced to find a model more dynamic than "personality" to make sense of the findings. Based on the scholarship widely available at the time, they could have framed the findings in terms of an intelligence or aptitude model, arguing that students simply got "smarter," or a remediation model, in which students gained more knowledge (became informed) and/or skills (became competent). Instead, they chose a developmental model, based loosely on the best-known framework at the time, Jean Piaget's, and thus emphasized the structural coherence of an individual's perspectives at any given time as well as the ongoing evolution of these perspectives in a relatively predictable and patterned way.

Now, after some thirty-odd years of wide-ranging scholarship and changing sensibilities, at least two other alternative explanatory models have emerged, as suggested in the earlier discussions of knowledge, learning, and assessment:

- Expertise model—movement from novices to experts regarding learning itself or, more likely, in the context of specific discipline or program areas (e.g., Brown, Collins and Duguid's, 1989, notion of "cognitive apprenticeship"; Niemi, 1997)
- Enculturation/socialization model—process of inculcating students into interpretive discourse communities as represented by the disciplines (the sociocultural perspective, Lave, 1988; Wertsch, 1991; O'Loughlin, 1992; or what Williams, 1989 refers to as an "outsider to insider" framework)

These frameworks offer heuristic alternatives to the developmental model, and have spawned solid lines of research. Taken in conjunction with the extensions of Perry's model within a developmental framework (e.g., Baxter Magolda, 1992; Belenky et al., 1986; King & Kitchener, 1994), this work can help refine, extend, and if necessary modify the essential "truths" of the Perry scheme. Certainly, as both the times and student populations change, ongoing open-ended explorations of these different frameworks are needed. More specifically, some of the key questions that need to be explored include:

- How much, and in what specific ways, do learners' conceptions vary across learning contexts, and across various subgroups of students (race, class, culture, aptitude, etc.)?
- In what ways do epistemological beliefs influence the nature and development of expertise in various learning contexts?

- How do teachers view the process of learning for their students, in what ways do those perspectives reflect the conceptual framework of socialization described in the literature, and how does that relate to/interact with the meaning-making of individual students?
- What are the critical aspects of teaching/learning environments promoting deep learning and qualitative changes in the complexity of student thinking, and how do they vary across both learning contexts and student subgroups?

For now, however, a careful reading of a wide array of recent scholarship on learning and development suggests strongly that Perry's model continues to provide a meaningful and heuristically powerful understanding of learning and students' approaches to learning. In Perry's own words:

> . . . [For] providing students with opportunities to discover and refine their own powers . . . the first prerequisite is the student's experience of being *met* . . . If a model of development helps portray the successive shapes of students' worlds, we can state a primary issue this way: what assessments, applications and contexts contribute toward such moments of meeting, and what distinguishes them from others that may detract from this potential? What greater community of care could we need? (1985, p. 5)

REFERENCES

Adorno, T. W., Frenkel–Brunswick, E., Levinson, D. J., and Sanford, R. N. (1950). *The authoritarian personality.* New York: Harper & Row.

Airasian, P. W. & Walsh, M. E. (1997). Constructivist cautions. *Phi Delta Kappan,* February, 444–449.

Banks, J. (1994). *Multiethnic education: Theory and practice (3rd ed.).* Boston: Allyn and Bacon.

Barr, R. & Tagg, J. (1995). From teaching to learning—a new paradigm for undergraduate education. *Change,* November/December, 1995, 13–25.

Baxter Magolda, M. B. (1992). *Knowing and reasoning in college: Gender-related patterns in students' intellectual development.* San Francisco: Jossey-Bass.

Baxter Magolda, M., & Porterfield, W. (1985). A new approach to assess intellectual development on the Perry scheme. *Journal of College Student Personnel, 26* (4), 343–351.

Belenky, M. F., Clinchy, B. M., Goldberger, N. R., & Tarule, J. M. (1986). *Women's ways of knowing: The development of self, voice, and mind.* New York: Basic Books.

Benack, S. (1982). The coding of dimensions of epistemological thought in young men and women. *Moral Education Forum, 7* (2), 3–23.

Bereiter, C. (1994). Implications of postmodernism for science, or science as progressive discourse. *Educational Psychologist, 29,* 3–12.

Berlak, H., Newmann, F. M., Adams. E., Archbald, D. A., Burgess, T., Raven, J. & Romberg, T. A. (1992). *Toward a new science of educational testing and assessment.* Albany, NY: SUNY Press.

Biggs, J. (1987). *Student approaches to learning and studying.* Hawthorne, Victoria (Australia): Australian Council for Educational Research.

Bloom, A. (1987). *The closing of the American mind: How higher education has failed democracy and impoverished the souls of today's students.* New York: Simon and Schuster.

Brooks, J. G., & Brooks, M. G. (1993). *In search of understanding: The case for constructivist classrooms.* Alexandria, VA: Association for Supervision and Curriculum Development.

Brown, J. S., Collins, A., & Duguid, P. (1989). Situated cognition and the culture of learning. *Educational Researcher,* January–February, 1989, 32–42.

Brown, J. S. & Duguid, P. (1996). Stolen knowledge. In H. McLellan (Ed.), *Situated learning perspectives.* (pp. 47–56). Englewood Cliffs, New Jersey: Educational Technology Publications.

Bruffee, K. (1993). *Collaborative learning: Higher education, interdependence, and the authority of knowledge.* Baltimore: Johns Hopkins University Press.

Burbules, N. C., & Rice, S. (1991). Dialogue across differences: Continuing the conversation. *Harvard Educational Review, 61*(4), November, 393–416.

Collins, P. H. (1990). *Black feminist thought: Knowledge, consciousness, and the politics of empowerment.* Boston: Unwin Hyman.

Commons, M., Richards, F., & Armon, C. (1984). *Beyond formal operations: Late adolescent and adult cognitive development.* New York: Praeger Press.

Commons, M. L., Sinnott, J. D., Richards, F. A., & Armon, C. (1989, 1990). *Adult development, Vol. 1 & 2.* New York: Praeger.

Cross, K. P. 1998. *Opening windows on learning. The Cross Papers # 2.* League for Innovation in the Community College & Educational Testing Service. *http://www.league.org*

Damarin, S. K. (1996). Schooling and situated knowledge: Travel or tourism? In H. McLellan (Ed.), *Situated learning perspectives* (p. 77–87). Englewood Cliffs, New Jersey: Educational Technology Publications.

Driver, R., Asoko, H., Leach, J., Mortimer, E., & Scott, P. (1994). Constructing scientific knowledge in the classroom. *Educational Researcher, 23* (7), 5–12.

Entwistle, N., & Ramsden, P. (1983). *Understanding Student Learning.* New York: Nichols Publishing Company.

Fosnot, C. (1989). *Enquiring teachers, enquiring learners: A constructivist approach to teaching.* New York: Teachers College Press.

Fowler, J. (1981). Stages of faith: The psychology of human development and the quest for meaning. San Francisco: Harper & Row.

Gergen, K. J. (1991). *The saturated self.* New York: Basic Books, Inc.

Gifford, B. R., & O'Connor, M. C. (Eds.). (1992). *Changing assessments: Alternative views of aptitude, achievement and instruction.* Boston: Kluwer Academic Publishers.

Gilligan, C. (1982). *In a different voice: Psychological theory and women's development.* Cambridge, MA: Harvard University Press.

Gray, H. H. (1982). Five ways to wisdom. *Time* magazine, September 11, p. 70.

Harding, S. (1991). *Whose science? Whose knowledge?* Ithaca, New York: Cornell University Press.

Harding, S., & Hintikka, M. (Eds.). (1983). *Discovering reality: Feminist perspectives on epistemology, metaphysics, methodology, and philosophy of science.* Dordrecht, Holland: D. Reidel Publishing Co.

Hofer, B. K. & Pintrich, P. R. (1997). The development of epistemological theories: Beliefs about knowledge and knowing and their relation to learning. *Review of Educational Research, 67* (1), 88–140.

Johnson, M. H. (1981). Some new thoughts on the Perry scheme. *The Perry Newsletter,* Spring, p. 1–3.

Kegan, R. (1983). *The evolving self.* Cambridge, MA: Harvard University Press.

Kegan, R. (1994). *In over our heads: The mental demands of modern life.* Cambridge, MA: Harvard University Press.

King, P. & Kitchener, K. S. (1993). The development of reflective thinking in the college years: The mixed results. In C. G. Schneider (Ed.), *Strengthening the college major* (pp. 25–42). *New Directions for Higher Education,* #84, Winter. San Francisco: Jossey-Bass.

King, P. M. & Kitchener, K. S. (1994). *Developing reflective judgment: understanding and promoting intellectual growth and critical thinking in adolescents and adults.* San Francisco: Jossey-Bass.

Knefelkamp, L. L. (1974). Developmental instruction: Fostering intellectual and personal growth of college students. Doctoral dissertation, University of Minnesota, Minneapolis. (Dissertation Abstracts 36,3: 1271A. 1975.)

Knefelkamp, L. L. (1998). Introduction. In William G. Perry, Jr. *Forms of ethical and intellectual development in the college years: A scheme.* (p. xi–xxxviii). San Francisco: Jossey-Bass.

Knefelkamp, L. L. & Slepitza, R. L. (1978). A cognitive-developmental model of career development: An adaptation of the Perry scheme. In C. A. Parker (Ed.), *Encouraging development in college students* (pp. 135–150). Minneapolis: University of Minnesota Press.

Kohlberg, L. (1981). *The philosophy of moral development.* San Francisco: Harper and Row.

Kohlberg, L. (1969). Stage and sequence: The cognitive developmental approach to socialization. In D. Goslin (ed.), *Handbook of socialization: Theory and research* (pp. 347–480). New York: Rand-McNally.

Kohlberg, L., & Armon, C. (1984). Three types of stage models used in the study of adult development. In M. Commons, F. Richards, & C. Armon, *Beyond formal operations* (pp. 383–394). New York: Praeger Press.

Laurillard, D. (1979). The process of student learning. *Higher Education, 8,* 395–409.

Laurillard, D. (1993). *Rethinking university teaching: A framework for the effective use of educational technology.* London & New York: Routledge.

Lave, J. (1988). *Cognition in practice: Mind, mathematics, and culture in everyday life.* Cambridge: Cambridge University Press.

Lave, J. & Wenger, E. (1991). *Situated learning: Legitimate peripheral participation.* Cambridge: Cambridge University Press.

MacGregor, J. (Ed.) (1994). *Student self-evaluations: Fostering reflective learning, New Directions for Teaching and Learning.* San Francisco: Jossey-Bass.

Marton, F. (1981). Phenomenography: Describing conceptions of the world around us. *Instructional Science, 10,* 177–200.

Marton, F., & Saljo, R. (1976). On qualitative differences in learning: Outcome and process. *British Journal of Educational Psychology, 46,* 4–11.

Marton, F., Dall'Alba, G., & Beaty, E. (1993). Conceptions of learning. *International Journal of Educational Research,* 277–300.

Marton, F., Hounsell, D., & Entwistle, N. J. (Eds.). (1984). *The experience of learning.* Edinburgh: Scottish Academic Press.

McLellan, H. (1996). Situated learning: Multiple perspectives. In H. McLellan (Ed.), *Situated learning perspectives* (pp. 5–17). Englewood Cliffs, New Jersey: Educational Technology Publications.

Mines, R. A., & Kitchener, K. S. (Eds.). (1986). *Adult cognitive development: Methods and models.* New York: Praeger Press.

Minnich, E. K. (1990). *Transforming knowledge.* Philadelphia: Temple University Press.

Moore, W.S. (1991). The Perry scheme of intellectual and ethical development: An introduction to the model and two major assessment approaches. Paper prepared for the annual meeting of the American Educational Research Association, Chicago, IL.

Moore, W. S. (1994). Student and Faculty Epistemology in the College Classroom: The Perry Scheme of Intellectual and Ethical Development. In K. Pritchard & R. M. Sawyer (Eds.), *Handbook of College Teaching* (pp. 45–67). Westport, CT: Greenwood Press.

Moore, W. S. (1999). A developmental perspective on the theology of assessment: Moving from received belief to creative faith. *Washington Assessment Group Newsletter, 8* (2), February, 1–6. *(http://www.sbctc.ctc.edu/Board/Ed/Outcomes/outcome.htm)*

Musil, C. M. (Ed.). (1992). *Students at the center: Feminist assessment.* Washington, DC: Association of American Colleges.

National Research Council (Bransford, J. D., Brown, A. L., & Cocking, R. R., (Eds.). (1999). *How people learn: Brain, mind, experience, and school.* Washington, D.C.: National Academy Press.

Newmann, F. & Associates. (1996). *Authentic achievement: Restructuring schools for intellectual quality.* San Francisco: Jossey-Bass.

Niemi, D. (1997). Cognitive science, expert-novice research, and performance assessment. *Theory into Practice, 36* (4), Autumn, 239–246.

O'Loughlin, M. (1992). Rethinking science education: Beyond Piagetian constructivism toward a sociocultural model of teaching and learning. *Journal of Research in Science Teaching, 29* (8), 791–820.

Perry, W. G. (1974). Students as makers of meaning. Annual report of the Bureau of Study Counsel, Harvard University.

Perry, W. G. (1981). Cognitive and ethical growth: The making of meaning. In A. Chickering & Associates (Eds.), *The Modern American College* (pp. 76–116). San Francisco: Jossey-Bass.

Perry, W. G. Jr. (1985). Perry's perplex: Issues unresolved and irresolvable. Notes to participants in the Project Match Conference, Davidson College, North Carolina, June, 1985. (Published in *Perry Newsletter,* Fall, 1985, p. 1–5).

Perry, W. G. Jr. (1998). *Forms of intellectual and ethical development in the college years: A scheme.* San Francisco: Jossey-Bass. (Originally published in 1970. New York: Holt, Rinehart & Winston.)

Piaget, J. (1977). *The development of thought: Equilibrium of cognitive structures.* New York: Viking Press.

Ramsden, P. (1988) *Improving learning: New perspectives.* London: Kogan Page.

Ramsden, P. (1992). *Learning to Teach in Higher Education.* New York: Routledge.

Resnick, L. B. (1987). *Education and learning to think.* Washington, D.C.: National Academy Press.

Rorty, R. (1991). *Objectivity, relativism, and truth.* Cambridge: Cambridge University Press.

Saljo, R. (1979). Learning in the learner's perspective: Some commonsense conceptions. *Reports from the Department of Education, University of Goteborg* (Sweden), Number 76

Sanford, N. (1969). *Why Colleges Fail.* San Francisco: Jossey-Bass.

Sass, L. (1990). Anthropology's native problems: revisionism in the field. *Harper's* magazine, May, 49–57.

Sigel, I. E., & Cocking, R. R. (1977). *Cognitive development from childhood to adolescence: A constructivist perspective.* New York: Holt, Rinehart, & Winston.

Slepitza, R. (1984). Commitment within the Perry Scheme: A question of structural change. Doctoral dissertation, University of Maryland. 1983. *(Dissertation Abstracts,* 45,2:448A.)

Steffe, L. P., & Gale, J. (Eds.). (1995). *Constructivism in education.* Hillsdale, New Jersey: Erlbaum Press.

Thompson, K. (1990). Learning at Evergreen: A study of cognitive development using the Perry model. Olympia, WA: The Evergreen State College Assessment Study Group, Report Number 1.

Torosyan, R. (1999). Applying learning to life: a theoretical framework in context. *Et cetera , 56* (1), Spring, 3–24.

Van Hecke, M. L. (1990). Critical thinking and the Perry scheme: tangled spirals. Paper presented at the "Reflection and Anticipation: A Celebration of Two Decades of Work with the 'Perry Scheme'" conference. Washington, D.C., December, 1990.

van Rossum, Erik J., & Diejkers, Rien A. (1984). Learning: Qualitative differences between novices and experts. Unpublished paper, Dept. of Educational Psychology, Tilburg University, the Netherlands, February, 1984.

van Rossum, E. J., Diejkers, R. A. & Hamer, R. (1985). Students' learning conceptions and their interpretation of significant educational concepts. *Higher Education, 14,* 617–641.

Wertsch, J. V. (1991). *Voices of the Mind: A sociocultural approach to mediated action.* Cambridge, MA: Harvard University Press.

Wiggins, G. P. (1993). *Assessing student performance: Exploring the purpose and limits of testing.* San Francisco, CA: Jossey-Bass.

Wiggins, G. (1998). *Educative assessment.* San Francisco: Jossey-Bass.

Williams, J. M. (1989). Afterword: Two ways of thinking about growth. In E. P. Maimon & B. F. Nodine (Eds.), *Thinking, reasoning, and writing* (pp. 245–255). New York: Longman.

Wilson, B. G. (1998). *Constructivist learning environments: Case studies in instructional design.* Englewood Cliffs, New Jersey: Educational Technology Publications.

Wineburg, S. (1991). Historical problem solving: A study of the cognitive processes used in the evaluation of documentary and pictorial evidence. *Journal of Educational Psychology, 83* (1), 73–83.

Wineburg, S. (1997). Beyond breadth and depth: Subject matter knowledge and assessment. *Theory into Practice, 36* (4), 255–261.

Wolf, D., Bixby, J., Glenn III, J., & Gardner, H. (1991). To use their minds well: Investigating new forms of student assessment. *Review of Research in Education, 17,* 31–74.

3

The Reflective Judgment Model: Twenty Years of Research on Epistemic Cognition

Patricia M. King*
University of Michigan

Karen Strohm Kitchener
University of Denver

Over 15 years ago, Kitchener (1983) suggested that a three-level model of cognitive processing was necessary to account for the complex monitoring that is involved when older adolescents and adults are faced with ill-structured problems (Churchman, 1971; Wood, 1983). These are problems about which "reasonable people reasonably disagree." These problems cannot be solved by the mechanical application of an algorithm; they require making judgments based on the strength of available evidence and the adequacy of argument. For example, citizens are asked to vote on ballot issues such as whether the benefits of spraying for mosquitoes outweighs the health risks, whether a proposed urban growth policy will protect farm land while spurring economic development, and the degree to which a culture of violence and availability of guns contributes to tragedies such as school shootings by teenage boys. People hold opposing and contradictory views about such truly vexing problems, and even the most conscientious parents and involved community leaders become perplexed when trying to decide how to address such issues in responsible, defensible ways.

At the first level of Kitchener's (1983) cognitive processing model, individuals engage in processes like computing, memorizing, reading, and perceiving;

---

*Both authors contributed equally to the preparation of this manuscript.

this level is called "cognition." Being able to monitor one's progress when engaged in level one tasks requires metacognitive processing, which is described in the model's second level. At the third level, labeled "epistemic cognition," individuals consider "the limits of knowing, the certainty of knowing, and the criteria for knowing" (Kitchener, 1983, p. 222). These skills allow individuals to monitor the epistemic nature of problems, such as whether they are solvable and the truth value of different solutions. While metacognition allows one to monitor Level 1 and Level 2 processes, epistemic cognition allows the monitoring of problem types and the evaluation of proposed solutions. We have argued that epistemic cognition is the foundation of critical thinking when individuals are engaged in ill-structured problem solving (King & Kitchener, 1994). More recently, Kuhn (1999) has made similar claims. It is the development of epistemic cognition that provides the focus of this volume and this chapter.

In the following pages, we first articulate our model of the development of epistemic cognition, which we call the Reflective Judgment Model. In doing so, we will explicate the roots of the concept of reflective judgment and how it is tied to epistemic cognition. Second, we provide a description of the model with illustrations from interviews with participants. Third, we discuss the longitudinal and cross-sectional data on the model and last, we suggest directions for future research.

THE DEVELOPMENT OF EPISTEMIC COGNITION: THE REFLECTIVE JUDGMENT MODEL

For the last 20 years, we have studied the development of epistemic cognition and found that is intrinsically tied to the ability to understand the nature of ill-structured problems and to construct solutions for them. Making interpretive judgments about ill-structured problems involves constructing beliefs, a task that requires people to wrestle with questions about the limits, certainty, and criteria for knowing, factors that comprise "epistemic cognition" (Kitchener, 1983). Both cross-sectional and longitudinal studies have shown that people's epistemic assumptions change over time in a developmental fashion from early adolescence to adulthood. Furthermore, there is a growing body of research suggesting that people's concepts of how to justify beliefs when faced with ill-structured problems change concurrently as part of an underlying developmental structure. (For summaries, see Hofer & Pintrich, 1997, King & Kitchener, 1994, Kitchener & Fischer, 1990, and chapters in Section I of this volume.) It is this developmental sequence that we have described in the Reflective Judgment Model. As we have discussed elsewhere (King & Kitchener, 1994), we chose the term "reflective judgment" (RJ) based on Dewey's (1933, 1938) observation that reflective thinking is called for when people recognize that some problems cannot be solved with certainty. In other words, they require a certain kind of epistemic cognition, one that includes the recognition that real uncertainty exists about some issues.

We have described the development of reflective thinking by reference to seven distinct but developmentally related sets of assumptions about the process of knowing (view of knowledge) and how it is acquired (justification of beliefs). Each successive set of epistemological assumptions is characterized by a more complex and effective form of justification (King & Kitchener, 1994). For purposes of brevity, we have summarized the model into three major periods: the prereflective (Stages 1–3), the quasi-reflective (Stages 4 and 5), and the reflective (Stages 6 and 7).

Studies supporting the claims are summarized next. First, however, we present a brief description of the changing assumptions of three stages representing the prereflective, quasi-reflective, and reflective periods (King & Kitchener, 1994; Kitchener & King, 1981). They are illustrated by statements that were made in response to interview questions that were designed to elicit information about participants' epistemic assumptions. In these excerpts, "I" stands for interviewer; "R" stands for respondent.

Example of Prereflective Reasoning (Stage 2)

I: Can you ever know for sure that your position on this issue is correct?

R: Well, some people believe that we evolved from apes and that's the way they want to believe. But I would never believe that way and nobody could talk me out of the way I believe because I believe the way that it's told in the Bible.

I: In this case, then, is one view right and one point of view wrong?

R: Well, I think the evolved one is wrong. (King & Kitchener, 1994, p. 53)

People who hold epistemic assumptions related to prereflective thinking believe that knowledge is gained through the word of an authority figure or through firsthand observation, rather than, for example, through the evaluation of evidence. They believe that what they know is absolutely correct, and that they know with complete certainty. People who hold these assumptions treat all problems as though they were well-structured (defined completely and resolved with certainty).

Example of Quasi–Reflective Reasoning (Stage 4)

R: I'd be more inclined to believe it [evolution] if they had proof. It's just like the pyramids. I don't think we'll ever know. People will come up with different interpretations because people differ. Who are you going to ask? Because no one was there. (King & Kitchener, 1994, p. 60)

People who reason using the assumptions of quasi-reflective thinking recognize that knowledge—or more accurately, knowledge claims—contain elements of uncertainty, which they attribute to missing information or to methods of obtaining the evidence. Although they use evidence, they do not understand how evidence entails a conclusion (especially in light of the acknowledged uncertainty), and thus tend to view judgments as highly idiosyncratic.

Example of Reflective Reasoning (Stage 7)

I: Can you ever say you know for sure about this issue?

R: It [the view that the Egyptians build the pyramids] is very far along the continuum of what is probable.

I: Can you say that one point of view is right and one is wrong?

R: Right and wrong are not comfortable categories to assign to this kind of item. It's more or less likely or reasonable, more or less in keeping with what the facts seem to be. (King & Kitchener, 1994, p. 72)

People who reason using reflective thinking assumptions accept that knowledge claims cannot be made with certainty, but are not immobilized by it; rather, they make judgments that are "most reasonable" and about which they are "reasonably certain," based on their evaluation of the available data. They believe they must actively construct their decisions, and that knowledge claims must be evaluated in relationship to the context in which they were generated to determine their validity. They also readily admit their willingness to reevaluate the adequacy of their judgments as new data or new methodologies become available. This kind of critical thinking about ill-structured problems illustrates the kind of thinking that Dewey (1933) referred to as involving reflective judgment.

As these brief descriptions show, the way respondents defend their points of view about controversial issues is tied to their assumptions about knowledge, such as the certainty of knowledge claims (Kitchener & King, 1981). For example, those who stated that their beliefs were derived directly from the words of authority figures also believed that knowledge existed with absolute certainty. By contrast, those who stated that their beliefs were based on their own evaluation of the evidence also believed that their own perspectives affected the kind of evidence they valued and that absolute knowledge claims were suspect.

A brief summary of the seven stages of the Reflective Judgment (RJ) Model, including both of these elements (concept of justification and assumptions of knowledge) appears in Table 3.1. For a detailed presentation of the RJ model and many more examples, see King and Kitchener (1994).

Several factors led us to select and retain a stage model as the most useful framework for capturing our observations. These included the observed consistency between defining components of the model that reflect an underlying, organized structure (e.g., concept of justification and view of knowledge), the

TABLE 3.1

Summary of Reflective Judgment Stages

Pre-Reflective Thinking (Stages 1, 2, and 3)

Stage 1

View of knowledge: Knowledge is assumed to exist absolutely and concretely; it is not understood as an abstraction. It can be obtained with certainty by direct observation.

Concept of justification: Beliefs need no justification since there is assumed to be an absolute correspondence between what is believed to be true and what is true. Alternate beliefs are not perceived.

"I know what I have seen."

Stage 2

View of knowledge: Knowledge is assumed to be absolutely certain or certain but not immediately available. Knowledge can be obtained directly through the senses (as in direct observation) or via authority figures.

Concept of justification: Beliefs are unexamined and unjustified or justified by their correspondence with the beliefs of an authority figure (such as a teacher or parent). Most issues are assumed to have a right answer, so there is little or no conflict in making decisions about disputed issues.

"If it is on the news, it has to be true."

Stage 3

View of knowledge: Knowledge is assumed to be absolutely certain or temporarily uncertain. In areas of temporary uncertainty, only personal beliefs can be known until absolute knowledge is obtained. In areas of absolute certainty, knowledge is obtained from authorities.

Concept of justification: In areas in which certain answers exist, beliefs are justified by reference to authorities' views. In areas in which answers do not exist, beliefs are defended as personal opinion since the link between evidence and beliefs is unclear.

"When there is evidence that people can give to convince everybody one way or another, then it will be knowledge, until then, it's just a guess."

Quasi-Reflective Thinking (Stages 4 and 5)

Stage 4

View of knowledge: Knowledge is uncertain and knowledge claims are idiosyncratic to the individual since situational variables (such as incorrect reporting of data, data lost over time, or disparities in access to information) dictate that knowing always involves an element of ambiguity.

Concept of justification: Beliefs are justified by giving reasons and using evidence, but the arguments and choice of evidence are idiosyncratic (for example, choosing evidence that fits an established belief).

"I'd be more inclined to believe evolution if they had proof. It's just like the pyramids: I don't think we'll ever know. Who are you going to ask? No one was there."

(Continued)

TABLE 3.1
(Continued)

Stage 5

View of knowledge: Knowledge is contextual and subjective since it is filtered through a person's perceptions and criteria for judgment. Only interpretations of evidence, events, or issues may be known.

Concept of justification: Beliefs are justified within a particular context by means of the rules of inquiry for that context and by the context-specific interpretations as evidence. Specific beliefs are assumed to be context specific or are balanced against other interpretations, which complicates (and sometimes delays) conclusions.

> *"People think differently and so they attaack the problem differently. Other theories could be as true as my own, but based on different evidence."*

Refective Thinking (Stages 6 and 7)

Stage 6

View of knowledge: Knowledge is constructed into individual conclusions about ill-structured problems on the basis of information from a variety of sources. Interpretations that are based on evaluations of evidence across contexts and on the evaluated opinions of reputable others can be known.

Concept of justification: Beliefs are justified by comparing evidence and opinion from different perspectives on an issue or across different contexts and by constructing solutions that are evaluated by criteria such as the weight of the evidence, the utility of the solution, or the pragmatic need for action.

> *"It's very difficult in this life to be sure. There are degrees of sureness. You come to a point at which you are sure enough for a personal stance on the issue."*

Stage 7

View of knowledge: Knowledge is the outcome of a process of reasonable inquiry in which solutions to ill-structured problems are constructed. The adequacy of those solutions is evaluated in terms of what is most reasonable or probable according to the current evidence, and it is reevaluated when relevant new evidence, perspectives, or tools of inquiry become available.

Concept of justification: Beliefs are justified probabilistically on the basis of a variety of interpretive considerations, such as the weight of the evidence, the explanatory value of the interpretations, the risk of erroneous conclusions, consequences of alternative judgments, and the interrelationships of these factors. Conclusions are defended as representing the most complete, plausible, or compelling understanding of an issue on the basis of the available evidence.

> *"One can judge an argument by how well thought-out the positions are, what kinds of reasoning and evidence are used to support it, and how consistent the way one argues on this topic is as compared with other topics."*

qualitative differences between the seven sets of assumptions, and the documented sequential changes in the emergence of epistemic assumptions. Furthermore, when the RJ model was juxtaposed with Fischer's (1980; Fischer & Pipp, 1984) cognitive skill theory model of the development of complex reasoning, additional evidence supporting stagelike development emerged. Comparing the two models revealed a striking degree of correspondence between the representational and abstract levels of Fischer's model and the underlying structure of the RJ stages (Kitchener & Fischer, 1990). For an extended discussion of the meaning of stages in the Reflective Judgment Model and how complex stage models differ from simple stage models, see King and Kitchener, 1994.

This description of a major aspect of the development of reasoning from adolescence to adulthood has provided researchers in many fields of study—from developmental psychology to educational psychology to student affairs in higher education to college outcomes assessment—with a conceptual frame of reference in which to ground their work. The Reflective Judgment Model is distinguished by its extensive database that includes both longitudinal and cross-sectional research that has been conducted over the last 20 years. It has been used extensively in studies of the development of critical or reflective thinking skills and related constructs in young adults and adults, especially college students. In their massive review of twenty years of educational research on collegiate outcomes, Pascarella and Terenzini (1991) referred to this collection of studies by concluding that the RJ model was ". . . the best known and most extensively studied" (p. 123) model of adult cognitive development. We next provide a summary of this body of research.

RESEARCH ON THE REFLECTIVE JUDGMENT MODEL

Most of the studies conducted through the early 1990s on the Reflective Judgment model are reported in detail in *Developing Reflective Judgment* (King & Kitchener, 1994), a major compendium of theory and research on this model. The centerpiece of this book is its review of research based on the responses of over 1,700 participants who completed the Reflective Judgment Interview (RJI) and the results of a 10-year longitudinal study of three different cohorts. Since the publication of that volume, Wood (1997) has completed a comprehensive secondary analysis of all available RJI data, and several additional studies have been completed. This review summarizes major results from this book, and updates it with reference to more recent studies.

To date, most RJ research has used the RJI, a one-hour, semistructured discussion of four ill-structured problems. In addition to the standard problems, problems in specific disciplines (e.g., business, chemistry, psychology) or about specific issues (e.g., sexual orientation) have also been successfully used to assess RJ. (See King & Kitchener, 1994, Resource A, pp. 259–265 for details.)

Standardized probe questions are posed to the respondent by a trained interviewer, who asks follow-up questions to clarify and focus a response. Each question is designed to elicit information about a particular concept of the RJ model. Trained raters evaluate the transcribed responses for their consistency with the Reflective Judgment Scoring Rules (Kitchener & King, 1985). For an extensive review of the psychometric properties of the RJI, see Wood (1997).

Although the vast majority of the research reported next has used the RJI for assessment purposes, we have been engaged in an ongoing effort to develop an objectively scored measure (Kitchener, King, Wood, & Lynch, 1994; Wood, Kitchener, Jensen, chap. 14, this volume). A few studies were completed in the early 1990s using the Reflective Thinking Appraisal (RTA); this instrument was replaced in 1996 by the Reasoning about Current Issues Test (RCI). Over 5,000 individuals have now completed the RCI. A description of the format, scoring, and findings to date on the RCI appears elsewhere in this volume (Wood, Kitchener, & Jensen, chap. 14, this volume).

The research summary that follows is divided into five sections. The first two examine whether the ability to make reflective judgments develops over time, which is a key attribute of a developmental model. The first of these also addresses the question of whether RJ stages form a developmental sequence using the most stringent test based on longitudinal data; the second section uses cross-sectional data to examine differences by age-educational levels. Third, we turn to studies that have compared RJ with other constructs in the intellectual domain; this is followed by a comparison with personality constructs. Last, we summarize the educational implications that have been suggested.

Do Reflective Judgment Stages Form a Developmental Sequence?

Validating a model of adolescent and adult cognitive development requires evidence that the stages in the model form a developmental sequence. While this can be inferred from cross-sectional data, longitudinal data are required to assess changes in individuals' reasoning over time. Such data also allow for a stricter test of the impact of educational experiences, which is of particular interest to educators seeking to teach students to reason more reflectively and to evaluators seeking to document the effectiveness of educational programs. Unfortunately, as Brabeck (1984) pointed out, this key piece of evidence is lacking for many cognitive developmental models.

The major longitudinal study of reflective judgment (Kitchener & King, 1981; King, Kitchener, Davison, Parker, & Wood, 1983; Kitchener, King, Wood, & Davison, 1989; Kitchener & King, 1990a; King & Kitchener, 1994) took place over ten years, with testings in 1977, 1979, 1983, and 1987. In addition, six other longitudinal studies ranging in duration from three months to four years have been conducted by other researchers. (See King & Kitchener, 1994, and Wood, 1997 for detailed reviews.) Since this study begun by Kitchener & King (1981) had the most testing times, largest sample, and was of the longest duration, it is summarized in more detail.

The original sample consisted of three age-educational level groups, twenty 16-year-old high school juniors, forty 21-year-old college juniors, and twenty third-year doctoral students with an average age of 28. The younger two groups were matched to the doctoral group on gender (half male, half female) and academic aptitude; the latter was included as a check against the possibility that obtained differences in RJ could be attributed to scholastic aptitude. Participation in subsequent retests was 74% in 1979, 69% in 1983, and 66% in 1987. Over this period of time, many participants remained engaged in educational pursuits and completed advanced degrees.

King, Kitchener, and Wood (1994) reported individual mean and modal scores for each participant at each time of testing. A pervasive pattern of upward change was observed: The RJI scores of virtually all participants (92%) increased between 1977 and 1987; between each testing interval, scores increased or remained stable for over two-thirds of the sample. Further, the upward changes in RJI scores generally followed the sequence of stages described in the model, with higher-stage usage following lower-stage usage. For example, using modal scores to yield dominant (modal) and subdominant (second most-frequently assigned) stage scores yielded scores that were almost always at adjacent stages. One participant's pattern is as follows, ordered by time of testing: 2(3), 4(3), 4(5) and 5(4), showing the slow, steady, and ordered emergence of reflective thinking over time. Few examples of stage skipping or regressions were observed.

Variability of stage reasoning (that is, evidence of reasoning that is characteristic of more than one stage at a time) was the norm in these scores. This mixture of scores led King, Kitchener, and Wood (1994) to characterize development as:

> . . . waves across a mixture of stages, where the peak of a wave is the most commonly used set of assumptions. While there is still an observable pattern to the movement between stages, this developmental movement is better described as the changing shape of the wave rather than as a pattern of uniform steps interspersed with plateaus. (p. 140)

Further, they found that the shape of the wave was different across stages. For example, for those whose modal score was Stage 2, 70% of the assigned ratings were Stage 2, for Stage 3, this proportion fell to two-thirds, and for Stage 5, only 50% of the ratings were at Stage 5. The curve of the wave was flatter for this stage than any other, as the remainder of the scores indicated reasoning characteristics of Stages 3, 4, 6, and 7. (For a summary of stage utilization based on all available studies, see Wood, 1997.) This pattern is consistent with the complex stage theory proposed by Rest (1979), and provides further evidence that characterizing individuals as being "in" or "at" a single stage is clearly erroneous and should be avoided.

Findings from the other longitudinal studies (Brabeck & Wood, 1990; Sakalys, 1984; Schmidt, 1985; Van Tine, 1990; Welfel & Davison, 1986) provide additional evidence of the slow, steady pace of this aspect of development. In every sample tested, changes over time reflected stability and development rather than regression to less complex stages of reflective thinking characterized by more absolutistic epistemic assumptions. Not surprisingly, the amount of change was proportional to the amount of time between testings. Significant increases over time were found in studies of at least a year's duration.

Educational Level Differences in Reflective Judgment

Another way of examining the question of whether epistemic cognition as measured by the reflective judgment model develops over time is to examine educational level differences. Since teaching critical reasoning skills (e.g., acquisition, analysis, and utilization of knowledge) is a common educational goal, improvements in reflective thinking across educational levels would be expected, and lack of progress would be problematic. Cross-sectional data can also be used to examine this question. King, Kitchener, and Wood (1994) reviewed a collection of studies in which the RJI was administered to about 1,500 students who ranged in age from the teenage years to middle adulthood, who were in high school through advanced doctoral programs, and who were at schools and colleges across the United States. The following data are from this chapter unless noted otherwise.

The high school students ($n = 172$, 11 samples, 5 studies) consistently evidenced prereflective thinking, such as believing knowledge was certain, making decisions about the problems presented based on what they "want to believe" or "what felt right." The average RJI score for this group was 3.2.

By contrast, traditional-age college students ($n = 966$, 44 samples, 20 studies) evidenced the use of Stage 3 and 4 assumptions, with the average mean score increasing from 3.6 to 4.0 between freshman and senior classes; the overall mean score was 3.8. A similar pattern of scores was found for samples of adult learners ($n = 137$, 9 samples, 5 studies). While the numerical difference between freshmen and seniors is small (about a half-stage), the shift to Stage 4 reasoning is noteworthy because it signifies the use of a qualitatively different set of epistemic assumptions. Specifically, Stage 4 reasoning reflects the acknowledgment that uncertainty is a natural part of the knowing process, and that evidence should play an important role in decision making. Indeed, with Stage 4 comes the cognitive capacity to recognize the existence and basis of ill-structured problems. So while Stage 4 reasoning does not reflect the sophistication of reasoning that is commonly expected of college students, it does represent an essential step forward toward this goal. Furthermore, while the numeric difference between freshmen and seniors is not large, it is an increase of about one standard deviation; this fairly large effect size has been consistent across studies.

To examine the role that different kinds of educational environments play in the development of reflective judgment, Dale (1995) assessed RJ levels of male students and faculty at a conservative Christian college for clergy. Although freshmen scored lower (3.65) than seniors (4.0), these class differences were not significant. She also found that students scored significantly lower on a problem focusing in the issue of creation and evolution than they did on the chemical additives to foods problem, suggesting that this educational environment might not be conducive to the development of RJ in some areas. Furthermore, the greater students' tendency to believe in God's revealed knowledge, the lower their scores on the creation-evolution problem. Interestingly, although the faculty scored significantly higher than the undergraduates, there was considerable variability in the faculty scores, with some scoring at the quasi-reflective level.

Graduate students have consistently earned the highest RJI scores: mean scores for early level graduate students tended to fall at Stages 4 and 5, and scores for advanced level graduate students clustered between Stages 5 and 6. The average RJI score for all graduate students was 4.76 ($n = 196$, 12 samples, 7 studies). It is noteworthy that the consistent use of Stage 5 reasoning (e.g., acknowledging the basis for different perspectives on a controversial issue) was first observed among graduate students, and Stage 6 reasoning has only been consistently observed among advanced doctoral students. A similar pattern of higher RJI scores has also been found for nonstudent adults with advanced degrees.

Two studies completed since 1994 have examined the effects of discipline on RJI scores. DeBord (1993) examined the differences between the RJ scores of undergraduate and graduate students in psychology on two traditional RJI dilemmas and two that addressed topics in psychology (the causes of alcoholism and depression). He found educational level differences as well as dilemma differences in the graduate students' scores, but not in the undergraduates' scores. Graduate students scored significantly higher on the psychology problems than they did on the traditional problems, which is consistent with data reported by King, Wood, and Mines (1990). This suggests that intense study in a discipline may provide the leading edge for the development of more complex epistemic cognition and true reflective thinking.

Friedman (1995) compared the RJI scores of 14 seniors, 15 master's level students, and 14 doctoral students who intended to pursue careers in education. She found a consistent pattern of upward scores across educational levels. Differences were significant between seniors and doctoral students, but not between the other groups. (Scores are not reported here since Wood [1997] found some discrepancies in the original scores. However, the pattern and significance of scores remained the same.) She then compared the scores of students who had completed undergraduate majors in education and in the humanities, and found that those with humanities majors scored significantly higher. However, since academic aptitude was not controlled in this study, it may have also contributed to this difference.

Wood (1997) reported that differences by area of study were greater for graduate students in different disciplines than they were for undergraduate samples: students at lower collegiate levels were more consistent in their RJ scores across domains than were those who were more highly educated. He cautioned readers that the results may be an artifact of the topics used on the RJI. These findings are consistent with DeBord's (1993) study regarding the role that intense study in a discipline may play in the development of advanced levels of epistemic cognition (i.e., Stages 6 and 7 in the RJ model). They offer support for the idea that there may be a relationship between domain-specific epistemological assumptions and more generalized assumptions, as suggested by Sternberg (1989) and by Hofer and Pintrich (1997). Reflective thinking (Stages 6 and 7) may first develop in a domain in which individuals are more familiar with the complexity of the issues and then be generalized to other related domains.

While the mean scores differ across samples and institutions, a clear upward trend in RJ scores over age and educational levels has been documented across baccalaureate degree institutions of higher education in the United States. Entry-level college students hold assumptions more like those described in the earlier stages of the model, while students who are farther along in their collegiate studies hold assumptions consistent with the more advanced stages of Reflective Judgment. Since collegiate environments focus on the acquisition, interpretation, and utilization of knowledge, it is both predictable and reassuring that such differences have been found. It should also be noted that because of differences in sampling procedures across these studies, specific predictions of students' reasoning based solely on their educational levels is problematic and is not recommended. Wood's (1997) finding of considerable variability in RJI scores within educational levels both within and across institutions emphasizes this point. Wood also pointed out that when sample size is small (as is often the case when assessment requires individual interviews), having adequate statistical power to find significant differences between educational levels is problematic. Wood and Conner (1999) have estimated the sample size needed to detect differences in RJ; we recommend that researchers consider their advice on this question before using small samples.

Are There Differences in Reflective Judgment by Gender and Ethnicity?

This section summarizes RJ studies that have examined differences by gender and ethnicity. Questions about gender differences are often raised in an attempt to ascertain bias in psychological models (Brabeck, 1983, 1993; Mednick, 1989). In light of this interest, King and Kitchener (1994) reported that 14 cross-sectional studies had examined gender differences in reflective thinking. Half of these studies reported no differences; the pattern of the other seven studies was mixed, and while these differences appeared to be sample-specific, we more often favored men. At the fourth testing, a gender difference was observed (males scored higher), along with a gender by educational level interaction. However, since we also observed that many more males than females had obtained graduate degrees, we suggested that the gender differences may be accounted for by educational level differences. More recent studies (Jensen, 1998; Guthrie, King,

& Palmer, 1999) found no differences by gender, and females in Thompson's (1995) studies scored higher than males. As a result of the patterns of gender differences over time reported by King, Kitchener, and Wood (1994), we would also like to caution readers that samples differ on many variables beyond gender (such as ability and educational level), and suggest that these should be examined when interpreting gender differences.

A provocative pattern of gender differences was discerned by Wood (1993), who found gender differences in growth spurts between the late teens and early adulthood. Females showed dramatic growth in RJI scores in their late teens; males' growth spurts occurred several years later when they were completing their college degrees and enrolling for post-baccalaureate degrees. We encourage researchers to investigate this finding more systematically to see if it is evident in other samples, and if so, how the timing of developmental growth spurts affects growth in RJI scores.

Brabeck and Larned (1996) suggested that three questions must be asked pertaining to claims of gender differences and how such claims are studied:

Is there a difference between men and women's ways of knowing? Only if the first question is affirmative must one address the second: What is the basis, the source, or the factors responsible for the observed differences? Finally, when one understands the origin of the observed difference, one can and must address the "so what?" question: What are the educational, occupational, and social implications of an observed difference? (p. 267)

They go on to argue that there is insufficient evidence for claims of a separate epistemology for women, a "women's way of knowing." Data on the Reflective Judgment Model supports their conclusion.

A second set of issues regarding the generalizability of any model involves its applicability to groups other than the ones on which it was initially developed. Since the RJ model was based on data drawn primarily from Euro-Americans, it has been important to ask whether development in epistemic cognition is similar for other ethnic groups. King and Taylor (1992) found that African American seniors scored significantly higher than freshmen and juniors and that RJI scores were found to predict college grade point average and college graduation. Samson (1999) recently found that Latino college seniors of Central American, South American, Puerto Rican and Cuban ancestry scored higher than freshmen and did not differ significantly from the general samples reported in King and Kitchener (1994) on the total RJI score. Findings from these two studies are consistent with findings from recent research using the RCI, which found that gains in RJ were similar for Euro-American and African American college students (Kitchener, Wood, & Jensen, 1999).

In summary, consistent upward changes in epistemic cognition have been found across educational levels; these differences are not only significant, but have yielded a large effect size. Future research on the model should focus on questions that examine the factors associated with the observed growth, lack of growth, and insufficient growth among individuals and selected samples over time. In particular, what aspects of students' educational experiences (e.g., curricular or pedagogical emphases) promote more complex epistemic cognition? What other kinds of life experiences outside formal educational settings help individuals learn to make reflective judgments? Can we more precisely describe the within-stage developmental processes? In addition, the disparity in the research on gender differences needs to be pursued, particularly Wood's (1993) observation that the timing of growth spurts may differ for men and women. Furthermore, additional study is needed about the development of RJ among ethnic minority groups, and whether cultural values and practices affect the development of epistemic cognition. The question of statistical power needs to be considered when addressing all of these issues.

The Relationship of Reflective Judgment to Other Constructs in the Intellectual Domain

The RJ model does not claim to describe all aspects of intellectual development in adulthood. However, any construct in the intellectual domain must be differentiated from other constructs that are better established, such as intelligence. Given the general domain similarities with reflective thinking, it is particularly important to differentiate RJ from constructs like verbal ability, scholastic aptitude, formal operations, and traditional measures of critical thinking (King & Kitchener, 1994). Prior studies have shown that RJ is related to but not the same as academic aptitude, verbal ability, formal operations, or traditional measures of critical thinking. More specifically, RJ should be differentiated from these constructs since it involves ill-structured problem solving, while these other four constructs are typically assessed in relationship to well-structured problems. Furthermore, it appears that there may be a necessary but not sufficient relationship between well-structured problem solving and reflective judgment and that the skills necessary for solving ill-structured problems are not equivalent to the logical skills used when solving well-structured problems. (Since these studies on which these comments are based are reviewed in detail in King and Kitchener [1994], only more recent studies are summarized individually here.) Similarly, it is important for newer models of personal epistemology to be clearly differentiated from more standard models. If all are measuring the same construct, then there is little justification for the proliferation of assessment methods and models.

Several researchers have begun to address this latter question (see Wood & Kardash, chap. 12, this volume). Scott (1994) examined patterns of justification, specifically in reference to Stage 4 reasoning, asking whether observed differences in Stage 4 reasoning could be explained by other models of personal epistemology. One of the defining characteristics of Stage 4 is the acknowledgment of uncertainty (for an explication, see Dove, 1990). Scott (1994) observed that two patterns of justification about questions of uncertainty in knowing could be identified in the Reflective Judgment Scoring Rules (Kitchener & King, 1985). In one pattern, individuals held their points of view strongly, but were somewhat defensive about examining those beliefs. In the second pattern, they were very open to new input from many sources, easily swayed by this input, and did not hold their views as strongly. Scott hypothesized that this difference might reflect Belenky, Clinchy, Goldberger, and Tarule's (1986) observations about gender differences in separate and connected styles of knowing. For example, using personal experience or beliefs to justify one's stance on an issue would be consistent with a connected knowing approach and using facts or other evidence to justify one's views would be consistent with a separate knowing approach. A finding of within-stage differences in reasoning styles at Stage 4 would be consistent with Baxter Magolda's (1992) findings of interindividual and individual patterns within her Independent Knowing style.

Scott (1994) examined 60 RJI transcripts that had been previously rated by two certified RJI raters as evidencing predominantly Stage 4 reasoning (thereby controlling for assumptions about knowledge). Half of the transcripts discussed the chemicals in foods problem, and half discussed the Egyptian pyramids problem. These transcripts were then re-rated by two new raters based on categories of separate and connected knowing. Scott found that both separate and connected knowing could be reliably discerned within these Stage 4 transcripts: interrater reliability was .90. These patterns were not, however, related to gender, as claimed by Belenky, et al. (1986): About two-thirds of both males and females used separate knowing styles and about one-third used connected knowing styles. However, like Baxter Magolda (1992), Scott found that many participants used both styles. No differences were found by problem. Scott concluded, however, that educational interventions designed to promote development should consider the difference between these styles of knowing within Stage 4.

Brabeck, Simi, and King (1996) examined whether the Belenky et al. (1986) model of "women's ways of knowing" matched the developmental stages of the Reflective Judgment model. A sample of undergraduate and graduate female students completed both the RJI and the Belenky et al. Interview Schedule, which were scored according to both sets of scoring rules. Raters were blind to the participants' educational level, gender, and to their scores on the other model. A consistent pattern of stage-related reasoning was found across age/educational levels. They concluded that overlap between the models may be found, but only to the extent that the Belenky et al. interview asks epistemic questions and scores for that category.

Another attribute in the intellectual domain is called "need for cognition," which is defined as the tendency "to engage in and enjoy effortful cognitive endeavors" (Cacioppo, Petty, Feinstein, & Jarvis, 1996, p. 197). Jensen (1998) investigated the relationship between Reflective Judgment and need for cognition in a sample of 81 students who ranged from undergraduate freshmen to advanced graduate students. She reasoned that higher Reflective Judgment scores might be explained by the fact that some people are simply more disposed toward thinking seriously about ideas and that educational level differences in Reflective Judgment exist because those high in need for cognition have a tendency to enroll in school longer. Because the RJI involves an interaction between two people, she also investigated the role of social desirability in RJ scores. Although she found significant correlations between RJ and both need for cognition ($r = .41$) and social desirability ($r = -.43$), these variables did not account for educational level differences in RJ scores, either in combination with each other or with age and verbal ability. However, her findings do suggest that a disposition toward engaging in intellectual endeavors may play a role in developing more advanced epistemic assumptions. This supposition is supported by Friedman's (1995) finding that the Intellectual Disposition Scales on the Omnibus Personality Inventory correlated positively and significantly with RJ scores ($r = .39$). These scales assess a person's disposition for reflective thought and developing knowledge through inquiry.

Of all the issues facing researchers in the area of personal epistemology, empirically differentiating their models from each other and from other constructs in the intellectual domain is critical. As we have noted elsewhere (Kitchener & King, 1990a), if we are simply finding a new vocabulary to discuss long-standing constructs like crystallized intelligence and the need for cognition, then complex and expensive measurement tools like the RJI are hard to justify when more efficient measures exist. Similarly, it is important to empirically test claims about differences in models of personal epistemology to further clarify the constructs.

The Relationship of Reflective Judgment to Personality Constructs

This section summarizes studies that relate Reflective Judgment to a variety of other attributes. The specific attributes discussed here include moral development, psychosocial development, and other personality variables.

Like the complex intellectual problems that adults encounter, the personal and moral problems they face are also ill-structured, and call for informed, thoughtful choices. Given these similarities, several studies have examined the relationship between reasoning in the intellectual and moral domains, that is, between individuals' epistemic assumptions and their assumptions about what is right, fair, and good. This relationship is of special interest to college educators, as the development of both reflective thinking and character are desired outcomes of higher education.

Moral judgment, as measured by Rest's (1979, 1986) Defining Issues Test (DIT) was used to measure moral reasoning in the 10-year longitudinal study of Reflective Judgment described earlier. The RJI and DIT scores correlated moderately (between .46 and .58) at all four testings (King, Kitchener, Wood, & Davison, 1989; King, Kitchener, & Wood, 1991). A significant time main effect on the DIT was attributed to increases in moral judgment scores between Times 1 and

2. However, when RJI scores were statistically removed, the time effect was not significant for the DIT scores (King & Kitchener, 1994).

Guthrie, King, and Palmer (1999) investigated the relationship between Reflective Judgment and tolerance for diversity, an attribute that is often associated with morality and fairness. Tolerance was measured using combined scores from two instruments, the New Racism Scale (Jacobson, 1985) and Heterosexuals' Attitudes Toward Lesbians and Gay Men Scale (Herek, 1988). They found moderate, positive correlations ($r = .45, .56, .58$) between tolerance and three measures of reflective judgment, RTA-chemicals, RTA-homosexuality, and RJI-homosexuality, respectively. (The sexual orientation problems were designed for this study to tap a tolerance-related issue.) Scores on the RJI dilemma on homosexuality correlated most highly with tolerance, accounting for 33% of the variance in tolerance scores using a linear regression, and 44% of the variance using a nonlinear binomial regression equation. There was a strong propensity for participants in this study who reasoned at quasi- and reflective thinking levels to hold tolerant viewpoints in the areas of race and sexual orientation.

To our knowledge, no studies have been completed since 1994 on the relationship between RJ and identity development. Prior studies found very low, nonsignificant correlations between RJ and Loevinger and Wessler's (1970) measure of ego development (King & Kitchener, 1994). However, when Glatfelter (1982) investigated the relationship between Marcia's (1967) identity statuses and RJI scores, she found that those in identity-achieved status had the highest RJI scores, and those in moratorium, foreclosed, and diffused categories had successively lower RJI scores. Polkosnik and Winston (1989) found low to moderate correlations between RJ and three other aspects of identity development, developing autonomy, purpose, and mature interpersonal relationships (Chickering, 1969).

A more recent study of the relationship between reflective judgment and two other personality variables, affect-tolerance and stressful affect, was conducted by Kozak, (1996), who used the RTA as a measure of Reflective Judgment. Using an experimental design, he divided 100 college students into two groups based on their RJ score; the average RJ score of the low RJ group was 4.23 and the average score of the high RJ group was 4.98. Stressful affect was induced in half of each group. Kozak found that those with higher RJ scores reported more feelings, physical sensations, and intrusions of thought, and also used more avoidance actions to control the intrusions. He concluded that those higher in RJ can access their feelings in the process of decision making, but aren't ruled by their feelings. The greater access to affect was not related to psychological maladaptations.

Research on the relationship between the development of epistemic cognition and personality constructs is in its infancy. What exists suggests the relationship may be important to understanding constructs like tolerance, moral development, and the relationship between affect, tolerance, and stress. However, there is a danger in drawing firm conclusions about such important issues on single, unreplicated findings. Additional longitudinal studies are needed to examine the complex interrelationships between development of epistemic cognition, identity, and constructs in the moral domain. Further examination of possible causal relationships between the recognition and acceptance of uncertainty and tolerance as well as the emotional ability to deal with intense stress is also needed. New lines of research should more explicitly examine Kegan's (1994) claims that adults trying to cope with the mental demands of modern life often find ourselves "in over our heads" when our mental capacities do not match the complexities of the challenges we face. He emphasized the connections between interpersonal, intrapersonal, and cognitive dimensions, which provides another fruitful area for research on epistemic cognition as well. Baxter Magolda's analysis of her longitudinal interviews with adults (2001; this volume, chap. 5) offers rich and insightful examples of the links between these dimensions.

Taken together, the body of evidence summarized here strongly supports the claim that epistemic cognition as described by the RJ model develops during adolescence and adulthood. Studies relating RJ to other aspects of intellectual development as well as to other personality variables have shown that it is related to but distinct from these other constructs. Neither personality variables researched to date nor development in other areas account for the development of epistemic cognition as conceptualized by the RJ model.

EDUCATIONAL IMPLICATIONS

Finding ways of improving students' reasoning is of great interest to educators, policy makers, and state legislators, among others; all have a vested interest in having adults be able to make informed decisions in their personal lives, in the workplace, and in their communities. However, as noted previously, the reasoning of many college seniors is characteristic of RJ Stage 4. Although individuals who reason at this level acknowledge elements of uncertainty, their arguments are not consistently based on evidence. Furthermore, data reported earlier suggest that many college-educated adults do not fully acknowledge uncertainty as part of the knowing process, and thus may look to authorities for firm, unqualified answers. This suggests that there is not only room for improvement, but that there is an urgent need to address this situation.

Several authors have addressed concerns like these by identifying instructional strategies that can be used to promote the development of epistemic cognition (King, 1992; King & Baxter Magolda, 1996; Kitchener & King, 1990b; Davison, King, & Kitchener, 1990; King & Wood, 1999; Kitchener, Lynch, Fischer, & Wood, 1993; Kroll, 1992a,b; Kronholm, 1993; Lynch, 1996; Lynch, Kitchener, & King, 1994; Thompson, 1995; Wood & Lynch, 1998). Although an extended review of these projects is beyond the scope of this chapter, we list them here to encourage those interested in educational applications to consult the primary sources. The most comprehensive of these projects have been undertaken by Kroll (1992b), Kronholm (1996), and Lynch, Kitchener, and King (1994).

The theoretical foundation underlying each of these projects is grounded in two major assumptions, that students' understanding of the nature, limits, and certainty of knowledge affects how they approach the process of learning, and that their epistemic assumptions change over time in a developmentally related fashion. A third (but less explicit) assumption is that learners' epistemic assumptions are tied to their sense of self (Baxter Magolda, 1999; Kegan, 1994; King & Baxter Magolda, 1996; Palmer, 1998). Common suggestions in the projects referenced here include the following.

1. Show respect for students' assumptions, regardless of the developmental stage(s) they exhibit. Their assumptions are genuine, sincere reflections of their ways of making meaning, and are steps in a developmental progression. If students perceive disrespect or lack of emotional support, they may be less willing to engage in challenging discussions or to take the intellectual and personal risks required for development.
2. Discuss controversial, ill-structured issues with students throughout their educational activities, and make available resources that show the factual basis and lines of reasoning for several perspectives.
3. Create many opportunities for students to analyze others' points of view for their evidentiary adequacy and to develop and defend their own points of view about controversial issues.
4. Teach students strategies for systematically gathering data, assessing the relevance of the data, evaluating data sources, and making interpretive judgments based on the available data.
5. Give students frequent feedback, and provide both cognitive and emotional support for their efforts.
6. Help students explicitly address issues of uncertainty in judgment-making and to examine their assumptions about knowledge and how it is gained.
7. Encourage students to practice their reasoning skills in many settings, from their other classes to their practicum sites, student organizations, residence hall councils, and elsewhere, to gain practice and confidence applying their thinking skills.

As Wood (1997) suggested, it may also be important to show how ill-structured problems in one area are similar to those in other areas, and that the nature of reasoning across problems in different areas depends on similar epistemic assumptions.

These suggestions are designed to help educators teach students how to actively construct their own beliefs and knowledge claims about the world in which they live. They are inconsistent with the "I pitch, you catch" view of knowledge acquisition, which is ineffective for teaching students how to make reflective judgments because it fails to take into account their epistemic assumptions, their role in interpreting information, and the uncertainty in judgment-making.

CONCLUSION

Adults are asked to make decisions about many types of issues, in their jobs, in their communities, and in their personal lives. Many of these will be based on incomplete information or evidence that is subject to multiple interpretations (i.e., "ill-structured problems") but that nevertheless require a judgment. Studies reported here suggest such judgments are tied to the development of a kind of epistemic cognition that both allows for real uncertainty in knowing and in which evidence plays a strong role in drawing conclusions, however tentative. Furthermore, these data also suggest that such development is sequential, thus offering a "road map" for those interested in charting and influencing its development. The fact that increases are strongly related to educational level should be encouraging for educators and policy makers who have committed their energies and resources to improving students' reasoning and decision-making skills. Despite consistent evidence of growth in RJ over time and across educational levels, the developmental levels of college graduates probably will not be sufficient for the kinds of problems they will be asked to address in a myriad of adult roles.

However, it is also important to note in this regard that the data reported here may underestimate students' cognitive abilities. That is, most are based on a difficult production task, the RJI. This assessment approach places demands of high difficulty on students as they construct responses "de novo" and without practice or even much time to collect their thoughts. It also measures their typical level of functioning, that is, the skills they draw on in "everyday" functioning. Kitchener and Fischer (1990) differentiate this from respondents' optimal level of functioning, which is similar to the kind of peak performance they could produce under optimal conditions. Kitchener et al. (1993) describe optimal conditions as including contextual feedback and emotional support for their efforts. They demonstrated that offering contextual support provided a mechanism for students to reach beyond their typical modes and respond at higher developmental levels.

Recent research reported here has extended the study of epistemic cognition in some important new directions. For example, the research on underrepresented groups is particularly important. Although the development of epistemic cognition described by the RJ model appears to be applicable beyond samples of Euro-Americans, the research base on this question is small. In addition, the relationships between epistemic cognition and the development of tolerance for diversity and affect-tolerance suggest that its implications extend beyond the intellectual domain to affective issues as well; but again, researchers have only begun to explore these relationships.

Although recent research has been encouraging, many theoretical and applied questions remain. Theoretically, many questions about the internal coherence of the RJ model of epistemic cognition remain unanswered. For example, Dove (1990) independently examined scores on concepts of justification and assumptions about knowledge in the early stages of the RJ model, and found the predicted consistency across stages. However, the issue has not been independently explored in the later stages. Similarly, Scott's (1994) work suggests there may be stylistic differences in individuals' approaches to epistemic assumptions within levels. Furthermore, Wood's (1997) extensive secondary analysis and findings from De-Bord's (1993) study suggest there may be a context effect for some dilemmas for some individuals. Again, these data bear verifying and extending to other stages.

Future research should attempt to identify the kinds of experiences that are related to the development of advanced epistemic assumptions for students at different levels of epistemic development, and for majority as well as for ethnic minority students. Stylistic differences may also prove important and merit further exploration; however, these may not be as clearly gender-linked as some (Belenky et al. 1986) once claimed. Research on the importance of providing feedback and contextual support (Kitchener et al, 1993) suggests that this strategy may help students consolidate the reasoning skills they will need to more effectively address a myriad of adult issues.

Educators have become increasingly interested in the RJ model because of its implications for helping students improve their critical thinking skills and its relatively strong empirical base. Although we have offered some general suggestions about how to encourage the ability to think reflectively about ill-structured problems, it is important to remember that each developmental journey is the student's own journey, not the teacher's. And while some major changes in epistemic development may be observed across individuals, it is important to remember that each journey is idiosyncratic to the individual experiencing and helping create it, based on the sum of his or her prior experiences, personal attributes, future goals, and so on. Therefore any general approach based only on the major similarities will probably have minimal impact in promoting development. A more effective approach will not only allow for but also encourage students to build on their prior experiences in meaningful ways.

Whether the issues are theoretical or applied, whether the samples are college students or noncollege adults, and regardless of the settings (educational, social service, therapeutic, etc.), researchers in the areas of personal epistemology must conscientiously and thoroughly conduct the research that is essential to answering these questions. It is our hope that this body of research on the Reflective Judgment Model has laid a firm foundation for further exploration of the development of personal epistemology.

REFERENCES

Baxter Magolda, M. B. (2001). *Making their own way: Narratives to transform higher education to promote self-development.* Sterling, VA: Stylus Press.

Baxter Magolda, M. B. (this volume). Epistemological reflection: The evolution of epistemological assumptions from age 18 to 30. In B. Hofer and P. Pintrich (Eds.), *Personal epistomology: The psychology of beliefs about knowledge and knowing.* Mahwah, NJ: Lawrence Erlbaum Associates.

Baxter Magolda, M. B. (1999). *Creating contexts for learning and self-authorship: Constructive-developmental pedagogy.* Nashville, TN: Vanderbilt University Press.

Baxter Magolda, M. B. (1992). *Knowing and reasoning in college: Gender-related patterns in students' intellectual development.* San Francisco: Jossey-Bass.

Belenky, M. F., Clinchy, B. M., Goldberger, N. R. & Tarule, J. M. (1986). *Women's ways of knowing: The development of self, voice, and mind.* New York: Basic Books.

Brabeck, M. M. (1983). Moral judgment: Theory and research on differences between males and females. *Developmental Review, 3,* 274–291.

Brabeck, M. M. (1984). Longitudinal studies of intellectual development during adulthood: Theoretical and research models. *Journal of Research and Development in Education, 17* (3), 12–27.

Brabeck, M. M. (1993). Recommendations for re-examining *Women's Ways of Knowing*: A response to Handlin's interview with Belenky and Clinchy. *New Ideas in Psychology, 11* (2), 253–258.

Brabeck, M. M. & Larned, A. (1996). What we do not know about women's ways of knowing. In Mary Roth Walsh (Ed.), *Women, men, and gender: Ongoing debates.* Hartford, CT: Yale University Press.

Brabeck, M., Simi, N. L. & King, I. C. (1996, August). Are women's ways of knowing and reflective judgment the same? Presentation made at the Annual Meeting of the American Psychological Association, Toronto, Canada.

Brabeck, M. & Wood, P. K. (1990). Cross-sectional and longitudinal evidence for differences between well-structured and ill-structured problem solving abilities. In M. L. Commons, C. Armon, L. Kohlberg, F. A. Richards, T. A. Grotzer, and J. D. Sinnott (Eds.), *Adult development 2: Models and methods in the study of adolescent and adult thought.* New York: Praeger.

Cacioppo, J. T., Petty, R. E., Feinstein, J. A., & Jarvis, W. B. G. (1996). Dispositional differences in cognitive motivation: The life and time of individuals varying in need for cognition. *Psychological Bulletin, 119,* 197–253.

Chickering. A. (1969). *Education and identity.* San Francisco: Jossey-Bass.

Churchman, C. W. (1971). *The design of inquiring systems: Basic concepts of systems and organizations.* New York: Basic Books.

Dale, J. L. (1995). *Reflective Judgment in a conservative, Christian college for clergy education.* Unpublished doctoral dissertation, University of Denver.

Davison, M. L., King, P. M., & Kitchener, K. S. (1990). Developing reflective thinking and writing. In R. Beach and S. Hynds (Eds.), *Developing discourse practices in adolescence and adulthood.* Norwood, NJ: Ablex.

DeBord, K. (1993). *Promoting Reflective Judgment in counseling psychology graduate education.* Unpublished master's thesis. University of Missouri-Columbia.

Dewey, J. (1933). *How we think: A restatement of the relation of reflective thinking to the educative process.* Lexington, Massachusetts: Heath.

Dewey, J. (1938). *Logic: The theory of inquiry.* Troy, Missouri: Holt, Rinehart & Winston.

Dove, W. R. (1990). The identification of ill-structured problems by young adults (Doctoral dissertation, University of Denver, 1990). *Dissertation Abstracts International, 51/06B,* 3156.

Fischer, K. W. (1980). A theory of cognitive development: The control and construction of hierarchies of skills. *Psychological Review, 87,* 477–531.

Fischer, K. W. & Pipp, S. L. (1984). Processes of cognitive development: Optimal level and skill acquisition. In R. J. Sternberg (Ed.), *Mechanisms of cognitive development.* New York: Freeman.

Friedman, A. A. (1995*). The relationship between intellectual disposition and reflective judgment in college women.* Unpublished doctoral dissertation, Boston College.

Glatfelter, M. (1982). Identity development, intellectual development, and their relationship in reentry women students. *Dissertation Abstracts International, 43,* 3543A.

Guthrie, V. L., King, P. M., & Palmer, C. P. (1999*). Cognitive capabilities underlying tolerance for diversity among college students.* Manuscript submitted for publication.

Herek, G. M. (1988). Heterosexuals' attitudes toward lesbians and gay men: Correlates and gender differences. *Journal of Sex Research, 25,* 451–477.

Hofer, B. K. & Pintrich, P. R. (1997). The development of epistemological theories: Beliefs about knowledge and knowing and their relation to learning. *Review of Educational Research, 67,* 88–140.

Jensen, L. L. (1998*). The role of need for cognition in the development of reflective judgment.* Unpublished doctoral dissertation, University of Denver.

Jacobson, C. K. (1985). Resistance to affirmative action: Self-interest or racism. *Journal of Conflict Resolution, 29,* 306–329.

Kegan, R. (1994). *In over our heads: The mental demands of modern life.* Cambridge, Mass.: Harvard University Press.

King, P. M. (Ed.) (1992). Special issue on Reflective Judgment, *Journal of Liberal Education, 78,* Whole number 1.

King, P. M. & Baxter Magolda, M. B. (1996). A developmental perspective on learning. *Journal of College Student Development, 37,* 163–173.

King, P. M., Kitchener, K. S., Davison, M. L., Parker, C. A., & Wood, P. K. (1983). The justification of beliefs in young adults: A longitudinal study. *Human Development, 26,* 106–116.

King, P. M. & Kitchener, K. S. (1994). *Developing reflective judgment: Understanding and promoting intellectual growth and critical thinking in adolescents and adults.* San Francisco: Jossey-Bass.

King, P. M., Kitchener, K. S., & Wood, P. K. (1991). Moral and intellectual development beyond the college years: A ten-year study. Paper presented at the Annual Meeting of the Association for Moral Education. Athens, Georgia.

King, P. M., Kitchener, K. S. & Wood, P. K. (1994). Research on the reflective judgment model. In King, P. M. & Kitchener, K. S., *Developing reflective judgment: Understanding and promoting intellectual growth and critical thinking in adolescents and adults* (pp. 124–202) . San Francisco: Jossey-Bass.

King, P. M., Kitchener, K. S., Wood, P. K., & Davison, M. L. (1989). Relationships across developmental domains: A longitudinal study of intellectual, moral, and ego development. In M. L. Commons, J. D. Sinnott, F. A. Richards & C. Armon (Eds.), *Adult development: Vol. I: Comparisons and applications of developmental models* (pp. 57–72). New York: Praeger.

King, P. M., & Taylor, J. A. (1992). Intellectual development and academic integration of African American students at Bowling Green State University. [Adaptation of King, P. M., Taylor, J., & Ottinger, D. (1989), Intellectual development of Black college students on a predominantly White campus. Paper presented at the Annual Meeting of the Association for the Study of Higher Education, Atlanta, Georgia, 1989.]

King, P. M., Wood, P. K., & Mines, R. A. (1990). Critical thinking among college and graduate students. *The Review of Higher Education, 13* (3), 167–186.

King, P. M. & Wood, P. K. (1999). Teaching for reflective thinking: Why students may not be learning what we try to teach. Manuscript in preparation.

Kitchener, K. S. (1983). Cognition, metacognition and epistemic cognition: A three-level model of cognitive processing. *Human Development, 4,* 222–232.

Kitchener, K. S. & Fischer, K.W. (1990). A skill approach to the development of reflective thinking. In D. Kuhn (Ed.), *Contributions to human development: Developmental perspectives on teaching and learning, Vol. 21.* Basel, Switzerland: Karger.

Kitchener, K. S. & King, P. M. (1985). Reflective judgment scoring manual. (Available from K. S. Kitchener, School of Education, University of Denver, Denver, CO 80208 or P. M. King, School of Policy and Leadership Studies, Bowling Green State University, Bowling Green, OH 43403.)

Kitchener, K. S. & King, P. M. (1981). Reflective Judgment: Concepts of justification and their relationship to age and education. *Journal of Applied Developmental Psychology, 2,* 89–116.

Kitchener, K. S., & King, P. M. (1990a). The reflective judgment model: Ten years of research. In M. L. Commons, C. Armon, L. Kohlberg, F. A. Richards, T. A. Grotzer & J. Sinnott (Eds.), *Adult development: Models and methods in the study of adolescent and adult thought.* Volume 2, (pp. 63–78). New York: Praeger.

Kitchener, K. S. & King, P. M. (1990b). The reflective judgment model: Transforming assumptions about knowing. In J. Mesirow and Associates (Eds.), *Fostering critical reflection in adulthood: A guide to transformative and emancipatory learning* (pp. 157–176). San Francisco: Jossey-Bass.

Kitchener, K. S., King, P. M., Wood, P. K., & Davison, M. L. (1989). Sequentiality and consistency in the development of Reflective Judgment: A six-year longitudinal study. *Journal of Applied Developmental Psychology, 10*, 73–95.

Kitchener, K. S., King, P. M., Wood, P. K, & Lynch, C. L. (1994). "Assessing reflective thinking in curricular contexts." Technical Report of the Reflective Thinking Appraisal, Fund for the Improvement of Postsecondary Education, Application No. P116B00926.

Kitchener, K. S., Lynch, C. L., Fischer, K. W. & Wood, P. K. (1993). Developmental range of Reflective Judgment: The effect of contextual support and practice on developmental stage. *Developmental Psychology, 29*, 893–906.

Kitchener, K. S., Wood, P. K. & Jensen, L. (1999, August). *Curricular, co-curricular, and institutional influences on real-world problem solving.* Paper presented at the Annual Meeting of the American Psychological Association, Boston, Massachusetts.

Kozak, A. I. (1996). *Epistemological development and adaptation: Reflective judgment and stressful affect and their relationship to affect-tolerance and attribution of pragmatic structure.* Unpublished doctoral dissertation: The State University of New York at Buffalo.

Kroll, B. M. (1992a). Reflective inquiry in a college English class. *Liberal Education, 78*, 10–13.

Kroll, B. M. (1992b). *Teaching hearts and minds: College students reflect on the Vietnam War in literature.* Carbondale: Southern Illinois University Press.

Kronholm, M. M. (1993). The impact of developmental instruction on reflective judgment. *Review of Higher Education, 19* (2), 199–225.

Kuhn, D. (1999). A developmental model of critical thinking. *Educational Researcher, 28*, 16–25, 46.

Loevinger, J. & Wessler, R. (1970). *Measuring ego development. Volume 1: Construction and use of a Sentence Completion Test.* San Francisco: Jossey-Bass.

Lynch, C. L. (1996). Facilitating and assessing unstructured problem solving. *Journal of College Reading and Learning, 27* (2), 16–27.

Lynch, C. L., Kitchener, K. S., & King, P. M. (1994). *Developing reflective judgment in the classroom: A manual for faculty.* Report of FIPSE Project #P116B00926. Available from Cindy Lynch, HCR75, Box 91, New Concord, KY 42076.

Marcia, J. E. (1967). Ego identity status: Relationship to self-esteem, 'general maladjustment,' and authoritarianism. *Journal of Personality, 35*, 119–133.

Mednick, M. T. (1989). On the politics of psychological constructs: Stop the bandwagon, I want to get off. *American Psychologist, 44* (8), 1118–1123.

Palmer, P. J. (1998). *The courage to teach.* San Francisco: Jossey-Bass.

Pascarella, E. T. & Terenzini, P. T. (1991). *How college affects students.* San Francisco: Jossey-Bass.

Polkosnik, M. C., & Winston, R. B. (1989). Relationships between students' intellectual and psychological development: An exploratory investigation. *Journal of College Student Development, 30*, 10–19.

Rest, J. R. (1979). *Development in judging moral issues.* Minneapolis: University of Minnesota Press.

Rest, J. R. (1986). *Moral development: Advances in research and theory.* New York: Praeger.

Sakalys, J. (1984). Effects of an undergraduate research course on cognitive development. *Nursing Research, 33*, 290–295.

Samson, A. W. (1999). *Latino college students and reflective judgment.* Unpublished doctoral dissertation, University of Denver.

Schmidt, J. A. (1985). Older and wiser? A longitudinal study of the impact of college on intellectual development. *Journal of College Student Personnel, 26*, 388–394.

Scott, R. (1994). Separate and connected knowing within Reflective Judgment data. Unpublished master's thesis, University of Denver.

Sternberg, R. (1989). Domain generality vs. domain specificity: The life and impending death of a false dichotomy. *Merrill-Palmer Quarterly, 35*, 115–130.

Thompson, S. S. (1995). *Techniques for assessing general education outcomes: The natural sciences core at the University of Denver.* Unpublished doctoral dissertation, University of Denver.

Van Tine, N. B. (1990). The development of reflective judgment in adolescents. *Dissertations Abstracts International, 51*, 2659.

Welfel, E. R. & Davison, M. L. (1986). How students make judgments: Do educational level and academic major make a difference? *Journal of College Student Personnel, 23*, 490–497.

Wood, P. K. (1983). Inquiring systems and problem structure: Implications for cognitive development. *Human Development, 26*, 249–265.

Wood, P. K. (1993). *Generalized growth curve analysis for cross-sectional skill theory.* Unpublished manuscript, University of Minnesota.

Wood, P. K. (1997). A secondary analysis of claims regarding the Reflective Judgment Interview: Internal consistency, sequentiality, and intra–individual differences in ill-structured problem solving. In J. C. Smart (Ed.), *Higher Education: Handbook of Theory and Research*, volume. XII, 243–312. Edison, N.Y.: Agathon Press.

Wood, P. K. & Conner, J. (1999). Deciding how many participants to use in assessment research. *Assessment Update, 11*, (4), 8–9,11.

Wood, P. K. & Kardash, C. A. (in press). Critical elements in the design and analysis of critical thinking studies. In B. Hofer & P. Pintrich (Eds.), *Personal epistemology: The psychology of beliefs about knowledge and knowing.* Mahwah, NJ: Lawrence Erlbaum Associates.

Wood, P. K., Kitchener, K. S., & Jensen, L. (in press). Considerations in the design and evaluation of a paper-and-pencil measure of reflective thinking. In B. Hofer and P. Pintrich (Eds.), *Personal epistemology: The psychology of beliefs about knowledge and knowing.* Mahwah, NJ: Lawrence Erlbaum Associates.

Wood, P. K. & Lynch, C. L. (1998). Using guided essays to assess and encourage reflective thinking. *Assessment Update, 10* (2), 14–15.

4

Revisiting *Women's Ways of Knowing*

Blythe McVicker Clinchy
Wellesley College

When Mary Belenky, Nancy Goldberger, Jill Tarule, and I began the project that led eventually to our book on *Women's Ways of Knowing* (WWK, 1986/1997), we called it Education for Women's Development. We set out to interview women varying widely in age, ethnicity, and social class, women who had attended or were attending a variety of educational institutions ranging from small, selective liberal arts colleges to inner city community colleges, as well as several "invisible colleges," social agencies serving mothers of young children living in rural poverty. The question that guided our research continues to guide my research today. I like the way Mary Belenky words the question: "How come so many smart women feel so dumb?" Based on our own experiences in college and graduate school, and experiences recounted by our friends and our students, the four of us suspected that part of the answer might lie in the structure and practices of these educational institutions. Thus, we shared with earlier psychologists such as G. Stanley Hall a concern that higher education might be harmful to women's health. Hall worried that college might shrink women's wombs, rendering them infertile or "functionally castrated" (1917, p. 634); we worried that it might shrink their minds, or at least fail to expand them to their full potential.

In an attempt to explore the nature of the problem and to consider how institutions might be modified to better serve the needs and interests of women, we developed an extensive interview and administered it to 135 women, along with several standard developmental measures. The interview included sections dealing with self-concept, moral judgment, relationships, and educational experiences, as well as one ultimately labeled "ways of knowing." Although, like all of the contributors to this volume, we were familiar with William Perry's "scheme" tracing epistemological development in the college years (1970), and Nancy Goldberger (1981) and I (Clinchy & Zimmerman,1982; 1985) had used it in previous longitudinal research, epistemology was at first no more salient in our thinking than any other aspect of development. Gradually, however, as we coded responses to what we then called the "Perry part" of the interview and then reread the rest of each woman's interview in the light of the coding, we came to believe, as we say in the preface to the second edition of the book, "that the women's epistemological assumptions were central to their perceptions of themselves and their worlds," and so "epistemology became the organizing principle for our data analysis and for the book that we were beginning to imagine" (WWK, 1997, xviii).

In the book we describe five different perspectives from which women view the world of truth, knowledge, and authority. Perry's scheme provided the scaffolding we used in coding the women's responses, and the perspectives we present are deeply grounded in his "positions," although we emphasize slightly different aspects of epistemology. Perry's positions are defined mainly in terms of the nature of knowledge and truth (truth as absolute, for example, versus multiple), whereas we stress the women's relation to knowledge and truth, their conceptions of themselves as knowers. For instance, do they conceive of the source of knowledge as internal or external, and do they experience themselves as receiving or as creating truth? We listened, too, for deviations from Perry's scheme, for one would not expect the responses of women varying widely in age, class, and educational background to be identical to those of Perry's largely privileged and largely male undergraduate sample. Indeed, we found that while the general outline of Perry's scheme survived, many of the answers the women gave could not be wedged into it, and so, "In this instance, as in others, when the data the women provided diverged from the theories we had brought to the project, we forced ourselves to believe the women and let go of the theories" (WWK, 1997, pp. xii-xiv).

The book plunged us into a lively, wide-ranging conversation: It drew serious attention, often intensely critical, among scholars and researchers from a variety of disciplines, as well as moving testimonials from hundreds of "ordinary" women who saw parallels between their own stories and the stories in the book. I intend this chapter to be a contribution to this continuing conversation. I shall discuss some salient and controversial aspects of each of the perspectives we defined, drawing on the original text and also on research and theoretical speculations that have emerged in the years since its publication.

SILENCE

We named this, the least adequate perspective we could discern, "Silence," signi-fying the voicelessness of women at this position. Asked, "How do you feel about speaking?", Trish responds, "Um. I wonder if I'm using the right words. I can't do it anywhere." These women have difficulty hearing as well as speaking. As Belenky writes, they "see words more as weapons than as a means of passing meanings back and forth between people. They do not believe themselves capa-ble of understanding and remembering what the authorities or anyone else might say to them" (Belenky, 1996, p. 394). Lacking "the most basic tools for dialogue, the Silenced feel voiceless and excluded from the community" (Belenky, 1996, p. 394). They have been excluded, also, from theories of epistemological devel-opment, for these theories are based on words—oral or written accounts—produced mainly by people with considerable formal education. Silent women, feeling "incapable of articulating their own thoughts and feelings to others," (Be-lenky, 1996) make poor research subjects, and they rarely wend their way into in-stitutions of higher learning. All of the women who taught us about Silence came from the invisible colleges, not the visible ones, and most of them could describe the position only because, having moved somewhat beyond it, they could view it retrospectively. For example, Ann said:

> I could never understand what they were talking about. My schooling was very limited. I didn't learn anything. I would just sit there and let people ramble on about something I didn't understand, and I would say "Yup, yup." I would be too embarrassed to ask, "What do you really mean?" . . . I had trouble talking. If I tried to explain something and someone told me that it was wrong . . . I'd just fall apart. (WWK, p. 23)

In fact, the Silence perspective does not belong in accounts of epistemological "development." Silence grows out of a background of poverty, isolation, subordi-nation, rejection, and, often, violence. It is not a step in "normal" development but a failure to develop, "a position of not knowing" (Goldberger, 1996b, p. 4) im-posed by a society inattentive to the needs of its members.[1] It should not be seen, as some readers have interpreted it, as the first stage in a developmental sequence.

Still, since the publication of WWK, I have learned that the position, although "abnormal," may not be as rare as I once thought. A few years ago, while outlin-ing the WWK positions for a group of community college faculty, I remarked that we could skip quickly over "Silence" because such people were unlikely to ap-pear in their classes. A flurry of hands went up, and the participants proceeded to disabuse me of my assumption. The position was heavily represented, they said, among the many very poor people who had recently entered their colleges, mostly perforce, as a result of changes in welfare regulations.

---

[1] In this respect, Belenky's (1996) renaming of the position as Silenced seems appropriate.

Even highly educated articulate women, some of whom make a profession of speaking and writing, have testified to us in hundreds of letters that they resonate to the description of this perspective. Although they are by no means entrapped in (capital "S") Silence, they report that they frequently find themselves in situations in which they are (lowercase "s") silenced. Lewis and Simon offer a fascinating account of a graduate course taught by Simon in which Lewis and the other women students felt silenced by the males in the class. They quote an account by one student that is remarkably similar to Ann's:

> I don't understand what they [the men] are talking about. I feel like I'm not as well educated as them. I haven't done too much reading in this area. They know so much more than I. I just feel that if I said anything, they'd say, what is she doing in this class, she doesn't know anything, so I keep my mouth shut. (Lewis & Simon, 1986, p. 466)

As Simon says,

> Being muted is not just a matter of being unable to claim a space and time within which to enter a conversation. Being muted also occurs when one cannot discover forms of speech within conversation to express meanings and to find validation from others. (Lewis & Simon, 1986, p. 464)

The muting of the women in Simon's class was confined to a particular (although not uncommon) situation, and the women were able to devise strategies for eliminating it. The muting of the profoundly Silent women pervades their entire lives and is much less tractable, but it is not irreversible: The invisible colleges and programs like the "Learning Partners" project directed by Belenky and her colleagues (Belenky, 1996; Belenky, Bond, & Weinstock, 1998), have succeeded in providing settings in which Silent women can "express meanings and find validation from others."

RECEIVED KNOWING[2]

From this perspective, built on Perry's (1970) Dualism, truth is absolute and unambiguous. Received Knowers[3] believe that for every question there is a single, correct answer. They see the world in terms of black and white, right and wrong, true and false, good and bad; there is no room for ambiguity. "The stars twinkle for one reason," a student said. "That's why they do it. If something is proven, then there is no other way it could happen." Truth is external; it lies in the hands

---

[2]In WWK we call this position "Received Knowledge." All four of the coauthors now prefer the more active verbal form for each of the positions.

[3]For convenience, I refer to Received "Knowers" rather than "Knowing," but I do not mean to imply that a given individual always operates out of a single perspective.

of Authorities, and one is utterly dependent on Them to dispense it:[4] "How can you learn if the teacher isn't telling you?" In the course of a longitudinal study of epistemological development in young women, based on Perry's scheme, (Clinchy & Zimmerman, 1982; 1985), Claire Zimmerman and I asked Wellesley undergraduates, "Suppose two people disagree on the interpretation of a poem. How would you decide which one is right?" A sophomore replied, "You'd have to ask the poet. It's his poem."

Like many of my colleagues, I grow impatient with students who behave as Received Knowers. These are the students who sit, pencils poised, prepared to record the truths I dispense, the ones who ask exactly how long the paper should be, and exactly which topics will appear on the exam. These students are willing to regurgitate the information they have stored in their heads on a test, but they don't like being asked to apply it. They tend to see knowledge as something to be stored and reproduced, but not to be used and never to be questioned. They like multiple choice exams, and I don't. I can muster some compassion for Received Knowers by recalling how I revert to this position whenever I am faced with something novel, complex, and incomprehensible, like the first time I saw a game of cricket or heard a piece of atonal music. On such occasions I yearn for an expert who will just tell me what it all means.

It was not until I embarked on the WWK research however, that I came to feel genuine respect for Received Knowing. I teach at an academically selective, academically rigorous college, and I see it as my task to help students move beyond received knowing and on to more active, reflective modes of thinking. But through this project we met women for whom Received Knowing was an achievement, rather then something to be "got over," like measles or chicken pox or adolescence. They showed us that the position has virtues. The chief virtue of the Received Knower is that she is receptive. She can listen, even if the listening seems hardly more active than the listening a tape recorder does. Women who rely on received knowledge can take in information, while Ann, looking back on a life in Silence, recalls that she "could never understand what they were talking about." Received Knowers can appreciate expertise and make use of it. Silent women do not perceive authorities as sources of knowledge. "Authorities bellow but do not explain;" although they must be obeyed; they cannot be understood.

Ann began to emerge as a knower when she became a mother. She needed to know how to take care of her baby, and she was lucky enough to live in an area serviced by a Children's Health Program, where the staff "knew all the answers," and took the time to spell them out in language she could understand. Unlike many professionals, they continually emphasized her competence, rather than their own.

> I'd walk in there and they would say, "You're wonderful. You're a great mother." . . . I'd walk out of there feeling so good. I'd feel like I could tame

---

[4]I borrow the uppercase (A and T) from Perry to connote the power of Authority and the nature of Truth as conceived at this position.

the world. . . . I feel like I could go in there and they could hire me, you know, that's how much knowledge they have given me.

While recognizing the virtues of Received Knowing, it is important, also to see its limitations. For Received Knowers, as we defined the position, Authority is the only source of knowledge. Judging by the comments of some of our critics, we did not make the "only" point clear. The feminist literary theorist Patrocinio Schweickart, for instance, recalls herself as listening intently and taking careful notes in college and graduate school. We "miss something important," she says, if we assume that in this case she was behaving as a Silent woman or a Received Knower. But the authors of WWK would make no such assumption; we would agree with Schweickart that "silence" in this case might well be "a sign not of passivity, but of the most intense intellectual engagement" (1996, p. 307). It is important to distinguish between (lowercase) received knowing as a "strategy" (Goldberger, 1996a) that one chooses to deploy in a particular situation (during a lecture, say, or a cricket game), because of its adaptive value, and (uppercase) Received Knowing as a compulsory position from which authorities are viewed as the sole source of knowledge, knowledge that is assumed to be absolutely true, and which one simply ingests "as is" without any awareness of active processing. Similarly, we do not assume, of course, that simply because a person is not speaking, she is operating from a position of Silence.

As Goldberger points out, "Relying on experts or yielding to the knowledge of others is not necessarily indicative of the narrowly defined version of Received Knowing we present in WWK. . . . It is the way in which a person 'constructs' authority and expert that helps us understand more fully his or her epistemological stance" (1996a, p. 347). For instance, in her own research with "bicultural" Americans, Goldberger found that although African Americans stressed in their stories the importance of relying on God, "their construal of God as authority is more one of Collaborator and Coknower than Dictator" (1996a, p. 347). Goldberger implies that WWK's treatment of Received Knowledge is culture bound: "Yielding to authorities external to oneself is often characterized in Western culture, which values autonomy and independent judgment, as 'childlike,' 'passive,' or 'dependent'" (1996a, p. 347). I agree, and I think, too, that we were "bound" by the limits of our sample. Most of the women we coded as Received Knowers occupied relatively subordinate positions in terms of age or social class, being either very young undergraduates or very poor older women. Received Knowing might take a different form among, say, a sample of prosperous middle-aged people.

I believe, now, that we paid too little attention to distinctions within our sample of Received Knowers. As it is, our construction of this and the other positions partakes of what might be called "epistemological (or perhaps "positional") essentialism," lumping into the same category perspectives that may differ in significant ways. Received Knowing cannot be quite the same for a first-year student in an elite college who depends on the words of a presumably benign professor, and a fifty-year-old with minimal formal education who is at the mercy of the "information" supplied by an abusive mate. Or consider a milder, but not insignificant contrast: the experiences of a male and a female Received Knower in Perry's sample (Harvard undergraduates in the 1960s) might also differ, for the male knew that he might someday be one of Them, while the female could envision no such possibility.[5]

SUBJECTIVISM

Subjective knowing is in some respects the opposite of received knowledge. Received Knowers believe in universally valid Absolute Truths. Subjectivists adhere to the doctrines of "Multiplicity" (Perry, 1970) and "Subjective Validity" (Clinchy & Zimmerman, 1982): truth (lowercase t) is personal and individual, all opinions are equally valid, and everyone's opinions are right for them. While Received Knowers see knowledge as external and utterly objective, subjectivists look inside themselves for knowledge; for them, truth springs from the heart or the gut. In WWK we tell the story of Inez, a young single mother of three, who (in our terms), had lately moved out of Received Knowing into Subjectivism. She told us, "There's a part of me that I didn't even know I had until recently— instinct, intuition, whatever. It helps me and protects me. It's perceptive and astute. I just listen to the inside of me and I know what to do."

Unlike Received Knowers, Subjectivists tend to be deeply suspicious of the information dispensed by authorities. For most of her life Inez had been abused and exploited by powerful males, first her father and brothers, then her husband. She grew up believing that, as she put it, no woman could "think and be smart." Inez no longer pays any attention to external authorities; she is her own authority. "I can only know with my gut," she said. "I've got it tuned to a point where I think and feel all at the same time and I know what is right. My gut is my best friend—the one thing in the world that won't let me down or lie to me or back away from me."

For Inez, Subjectivism spells liberation, but for Kim, a first-year African American student at a traditional elite college, it almost certainly spells trouble. I asked Kim to read and respond to the following statement: "In areas where the rights answers are known, I think the experts should tell us what is right. But in areas where there are no right answers I think anybody's opinion is as good as another's." Kim didn't just agree with the second sentence; she also *dis*agreed with the first, the notion that there are in any area "right answers" that are "known." "I don't like that," she said. "I just don't like that. Who's to say what answer is right and what answer is wrong? They could have been given the wrong information. I'm sure there are a helluva lot of teachers who are walking around being misinformed. . . . I very seldom go by what people say."

---

[5]Even today, women constitute only about 12% of Harvard's faculty of Arts and Sciences.

Like other Subjectivists, Kim relied on the data supplied by first-hand experience rather than the second-hand information offered by authorities:

> If they were to tell me that there was going to be an earthquake tomorrow, that scientists had gone and studied all the scales and said this, I wouldn't believe them. I'd have to wait and see. The only way I could believe it is for it to actually happen. It is said that the earth goes around the sun. I don't have any proof. It is written in books, sure. But the person who wrote it in books could have been misinformed.

A Subjectivist would not dream of "asking the poet" how to interpret his poem. In her view, it isn't "his poem;" it's hers, and "there isn't any right or wrong. We're all allowed to read into a poem any meaning we want." As one woman said, "Whatever you see in the poem, it's got to be there." Here, the external world seems almost to disappear. The words on the page dissolve into a sort of Rorschach inkblot exerting little constraint on the meaning the reader projects onto the page. What the Subjectivist reader "sees" is likely to resemble closely what she already "knows." Asked how she decided among competing interpretations being discussed in English class, one student said, "I usually find that when ideas are being tossed around I'm usually more akin to one than another. I don't know—my opinions are just sort of there." And another said, "Well, with me it's almost more a matter of liking one more than another. I mean, I happen to agree with one or identify with it more."

Unless she can "identify" with a phenomenon, the Subjectivist cannot deal with it. "I cannot relate to an atom," Kim told me. Asked what she meant by "relate," she said, "I can comprehend it, I can feel it." Some of her classmates, she said, "can see why two positives would connect. I can't see that force, but I can see anger and emotions." How, I wondered, was this young woman going to pass the science distribution requirement?

Subjectivists "just know" what they know; their knowledge is based not on words or inferences but on the immediate apprehension of reality. Mrs. Spender, a character in Angela Thirkell's novel, *Growing Up*, says, "You only have to mention a thing to me and I seem to see it . . . I don't need to read, I just sense what things are about." Mrs. Spender does not question the validity of her perceptions, nor does she leave room for others to question them. "A person's experience can't be wrong," as one young woman said, and "an idea is right if it feels right"—right for herself, although not necessarily for anyone else. Subjectivists are as tolerant of others' opinions as they are of their own: judge not, that ye not be judged. When Kim told me that she didn't like to call people wrong, I asked, "Would that extend to people like Hitler?" "Absolutely," she replied. "I would never, no—I wouldn't call him wrong. Whatever he has done, I would not call him wrong . . . I value my opinion. I value what I do. I have no right whatsoever to go out and call somebody wrong because it is different from what I do."

At first glance, this passage may strike the reader, as it did me, as amoral mindless relativism. But Kim's next sentence makes it clear that she does have values of her own: "Now I think that the extermination of the Jews was wrong. I am not saying that he was wrong." It is not clear whether Kim means that Hitler's opinion is wrong in some objective or absolute sense, or whether it is simply wrong for her, but it is clear that she distinguishes between persons and the opinions they hold. She knows that, as the anthropologist Clifford Geertz puts it, differences of opinion are not just "clashes of ideas," that "there are people attached to those ideas" (Geertz, quoted in Berreby, 1995). Only if you realize that, Geertz maintains, can you be "open to dialogue with other people."

Kim realizes it, but she is not open to dialogue with other people. She disagrees with Hitler, but she would see no point in exploring the issue with him. She is not interested in why he believes in the extermination of Jews, nor would she care to argue the point: Hitler's opinion may be right for him, but it is irrelevant to her. Subjectivists do not see values—their own or anyone else's—as a subject for reflection, and without reflection there can be no genuine dialogue. Their anemic "discussions" are like parallel play: based on "mere unlikeness" of views, in Geertz's phrase, they are characterized by a "vacuous tolerance that, engaging nothing, changes nothing" (Geertz, 1986, p. 113). As the philosopher Elizabeth Spelman wrote:

> Tolerance is . . . the least of the virtues of people who really want to learn about others and about their lives: to tolerate someone is simply to let her have her say; I needn't listen to her, I needn't respond to her, I needn't engage with her in any way at all. All I have to do is not interfere with her. Prior to and after I've allowed her to make her presence known, I can blot her out of my consciousness. (Spelman, 1988, p. 181)

Although Subjectivists preach "openness," they actually practice a sort of aloof tolerance toward other points of view; they listen politely, but they do not really hear. As the philosopher Iris Murdoch might put it, they are unable to love. "Love," Murdoch said, "is the extremely difficult realisation that something other than oneself is real. Love . . . is the discovery of reality" (1970/1985, p. 51). Genuine dialogue, Geertz says, requires the realization that "other people are as real as you are" (quoted in Berreby, 1995). In some sense, the Subjectivist lacks this realization; she is lost in her own subjectivity. Although she acknowledges in theory the existence and validity of other realities, only her own is really real to her. She can only look out through this subjective reality; she cannot transcend it or detach herself from it.

Subjectivists perceive the world in terms of themselves, ignoring its otherness. The writer/teacher Peter Elbow calls this "projection in the bad sense" (Elbow, 1973, p.149). They hear a person (or a poem) meaning what they would mean, if they said those words, or else they do not hear it at all. In order to perceive otherness, one must acquire a degree of objectivity. To avoid projection in the bad sense, Subjectivists need to acquire techniques for "imaginative entry . . . into an alien turn of mind" (Geertz, 1986, p. 118). They need to learn how to explore and examine ideas—their own and other people's. They must rediscover on a higher plane the insight achieved by children of four and five, that belief and reality do not always coincide.

The Limits of Preprocedural Knowing

At my college, many students, especially in the first year or two, exhibit a split epistemology. Typically, they perceive science and mathematics from a Received Knowing perspective, and the humanities from a Subjectivist perspective. Students with a strong proclivity for Received Knowledge gravitate toward the first domain, and those who are strongly tilted toward Subjectivism gravitate toward the latter.[6] If they persist in these positions, both groups will run into trouble, especially in advanced courses: Received Knowers may be confronted with Heisenberg's uncertainty principle and Bohr's principle of complementary, and Subjectivists will certainly encounter teachers who insist that only those interpretations that are thoroughly grounded in the text deserve consideration. Unless they are to find themselves "in over their heads" in the psychologist Robert Kegan's (1994) phrase, in college and beyond, they will need to develop more powerful ways of knowing, for both these perspectives, although seemingly so different, share similar serious deficiencies.

Both are uncritical ways of knowing. Ann, the Received Knower, perceives the staff at her invisible college to be infallible, and Inez, the Subjectivist, perceives her own gut as infallible. They do not examine their knowledge; they simply accept it as true and act on it with unquestioning obedience. Both modes are relatively passive. Ann and Inez do not create their knowledge. Ann's opinions come ready-made from the agency; Inez's opinions are, as that student put it, "just there." People who rely solely on received or subjective knowledge are in some sense not really thinking. They have no systematic, deliberate procedures for developing new ideas or for testing the validity of ideas. Judging from longitudinal data and the women's retrospective accounts, this "Procedural Knowing" is for some the next step in development.

PROCEDURAL KNOWING

Procedural Knowers no longer believe that one can acquire knowledge or arrive at truth through immediate apprehension. Knowledge does not consist of facts to be stored "as is," nor of the static residue of direct experience. Knowledge is a

---

[6]In a survey distributed as part of the "Pathways Project" (Rayman & Brett, 1993) at Wellesley, students were asked to respond to the statement, "I prefer subject matter with precise answers to subject matter with multiple interpretations." This question discriminated significantly, and more than any other, (a) between those students who said on entering the college that they planned to major in math or science from those who said they planned to major in social sciences or humanities; and (b) between those who at the end of the sophomore year stuck with their plan to major in math or science and those who switched to a nonscience major.

process, and it requires work. Although no single "answer" may be "right," all interpretations are not equally valid. Knowing requires the application of procedures for comparing and contrasting and constructing interpretations, and the quality of the knowledge depends on the skill of the knower.

In WWK we described two sorts of procedures that we called "separate" and "connected" knowing. Separate Knowing is a detached, impersonal, objective, critical approach, best typified, perhaps, by the model of "hard science." Many people would call it simply "thinking," or maybe "good thinking." Once upon a time, so did I. Elsewhere, I have told how Zimmerman and I stumbled on what we now call "connected knowing" while searching for evidence of what we now call "separate knowing" among Wellesley undergraduates. Some of our interview questions were designed to ascertain whether the students had acquired an appreciation of critical thinking, a component of Perry's Position 4. For example, we asked them to respond to a statement another student had made in an earlier interview that seemed to provide evidence of critical thinking: "As soon as someone tells me his point of view, I immediately start arguing in my head the opposite point of view. When someone is saying something, I can't help turning it upside down" (Clinchy, 1998, p. 770).

Although some of the women agreed heartily with the quotation, some disagreed. One said, "When I have an idea about something, and it differs from the way another person's thinking about it, I'll usually try to look at it from that person's point of view, see how they could say that, why they think they're right, why it makes sense." And another said,

> If you listen to people and listen to what they have to say, maybe you can understand why they feel the way they do. There are reasons. They're not just being irrational. When I read a philosopher I try to think as the author does. It's hard, but I try not to bias the train of thought with my own impressions. I try to just pretend that I'm the author. I try to really just put myself in that person's place and feel why is it that they believe this way.

This young woman would agree with Virginia Woolf (1932/1948) that in reading a book one should "try to become" the author, his "fellow worker" and "accomplice."

In time, as my colleagues and I accumulated more and more responses like these, we began to think that connected knowing might constitute a genuine procedure, and this is how we present it in WWK. In retrospect, this seems to me to have been an audacious, perhaps presumptuous move. Because we had little empirical data of our own to use in constructing the concept, having never asked a single question designed to elicit it, in a sense we "made it up"—not out of whole cloth, to be sure, but out of a necessarily eclectic assortment of ideas. Since the publication of the book, along with various collaborators, I have been attempting through systematic research and conversations with colleagues (alive and dead, in person and in print) to define the components of connected knowing and separate knowing more clearly and to ascertain how the two procedures (or various versions thereof) play out in actual practice. Annick Mansfield and I (1992) developed an interview designed to elicit the ways in which men and women define the two procedures, how they feel about them, what they see as their benefits, drawbacks, and purposes, when and where and with whom they do and do not use each procedure, and how their use of them has changed over time. A number of researchers, including my own students as well as other investigators at various institutions working with widely varying populations, have also used some version of this interview. Because most of this research is still in progress, and because of limitations of space, I shall not dwell on it in detail here, but I have drawn on it in developing the description of the two procedures that I present here.

Table 4.1 summarizes some contrasting features of separate and connected knowing. The two modes have somewhat different purposes: while Connected Knowers are primarily interested in understanding the object of attention, Separate Knowers are primarily oriented toward its validity. The Connected Knower asks, "What does this poem (person, idea, etc.) mean?" The Separate Knower might ask, "How good is this poem? What are its strengths and weaknesses?"

TABLE 4.1
Characteristics of Connected and Separate Knowing

Aspect	Connected Knowing	Separate Knowing
The name of the game:	The "Believing Game": looking for what is right; accepting	The "Doubting Game": looking for what is wrong; critical
Goals:	Emphasis on meaning: to understand and be understood	Emphasis on validity: to justify, test, refine, convince, and be convinced
The relationship between the knowers:	Supportive: reasoning *with* the other	Adversarial, challenging: reasoning *against* the other
The knower's relation to the known:	Personal. Attachment & intimacy: "stepping in"	Impersonal. Detachment and distance: "stepping back"
The nature of agency:	Active surrender	Mastery and control
The nature of discourse:	Narrative	Argument
The role of emotion:	Feelings illuminate thought	Feelings cloud thought
Procedure for achieving (approximating) "objectivity":	Adopting the perspective of the particular other; empathy	Adopting a neutral perspective,"from no position in particular;" adhering to rules for avoiding bias
Basis of authority:	Personal experience (own or vicarious)	Mastery of relevant knowledge and methodology
Strengths:	Holistic, inclusive	Narrowing, discriminating
Vulnerabilities:	Absence of conviction; loss of identity, autonomy, and power. Danger of always being the listener	Absence of conviction; alienation and absence of care and intimacy. Danger of never listening

"What is the evidence for and against this theory?" In attempting to get at the meaning of an idea, the Connected Knower adopts a "believing" stance (Elbow, 1973; 1986), using empathy in an attempt to share the experience behind the idea, "feeling with" and "thinking with" the author of the idea. One woman told us that in counseling undergraduates, she is "usually a bit of a chameleon. I try to look for pieces of the truth in what the person's saying instead of going contrary to them, sort of collaborate with them." In contrast, Separate Knowers take a critical stance, acting as adversaries rather than allies. Instead of stepping into the other's shoes they step back, measuring the quality of the object against impersonal criteria such as the logic of the argument or the fit between the theory and the data.

Both Separate and Connected Knowers exhibit objectivity, but of a different sort. Separate Knowers believe in separating the knower from the known, so as to avoid "contamination." In searching for truth, they try to "weed out the self" using Elbow's (1973, p. 149) phrase, putting their own feelings and values aside and adopting a neutral perspective, "from no position in particular." To avoid bias, they adopt procedures such as "double-blinding" in conducting experiments and "blind grading" in assessing students' work. Connected Knowers also attempt to suspend their own beliefs, but instead of adopting a neutral perspective, they adopt the perspective of the other. When we asked women what "objectivity"meant to them, and why one should be objective, they often said something like, "When you're trying to help a friend decide whether to get an abortion, you have to forget what you think about abortion and see it from her point of view, given her assumptions." Connected Knowers do not "extricate" (Elbow, 1973) the self: convinced that the knower and the known are inextricably related, they use the self to help them connect with the other. To "the strong democrat," wrote the political scientist Benjamin Barber:

> "I will listen" means not that I will scan my adversary's position for weaknesses and potential trade-offs, nor even . . . that I will tolerantly permit him to say whatever he chooses. It means, rather, "I will put myself in his place. I will try to understand, *I will strain to hear what makes us alike* (1984, p. 175; emphasis added).

Connected Knowers take this approach not only to people but to relatively "impersonal" objects. "To understand a poem," an undergraduate said, "You must let the poem pass into you and become part of yourself, rather than something you see outside yourself. . . . there has to be some parallel between you and the poem." And the biochemist portrayed by June Goodfield in *An Imagined World* says, "If you really want to understand about a tumor you've got to *be* a tumor" (Goodfield, 1991/1994, p. 226). In contrast, Separate Knowers adhere to what the feminist philosopher Susan Bordo calls "the Cartesian masculinization of thought;" for them it is "the otherness of nature [that] allows it to be known," and "empathic, associational, or emotional response obscures objectivity, feeling for nature muddies the clear lake of the mind" (Bordo, 1986, p. 452). Connected Knowers, in contrast, believe that emotions can serve as clues. A nursery school teacher once told me that in trying to understand a particular child, she asks herself, "How does this child make me feel?" "I know my reaction says something about me," she says, "and I have to sort that out, but it also tells me something about him."

Separate and connected knowing, as presented here, are inventions, something like ideal types. In our work we have never encountered an individual who exhibited all the aspects of either mode, and it is possible that different categories of individuals will show different patterns, containing some components of a mode and excluding others. In a study of attitudes toward separate and connected knowing among Wellesley and MIT undergraduates, Mansfield and I found that many of the Wellesley undergraduates we interviewed embraced some aspects of Separate Knowing as we presented it (impartial analysis, for example) but strongly objected to its more oppositional aspects, such as playing "devil's advocate," and while most of the women included empathy in delineating their own versions of "connected knowing," not one of the men referred to empathy or, indeed, made any mention of affect (Rabin, 1994). (We suspect that the difference has as much or more to do with the cultural norms of the two institutions as with gender.)

Some of our research participants seem to express more complex versions of the modes than others. As the philosopher Sara Ruddick reminds us, "a 'position' or 'way' allows development within its modality" (Ruddick, 1996, p. 255). In an attempt to trace this development, Mansfield and I are looking for specific differences between versions that seem intuitively more or less sophisticated, and we are examining longitudinal data collected from adolescents in search of developmental change, asking, for instance, whether some components appear to come in earlier than others.

As work continues, particularly in different cultures and subcultures, researchers will surely deconstruct the crude dichotomy presented in Table 4.1, identifying configurations that contain elements from both its columns. Consider, for instance, Kochman's (1981) intriguing account of the distinctive ways in which urban community Black students and White middle-class students in his Chicago college classroom deal with conflict. The White students seem to adopt a prototypical detached Separate Knowing style: They "relate to their material as spokesmen, not advocates . . . They believe that the . . . merits of an idea are intrinsic to the idea itself. How deeply a person cares about or believes in the idea is considered irrelevant to its fundamental value." Blacks, on the other hand, use an approach that is adversarial, but neither disinterested nor unemotional. They "present their views as advocates. They take a position and show that they care about this position" (p. 20)." Whites believe that "caring about one's own ideas" makes a person "less receptive to opposing ideas," but Blacks see no contradiction between attachment to one's own ideas and openness to alternative ideas, which they also value; in fact, they are suspicious of people who present an argument as if they had no personal stake in it. "Whites believe that opinions should be evaluated on their own merits: they are taught to present ideas as though the ideas had an objective life, existing independent of any person expressing them," but Blacks, "because they feel that all views . . . derive from a central set of core beliefs that cannot be other than personal . . . often probe beyond a given statement to find out where a person is 'coming from' in order to clarify [its] meaning and value" (Kochman, 1981, pp. 20–23).

Connected Knowing Versus Subjectivism

Of all the themes presented in WWK, the concept of Connected Knowing has provoked the most interest, probably the most research, certainly the most controversy, and—in my defensive opinion—the most misunderstanding. As I have written:

> In WWK we defined connected knowing as a rigorous, deliberate, and demanding procedure, a way of knowing that requires work. Contrasting it with . . . "subjectivism," we said, "It is important to distinguish between the effortless intuition of subjectivism (in which one identifies with positions that feel right) and the deliberate imaginative extension of one's understanding into positions that initially feel wrong or remote." (WWK, 1986, p. 121). Many of our readers—friends and foes alike—have ignored the distinction, conflating connected knowing with subjectivism by treating it more as a reflex than a procedure. (Clinchy, 1996, p. 209)

Connected Knowing builds on the positive qualities of Subjectivism, but it transcends its limits. Table 4.2 presents some of the similarities and differences between the two modes. Connected Knowers retain the Subjectivist's respect for subjectivity and for the lessons that can be learned from first-hand experience, but they are not imprisoned within their own subjectivity or confined to their own narrow slice of experience; they develop techniques for entering into alien subjectivities and making use of vicarious experience. Connected Knowers, like Subjectivists, are reluctant to make judgments; they are in this sense "accepting," but theirs is not the passive acceptance, the "to-each-his-own-indifferentism" (Geertz, 1986, p. 122) of the Subjectivist. Fully developed Connected Knowing requires that one "affirm" or "confirm" the subjective reality of the other, and affirmation is not merely the absence of negative evaluation; it is a positive effortful act. Affirmation of a person or a position means "saying Yes to it" (Elbow, 1986, p. 279), rather than merely offering sympathetic understanding. Confirmation means, in the theologian Martin Buber's wonderful phrases, to "imagine the real," to "make the other present" (Buber, quoted by Friedman, 1985, p. 4). It involves "a bold swinging . . . into the life of the other" (Buber, quoted by Kohn, 1990, p. 112).

We saw that Subjectivists cannot engage in genuine dialogue; although they speak, often they cannot really hear. "What's the point of class discussion," one student asked, "when you have your own thoughts that feel right?" For

TABLE 4.2
Subjectivism and Connected Knowing
Similarities and Differences

Subjectivism	Connected Knowing
reflexive, reactive, spontaneous	deliberate, effortful; midwifery
locked in one's own perspective	entering another perspective
often, "projection in the bad sense" (Elbow): egocentric assumption that others share one's view	suspending, "bracketing" one's own view
Everyone has a right to their own opinion and everyone's opinion is right for them.	Everyone has a right to a considered opinion. People are responsible for their opinions.
All opinions are equally valid; an opinion has validity simply because someone holds it. Assertion of validity of one's own opinionfor one's self, but only for one's self.	Some opinions are better than others, but one should not evaluate an opinion unless one has tried hard to understand it.
Knowledge is derived from first-hand experience.	Knowledge can be acquired through vicarious experience.
Only my own subjectivity is really real to me.	One can enter into other subjectivities.
One should show tolerance and respect for views that differ from one's own.	One should try to imagine, explore, and understand views that differ from one's own
Intuition and feeling are involved, but not empathy. (feeling, but not feeling with)	Intuition and feeling may be involved, especially empathy.
little or no reasoning involved; the "gut" or "the heart" predominate.	"thinking with" as well as "feeling with" the other.
One need not entertain other views as possible options for the self. (Resistant to change)	One should entertain other people's opinions as possibilities for the self. (Open to transformation)

Connected Knowers knowledge is neither absolutely private nor absolutely certain; hearing other voices becomes not only possible but, because truth is now problematic rather than transparent, essential. Connected Knowers begin to perceive other people's realities not just as "alternatives to" themselves, as Subjectivists do, but as "alternatives for" themselves (Geertz, 1986, p. 111, citing Bernard Williams). Other people's realities become possibilities for them.

Connected Knowers develop techniques for facilitating and eliciting these realities through "active listening" (Rogers & Farson, 1967). Active listening is not a natural capacity, but in Geertz's phrase, a "skill arduously to be learned" (Geertz, 1986, p. 122), one that is rarely practiced in daily life. Having tried for years with more and less success to learn and to teach the art of interviewing, I know how difficult it is to listen "objectively" in the connected sense, that is, to hear the other in the other's own terms, to act, as the psychoanalyst Evelyne Schwaber puts it, as "an observer from within" (Schwaber, 1983, p. 274). Connected Knowers achieve skill, too, in making themselves understood by finding a route into the other's subjectivity: Kim, the African American student we met earlier, seemed to move outside her normally

Subjectivist frame when, in the midst of describing an experience of racial discrimination, she suddenly leaned across the desk and asked, "Are you Jewish?"—searching, it seemed, for some "parallel" between us that would allow her experience to "pass into" me.

Connected Knowing, like Subjectivism (and unlike Separate Knowing), attends to feelings as sources of insight, but it also involves reasoning—feeling with and thinking with. This point is often overlooked, perhaps because the dichotomy between separate and connected knowing that we present is assimilated into the dualism between thinking and feeling that pervades this culture, leading to a fallacious syllogism: If separate knowing involves thinking, and connected knowing involves feeling, connected knowing must not involve thinking. We say that although connected knowing is uncritical it is not unthinking, but in a culture in which the predominant view is that thinking *is* critical thinking, "uncritical thinking" becomes an oxymoron.

Issues of Gender

Although WWK is based entirely on interviews with women, it has been widely described as a study of "sex differences," perhaps partly because when male and female are perceived as binary opposites, as they typically are, it is difficult to see why one would speak of "women's" ways of knowing except to distinguish them from men's ways. We did not argue that the positions we described applied only to women, although we speculated that for various reasons, the positions might take somewhat different form in men; Marcia Baxter Magolda's research (chap. 5, this volume) suggests that this might be so. In particular, we did not mean to imply that all women, and only women, are Connected Knowers or that all men, and only men, are Separate Knowers. Because we interviewed only women, the voices we used to illustrate both modes were largely , of course, women's voices. Indeed, we did not attempt to "code" participants as Connected or Separate Knowers, but only as Procedural Knowers, for, having not yet clearly defined the two modes when we began the research, we had asked no questions designed to elicit the relevant data.

Subsequent research, involving men as well as women, and using recently developed survey measures as well as interviews focusing directly on separate and connected knowing, suggests that the two modes may be gender-related, but not gender exclusive. For instance, in two studies involving undergraduates at academically selective colleges, females consistently rated connected knowing statements higher than separate knowing statements, while males' ratings of the two modes did not differ (Galotti, Clinchy, Ainsworth, Lavin, & Mansfield, 1999; Galotti, Drebus, & Reimer, 1999). I know of no studies comparing the frequency of use of the two modes by males and females except in terms of self-report; more objective (observer-based) data would be useful.

However, sex differences were not then and are not now a central interest for me. I resonate to the words of Carol Gilligan: "When I hear my work being cast in terms of whether women and men are really (essentially) different or who is better than whom, I know that I have lost my voice, because these are not my questions" (1993, xiii). They were not our questions either. We did not mean to assert that connected knowing was "better" than separate knowing, only that it was "a different voice," a legitimate and effective voice that deserved to be heard. Like Gilligan and other "different voice" theorists, we "wished to repair an omission in psychological theory and in the society, by bringing into public consciousness a way of seeing, speaking, and knowing that emphasized attachment and interdependence rather than detachment and autonomy" (Clinchy & Norem, 1998, p. 785).

Critics contend that connected knowing is essentially a powerless way of knowing. I argue that it can be a powerful way of constructing knowledge (Clinchy, 1998), but I acknowledge that a society that devalues it will devalue the person who uses it. Until the "omission" of that voice in the institutions of this society is repaired, those who use it will suffer. I was reminded of this recently when I heard a colleague in economics tell how she insists that her students develop " a public voice" for use in class, a confident, decisive, authoritative voice that differs from the hesitant, groping, vague, and uncertain "private" voice they use in the residence hall. "I tell them," she said, "that if the CEO asks them how many factories they should build, and they says "F-i-i—i-ve. . . .? (with rising inflection), while the guy next to her says firmly "Seven!," seven will be built and the guy will be promoted above them." A bit shaken, I recalled how that very morning I had been urging the students in my seminar not to conduct an interview as if it were an exam, but to say things like "So - o - - o, you mean . . . ? . . . I'm not sure I understand . . . I think maybe . . ." In effect I was asking them to bring their private voices into the public domain. Which of us was right, I asked myself, the economist or me? Both. One voice is more effective in one context, the other in the other. We know from research that these procedures are not mutually exclusive, indeed, measures of the two appear to be orthogonal (David, 1999; Galotti, Clinchy, Ainsworth, Lavin, & Mansfield, 1999; Galotti, Drebus, & Reimer, 1999). Students need to develop skill in both modes, so that they can deploy whichever is appropriate for a given occasion. In time, we might even envision their achieving a way of knowing that integrates the two voices into one. What would such a voice sound like? In WWK, we weren't sure, but, we began to sketch it out, and we called it Constructed Knowing.

CONSTRUCTED KNOWING

The chapter on Constructed Knowing in WWK was by far the most difficult to write. It passed from hand to hand among us for months, as we wrote and revised it, and I, for one, have never been satisfied with it. Because this is the most complex of the positions, it is the most difficult to construct, and because our sample contained so few Constructed Knowers, we had little data to work with. Since the publication of WWK, my students and I have sought out research participants who we believed might help us in constructing a richer portrait of the position—for instance, relatively privileged adults active in professional and community life, and a sample of undergraduates nominated by their professors as "complex thinkers" in their fields (Arch, 1998). In this section, I rely largely on their words, elaborating on several aspects of the position presented in WWK. This research is in its infancy, and my comments should be read as highly speculative.

Constructed knowing has much in common with Perry's Position 5. Complexity and ambiguity are assumed, and "right answers are a special case." Anna, a senior honors student majoring in history, said that in her field, although there were some questions such as "Did this happen on this day?" to which an answer could be true or false, "those aren't the questions that are the important questions." For Amy, another senior, the epistemological "revolution" described by Perry, has clearly occurred: "There's a state of creative confusion, or at least doubt. I think it's always going to be that way." When last she encountered math and science, Amy had assumed that they contained "Truth with a capital T:"

> My experience with [science and math] has been on such a basic level that it's almost like spelling. You can spell right and you can spell wrong . . . I have a sense, though, that [in] higher level mathematics and stuff you get into things where just one answer isn't sufficient or isn't the only way. Things can sort of just diverge off, and there is more than one possibility. . . . I think that exists, you know, it must. Can't all be '2 and 2 is 4.'

When we ask Procedural Knowers to describe their ways of learning and thinking, they often enumerate a linear step-by-step program. Constructivists are less articulate; they struggle to find images to express the process, and the images are more often circular than linear. Amy says "it's hard to explain:"

> You proceed out of confusion. . . . There's just sort of a sense of a mixing bowl where you sort of let—where you are confused and you don't have any solid or stable. . . . I think it's sort of like a whirlpool or something like that. Where you've got a lot of ideas zooming around, and you haven't yet affixed any of them to being right or wrong in your head yet or meshing with all the others. Things are still just sort of whirling around; then you start, pulling them out and filtering things out and making sense out of them.

Similarly, Marie said:

> A lot of it has been lots of passive and then 'Boom!', all of a sudden something comes and really sticks, and I'm very active, and [then] lots of passive again, and then 'Boom!' again. It's like I have to take in a whole lot and sift it all down. You know, put it all in a big sieve and sift it all down

and the stuff that falls through I collect and start building with, and then 'Wham!'—all of a sudden the right piece will fall into the sieve and something will be completed.

We gave the Constructed Knowing chapter the subtitle, Integrating the Voices, to capture the women's tales of "weaving together the strands of rational and emotive thought and of integrating objective and subjective knowing" (WWK, p. 134). Amy and Marie weave together the "active surrender" of connected knowing with the "mastery and control" of separate knowing into a single way of knowing. In her practice as a family counselor, Sara tries to combine the empathy of connected knowing with the detachment of separate knowing. Recently, she told us, she canceled an appointment with a client in order to take a needed vacation with her daughter, and the client felt betrayed. "I'm working hard to get to a place where I can really understand how tortured she feels by this," she said. "I want to stay right with her as much as I can. I also have to keep monitoring this whole thing from a professional stance, trying to see it all and keep it all in perspective." Aware that she herself is tilted toward connection, she observes herself carefully: "If I find myself being too much into that close-up stance where I'm completely involved in that person's perspective and maybe lose touch with the professional stance, I need to scramble to get my professional stance back." Although Sara is aware that some therapists find an aggressive approach effective, she knows that it would not work for her. "Even if I have to confront sometimes, I still want to do that within a relationship that I feel is viable and trusting." She has evolved an approach that blends aspects of separate and connected knowing: she will "take an oppositional stance," voicing exceptions to a client's interpretations, but she phrases her comments in connected language, "in a way that hopefully isn't argumentative, but sort of like a confused statement." No one taught Sara this technique; she developed it herself to suit the sort of person she is. As Kegan might put it, while Procedural Knowers are "subject" to their procedures, Constructed Knowers are in control of them; they own them.

At the heart of constructed knowing, as is implicit in Perry's Position 5, is the belief that "All knowledge is constructed, and the knower is an intimate part of the known" (WWK, p. 137). Kegan asks, "Having put our world together, are we awake to the fact that it is an invented reality, a made world? Do we regularly look for some quite different way the same experience could cohere and so render a whole different meaning?" "[W]e 'make sense,'" he goes on, "but we do not always take responsibility for it as made" (Kegan, 1994, p. 205). Although none of us, of course, is always conscious of inventing reality, Constructivists often are, and at least on reflection, they recognize that they are responsible for their constructions and that it is their duty—"an ethical imperative," as one woman put it—to consider alternative constructions. If truth is "an increasing complexity," as the poet Adrienne Rich (1979, p. 187) said, and as our Constructivists believe, there is never a single, crucial experiment or a perfect, "impregnable" argument that will settle the matter. Procedural Knowers stay within a given system—the viewpoint of a particular person or a particular discipline, for example. Constructivists move among systems. Amy, who worried during her sophomore year that she might "mix up" the material from one course with the material from another, and "say the wrong things on the exam," told us, as a senior:

> I think one of the most exciting things is when you're getting different insights into a similar thing. Like when you're taking seventeenth-century literature as well as art you have a sense of a lot of things coming together, a lot of different things that explain each other sometimes . . . And you start getting a much greater sense of what was happening, and why each thing in turn produced the other, and how they all interact.

In WWK we wrote, "[C]onstructivists show a high tolerance for internal contradiction and ambiguity" (p. 137). "'Dialogue' and 'balance' were key words in [the] epistemological vocabulary" of the "complex thinkers" interviewed by Joanna Arch (1998, p. 53). For example, Karen approaches history, her field of concentration, as "a dialogue" between past and present; although it is important for historians to avoid projecting current assumptions and concerns "blindly back into the past," she said, it is important also to keep them in mind. Philosophers and psychologists refer to this sort of approach as "dialectical thinking" (e.g., Basseches, 1986; Clayton & Birren, 1980; also see Oser & Reich, 1987, on "complementarity"), Karen calls it "my little two-direction thing." (Notice that, like Sara, she "owns" the approach.)

When Constructed Knowers find their thoughts and feelings in conflict, they try to cultivate a "conversation" between the two, instead of allowing one to silence the other. In her "rational mind," Karen said, she is opposed to censorship, but, "intuitively," because of an experience involving the attempted suicide of a friend after reading an assigned book, she is in favor of it:

> There has to be a way for that experience to coincide with thought. And be more than a gut reaction, even though the gut reaction is the strongest thing about it. And I think that's true of all sorts of things.. . . I remain convinced . . . that what's truly right will work on both an emotional and a logical level. And maybe that's not true. But I'd like to think that and pursue that thought.

Although barely twenty one years old, Karen seems to have the beginnings of "wisdom," as defined by Labouvie-Vief: "While *logos* has insisted on the separation of such realms as reason and faith, thinking versus feeling, outer versus inner, or mind versus body, wisdom maintains that these two realms constitute but complementary and interacting poles of thought (1990, p. 78)."

Interviews with older, seemingly "wise" women like Sara have led me to suspect that when constructed knowing reaches its fullest development (probably not before middle age, I would guess), the construction of self and other might look something like Kegan's (1994) "fifth order consciousness." To illustrate the difference between fourth and fifth order consciousness, respectively, Kegan invents two couples, the Ables and the Bakers, both of whom have been married for many years. The Ables respect their differences, and most of the time they are "comfortable" with them. "We're probably more comfortable with each other," they said, "because we're a lot more comfortable with ourselves. . . . Anyway, we've become a good team. We find that our differences are often complementary. One picks up what the other one misses." For each of the Ables, the self is single and complete: "Mr. Able comes over to discover the world of Mrs. Able, but in all his respectful discovering he never questions the premise that this is not his world." For each of the Bakers, on the other hand, the self is multiple and incomplete, an "evolving self" (Kegan, 1982) composed of contradictory parts. The Bakers have come to see that the differences each experiences between the self and the other are also differences within the self and the other. "When Mr. Baker comes over to try on the perspective he has identified with Mrs. Baker, . . . he is vulnerable to discovering another world within himself." For instance, to an outsider it may appear that one of the Bakers is an activist and the other a contemplative. But "when we are at our best," said the Bakers themselves, "we get a good glimpse of the fact that the activist . . . also has a contemplative living inside him." And when they have a fight, if it's a good fight, "the fight becomes a way for us to recover our own complexity, . . . to leave off making the other into our opposite and face up to our own oppositeness."

The Ables have learned to avoid destructive conflict by treating each other as complements rather than enemies; through respecting each other's points of view, compromising, and taking turns, they have become "a good problem-solving team." But their relationship is not a source of growth: "We are who we are," they say (Kegan, 1994, p. 308). The Bakers' relationship is a source of growth, "a context for a sharing and an interacting in which both are helped to experience their 'multipleness,' in which the many forms or systems that each self is are helped to emerge" (Kegan, 1994, p. 313). When differences between partners are acknowledged as differences within each of the partners, they become similarities between them, and the apparent opposition between similarity and difference is dissolved. Piaget was right, I think, in positing difference and contradiction as powerful forces in development, but I believe that similarity and coincidence can be equally powerful, and that the integration of the two, in constructed knowing, is more powerful still.

CONCLUSION

In WWK we could not assert with confidence that the epistemological positions we defined represented a developmental progression, for we had longitudinal data for only the small proportion of our sample whom we had also interviewed in earlier studies; otherwise, we had to rely on retrospective accounts. In any case, I now believe that we should be wary of moving too quickly to embrace theories that postulate a single, acontextual linear direction in epistemological development. Such global theories have been useful in the past, but, the pervasiveness of "domain specificity" has led me to believe that we need to examine development within rather than across domains. For instance, it seems likely that, while in approaching the humanities, students often move from a Subjectivist to a Procedural position, in approaching science they may "skip" Subjectivism, going directly from Received to Procedural Knowing. I believe that microanalytic longitudinal investigations of individuals grappling with a particular discipline or set of issues can be especially illuminating, for example, studies of changes over months or years in students' conceptions of truth within a particular course, as revealed through interviews and essays (e.g., McCarthy, 1987; McCarthy & Fishman, 1991). Besides providing a more detailed account of the nature of development, longitudinal "case studies" of this sort can lead to hypotheses about the kinds of experiences that facilitate epistemological development, for example, Haviland and Kramer's (1991) analysis of the diary of Anne Frank suggests that intensity of emotion about a particular issue can serve as a stimulus to more complex constructions of the issue.

REFERENCES

Arch, J. (1998). Epistemological assumptions and approaches to learning in three academic disciplines. Unpublished undergraduate honors thesis. Wellesley College, Wellesley, MA.

Barber, B. (1984). *Strong democracy: Participatory politics for a new age.* Berkeley: University of California Press.

Basseches, M. (1986). Dialectical thinking and young adult cognitive development. In R. A. Mines & K. S. Kitchener (Eds.), *Adult cognitive development: Methods and models.* New York: Praeger.

Belenky, M. (1996). Public homeplaces: Nurturing the development of people, families, and communities. In *Knowledge, difference, and power: Essays inspired by* Women's Ways of Knowing, 393–440. New York: Basic Books.

Belenky, M., Bond, L., & Weinstock, J. (1997). *A tradition that has no name: Public homeplaces and the development of people, families, and communities.* New York: Basic Books.

Belenky, M., Clinchy, B., Goldberger, N., R., & Tarule, J. (1986/1997). *Women's ways of knowing: The development of self, mind, and voice.* New York: Basic Books.

Berreby, D. (1995, April 9). Unabsolute truths: Clifford Geertz. *The New York Times Magazine.*

Bordo, S. (1986). The Cartesian masculinization of thought. *Signs, 11,* 439–456. Reprinted in S. Harding, & J. O'Barr (Eds.) (1987). *Sex and scientific inquiry* (pp. 247–264). Chicago: University of Chicago Press.

Clayton, V. & Birren, J. (1980). The development of wisdom across the life span: A reexamination of an ancient topic. *Life span development and behavior, 3,* 103–135.

Clinchy, B. (1996). Connected and separate knowing: Toward a marriage of two minds. In N. Goldberger, J. Tarule, B. Clinchy, & M.. Belenky (Eds.), *Knowledge, difference, and power: Essays inspired by* Women's Ways of Knowing (pp. 205–247). New York: Basic Books.

Clinchy, B. (1998). A plea for epistemological pluralism. In B. Clinchy and J. Norem (Eds.), *Readings in gender and psychology* (760–777). New York: New York University Press.

Clinchy, B. & Norem, J. (1998). Coda: In-Conclusion . . . In B. Clinchy and J. Norem (Eds.), *Readings in gender and psychology* (778–798). New York: New York University Press.

Clinchy, B., & Zimmerman, C. (1982). Epistemology and agency in the development of undergraduate women. In P. Perun (Ed.), *The undergraduate woman: Issues in educational equity*. Lexington, MA: D. C. Heath.

Clinchy, B., & Zimmerman, C. (1985). Growing up intellectually: Issues for college women. *Work in Progress*, No. 19. Wellesley, MA: Stone Center Working Papers Series.

David, C. (1999). Fear of success and cognitive styles in college women. Unpublished undergraduate honors thesis. Wellesley College, Wellesley, MA.

Elbow, P. (1986). *Embracing contraries*. New York: Oxford University Press.

Elbow, P. (1973). Appendix Essay: The doubting game and the believing game—An analysis of the intellectual enterprise. In *Writing without teachers*. London: Oxford University Press.

Friedman, M. (1985). *The healing dialogue in psychotherapy*. New York: Jason Aronson.

Galotti, K., Drebus, D., & Reimer, R. (1999, April). Ways of knowing as learning styles. Research Display presented at the Biennial Meeting of the Society for Research in Child Development, Albuquerque, NM.

Galotti, K., Clinchy, B., Ainsworth, K., Lavin, B., & Mansfield, A. (1999). A new way of assessing ways of knowing: The attitudes toward thinking and learning survey (ATTLS). *Sex Roles, 40*, 745–766.

Geertz, C. (1986, Winter). The uses of diversity. *Michigan Quarterly Review*, 105–123.

Gilligan, C. (1993). Letter to readers, 1993. In *In a different voice: Psychological theory and women's development*, 2nd ed., ix–xxvii. Cambridge: Harvard University Press.

Goldberger, N. (1981). *Meeting the developmental needs of college students*. Final report presented to the Fund for the Improvement of Post-Secondary Education (FIPSE), Simon's Rock of Bard College, Great Barrington, MA.

Goldberger, N. (1996a). Cultural imperatives and diversity in ways of knowing. In *Knowledge, difference, and power: Essays inspired by* Women's Ways of Knowing, 335–371. New York: Basic Books.

Goldberger, N. (1996b). Looking backward, looking forward. In *Knowledge, difference, and power: Essays inspired by* Women's Ways of Knowing, 1–21. New York: Basic Books.

Goodfield, J. (1991/1994). *An imagined world: A story of scientific discovery*. Ann Arbor: University of Michigan Press.

Hall, G. S. (1917). *Adolescence: Its psychology and its relations to physiology, anthropology, sociology, sex, crime, religion, and education*. New York: D. Appleton & Co.

Haviland, J. M., & Kramer, D. A. (1991). Affect-cognition relationships in adolescent diaries: The case of Anne Frank. *Human Development, 34*, 143–159.

Kegan, R. (1982). *The evolving self*. Cambridge, MA: Harvard University Press.

Kegan, R. (1994). *In over our heads: The mental demands of modern life*. Cambridge, MA: Harvard University Press.

Kochman, T. (1981). *Black and white styles in conflict*. Chicago: University of Chicago Press.

Kohn, A. (1990). *The brighter side of human nature: Altruism and empathy in everyday life*. New York: Basic Books.

Labouvie-Vief, G. (1990). Wisdom as integrated thought: Historical and developmental perspectives. In R. Sternberg (Ed.), *Wisdom: Its nature, origins, and development* (pp. 52–83). Cambridge: Cambridge University Press.

Lewis, M., & Simon, R. (1986). Discourse not intended for her: Learning and thinking within patriarchy. *Harvard Educational Review, 56*, 457–471.

Mansfield, A., & Clinchy, B. (1992, May 28). *The influence of different kinds of relationships on the development and expression of "separate" and "connected" knowing in undergraduate women*. Paper presented as part of a symposium, *Voicing relationships, knowing connection: Exploring girls' and women's development*, at the 22nd Annual Symposium of the Jean Piaget Society: Development and vulnerability in close relationships. Montreal, Québec, Canada.

McCarthy, Lucille P. (1987). A stranger in strange lands: A college student writing across the curriculum. *Research in the Teaching of English, 21*, 233–265.

McCarthy, Lucille P., & Fishman, Stephen M. (1991). Boundary conversations: Conflicting ways of knowing in philosophy and interdisciplinary research. *Research in the Teaching of English, 25,* 419–468.

Murdoch, I. (1970/1985). *The sovereignty of good.* London: ARK Paperbacks, Routledge & Kegan Paul.

Oser, F., & Reich, K. (1987). The challenge of competing explanations: The development of thinking in terms of complementarity of 'theories.' *Human Development, 30,* 178–186.

Perry, W. (1970/1999). *Forms of intellectual and ethical development in the college years.* New York: Holt, Rinehart, and Winston.

Rabin, C. (1994). *Separate and connected knowing in undergraduate men and women.* Unpublished undergraduate honors thesis. Wellesley College, Wellesley, MA.

Rayman, P., & Brett, B. (1993). *Pathways for women in science: The Wellesley report.* Wellesley, MA: Wellesley College.

Rich, A. (1979). *On lies, secrets, and silence: Selected prose (1966–1978).* New York: Norton.

Rogers, C, & Farson, R. (1967). Active listening. In Haney, W. *Communication and organizational behavior: Text and cases,* (81–97). Homewood, IL: Richard D. Irwin, Inc.

Ruddick, S. (1996). Reason's femininity: A case for connected knowing. In *Knowledge, difference, and power: Essays inspired by* Women's Ways of Knowing, 248–273. New York: Basic Books.

Schwaber, E. (1983). Schwaber, E. (1983). Construction, reconstruction, and the mode of clinical attunement. In A. Goldberg , *The future of psychoanalysis.* (pp. 273–291). New York: International Universities Press.

Schweickart, P. (1996). Speech is silver, silence is gold: The assymetrical intersubjectivity of communicative action. In *Knowledge, difference, and power: Essays inspired by* Women's Ways of Knowing, 305–331. New York: Basic Books.

Spelman, E. (1988). *Inessential woman: Problems of exclusion in feminist thought.* Boston: Beacon Press.

Woolf, V. (1932/1948). How should one read a book? In *The common reader, Series 1 and 2* (pp. 281–295). New York: Harcourt Brace.

5

Epistemological Reflection: The Evolution of Epistemological Assumptions from Age 18 to 30

Marcia B. Baxter Magolda
Miami University (Ohio)

During his sophomore year of college, Ned (age 19) told me that when confronted with discrepancies in his studies "you have to trust the author" because "at a freshmen-sophomore level as I am, I don't know enough about these things." At age 26 he described learning on his job like this:

> I figure things out as I go along and adapt, change, redefine, until you get to the final conclusion. I approach it based on other past histories or experiences I've had that lead me to a more accurate hypothesis of what's going to happen. You read a couple of lines in a book saying [it] should do this, but it never happens that way and there's always some good reasons why it doesn't.

At the outset of his college experience Ned believed that authority figures knew the truth. Over time he came to believe that knowledge is contextual, constructed by persons with appropriate expertise. Why did Ned, at 19, regard himself as insufficiently knowledgeable? What occurred over the next seven years that altered his perspective? Could educators create conditions that would have helped Ned at an earlier age construct the self-authorship he exhibits at age 26? Does gender play a role in young adults' view of knowledge and their role in constructing it? Curiosity about answers to questions like these led me to initiate a longitudinal study of college students' epistemological development in 1986.

Ned's story, and those of one hundred of his college peers, yielded the Epistemological Reflection Model (Baxter Magolda, 1992)—one theory of how assumptions about the nature, limits, and certainty of knowledge evolve during young adulthood. Eight years of postcollege participant stories refined and extended the theory. This chapter offers one portrait of epistemological development in young adults age 18 to 30 and possibilities for the role of gender in epistemological development.

GUIDING ASSUMPTIONS

As a social constructivist, I am compelled to share the theoretical underpinnings and assumptions that guide my interpretations in the longitudinal study. My view of cognitive development is grounded in the constructive-developmental tradition. Constructivism refers to the belief that persons actively construct their perspectives by interpreting their experience; developmentalism refers to the belief that these constructions evolve through eras marked by principles of stability and change (Kegan, 1982; 1994). Piaget's (1950) notion of cognitive structures that change through equilibration stands at the core of this tradition. Cognitive structures are sets of assumptions we use to make meaning of our experience. When we encounter experiences that are discrepant with our structures, we either assimilate the new experience into the current structure (what Piaget called assimilation) or alter the structure to account for the new experience (what Piaget called accommodation). The need to keep our meaning-making structures and experience coherent and the ongoing balancing of the two constitutes the equilibration process. The continual interaction between us and our world, during which we make meaning of what happens to us, is marked by stability or balance when we can assimilate our experience into current structures. Instability and change to a qualitatively new balance mark it when we accommodate our structures to account for new experience. Kegan's (1982) notion that meaning is made in the space between persons and events they experience captures the dynamic interplay between the individual and the social in epistemological development.

These qualitative structures through which meaning is made are characterized in part by particular assumptions about the nature, limits, and certainty of knowledge that Kitchener (1983) labeled epistemic assumptions. William Perry's (1970) pioneering work in articulating these structures during the college years formed the foundation for my thinking about college students' epistemological development. The questions raised by Belenky, Clinchy, Goldberger, and Tarule (1986) about the dynamics of such development for women played a substantial role in using gender as a central dimension of the longitudinal study. They also highlighted the role of assumptions about the self in epistemology, a dimension also central in Kegan's notion that epistemological, intrapersonal, and interpersonal dimensions of development are integrally intertwined. Although the epistemological dimension stands at the forefront of my study, the other dimensions have become increasingly salient as participants move through their twenties.

This foundation yields particular assumptions that guide my theory construction. First, epistemic assumptions and the structures they constitute are socially constructed. The meaning we make of our experiences depends partially on our initial epistemic assumptions, partially on the nature of dissonance we experience when we encounter others with different assumptions, and partially on the context in which the dissonance occurs. This leads to a second assumption, that my longitudinal participants' stories are context-bound. The meaning they make of their experience is grounded in the context of their epistemic assumptions and particular experiences. These two assumptions led to my description of epistemic structures and gender-related patterns within them as possibility, learned via context, and fluid depending on context, rather than essentialist, enduring states generalizable to others beyond my particular participants. Viewing epistemological development as socially constructed, context-bound, fluid, and constituted by multiple realities requires qualitative inquiry to access and respect this complexity. Thus despite the theoretical grounding of Piaget, Perry, Belenky et al., and Kegan, I pursued an inductive or discovery approach (as had these theorists) rather than one of confirmation. I explain this approach and the nature of my study next as context for the Epistemological Reflection model.

MODE OF INQUIRY

The primary goal of the college phase (Phase 1) was to describe a gender-inclusive model of epistemological development. The goal of the postcollege phase (Phase 2) was to explore epistemological development, including the role of gender, through the twenties. Both phases involved annual interviews to explore participants' assumptions about the nature, limits, and certainty of knowledge.

Participants

The study began with 101 traditional-age college students (51 women and 50 men) who attended a state institution with a liberal arts focus. Admission is competitive and the entering class of which the study participants were a part had a mean ACT score of 25.8 and 70% ranked in the top 20% of their high school class. Their majors included all six divisions within the institution and involvement in college was high. Eighty students participated through their four years of college.

Of the 70 participants continuing in Phase 2, 59 graduated within four years and the remaining 11 in five years. One dynamic of this context is the small number of students from underrepresented groups on the campus. Only three of the original 101 participants were members of underrepresented groups; two of whom continued into the postcollege phase. Although none of these three withdrew from the study, all were unreachable by Year 10 due to changing addresses.

By Year 10 participation included 39 people. During the previous five years, 7 participants withdrew and 24 participants were lost due to address changes or inability to schedule interviews after repeated attempts.

Of the 39 who remained through Year 12, 27 were married, 2 were divorced, and 11 had children. Sixteen were involved in advanced education: 11 had received master's degrees in education, psychology, social work, business administration, and economics. One had completed seminary, two had received their J.D., and one had completed a Ph.D. program. One was in medical school. The most prevalent occupations of these 39 participants were business (19) and education (8). Areas within business included sales in varied industries, financial work, public services, real estate, and marketing. The remaining participants were in social work, law, homemaking, and the Christian ministry. Gender remained balanced over the years with 20 women and 19 men remaining by year 12.

Interviews

During the college interviews, I invited students to talk freely about their role as learners, the role of instructors and peers in learning, their perception of evaluation of their work, the nature of knowledge, and educational decision making. These six areas revealed epistemic assumptions, as well as experiences that affected those assumptions. The question in each area introduced the topic but did nothing beyond that to frame the response. For example, I introduced the nature of knowledge with, "Have you ever encountered a situation in which you heard two explanations for the same idea?" When students said yes, I invited them to describe the experience, their reaction to it, and the way they decided what to believe. Follow-up questions clarified each student's responses, and I routinely summarized the responses to make sure I understood the perspective. The interviews were recorded and transcribed verbatim. Students also completed the Measure of Epistemological Reflection (Baxter Magolda & Porterfield, 1988) as another means to acquire their epistemic assumptions.

Phase 2 interviews are best characterized as informal and conversational (Patton, 1990). Because few researchers have explored epistemological development after college via a longitudinal approach, the method especially needed to allow insights to emerge from the learners' experiences. The annual interview began with a summary of the focus of Phase 2 of the project; to continue to explore how participants learn and come to know. The participant was then asked to think about important learning experiences that took place since the previous interview. The participant volunteered those experiences, described them, and described their impact on her or his thinking. I asked questions to pursue why these experiences were important, factors that influenced the experiences, and how the learner was affected. Each year, I noted participants' reactions to the conversation to routinely enhance the interview process. By Year 9, the interview cast a wider net in response to participants' views regarding effective techniques for accessing their thinking. After the introduction, I asked grand tour questions such as what life had been like for them since we talked last. These conversations included discussion of the dimensions of life they felt were most relevant, the demands of adult life they were experiencing, how they made meaning of these dimensions and demands, their sense of themselves, and how they decided what to believe. Interviews were conducted by telephone and ranged from 60 to 90 minutes.

Interpretation

Interview responses were analyzed using grounded theory methodology (Glaser & Strauss, 1967; Strauss & Corbin, 1994). Transcriptions of the taped interviews were reviewed and divided into units. The units were then sorted into categories to allow themes and patterns to emerge from the data. Credibility of the themes and patterns is addressed through prolonged engagement to build trust and understanding and member checking to assure accuracy of interpretations.

EPISTEMOLOGICAL REFLECTION

Marilyn Frye wrote, "Naming patterns is like charting the prevailing winds over a continent, which does not imply that every individual and item in the landscape is identically affected" (1990, p. 180). The structures and patterns I have named in the Epistemological Reflection Model are prevailing winds that do not affect all young adults identically. The structures and patterns that follow are possible social constructions young adults use to move from dependence on authority to self-authorship.

Absolute Knowing: Receiving or Mastering Knowledge

Eileen preferred classes based on factual information during her first year in college. She explained, "It's very easy for me to memorize facts. The advantage is that it is kind of cut and dried. The information is there—all you have to do is soak it into your brain." I came to understand this perspective as absolute knowing, characterized by the assumption that knowledge is certain and people designated as authorities know the truth. Based on these epistemic assumptions, absolute knowers believed that: (a) teachers were responsible for communicating knowledge effectively and making sure students understood it, (b) students were responsible for obtaining knowledge from teachers, (c) peers could contribute to learning by sharing materials and explaining material to each other, and (d) evaluation was a means to show the teacher that students had acquired knowledge.

Within the absolute knowing structure, two distinct gender-related patterns were evident. I use the term gender-related to convey that women or men used one pattern more than the other but patterns were not exclusive to one gender. More women than men used the receiving pattern, characterized by listening and recording information to acquire knowledge. More men than women used the mastery pattern, characterized by active involvement to maintain attention and remember the material. Receiving pattern students expected their peers to be supportive by asking questions; mastery pattern students expected their peers to debate and quiz each other to promote mastery. Students in both patterns shared the same basic assumptions about the nature of knowledge; they differed only in the style through which they approached knowledge acquisition.

Absolute knowing was prevalent during the first two years of college. Sixty-eight percent of my participants used absolute knowing their first year; 46% continued to use it as sophomores. After the sophomore year absolute knowing became rare. Students altered their epistemic assumptions as they encountered experiences that called the certainty of knowledge into question.

Transitional Knowing: Interpersonal and Impersonal Patterns

Bob described the experience that moved him into transitional knowing:

> I took a different teacher in the sophomore level of the subject, and I learned to interpret things differently. When you have someone else give you a different interpretation of the same subject, you're forced to go back and make comparisons. It begins to change you a little bit.

Experiences like this one prompted students to assume that knowledge was uncertain in the areas where different interpretations were offered. Transitional Knowers kept their assumption that knowledge was certain in areas like mathematics and science yet saw areas such as humanities and social science as uncertain. In these uncertain areas students focused on understanding rather than acquiring knowledge, expected teachers to help with understanding and application of knowledge, preferred tests focused on understanding rather than memorizing, and viewed peers as helpful in exploring different interpretations.

Two gender-related patterns emerged within the transitional structure. The interpersonal pattern entailed connecting to others and the subject in order to sort out opinions in the uncertain areas. Interpersonal pattern knowers, primarily women, enjoyed the uncertain areas more than the certain ones and emphasized using personal judgment to decide on opinions. In contrast, Impersonal pattern knowers stood at arm's length from the subject and others in learning. They were interested in others' views and discussion because these forced them to think. Impersonal pattern students, primarily men, focused on defending their views; interpersonal pattern students focused on sharing views. Impersonal pattern knowers focused on being challenged to think and resolved uncertainty via logic.

Transitional knowing dominated the college years of these students. It was used by 32% of the first-year students. Fifty-three percent continued to use it as sophomores, 83% as juniors, and 80% as seniors. Their college experience reinforced the dichotomy of certainty and uncertainty and offered few experiences to move to self-authorship.

Independent Knowing: Interindividual and Individual Patterns

Laura was one of the few students who encountered experiences during college that prompted the move to independent knowing, characterized by the assumption that most, if not all, knowledge was uncertain. She described the experience in a statistics course that prompted her discovery:

> I became very skeptical about what the "truth" was. It's amazing how you can influence statistics. Statistics are supposed to be really the truth. You can't manipulate statistics. But then I learned that you really can manipulate statistics to have a point of view to be the truth.

This experience led Laura to conclude, "Everything's relative; there's no truth in the world. Each individual has their own truth." This new core assumption about the nature of knowledge led independent knowers to focus on thinking for themselves, expecting teachers to promote independent thinking and avoid judging students' opinions, and exchanging views with peers to expand possibilities. Despite this core structure, independent knowers differed in how they balanced their own and others' voices in thinking for themselves.

Participants who had perfected listening to others in earlier structures (those using the receiving and interpersonal patterns) struggled to establish their own voice alongside those of others. Interindividual pattern knowers, primarily women, were quick to see how others' views could be right and amenable to changing their views accordingly. In contrast, individual pattern knowers held more tightly to their own views and struggled to hear the views of others. These students, most often men, had perfected their own voices in earlier structures (mastery and impersonal patterns). Thus the gender-related patterns used in earlier ways of knowing mediated the transition to authoring one's own views.

Independent knowing was minimally used in college; only 16% of seniors exhibited this set of assumptions. It became prevalent quickly after college, with 57% of the participants using it in their first year out of school. In most cases this dramatic shift was due to work and graduate school contexts in which participants were expected to function independently. Megan's report on expectations in her public relations position was typical of what participants encountered after college. She said, "It's up to me how, what approach I take to do it, and different angles for things. It's expected for me to improve, but . . . the way I do it is my choice. This gives me a lot of flexibility and creativity, which I like. There's no right or wrong to it, they are my ideas." These contexts offered the first substantive opportunity for self-authorship. However, participants initially interpreted these expectations as total freedom; they did not realize the need for rationale for work decisions or stances taken in graduate courses. It was not long before issues of better or worse arose in their work and school contexts.

Contextual Knowing: Integrating Relational and Impersonal Knowing in the Postcollege Years

Postcollege contexts and expectations differed substantially from those participants experienced during college. This created dissonance that led to another shift in epistemic assumptions. Anne's experience was typical of what my participants reported as they made their way in the world after college graduation. After two years of experience as an accountant, Anne told me, "I wish teachers wouldn't do so many multiple-choice questions and have some more thinking type things because life is not multiple choice. I've been realizing out here, there's so many things I have to think about and look up and research and think about more." Anne reported learning to think through the questions her boss asked and her initial embarrassment at not having thought about them prior to making a decision. She explained:

> I guess you just do it because you have to . . . just kind of bumble through it I guess, try to rationalize things out. I wrote down some solutions and wrote down plusses of the solutions. Then I'd try to think of what kind of questions my boss would ask, like "What would happen if we did this?" and "Where did you get these numbers?" Before I would make a decision; now I've learned to say to myself, "What kind of questions are you going to get?" And it's made me go back and rethink everything and come up with some other alternatives too and just make sure what I'm thinking is good.

Anne learned that all solutions were not equally valid; good solutions existed in particular contexts and were based on relevant information. The shift to assuming that knowledge is constructed in a context led participants to learn how to think through problems, integrate and apply knowledge in particular contexts, and make judgments based on evidence. Contextual knowing was rare in college, used by only 2% of the seniors in the study. It became prevalent as participants engaged in advanced education, professional work roles, and complex personal relationships.

Knowing contextually was more difficult than any previous epistemic structure. Although independent knowing required use of multiple perspectives and making one's own choices, it did not require making judgments about multiple perspectives and using criteria to determine better or worse choices. Realizing the need to make good judgments, or make sure one's thinking was good as Anne suggested, did not automatically make it clear how to do so. Although some participants were taught this process in advanced education, most learned it by watching supervisors, coworkers, and significant others in their lives.

Making sense of multiple perspectives and judgments about what to believe led to a merger of the gender-related patterns evident in earlier epistemic structures (Baxter Magolda, 1995). As participants watched others learn to make judgments, they often saw the other pattern and discovered it could augment the pattern they used. Sheila, who had used the relational patterns during college, described learning a logical approach from her husband. She said, "I need to be a little bit more logical. So I can have a basis for my feeling on this situation. I think it is intelligent both ways, but I've come to see how important it is to have both things." She saw his ability to stand apart from something to analyze it as a way to augment her preference to stand inside of it. Sandra found herself in the opposite situation, having relied on the logical, separate pattern during college. As a professional counselor she had amassed first-hand experience in various contexts and described how this affected her decision making:

> I like to hear different viewpoints. I guess I already have—especially from experience—a pretty solid idea of how I think it should be. I'm willing to listen and hear what they have to say, but if it doesn't feel comfortable, I guess, sort of at a gut level, then I just figure, "Well, I'll stick with what I've got."

Sandra made it clear that she still used logic to analyze a viewpoint but that she simultaneously used the gut feeling that had emerged from her connection to counseling through first-hand experience. The role of gender appeared to dissipate in the postcollege years as participants integrated relational and impersonal patterns.

Phases of Contextual Knowing in the Postcollege Years

Contextual knowing also led to a shift from external to internal sources of knowing. Three distinct phases of this shift emerged in the postcollege interviews: using external formulas to make decisions, searching for internal authority, and establishing an internal foundation for belief (Baxter Magolda, 1999a, 2001).

External Formulas. In the initial phase of contextual knowing, participants realized their responsibility to decide what to believe, but having no internal system from which to choose, relied on external formulas. This was most evident in career and personal life choices in which participants did what they thought was expected of them without serious consideration of whether they would be satisfied with the choice. Anne explained her decision to work on becoming a CPA in this vein:

> The company wants you to do it; they'll pay for it. But most of the accountants in my company aren't CPAs. I think it kind of matters a little bit, like if there are two equal people up for a job and you're a CPA, you'd probably have a better chance. There are a couple of jobs in my department that are really technical and you have to have a CPA. So if I ever wanted one of those jobs, I mean, they're probably ten years from now jobs I would want to have, I would need it. I figure if I'm going to be an accountant I might as well be the best one and—I think people respect you a little more when you have that title. They think you know what you're doing. In today's world

with companies and mergers, I just figure it would make me more mar-
ketable if I needed to move sometime. . . . I felt useful and felt like I was
doing something to better myself.

Anne's description of her choice is based primarily on how others perceive the
CPA title and its utility for career advancement. Although she sees it as bettering
herself, she does not articulate what she might learn or how it will enhance her
vision of herself as an accountant.

Reliance on external formulas stemmed in part from participants' intrapersonal and interpersonal—as well as from their epistemological—development.
The strength of their sense of self in contrast to their need to please others contributed to reliance on external others, as Genesse described:

I loved working on the major account. I dealt with customers on a daily
basis, they were fun to talk to, and I dealt with internal people at the company. It was a high profile account, so I was invited to meetings and activities that were interesting. Then [the company] wanted me to take my own
set of accounts. I felt I couldn't say no. I cut off my nose to spite my face.
I interviewed and they picked me to take over a key account. It proved to
be more than what I felt I could handle. There were all sorts of problems
and I was unhappy. They offered me the option to go back to the major account and I did. Getting off the other account was good, but I feel like—
I sort of failed.

Genesse knew she was not ready for the new assignment but allowed others'
voices to overrun hers because she did not have a strong sense of self. Part of her
feeling of failure was from lack of success on the new accounts and part was
from disappointing external others. As in Genesse's case, doing what the external
world expected of them resulted in participants' disillusionment. The emerging
tension between external formulas and personal happiness brought them to a
crossroads between external and internal sources of knowing and choosing.

In Search of Internal Authority.   Kelly, at age 26, articulated arriving at the
crossroads and its implications:

I thought, "By the time I'm 25 I'll know it all; I'll have it all. It will all be
straight. My life will be set." Well, of course, we know that's not true. So
I've kind of accepted the fact that I don't know what's going on, just have
to take it as it comes and do the best I can. I've accepted the fact that I'm
never going to have it all straightened out. You just have to take each day,
each year, and do the best you can to educate yourself and do the best you
can in your work and your life.

Letting go of the external formula often resulted in the feeling of "not knowing
what is going on." Participants looked inward for a source of knowledge to re-

place the external one. Jim was experiencing this search for internal authority in both his work and personal life:

> I got engaged, then unengaged. Since I left college my focus has been getting to the top. Quality of life wasn't an issue; I wanted power. I'm realizing there is more to life than working. Scary—work has been my motivation. Now I'm considering more variables. I'm rethinking power, money, et cetera. Work was number one; fiancee was number two. I understand that now. Her moving out forced me into thinking more about what I am going after.

The need for internal authority usually stemmed from unhappiness. Participants used books as resources to develop their internal voices; some had encouragement from mentors who emphasized the importance of internal perspectives. Some engaged in professional counseling to solidify their own voices. Others found the value of genuine self-authorship when they experienced the positive consequences of acting on their own needs. By the mid to late twenties for most participants, the strength of the growing internal belief system prevailed over external influences.

Developing this internal belief system also required a shift in the intrapersonal and interpersonal dimensions of development (Baxter Magolda, 1999b). To adopt and act on internally derived beliefs, participants needed a coherent sense of self that could be influenced but not overwhelmed by others' perceptions and approval. Gavin articulated this succinctly in explaining a career change:

> [It was a] shift from what do my friends and relatives think versus what do I think. If my friend is a market analyst for Arthur Andersen, and I'm a social worker, what will people think? I am the only one who has to worry about what I think.

Gavin reported that it took him three years after college to come to this point and to act on his own interests without worrying about how he would be perceived.

The Foundation.   By their late twenties and early thirties, many participants had established an internally generated belief system that served as the foundation for self-authorship. Ned, quoted at the outset of this chapter, described how this foundation functioned to guide his work life in his early thirties. Reporting directly to the president of his company and supervising 50 people, Ned has significant responsibility and complex tasks:

> I am faced, on a daily basis, with situations or issues that I'm not prepared to answer or haven't thought about. How to run this project? What to do with this person? I have no idea. What I always do is fall back on basic life principles—all kinds of them—people are important, don't lie, do more for others than they expect, assume people are smart and will find an answer, hard work is important—those golden rules for the way you live your life—personal philosophies. When faced with a gray area, I fall back on

principles. Where did I get them? Parents, upbringing. What made that strong is that they have been accurate day to day. I've been able to practice them, they haven't failed me, so that emboldens me to rely on them more. Maybe it's called security, or confidence; it works for me.

Although Ned describes acquiring these principles from his parents and upbringing, they were solidified through his own success with them. As he has gained confidence with these principles, they became the core from which he operates. Despite having amassed extensive tecnhical knowledge and management expertise, he points to this foundation as the core of his functioning. It also guides his personal life, as he described balancing it with work:

One of my strongest internal drives is to succeed. I could be faulted for—my wife would say this—being unbalanced in approach to work versus free time. My dad was success-oriented; I've subconsciously held that model up. I am aware of the potential drawbacks; it is a delicate balance all the time. I tinker with it based on a keen sense of what is going on. My wife and I are close and talk a lot. I know when things need to be propped up at home versus what needs to be done in the business. Having a pulse on what's going on. My overall success is based on happiness in my relationship with my wife. Business is a secondary factor. We both want to be successful in the relationship and our careers, and want a family too. We want a rich and rewarding life together. Everyday we talk about it, reprioritizing goals. It is workable; it just takes a high amount of planning and constant communication.

Ned's sense of self is evident in these comments. He is aware of what influences him and the need to have a pulse on what is going on. He is willing to negotiate his needs and desires with those of his wife, illustrating interpersonal maturity. He realizes it is up to him and his wife to make the decisions that will lead to a rich and rewarding life. Ned's story conveys that this third phase of contextual knowing integrates the epistemic assumption that knowledge is contextual, the intellectual process of determining what to believe, and the integral role of the internally defined self in the knowledge construction process.

FUTURE DIRECTIONS

My longitudinal participants' stories offer one account of the journey from external to internal meaning-making. I emphasize this account as a possibility rather than a generalization because it is based on one group of predominantly White students who attended one university. Yet the trajectory they describe is not new. The Harvard men Perry (1970) studied in the 1950s traveled a similar path, as did the women Belenky, Clinchy, Goldberger, and Tarule (1986) studied in the 1980s. Perry's relativism, Belenky et al.'s constructed knowing, and my term contextual knowing all reflect the same core epistemic assumption. The four ways of knowing I have described also resemble the trajectory King and Kitchener (1994) describe in their Reflective Judgment Model. Similarities with these theories lend credibility to my longitudinal participants' account as a reasonable possibility for epistemological development in young adulthood.

What the Epistemological Reflection (ER) Model adds to our understanding is gender-related patterns across ways of knowing. Many of the nuances Belenky et al. pointed out in contrasting their women participants to Perry's scheme are evident in the gender-related patterns of the Epistemological Reflection Model. The relational patterns—receiving, interpersonal, and interindividual—reflect the core characteristics of Belenky et al.'s connected knowing while the separate patterns—mastery, impersonal, and individual—reflect their separate knowing. The ER data extend those concepts to earlier ways of knowing (Belenky et al. noted them in procedural knowing) and trace their integration in contextual knowing.

One limitation of the ER model is the minimal number of students of color in the study. Thus while these ways of knowing and patterns within them could be relevant to students of color, that judgment is not possible without further research. The existence of a connected pattern across ways of knowing, however, heightens the probability that the ER model reflects the experience of a broader population of students, in particular students of color who have been portrayed as connected (e.g., Branch-Simpson, 1984; Taub & McEwen, 1991; Ward, 1989)

Further research is needed to 1) determine the extent to which this portrayal of epistemological development transfers to other populations, 2) continue tracing development into adulthood, and 3) further integrate the intrapersonal, interpersonal, and epistemological dimensions of development into a holistic picture. Conducting a longitudinal, intensive interview study of young adults of color would be a major addition to the ER model and to the epistemological development literature in general. More longitudinal studies of various populations in which participants share their thinking in in-depth interviews are needed to access the complexities of development. Although I plan to continue my longitudinal project for this reason, similar work with diverse students is also needed. In the postcollege phase of my study, the intrapersonal and interpersonal dimensions of development began to surface in the interviews. I now try to incorporate those dimensions with the epistemic dimension to pursue an integrated theory of development. Future research would access complexity more readily if it focused on integration rather than isolation of one dimension. This shift is consistent with the shift in human development theory from positivist to constructivist approaches to understanding.

The value of the ER model is its emergence from longitudinal data. Following participants from age 18 to their early thirties via intensive annual interviews yielded rich data from which to interpret their experience. Including both women and men made seeing gender-related patterns across the developmental trajectory possible and yielded the important insight that the patterns are stylistic rather than structural characteristics. Rich descriptions of the participants' college experience also produced insights into contexts that promote self-authorship. Continuing the study into participants' twenties revealed possible effects of work, personal, and advanced educational environments on development, as well as the complexities of contextual knowing. Descriptions of contexts that promote self-authorship appear elsewhere (Baxter Magolda, 1992, 1999c, 2001). Finding ways to help young adults achieve self-authorship is another much needed line of research as contemporary society increasingly demands maturity for success in adult life.

REFERENCES

Baxter Magolda, M. B. (1992). *Knowing and reasoning in college: Gender-related patterns in students' intellectual development.* San Francisco, CA: Jossey-Bass.

Baxter Magolda, M. B. (1995). The integration of relational and impersonal knowing in young adults' epistemological development. *Journal of College Student Development, 36*(3), 205–216.

Baxter Magolda, M. B. (1999a). The evolution of epistemology: Refining contextual knowing at twentysomething. *Journal of College Student Development, 40* (4), 333–344.

Baxter Magolda, M. B. (1999b). Constructing adult identities. *Journal of College Student Development, 40* (6), 629–644.

Baxter Magolda, M. B. (1999c). *Creating contexts for learning and self-authorship: Constructive-developmental pedagogy.* Nashville, TN: Vanderbilt University Press.

Baxter Magolda, M.B. (2001). *Making their own way: Narratives to transform higher education to promote self-development.* Sterling, VA: Stylus Publishing.

Baxter Magolda, M. B., & Porterfield, W. D. (1988). *Assessing intellectual development: The link between theory and practice.* Alexandria, VA: American College Personnel Association.

Belenky, M., Clinchy, B., Goldberger, N., & Tarule, J. (1986). *Women's ways of knowing: The development of self, voice, and mind.* New York: Basic Books.

Branch-Simpson, G. E. (1984). *A study of the patterns in the development of black students at the Ohio State University.* Unpublished doctoral dissertation, Department of Educational Policy and Leadership, The Ohio State University.

Frye, M. (1990). The possibility of feminist theory. In D. L. Rhode (Ed.), *Theoretical perspectives on sexual difference* (pp. 174–184). New Haven. CT: Yale University Press.

Glaser, B., & Strauss, A. (1967). *The discovery of grounded theory: Strategies for qualitative research.* Chicago, IL: Aldine.

Kegan, R. (1982). *The evolving self: Problem and process in human development.* Cambridge, MA: Harvard University Press.

Kegan, R. (1994). *In over our heads: The mental demands of modern life.* Cambridge, Massachusetts: Harvard University Press.

King, P. M., & Kitchener, K. S. (1994). *Developing Reflective Judgment.* San Francisco: Jossey-Bass.

Kitchener, K. S. (1983). Cognition, metacognition, and epistemic cognition. *Human Development, 26,* 222–232.

Patton, M. Q. (1990). *Qualitative evaluation and research methods.* Newbury Park, CA: Sage.

Perry, W. G. (1970). *Forms of intellectual and ethical development in the college years: A scheme.* Troy, MO: Holt, Rinehart, & Winston.

Piaget, J. (1950). *The psychology of intelligence* (M. Piercy and D. Berlyne, Trans.). London: Routledge & Kegan Paul.

Strauss, A., & Corbin, J. (1994). Grounded theory methodology: An overview. In N. Denzin & Y. Lincoln (Eds.), *Handbook of qualitative research* (pp. 273–285). Thousand Oaks, CA: Sage.

Taub, D. J., & McEwen, M. K. (1991). Patterns of development of autonomy and mature interpersonal relationships in black and white undergraduate women. *Journal of College Student Development, 32,* 502–508.

Ward, J. V. (1989). Racial identity formation and transformation. In C. Gilligan, N. P. Lyons, & T. J. Hanmer (Eds.), *Making connections: The relational worlds of adolescent girls at Emma Willard School.* Troy, NY: Emma Willard School.

6

An Evolving Theoretical Framework for an Epistemological Belief System

Marlene Schommer-Aikins
Wichita State University

This chapter describes the study of epistemological beliefs as an epistemological belief system over the last ten years. If you are new to the field of epistemological belief inquiry, be forewarned. Some of the challenges of studying epistemological beliefs are: (a) facing your own epistemological beliefs, (b) wrestling with your own epistemological beliefs as they come to your consciousness, and (c) realizing that your present-day thinking is only one more step down the road of understanding.

In many ways this is a story about a journey; a journey in the development of thought regarding epistemological beliefs. In sharing my story, I hope to let budding researchers be aware of some of the adventures and pitfalls of the research process. For those more seasoned researchers, educators, and business leaders, I hope the journey will provide insight into your own thinking.

The following sections present a brief summary of my thinking in 1990, recapitulate my theoretical framework as of 1994, and present my most recent reflections of the conception and study of epistemological beliefs.

103

1990: INTRODUCING THE IDEA OF
AN EPISTEMOLOGICAL BELIEF SYSTEM

In the late 1980s a review of the epistemological research revealed that researchers who were studying learners' beliefs about the nature of knowledge and the nature of learning, or epistemological beliefs, were either followers of William Perry's (1968) work or, for the most part, engaged in unique lines of research. Perry is the pioneer researcher who examined Harvard undergraduates' epistemological beliefs using interviews and questionnaires. He concluded that students entering college tended to believe in simple, certain knowledge that is handed down by authority. By the time they reached their senior year, most students believed in tentative, complex knowledge that is derived from reason and observation.

Researchers following Perry's thinking provided greater insight into the notion of epistemological beliefs through lines of research with special focus. For example, Kitchener and King (1981) introduced the Reflective Judgment Model. Their 20 plus years of research have characterized the development of individuals' justification of knowledge. They suggest that learners move from the early stage of believing in absolute, concrete knowledge that is justified by acclamation of authority to a final stage of believing in tentative, context dependent knowledge that is justified with reason as well as expertise.

Researchers working independently of Perry were studying epistemological beliefs with a special interest in examining the relationship between epistemological beliefs and aspects of learning. Dweck and Bempechat (1983) ascertained that children have beliefs about the ability to learn. Children who believe the ability to learn is fixed at birth will display helpless behavior in the face of a difficult academic task. Children who believe the ability to learn can actually improve over time will stand up to the task by trying alternative paths to learning and continuing to persist. Schoenfeld (1983; 1985) has investigated high school students' beliefs about the nature of mathematics. His findings indicated that students with poor problem-solving skills tend to believe that mathematical knowledge is handed down by an omniscient authority and that solving mathematical problems should not take longer than about 12 minutes.

Hence, epistemological research extending from the late 1960s to the mid 1980s was being conducted by researchers with unique focuses of investigation and, to a certain extent, without knowledge of each other. With a synthesis of these ideas and the desire to capture the complexity of personal epistemology, the idea of an epistemological belief system was born.

In 1990 I reported the first major study attempting to test the conceptualization of personal epistemology as a system of more or less independent beliefs. By system of beliefs it is meant that there is more than one belief to consider in personal epistemology. The beliefs that were hypothesized included beliefs about: (a) the stability of knowledge, ranging from tentative to unchanging; (b) the structure of knowledge, ranging from isolated bits to integrated concepts;

(c) the source of knowledge, ranging from handed down by authority to gleaned from observation and reason, (d) the speed of knowledge acquisition, ranging from quick-all-or-none learning to gradual learning, and (e) the control of knowledge acquisition, ranging from fixed at birth to life-long improvement.

In order to assess these beliefs, a questionnaire was developed. Participants responded to statements such as "Scientists can ultimately get to the truth," and "Successful students learn things quickly," on a Likert scale from 1 (strongly disagree) to 5 (strongly agree). Using exploratory factor analysis, four of the five hypothesized beliefs were generated: structure and stability of knowledge, as well as the speed and control of learning.

In order to provide predictive validity, students were asked to read a passage (either in the social sciences or the physical sciences) and write a concluding paragraph. They also completed a passage content test and rated their confidence in their understanding of the passage. Regression analyses indicated that the more students believed in quick learning, the more likely they were to write oversimplified conclusions, perform poorly on the content test, and be overconfident in their understanding of the material. The more students believed in certain knowledge, the more likely they were to write definitive conclusions for tentative passages. These findings set the stage for further investigation into the idea of an epistemological belief system

1994: DEVELOPING A
THEORETICAL FRAMEWORK

The early 1990s was a time when researchers continued to test the notion of an epistemological belief system. The four-factor structure was replicated with additional samples of college students (Schommer, Crouse, & Rhodes, 1992) and with high school students (Schommer, 1993). Other researchers (Dunkle, Schraw, & Bendixen, 1993; Jehng, Johnson, & Anderson, 1993) revised the questionnaire. Factor analysis of the revised questionnaires generated five-factor models.

Although identifying multiple beliefs was important in the investigations of an epistemological belief system, linking epistemological beliefs to unique aspects of learning was essential. The early 90s research revealed that belief in quick learning related to students' grade point average (Schommer, 1993; Schommer & Dunnell, 1994). Belief in simple knowledge related to students' study strategies and comprehension of complex text (Schommer et al., 1992). Beliefs in simple and certain knowledge related to students' problem solving of ill-structured content (Schraw, Dunkle, & Bendixen, 1995). Belief in quick learning predicted problem solving in well-structured content (Schraw et al., 1995). Furthermore, the notion of epistemological beliefs was being incorporated into more encompassing theories. For example, Pajares (1992) considered epistemological beliefs to be an important aspect in teachers' instructional beliefs and Winne (1995) theorized that epistemological beliefs serve an important role of setting standards for students' self-regulated learning.

In 1994 I published a loose-knit theoretical framework describing the episte-mological belief system based on accumulating evidence and reflection. A brief summary follows. For more details, see Schommer (1994).

1. Personal epistemology may be conceptualized as a system of beliefs. That is, personal epistemology is composed of more than one belief. (Neither four nor five beliefs is considered a sacred number. This will be discussed later in this chapter.)
2. Beliefs within the system are more or less independent, that is, it cannot be assumed that beliefs will be maturing in synchrony. First, it is important to understand that among many epistemological belief researchers, epistemo-logical maturity was presumed to be indicated by learners' propensity to believe that knowledge is tentative and complex and that learning is grad-ual and controllable. To be in synchrony would mean that learners believe all four of these attributes. As an example of asynchrony, at some point in time an individual may strongly believe in complex knowledge (consid-ered a more mature belief) and simultaneously strongly believe in un-changing knowledge (considered a less mature belief). My point of more or less independent is that learners may, or may not, be in synchrony. It simply cannot be assumed one way or the other; Rather, in practice devel-opment should be determined on a case-by-case basis.
3. Epistemological beliefs are better characterized as frequency distributions rather than dichotomies or continuums. For example, it is likely that a ma-ture learner believes that a small percentage of knowledge is unchanging and a substantial percentage of knowledge is evolving.
4. Epistemological beliefs have both indirect and direct effects. By indirect effect it is meant that epistemological beliefs mediate learning. For exam-ple, a strong belief in isolated knowledge could set the standard for what it means to learn, in this case, learning would mean being able to recall a list of facts. This standard in turn leads the learner to select only memo-rizing as a study strategy. This single, limited study strategy would result in an impoverished mental representation of the content. Ultimately this leads to inert knowledge. As an example of a more direct effect, strong belief in certain knowledge may serve as a filter in interpreting tentative text as if it were definitive.
5. Whether epistemological beliefs are domain general or domain independent will vary over time for any particular individual. (More about this later.)
6. Epistemological belief development and change is influenced by experi-ence. These experiences include engaging in problem solving and learn-ing from family, friends, formal education, and life experiences.
7. The final point in my 1994 presentation of a theoretical framework was an invitation. I wrote at that time, "If you . . . are now convinced that epis-

temological beliefs, as difficult as they may be to conceive and measure, are too important to ignore, then I have achieved my most important goal. If you find yourself in doubt about the conception, the measure, and the findings of epistemological beliefs to date, then I have achieved another goal, to entice you to reflect, research, and revise the conceptualization of epistemological beliefs" (Schommer, 1994, p. 38). The contributors to this book are participating in the ongoing pursuit of this challenging task.

2000: IT IS TIME TO CLARIFY AND ELABORATE

In the decade of the 90s interest in epistemological belief research has risen dramatically. I receive manuscripts to review on a regular basis. E-mail from around the world enters my electronic mailbox frequently. I have had the opportunity to see the bigger picture of the research process in action.

I have not seen a direct reference to my invitation quoted previously. I can only infer that many are responding to it. I have seen reviews of my work, applications of my work, misunderstandings of my work, or misinterpretations of my words. As I have interacted with veteran researchers, I have learned that all of these events are likely to occur over time. They have provided the impetus for me to rethink what I write and provide guidance as to what needs to be clarified.

Researchers have started to examine the notion of a system of epistemological beliefs. For example, some researchers have used the theory and/or the questionnaire to study epistemological beliefs in situ of their own existing line of researcher (e.g., Hall, Chiarello, & Edmonson, 1996; Kardash & Scholes, 1996; Winne, 1995). That is, they are identifying the role of epistemological beliefs in the larger picture of cognition and/or affect.

Some researchers have tried to develop new means of assessing epistemological beliefs. New questionnaires are being developed (see King & Kitchener, chap. 3, this volume; Schraw, Bendixen, & Dunkle, chap. 13, this volume; Wood & Kardash, chap. 12, this volume). There are those pushing harder for the qualitative approach (Hammer & Elby, chap. 9, this volume). In addition, some researchers are trying to revise the theory I have proposed by adding some beliefs, subtracting other beliefs, and elaborating on their own theory (Hofer & Pintrich, 1997). All of these are exciting developments that should ultimately lead to better epistemological belief theories, measurement, and instruction.

Furthermore, the last ten years has been marked by the consistent development of earlier conceptions of epistemological belief, which is readily apparent by some of the contributors to this volume (e.g., Baxter Magolda; Chandler; Clinchy; King & Kitchener). After taking the time to reflect on other's work, that is, those who influenced me in the first place, and to consider the challenges more recent researchers have generated, the following are reflections that help clarify some issues of conception of an epistemological belief system.

RECENT REFLECTIONS

Why Is the Study of Epistemological Beliefs Important?

One of the most basic questions that can be asked of any line of research is, "Why is it important?" A traditional response to the need of a theory is that the theory allows us to explain, predict, and modify thinking. But to sharpen that pat answer, it's important to be reminded of what is really the underlying theme of the study of epistemological beliefs. It is an attempt to understand the learner's perspective. Why would the learner say, "Which theory is the right theory?" immediately after the teacher finished clarifying that the issue is still unresolved? Why will students fail to integrate ideas unless instruction "forces" them to integrate? From an applied point of view, it may not seem necessary to understand the student's perspective as long as the student is learning. It's when the student's thinking goes awry that the teacher must pinpoint the source of the problem. The study of epistemological beliefs may serve to identify some critical sources of the problem. The study of epistemological beliefs may also serve to guide us in modifying the instruction to be more amenable to students' ways of thinking.

I bring this issue to the forefront; because once immersed in the study of epistemological beliefs, it is easy to become lost in the sea of philosophical quandaries, debates over definitions and contentions over measures. It is important to keep the ultimate goals in mind: to understand learners, to help teachers help learners, and to inform other theories of cognition and affect.

What Is Personal Epistemology?

Defining personal epistemology is highly complex. The fine work of others in developing conceptions notwithstanding, I will attempt to clarify the notion of an epistemological belief system. For a more precise definition of an epistemological belief system, other issues must be incorporated including: (a) the multiplicity and singularity of beliefs, (b) the independence and dependence among beliefs, and (c) the domain specificity and generality of beliefs. Before answering the question, "What is personal epistemology?," some underlying concepts need elucidation.

Theme of Balance. One of the key themes throughout my more recent thinking is balance. You will note for example that I used the conjunction "and" among the issues to be incorporated. It has never been my intention to assert that epistemological beliefs are completely independent or that epistemological beliefs are only domain general. Personal epistemology is far too complex to be defined in either/or terms.

There is a caveat with regard to understanding what I mean by balance. The theme of balance does not imply falling into an abyss of relativism. You will see in the following clarification that I do not waffle on issues. Rather, I argue that epistemological beliefs will vary in multiplicity, generality, and independence over time. This variation adds to the challenge of attempting to define and measure epistemological beliefs. Presently in my thinking, what I reject are definitions of epistemological beliefs that adamantly eliminate the possibility of variation in the nature of epistemological beliefs or that adamantly dismiss the possibility of measuring epistemological beliefs at least to a limited degree.

What Is Included in Personal Epistemology?   The very definition of personal epistemology remains controversial among epistemological belief researchers. If driven from a purely philosophical stance, one might suggest that the definition of personal epistemology is limited to beliefs about the nature of knowledge (e.g., Hofer & Pintrich. 1997). What constitutes knowledge? What serves as justification of knowledge? What is the source of knowledge? Although this is epistemology in its philosophical sense, it does not capture other epistemic issues that are intimately related. Hence, I have included two beliefs about learning, beliefs about the speed of learning and the control of learning. From a practical stance, these two beliefs about learning have been found to be related to numerous aspects of learning, such as persistence in the face of a difficult task (Dweck & Leggett, 1988), planned thinking time (Schoenfeld, 1983), and the valuing of education (Schommer & Walker, 1997). From a theoretical stance, a preponderance of epistemological belief researchers would agree that it is the role of epistemological beliefs in other cognitions and affect that make it important and beliefs about learning qualify in this respect.

Although Hofer and Pintrich chose to define personal epistemology in its purest form, they acknowledge the importance of beliefs about learning. Indeed, they offer an alternative notion that beliefs about learning may be a precursor to beliefs about knowing. I am not opposed to that idea. On the other hand, if beliefs about knowledge are born from beliefs about learning, then I suggest this is evidence of the intimacy among the beliefs. Recent investigations hint at this precursor relationship. Factor analysis based on middle school students' responses to an epistemological questionnaire suggests that these young students have undifferentiated beliefs about learning, and a very limited, simplistic understanding about the nature of knowledge per se (Schommer-Aikins, Mau, Brookhart, & Hutter, 2000). Older students' data generate multiple, differentiated beliefs about knowledge and learning (e.g., Jehng et al., 1993; Schommer, 1990). This cross-sectional view of epistemological beliefs suggests the developmental trend from acquiring beliefs about learning to acquiring beliefs about knowledge per se. I remain particularly tentative on this issue. Much more evidence is needed. Furthermore, Chandler's evidence (in this volume) of the early development of beliefs about the certainty of knowledge challenge this notion. Obviously more inquiries are needed to determine the adequacy of this hypothesized developmental trend.

Some epistemological belief researchers chose to focus their research on a single belief or a subset of beliefs (see contributors to this volume). This focus allows them to probe more deeply into the details of specific beliefs. On the other hand, if researchers arc attempting to look at the bigger picture, they need to include beliefs about learning. An even more encompassing picture will include other beliefs, for example beliefs about self and beliefs about domains, (see De Corte, Eynde, & Verschaffel, chap. 15, this volume). In sum, it would appear that the question of what should be included in the definition of personal epistemology involves the determination of the relationship between beliefs about learning and beliefs about knowledge, and the scope of research interest.

The Role of Development in the Dimensionality and Level of Specificity of Personal Epistemology

You will note that in my recent reflections I have already implied that there is more than one belief to be considered in the conception of personal epistemology. To me, personal epistemology is too complex to be captured as a single belief. To be discussed in more detail later, it is quite possible that this set of beliefs is functioning in unison at certain times in one's life, but not all of the time. Furthermore, from a practical point of view, teachers would find diagnosing students' cognition and affect easier if they could pinpoint strengths and weaknesses in specific areas of a students' epistemological beliefs. In other words, detailed information as well as global information is important for teachers to understand students' epistemological beliefs.

Furthermore, I continue to entertain the notion that epistemological beliefs are more or less independent. Let me try to clarify the thinking behind this concept. By more or less independent, I mean that individual beliefs within a system of beliefs do not develop in synchrony. That is, there are times during development that an individual may believe that knowledge is highly complex, yet simultaneously believe that knowledge is highly certain. What is key here is that this synchrony or asynchrony will vary depending at what point in development an individual is. This same phenomenon may also be occurring with regard to the domain specificity issue. Personal epistemology may be predominately domain general or domain specific depending on where one is developmentally.

With regard to the dimensionality of an epistemological belief system, it may be that early in life epistemological beliefs are undifferentiated. As children gain input from parents, peers, culture, and education, they begin to differentiate among different aspects of knowledge, for example, beliefs about the certainty of knowledge, source of knowledge, and the structure of knowledge.

As learners continue to develop, individual beliefs may begin to merge, blur, and finally combine symbiotically, or in the case of the confused or anxious individual, combine in discord. I use the words merge and blur to suggest that part of epistemological belief development involves the experience of a state of confusion. In the best of all worlds, on the other side of confusion comes the symbiotic synthesis of beliefs in the system, for example that knowledge may be seen as complex, evolving, and being derived from self, interaction with others, and empirical evidence. Furthermore, acquiring knowledge is ongoing, gradual, and ever improving. In terms of Hofer and Pintrich (1997), this may be the development of a personal theory of epistemology.

Similar to Chandler's thinking (chap. 8, this volume), I do entertain the idea that the development of epistemological beliefs may be recursive. In my own opinion, this recursive process of revisiting, revising, and honing our beliefs within a system of epistemological beliefs is likely to be a life-long process. The only time this process would end would be at the end of our lives, or at the demise of our ability to think. What would be most informative would be to study the epistemological belief researchers contributing to this volume when they are near the end of their lives. How much will they have learned? How much will their conceptualizations have changed? How many ideas will they have held onto tenaciously?

Attempting to determine if learners' epistemological beliefs develop in synchrony or asynchrony is related to whether one conceives of epistemological beliefs as unidimensional or multidimensional. Imagine a researcher entertains the idea of multiple beliefs. If one is using a quantitative instrument and the participants' beliefs are synchronous, then factor scores will be highly correlated and factor analysis will generate only one or two factors. When participants' beliefs are differentiated, factors scores will be less correlated and factor analyses will generate multiple factors. Up to five factors have been discerned to date (e.g., Jehng et al., 1993). On the other hand, the researcher who rejects, for example a five-belief system, would interpret correlated data as evidence of fewer beliefs, not as evidence of synchronous development.

The point is that it is possible that the number of dimensions one finds with quantitative measures may vary depending on the developmental level of the participants. To make sure that the variation is not due to inadequate measurement, it is advisable to re-administer the assessment to the same group of participants within a short amount of time and see if the findings are replicable (test–retest reliability). Furthermore, comparisons to comparable groups with the exact same version of the measuring instrument and with comparable administration procedures would be useful.

If one is using qualitative measures, it is possible to examine epistemological beliefs in more detail. The researcher is not limited to looking at beliefs along a continuum. Rather, if researchers choose to look at personal epistemology in a more diagnostic, detailed way, they can examine individuals' epistemological beliefs by gleaning them from general questions or asking more pointed questions. Hence, even if individual beliefs within the learners' system of epistemological beliefs are at similar levels of development (as assessed by a quantitative instrument), the qualitative nuances of each belief can be captured by the careful, pinpointed characterization of each belief through phenomenological descriptions. If learners cannot respond to specific questions or researchers cannot glean different beliefs within the system of beliefs, then participants may be in an undifferentiated point of development.

In a similar vein, the issue of domain specificity may vary over development. Again, the exact nature of this development is difficult to discern. One possibility is that personal epistemology may be domain general very early in life. As children are exposed to ideas from family, peers, culture, and formal education, their personal epistemology may become more domain specific. And, a point that I would like to stress, it is likely that as learners progress in their development they will acquire both domain specific and domain general epistemological beliefs.

On the surface, the assertion of the existence of both domain specific and domain general epistemological beliefs may sound like the bottomless well of relativism. It is not. Rather, this notion echoes the theme of balance. For example, mathematics is generally taught on the basis of well-established rules, while social studies focuses on ill-structured problems. This does not mean that certainty and structuredness does not vary within both domains (Alexander, 1992). For example, learners are likely to encounter both tentative and ill-structured problems in advanced mathematics (Schommer, 1998).

Furthermore, to assume there is no domain generality of epistemological beliefs is like assuming we change like a chameleon from environment to environment. Even a chameleon only changes its color to fit in. It does not change its essence. I suggest that mature individuals have a sense of self that is core. And that part of this sense of self is personal epistemology, an aspect of their epistemological beliefs that is domain general. This general core of epistemological beliefs may serve as the foundation from where their domain specific epistemological beliefs spring forth. More importantly, this general core of epistemological beliefs will serve them well when they are initially learning a new domain, particularly when learners cannot readily relate the new domain to a domain with which they are already familiar.

What Is This Talk About Sophisticated Beliefs?

Understandably so, a few people have been disgruntled by the use of the term "sophisticated" or mature epistemological beliefs. To be sure, it is audacious to assume that one has the omniscient vision to know what is precisely the best epistemological stance. Sometimes this language is used as a consequence of the means of measurement. For example, when researchers are using quantitative instruments, they symbolize the learners' epistemological beliefs with a number. A higher value means "A" and a lower number means "B." It is inherent in the numerical system to imply one value is preferred over another. As we become more sophisticated in our quantitative approaches, this simplistic interpretation may be replaced with a more refined, accurate, and flexible means of interpreting scores.

This implicit assumption of a hierarchical system of epistemological beliefs is not limited to quantitative investigations. Researchers using qualitative measures clearly assert upward change in either stages of development, e.g., the Reflective Judgment Model, or positions of development, Perry's model. It is clear from work using either research methodology that the idea of sophisticated beliefs embraces evolving knowledge, multiple approaches to the justification of knowledge, integration of knowledge, and for those willing to entertain a broader conception of epistemological beliefs, gradual learning, and ever growing ability to learn.

Among my reflections the key word, again, is balance. I will not sit comfortably on a fence and deny that there is such thing as mature epistemological beliefs. The denial of a preferred epistemological perspective throws me into the deep well of excessive relativism. Furthermore, Perry (1968) also suggested balance in his thinking when he described the more advanced learner, for example, as believing in tentative, complex knowledge as the rule. At the same time the learner could also entertain the idea of either solid, unchangeable knowledge and/or isolated knowledge. The difference between the advanced thinking and unadvanced is that the unchangeable, isolated beliefs in knowledge are predominant for the less mature thinker and are the exception for the more mature thinker.

In terms of the frequency distributions that I suggested in the 1990s, the unchangeable, isolated beliefs are given a large share of the frequency distribution for the less mature learner and small share of the frequency distribution for the more mature learner. Recent research tends to be consistent with this notion. One approach to testing this notion is to compare expert and novice learners. For example, in epistemological interviews in which students and mathematics professors were asked to assign frequencies to the amount of mathematical knowledge that is evolving and the amount of mathematical knowledge that will change, undergraduates on the average attributed 78% of mathematical knowledge as unchanging, while professors attributed on the average 36% of mathematical knowledge as unchanging (Schommer, 1998).

Obviously the rationale used in designating epistemological sophistication is that the beliefs support quality study strategies, quality comprehension, quality interpretation, and quality problem solving. That is, those qualities presumably are the basis on which epistemological belief researchers have either implicitly or explicitly defined sophisticated epistemological beliefs. I realize as I write this that the paradigms that are prevalent today are serving as the assumed qualities, e.g., domain specificity, social discourse, situated cognition, and multicultural education.

Here is where I must be bold and step off the easy ride of unbridled relativism. As of this writing I will suggest that there really is a difference between the sophisticated learner and the unsophisticated learner. There is a difference between sophisticated epistemological beliefs and less sophisticated epistemological beliefs. The sophisticated learner will maintain epistemological beliefs that support flexible thinking, yet underlying that ability to take in new ideas or change old ideas, will be a steadfastness of core concepts. It's back to the issues of balance and development.

In the very early years a child perhaps with little knowledge base must of necessity ebb and flow with incoming information. It is as if life is handing them bricks and mortar for the first time and children begin to build their thinking. This early-in-life foundational groundwork is but one part of the solid core to which I refer. Another part of this core is the idea of stability in life. Please do not confuse stability in life as rigidity or being "stuck in one's ways." That is the negative interpretation of stability. Rather, from a positive perspective, stability in life means knowing who you are and believing that some knowledge is reliable. Without some aspect of knowledge being stable, learners could not make decisions, learners would live in constant fear of the unknown, and values in life could not be established. As I have suggested in my earlier work, one could feel insane, suicidal, or in the vernacular of Boyes and Chandler (1992), a life long skeptic.

Again, as you read this, think balance. I am not saying the solid core dominates the learners' thinking. Rather, it may be a small core that allows one to build on and around that one entertains new ideas and modifies old ideas. Can the core ever change? I would suggest that, yes, it probably can change through traumatic experiences or extreme challenges to one's thinking.

Nevertheless, even with the presence of the solid core, on the surface—to most other onlookers—the sophisticated learner will appear flexible, evolving, the seeker of complexities, the ever patient learner who takes his or her time to learn. And indeed, it is true that these modes of thinking and affect driven by epistemological beliefs will be the learner's dominant force.

As one last effort to express this thought, to me this is like the nature versus nurture argument. It makes little sense to deny either influence. The difficult part is to ascertain which aspect is dominating. And that dominating factor may vary from time to time or situation to situation. The important point is that both the factors are functioning.

How Do We Measure Personal Epistemology?

It has been interesting to see what researchers have done with the epistemological questionnaire that I developed in 1990. Some have found the instrument as a useful predictor (e.g., Hall et al., 1996; Windschitl & Andre, 1998). Some have worked diligently to revise it and develop a more psychometrically sound instrument (Jehng et al., 1993). Still others have used it as a springboard to develop their own measures (e.g., Schraw et al., chap. 13, this volume; Wood & Kardash, chap. 12, this volume).

I would hope that we wouldn't consider this 1990 instrument to be the final assessment tool of all times. Would we be happy if we were all using the first phone that was invented, the first measure of psychological thinking, or the first assessment of disease? Rather, the basic ideas behind the first tools serve as the foundation for future inventions. So it is with the 1990 Schommer Epistemological Questionnaire.

Let me share some of the thinking that went into the development of this instrument. This may help others as they attempt to develop improved assessments. First, I gathered ideas from respected researchers that proceeded me (e.g., Kitchener & King, 1981; Perry, 1968; Ryan, 1984; Schoenfeld, 1983). Second, in attempting to synthesize their work, the idea of multiple dimensions was implicit.

Part of the challenge of assessing epistemological beliefs was dealing with the idea that epistemological beliefs are for the most part unconscious, if not tacit. How does one assess these beliefs that are so deeply imbedded in the mind and spirit? My attempt was to cast a net of inquiry in order to capture an array of beliefs by constructing a questionnaire that probed in different ways at the same concepts. That is, I had learners respond in numerous situations by asking questions that varied in person (first, second, and third person) and varied in directness and/or situation (study strategies, educational settings, life in general, and content—science and reading). A natural consequence is that the questionnaire is long. I have not found the 63 items to be excessive for high school, college, or adult participants. I do not assume young participants would be comfortable with this many items.

I found some intriguing reactions to the survey. The change of person and the varying of directness has been criticized because it does not follow intuitive notions of parsimony (Hofer & Pintrich, 1997). Consider the possibility that the more clean and parsimonious we make a questionnaire, the less we will capture when we are assessing concepts in ill-structured domain, such as beliefs. There is a trade-off between breadth and depth, between complex and simple, between ill-structuredness and well-structuredness. My response is that we need both.

Others reactions have focused on the length of the questionnaire. Although I certainly prefer a shorter questionnaire and am working on it, this length is not unusual. It should also be noted that the items are in random order to serve as a safeguard for potential fatigue effect. Furthermore, psychometricians would agree that assessing complex concepts with a handful of items is not advisable.

What I would hope is that in the future we continue to improve on the quantitative approaches to the assessment of epistemological beliefs. These tools will facilitate gathering data from large samples, assessing expeditiously, and serve as an assessment tool for teachers to use.

Furthermore, it is critical that we continue to develop qualitative approaches. It is likely that we need fresh approaches to qualitative methodologies as well (Hammer & Elby, chap. 9, this volume). It would seem that ideally, we will develop combination assessments, that is, in a single assessment tool we will have both qualitative and quantitative measures. In this way, we can get a notion of the big picture and simultaneously delve into individuals' nuances. Furthermore, if these two measures within the same tool sharply contrast, we will be forced to reconcile the differences or understand why such differences coexist.

With the ongoing development of computer technology, it is likely that we will be able to capture the dynamic nature of epistemological beliefs as well as the small stable core. This technology may also help us cope with the complexity and time-consuming process of data analysis.

FINAL THOUGHTS

In brief, this journey of epistemological belief research has provided an overview of ten years of research. In the early 1990s epistemological beliefs were reconceptualized as a system of multiple beliefs that developed more or less independently. By 1994 it was proposed that each belief be considered more complexly by using a frequency distribution metaphor, asserting indirect and direct effects, and considering the complex relationship of development with issues such as domain specificity and synchrony of development. Table 6.1 summarizes some of the key points that I have tried to make in this chapter.

This theory, as does any theory, has its limitations. Many questions remain unaddressed. Although only a small list will be presented here, each question can serve as the impetus of future research. Do learning beliefs lead to knowledge beliefs or vice versa? Do two or more beliefs effect learning concurrently? In other

TABLE 6.1
Summarizing Main Points of the
Conceptualization of an Epistemological Belief System

1990

1. Prior epistemological belief research is synthesized.
2. Five epistemological beliefs are hypothesized.
3. Four epistemological beliefs are derived.
4. Epistemological beliefs examined along continuums.
5. Links between epistemological beliefs and learning are found.

1994

1. A system of epistemological beliefs is proposed.
2. Epistemological beliefs are considered more or less independent.
3. The nature of each epistemological belief is characterized as frequency distributions.
4. Epistemological beliefs have indirect and direct effects.
5. Domain scope of epistemological beliefs varies over time.
6. Development and change of epistemological beliefs are influenced by experience.

2000

1. The overall theme is balance.
2. An antithesis is unbridled relativism.
3. Development is key to other aspects of the theory of an epistemological belief system.
4. The number of epistemological beliefs may vary over time.
5. Domain scope of epistemological beliefs may vary over time.
6. Epistemological belief development is a lifelong process.
7. A small core of epistemological belief distributions may provide stability and foundation for growth.
8. Multiple approaches to assessment are needed.
9. Measurement should consider the developmental level of the individual.
10. Do not forget the goal of understanding the students' perspective.

words, how do combinations of beliefs affect learning? If it is assumed that epistemological beliefs are tacit, can individuals articulate their beliefs in response to researchers' direct inquiries? Are the epistemological beliefs hypothesized in this theory applicable across cultures? Is there any reason we should assume universality? Are the epistemological beliefs of experts within a domain the same? Are the epistemological beliefs of experts between domains the same? These are but a few questions that the theory does not address nor does data yet answer.

If there is but one message you retain from this work, the key idea to remember is "balance," but not at the price of unbridled relativism. And let it not be forgotten that all of us, we the contributors to the text and you the readers, will continue to grow and develop epistemologically. We must ask ourselves, where will our thinking be in 10 years, 20 years, 30 years, or longer? If we think to the future, perhaps it will help us in the present.

REFERENCES

Alexander, P. A. (1992). Domain knowledge: Evolving themes and emerging concerns. *Educational Psychologist, 27*, 33–51.

Boyes, M. C., & Chandler, M. (1992). Cognitive development, epistemic doubt, and identity formation in adolescence. *Journal of Youth and Adolescence, 21*, 211–303.

Dunkle, M. E., Schraw, G. J., & Bendixen, L. (1993). *The relationship between epistemological beliefs, causal attributions, and reflective judgment.* Paper presented at the Annual Meeting of the American Educational Research Association, Atlanta, GA.

Dweck, C. S., & Bempechat, J. (1983). Children's theories of intelligence: Consequences for learning. In S. G. Paris, G. M. Olson, & H. W. Stevenson (eds.), *Learning and motivation in the classroom* (pp. 239–256). Hillsdale, NJ: Erlbaum.

Dweck, C. S., & Leggett, E. L. (1988). A social-cognitive approach to motivation and personality. *Psychological Review, 95*, 256–273.

Hall, V. C., Chiarello, K. S., & Edmonson, B. (1996). Deciding where knowledge comes from depends on where you look. *Journal of Educational Psychology, 88*, 305–313.

Hammer, D. (1994). Epistemological belief in introductory physics. *Cognition and Instruction, 12*, 151–183.

Hofer, B. K., & Pintrich, P. R. (1997). The development of epistemological theories: Beliefs about knowledge and knowing and their relation to learning. *Review of Educational Research, 67*, 88–140.

Jehng, J. J., Johnson, S. D., & Anderson, R. C. (1993). Schooling and student's epistemological beliefs about learning. *Contemporary Educational Psychology, 18*, 23–35.

Kardash, C. M., & Scholes, R. J. (1996). Effects of preexisting beliefs, epistemological beliefs, and need for cognition on interpretation of controversial issues. *Journal of Educational Psychology, 88*, 260–271.

Kitchener, K. S., & King, P. M. (1981). Reflective judgment: Concepts of justification and their relationship to age and education. *Journal of Applied Developmental Psychology, 2*, 89–116.

Ryan, M. P. (1984). Monitoring text comprehension: Individual differences in epistemological standards. *Journal of Educational Psychology, 76*, 248–258.

Pajares, F. (1992). Teachers' beliefs and educational research: Cleaning up a messy construct. *Review of Educational Research, 62*, 307–332.

Perry, W. G., Jr. (1968). *Patterns of development in thought and values of students in a liberal arts college: A validation of a scheme.* Cambridge, MA: Bureau of Study Counsel, Harvard University (ERIC Document Reproduction Service No. ED 024315).

Ryan, M. P. (1984). Monitoring text comprehension: Individual differences in epistemological standards. *Journal of Educational Psychology.* 76, 248–258.

Schoenfeld, A. H. (1983). Beyond the purely cognitive: Beliefs systems, social conditions, and metacognitions as driving forces in intellectual performance. *Cognitive Science, 7,* 329–363.

Schoenfeld, A. H. (1985). *Mathematical problem solving.* New York: Academic Press.

Schommer, M. (1990). Effects of beliefs about the nature of knowledge on comprehension. *Journal of Educational Psychology, 82,* 498–504.

Schommer, M. (1993). Epistemological development and academic performance among secondary students. *Journal of Educational Psychology, 85,* 1–6.

Schommer, M. (1994). An emerging conceptualization of epistemological beliefs and their role in learning. In R. Garner and P. Alexander (Eds.), *Beliefs about text and about text instruction* (pp. 25–39). Hillsdale, NJ: Erlbaum.

Schommer, M. (1998, April). *Comparing professors and students on their epistemological beliefs.* Contribution to a symposium presented at the annual conference of the American Educational Research Association, San Diego, CA.

Schommer, M., Crouse, A., & Rhodes, N. (1992). Epistemological beliefs and mathematical text comprehension: Believing it's simple doesn't make it so. *Journal of Educational Psychology, 84,* 435–443.

Schommer, M., & Dunnell, P. A. (1994). A comparison of epistemological beliefs between gifted and nongifted high school students. *Roeper Review, 16,* 207–210.

Schommer, M., Mau, W., & Brookhart, S., & Hutter, R. (2000). Understanding middle students' beliefs about knowledge and learning using a multidimensional paradigm. *Journal of Educational Research, 94,* 120–127.

Schommer, M., & Walker, K. (1997). Epistemological beliefs and valuing school: Considerations for college admissions and retention. *Research in Higher Education, 38,* 173–185.

Schraw, G., Dunkle, M. E., & Bendixen, L. D. (1995). Cognitive processes in well-defined and ill-defined problem solving. *Applied Cognitive Psychology, 9,* 523–538.

Windschitl, M. & Andre, T. (1998). Using computer simulations to enhance conceptual change: The roles of constructivist instruction and student epistemological beliefs. *Journal of Research in Science Teaching, 35,* 145–160.

Winne, P. H. (1995). Inherent details in self-regulated learning. *Educational Psychologist, 30,* 173–187.

II

Theoretical and
Conceptual Issues

7

What Is Epistemological Thinking and Why Does It Matter?

Deanna Kuhn
*Teachers College,
Columbia University*

Michael Weinstock
*Teachers College,
Columbia University*

The title of our contribution to this volume reflects our view that these two questions—first, what exactly is epistemological thinking, and, second, why does it matter—are the essential ones that must be answered if the objectives that the present volume represents are to be realized. Until very recently, the study of epistemological thinking has held more or less orphan status in the field of cognitive development. A handful of different research groups have worked on the topic for a number of years and produced broadly consistent findings. These findings, however, elicited little reaction on the part of others in the field of cognitive development, and scarcely any connections have been made to other dimensions of cognitive development, either by those conducting this research or by its potential audience.

Possible reasons that we have proposed as to why there has not been broader interest in the topic are its conceptual ambiguity and complexity (Kuhn, Cheney, & Weinstock, in press). As Hofer and Pintrich (1997) note in their comprehensive review, "Defining the construct [of epistemological understanding] is problematic, as there are discrepancies in naming the construct as well as in defining the construct, to the extent that it is sometimes unclear to what degree researchers are discussing the same intellectual territory" (p. 111). Moreover, previous attempts to define the construct have been of a sort that have limited its accessibility. King and Kitchener's (1994) model, as the most well-known example, contains seven distinct levels, with each of these levels defined in terms of multiple dimensions and a complex coding system employed to assess an individual's level. As a result, the casual interest of someone seeking an overview of the development of epistemological thinking is not readily rewarded.

On the positive side, however, the largely independent research groups working on the topic have in fact produced a broadly consistent picture of what it is that develops. A major goal of our own recent work (Kuhn et al., in press) has been to clarify this picture by attempting to define what develops in the epistemological domain in the simplest possible theoretical and empirical terms. Doing so, we believe, has the potential benefit of facilitating the "anchoring" of epistemological development in a broader context of what has preceded it developmentally and what else is developing cognitively during the adolescent and early adulthood period of the life span when epistemological development is most likely to take place. This anchoring is essential, we believe, if the topic is to receive the attention it deserves and its significance is to be fully appreciated.

A related, and, in our view, equally critical condition for this objective to be met is to establish not just how epistemological development is connected to other areas of cognitive or social development but to ascertain what impact if any it might have on these other dimensions of development. If development in epistemological thinking does in fact occur but proceeds as an isolated strand of development, with no consequences extending beyond its own development, it may still remain an interesting phenomenon to study—the adolescent or young adult as amateur philosopher—but its significance is vastly reduced.

We believe this not to be the case, and in this chapter we describe the results of our own efforts to identify exactly what epistemological thinking and its development entail and to identify the possible consequences of such development (or lack of it)—in other words, to establish what difference it makes.

WHAT IS DEVELOPING?

Theoretical efforts to characterize the development of epistemological thinking have largely adhered to a stage model. In other words, a sequence of some number of distinct stages is proposed, with each stage identified by multiple characteristics that serve to define that stage. A common set of dimensions may or may not run through these characteristics, or may do so partially. In other words, some characteristics may be points along a common dimension identified at every stage, while other characteristics are unique to a single stage and appear only in the definition of that stage.

The strengths and weaknesses of stage models have been widely discussed in the cognitive development literature. Certainly among the significant strengths is the qualitative description of a developmental course (in contrast to a quantitative characterization of "how much" of various attributes are present). A significant weakness of stage models that depend on multiple, diverse characteristics to define each stage, however, is a lack of cohesion with respect to these characteristics, such that it is not clear what defines the "essence" of the stage, and particularly, what drives the movement from the diversity of characteristics defining one stage to those defining the next.

In our view this negative feature of traditional stage models has been a liability limiting the expansion of research on the development of epistemological thinking. In our own work on the topic, therefore, we have sought to identify the underlying essence of what is developing in the simplest, most parsimonious terms possible. We have done so at the risk of oversimplifying a complex phenomenon but with the potential benefit of making this developmental course more accessible to theoretical and empirical analysis.

The core question we ask is this: What is the developmental task to be achieved or the developmental goal toward which changes in epistemological understanding are directed? The answer we propose is that the developmental task that underlies the achievement of mature epistemological understanding is the coordination of the subjective and objective dimensions of knowing. Initially, the objective dimension dominates to the exclusion of subjectivity. Subsequently, in a radical shift, the subjective dimension assumes an ascendant position and the objective is abandoned. Finally, the two are coordinated, with a balance achieved in which neither overpowers the other.

This progression is reflected in the sequence of levels depicted in Table 7.1. Someone at the absolutist (as well as the pre-absolutist realist) level sees knowledge in largely objective terms, as located in the external world and knowable with certainty. In what we take to be a key event in the development of epistemological thought, fostered in large degree we think by discovery of the ubiquity of conflicting assertions, the multiplist relocates the source of knowledge from the known object to the knowing subject, hence becoming aware of the uncertain, subjective nature of knowing. This awareness initially assumes such proportions, however, that it overpowers and obliterates any objective standard that could serve as a basis for comparison or evaluation of conflicting claims. Because claims are subjective opinions freely chosen by their holders and everyone has a right to his or her opinion, all opinions are equally right.

The evaluativist reintegrates the objective dimension of knowing by acknowledging uncertainty without forsaking evaluation. Thus, two people can both have legitimate positions—they can both "be right"—but one position can have more merit ("be more right") than the other to the extent that that position is better supported by argument and evidence.

The sequence depicted in Table 7.1 is consistent with the broadly similar levels that appear in the work of independent researchers who have studied the development of epistemological thinking and that have been identified in Hofer and Pintrich's (1997) comprehensive review. The coordination of subjective and objective dimensions of knowing, we maintain, is the singular dimension that

TABLE 7.1

Levels of Epistemological Understanding

Level	Assertions	Reality	Knowledge	Critical Thinking
Realist	Assertions are COPIES of an external reality.	Reality is directly knowable.	Knowledge comes from external source and is certain.	Critical thinking is unnecessaary.
Absolutist	Assertions are FACTS that are correct or incorrect in their representation of reality (possibility of false belief).	Reality is directly knowable.	Knowledge comes from external source and is certain.	Critical thinking is a vehicle for comparing assertions to reality and determining their truth or falsehood.
Multiplist	Assertions are OPINIONS freely chosen by and accountable only to their owners.	Reality is not directly knowable.	Knowledge is generated by human minds and is uncertain.	Critical thinking is irrelevant.
Evaluativist	Assertions are JUDGMENTS that can be evaluated and compared according to criteria of argument and evidence.	Reality is not directly knowable.	Knowledge is generated by human minds and is uncertain.	Critical thinking is valued as a vehicle that promotes sound assertions and enhances understanding

drives this progression. The product, however, is a sequence of qualitatively distinct understandings of what it means to make a claim. The progression from claims as copies to claims as facts, opinions, and finally judgments (Table 7.1) defines the essence of epistemological development.

DEVELOPMENTAL ORIGINS OF EPISTEMOLOGICAL THINKING

The literature on epistemological thinking focuses almost entirely on the age range of adolescence and adulthood. Thinking of an epistemological nature almost certainly does not spring up from nothing, at an advanced age (cf. Chandler, chap. 8, this volume). When, where, and how does it originate? Conceptualizing the developmental endpoint or goal of epistemological understanding as the coordination of subjective and objective dimensions of knowing is helpful in tracing its developmental origins—an objective we see as equally important in fully understanding a developmental phenomenon. This endeavor has been facilitated by the recent wave of research on children's theory of mind.

Children by age 3 show some epistemological awareness in making reference to their own knowledge states, using verbs such as think and know (Olson & Astington, 1986). However, much evidence now exists that children below the age of 4 regard people's claims as isomorphic to an external reality. The most familiar source of evidence for this characterization is young children's poor performance in the now classic false-belief task. Three-year-olds believe that newcomers will share their own accurate knowledge that a candy container in fact holds pencils (Perner, 1991). It is impossible that the other person could hold a belief that the child knows to be false.

Less widely cited is the finding that this refusal to attribute false knowledge to another extends beyond the realm of factual knowledge to values, social conventions, and moral rules that the child takes to be valid or true claims. In a study by Flavell, Mumme, Green, and Flavell (1992), preschool children were told, for example, about a girl Robin who thinks that it is okay to put her feet on the dinner table, and then immediately asked, "Does Robin think that it is okay to put her feet on the dinner table?" Strikingly, a majority of 3-year-olds responded negatively to such questions, as well as to parallel questions about whether someone could hold non-normative beliefs regarding moral rules (e.g., breaking a toy), values (e.g., eating grass), and facts (e.g., whether cats can read books). Performance improved (although remaining below ceiling) among 4-year-olds.

Children at age 3, then, are realists (Table 7.1). Although they have some appreciation of mental phenomena, the assertions that people make are assumed to mirror an objective reality. There are no inaccurate renderings of events. Beginning at about age 4, children begin to recognize assertions as the expression of someone's belief—a milestone in their cognitive development that paves the way for further achievement in epistemological understanding. This initial connection of knowing to its subjective or human source, with its implication that assertions may not correspond to reality, renders assertions susceptible to evaluation vis-à-vis the reality from which they are now distinguished. Although this progression from the realist level to the absolutist level of epistemological understanding achieves no more than the capacity for simple comparison of an assertion to an alleged reality and declaration of it as true or false, it is a critical step in the development of epistemological understanding a transition from simple, unconscious, unreflective knowing about the world to a second-order, or metacognitive, reflection on the knowing claims of self and others (Kuhn, 1999).

Once the false belief concept is fully developed, and the products of knowing connected to their generative source, a child of 5 or 6 would appear to be well on the way to the multiplist epistemological level, in which conflicting beliefs are accepted as the legitimate product of people's differing experiential and knowing histories. Children of this age, however, appear to have not progressed sufficiently in locating the source of knowing in the knower rather than the known to understand differences in knowledge claims as legitimate reflections of the subjective dimension of knowing. Instead, they remain at an absolutist level of epistemological understanding, with knowledge claims judged exclusively against a standard of truth dictated by an objective external reality: To the extent others judge differently than I do, it is because they are in a state of misinformation or misunderstanding; they have not seen the reality that is there to be seen. By school age, children recognize that exposures to different information may lead to different knowledge claims (Carpendale & Chandler, 1996; Pillow & Henrichon, 1996; Taylor, Cartwright, & Bowden, 1991). The source of these differences, however, remains firmly fixed in the external world. There exists a single, externally defined reality, which, once apprehended, yields only one valid conclusion. If we come to different conclusions, it is because one of us fails to have the full or correct story.

It is not before middle to late childhood that there begins to emerge what Carpendale and Chandler (1996) call a "constructivist theory of mind." Conflicting representations of the same event come to be understood as legitimate products of individuals' unique meaning-making efforts—because interpretive mental processes vary across individuals, their products may also differ. It is at this point that the multiplist level of epistemological understanding emerges, leading eventually to the idea that knowing can never be more than subjective opinion.

Remaining is the most fragile developmental transition—the one most likely never to be achieved. We refer to the transition from the multiplist's equation of all claims as equally valid reflections of their owners' subjective perspectives to the evaluativist's reintegration of objectivity into knowing. The latter is reflected in the evaluativist's belief that, despite the respect accorded to people's rights to their own views, criteria exist for judging some claims to have more merit than others.

EMPIRICAL ASSESSMENT OF
EPISTEMOLOGICAL THINKING

Consistent with our conceptualization of the essence of developing epistemological understanding as the coordination of objective and subjective dimensions of knowing, the instrument we have used most recently (Kuhn, Cheney, & Weinstock, in press) to assess epistemological understanding was designed to focus on what we propose to be the key elements in achieving this coordination for each of the transitions (from absolutist to multiplist and from multiplist to evaluativist) examined. To assess the transition from absolutist to multiplist, two contrasting claims within a particular knowledge domain are presented and the individual is asked whether only one could be right or whether "both could have some rightness," with the first option taken as indicating an absolutist level of epistemological understanding. To assess the subsequent transition from multiplist to evaluativist (given the second option is chosen in response to the initial question), the individual is asked whether one judgment (regarding the same knowledge object) might be regarded as having more merit than another.

The resulting simplicity of the instrument, while sacrificing examination of many of the nuances and range of thinking about epistemological issues, has the practical advantage of making it feasible to assess epistemological understanding across multiple kinds of judgments as well as multiple content within these judgment domains. (See Tables 7.2 and 7.3 for the item format and item content across five types of judgment domains.) In addition, its simplicity makes it more appropriate for children than the long and complex interview format in which epistemological thinking has typically been assessed. More fundamentally, however, it offers the theoretical benefit of conceptual (as well as empirical) clarity as to what is being alleged to develop.

To lend support to our claim that this instrument captures the essence of development in epistemological understanding, we examined the relation between it and a more traditional extended interview, the Livia problem used in our earlier work (Kuhn, Pennington, & Leadbeater, 1983; Leadbeater & Kuhn, 1989; Weinstock, 1999). The Livia problem poses two conflicting accounts of the fictitious "fifth Livian war," one allegedly written by a historian from North Livia and the other by a historian from South Livia. After reading the accounts, respondents are asked to summarize what the fifth Livian war was about and what happened. In addition they are asked: (a) if the accounts were different and, if so, how; (b) whether both accounts could be correct, and, if so, whether one could be more true than the other; (c) whether anyone could be certain of what happened and, if not, why not; and (d) whether a third historian's account might be different and, if so, why.

Responses to the Livia interview are codable in terms of the 22 dimensions listed in Appendix A, along with the levels of reasoning (from 0 to 5) that the alternatives shown under each dimension correspond to. (Overall level is assigned

TABLE 7.2
Assessment Items by Domain

Judgments of Personal Taste

Robin says warm summer days are nicest.
Chris says cool autumn days are nicest.

Robin says the stew is spicy.
Chris says the stew is not spicy at all.

Robin thinks weddings should be held in the afternoon.
Chris thinks weddings should be held in the evening.

Aesthetic Judgments

Robin thinks the first piece of music they listen to is better.
Chris thinks the second piece of music they listen to is better.

Robin thinks the first painting they look at is better.
Chris thinks the second painting they look at is better.

Robin thinks the first book they both read is better.
Chris thinks the second book they both read is better.

Value Judgments

Robin thinks people should take responsibility for themselves.
Chris thinks people should work together to take care of each other.

Robin thinks lying is wrong.
Chris thinks lying is permissible in certain situations.

Robin thinks the government should limit the number of children families
are allowed to have to keep the population from getting too big.
Chris thinks families should have as many children as they choose.

Judgments of Fact About the Social World

Robin has one view of why criminals keep going back to crime.
Chris has a different view of why criminals keep going back to crime.

Robin thinks one book's explanation of why the Crimean wars began is right.
Chris thinks another book's explanation of why the Crimean wars began is right.

Robin agrees with one book's explanation of how children learn language.
Chris agrees with another book's explanation of how children learn language.

Judgments of Fact About the Physical World

Robin believes one book's explanation of what atoms are made up of.
Chris believes another book's explanation of what atoms are made up of.

Robin believes one book's explanation of how the brain works.
Chris believes another book's explanation of how the brain works.

Robin believes one mathematician's proof of the math formula is right.
Chris believes another mathematician's proof of the math formula is right.

TABLE 7.3
Item Format for Epistemological Thinking Assessment

Each item consisted of a pair of contrasting statements attributed to two individuals, Robin and Chris (see Table 7.2). Following each pair of statements, the following questions appear:

Can only one of their views be right, or could both have some rightness? (circle one)

Only one right
Both could have some rightness

If both could be right:

Could one view be better or more right than the other? (circle one)

One could be more right
One could be more right than the other

based on the modal level scores across the 22 dimensions.) Note that this scheme permits subdivision of the absolutist level, as well as the evaluativist level, into two sublevels. The resulting six levels can be briefly summarized as follows:

Level 0. Realist. No differences between the two accounts are acknowledged.

Level 1. Simple absolutist. Differences between the accounts are acknowledged and attributed to incompleteness of one or both accounts. One historian either did not see or did not include what the other did. Adding the two accounts together produces a more correct account.

Level 2. Dual absolutist. A distinction is made between fact and interpretation. Discrepancies between accounts are attributed to each historian's subjective bias and consequent distortion of the facts. An unbiased third historian could provide a certain account.

Level 3. Multiplist. The conflicting accounts are seen as entirely the product of each historian's subjective interpretation, with no underlying factual reality, no basis for judging one account as superior to the other, and no basis for reconciling them.

Level 4. Objective evaluativist. Discrepancies are attributed to the historians' subjective emphases, but the accounts can be largely reconciled by comparing them, evaluating their consistency, and finding points of agreement, although some questions may remain unanswered.

Level 5. Conceptual evaluativist. Discrepancies are attributed to the historians each reporting facts from their own respective frame of reference. Although the accounts can be interpreted and evaluated, their differences are only partially reconcilable and no single true account exists.

Weinstock (1998) reports a percentage–agreement inter-rater reliability of 88% for these levels. In a study of 33 young adults who were adminstered both the Livia problem and the short instrument shown in Table 7.2 (Kuhn, Cheney, & Weinstock, in press), 24 of the 33 scored at the same overall level (absolutist, multiplist, or evaluativist) on both long and short instruments (there were no scores at the realist level in the Livia problem), a highly statistically significant association. Only two participants not scoring at the same level on both scored at the highest level on one and the lowest on the other; the remaining seven scored at adjacent levels.

The short instrument, then, in most cases offers a good indication of roughly where an individual falls in the broad progression from absolutist to multiplist to evaluativist thought. It obviously does not provide a full, or nuanced, picture of an individual's thinking in the epistemological domain, and we do not wish to minimize the value of such a picture. When it is the goal, a more extensive, in-depth interview becomes the method of choice, and, indeed, this is the method we chose in work described later in this chapter. Nonetheless, the short instrument, we believe, offers the theoretical and empirical benefits that we have indicated.

LEVELS OF EPISTEMOLOGICAL THINKING ACROSS AGE AND EXPERIENCE GROUPS

Since previous research has shown epistemological understanding to be highly sensitive to education level as well as age, in our research we have included multiple adult groups varying along these dimensions, as well as younger groups covering the period from middle childhood through adolescence. Specifically, in addition to elementary and high school students in fifth, eighth, and twelfth grades, we have examined four adult groups. One consists of undergraduates at a selective private university. This population was chosen to be of high intellectual ability but limited life experience.

Two mature adult groups were chosen to be older and therefore have a richer background of life experience, relative to the undergraduates, but to differ from one another in terms of educational and socioeconomic background. The two groups were of an equivalent age range (mid twenties to late thirties) but had little else in common. The community college group, primarily of Hispanic-American ethnicity, was enrolled in largely vocational programs at an urban public community college serving an inner-city, low-income population. The professional group was enrolled in a highly selective degree program for business executives (executive MBA) at a major business school, in addition to holding high-level full-time positions in the business world. Finally, a small expert group, comparable in age to the mature adult groups, were Ph.D. candidates in educational philosophy.

Patterns of performance by participant group are summarized in Table 7.4 (from Kuhn et al., in press). The top portion of Table 7.4 shows the percentages of participants in each group who were classified as at a predominantly absolutist level for each judgment type. (No participants were classified at the realist level.) Some members of all groups except the expert group, it is seen, remain at an absolutist level in at least some domains. Some developmental trend in the direction of declining absolutism appears between fifth grade and adulthood, although not a pronounced one.

The percentages of participants of each group who were classified as at a predominantly evaluativist level appear in the bottom portion of Table 7.4. These percentages, it is seen, are at a low among fifth graders and increase modestly up to the college level, where they are the highest, except for the expert group. Differences among the adult groups, except for the expert group, are slight. Across

TABLE 7.4

Epistemological Levels Across Judgment Domains by Participant Group

Percentages of Participants Showing a Predominantly Absolutist Level

| | Judgment Domain | | | | |
	Taste	Aesthetic	Value	Social fact	Physical fact
Fifth grade	—	—	30	—	30
Eighth grade	—	—	16	—	12
Twelfth grade	—	14	33	14	19
Undergraduate	—	—	—	—	10
Community College	—	10	10	—	10
Professional	—	—	—	—	22
Expert	—	—	—	—	—

Percentages of Participants Showing a Predominantly Evaluativist Level

| | Judgment Domain | | | | |
	Taste	Aesthetic	Value	Social fact	Physical fact
Fifth grade	10	—	10	35	20
Eighth grade	16	16	20	40	32
Twelfth grade	19	29	29	39	38
Undergraduate	25	25	45	45	40
Community College	35	10	25	40	45
Professional	11	—	22	50	44
Expert	20	60	80	100	100

domains, mature adults, it is seen, are more likely than young college adults to remain multiplists in the values domain, as well as in the aesthetic domain (although
some community college adults, as seen in Table 7.4, remain at the absolutist
level).

Differences across participant groups, as observed in Table 7.4, are modest.
Performance of the expert group, nonetheless, establishes the evaluativist position
as a developmental endpoint. Group comparisons were made separately for the
two major transitions, reflected in the upper and lower portions of Table 7.4. The
comparison of adults to younger participants was statistically significant with respect to the first transition, reflected in the proportion of responses conforming to
the absolutist pattern but not the second (reflected in the proportion of responses
conforming to the evaluativist pattern). Individual comparisons of the younger
groups to the undergraduates (the most developmentally advanced group, except
for the experts) showed significant differences between fifth graders and undergraduates and between twelfth graders and undergraduates and a marginally significant difference between eighth graders and undergraduates with respect to the
proportion of responses conforming to the absolutist pattern. With respect to the
second transition, reflected in the proportion of responses conforming to the evaluativist pattern, only the difference between the fifth graders and undergraduates
reached statistical significance. No sex differences appeared.

EPISTEMOLOGICAL UNDERSTANDING
ACROSS CONTENT DOMAINS

Our earlier account of the developmental origins and subsequent evolution of
epistemological understanding led us to the question of whether the transitions
from absolutist to multiplist and from multiplist to evaluativist levels of epistemological understanding occur in a domain-dependent manner. The judgments
that we make in the process of knowing are of distinctly different types—judgments of personal preference or taste, aesthetic judgments, value judgments, and
judgments of fact, which in turn can be further categorized by content domain,
for example judgments about the physical world versus the social world. If the
development of epistemological understanding is conceptualized as we have proposed, i.e., as a task in coordinating the subjective and objective dimensions of
knowing, it is possible that this coordination is more readily achieved with respect to some kinds of judgments than others. In fact, the Flavell et al. (1992)
study described earlier hints at this possibility of domain specificity in the early
childhood transition from realist to the recognition of false belief that marks attainment of the absolutist level.

Recall that the developmental task is different at each of the subsequent transitions in epistemological level. In the transition from absolutist to multiplist
levels, the task is one of recognizing the subjective dimension of knowing. In this
case, then, it might be hypothesized to be easiest to recognize this subjectivity in

the realm of judgments of personal taste. These are the kinds of judgments most closely connected to the human as a subjective being and may follow from young children's observation that people have different emotional reactions to the same event (what makes you angry, I find comical). So then may people be recognized as having legitimately different preferences (in everything from food to friends) and tastes (the clothing you regard as tasteful, I find dull). Aesthetic judgments might follow, as having a strong component of personal preference (we differ in our judgments of whether the Spice Girls are a talented musical group). Value (including moral) judgments, in contrast, may be a domain in which the concept of absolute standards is not as readily relinquished. Lastly, judgments of fact may be the most difficult judgment domain in which to forego the concept of a single absolute truth and to accept that conflicting claims may both have some truth, especially in judgments pertaining to the physical world.

In the transition from multiplist to evaluativist, in contrast, the developmental task is one of recognizing and reintegrating the objective dimension of knowing. Hence a reverse order might be predicted. It may be easiest to recognize the possibility of objective criteria in the face of multiplicity in the domain of factual judgments: Scientists are recognized as having divergent views, but evidence suggests one scientist's model to be more accurate ("closer to the truth") than another's, with the further possibility of such distinctions being more readily accepted when claims are about the physical world than when they are about the social world. Values may be the next easiest judgment domain in which to progress beyond the radical relativism of the multiplist to embrace objective criteria for comparison of divergent views (can some behaviors be judged less moral than others, despite their acceptability within the cultural groups that practice them?), with aesthetic judgments more difficult still in this respect (can one legitimately regard one piece of music or art as objectively superior to another?). Finally, personal taste is a judgment domain where it would be predicted that this transition would fail to occur at all: There is little, if any, basis for judging one person's personal tastes as having more merit than another's. In this judgment domain, we all can (and should) remain content to be multiplists.

The predicted orders for the two major transitions in the development of epistemological understanding, then, are exactly the reverse of one another. (See Table 7.5 for summary.) In our recent research, these predictions were largely supported among the various child, adolescent, and adult groups described earlier (see Kuhn et al., in press, for details). Counter to our expectation, and reflected in Table 7.4, some individuals in all groups showed the evaluativist pattern in the domain of personal taste, maintaining, for example, that some argument could be constructed to support the superiority of afternoon over evening weddings. It is further worthy of note that in no group, with the exception of the experts, does the frequency of an evaluativist pattern in the aesthetic domain significantly exceed its frequency in the domain of personal taste. The relative merits of works of musical, literary, or visual art, in other words, are no more judgeable than those of simple personal tastes.

TABLE 7.5
Predicted Sequence of Attainment of
Levels of Epistemological Understanding by Judgment Domain

Transition from Absolutist to Multiplist

Judgments of personal taste
Aesthetic judgments
Value judgments
Judgments of fact about the social world
Judgments of fact about the physical world

Transition from Multiplist to Evaluativist

Judgments of fact about the physical world
Judgments of fact about the social world
Value judgments
Aesthetic judgments
(Transition predicted not to occur for judgments of personal taste)

DOES EPISTEMOLOGICAL
THINKING MATTER?

A broad conclusion to be drawn from Table 7.4 is that even well into adulthood, not as much progress toward an evaluativist epistemology has been made as ideally might be. Among both adults and adolescents, significant variability exists in level of epistemological understanding. A second objective of our work has been to examine the implications of this variability. Does an evaluativist, versus a multiplist or absolutist, epistemology make any significant difference in how an individual functions in any important arenas of everyday life?

Conceptually, the case is compelling that it should. Epistemological theories are "theories in action" in the sense that we all are required to make knowledge judgments in our everyday lives. Whether people understand such judgments to be certain facts, mere opinions, or genuine considered, though fallible, judgments should make an enormous difference in how people make and make use of them.

Empirically, we have sought to document associations between the level of epistemological understanding individuals possess and the kinds of thinking they display in everyday reasoning tasks. Kuhn's (1991) study of adolescents' and adults' argumentive reasoning skills included assessment of epistemological understanding and was encouraging in suggesting that such associations exist. More recently, we have undertaken to examine this relationship with respect to an everyday reasoning task in which we thought it would be particularly salient— that of juror reasoning (Kuhn, Weinstock, & Flaton, 1994; Weinstock, 1999).

The juror's task requires an individual to coordinate a body of evidence with multiple theories (in this case, competing theories of what happened that correspond to different verdict choices), in order to reach a verdict judgment. An epistemological theory in action should inform the way in which an individual juror conceives and approaches the task. Does the juror see him- or herself as ascertaining a certain truth, as registering a personal preference among equally likely alternatives, or as evaluating and weighing evidence with respect to its bearing on alternative theories, as a way of identifying the best supported theory?

Weinstock (1998) sought to determine the extent to which jurors' level of epistemological understanding would be evidenced in a juror reasoning task. Following our earlier work on the topic (Kuhn, Weinstock, & Flaton, 1994), real jurors awaiting trial assignment at the New York Supreme Court in Brooklyn, New York, were presented audiotaped reenactments of the highlights of two criminal trials offering verdict alternatives ranging from first-degree murder through second-degree murder, manslaughter, and self-defense (Weinstock, 1999). After listening to each reenactment, in an individual interview the juror was asked to make and justify a verdict choice, with the justification elaborated by responses to several probing questions, including degree of certainty, whether any evidence existed countersupportive of the chosen verdict, and how alternative verdicts might be supported or discounted.

Table 7.6 shows the eight dimensions in terms of which jurors' reasoning was classified. Jurors participating in the study were also classified based on their responses to the Livia problem. Overall, 47% of the 173 participants were classified at the absolutist level, 39% at the multiplist level, and 14% at the evaluativist level. Scores on the Livia problem (see Appendix A for a detailed version of the coding scheme) were predictive of performance on seven of the eight dimensions of juror reasoning in Table 7.6. (Counterargument was the one exception.) Cross-tabulations across the Livia and juror reasoning levels showed individuals at the higher levels on the Livia problem more likely to exhibit higher levels of juror reasoning.

Interpretation of these kinds of correspondences, of course, is limited when the two dimensions in question share a common association with age or, in this case, education (Kuhn et al., 1994; Weinstock, 1999). They fall short of demonstrating that one dimension psychologically informs or explains the other. For this reason, it is desirable to identify specific correspondences in reasoning across the two domains, increasing confidence that the association is more than one mediated by a common third variable. Weinstock (1999) reports a number of such specific correspondences, for example between the judgment in the Livia problem that one historian's account had to be the true or correct one (Dimension 5, Appendix A) and the ability to support or discount alternative verdict choices (Dimensions III C&D, Table 7.6) in the juror task. Another example of a specific correspondence is whether the historians' accounts were treated as facts, opinions, or interpretations (Dimensions 19 and 22, Appendix A), and judgmental use of evidence (Dimension II B, Table 7.6) in the juror task. Most interesting, perhaps, is the correspondence with respect to certainty: Those who believed certainty to be achievable with respect to the historical narrative were most likely to be highly certain that their own verdict decisions were correct in the juror task.

TABLE 7.6

Dimensions of Juror Reasoning

I. *Representation of verdict criteria.* Did the juror correctly represent the category criteria for each verdict as presented in the judge's instructions? A score from 0–4 was assigned based on the number of possible verdicts whose criteria were correctly represented.

II. Use of *evidence*

II A. *Representation of evidence.* Testimony for each trial was analyzed with respect to the number of distinct pieces of direct evidence it contained, and the number of these mentioned by the juror was counted. Scores of 0–3 were assigned for this dimension by placing individuals into the low, low-middle, high-middle, or high quartiles of the distribution on this dimension.

II B. *Judgmental use of evidence.* Utterances including references to evidence were categorized based on whether they reflected direct acceptance of the evidence as fact or reflected some effort to evaluate the evidence, by assessing its credibility or meaning in relation to external, real-world knowledge, in relation to other evidence, or in relation to the witness providing it. A score of 0 was assigned if the juror never showed judgmental use of evidence. A score of 1 was assigned if a minority of references to evidence were judgmental, and a score of 2 was assigned if a majority of references to evidence were judgmental.

II C. *Synthesis of evidence.* Five types were distinguished: (a) *no synthesis* of evidence—the juror cited only single pieces of evidence with no attempt to connect them; (b) *narrative* synthesis—multiple pieces of evidence were combined into a narrative (that then served as the rationale for verdict choice); (c) *simple corroboration*— two or more pieces of evidence were connected in an attempt to corroborate a specific claim; (d) *integration*—multiple pieces of evidence were connected to build an argument that served either to support a verdict or to aid in the evaluation of other evidence. (e) A fifth type, *combination*, consisted of integration in conjunction with either corroboration and/or narrative. Scores ranged from 0–4, based on the highest category observed.

III. *Relation of evidence to verdict*

III A. *Simple argument.* An argument was offered in which accurately represented evidence was drawn on to support or discount a verdict. Possible number ranged from 0 to the number of such distinct arguments made. Scores of 0–3 were assigned for this dimension by placing individuals into the low, low-middle, high-middle, or high quartiles of the distribution on this dimension.

III B. *Counterargument.* Evidence was cited (either spontaneously or in response to Question 5) that was not consistent with the juror's own verdict choice. Possible scores were 0 (no attempt), 1 (unsuccessful attempt), 2 (partially successful attempt, because representation of evidence or of verdict criteria was faulty), and 3 (successful attempt).

III C. *Discounting of alternative verdicts.* An argument was made (either spontaneously or in response to questioning) as to why verdicts not chosen were incorrect. For each alternative (non-chosen) verdict, possible scores were 0 (no attempt), 1 (unsuccessful attempt), 2 (partially successful attempt, because representation of evidence or of verdict criteria was faulty), and 3 (successful attempt).

III D. *Justification of alternative verdicts.* An argument was made (either spontaneously or in response to questioning) as to how an alternative verdict might be supported. For each alternative (nonchosen) verdict, possible scores were 0 (no attempt), 1 (unsuccessful attempt), 2 (partially successful attempt, because representation of evidence or of verdict criteria was faulty), and 3 (successful attempt).

A qualitative sense of these correspondences is obtainable from case studies of individuals' reasoning across the two tasks. Some excerpts are presented in Table 7.7. Subject 53, note, who shows the absolutist's certainty in her epistemological reasoning, in her reasoning as a juror demonstrates great trust in the absolute truth of a story. She does not acknowledge the possibility of the evidence being used to tell a different story. Rather, the story she tells constitutes a single unassailable piece of evidence that dictates the conclusion. Subject 96, in contrast, who in her epistemological reasoning recognizes claims as judgments,

TABLE 7.7

Illustrations of Correspondences Between Epistemological
and Juror Reasoning

Subject 53

Epistemological reasoning

(Are the accounts different?) No, they seem like they're the same . . .
(Can someone be certain the accounts are correct?) By reading this they can be
  certain. It really explains. It gives details on what happens.

Juror reasoning

. . . when the father went out to go to the store, he went right upstairs to get the
  gun and . . . they started fighting again when his father came back into the
  house and he just, he shot him right there, and then he shot him not once—he
  shot him four times—so he really meant to kill him.

Subject 96

Epistemological reasoning

(Could both be right?) They could because the North Livian talks about early set-
  backs, and his emphasis is on the later battles . . . when the North Livians won
  . . . But the South Livian . . . stresses the earlier wins . . . Neither one is a reality, each one is making a judgment . . .

(Could one be more right?) . . . the accounts are based on their perspective. It
  would be interesting to see how somebody who is not either North or South
  Livian would see it.

Juror reasoning

. . . it wasn't like this was a situation where he had been fighting back. The only
  thing he had done was to have guns, but I saw that as an attempt to protect himself as well, not necessarily intent to kill . . . I thought about the part about him
  getting the pets downstairs. I felt that that was not clear evidence that he meant
  to kill the father, that there was premeditation. He may have felt that whatever
  happened between him and the father . . . that he wanted them out of the way
  for their own protection . . . The mother's testimony, at one point when the
  lawyer asked her whether she had seen the husband with a weapon . . . she
  said she didn't see him holding a gun. But somebody else did report he did
  have a gun.

---

in her juror reasoning differentiates the evidence from theories of what might have happened and uses the evidence critically to construct and evaluate theories.

In sum, although much remains to be done in this vein, we see a "theory in action" emphasis as reflecting a very important and potentially fruitful approach in the future investigation of epistemological thinking. The task is to identify the kinds of real-world cognitive activities in which we would expect epistemological understanding to figure heavily. As our juror research illustrates, such activities include certainly, but are not confined to, the academic sphere. Even within academic domains, people are likely to be casual consumers, as well as serious students, of topics in both physical and social sciences. How they understand the enterprise of science, as an epistemological endeavor, should be as apparent in the consumer role as it is in formal academic pursuits. In sum, it is in real-world cognitive activities of the sort we have illustrated that we would expect epistemological understanding to make a difference, and this is the place, we believe, that it is most important to explore that difference.

HOW CAN WE BEST ADVANCE
EPISTEMOLOGICAL UNDERSTANDING?

Further exploration of what difference epistemological understanding makes, we have suggested, is an important direction for future research. Another important direction for future researchers to pursue is investigation of the mechanisms that are responsible for advances in epistemological understanding. If epistemological understanding makes a difference, as we have claimed it does, we need to be concerned about the scarcity of evaluativist epistemological thinking in the adult population, a scarcity that our own and others' data consistently have pointed to.

Maturity and life experience, particularly educational experience, are often mentioned as the most likely contributors to the development of epistemological understanding. Yet, our research showed negligible progression toward the evaluativist level of understanding with the increase in age and experience represented in the comparison between the undergraduate and mature adult groups. To the extent that increasing age and education are not sufficient to effect the transition to an evaluativist level of epistemological understanding, except among a small proportion of the population who are exceptionally highly educated, then other experiential factors need to be considered as possibly implicated in this transition (or, more precisely, in its failure to occur).

One factor we would point to as salient is the intellectual climate and values that are ascendant in modern American culture. At the heart of the evaluativist epistemological position is the view that reasoned argument is worthwhile and the most productive path to knowledge and informed understanding, as well as to resolution of human conflict. Competing to some degree with this set of values in modern society are the values of social tolerance and acceptance—reflected in the "live and let live" and "to each his own" adages. There is much in modern society to suggest that the latter set of values overpower the former, with the result being an inhibition of intellectual development beyond the multiplist level. Choice of political candidates, to cite just one example, tends to be treated as a matter of personal taste and opinion, rather than comparison on the basis of positions supported by reasoned argument.

Our empirical data are consistent with this interpretation. Mature adults, our results show, are even more likely than undergraduates to show the multiplist's "tolerance" of treating contrasting aesthetic judgments and value judgments as equally worthy. Their additional life experience has not fostered the view that discriminations are worth making or that there exists any basis for making them. As others' choices are respected in the realms of aesthetic preferences and values, similar to the respect accorded their preferences in personal tastes, so should their opinions about the nature of the physical and social world be accorded a similar respect. As noted earlier, it is a deceptively simple step down a slippery slope from the belief that everyone has a right to his or her opinion to the belief that all opinions are equally right. Tolerance of multiple positions, in other words, becomes confused with discriminability among them.

How, when, and where, then, can we promote epistemological development? Adolescence may in fact be a critical period in the development of the intellectual skills of inquiry, analysis, and argument, as well as the intellectual values and epistemological understanding that we would claim develop in tandem with skills—both supporting and being supported by developments in skill (Kuhn, 2001). If so, children, as well as adolescents, from an early age need practice in making and defending claims, especially in social contexts where claims must be examined and debated in a framework of alternatives and evidence. But they also need to grow up in a climate in which such activities are valued, which can only be the case if the epistemological rationale for reasoned debate is understood and appreciated. In sum, we need to foster individual growth by providing frequent opportunities for the exercise of judgment, but we also need to work toward creating the kind of society in which thinking and judgment are widely regarded as worth the effort they entail.

REFERENCES

Carpendale, J., & Chandler, M. (1996). On the distinction between false belief understanding and subscribing to an interpretive theory of mind. *Child Development, 67,* 1686–1706.

Flavell, J., Mumme, D., Green, F., & Flavell, E. (1992). Young children's understanding of different types of beliefs. *Child Development, 63,* 960–977.

Hofer, B., & Pintrich, P. (1997). The development of epistemological theories: Beliefs about knowledge and knowing and their relation to learning. *Review of Educational Research, 67,* 88–140.

King, P., & Kitchener, K. (1994). Developing reflective judgment: *Understanding and promoting intellectual growth and critical thinking in adolescents and adults.* San Francisco: Jossey-Bass.

Kuhn, D., (1991). *The skills of argument.* Cambridge: Cambridge University Press.

Kuhn, D. (1999). Metacognitive development. In L. Baltcr & C. Tamis Le-Monda (Eds.), *Child psychology: A handbook of contemporary issues.* Philadelphia: Psychology Press.

Kuhn, D. (2001). Why development does (and doesn't) occur: Evidence from the domain of inductive reasoning. In R. Siegler & J. McClelland (Eds.), *Mechanisms of cognitive development: Neural and behavioral perspectives.* Mahwah, NJ: Erlbaum.

Kuhn, D., Cheney, R., & Weinstock, M. (in press). The development of epistemological understanding. *Cognitive Development.*

Kuhn, D., Pennington, N., & Leadbeater, B. (1983). Adult thinking in developmental perspective: The sample case of juror reasoning. In P. Baltes & O. Brim (Eds.), *Life-span development and behavior,* Vol. 5. New York: Academic Press.

Kuhn, D., Weinstock, M., & Flaton, R. (1994). How well do jurors reason? Competence dimensions of individual variation in a juror reasoning task. *Psychological Science, 5,* 289–296.

Leadbeater, B., & Kuhn, D. (1989). Interpreting discrepant narratives: Hermeneutics and adult cognition. In J. Sinnott (Ed.), *Everyday problem solving: Theory and application.* New York: Praeger.

Olson, D., & Astington, J. (1986). Children's acquisition of metalinguistic and metacognitive verbs. In W. Demopoulos & A. Marras (Eds.), *Language learning and concept acquisition.* Norwood, NJ: Ablex.

Perner, J. (1991). *Understanding the representational mind.* Cambridge, MA: MIT Press.

Pillow, B., & Henrichon, A. (1996). There's more to the picture than meets the eye: Young children's difficulty understanding biased interpretation. *Child Development, 67* (3), 803–819.

Taylor, M., Cartwright, B., & Bowden, T. (1991). Perspective taking and theory of mind: Do children predict interpretive diversity as a function of differences in observers' knowledge? *Child Development, 62,* 1334–1351.

Weinstock, M. (1999). *Epistemological understanding and argumentive competence as foundations of juror reasoning skill.* Unpublished doctoral dissertation, Teachers College, Columbia University.

APPENDIX A

Dimensions of Epistemological Reasoning Coded on the Livia Problem

1. What is subject's core explanation of what differs?
   No difference (0)
   Difference noted (1-5)
      Content of accounts of events differ (1,2)
      Historians' perceptions of events differ (3-5)
         Historians have different opinions (3)
         Conditions under which historians conclude what happened differ (4,5)
         Emphasis on different facts (4,5)
2. Structural reasons for difference?
   No difference (0)
   Different content available to different people (1,2)
   Logical contradiction, only one set of facts or conclusions can be right (2)
   Different people—each has own ideas (2,3)
   Different context in which historians operate, different perspectives on content (4,5)
3. Both Right
   Yes (0,1,3,5)
      No real differences (0,1)
      Both equally right or wrong (may read: No, both biased and wrong) (3)
      Yes, from own perspective (3,5)
   No (2,3,4)
      One closer to truth (2,4)
4. One Account More True?
   No (0,1,3)
      They are both accurate reports of the events (0,1)
      They are both equally biased, or there is no way to judge (3)
   Yes (2,4,5)
      One account is a better fit and/or more probable (2,4,5)
      Maybe, not without overall perspective, but interpretation still must fit evidence (5)
5. Reconcilability Between Accounts?
   Stories/facts not contradictory (0,1)
   Stories/some facts are contradictory (2-5)
      one right, one wrong (2)
      stories, the framework for facts, are basically incompatible (3,5)
      some parts of the story/facts can be agreed upon or brought into agreement (4,5)

6. Number of Accounts

One (0,1)

Two (2)

   Three (with the third historian) (2,3)

   Multiple or indeterminate number more than 2 (3-5)

7. Explanation of how two accounts emerge?

Both people report what happened as far as the subject knows (0)

One person collected some facts, the other collected other facts—some overlap (1)

They use different facts to tell the story with no judgment about facts (1,2)

One person had access to correct facts; other in error or bias distorts one story (2)

Each tells story based on biased opinion or perception (3)

Each has different access to facts, different facts emphasized due to perspective (4)

Each approaches question of what happened from different subjective perspective (5)

8. Certainty?

Yes, with access to facts (0-2)

No (2-5)

   Not from the given accounts (2,3)

   All views equal without possibility of adjudication (3)

   That is the condition of knowing—but degree of confidence may be possible (4,5)

9. Determining factor in account?

What happened (0,1,2)

Belief, or biased perspective of teller (2,3)

Both evidence and perspective (4,5)

10. Account as?

Report of what happened (0-2)

Opinion of teller (3)

Construction from evidence from a particular perspective (4,5)

11. Bias?

Not considered (0,1)

Responsible for distortion, or way evidence reported, by at least one historian (2,3)

One possible factor in construction of account that may affect interpretation (4,5)

12. Person who was there?

Would know what happened (0-2)

Would provide yet another, no more definitive perspective (3,5)

Would not know whole story, could provide firsthand account as evidence (4,5)

No mention

13. What Mediates Knowledge?
    Nothing (0)
    Available information (1,2)
    Bias, opinion (2,3)
    Perspective; incomplete/unreliable evidence; methods of inquiry; inter-
    pretation (4,5)
14. Is at least one account reliable source?
    Yes (0-2)
      Both (0)
      Insofar as the accounts are accurate but incomplete (1)
      But only one is (2)
    No (3-5)
      Neither could be (3)
      Neither completely reliable (4,5)
      One could be found to be more reliable (4)
      Each could be more or less reliable within perspective (5)
15. Means of Assessing Accuracy of Facts from Account
    At least one account reports facts which are accepted at face value (0-2)
    One account is more persuasive, convincing, credible (2)
    Isn't really one (3,5)
    The accounts agree on facts (4,5)
    Qualified corroboration of by another historian (4,5)
16. Accuracy Possible
    Yes (0-2, 4,5)
      Without qualification (0-2)
      To a degree (4,5)
    No (3,5)
17. Best indicator of accuracy
    It's appearance in accounts (0)
    Most facts (1)
    Story that makes most sense (2)
    No indicator (3,5)
    Good evaluation of evidence (4,5)
18. Assumption of Underlying Actuality
    Yes (0,1,2,4)
      Knowable (0-2, 4)
      Completely (0-2)
      Only in part (4)
    No (3,5)
      There is no underlying, knowable reality (3,5)
      Not a single actuality (5)
19. Fact and Interpretation
    No distinction made between fact and interpretation (0-1)
    Distinction made between fact and interpretation (2-5)

Interpretation separate from fact, but facts determine correct account (2)
Interpretation determines construction of accounts (3-5)
Interpretation predominates to degree that facts are basically irrelevant (3)
Interpretation depends on evidence and is necessary (4,5)

20. Subjective Element in Interpretation
No (0,1)
Yes (2-5)
Objective predominates (2,4)
Subjective predominates (3,5)

21. Subjective Emphasis
None (0,1)
Mistaken on facts (2)
Distortion of facts, or highly selective, slanted choice of facts (3)
Facts interpreted, receive different emphasis (4)
Facts selected and interpreted coinciding with perspective (5)

22. Understanding of Nature of Information Presented
Information presented as fact (although possibly incorrect) (0-2)
Information is opinion (3)
Information is interpretation and fact (4,5)

8

Competing Claims About Competing Knowledge Claims

Michael J. Chandler
The University of British Columbia

Darcy Hallett
The University of British Columbia

Bryan W. Sokol
The University of British Columbia

Remember repeatedly falling in love for the first time? Well, if the relevant research literature is to be believed, then the story about your—about our—loss of epistemic innocence is rather like that. That is, seemingly without reference to the particular age group being studied, effectively everyone who has ever gone out in search of possible differences in the ways that older, as opposed to younger, persons think about matters of belief entitlement has miraculously ended up reporting what amounts to the same thing. The recurrent story goes like this: The youngest of available subjects (whatever their actual age might happen to be), enter stage-left as naïve realists—objectivists at heart, only to shortly find themselves inextricably drawn toward some waiting pit of nihilism. As the plot thickens and skeptical doubts progressively overtake them, these previously committed foundationalists lose their ability to act on the basis of reason, and so, for a time, remain stupefied and lost in a directionless moratorium where blind intuitionism, or simply doing the done thing, is all that is left of choice. Finally, just before exiting stage-right, the best and brightest among this temporarily dispirited group is shown to come to a new "postskeptical" insight, as some beliefs are recognized as better grounded than are others, and the cautious possibility of rational choice is triumphantly restored. That is the Procrustean bed, and the good news is that one size is argued to conveniently fit all.

The bad news is that these more or less identical claims about the supposed course of epistemic development are all made about research participants of wildly different ages. Some report that this reliable pattern of shifting beliefs about belief occurs only in adulthood (Gilligan & Murphy, 1979; Sinnot, 1989). Many more find essentially the same "developmental" sequence unfolding during the early college years (e.g., Perry, 1970; Kitchener & King, 1981). Still others make indistinguishable claims for young adolescents (Reich, Oser, & Valentin, 1994; Chandler, Boyes, & Ball, 1990; Boyes & Chandler, 1992), or even preadolescents (Mansfield & Clinchy, 1997; Benack & Basseches, 1989; Walton, 2000). Most recently, a new phalanx of "theory-theorists" (for whom "young" typically means 3 or 4, and "old" 6 or 7) have alleged that many of these same changes can be observed in the "naive" or "folk" epistemologies of youngsters who are scarcely out of short pants. Obviously, not everyone can be right about all of this.

Accustomed as we are to ferreting out common denominators in what, to less practiced eyes, wrongly appear to be different things, no one is surprised at hearing that what blind men variously regard as vines and tree trunks are actually better seen as fractional parts of one and the same elephant. What we are not so good at, or so the present case would suggest, is avoiding the opposite error. Here, some clearly appear to have hold of the front end of what might well prove to be a whole congaline of developments, while others are just as obviously hanging onto the back, and yet everyone is talking one elephant. The purpose of this chapter is to attempt to make real heads or tails out of this topsy-turvy situation.

We mean to go about doing this in several short steps. First, we intend to begin, in Part I, by working to persuade you that we are not simply making up this whole improbable state of affairs. That is, we plan to start by laying out what is, in fact, a rather staggering array of contradictory claims currently being advanced about just how old people ordinarily need to get before they first come to the insight that truth is not simply revealed, or that knowledge is unavoidably subjective, or that commitments and reasoned choices are necessarily made against a back cloth of unredeemable uncertainty. It will not be our intention here to attempt to cast doubts on the authenticity of anyone's data—that is, we are prepared to stipulate that all of the subjects of all of the ages typically described in all of the relevant research to be cited actually do say the sorts of things that have gotten them consistently coded as (for example) epistemic "realists" or "objectivists" or "relativists." Instead, our aim will simply be to convince you that it just can't possibly be true that the self-same threshold insights about representational diversity, or the identical epistemic doubts that such insights naturally engender, do in fact naturally crop up, for the very first time, at the age of 4, and then (miraculously) again at 7, and at 14 and 21. Someone—actually several someones—will obviously need to take back some of what they have said.

We are not, of course, the first to have noticed that the developmental milestones that some count as first passed only in adulthood actually look remarkably like still other waystations that others insist have already been left behind. Although there are not, to our knowledge, any published accounts pointing to the full length and breadth of the confusion that evidently surrounds these matters, note has sometimes been taken of the fact that apparently similar epistemic claims are being made in behalf of subjects slightly younger or somewhat older than those whose beliefs about belief happen to be the subject of immediate research concern. Part II of this chapter is given over to a short listing of some of the discounting strategies already employed by others who are evidently troubled by even the localized prospect that what growing persons are supposedly doing for the very first time they have already been credited with doing by others. As it will be shown to turn out, of the various reasons that have been offered up as ways of accounting for such apparent redundancies, some are primarily procedural or methodological. Arguments of this technical sort are typically meant to work by showing either: a) that what sometimes mistakenly pass for especially early epistemic competence are actually better understood as some simpler but analogous ability in masquerade; or b) that the alleged late appearance of abilities, personally hypothesized to have a still earlier onset, are actually the artificial by-product of some unnecessarily cumbersome measurement technique. Other proposals are more substantive, and allege a real revisiting of the same issues at a "higher" or more abstract level. An especially warm reception is planned for arguments of this second sort.

Finally, in Part III, an attempt will be made to envision the whole range of competing claims about the train of developmental changes that moves growing persons from an original place of epistemic realism to some alternative station that allows for the possibility of seriously entertaining competing knowledge claims. Central to this account will be an examination of different understandings of the meaning of psychological competencies in general (Chandler, 1991), and of epistemic development in particular (Chandler, 1975, 1987). The conclusion toward which this discussion is meant to move is that new and improved understandings of representational diversity occur, and then reoccur, first at what will be marketed as a "retail," and then a "wholesale" level. Otherwise, as this final part will seek to make clear, everything else is methodological sound and fury that, while signifying more than "nothing," is not the expression of the fundamental restructuring of beliefs about beliefs that it is regularly held out to be.

PART I: HE SAID, SHE SAID

A. The College Years

What immediately follows amounts to a simple lining out of various "proofs," meant to demonstrate that the available literature concerned with the growth of epistemic understanding really is the dog's breakfast of contradictory claims already alleged in the introduction. Because one can allege just about anything, what seems best, if you are to end up convinced that there really is a serious disagreement here, is to allow each of the accused (ourselves included) to be convicted out of their own mouths.

Perhaps the earliest, and still most authoritative, voice in the mounting chorus of investigators who have spoken directly to questions concerning the course of epistemic development is William Perry. Almost 30 years after the publication of his seminal 1970 book, *Forms of Intellectual and Ethical Development in the College Years: A Scheme,* the great bulk of what others have gone on to add can, without serious prejudice, be characterized as an elaborate footnote to Perry's original and richly detailed account. Without resorting to a full caricature of his well storied narrative, it is, perhaps, fair to say that the first four or five most talked about, and most explicitly epistemic "periods" within Perry's 9-level model were all thought to unfold within the four-year period that privileged North American youth ordinarily devote to getting a college education. Much of the special appeal of what he had to say about this age group arises out of the fact that most academics are quick to recognize their students in his writings. Many "freshmen" are, just as Perry described, naive realists—objectivists at heart—hopelessly committed to the idea that somewhere, waiting in the wings, there is a brute fact capable of resolving any competing knowledge claim. Similarly, who among us would fail on reading Perry to be reminded of all of those "multiplicitists" and uncommitted "relativists" who have riled their way through our second- and third-year classes, smugly insisting that everything is a matter of opinion, and that their own homespun opinions automatically have as much to recommend them as do the celebrated views of the famous authors whose work they are rudely obliged to read? Nor are there many instructors who are free of the special sin of pride experienced when the best senior students begin demonstrating some newfound appreciation of the "fact" that an allegiance to a constructive theory of mind need not be the same thing as concluding that one belief is as good as any other. In fact, Perry was so good at his job that many college students can even pick themselves out from among his various "period" descriptions, and are typically either prideful or crestfallen depending on whether their own personal epistemology garners a high or low number in his 9-point scale. Little wonder, then, that Perry's account of the course of epistemic development has come to be identified with the college years, or that those who make their living trying to teach and understand college youth should have counted his theory as a revelation, worthy of being studied and applied "six ways to Sunday."

While Perry's data naturally led him to insist that not everyone arrived at university in precisely the same epistemic state, and while it was equally evident that not everyone proceeded at the same pace through his various periods, no one familiar with his work would have the least reason to suspect anything like the possibility that 4-, 7-, or 14-year-olds might already be well on their way to an understanding of representational diversity, or that young teenagers might suffer the same "Cartesian anxiety" (Chandler, 1987) that evidently plagued the second and third-year college students in his study. Nor have similar thoughts much troubled the following army of educators or college counselors who have created something of a cottage industry out of Perry's ideas. Instead, whole careers have been built out of deciding whether some aspects of the standard curriculum better promotes epistemic development than do others (Schommer, 1990, 1993), or whether persons of certain epistemic persuasions are naturally drawn to one as opposed to another area of study (Paulsen & Wells, 1998). Still others have been led to explore the questions of whether students of this or that sex (Baxter Magolda & Porterfield, 1985), or persons with and without the benefit of a college education (Kuhn, 1991), might approach epistemic maturity differently, or move through Perry's several periods at different rates. Certain among these (e.g., Belenky, Clinchy, Goldberger, & Tarule, 1986; Baxter Magolda, 1992; Baxter Magolda & Porterfield, 1985; Clinchy, Belenky, Goldberger, & Tarule, 1985; Moore, 1994), although otherwise well within the orbit of Perry's model, have seriously challenged the legitimacy of generalizing from his original elite male sample to college populations, in general, and to women students, in particular. Over and above these and other content-bearing lines of inquiry concerning constraints and correlates of possible movement through Perry's hierarchy of epistemic levels, still more energy has been expended in an effort to develop various paper-and-pencil tests that avoid the necessity of conducting lengthy interviews of the sort that consumed so much of Perry's time, and that consequently allow whole student bodies to be tested en masse (for a recent summary of these measurement efforts, see Hofer & Pintrich, 1997).

In view of the fact that long stretches of the present volume are given over to an examination of all of these matters, there is hopefully no need to attempt still another detailed review of this literature here. If such an attempt were made, however, the thing that would stand out most clearly is that, because the large bulk of this work has been principally focused on how individuals interpret their postsecondary educational experiences (Hofer & Pintrich, 1997), it could tell us little about the real nature of epistemic development in the precollege years. Rather, by the lights provided by Perry's model, the length and breadth of epistemic development is made to appear to be contained within the horizon of the collegiate years, leaving few reasons left over to search for what must be the antecedents of such changes. Instead, we are all portrayed as arriving on campus still trailing vapors of our objectivist past, spend a few anxious years wrestling with relativism, and then graduate with a newly minted appreciation for the merits of reasoned argument, and something like the scientific method.

While we have no special quarrel with those investigators, or anyone else, who primarily study convenient samples of college students in the hopes of finding useful and generalizable things to say about their counterparts in similar academic settings, we do rather strenuously object to the use of such data as a springboard from which to launch generic claims about the whole course of epistemic development. The fact that college students are easily indentured into service as research subjects, often settle for being reimbursed in course credits, and can almost always be found and tested without venturing dangerously beyond the hallowed halls of the academy, naturally leaves those developmentalists who make a singular career out of studying only them open to the charge of searching for evidence (in this case evidence of epistemic growth) only where the light is brightest.

The best line of defense against such accusations would, of course, be to point convincingly to good reasons, or solid evidence, clearly showing that still younger persons simply lacked some prerequisite ability that would necessarily have to be in place before it would make any sort of reasonable sense to include them among the ranks of potential research participants. Few, we take it, would likely initiate a call to arms on learning that studies of the effects of puberty regularly excluded preschool subjects, or that word association studies enlisted no preverbal children in their samples. This is not like that. Most who have focused their research efforts on the epistemic orientations of college students have, it would seem, done so primarily out of some concern for the ways in which the natural epistemologies of such young adults potentially impact on the business of offering up a postsecondary education, or with the possibility that such epistemic matters could or should be taken into account in matters of student counseling or curricular reform. Driven by these practical concerns, and the untested conviction that they were already working on the ground floor, the large majority of contributors to this literature have had little or nothing to say about what might have transpired in the years before college admission, and have shown even less interest in detailing the sorts of cognitive limitations that are presumably responsible for preventing still younger persons from having already moved beyond the sorry absolutist and objectivist state thought to characterize standard issue college freshmen. Assuming any such thing, as we obviously mean to show, is a serious mistake that costs the larger developmental enterprise its opportunity to address a range of important questions.

Before turning attention to what is a much smaller group of investigators who have set out, with purpose of forethought, to target decidedly younger study populations, attention first needs to be drawn to another more loosely federated collection of research programs that, because they orbit at a greater distance from the gravitational center of Perry's model, have tended to include in their programs of research samples of either high school students, or persons beyond the usual college years. Well positioned at or near the head of this pack are Kitchener and King and their colleagues (e.g., King & Kitchener, 1994; King, Kitchener, Davidson, Parker, & Wood, 1983; Kitchener & King, 1981; Kitchener, King, Wood, & Davidson, 1989; Kitchener, Lynch, Fischer, & Wood, 1993; Kitchener & Wood, 1987), who have contributed greatly to the literature on epistemic development for almost 20 years. Although clearly influenced by the work of Perry, these authors have concentrated their efforts on detailing how a somewhat wider range of age groups (i.e., high school students, doctoral students, and even middle-aged adults) form and justify their beliefs about various ill-structured problems. While their research instrument—the Reflective Judgment Interview—

is better articulated than Perry's more open-ended approach, and while their 7-stage Reflective Judgment Model is more single-mindedly focused on explicitly epistemic matters, what they have to say about all of this is, in the end, much more like Perry's account than not. Nor do their results hold out any higher hopes regarding the epistemic accomplishments of the young. Rather, the bulk of the college freshmen and sophomores that they have tested seem only marginally aware that representational diversity may signal anything beyond the intrusion of remediable personal bias. Worse still, their adult subjects appear to succeed no better, and then only on the strength of whatever prior college experience they may have had. As it is, their third and final genuinely "reflective" level (i.e., their stages 6 and 7) is reached, if at all, only by the occasional advanced doctoral student. While there is much else to recommend their unique longitudinal effort, the evidence in hand does little to encourage the belief that their continuing program of research will ever tell us anything new about the early course of epistemic development.

Like Kitchener and King, Kuhn and her colleagues (Kuhn, 1991; Kuhn, Amsel, & O'Laughlin, 1988; Kuhn, Weinstock, & Flaton, 1994) have also explored dimensions of epistemic reasoning that interface, but only partially overlap with, the work of Perry and those more immediately within his orbit. Kuhn's 1991 book, which usefully focuses on subjects in their 40s and 60s, as well as more usual 20-year-olds, is primarily about argumentative reasoning regarding various ill-formed, but everyday social problems. That portion of her work that focuses most directly on epistemic issues is relevant to the present discussion only in that no clear age differences were observed in the frequency with which her broad sample of subjects endorsed what she described as absolutist, multiplist, and evaluative epistemic views. By contrast, her earlier work with Amsel and O'Laughlin (Kuhn et al., 1988) included sixth-, ninth-, and twelfth-graders, as well as nonstudent adults and graduate students. Again, however, almost all of the sixth- and ninth-graders tested scored at levels 0, 1, and 2 in their 6-stage model, and were seemingly committed to the view that a given event could support one and only one defensible interpretation. In keeping with the work emanating out of Perry's model, any appreciation of the inherently subjective or interpretive nature of the knowing process only began to appear for the first time among their twelfth graders, and was only found to be well consolidated in their sample of graduate student subjects. Although Kuhn and her colleagues do make some effort to interpret progress through their proposed stage sequence as necessarily turning on the achievement of something like Piagetian Formal Operations (Inhelder & Piaget, 1958), their previously published data, like that of Kitchener and King, contain little to suggest that epistemic development gets seriously off the ground before the college years. Interestingly, Kuhn's most recent efforts (chap. 7, this volume) move strongly in the directions being advocated here, and detail interesting changes in the epistemic presumptions of even middle school children.

B. The Adolescent and Preadolescent Years

Although, as just outlined, a small fraction of the many studies centrally concerned with possible changes in the natural epistemologies of young adults have
also included samples of primary and secondary school students, none previously
did so with any serious expectation that such young persons would score beyond
the lowest entry levels of their respective stage theories. Not surprisingly, they all
proved themselves to be right. In contrast to all such self-fulfilling prophesies,
there also exists a scattered and still smaller handful of studies, most of which
have their intellectual roots in soil different from that which has nourished work
in the Perry tradition, that also went about testing various groups of adolescents
and preadolescents, but this time full of high hopes that such young persons
would have already made some real progress toward epistemic maturity. That is,
in opposition to Perry (1970), who described the typical undergraduate male as
beginning his college career still committed to a "simplistic form of understanding [in which he continues to] construe his world in unqualified polar terms of
absolute right-wrong . . ." (p. 3), or Kitchener and King (1981), who state that
even senior "high school students tend to justify their beliefs with an absolute assumption about knowledge . . ." (p. 12), the studies to be listed out here make
more or less the same claims, but this time make them on behalf of preadolescents, and sometimes even preschool children. Advocates of this "early-onset"
view are broadly committed to the ideas: a) that progress in epistemic understanding is a fundamental part of all social-cognitive development (Broughton,
1978); b) that an awareness of representational diversity is a natural by-product
of the fading of egocentrism and the growth of those role-taking abilities common to the middle school years (Selman, 1980; Elkind, 1967); and c) that the capacities for abstraction and the metarepresentational skills that help to define
even early Formal Operational thought are sufficient to standardly move young
adolescents to an early appreciation of the subjective (and therefore relativised)
character of all knowledge (Boyes & Chandler, 1992; Chandler, 1975, 1987,
1988; Chandler, Boyes, & Ball, 1990). On these accounts, advocates of such
views are quick to argue that there is nothing in principle to prevent young rank-
and-file adolescents from all coming to those same insights about the subjective
nature of belief entitlement that others steadfastly reserve for only the most deserving of college graduates. Of course, there is no end to the list of possible mit-
igating factors that might intrude in ways that could prevent the typical adolescent from showcasing their best understanding of such heady epistemic matters,
but it is one thing to argue that such young persons own epistemic insights that
are not always in evidence, and quite another to suppose that they are bereft of
any such intuitions until they can confidently throw such doubts into the face of
their teachers and other "experts" who are broadly acknowledged to have a patent
on the scientific method, and who are seen as possessing clear title to the true
means of knowledge production. What is obviously needed, if such a looming de-

bate is to successfully get off the ground, is some line of evidence that purports to show that real flesh-and-blood adolescents actually do, as a matter of empirical fact, possess at least some of the epistemic abilities that their advocates claim for them in principle.

At least some of the work that claims to have provided such an empirical demonstration is a product of our own laboratory (Boyes, 1987; Boyes & Chandler, 1992; Chandler, 1975, 1987, 1988; Chandler et al., 1990). For example, by presenting eighth through twelfth graders with story problems involving competing knowledge claims about what were for them "live" matters of serious personal concern (i.e., whether 16-year-olds are responsible enough to drive), Boyes and Chandler (1992) and Chandler, Boyes, and Ball (1990) found that more than half of their high school samples already evidenced a clear appreciation of the relativised or subjective nature of beliefs, while fewer than a third responded in ways that still betrayed anything like a consistently "objectivist" or "absolutist," or "naively realistic" commitment to the idea that there is always some singular truth of the matter hiding behind every difference of opinion.

Although these findings pose an interesting challenge to all those who remain committed to the idea that such accomplishments are still at least a college education away, they, nevertheless, appear to fit quite comfortably with a good deal of other data about the usual course of adolescent cognitive and identity development. That is, in addition to following rather directly from what is otherwise understood about the ability of adolescents to think abstractly, and in terms of possibility and necessity (e.g., Chapman, 1988; Piaget, 1983), the sequence of epistemic stances identified in this program of research has been shown to bear directly on other intuitively related matters central to the study of the adolescent period. For example, readers familiar with the "ego-identity statuses" literature, and the ongoing efforts of Marcia (e.g., 1980), and others (e.g., Grotevant & Cooper, 1985; Waterman, 1985) to further systematize Erikson's classic writings on the subject of adolescent identity formation, would hardly be surprised to learn that the minority of young persons still comfortably committed to an objectivist epistemology rarely concern themselves with the problem of choosing among alternative conceptions of selfhood, or that those classified as still hiding out in the skeptical purgatory of an adolescent "Moratorium" remain stuck there largely for the relativised reason that they can find no good reasons for supposing that one life course has more to recommend it than another. Although mainly out of an obligation to ensure that at least some of their subjects will have already moved on to a status of "Identity Achievement," much of this work has also included the study of college-age students, the real conceptual center of gravity of these efforts, as Erikson originally imagined, has always remained in adolescence (see Grotevant & Cooper, 1985; Waterman, 1985 for reviews), where related matters of initial epistemic uncertainty also prevail. Consistent with this picture, our own preliminary results (i.e., Boyes & Chandler, 1992; Chandler, et al., 1990) demonstrate that, quite independent of age, only subjects who have already come to a "relativised" understanding of the process of belief entitlement also ordinarily score in the higher, or later arriving, stages of "Moratorium" or "Identity Achievement," as measured by procedures of the sort introduced by Adams and his colleagues (e.g., Adams, Shea, & Fitch, 1979).

Similarly, there would seem to be good reasons to assume that those adolescents who have already come to some relativised view of representational diversity would also find more adaptive ways of responding to the otherwise confusing swirl of competing knowledge claims that naturally surround them than those committed to some form of epistemic realism—a perspective that automatically renders views other than one's own as (at best) wrong-headed, and (at worst) mean-spirited. These expectations are largely born out by our own research (e.g., Chandler, et al., 1990) that shows that, in contrast to a comparison group of rank-and-file adolescents, the large bulk of whom already evidenced some commitment to a relativised view of belief entitlement, more than three-quarters of a matched sample of troubled adolescents, temporarily hospitalized as a result of antisocial and self-destructive behaviors, persisted in their commitments to a less mature form of "defended realism." Similar findings have recently been reported by Beaudoin (1998), who has also shown that adolescents removed from public schools as a result of chronic antisocial behavior are characteristically slow to envision the possibility that different persons might legitimately hold to different beliefs about one and the same event.

In a related series of studies, Oser and Reich (1987; Reich, 1998; Reich, Oser, & Valentin, 1994), working with a group of 9- to 22-year-old Swiss youth, report that recognition of the active contribution of the knower to the known begins to emerge in preadolescence, and that even the youngest of their subjects recognized the contribution of internal as well as external features of the knowing process. Similarly, Broughton (1978) reports evidence of "nascent skepticism" among his 12-year-old subjects, and that, by 18, respondents regularly voiced the view that knowing is a "constructive" enterprise guaranteed only by social convention. Clinchy and Mansfield (1985, 1986) and Mansfield and Clinchy (1987, 1997), who tracked the "natural epistemologies" of children from their preschool years through adolescence, also report that children as young as 4 already realize that knowledge is not simply absorbed, but is rather constructed by people with individual personalities and unique pasts; that as many as half of their 7-year-olds, and nearly all of their 10-year-olds, believed that diversity of opinion was legitimate; and that between 9 and 13 participants in their studies regularly came to "portray the knower as an active constructor rather than a passive receiver of knowledge" (Mansfield & Clinchy, 1997, p.1). As they put it, "by 13, not a single objectivist was left" (p. 10) in their sample. In much the same vein, Schwanenflugel, Fabricius, and their colleagues (e.g., Fabricius & Schwanenflugel, 1994; Schwanenflugel, Fabricius, & Alexander, 1994; Schwanenflugel, Fabricius, & Noyes, 1996) report that children of 8 or 10 regularly "move toward a constructivist theory of mind" in which they recognize that the same event may be interpreted differently because of differences in the minds that process the information. Similarly, Kuhn and her colleagues (chap. 7, this volume) have also demonstrated that, particularly in domains removed from the imagined certainty of "hard" or impersonal facts, even middle school children are often quick to entertain the possibility that equally well-informed others are free to differ in their beliefs about what is right or true. Finally, Walton (2000), who examined the epistemological expressions present in the spontaneous utterances of kindergarten through fourth grade children, also reports that, in talking about knowing and believing, all of her especially young subjects commonly employed epistemological expressions that "concerned certainty, contrasting knowledge with belief."

While it is possible to go on piling up more such examples, the point to be made here is hopefully already clear enough. At least in the minds of many investigators who have directly explored the natural or personal epistemologies of adolescents and preadolescents, it hardly seems necessary to hang back until they have entered college before observing that young people take note of, and struggle to comprehend, what they take to be legitimate interpretive diversity. If the data these authors present really does mean what they take it to mean, then it is elementary school students, and not college freshmen, who are first beginning to put their earlier objectivistic or naively realistic beliefs about belief behind them, and that it is young high school students, and not college seniors or advanced doctoral students, who first find themselves dangling above the pit of relativism, and who are newly scrapping for reasons to favor one necessarily subjective view of reality over another. All of this is not simply to say that the investigator who succeeds in unearthing the youngest epistemically active subject should be automatically declared the winner. Kitchener and King (1994), to take only one example, report that they have tested in excess of 1,700, mostly college-aged, students with their Reflective Judgment Interview, and there is every reason to believe that their responses actually do show them to be just exactly as epistemically obtuse as they are purported to be. Hoping to bury all of these respondents under a pile of counterexamples is hardly the way to model how best to deal with competing knowledge claims. Still, we have a real problem here, and, as the following section is meant to suggest, the problems are only beginning.

C. The Preschool and Primary School Years

As if the interpretive waters were not already murky enough, there has, over the last 15 years, been a virtual flood of new research concerned with young children's so-called "theories of mind," all of which speaks more or less directly to the questions of epistemic development. While neither space nor personal inclination permit yet another summary of this over-reviewed topic (interested parties might wish to consult, for example: Chandler & Carpendale, 1998; or Chandler & Sokol, 1999; or Moses & Chandler 1992), just enough does need to be said about its main lines to make it clear how this work bears on the question at hand. Here, more or less, is how such research goes. Some child (most often a preschooler) is made to watch as some target character (most often a puppet) has her or his prior belief about some material state of affairs (most often the whereabouts of a chocolate bar) rendered obsolete by some surreptitious and unexpected change (most often the relocation of the candy) that works behind the back of that story character to mark their initial belief as now false. The business end of this procedure—the litmus test of false belief understanding (Wellman, 1990), as it is commonly understood—comes when the child subject is asked to predict (i.e., show or tell) whether the target character: a) will now act on his or her original, but now sadly mistaken, belief (thereby demonstrating an appreciation of the fact that people who have no reason to know better often get things wrong); or, alternatively, b) will wrongly be thought to behave with reference to the way the world currently is, despite having no understandable reason for doing so (thereby demonstrating a failure to recognize the possibility of beliefs that are "false" or different from the reality they are meant to "represent").

As things usually turn out, children younger than 4 (some say 3 or even 2.5) typically fail such false belief tasks, supposedly marking themselves in the process as persons who are unable to separate the world from the beliefs that are had about it. Children of this immature sort are typically said to be suffering some otherwise unspecified "cognitive deficit" (Perner, 1991), and to fail to qualify as having a "representational" view of mental life. Except for the "cognitive deficit" part, which seems unnecessarily harsh, there are no real surprises here. What may surprise you, and certainly initially surprised us, is what is standardly said about those who take this litmus test and pass. Despite having really managed only a first approximation to the insight that those who have all of the relevant facts at their disposal tend to believe one thing, while those kept in the dark tend to believe something else, all of the 3- and 4-year-olds who succeed in working out whose beliefs are true as opposed to false are widely characterized as having already come to an "interpretive," or "constructive," or genuinely representational theory of mind—a theory said to be different from that subscribed to by adults in only quantitative ways (Chandler & Sokol, 1999). Extravagant as this may sound to those who are not themselves "theory-theorists" (e.g., Gopnik & Wellman, 1992), those who are seem quick to agree. As Perner (1991) put it, preschoolers who pass such false belief measures show en route that they have begun "to understand knowledge as representation with all its essential characteristics"(p. 275). "One such characteristic," he insists, "is interpretation" (p. 275, italics original). Many others appear to have followed Perner's lead here. Wellman, for example, not only describes preschool children as having already come to "an interpretive or constructive understanding of representation" (Wellman, 1990, p. 244), but further characterizes them as having already acquired the view that the contents of mental life are actively constructed "on the basis of inference and subject biases, misrepresentations, and active interpretations" (Wellman & Hickling, 1994, p. 1578). In similar fashion, Ruffman, Olson, and Astington (1991) also explicitly dismiss the possibility of any, let alone an "interpretive," stage in children's understanding of representation beyond straightforward false belief understanding. Similarly, Meltzoff and Gopnik (1993) argue that 5-year-olds already understand that beliefs are "active interpretations or construals of them from a given perspective" (p. 335).

Although we mean to have something to say in the section to follow about whether such comments actually credit preschoolers with too much, it is enough for present purposes to draw attention to the fact that what is being said about them is similar in most important respects to what others have reserved to say about young persons of 7 or 14 or 21, and who are also variously credited with having just come to an active, or constructive, or interpretive understanding of the knowing process. However this sorry state of affairs may have come about, it obviously just won't do to have more or less everyone making more or less the same claims about more or less everybody. What follows is a second listing out, this time of various lines of argument meant to demonstrate why it follows that one's own claims about one's own research subjects are true, while the same claims made by others about their own much younger or older subjects deserve to be branded as false.

PART II: DISCOUNTING STRATEGIES

If, after having devoted a sizeable chunk of your professional lifetime to tracking the onset of some competence in young adults, the next person in line announces that what you thought you saw for the first time was actually quite old hat, and was already plainly apparent half a childhood earlier; or if, after having struggled to work out just the right procedural means for allowing young persons to showcase abilities commonly thought by some to be still decades in the making, you were told that what you were panning was actually fool's gold—if this happened to you, then, of course, you would want and need a really good comeback. Because this is precisely the situation in which we find ourselves here, and because the number of possible retorts at our collective disposal is not only finite, but can be counted on the fingers of one hand, trying to list out what they might be is an exercise worth attempting. Here is such an attempt.

Clearly the easiest, and it would seem the most popular, way of managing the startling array of competing claims about knowledge claims currently afoot is to simply keep one's eyes on one's own work. That is, by averting one's gaze by reading only in our own specialized journals, it is evidently possible to scotomatize whole domains of research that manage to voice what may be our own question in different dialects. For example, with the occasional rare exception (e.g., Hofer & Pintrich, 1997; Kuhn, chap. 7, this volume; Mansfield & Clinchy, 1997), almost no one who writes about the epistemic development of college students gives any indication of also having read the literature on children's so-called theories of mind. No less guilty of surviving only by taking in one another's laundry, contemporary theory-theorists have grown equally notorious for living so surrounded by a thicket of self-citations that only light from other theory-of-mind

fires has any hope of getting through (Chandler & Sokol, 1999). Under insular circumstances such as these it would not be unheard of for a kiss-and-tell chapter
such as this to actually contain elements of surprise. Still, absolute denial is hardly
a sophisticated defense, and barely deserves its place on any list (such as this) of
workable discounting strategies. Beyond simply turning a blind eye, then, the
usual alternatives open to anyone accused of championing the wrong age group
generally break down along the lines of whether one is said to be mistakenly back-
ing children who are too young, or wrongly advocating for adults who are too old.

A. Early Onset Arguments

On its face, the easiest case to be won would appear to be that of those who insist
that others are mistaken for having attributed only to adults, or older adolescents,
epistemic competencies that, in their own more generous view, are actually within
the competence range of much younger persons. Here the standard ploy is to fault
the measurement strategies employed by others, claiming that they are somehow
just too cumbersome or obscure for words. By way of example, we adopted a variant of this strategy in some of our own earlier research (e.g., Boyes & Chandler,
1992; Chandler, 1987; Chandler et al., 1990), where it was argued that adolescent
participants had often been mischaracterized as the result of an overreliance on
procedures that required them to arbitrate the competing knowledge claims of "experts," or that obliged them to enter into debates about esoteric matters that more
typically concern only salaried epistemologists and metaphysicians. Unfortunately, whatever new meaning might have been taken from the fact that our own
adolescent subjects performed much better when presented with study problems
that involved issues that were much closer to home, it was later contradicted by
others (e.g., Kuhn, 1991), who used similarly scaled down and everyday study
problems, and got just the opposite effect. Here, then, as elsewhere, while no one
doubts the importance of presenting subjects with problems they are interested in
and feel qualified to address, it seems unlikely that the considerable epistemic differences so often observed between the performances of the young and old can, in
the end, be successfully laid off to some poor choice of stimulus materials.
Frankly, the child-friendly study problems on which the young are sometimes
found to succeed, and the supposedly more obscure standard issue tasks on which
adults continue to fail, often just don't seem sufficiently different to justify all of
the high hopes that are sometimes hung on the little light between them. What really seems required instead, if interpretable sense is to be made out of such age
differences, is to somehow get really clear about the underlying cognitive mechanisms that are thought to make the difference between this epistemic stance and
that—a task that, awkwardly, no one seems particularly keen to get involved in.
Until this is accomplished—as we have sought to do by distinguishing between
simple false belief understanding and adopting a bona fide interpretive theory of
mind—local repairs on the supposed procedural shortcomings of your test versus
mine will continue to amount to only tinkering.

B. Late Onset Arguments

For those committed to some variant of the "late onset" position (i.e., the position that has it that epistemic advancement requires a higher education), the standard method for discounting the early onset claims of others is to dismiss them as having accepted as the genuine article what are in fact mere homologies—counterfeits that manage to look like one thing, but are, in reality, something else entirely. Again, a working example of this discounting strategy can be found in our own earlier efforts to discredit the assumption, common within the theories-of-mind literature, that success on standard measures of "false belief understanding" should actually count as a "proof" that one has already come to an interpretive or constructive understanding of mental life. By our own more demanding account, the simple recognition (common to 3-and 4-year-olds) that people who are well or badly informed (about, for example, the current whereabouts of a chocolate bar) will naturally subscribe to different beliefs, is still a far cry from having already proven one's self to be one of those, typically older, individuals who are fairly judged to grasp the idea that one and the same thing may legitimately admit to more than a single interpretation. On this logic, those story characters who are left in ignorance as a result of having been in the wrong place at the wrong time (as is routinely the case in standard false-belief measures) simply have access to a different slice of reality than do those whose knowledge is more up to date. The fact that even preschoolers are able to understand such arrangements, and successfully mark as "false" the beliefs of others less well informed than themselves, is, we insist, entirely beside the point when it comes to deciding when young persons first understand that two people can both fairly and differently represent the same thing, and so legitimately deserve to be credited with subscribing to something like a constructivistic or interpretive theory of mind. Although it offers only cold comfort to those (e.g., Belenky et al., 1986; Clinchy, 1990) that imagine that one must be a high school or perhaps a college student before first learning that knowledge is an interpretive achievement, our own research (Carpendale & Chandler, 1996; Chandler & Lalonde, 1996), and that of others (e.g., Fabricius & Schwanenflugel, 1994) does go some distance toward demonstrating that children typically need to be 7 or 8 (rather than 3 or 4, as rumored by most theory-theorists) before first coming to this insight.

In a somewhat different pass at essentially the same issue, Kuhn and her colleagues (Kuhn et al., 1988) report that, while their own sixth grade subjects did acknowledge that persons may hold to different beliefs when they are differently informed, it was not until grade nine that they fully appreciated that people were within their rights for doing so. Like Mansfield and Clinchy (1997), who report similar results, Kuhn and her colleagues argue that their data support the idea that an important distinction needs to be drawn between simply marking the existence of representational diversity, and its later legitimization. Whether or not it eventually proves to be second, or sixth, or ninth graders who first deserve to be credited with an understanding to the subjective nature of all knowing, it is not, by any of these accounts, the rarified by-product of doctoral training, or the exclusive province of adult thought.

C. Arguments for Recursion

The prospect that is raised by findings of the sort just reported is the possibility of a third reading of the apparent contradictions afoot in the contemporary literature on epistemic development. On this view, the fact that evidence for "the same" achievement is said to emerge at radically different times is less an indication of sloppy craftsmanship, or that some people wouldn't recognize a legitimate epistemic achievement if it bit them, than it is of the serious possibility that the sweep of development is more spiral than linear (Chandler, 1987; Eckensberger, 1983; Overton, 1998; Zelazo, 1999), and that individuals must often confront and re-confront the same epistemic issue at different junctures along the path toward maturity. More will be said about this prospect in Part III to follow.

D. Arguments for Suppression

Before turning to the last section, however, a fourth and last possible reading of the contradictory character of the literature on epistemic development needs to be raised, less because we are certain that it is right than because, if it is, we all have a great number of amends to make. This somewhat demoralizing prospect is raised in interesting ways by some recent data reported by Walton (2000). In her study of the frequency with which kindergarten through fourth graders spontaneously employ various verbs of knowing, she notes two things of special interest. One of these is that, while such expressions increased in frequency across the ages studied, even kindergartners used such epistemological terms to express degrees of certainty and contrasting knowledge claims. The second is about teachers, and concerns the fact that, while producing a greater preponderance of such verbs of knowing than do their young pupils, they tended to use them almost exclusively as tools for classroom management rather than as a way to encourage children to understand knowledge as negotiated, speculative, and contextual. That is, Walton's teachers used terms such as "I think" almost exclusively to mean "You must," as in "I think you need to get to work on your math," or used "I guess," as in "I guess you'll have to lose your outside time." The unhappy prospect that all of this raises is that, while even very young primary school children may already be well on their way toward acquiring a fledging constructivist epistemology, their classroom experiences do little to encourage them to develop that understanding. Instead, as Walton points out, teachers often appear to be working behind the back of such accomplishments by encouraging or perpetuating beliefs in the objectivity of knowledge as delivered by true authorities. To the degree that this is true, it offers a final and especially dark explanation for why epistemic insights ordinarily appear only at the beginning and at the end of the public schooling process. That is, we may so thoroughly discourage and punish their use that such thoughts simply go underground until our children have grown too big to any longer take us seriously.

PART III: RECURSION RECURSION

If, as has already been demonstrated, evidence for just about every conceivable sort of epistemic development has been shown to characterize persons of just about every conceivable age, and if all of this variability cannot be easily written off to bad methodologies, or to some predilection for accepting counterfeits, then we are obviously stuck with a great diversity that simply refuses to go away. In view of this irreducible divergence of opinion, the most plausible explanation, we mean to argue, is that much of epistemic development is recursive (Boyes & Chandler, 1992; Chandler, 1987), and that much of what is imagined to be novel in adolescence or young adulthood actually represents some second, or perhaps even third, pass through "the same" epistemic levels. If something like this should prove to be the case, it would not be for the first time. As Kuhn (1989) and others (e g , Boyes & Chandler, 1992; Chandler, 1975, 1987; Eckensberger, 1983; Zelazo, 1999) point out, children, like scientists, often appear to "gain understanding of the world through construction and revision of mental models" that cause development to "[occur] not once but many times over" (Kuhn, 1989, pp. 687–688).

While it is perhaps reassuring to learn that children and scientists may both be adrift in the same boat, all such easy talk about the recycling of claims about competing knowledge risks being empty without our first having some firm idea about just how many such recursions are meant to be involved, and some specific criteria for deciding what is to count as a manifestation of one, as opposed to another, of these levels (Chandler & Chapman, 1991). As a way of addressing these needs, we mean to end this chapter with the following telegraphic proposals: the right number of recursions is two; and the operative criteria for deciding which is which is "wholesale versus retail" (Chandler, 1987).

The first of these propositions is straightforward enough. The number of years intervening between the point at which growing persons first begin to entertain the idea that people seriously and soberly hold to different beliefs about one and the same thing, and the age by which they eventually arrive at some coherent understanding of the fact that this insight need not do away with the very possibility of warranted belief, is simply too large to be comfortably contained within one followable story about the course of epistemic development. We get from here to the number "two" (as opposed, for example, to three or four) through a battle of attrition that discounts the bid that theorists of mind have made in behalf of preschoolers as an unacceptable low-ball offering (Chandler & Sokol, 1999), and by persuading at least ourselves that there is nothing of substance standing between the epistemic offerings of high school students and their college-age counterparts that cannot be written of to the different complexities of the competing knowledge claims that they are asked to arbitrate. Even so, we are still looking at a 10- or 12-year period between the ages of roughly 8 and 20—a period that is neatly bisected by an emerging capacity for abstraction (Eckensberger, 1983), or the onset of Piaget and Inhelder's (1958) Formal Operations. All of this naturally leads, as we will go on to show, to talk about "wholesale and retail." For the moment, though, it is enough if, by pruning away years as we have just done, it simply grows more plausible that we are not obliged to go on endlessly multiplying possible recursions just to fit everything in.

Of course, the possibility that formal operations may bear on matters of epistemic development has already been raised elsewhere, and, as no one will be surprised to learn, is not without its defenders (e.g., Chandler, et al., 1990; Reich, 1991) and detractors (e.g., King, 1977). Still, when what is had in mind by epistemic development is only that usually truncated bit that balances on the cusp of college admission, then we are naturally in a "no variance situation," and the best that can usually be said is that formal operations is a necessary but not sufficient condition for epistemic growth, at least during the late high school and college years. When, by contrast, the possible horizon of relevant behaviors is opened up to include some or all of the expressions of epistemic competence of interest to others such as Broughton (1978), Subbotsky (1996), Walton (2000), and the whole theories of mind crowd, then the possible stock of something like formal operations' potential cutting edge goes up considerably.

At the same time, we do not mean to be taken too literally with our talk of "something like formal operations." Rather, what we do intend is something closer to what Piaget (1983) meant in *L'evolution du necessaire chez l'enfant* when he argued that, not until the formal operational period do children ordinarily become capable of appreciating that "the real is . . . only one possibility among others . . . because the subject of knowledge is recognized as part of reality even as that reality is known only in terms of the subject's constructions" (Chapman, 1988, p. 321). It is, we mean to argue, this insight that drives a wedge between the case-specific, or "retail," doubts of young preadolescents, and the generic, or "wholesale," doubts of adolescents and young adults (Chandler, 1988). Certainly well before adolescence, and perhaps as early as 6 or 8, young school-age children already appreciate that different persons can hold different beliefs about one and the same thing (Carpendale & Chandler, 1996; Chandler & Lalonde, 1996), and they obviously worry about and quarrel over these different interpretations (Walton, 2000). What they do not do, or so we would argue, is see in these localized and case-specific doubts the dangerous prospect that diversity of opinion is somehow intrinsic to the knowing process that the resulting plurality of available opinion is nonreducible (Habermas, 1971), that rooted in the unavoidable necessity of interpretation is a fundamental ambiguity in all knowledge

(Sass & Woolfolk, 1985), or that with the recognition of the essential subjectivity of all truth the possibility of shareable and demonstrable knowledge may have been irreparably destroyed (Douglas, 1971). In short, what they do not yet do, but will ordinarily come to in adolescence, is wholesale out their initial insight that the criteria for knowledge are indeterminate and ambiguous, and do so in ways that often ends up poisoning their own well of epistemic certainty. To do so, as their older counterparts often learn to their dismay, is to invite the prospect of 'epistemological loneliness' (Chandler, 1975), to suffer 'a loss of epistemic community' (Rescher, 1980), and to enter a 'relativistic hall of mirrors' (Laing & Cooper, 1964) where everyone is seen to occupy eternally separated solipsistic worlds (Wittgenstein, 1969), and where the best warrant for any belief is no better than a blind liking (Perry, 1970).

These fearsome prospects—this first peek into the deepest part of the pit of relativism, and the resulting struggles for grounded conviction that it engenders—may well constitute defining episodes in the lives of adolescents and young adults, but they are not their first such encounters with representational diversity. They are their second. Keeping these two recursive moments well separated in our thinking is, we urge, the first step toward making a new kind of sense out of the confusion that plagues the current literature on epistemic development.

SUGGESTIONS FOR FUTURE RESEARCH

We mean to have already been clear enough that there is a heavy obligation on anyone concerned with the course of epistemic development in college-age youth to explain how the accomplishments that they report are similar to and different from the counterpart changes that occur in the lives of much younger persons. Meeting this obligation naturally requires a commitment to abandoning what otherwise risks being coded as just another lamentable instance of looking only where the light is brightest. Consequently, our strongest recommendation for future research is that anyone who imagines themselves to have detected some new and previously unheard of epistemic joint in the student body of their own university should—before rushing into print—pause long enough to first explore the possibility that what they are heralding may well have already come up on some still earlier turn of the developmental wheel. If this were done, then there would no longer be a need to just theorize about just how many recursions fit into the course of epistemic development.

Second, the current research literature concerned with possible changes in the way that young adults think about matters of belief entitlement parallels in many ways a counterpart literature concerned with those early "theories of mind" thought to unfold during the preschool and primary school years. In both cases, contributors to these distinct research enterprises have trenched their way deep into a narrowing vein of development, all on the promissory note that knowing exactly where others stand epistemically will somehow clarify much that is otherwise left obscure. By and large, bystanders to these efforts have remained optimistic. Whether young children have or have not yet come to some fledgling theory of mind, and whether young adults do or do not appreciate the ineluctably subjective nature of the knowing process, strikes just about everyone as matters pregnant with possibilities. All of these expectations not withstanding, the real truth is that there is as yet precious little in the way of hard evidence to warrant our faith that there is some real upshot to the fine-grained differences being described. What, consequently, seems required, in both cases, is some serious effort meant to demonstrate that changes in people's tacit epistemologies actually impact on the ways in which they run their lives. Our own efforts to show that changes in the way that adolescents understand competing knowledge claims actually make a difference in their efforts to secure a stable sense of identity (Boyes & Chandler, 1992), or to hammer out some sociable and adaptive way of responding to the competing beliefs of others (Chandler et al., 1990), are small steps in a direction that we regard as crucial.

ACKNOWLEDGMENTS

The preparation of this chapter was supported by a Natural Sciences and Engineering Research Council of Canada operating grant to the first author, by a University Graduate Fellowship to the second author, and by a Natural Sciences and Engineering Research Council of Canada Graduate Fellowship to the third author.

REFERENCES

Adams, R., Shea, J. A., & Fitch, S. A. (1979). Toward the development of an objective assessment of ego-identity status. *Journal of Youth and Adolescence, 2,* 223–237.

Baxter Magolda, M. B. (1992). *Knowing and reasoning in college: Gender-related patterns in students' intellectual development.* San Francisco: Jossey-Bass.

Baxter Magolda, M. B., & Porterfield, W. D. (1985). *Assessing intellectual development: The link between theory and practice.* Alexandria, VA: American College Personnel Association.

Beaudoin, K. M. (1998). *Adolescent egocentrism and epistemic development among adolescents with behavior disorders and their nondisordered peers.* Unpublished doctoral dissertation, University of British Columbia, Vancouver, BC.

Belenky, M. F., Clinchy, B. M., Goldberger, N. R., & Tarule, J. M. (1986). *Women's way's of knowing: The development of self, voice, and mind.* New York: Basic Books.

Benack, S., & Basseches, M. A. (1989). Dialectical thinking and relativistic epistemology: Their relation in adult development. In M. L. Commons, J. D. Sinnott, F. A. Richards, & C. Armon (Eds.), *Adult development: Comparisons and applications of developmental models* (pp. 95–109). New York: Praeger.

Boyes, M. (1987). *Epistemic development and identity formation in adolescence*. Unpublished doctoral dissertation, University of British Columbia, Vancouver, BC.

Boyes, M. & Chandler, M. J. (1992). Cognitive development, epistemic doubt, and identity formation in adolescence. *Journal of Youth and Adolescence, 21(3)*, 277–304.

Broughton, J. (1978). Development of concepts of self, mind, reality, and knowledge. *New Directions for Child Development, 1*, 70–100.

Carpendale, J. I. M. & Chandler, M. J. (1996). On the distinction between false belief understanding and the acquisition of an interpretive theory of mind. *Child Development, 66*, 1686–1706.

Chandler, M. J. (1975). Relativism and the problem of epistemological loneliness. *Human Development, 18*, 171–180.

Chandler, M. J. (1987). The Othello effect: Essay on the emergence and eclipse of skeptical doubt. *Human Development, 30*, 137–159.

Chandler, M. J. (1988). Doubt and developing theories of mind. In J. W. Astington, P. L. Harris, & D. R. Olson (Eds.), *Developing theories of mind* (pp. 387–413). New York: Cambridge University Press.

Chandler, M. J. (1991). Alternative readings of the competence-performance relation. In M. J. Chandler & M. Chapman (Eds.), *Criteria for competence: Controversies in the conceptualization and assessment of children's abilities* (pp. 5–18). Hillsdale, NJ: Erlbaum.

Chandler, M. J., & Ball, L. (1989). Continuity and commitment: A developmental analysis of identity formation process in suicidal and nonsuicidal youth. In H. Bosma & S. Jackson (Eds.), *Coping and self-concept in adolescence* (pp. 149–166). Heidelberg: Springer Verlag.

Chandler, M. J., Boyes, M. C., & Ball, L. (1990). Relativism and stations of epistemic doubt. *Journal of Experimental Child Psychology, 50*, 370–395.

Chandler, M. J., & Carpendale, J. I. M. (1998). Inching toward a mature theory of mind. In M. Ferrari & R. Sternberg (Eds.), *Self-awareness: Its nature and development* (pp. 148–190). New York: Guilford Publications.

Chandler, M. J. & Chapman, M. (Eds.). (1991). *Criteria for competence: Controversies in the conceptualization and assessment of children's abilities*. Hillsdale, NJ: Erlbaum.

Chandler, M. J. & Lalonde, C. E. (1996). Shifting to an interpretive theory of mind: 5- to 7-year-olds changing conceptions of mental life. In A. Sameroff & M. Haith (Eds.), *The five to seven year shift: The age of reason and responsibility*. (pp. 111–139) Chicago, IL: University of Chicago Press.

Chandler, M. J., & Sokol, B. W. (1999). Representation once removed: Children's developing conceptions of representational life. In I. E. Sigel (Ed.), *Development of mental representation: Theories and applications* (pp. 201–230). Mahway, NJ: Erlbaum.

Chapman, M. (1988). *Constructive evolution: Origins and development of Piaget's thought*. Cambridge: Cambridge University Press.

Clinchy, B. M. (1990). Issues of gender in teaching and learning. *Journal on Excellence in College Teaching, 1*, 52–67.

Clinchy, B. M., Belenky, M. F., Goldberger, N., & Tarule, J. M. (1985). Connected education for women. *Journal of Education, 167(3)*, 28–45.

Clinchy, B. M. & Mansfield, A. F. (1985, March). Justifications offered by children to support positions on issues of "fact" and "opinion." Paper presented that the 56th annual meeting of the (U.S.) *Eastern Psychological Association*, Philadelphia.

Clinchy, B. M. & Mansfield, A. F. (1986, May). The child's discovery of the role of the knower in the known. Paper presented that the 16th annual symposium of the *Jean Piaget Society*, Boston.

Douglas, J. (1971). *Understanding everyday life: Toward the reconstruction of sociological knowledge*. Chicago: Aldine.

Eckensberger, L. H. (1983). Research on moral development. *German Journal of Psychology, 7*, 195–244.

Elkind, D. (1967). Egocentrism in adolescence. *Child Development, 38*, 1025–1034.

Fabricius, W. V. & Schwanenflugel, P. J. (1994). The older child's theory of mind. In A. Demetriou, and A. Efkildes (Eds.), Intelligence, mind, and reasoning: Structure and development. *Advances in psychology, 106*, 111–132. Amsterdam: Elsevier Science.

Gilligan, C. & Murphy, J. M. (1979). Development from adolescence to adulthood: The philosopher and the dilemma of the fact. *New Directions for Child Development, 5*, 85–99.

Gopnik, A., & Wellman, H. M. (1992). Why the child's theory of mind really is a theory. *Mind and Language, 7*, 145–171.

Grotevant, H. D. & Cooper, C. (1985). Patterns of interaction in family relationships and the development of identity exploration in adolescence. *Developmental Psychology, 56*, 415–428.

Habermas, J. (1971). *Knowledge and human interests*. Boston: Beacon.

Hofer, B. K. & Pintrich, P. R. (1997). The development of epistemological theories: Beliefs about knowledge and knowing and their relation to learning. *Review of Educational Research, 67(1)*, 88–140.

Inhelder, B., & Piaget, J. (1958). *The growth of logical thinking*. London: Routledge & Kegan Paul.

King, P. M. (1977). The development of reflective judgment and formal operational thinking in adolescents and young adults. *Dissertation Abstracts International, 38*, 7233A.

King, P. M., & Kitchener, K. S. (1994). *Developing reflective judgment: Understanding and promoting intellectual growth and critical thinking in adolescents and adults*. San Francisco: Jossey-Bass.

King, P. M., Kitchener, K. S., Davison, M. L., Parker C. A., & Wood, P. K. (1983). The justification of beliefs in young adults: A longitudinal study. *Human Development, 26*, 106–116.

Kitchener, K. S., & King, P. M. (1981). Reflective judgment: Concepts of justification and their relationship to age and education. *Journal of Applied Developmental Psychology, 2*, 89–116.

Kitchener, K. S., King, P. M., Wood, P. K., & Davison, M. L. (1989). Sequentiality and consistency in the development of reflective judgment: A six-year longitudinal study. *Journal of Applied Developmental Psychology, 10*, 73–95.

Kitchener, K. S., Lynch, C. L., Fischer, K. W., & Wood, P. K. (1993). Developmental range of reflective judgment: The effect of contextual support and practice on developmental stage. *Developmental Psychology, 29(5)*, 893–906.

Kitchener, K. S. & Wood, P. K. (1987). Development of concepts of justification in German university students. *International Journal for Behavioral Development, 10*, 171–185.

Kuhn, D. (1989). Children and adults as intuitive scientists. *Psychological Review, 96*, 674–689.

Kuhn, D. (1991). *The skills of argument*. Cambridge: Cambridge University Press.

Kuhn, D., Amsel, E., & O'Laughlin, M. (1988*). The development of scientific thinking skills*. Orlando, FL: Academic Press.

Kuhn, D., Weinstock, M. & Flaton, R. (1994). Historical reasoning as theory-evidence coordination. In M. Carretero, M. & J. F. Voss (Eds.), *Cognitive and instructional processes in history and the social sciences* (pp. 377–401). Hillsdale, NJ: Erlbaum.

Laing, R. D. & Cooper, D. (1964). *Reason and violence*. London: Tavistock.

Mansfield, A. F., & Clinchy, B. (1987). The child's discovery of authoritative judgment. Paper presented at the biennial meeting of the *Society for Research in Child Development*, Baltimore, MD.

Mansfield, A. F., & Clinchy, B. (1997). Toward the integration of objectivity and subjectivity: A longitudinal study of epistemological development between the ages of 9 and 13. Paper presented at the biennial meeting of the *Society for Research in Child Development*, Washington, DC.

Marcia, J. E. (1980). Identity in adolescence. In J. Adelson (Ed.), *Handbook of adolescent psychology*. New York: Wiley.

Meltzoff, A., & Gopnik, A. (1993). The role of imitation in understanding persons and developing a theory of mind. In S. Baron-Cohen, H. Tager-Flusberg, & D. J. Cohen (Eds.), *Understanding other minds: Perspectives from autism* (pp. 335–366). Oxford: Oxford University Press.

Moore, W. S. (1994). Student and faculty epistemology in the college classroom: The Perry schema of intellectual and ethical development. In K. W. Prichard & R. A. Sawyer (Eds.),

Handbook of college teaching: Theory and applications (pp. 45–67). Westport, CT: Greenwood Press.

Moses, L. J., & Chandler, M. J. (1992). Traveler's guide to children's theories of mind. *Psychological Inquiry, 3*, 286–301.

Oser, F. K. & Reich, K. H. (1987). The challenge of competing explanations: The development of thinking in terms of complementarity of "theories." *Human Development, 30*, 178–186.

Overton, W. F. (1998). Developmental psychology: Philosophy, concepts, and methodology. In W. Damon (Series Ed.) & R. M Lerner (Volume Ed.), *Handbook of child psychology: Vol. 1. Theoretical models of human development* (5th ed., pp. 107–188). New York: Wiley.

Paulsen, M. B. & Wells, C. T. (1998). Domain differences in the epistemological beliefs of college students. *Research in Higher Education, 39(4)*, 365–384.

Perner, J. (1991). *Understanding the representational mind.* Cambridge, MA: MIT Press.

Perry, W. G. (1970*). Forms of intellectual and ethical development in the college years: A scheme.* New York: Holt, Rinehart & Winston.

Piaget, J. (1983). *Le possible et le necessaire, Vol 2: L'evolution du necessaire chez l'enfant.* Paris: Presses Universitaires de France.

Reich, K. H. (1991). The role of complementarity reasoning in religious development. In F. K. Oser & W. G. Scarlett (Eds.), *Religious development in childhood and adolescence* (pp.77–89). Series: *New Direction for Child Development* (W. Damon, series ed.), CD 52. San Francisco: Jossey-Bass.

Reich, K. H. (1998). Relational and contextual reasoning and its relationships with other forms of thought. Poster presented at the 15th advanced course of the *Archives Jean Piaget*, Geneva, Sept. 21–24.

Reich, K. H., Oser, F. K., & Valentin, P. (1994). Knowing why I now know better: Children's and youth's explanations of their worldview changes. *Journal of Research on Adolescence, 4(1)*, 151–173.

Rescher, N. (1980). *Skepticism: A critical reappraisal.* Oxford: Blackwell.

Ruffman, T., Olson, D. R., & Astington, J. W. (1991). Children's understanding of visual ambiguity. *British Journal of Developmental Psychology, 9*, 89–102.

Sass, L. & Woolfolk, R. (1985). Psychoanalysis and the hermeneutic turn. Unpublished paper.

Schwanenflugel, P. J., Fabricius, W. V., & Alexander, J. (1994). Developing theories of mind: Understanding concepts and relations between mental activities, *Child Development, 65*, 1546–1563.

Schwanenflugel, P. J., Fabricius, W. V., & Noyes, C. R. (1996). Developing organization of mental verbs: Evidence for the development of a constructivist theory of mind in middle childhood, *Cognitive Development, 11*, 265–294.

Schommer, M. (1990). Effects of beliefs about the nature of knowledge on comprehension. *Journal of Educational Psychology, 82*, 498–504.

Schommer, M. (1993). Epistemological development and academic performance among secondary students. *Journal of Educational Psychology, 85(3)*, 406–411.

Selman, R. L. (1980). *The growth of interpersonal understanding: Developmental and clinical analyses.* New York: Academic Press.

Sinnot, J. D. (1989). Life-span relativistic postformal thought: Methodology and data from everyday problem-solving studies. In M. L. Commons, J. D. Sinnott, F. A. Richards, F. A., & C. Armon (Eds.). *Adult development: Vol. 1. Comparisons and applications of developmental models* (pp. 239–278). New York: Praeger.

Subbotsky, E. V. (1996). *The child as a Cartesian thinker: Children's reasonings about metaphysical aspects of reality.* East Sussex, UK: Psychology Press.

Walton, M. D. (2000). Say it's a lie or I'll punch you: Naïve epistemology in classroom conflict episodes. *Discourse Processes, 29(2), 113–136.*

Waterman, A. S. (1985). Identity in the context of adolescent psychology. In A. S. Waterman (Ed.), *Identity in adolescence: Progress and contents: (New directions for child development*, No. 30). San Francisco: Jossey-Bass.

Wellman, H. M. (1990). *The child's theory of mind.* Cambridge, MA: The MIT Press

Wellman, H. M., & Hickling, A. K. (1994). The mind's "I": Children's conceptions of the mind as an active agent. *Child Development, 65,* 1564–1580.

Wittgenstein, L. (1969). *On certainty.* London: Blackwell.

Zelazo, P. D. (1999). Language, levels of consciousness, and the development of intentional action. In P. D. Zelazo, J. W. Astington, & D. R. Olson (Eds.), *Developing theories of intention: Social understanding and self control* (pp. 95–117). Mahwah, NJ: Erlbaum.

9

On the Form of a Personal Epistemology

David Hammer
*University of Maryland
at College Park*

Andrew Elby
*University of Maryland
at College Park*

INTRODUCTION

Research on "epistemological beliefs" has made important contributions to education, most fundamentally in identifying epistemology as a category of informal knowledge that may play a role in students' knowledge, reasoning, study strategies, and participation. A perspective on students as having epistemological beliefs can provide an alternative interpretive lens for teachers to use in understanding their students' ideas and behavior, in assessing students' abilities and needs, and in adapting their plans and strategies for instruction.

This value of the perspective in opening a new category of instructional perception and intention has not been sensitive to the details of the perspective. At this point, however, further progress will depend on those details. In this chapter, we contend that current perspectives on epistemologies are problematic in their form, or "ontology." We will focus our arguments primarily on epistemological beliefs about science and science learning, specifically in introductory physics, but our contentions apply to beliefs in other disciplines as well.

The study of epistemologies has largely emulated the study of "conceptual understanding," which has established that students have informal knowledge, about physical phenomena for example, that strongly affects what they learn. It is not clear, however, with respect either to epistemological beliefs or to conceptual understanding, how best to model what takes place in an individual's mind. What is the internal form of an informal epistemology? In other words, tolerating a cumbersome alliteration, what ontology should we ascribe to epistemology?

For the most part, researchers have presumed an ontology of "beliefs" as essentially unitary components of essentially stable epistemologies. By "unitary" we mean that each belief corresponds to a unit of cognitive structure, which an individual either does or does not possess. Construed in this way, epistemological beliefs are analogous to the "concepts" or "conceptions" posited as elements of cognitive structure. Just as cognitive science has understood naïve physics to be made up largely of "misconceptions" (e.g., "motion requires force") that differ from expert conceptions ("acceleration is caused by force"), research on epistemologies has understood students to have "misbeliefs" (e.g., "scientific knowledge is certain") that differ from expert beliefs (e.g., "scientific knowledge is tentative"). It follows that, just as developing an understanding of Newtonian physics requires "conceptual change," developing a more sophisticated epistemology requires changing beliefs. In neither case could the naïve constructs—the misconceptions or misbeliefs—be understood to contribute to that development, because they are inherently inconsistent with expert thought.

Therein lies a fundamental theoretical difficulty, as Smith, diSessa, and Roschelle (1993/1994) have argued with respect to the misconceptions perspective: Although couched as "constructivist," it offers no account of productive resources for the construction of more sophisticated understanding. If conceptions are unitary elements of cognitive structure, then student conceptions must be replaced by expert conceptions. To suppose that they could evolve in some way is to suppose, at least, that they have some underlying structure, that they contain productive elements at a finer grain size; but the misconceptions perspective has not described what that underlying structure might be. Similarly, in considering naïve epistemologies to be made up of constructs such as "knowledge is certain," current perspectives on epistemology offer no account of what may be the raw material from which students could develop new structures, such as that "knowledge is contingent on context and perspective."

There is an empirical difficulty as well. To model students' understanding of physical phenomena in terms of misconceptions is to imply a consistency in their reasoning that is contradicted by evidence from interview protocols (Viennot, 1985; diSessa, 1993; Smith, diSessa, & Roschelle, 1993/1994). Similarly, to presume students' epistemologies exist in the form of beliefs as stable structures is to presume a consistency across contexts: If a belief such as "knowledge is certain" exists as a unitary component of a stable epistemology, an alternative component to an expert's "knowledge is tentative," then this difference between the student and the expert should be consistently evident.

This ontology, which we will refer to as "unitarity," has not to our knowledge been explicitly defended in the literature on epistemologies. It is a default presumption, not the result of a deliberate process of investigation, and we contend it is inadequate. We will argue in the following section that researchers are presuming unitarity, more specifically the consistency it implies, in studying students' beliefs through questionnaire and clinical interviews that are far removed from the contexts of learning in which the beliefs are supposed to apply. This assumption of consistency across such diverse contexts is neither evident nor, when made explicit, plausible. We will then sketch a framework of epistemological resources at a finer grain size than unitary beliefs, analogous to diSessa's (1993) account of phenomenological primitives at a finer grain size than unitary (mis)conceptions.

By "unitarity" here, it is important to specify, we are not referring to the idea that epistemological thinking develops in unidimensional stages, advanced by Perry (1970), King and Kitchener (1994), and others. Schommer (1990), Hofer and Pintrich (1997), and others have challenged this assumption, arguing that epistemologies are better modeled along multiple dimensions. We concur. However, as we now elaborate, even authors who reject stage theories of epistemological development continue to assume unitarity in the sense that we are using the term, the idea that personal epistemologies take the form of theories or traits.

THEORIES AND TRAITS

There are two (sometimes undifferentiated) versions of the presumption of unitarity in the literature. The first, most common, and most closely aligned with the usual connotation of "beliefs," is that individuals hold epistemological beliefs in the form of declarative knowledge to which they can have conscious, articulate access. Thus Hofer and Pintrich (1997b, p. 117) suggest these beliefs be seen as "epistemological theories," following research on conceptual understanding. If students are not ordinarily aware of their theories, they may become aware of them and report on their substance through well-designed questionnaires and interviews.

Most studies of epistemologies proceed in this way, by asking subjects direct questions about their beliefs, often by presenting epistemological statements and asking subjects to rate their agreement or disagreement on a Likert scale. Students are asked, for example, whether they agree or disagree that "the best thing about science courses is that most problems have only one right answer" (Schommer, 1990); whether "the science principles in the textbooks will always be true (Songer & Linn, 1991); whether "knowledge in physics consists of many pieces of information, each of which applies primarily to a specific situation" (Redish et al., 1998).

It is only by a presumption of unitarity that the results of these studies may be seen as applying to contexts of learning. Students do not typically reflect directly and explicitly on the nature of knowledge and learning in their science classes, where their attention is almost always focused on concepts and phenomena. Questioning students in these ways about their epistemologies may be, to borrow an old joke, like interviewing golfers about their swings, off the course and away from their clubs: "Do you inhale or exhale when you swing the club?" It is not something they think about, ordinarily, and they may not know the answer. There would probably be a correlation between what golfers say and what they are observed to do when they play, but the former would probably not reliably indicate the latter.

That is, it is at least plausible that students' epistemologies might not be accessible to conscious reflection and articulate reporting, and their epistemologies as revealed on surveys and questionnaires may not be reliably indicative of their epistemologies in contexts of learning. To expect that students' responses to direct questions accurately represent their epistemologies in the classroom is to presume a consistency across these very different contexts.

The second version of the presumption of unitarity is that individuals have epistemological beliefs as constitutional attributes, akin to "learning styles" or "personality traits." Seen in this way, students may not be aware of or able to discuss their epistemologies explicitly, but they could have access to other aspects of their preferences and habits from which one may infer these aspects of their personalities. Thus some studies of epistemologies pose to subjects questions about their much more general tastes and attitudes, deliberately shifting to contexts that may be more accessible to reflection than those of learning science, such as whether they "like movies that don't have endings," or whether they agree or disagree that "people who challenge authority are overconfident" (Schommer, 1990).

Again, to treat students' responses to these questions as reliably indicative of their beliefs about knowledge and learning is to presume a consistency across contexts. In this case, it is a consistency not only with respect to the context of the interview, but also with respect to the target of reflection. This is analogous to asking golfers about their techniques in other activities and using their responses to infer how they play golf. In some cases, no doubt, that would be a reasonable assumption: Someone who is right-handed on the guitar would be very likely to be right-handed with a golf club; there is a strong basis for attributing handedness as a trait.[1]

---

[1]Even in that case, however, it is clear that for individuals who are ambidextrous it is necessary to think of handedness as context-dependent. Moreover, even people who are clearly "right-handed" are likely to have specific tasks they perform best with their left hands. To account for these phenomena, an adequate theory of handedness must address context dependence, and a simple ontology of traits will not suffice.

However, while most people can be characterized consistently as right-or-left handed across a wide range of contexts, there is not a basis for a similar claim regarding their epistemologies. There is no reason to expect that what an individual believes about knowledge in the realm of interpersonal relations, for example, about knowing and learning how to get along with others, must be consistent with what he or she believes about knowing and learning in an introductory physics course.

REASONS TO DOUBT
UNITARY CONSISTENCY

In fact, there are good reasons to expect that beliefs about knowledge and learning vary with both domain and context. Most people would agree that what makes someone a good dancer need not make him or her a good scientist, that the nature of expertise in the one is quite different from the nature of expertise in the other. That this bit of epistemology seems a matter of common sense is reason enough to doubt that epistemologies are consistent across domains. There is formal evidence as well, such as Stodolsky, Salk, and Glaessner's (1991) study, which showed differences between middle school students' beliefs about learning in math and in social studies, and Hofer and Pintrich's (1997a) study, which showed differences between students' epistemological beliefs about psychology and science.

There must also be at least some variation with context, even holding the putative topic fixed. It would be strange to suppose that the beliefs a subject would express about the certainty of knowledge would not depend, for example, on whether the context is that of a philosophical discussion, a scientific debate, or an everyday exchange of information. The same person who adopts a critical stance toward claims made in the academic context of a psychology course may be inclined to accept without question the advice of a therapist. Such variation with context belies either theory-like or trait-like unitarity for a belief such as "knowledge is certain."

Again, there are indications from research that epistemologies may be sensitive to context. In their review, Hofer and Pintrich (1997b) point to a variety of inconsistencies within and between various measures of epistemologies, citing Moore (1991), for example, who found low correlations between scores from different epistemological assessments of subjects' beliefs along Perry's (1970) scheme, and noting that few subjects showed consistent epistemological reasoning across the different questions in Kuhn's (1991) study. Leach, Millar, Ryder, and Séré (1999) gave evidence of the sensitivity to context of high school and university students' epistemological reasoning, arguing that it would not be well understood as reflecting a consistent framework of beliefs.

We are not suggesting there can be no consistency in students' reasoning or epistemologies. Clearly there can be, as a number of studies have shown (King & Kitchener, 1994; Schommer, 1990). One of us has presented evidence to show that students in an introductory physics course could be characterized as having consistent epistemological beliefs *within the context of the course* (Hammer, 1994). The data for those characterizations came from series of interviews of six students. These interviews, following Perry (1970), had an open format and a conversational tone in an effort to keep the context of the interviews close to the context of the course.

To claim, however, that an epistemology is consistent within a given context, in this case that of a traditional introductory physics course, is not to claim that the consistency derives from a unitary ontology. We contend that it need not.[2] For instance, it would be a mistake to attribute someone's raucous behavior as a spectator at football games to an inherent "raucousness," even if their behavior is consistent in that context; in other contexts the same person's conduct may be reliably proper. Similarly, a student's epistemology as revealed by a survey or in a "Reflective Judgment Interview" (King & Kitchener, 1994), even if it is consistent in that context, may not coincide with that student's tacit epistemology in the context of a science class.[3]

Of course, classroom contexts may also vary. For us, the most compelling reasons to doubt unitarity come from our informal experience as teachers. It is possible to change, very quickly, how students participate in our physics classes. Students who arrive on the first day expecting a blackboard lecture replete with equations, who would appear to hold beliefs that scientific knowledge is formal, absolute, and received from authority, may by the end of the period be participating in heated debate, behaving as if they believe their own ideas and experiences matter. This does not reflect a sudden, global change in their epistemological beliefs; it reflects a local change in the context of the classroom, which engenders in students a more productive epistemological mode.

That this mode is available to students, even temporarily, implies that they have the epistemological resources needed to enter that mode. An adequate theory of epistemologies must account for those productive resources and for the contextual dependence of their activation.

AN ALTERNATIVE FRAMEWORK

Krieger (1992) described the development of theory in science as analogous to the design and production of machines: A scientific model is like a machine scientists assemble, from the various "parts" they have available, to produce the

---

[2]Indeed, a standard topic in psychology texts (e.g., Wortman, Loftus, & Marshall, 1988) is the "fundamental attribution error," the tendency to attribute a person's behavior to a general trait when contextual factors play a role.

[3]King and Kitchener, in fact, advise caution in applying the Reflective Judgment Interview on an individual basis (1994, p. 115).

same phenomena they observe in the physical world. On this analogy, theoretical advances often come from new choices of parts, or from the creation of new kinds of parts, just as technological advances often come from selection or development of new materials. Several hundred years ago, for example, physicists were trying to assemble a model of light out of conceptual parts they had available from their observation of balls and other bits of solid matter, namely small hard, solid particles. Much effort went into contriving different ways to assemble these parts into a model that would produce phenomena such as diffraction and interference. In the end, however, progress resulted from the use of different conceptual parts, namely "waves."

To frame our criticism in Krieger's language, we are questioning the use of "theories" and "traits" (or "styles") as the parts from which to assemble models of students' epistemologies. Certainly there have been advantages to their use. Notions of theories and traits fall within everyday lexicon, and that familiarity facilitates discussion. This is especially important in the case of students' epistemologies, where for many audiences the idea that students might have epistemological orientations in any form may be unfamiliar. "Theories" and "traits" are effective means of introducing epistemological considerations, just as "alternative conceptions" are effective means of introducing consideration of students' intuitive content knowledge.

With respect to advancing beyond these first models, however, they are limiting progress, making what Minsky (1986) called the "single-agent fallacy" in presuming epistemologies are comprised of unitary beliefs. Dennett (1991) has similarly described it as a fallacy to attribute the experience of consciousness to ontological unitarity, a mistake similar in kind to that of understanding complex behavior such as bird flocking as having a single, central, organizing source (see, e.g., Wilensky & Resnick, 1999). Our purpose in this section is to propose an alternative, manifold ontology, in the general class of models that has developed from Minsky's notion of multiple "agents" acting in a "complex society of processes" (Minsky, 1985).

diSessa (1993) has proposed such an ontology in his account of "phenomenological primitives," or "p-prims," the parts he proposed to assemble into a model of intuitive physics. To see how p-prims differ from theories or "alternative conceptions," consider a specific well-studied student difficulty. When asked about the forces involved in pushing a desk across the floor, many students say that there must be an overall forward force, i.e., the forward force must "beat" any backward ones, and as soon as the forward force turns off, the desk stops moving. Generally, this is explained by attributing to students the stable, context-independent misconception that motion requires force.[4]

---

[4]On a Newtonian account, a force is required to *initiate* or *change* an object's motion, but not to *maintain* motion.

In other contexts, such as when asked about a ball being thrown, students correctly answer that the ball continues to move in the absence of the forward force of the hand. On the misconceptions perspective, students must then be thinking of an internally stored force as responsible for the continued motion of the ball.

Rather than describing students' knowledge in terms of conceptions inherently inconsistent with experts', diSessa posited elements that, appropriately organized, contribute to expert understanding. By his account, attributing to students the unitary conception that *Motion requires force* confuses emergent knowledge, an act of conceiving in a particular situation, for a stable cognitive structure. On this view, students' reasoning about the desk and the ball can be understood in terms of the context-specific activation of the following p-prims. *Maintaining agency*[5] is an element of cognitive structure useful for understanding any continuing effect maintained by a continuing cause, such as a light bulb needing a continuous supply of energy to stay lit. *Actuating agency* is another p-prim, an element of cognitive structure involved in understanding an effect initiated by a cause when the effect outlasts the cause, such as the strike of a hammer causing a bell to ring. The desk question tends to activate *Maintaining agency*, and hence, the idea that a continued net forward force is needed to keep the desk moving forward. By contrast, the ball question tends to activate *Actuating agency*, and the idea that the ball's motion can outlast the force exerted by the thrower.[6] Unlike the misconception *Motion requires force*, the p-prims *Maintaining agency* and *Actuating agency* are not "incorrect." Neither are they correct; they are resources that can be activated under various circumstances, sometimes appropriately, sometimes not. Furthermore, while the misconception is an element of cognitive structure specifically tied to motion and force, the p-prims also apply to light bulbs, bells, and numerous other situations. In this sense, p-prims are both smaller and more general than unitary conceptions.

The ontology of p-prims has several advantages over the ontology of conceptions. First, it provides theoretical structure to account for the sensitivity to context of students' reasoning, as different p-prims are more and less likely to be activated in different circumstances. Second, it provides an account of productive cognitive resources from which students may construct more adequate understanding. Development toward expert understanding involves modifying which p-prims get activated in which situations, rather than replacing p-prims with other structures.

We seek, similarly, a framework of epistemological resources, smaller and more general than theories or traits, that can accommodate contextual dependence and provide an account of productive resources. For example, many students appear to view scientific knowledge as coming from authority. At the same

---

[5]diSessa (1993) called this p-prim *Continuing push*, but the word *push* in that name may be misleading, as the agency need not take the form of a force. We will also use the name *Actuating agency* instead of diSessa's *Force as mover*.

[6]In many contexts, the ball question may also activate *Maintaining agency*, which students attribute to an "internal force" that was impressed into the ball by the hand.

time, it is clear even small children have epistemological resources for understanding knowledge as invented ("How do you know your doll's name is Ann?" "I made it up!") or knowledge as inferred ("How do you know I have a present for you?" "Because I saw you hide something under your coat!").

Following Minsky (1986) and diSessa (1993), we are looking for epistemological resources that are naturally invoked in familiar circumstances, and for which we can describe plausible developmental origins. For now, we have focused on identifying resources that may reasonably be attributed to young children, and that have an everyday face validity. In other words, when described appropriately, they should be recognizable as part of common sense. We do not consider this set of resources to be established; it is certainly not complete. These are tentative ideas as we begin a new program of research. We cannot emphasize enough that the knowledge elements presented here are intended to demonstrate the kind of epistemological resources we view as alternative to unitary beliefs. Future research will undoubtedly reveal that many of the particular elements we list are not part of an adequate theory of naïve epistemology.

As we currently conceive it, the framework has four categories of epistemological resources. The first is of resources for understanding the general nature of knowledge and how it originates, beginning from a notion of "knowledge as stuff" (Lakoff & Johnson, 1980). The second and third categories are of resources for understanding epistemological activities and forms, such as *Brainstorming* and *Lists* respectively,[7] these following the notions of "epistemic games" and "epistemic forms" as developed by Collins and Ferguson (1993). The fourth category is of resources for understanding stances one may take toward knowledge, such as *Doubting* or *Accepting*.

We consider these categories to be useful in describing these resources, and useful at this stage of theory building, but we do not consider them to have ontological significance. The activation of a resource does not preclude the activation of other resources within that same category or, certainly, in other categories. In fact, as will be clear, there are close links between resources in different categories. It may well be that, in some cases, these close links would be better understood as single resources that lie across the categories we have drawn.

Resources for Understanding the Nature and Sources of Knowledge

In different contexts, children as young as 3 years old can be heard to speak of knowledge in several different ways, reflecting different resources for understanding what sort of thing knowledge is and how it arises. The following are examples of resources in this category.

---

[7]We will use italics and capitalization in this way to denote epistemological resources. Thus *Lists* refers to a resource for understanding lists as an epistemological form.

Knowledge as propagated stuff: The first of these is to treat knowledge as a kind of stuff that can be passed from one person to the next. Knowledge understood in this way has a source and a recipient, although it is not "conserved," because the source does not lose any knowledge in the process. Knowledge is not, in this sense, like money or material; it is more like fire, or the flu, or a state of dirtiness or contamination (as in, for example, the child's notion of "cooties"). Small children can understand the question "How do you know we're having soup for dinner?" and respond "Because Mommy told me."

Knowledge as free creation: Children also have other resources for understanding how knowledge may arise. Invention is a routine experience for children, and "I made it up" a routine explanation for the origin of many of their ideas, including stories, imaginary characters, and games. Knowledge by this resource, like the pictures a child draws on a blank page, does not have any source other than the child's own mind, where it arose spontaneously. Again, we are not claiming that this is correct—we would expect that children's creations arise from other knowledge they have. We are claiming only that this is an element of the children's epistemologies, a resource they invoke to understand how some of their ideas come to be.

Knowledge as fabricated stuff: Children may also think of knowledge as inferred or developed from other knowledge. This resource may be a metaphor for knowledge as a more familiar sort of stuff, something one creates, but out of other material. Thus it is not a free creation; it is constrained by the nature of the material. Thus the answer to the question "How do you know?" is "I figured it out from [the source material]." For example, asked "How do you know that $3 \times 5 = 15$?" a child may answer, "Because I added $5 + 5 + 5$," rather than "I made it up" or "My teacher told me." In this way, asking a child "How do you know this?" is analogous to asking "How did you make this?" about a physical object. To understand knowledge in this way, moreover, is to think that others can create the knowledge for themselves, as long as they have access to the same raw material. (By contrast, knowledge generated by *Free creation,* must be divulged by the creator.)

Other resources in this category would include *Knowledge as direct perception,* ("How do you know I'm in the room?" "I see you!"); and *Knowledge as inherent* ("How do you know this color is red?" "I just do!").

To be clear, we are not describing a progression of stages of increasing sophistication. We are describing a set of resources that are available from an early age for use, as needed, in various contexts. Moreover, these resources may be invoked in combination with each other. For example, an adult would be likely to invoke *Propagated stuff* to understand the spread of a rumor, in conjunction with *Fabricated stuff* to understand its evolution along the way. Or, a child who invokes *Free creation* to understand her authorship of a story would invoke *Propagated stuff* to understand how others come to know that story.

Resources for Understanding Epistemological Activities

Our principle strategy in the preceding category was to consider what resources may underlie children's various responses to the question "How do you know _____? Here, our principle strategy is to consider what resources may underlie their responses to the question "What are you doing?" to identify resources that allow children to understand and engage in familiar activities, such as telling and listening to stories, playing and inventing games, asking questions and guessing at answers, all of which involve the creation, manipulation, or application of knowledge.

As before, it is important to remember that what we are describing are not *activities,* but *resources for understanding* activities. Thus one may disagree over whether knowledge is ever simply "accumulated" but nevertheless agree that *Accumulation* is a resource people invoke in some contexts to understand what they are doing.

Accumulation: When asked "Is Mommy in the yard?" and not knowing the answer, a child could easily respond "I'll go find out." This reflects an understanding of "finding out" as a simple activity, the retrieval of information. *Accumulation* probably develops very early from experience with ordinary objects, with "get the toy" as the basis for "get the piece of information." It is reflected in everyday language, when we speak of "gathering" or "retrieving" information, and it may be invoked by children or adults to understand learning in many contexts.

Formation: Children also understand activities in which they construct ideas for themselves, whether in writing stories, composing songs, devising rules, or inventing games. There may be a resource of *Formation* they invoke in all of these contexts; but perhaps this is better described as a collection of more specific primitives, for example with *Forming rules* a distinct primitive from *Forming stories,* or *Guessing* and *Brainstorming* distinct from *Crafting* and *Adjusting.* In any case, it is clear that children have resources to understand the differences between *Accumulation* and what they are doing with knowledge in these more creative contexts. Again, *Formation* may develop, in conjunction with *Fabricated stuff,* from experience of making things out of everyday material.[8]

Checking: A child would also understand, for example, a request to "Check to make sure you put your book away," reflecting an understanding of "making sure" as an epistemological activity. *Checking* may evolve in response to early

---

[8]Here, then, is an example of a pair of closely linked resources, *Formation* and *Fabricated stuff,* that may be better understood as two views of the same resource.

experiences of error, in conjunction with *Doubting* as a stance (see the following section). In various contexts *Checking* may be invoked in conjunction with *Accumulation,* such as when the child goes to re-retrieve information regarding the location of the book, or in conjunction with *Formation,* such as when checking the conclusion that $3\times5=15$ by counting.

There must also be a resource, or set of resources, of *Application,* invoked in situations that involve using a piece of existing knowledge, such as in singing a song, telling information, or in following or enforcing a rule; other resources for understanding epistemological activity may include *Comparing, Sorting, Naming, Counting, Adding,* and so on. See Collins and Ferguson (1993) for a more detailed list.

Again, this is not a hierarchical list of greater and lesser sophistication. These resources are all available from an early age. Therefore, "development" would primarily consist of changes in their activation. In this way, a framework of this sort allows modeling of epistemological development as more "unique" to a context than "universal" (Feldman, 1994). For example, what the literature describes as the counterproductive epistemological belief that knowledge is received may be understood instead, roughly, as an overuse in the given context of some resources (*Accumulation, Propagated stuff*) and an underuse of others (*Formation, Checking, Fabricated stuff*). An epistemological intervention, then, could be conceived as modifying the activation of epistemological resources in that context, rather than as disestablishing an epistemological theory.

Resources for Understanding Epistemological Forms

Resources for understanding epistemological activities are not sufficient, inasmuch as these activities invariably involve epistemological forms. Thus the activity of writing a story requires resources for understanding the activity of writing, some version of *Formation* in conjunction with *Free Creation* or *Fabricated stuff,* as well as a resource for understanding the form of a story, which we will call, simply, *Stories.* The latter resource may of course also be invoked to understand the activity of listening to a story, in conjunction with *Application* and *Propagated stuff.*

In addition to *Stories,* we can also identify *Rules* as an epistemological resource available to young children, which they may invoke in activities of formation (inventing a new rule to a game) or of application (enforcing an existing rule). Both of these resources, *Stories* and *Rules,* seem to be primitive notions in the sense that, within informal epistemology, they cannot and do not need to be defined in any more basic terms.

Rule system is a resource for understanding a coherent set of rules that define a game, such as checkers or tic-tac-toe. *Facts* is a resource for understanding a piece of information, such as a phone number or an address. Other resources in this category would include *Songs, Lists, Pictures, Categories, Statements,*

Words, Names, and *Numbers;* again, Collins and Ferguson (1993) provide a more detailed list.

In this respect as well, an account of resources allows a reinterpretation of evidence from existing studies. Rather than attribute results of surveys and interviews to, for example, the presence of one unitary belief ("knowledge is simple") and the absence of another ("knowledge is complex"), we can view the results as evidence of the *activation,* in the context of that survey, of some resources (*Facts, Rules, Names*) and deactivation of others (*Categories, Rule systems*).

Resources for Understanding Epistemological Stances

We describe only briefly this fourth category of our draft framework of epistemological resources, those for understanding the stances one may take toward an epistemological form. Hearing something that does not seem reasonable, a child can say "I don't believe that," reflecting an understanding of *Belief* and *Disbelief* as alternative stances one can adopt toward a piece of information. *Doubting* seems another resource that is likely part of a school-age child's repertoire, to understand a stance one adopts toward a piece of information one has neither accepted nor rejected. There should also be resources for understanding experiences of an idea seeming right or making sense, *Understanding,* and experiences of an idea not making sense, *Puzzlement. Understanding* would generally trigger *Acceptance,* although perhaps not always: Someone may understand the experience of an idea seeming right but knowing it to be false. Educational problems may arise when, in the context of a course, *Acceptance* triggers *Understanding;* in other words, when students understand the experience of believing an idea is correct as implying that they understand the idea.

IMPLICATIONS FOR INSTRUCTION AND RESEARCH

The previous list of epistemological resources illustrates the shift in ontology we are proposing from unitary beliefs, attributed to students as traits or theories, to manifold resources, seen as activated within particular contexts. To reiterate, we are not arguing here for this particular list of resources; we are arguing for the shift in ontology they illustrate. However, this shift in itself has implications for instruction and for research.

Instructional Diagnoses and Strategies

These ontological considerations affect how we, as physics teachers, diagnose our students' strengths and needs. For instance, to understand their epistemologies as *traits* is to understand them, in some sense, as parts of who they are as people. In this case, we should try to accommodate different epistemologies, just as many teachers try to accommodate different learning styles. Expecting that epistemologies are general characteristics of students' personalities, we should have only modest hopes of inducing change. By contrast, if we understand students to have epistemological *theories,* then our approach to instruction should include some effort to disestablish theories that disagree with what we hope them to believe. Following the literature on conceptual change, we would likely pursue this by drawing out students' theories, trying to challenge or refute them, and finally offering better theories in their place.

An ontology of manifold resources affords a different perspective on students' epistemologies and a different approach to fostering epistemological change. If we understand students' epistemologies as specific to a context, we may expect that they have other resources tied to other contexts. Rather than think in terms of accommodating their traits or refuting their theories, we may think in terms of finding and animating the more productive epistemological resources the students invoke in other situations.

On this view, much may be achieved by manipulating the context of learning. If in class debates among students are more typical than lectures by the teacher, the class may become a context in which students naturally consider it important to explore a variety of perspectives. Therein may lie much of the benefit of innovative pedagogical approaches: They change the context in such a way as to invoke more productive epistemological resources. Another manipulation of context is to engage students in more activities of design and construction, such as building gadgets or writing computer programs that will accomplish some task. Contexts of design and construction are more likely than traditional classroom contexts to activate epistemological resources productive for learning (Harel & Papert, 1991).

Clement, Brown, and Zeitsman (1989) described one strategy instructors have for helping students draw on productive conceptual resources, that of "bridging analogies" to productive "anchoring conceptions" in more familiar situations. For example, students often have difficulty understanding how a "passive" object, such as a table, can exert an upward force on a book. Students do not, however, have trouble understanding how a hand, or a compressed spring, can exert a force. By helping students to think of the table as a very stiff spring, instructors can help them understand it as exerting an upward force (Minstrell, 1982).

Instructors may employ similar strategies to help students activate productive epistemological resources. In these cases, the analogies form a bridge from targeted, less familiar activities of learning to what we may call "epistemological anchors," familiar activities in which the productive resources are likely to be invoked.

One common example is the analogy many instructors draw between learning and physical exercise, comparing the mental benefits of thinking to the physical benefits of exercising. This bridge between exercise and learning helps students to think of knowledge and ability as developed through effort.

Another example is the following story we have used to promote metacognitive reflection in our physics students, a bridging analogy to what we expect are familiar experiences in context of interpersonal relationships:

> Imagine you have met a new person and he irritates you for some reason but you can't put your finger on it. So you think about it, trying to figure out what it is about him that bugs you, and eventually you realize that it's because he looks and sounds a bit like a character in a movie you saw recently. Having figured that out, you know that it's not really this new guy who irritates you, but that movie character, and you don't have to worry about it anymore. In another instance, you may realize that you've met him before and had an unpleasant interaction, in which case there's good reason for that feeling of irritation.

This may serve as an epistemological anchor to help students understand the phenomenon of having an intuitive sense that a physical object will behave in a certain way, but not being able to explain why. For example, although Newton's First Law says that an object moves at a constant velocity if there are no forces acting on it, most students have the intuitive sense that the motion will die away. The movie character analogy may help students understand the importance of looking into the experiential bases for that intuitive sense, to articulate them and assess how they might reconcile those experiences with Newton's laws.

We are certainly not suggesting that these are new ideas for instruction. In our experience, effective teachers already know, if tacitly, that students have productive epistemological resources (as well as productive conceptual resources, emotional resources, and physical resources), and that much of effective teaching is helping students find these resources and use them. However, this knowledge is not reflected in the status quo of formal research about epistemological beliefs.

Implications for Research

A shift in ontology from unitary theories or traits to finer-grained resources also has implications for research. We are proposing, first, a new emphasis in the study of personal epistemologies, the identification of naïve epistemological resources and the contexts in which they are invoked.

Like research on conceptions, research on epistemologies has focused almost exclusively on identifying the ways in which students' views differ from those educators wish them to develop. To understand epistemologies as made up of resources is to understand the need to develop an account of what those resources are. This is a more fundamentally constructivist agenda in that it aims to provide an account of resources from which students may construct more adequate epistemologies.

This is rich, relatively unexplored terrain. There are several ways to explore it; what we sketched previously is at best a beginning. To date, we have worked primarily by reflecting on what we know children to be capable of understanding based on everyday experience and supplemented by some informal interviews of a first grade student. That a young child is capable of answering "How do you know that?" with a variety of different responses suggests the existence of a variety of different epistemological resources.

Of course, more can be achieved through careful interviews. For instance, by carefully designing the tasks children are presented, Samarapungavan (1992; Samarapungavan & Westby, 1999) has provided convincing evidence that first graders are richly equipped with epistemological resources for scientific thought: When told that a certain theory about tigers is true, and then presented with evidence that seems to support a rival theory, most first graders concluded that another person looking at that same evidence would believe the false theory. That children and lay adults do not activate these resources in many contexts (Kuhn, 1989) may be understood in this way, rather than as a general developmental limitation.

Insights can also arise, we contend, through reflection on everyday adult activities. That an ordinary adult, for example, would be capable of understanding the notion that they may be irritated by someone they just met because that person reminds them of a movie character reflects epistemological resources for thinking about the existence and influence of inarticulate knowledge. No doubt there are many other examples of everyday competencies that suggest the existence of epistemological resources. It should also be possible to design tasks for formal protocols to reveal adult epistemological competence.

We have already alluded to methodological concerns regarding the use of large-scale questionnaire studies. Epistemology researchers should make greater use of naturalistic case studies, including open format interviews (Perry, 1970; Belenky et al., 1986) as well as classroom observations (Hogan, 1999). If the activation of epistemological resources depends on context, then to determine a student's epistemological stance in introductory physics, for instance, a study must be conducted in a manner that remains as close as possible to the contexts of learning introductory physics (Hammer, 1994).

The particular value of case studies, as opposed to paper-and-pencil surveys, is that they provide a depth of information about a small number of subjects, instead of a thin thread of information about a large number. Depth rather than breadth of information is particularly important when identifying which cognitive structures should be attributed to individual minds. By analogy, a biologist studying *e coli,* who wanted to claim there are within *e coli* certain structures, would be obligated to identify the structures within individuals. To insist that studies involve a large number of subjects may hinder an understanding of the nature of those structures.

Songer's and Linn's (1991, 1993) work has been effective in bringing wide attention to secondary school students' beliefs about the nature of scientific knowledge. However, their analysis illustrates how a commitment to unitary ontology can occlude alternative interpretation. In their framework, a "static" stance holds that scientific knowledge is certain and unchanging, mostly facts to be memorized. A "dynamic" stance holds that scientific knowledge stems from evidence, changes and expands, and relates to daily life. However, in response to seven survey questions, most students (63%) held "some static ideas, some dynamic ideas, and some ideas that were difficult to categorize" (Linn & Songer, 1993). In their 1991 article (Songer & Linn, 1991), the authors characterized these students as having mixed beliefs.

In a manifold ontology, the seemingly inconsistent and hard-to-categorize responses could indicate that different questions cued different epistemological resources. Researchers could explore these context-dependent patterns of activation using deeply contextualized interviews. By contrast, Linn and Songer (1993) conducted short interviews (15 minutes), simply asking students to explain their answers to the survey items. Based on students' brief responses, such as the idea that scientists can reach different conclusions about experimental results because "because everybody has a different opinion" or because "they can find something in the experiment, and then a week later they can find something else," Linn and Songer conclude that students with mixed beliefs are relativists, in some cases radical relativists: "Some students who abandoned a static view of scientific knowledge turned instead to a view that might be classified as radical relativism. These students had no criteria for comparing explanations and no ability to distinguish established and controversial ideas." A manifold ontology affords an alternative interpretation, that these were context-sensitive shifts. Interview questions set in the context of discussing whether the heart pumps blood, or whether the Earth is round, would undoubtedly activate epistemological resources corresponding to static beliefs. Our point is that a unitary ontology pushes researchers to place students into categories such as "relativist" or "radical relativist," rather than explore the possibility that students' "beliefs" *really are* mixed, due to the activation of different epistemological resources by different questions.

We do not suggest researchers should abandon surveys, however, nor do we suggest that any case study approach is sufficient. King and Kitchener (1994) designed their Reflective Judgement Interviews to address context by focusing on rich issues, such as the conflict between creationism and evolution. We contend, however, that a unitary ontology distorts their analyses. In particular, their scoring scheme focuses on the abstract form rather than the context-dependent meaning of their subjects' responses, and this context stripping leads to potentially misleading conclusions.

For instance, reflective judgment Stage 2 corresponds to an absolutist stance; knowledge is certain but not immediately available, and it generally comes from direct experience or from authority. The authors cite the following as a definitive Stage 2:

Interviewer: How do you decide?
    Subject: I decide what goes with my views.
Interviewer: Where do your views come from?
    Subject: My teachers and how I've been brought up. As you grow up, you automatically get certain views.

The subject may be more sophisticated than she appears. Her beliefs,[9] expressed in more academic language, could be:

When deciding what to believe about the origin of humanity, I take into account what fits with my religious beliefs. Those beliefs undoubtedly come from the way I was brought up, from my parents and teachers. When children are exposed to certain articles of faith over a long period, those beliefs get incorporated into the child's views.

If this rewording reflects the subject's views, then she holds some relativist ideas about the origin of religious beliefs, but it is a sophisticated relativism supported by developmental psychology. That is, we contend, this excerpt does not provide sufficient contextual information to characterize the subject's epistemology definitively.

These examples illustrate a further difficulty in the study of epistemologies. Within the literature on epistemologies in science education, there is the further, explicit consensus about what constitutes epistemological sophistication: beliefs that knowledge is tentative rather than certain, constructed rather than discovered, subjective rather than objective. We challenge this consensus elsewhere (Elby & Hammer, in press), largely on the grounds that in considering "knowledge is tentative" to be a desirable epistemological stance, researchers are neglecting context. It is hardly sophisticated, for example, to consider it "tentative" that the earth is round, that the heart pumps blood, or that living organisms evolve. A manifold ontology affords a view of epistemological sophistication as sensitive to the nuances of context.

---

[9]King and Kitchener did not specify the topic of discussion, but the interview snippet they presented immediately before this one concerned creationism versus evolution.

SUMMARY

Studies of beliefs have found statistical patterns in students' responses to questions designed to assess epistemology, as well as correlations between epistemological sophistication (as measured by these instruments) and academic performance. Such studies strongly suggest that there should be an epistemological contribution to the ecology of mind researchers and teachers attribute to students. What remains unclear is the form in which these epistemologies reside in students' minds. How researchers and teachers answer this question, whether implicitly or explicitly, affects the methods they use to study or influence these epistemologies.

The methods used by most researchers reflect a tacit presumption of unitarity, that students hold epistemological knowledge either as theories, the content of which can be probed by direct questions, or as traits that manifest themselves in students' behavior and preferences. As theories or as traits, students' epistemologies are understood to be consistent across contexts; thus, inferences about epistemologies as drawn from questionnaires and surveys are expected to be relevant to contexts of instruction.

We have suggested an alternative view of students' epistemological knowledge as made up of a range of epistemological resources, the activation of which depends on context. These resources differ from unitary epistemological (mis)beliefs in the same way that diSessa's p-prims (1993) differ from unitary (mis)conceptions. Although the specific resources we presented here are tentative, we suggested heuristics for identifying promising candidates. Naïve epistemological resources should:

- be possible to identify in young children;
- have plausible developmental origins;
- be recognizable, when articulated, as "commonsense" mini-generalizations about knowledge.

For instance, children's behavior suggests that they sometimes activate *Knowledge as propagated stuff,* understanding knowledge as something they receive ("I know the cat's name because Diana told it to me."). Other times, they activate *Knowledge as fabricated stuff,* understanding it as something they create from other knowledge ("I thought you had a present for me because I saw you hiding something under your coat!") Although *Knowledge as propagated stuff* seems to correspond to an authority-driven view of knowledge while *Knowledge as fabricated stuff* seems closer to a constructivist view, these epistemological primitives are not general beliefs. They are, in general, inarticulate and unstable in their activation, switching on or off beneath the child's conscious awareness.

This is not to disallow consistency, however. By this view, epistemological beliefs, when they exist within or across contexts, correspond to patterns of activation of epistemological resources, along with some kind of metacognitive awareness when the beliefs are articulate. A full-fledged authority-driven view of knowledge may well exist, in a given context, but it would also involve the sustained activation of other epistemological primitives beyond *Knowledge as propagated stuff,* such as *Accumulation* as a resource for understanding epistemological activity and *Acceptance* linked tightly with *Understanding* as an epistemological stance.

This shift in ontology suggests new directions for teachers and researchers. Accounts of students as having unitary misconceptions suggest the need for instruction to elicit, confront, and replace students' misconceptions with more appropriate conceptions. In contrast, to understand students' conceptual understanding in terms of a manifold ontology of resources, such as diSessa's (1993) p-prims, offers the possibility for instructors to conceptualize their agenda in terms of helping students draw on those resources more productively (Hammer, 1996). Similarly, accounts of students as having "misbeliefs" suggest the need to elicit, confront, and replace those beliefs. An account of students' epistemologies as made up of resources would suggest a different agenda for instruction, of helping students draw on their epistemological resources more productively.

REFERENCES

Belenky, M. F., Clinchy, B. M., Rule, G. N., & Tarule, J. M. (1986). *Women's Ways of Knowing: The Development of Self, Voice, and Mind.* New York: Basic Books.

Clement, J., Brown, D., & Zeitsman, A. (1989). Not all preconceptions are misconceptions: Finding 'anchoring conceptions' for grounding instruction on students' intuitions. *International Journal of Science Education, 11,* 554–565.

Collins, A. & Ferguson, W. (1993). Epistemic forms and epistemic games: Structures and strategies to guide inquiry. *Educational Psychologist, 28,* 25–42.

Dennet, D. C. (1991). Consciousness explained. Boston: Little, Brown.

diSessa, A. (1993). Towards an epistemology of physics. *Cognition and Instruction, 10,* 105–225.

Elby, A. (1999a). *A high school curriculum designed to nudge students' epistemological beliefs.* Paper presented at the Annual Meeting of the American Educational Research Association, Montreal.

Elby, A. (1999b). Another reason that physics students learn by rote. *American Journal of Physics, 67,* S53–S60.

Elby, A., & Hammer, D. (in press). On the substance of a sophisticated epistemology. *Science Education.*

Feldman, D. H. (1994). *Beyond universals in cognitive development,* Norwood, NJ: Ablex.

Hammer, D. (1989). Two approaches to learning physics. *The Physics Teacher, 27,* 664–670.

Hammer, D. (1994). Epistemological beliefs in introductory physics. *Cognition and Instruction, 12,* 151–183.

Hammer, D. (1995). Epistemological considerations in teaching introductory physics. *Science Education, 79,* 393–413.

Hammer, D. (1996). Misconceptions or p-prims: How may alternative perspectives of cognitive structure influence instructional perceptions and intentions? *Journal of the Learning Sciences, 5,* 97–127.

Harel, I., & Papert, S. (1991). *Constructionism: research reports, and essays, 1985–1990.* Norwood, NJ: Ablex.

Hofer, B. K., & Pintrich, P. R. (1997a). *Disciplinary ways of knowing: epistemological beliefs in science and psychology.* Paper presented at the Annual Meeting of the American Educational Research Association, Chicago.

Hofer, B. K., & Pintrich, P. R. (1997b). The development of epistemological theories: Beliefs about knowledge and knowing and their relation to learning. *Review of Educational Research, 67,* 88–140.

Hogan, K. (1999). Relating students' personal frameworks for science learning to their cognition in collaborative contexts. *Science Education, 83,* 1–32.

King, P. M., & Kitchener, K. S. (1994). *Developing Reflective Judgment: Understanding and promoting intellectual growth and critical thinking in adolescents and adults.* San Francisco: Jossey-Bass.

Krieger, M. H. (1992). Doing Physics: *How physicists take hold of the world.* Bloomington, IN: Indiana University Press.

Kuhn, D. (1989). Children and adults as intuitive scientists. *Psychological Review, 96,* 674–689.

Kuhn, D. (1991). *The skills of argument.* Cambridge: Cambridge University Press.

Lakoff, G., & Johnson, M. (1980). Metaphors we live by. Chicago: University of Chicago Press.

Leach, J., Millar, R., Ryder, J., & Séré, M. G. (1999). *An investigation of high school and university science majors' epistemological reasoning in the context of empirical investigations.* Paper presented at the Annual Meeting of the American Educational Research Association, Montréal.

Linn, M. C., & Songer, N. B. (1993). How do students make sense of science? *Merrill-Palmer Quarterly Journal of Developmental Psychology, 39,* 47–73.

Minsky, M. L. (1986). *Society of mind.* New York: Simon and Schuster.

Minstrell, J. (1982). Explaining the 'at rest' condition of an object. *The Physics Teacher, 20,* 10–20.

Moore, W. S. (1991). *The Perry scheme of intellectual and ethical development: An introduction to the model and major assessment approaches.* Paper presented at the Annual Meeting of the American Educational Research Association, Chicago.

Perry, W. B. (1970). *Forms of intellectual and ethical development in the college years: A scheme.* New York: Holt, Rinehart, and Winston.

Redish, E. F., Steinberg, R. N., & Saul, J. M. (1998). Student expectations in introductory physics. *American Journal of Physics, 66,* 212–224.

Samarapungavan, A. (1992). Children's judgments in theory choice tasks: Scientific rationality in childhood. *Cognition, 45,* 1–32.

Samarapungavan, A., & Westby, E. (1999). *Predicting and explaining how people form beliefs about the natural world: The development of epistemic knowledge in childhood.* Paper presented at the Annual Meeting of the American Educational Research Association, Montréal.

Schommer, M. (1990). The effects of beliefs about the nature of knowledge in comprehension. *Journal of Educational Psychology, 82,* 498–504.

Schommer, M., Crouse, A., & Rhodes, N. (1992). Epistemological beliefs and mathematical text comprehension: Believing it is simple does not make it so. *Journal of Educational Psychology, 84,* 435–443.

Smith, J., diSessa, A., & Roschelle, J. (1993/1994). Misconceptions reconceived: A constructivist analysis of knowledge in transition. *The Journal of the Learning Sciences, 3,* 115–163.

Songer, N. B., & Linn, M. C. (1991). How do students' views of science influence knowledge integration? In M. C. Linn, N. B. Songer, & E. L. Lewis (Eds.), Students' models and epistemologies of science, a special issue of the *Journal of Research in Science Teaching, 28,* 761–784.

Stodolsky, S. S., Salk, S., & Glaessner, B. (1991). Student views about learning math and social studies. *American Educational Research Journal, 28*, 89–116.

Viennot, L. (1985). Analyzing students' reasoning: Tendencies in interpretation. *American Journal of Physics, 53*, 432–436.

Wilensky, U., & Resnick, M. (1999). Thinking in levels: A dynamic systems perspective to making sense of the world. *Journal of Science Education and Technology, 8*, 3–19.

Wortman, C. B., Loftus, E. F. & Marshall, M. E. (1988). *Psychology* (3rd ed.). New York: Alfred A. Knopf.

10

A Process Model of Epistemic Belief Change

Lisa D. Bendixen
University of Nevada, Las Vegas

This chapter describes a process model of epistemic belief change and its implications for epistemological development. Epistemic beliefs are considered to be
an individual's beliefs about the nature of truth and knowledge. Educators have
been interested in epistemological development since the seminal work of Perry
(1970).

Epistemological Development

In a recent review of the theory and research associated with the development of personal epistemological theories, Hofer and Pintrich (1997) include
a discussion of the commonalities among theories of epistemological development. In general, there seems to be agreement in terms of the course of epistemological development. Perry and a number of other theorists believe that individuals pass through a predictable sequence of epistemological growth (e.g.,
Basseches, 1984; Chandler, 1987; King & Kitchener, 1994; Kuhn, 1991). In
early stages, individuals hold simple, dichotomous views of knowledge; reasoning then becomes increasingly more complex and relativistic. As students'
epistemological beliefs further develop, views about knowledge become

postrelativistic with a focus on the evaluation of different viewpoints (King & Kitchener, 1994).

In addition to the trends of epistemological development, there is general consensus in the consideration of a mechanism of change. The models of Perry (1970) and King and Kitchener (1994) are examples of theories reviewed by Hofer and Pintrich (1997) in this regard.

Perry (1970) is credited with being the first to observe that underlying assumptions about knowledge and learning make a difference in the reasoning of college students. Using open-ended interviews, Perry characterized students' epistemological development by describing a progression of nine different points of view, which he called positions. These positions traced the evolution of students' thinking about knowledge, truth, and values and their own responsibilities for their beliefs and actions. Students normally moved through these positions sequentially, but Perry also describes students who temporized in particular positions or "retreated" to earlier ones.

King and Kitchener (1994) have presented a stage model of epistemological development. In their model of Reflective Judgment they describe seven sequential stages, each characterized by different epistemological assumptions, as well as different approaches to justification. The stage descriptions are gleaned from their research examining the assumptions and reasoning styles that are apparent in an individual's reasoning about ill-structured problems.

For the purposes of this chapter, what is important about these models and other prominent models of epistemological development is their consideration of the process by which an individual moves through the various stages of epistemological development. In considering epistemological beliefs and how they are acquired and change over time, current models of epistemological development (e.g., King & Kitchener, 1994; Perry, 1970) would be considered consistent with the Piagetian notion of equilibration in cognitive development (Hofer & Pintrich, 1997).

According to Piaget (1985) knowledge is constructed through a process of equilibration. Piaget considers the equilibration process to be the mechanism by which the individual progresses through stages of cognitive development. He states that there must be a balance, or equilibrium, between the person and the environment and a balance between accommodation and assimilation (Piaget, 1985). When a person acts on the environment, they incorporate the external world into their already existing cognitive structure (assimilation). Alternatively, when the environment acts on the person, the person's cognitive structure is altered in order to adjust to the external world (accommodation). Within equilibration, both assimilation and accommodation are complementary processes that are always involved in cognitive development. To Piaget, the equilibration process is the moving force behind all cognition.

Other than a nod to Piagetian cognitive disequilibrium, most theories of epistemological development do not examine in depth a causal mechanism for change. For example, King and Kitchener (1994) consider epistemological development to be stimulated, "when an individual's experiences do not match his or her expectations" (p. 228). Contradictory experiences may provoke a person to "reconsider, reinterpret, or reject" prior assumptions or beliefs (p. 229). In reviewing current models of epistemological development, Kramer (1983) also discusses contradiction and the need for the reorganization of knowledge as being a common perspective among models.

In their consideration of epistemological development, Hofer and Pintrich (1997) speak of the need for the empirical study of "the mechanisms by which individuals acquire and change their perspectives on knowing" (p. 111). This chapter explores the process of change unique to epistemological development.

Conceptual Change

Turning to the literature on conceptual change offers some insight into the conditions necessary for epistemic belief change. The first condition for conceptual change is that individuals must feel that current beliefs are no longer working satisfactorily (i.e., dissatisfaction with current conceptions). The second condition is that individuals must be able to understand the new beliefs (i.e., new conception must be intelligible). The third condition is that the individual must be able to adequately apply the new beliefs (i.e., new concept must be plausible). The fourth condition states that new beliefs must stand up to challenges and lead to further learning (i.e., new concept must appear fruitful) (Pintrich, Marx, & Boyle, 1993). What is unknown at this time is whether or not conceptual change, as it is described, is consistent with belief change in epistemological development.

In considering the conditions for conceptual change, Pintrich et al.(1993) propose that along with these conditions, motivational and contextual factors need to be studied to complete the picture. Along these same lines, Schoenfeld (1985) proposes that affect may play an important role in the consideration of beliefs and cognition. Similarly, Hofer and Pintrich (1997) point to the need for investigations into the more affective side of epistemological development. In discussing the seeming regression of college students to lower levels of epistemological stages (from Boyes & Chandler, 1992), Hofer and Pintrich (1997) speak of the possibility of individuals retreating to "safer, more established positions when in new environments and that there may be affective issues involved, such as the effects of anxiety and negative feelings associated with challenges to strongly held ideas" (p. 122).

In summarizing the research in these areas, Hofer and Pintrich (1997) call for more qualitative studies examining the "affective dimensions" of epistemological theories. They also recommend research examining the "motivational mechanisms" and "contextual factors that can constrain or facilitate" the process of epistemological theory change. One of the aims of this chapter includes investigating the roles of affect and motivation in epistemological development.

Epistemic Doubt

The transitions that take place in epistemological development have been the focus of the research by Chandler and colleagues (e.g., Boyes & Chandler, 1992; Chandler, 1987; Chandler, Boyes, & Ball, 1990). Chandler's work has examined the particular levels that individuals pass through on their way to more sophisticated epistemological stances. One particular aspect of this theory is the concept of epistemic doubt. This is an important part of relativistic thinking where one continually questions the existence of absolute knowledge.

This chapter examines epistemic doubt using a broader perspective than Chandler's consideration. Rather than the epistemic doubt associated only with relativistic thinking that Chandler describes, the possibility of doubting one's beliefs at any stage of epistemological development is considered. For example, is it possible that those in early stages of epistemological development (i.e., Absolutists) doubt their beliefs at certain times? In addition, individuals in later stages (i.e., Post Relativists) may doubt their beliefs at a certain level on some occasions. Could this epistemic doubt play a role in epistemological development? This chapter explores this possibility.

Summary

In summary, a number of needs are apparent in the research associated with epistemological development. To date, little research has been done looking at the process of epistemological development, specifically, the explicit examination of a mechanism of change in epistemic beliefs. In addition, more information is needed in terms of the contributions of affect, motivation, and context in epistemic belief change. In addressing these needs, this chapter investigates the role of epistemic doubt in epistemological development.

The Current Chapter

This chapter explores epistemic doubt from an individual perspective. It is currently unknown what the experience of epistemic doubt is like for the person experiencing it. It is also unknown how one goes about resolving epistemic doubt. This chapter provides a phenomenological account of epistemic doubt. It focuses in particular on two aspects of epistemic doubt: (1) how adults perceive and describe their own epistemic doubt, and (2) how adults have resolved their epistemic doubt. Finding a coherent picture of the experience of epistemic doubt would be a crucial first step in examining the role that epistemic doubt plays in epistemological development.

METHOD

Participants

Twelve undergraduates from a large midwestern university were chosen to participate (7 females, 5 males). Ages ranged from 19 to 50 ($M = 26.5$). These individuals were chosen from a screening phase that took place approximately three weeks earlier and included a pool of 129 undergraduates. The rationale for the screening phase was to purposefully select certain individuals to be interviewed (Glaser & Strauss, 1967; Miles & Huberman, 1984).

Screening included a test of logical reasoning, a reading comprehension test, and the essay question, "Is truth unchanging?"

Materials and Procedure

Materials for the screening phase consisted of a packet including (a) a 12-item test of syllogistic reasoning, (b) a 36-item Nelson–Denny reading comprehension test (Brown, Bennett, & Hanna, 1981), (c) a brief demographic variable information sheet, and (d) an essay booklet in which participants were asked to write a response to the question, "Is truth unchanging?".

Materials in the screening phase (i.e., syllogisms, Nelson–Denny) were used to screen participants who would eventually be chosen to be interviewed. It was expected that differences in reading comprehension and reasoning skill would be minimal and this was the case. None of the participants chosen to be interviewed were significantly different from the mean on the screening measures used.

Participants were chosen to be interviewed according to their responses to the epistemological question, "Is truth unchanging?" This question was selected because Kitchener (1983) has identified assumptions about truth as a critical component of epistemic reasoning. This question has also been used successfully by the author and colleagues (e.g., Bendixen, Dunkle, & Schraw, 1994). Individuals were chosen to be interviewed based on their ability to articulate themselves in their essay and/or to provide interesting and relevant discussion of their epistemological beliefs.

Materials for the interview included a list of eight interview questions (see Appendix A) for the interviewer. The actual interview questions were developed through dialogue among the author and several coresearchers familiar with epistemological theory and research.

Another important function of the epistemological essay was to provide a starting point for the interview. At the beginning of the interview, participants were asked to discuss their responses to the essay. This was done to remind the participants of their epistemological beliefs and to clarify the kinds of beliefs that were to be discussed in the subsequent interview. The one-on-one interviews lasted approximately one hour, were audiotaped, and later transcribed.

RESULTS

This section presents results of the qualitative analysis of experiences related to epistemic doubt and belief change using the twelve interviews chosen. Epistemic beliefs were considered to be beliefs about the nature of truth and knowledge. In considering their beliefs about truth, two of the twelve participants considered aspects of truth to be a part of their religious beliefs and this may have had to do with their responses to the epistemological essay question, "Is truth unchanging?" that began the interview. "Truth" for these participants was God and vice versa. The remaining ten participants referred to more general beliefs about knowledge, and the doubting of them, in their descriptions of belief change.

Qualitative Analysis

In order to adequately explore the process of epistemic belief change from an individual perspective, the phenomenological method of inquiry described by Moustakas (1994) was employed. This methodology relies on one-on-one dialogue between a researcher and participant. The purpose of these dialogues is to provide an environment where participants can describe the phenomenon of study in considerable detail from their own perspective.

Specifically, eight steps of data reduction were used to qualitatively analyze the twelve participants' interviews (see Appendix B). The steps used are a modification of the Moustakas (1994) method of analysis of phenomenological data. It is the goal of this phenomenological analysis to begin with an objective description of participants' reported experiences related to epistemic doubt and move toward a more subjective or interpretive account of the meaning and essences of the experience of epistemic doubt as a whole.

The following section contains a description of the process model of epistemic belief change developed to represent the group's experiences as a whole. Participants felt that their experiences associated with epistemological belief change were a part of a "process" and this was the reason that this particular terminology was used for the model. The model is comprised of four components that describe the groups' experiences related to how epistemic doubt influenced their belief change (see Fig. 10.1). Included in each component description are sample themes gleaned from qualitative analysis to represent each component (see Appendix B).

Component 1: What Triggered Epistemic Doubt

Exposure and independence were catalysts of epistemic doubt. Beliefs long held by participants were disintegrating because of the people and experiences around them. Exposure to beliefs unlike their own made participants see their beliefs in a new light.

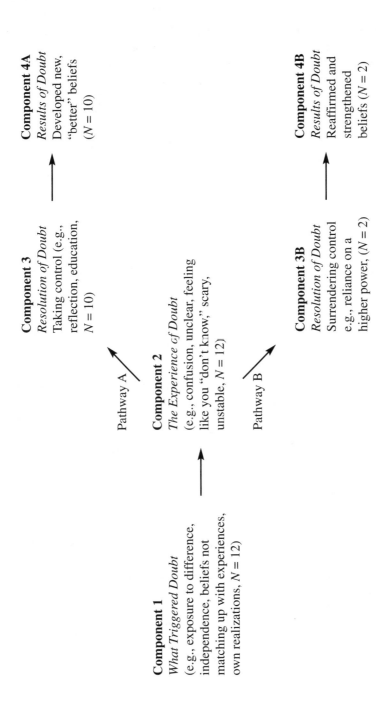

Component 4A
Results of Doubt
Developed new,
"better" beliefs
($N = 10$)

Component 3
Resolution of Doubt
Taking control (e.g.,
reflection, education,
$N = 10$)

Pathway A

Component 2
The Experience of Doubt
(e.g., confusion, unclear, feeling
like you "don't know," scary,
unstable, $N = 12$)

Pathway B

Component 1
What Triggered Doubt
(e.g., exposure to difference,
independence, beliefs not
matching up with experiences,
own realizations, $N = 12$)

Component 3B
Resolution of Doubt
Surrendering control
e.g., reliance on a
higher power, ($N = 2$)

Component 4B
Results of Doubt
Reaffirmed and
strengthened
beliefs ($N = 2$)

FIG. 10.1 A process model of epistemic belief change in which four components of the experience are described, including two pathways taken, and sample themes are given.

College was mentioned as a place where differing epistemological beliefs were encountered and these differences caused one to question the validity of the current beliefs held. For instance, one participant stated that, "A lot of people probably come to school and meet and get around people they're not used to being around and get exposed to an entirely different set of beliefs and ideals that they have never known and that changes them or challenges their beliefs."

Along theses same lines, the differing beliefs of friends were also mentioned as a cause for doubt. One participant stated, "This is where I kind of doubt because they really, my friends make good points and it pulls me to their side into their way of thinking and then I doubt . . . I want to be open-minded about it, I want to choose the best thing."

Participants stated that, gaining "independence" and experiencing the "shock" of "real life" prompted epistemic doubt as well. One participant said that, in experiencing real life, "You get around more people and your environments change more so you have a better perspective." Being out on one's own allowed participants to be "confronted with all sorts of experiences" and a part of these confrontations was doubt.

For participants who were grappling with their conceptions of truth, the fact that the beliefs that they held were not coinciding with what they were experiencing was important in their experience of doubt. These experiences caused what one participant called, "realizations" about their current beliefs and doubt was a result. For example, one participant started making "little realizations about things that I had always believed in, things I had been told were absolute truths and I thought 'These aren't really truths!'"

From the participants' own words, the essence of this transition was gaining a sense of independence and being exposed to differing viewpoints. Separation from the important figures in one's life, going to college, and working to pay bills were essential ingredients in triggering doubt.

Component 2: The Experience of Epistemic Doubt

Participants painted a very poignant picture of the experience of epistemic doubt. All participants felt that the actual experience of doubt was an obstacle not easily overcome. As can be seen in Fig. 10.1, this component was characterized by feelings of fear, anxiety, and confusion.

Confusion was a major part of the doubting experience as is evident in the following quote: "I would hear these voices in my head from my school teachers telling me that this is it, but no, this is it, no but, no this is . . . I guess it was a really confusing thing to me because I didn't know which voice to believe." Part of this confusion was related to feeling not very clear in one's beliefs. As one participant stated, "It's almost like you're in a cloud, like things are just foggy around you and not clear."

Participants stated that, feeling like you "don't know anything" or at the very least you are "wishy-washy" about your beliefs was a part of the experience. As one participant put it, "It makes me feel like I really haven't got it figured out and it makes me feel like I really don't know what to think."

Participants' not knowing what to do about the numerous unanswered questions encircling their epistemological beliefs brought about a sense of being adrift. Things were out of focus, unclear, and this caused a great deal of apprehension.

Component 3: Resolution of Epistemic Doubt

Despite the tumultuous feelings of epistemic doubt, participants showed that there is the potential to come to terms with doubt. Participants began to struggle forward and started searching for ways to resolve their doubt. Although what triggered doubt and the feelings associated with the experience of doubt (Components 1 and 2) were similar, participants differed in the path that they chose to resolve their epistemic doubt. As can be seen in Fig. 10.1, participants took one of two pathways to resolve their doubt. Component 3A describes participants choosing Pathway A, which includes taking control of beliefs to resolve their doubt. Component 3B describes participants who chose Pathway B and this includes surrendering control of beliefs to what some called a "higher power" to resolve doubt.

Component 3A: Taking control of beliefs. Most participants ($N = 10$) chose to take control of their epistemological beliefs to resolve doubt. The essence of the resolution process was reflection and through reflection came change. Reflecting on one's past, and analyzing beliefs and their implications was a way to begin resolving doubt. Instead of the mental blur of epistemic doubt, logic in the face of doubt brought clarity for participants. One participant summarized this by saying that he "Stopped everything and reassessed everything. The best way to put it to you is it's like building a scaffolding, just starting at the bottom and just building up slowly."

Education helped make the best decisions when it came to resolving epistemic doubt. Reading and taking classes about various things and discussion with others helped understand differing beliefs. This also helps understand new beliefs that are being developed. As one participant said, "Enhancing the process all along is education . . . it's the backbone of everything." Through educating oneself there is a logical way to resolve questions. Once knowledge was gained about different options, better choices could be made in good faith. This sentiment is obvious in the following quote: "I'm a very logical person and the most logical way to overcome some of your doubts is to find arguments for and against each thing and to see which is more accurate, more believable, more truthful."

Finally, a belief in one's ability to overcome epistemic doubt was important in getting through the process. Feeling the confidence to succeed independently was crucial for change to happen. For example, one participant stated that, "Talking yourself through it" and saying, "Okay this is a process I just have to get through it, I need to get on with life" gives one the confidence to succeed.

Personal growth pursuits such as classes and jobs aided in this transformation. Asking questions of others, having heated arguments with friends, reading, listening, and thereby learning from others were at the heart of the resolution process.

Component 3B: Surrendering control of beliefs.   A small number of participants ($N = 2$) felt that to resolve epistemic doubt one must give up control of their beliefs about truth to a higher power. Seeing the inadequacies of doing things on their own in the past, participants felt that to put their trust in something else alleviated the doubts they were experiencing. Faith and dependency were the essence of this resolution process. No longer were they lost in a sea of uncertainty and disorder. Faith brought with it a certain logic and ultimate answers to the questions that plagued them. Reliance on a power that is, in their words, "all-knowing" and "all truth" was not a sign of weakness or ignorance but a path toward fulfillment and contentment.

In essence, relying on a higher power took away their epistemic doubt. One participant summarized this by stating, "I can rely fully on and I can just surrender over every area of my life to God and say, 'God, I know you're there and that's what I needed to know, and you let me know.'" "Listening to him (God) say, 'This is what you should do,' has just been confirmed so many other times in my life I'm just . . . not going to listen to myself anymore."

Component 4: Results of the Doubting Process

As can be seen in Fig. 10.1, those who chose Pathways 3A and 3B continued on these different pathways in the beliefs that resulted from the doubting process.

Component 4A: Developed new, "better" beliefs.   Those who took control of resolving doubt developed new beliefs (see Fig. 10.1). After experiencing the struggle of epistemic doubt and taking steps to resolve it, new beliefs were chosen and/or developed and doubt was alleviated. The essence of this experience was struggle bringing forth something better. Emerging beliefs were viewed in a positive light by participants. They were much more clear on what they believed and why, and these feelings of confidence in what they were believing was evident. Many felt that these new beliefs were the right ones and were better than before. As one participant stated, "Just doubting myself and making myself come to different conclusions that these old beliefs were probably not the best . . . it makes me feel good."

A sense of assurance that beliefs were dependable and reliable was also a part of this component. Epistemic beliefs could be trusted in the face of argument and questioning from others. In essence, new beliefs had been, as one participant said, "road tested" and this brought a sense of security. One participant concluded that, "What you gain after you walk through it all and come out on the other side" is "knowing a little bit better about that belief . . . not saying that you never question it again but . . . it's a bit of a cycle I guess."

Component 4B: Reaffirmed and/or strengthened old beliefs. As can be seen in Fig. 10.1, those participants who turned to a higher power to resolve their epistemic doubt strengthened old beliefs rather than developed new ones. The doubting process was very useful to participants in that it refocused their faith and confirmed their beliefs in truth. Belief in truth was considered "stronger than it's ever been in my life" as one participant stated.

Results of the doubting process were considered wonderful and things were now easier because the struggle was over. As one participant stated, "I guess at the point I am right now my current feelings about" my beliefs "would be feelings of peace, joy, and happiness."

Overall, the essence of this component was truth as a result of the doubting process. Their's was not an unquestioning faith, but one that was confirmed through the process of doubt and the resolution of it. Beliefs that were held without question were reexamined and this was a crucial part of the process. For instance, one participant stated that, "I just didn't want to come at it with a blind faith-type attitude and think, 'Okay, everything is the truth.'" Participants stated that "Asking all the questions" and "doing research" and "listening to what people's answers were" were important resources in revamping beliefs about truth. Instead of new and completely different beliefs emerging, a confidence in the beliefs of the past was felt. As one participant concluded, "Now I'm back to my childhood faith and growing."

DISCUSSION

The current process model of epistemic belief change offers meaningful and significant details concerning the experience of epistemic doubt and its influence on epistemological development. This section will include a discussion of the four components of the model and their specific implications, the overall model and its implications for theory and research, conclusions, and ideas for future research.

The Model's Four Components

Component 1. Moving away from home and going to college were important arenas for triggering epistemic doubt. A number of researchers have noted that the college experience is an important factor in epistemological development (e.g, Benack & Basseches, 1989, Perry, 1970; see also Hofer & Pintrich, 1997). Chandler et al.(1990)have questioned when epistemic doubt first occurs. They have found in their research that students in middle school and high school report on the relativistic nature of knowledge. While the current model indicates that college was very important in triggering epistemic doubt, this does not exclude the possibility that young adolescents experience doubt as well.

Component 2. The experience of epistemic doubt related to relativistic thinking has been described as tumultuous, fraught with difficulty, worrisome, and lonely (Chandler, 1987). Although participants were considering a broader view of the nature of knowledge, they did offer similar insights regarding their own experiences of epistemic doubt. Indeed, participants likened their experiences of doubt to "crisis," a "kind of turmoil," a "sense of hopelessness," "terribleness and depression."

Components 3A and 4A. Reflection was a critical element to the resolution of epistemic doubt and subsequent belief change. "Looking back at the past" and "analyzing" the implications of their beliefs, and making educated choices were mentioned as examples of reflection. Reflection has been noted by researchers as important to development. In Piaget's (1985) theory of cognitive development, reflective abstraction is central to the equilibration process. Within this process, especially in formal operational thinking, individuals consciously reflect on information they have gleaned from the environment and their own learning.

Along with reflection, participants described the importance of social interaction in their resolution of epistemic doubt. Numerous researchers have noted the prominent role that social interaction and, more specifically, argumentation play in development (e.g., Kuhn, 1991; Lerner, 1982; Moshman, 1998; Vygotsky, 1978).

In a related discussion, Moshman (1998) proposed that dialectical reflection and argumentation are not only "contexts" for advanced development but are "developmental forces" in and of themselves (p. 968). Current findings related to reflection and social interaction are consistent with this view.

Components 3B and 4B. Turning over doubts to a higher power was a crucial aspect of these components. Chandler et al. (1990) describe three strategies to cope with relativism. One pathway, labeled Dogmatism, consists of a "blind leap of faith into the arms of some omniscient authority that is assumed to have better reason to know" (p. 380). It is important to note that this reinstatement of former beliefs of truth was not as "blind" in the current model as Chandler has described. Questioning and searching for answers before turning over beliefs was apparent. Similarly, this could be seen as a "retrenching" of former beliefs due to challenges that have been described previously (Hofer & Pintrich, 1997).

In considering aspects of truth, religious beliefs came into play for a small number of participants. Is doubt related to religious truth a subset of epistemological beliefs, or do they stand alone? Current findings are not clear in this regard and future studies may focus on this interesting question.

The Model

One major implication of the process model of epistemic belief change is that there was a systematic reaction to, and processing of, epistemic doubt. The four general components described were evident in all of the participants' descriptions of the experience. There also was a common sequence in the process of epistemic belief change. First came a trigger for doubt, second the experience of epistemic began, third a resolution of doubt occurred, and finally new beliefs were developed or former beliefs were reaffirmed.

Another major implication of the model was that epistemic doubt and its resolution comprised the mechanism for epistemic belief change. The idea of epistemic doubt as a mechanism for belief change is consistent with theories of epistemological development. While most theories of epistemological development do not investigate a mechanism for change directly, their reference to Piagetian cognitive disequilibrium coincides with the model offered in this chapter (e.g., King & Kitchener, 1994; Perry, 1970). Consistent with the equilibration process, disequilibrium, accommodation, and assimilation, the proposed model could be considered the more detailed and informative description of the mechanism for change specific to epistemological development. For example, the model provides explicit detail in the thought processes, and emotions associated with being in a state of disequilibrium and specific tactics that were used to reach a state of equilibrium in terms of epistemological beliefs.

Epistemic doubt was essential for epistemic belief change to occur. This finding mirrors conceptual change theory. As was stated previously, the four conditions for change include 1) a dissatisfaction with existing beliefs, 2) individuals must find new alternatives intelligible and useful, 3) individuals must find the new beliefs plausible, and 4) new conceptions must stand up to challenges and lead to new learning (Pintrich et al., 1993). Initial components of the model are a clear testament to the idea that dissatisfaction with existing beliefs was occurring. Coming in contact with individuals holding different viewpoints and having beliefs that were not working caused a sense of dissatisfaction to emerge.

Later components of the model are also consistent with the conceptual change conditions that alternatives must be intelligible and useful, and that new beliefs stand up to challenges. The resolution of doubt brought with it numerous strategies, including reflection and education. In terms of beliefs, these strategies made choices clear and beneficial to achieving "equilibrium." The beliefs that resulted either were a reaffirmation of former beliefs or the development of new ones. In either case, participants felt that beliefs that resulted from the doubting process (i.e., ones that had been "road tested") would stand up to future challenges.

The model also offers a glimpse into some of the affective and motivational dimensions of epistemological development that is needed in the literature (Hofer & Pintrich, 1997). The rich description of the experience of epistemic doubt allows a view into the more affective side of epistemic belief change. It is apparent that motivational and contextual considerations constrained and facilitated epistemic change as has been discussed in regard to conceptual change (Pintrich et al., 1993). For example, the struggle and anxiety associated with the experience of doubt caused some participants to ignore dealing with their doubts for a time. Others mentioned that these difficulties also led to a state of depression where nothing was accomplished in terms of resolving doubt. Therefore, the conditions for epistemic change described in this chapter did not take place in a vacuum, where influences related to affect and motivation are nonexistent. While the current model sheds some light in these particular areas, more research along these lines is warranted.

CONCLUSION

The process model of epistemic belief change offered in this chapter contributes to the understanding of epistemological development in several important ways. The crux of the current model is a detailed view into experiences associated with epistemic doubt. Using descriptions of this experience from individual participants, a four-component model of epistemic belief change was offered to represent the experience as whole.

The current model is a significant first step in exploring epistemic doubt and its contribution to epistemic change. The role of epistemic doubt as a mechanism of change was confirmed in the model.

The affective side of epistemological development was also illuminated. One of the more unique and compelling findings of this study was the window that was provided into the tumultuous experience of doubting one's epistemic beliefs.

An additional contribution of this study was a description of the various strategies employed by individuals to resolve their epistemic doubt successfully. Specifically, reflection and social interaction were mechanisms of change for participants' epistemological beliefs.

The importance of the doubting process to belief change and subsequent epistemological development was strongly communicated. In final testament to this idea, one participant succinctly stated that, "Without the pain of doubt I don't think you grow."

Future Research

There are a number of possibilities for future research derived from the model. Given that the phenomenological approach to explore the experience of epistemic doubt and belief change was used, the next logical "qualitative" step may be to use a grounded theory approach. This approach could broaden the base of the information gathered by generating hypotheses and theory regarding epistemic doubt and belief change (Strauss & Corbin, 1990).

Future studies could also examine the possible differences and similarities in the perception of doubt and its relation to specific levels of epistemological development. For example, those individuals who are considered Absolutists could take a very different approach to resolving doubt as compared to individuals who are labeled Relativists due to differing views of the nature of knowledge. In contrast, all individuals, regardless of their epistemological level, may have a difficult struggle with epistemic doubt.

Although college was an important breeding ground for doubt in the current chapter, it is unclear if epistemic doubt was nonexistent in participants' earlier years. Future research could examine whether or not the four components of the process of epistemic belief change exist in early adolescence. For example, it is possible that younger adolescents may differ from college-age individuals in terms of strategies for resolving epistemic doubt. In addition, longitudinal studies investigating the experience of epistemic doubt over time could be extremely informative.

A number of educational implications arise from this study that need to be studied empirically. Not only may the epistemological theories students hold influence learning as a few studies indicate (e.g., Ryan, 1984; Schommer, 1994), but experiencing doubt of these beliefs may also have similar and/or unique influences on learning and motivation. It is apparent that the experience of epistemic doubt is not an easy one, nor is the struggle to resolve epistemic doubt, and these could certainly have effects on learning as well. For example, student motivation could be adversely affected during the anxious period of epistemic doubt. On the other hand, student motivation to learn could be increased during the resolution phase when students may be turning to education for clarification of their questions.

The role of the instructor in students' epistemic belief change could also be examined. For instance, is it the role of the instructor to enhance epistemological development by conducting classes in such a way as to promote less naive epistemological theories in their students? If this is the case, should teachers be encouraged to induce epistemic doubt in their students? Or, if changes in epistemological theory occur more indirectly, should teachers be supportive of the possible tumultuous experience associated with the epistemic doubt of their students? More work investigating these questions is needed to better understand the educational issues associated with epistemological development and, more specifically, the influence of epistemic doubt in student motivation and learning.

REFERENCES

Bendixen, L. D., Dunkle, M. E., & Schraw, G. (1994). Epistemological beliefs and reflective judgment. *Psychological Reports,* 75, 1595–1600.

Basseches, M. (1984). *Dialectical thinking and adult development.* Norwood, NJ: Ablex Publishing Corporation.

Benack, S. & Basseches, M. A. (1989). Dialectical thinking and relativistic epistemology: Their relation in adult development. In M. L. Commons, J. Sinnott, F. A. Richards, & C. Armon (Eds.), *Adult Development, Vol. 1. Comparisons and applications of developmental models.* New York: Praeger.

Boyes, M. C., & Chandler, M. (1992). Cognitive development, epistemic doubt, and identity formation in adolescence. *Journal of Youth and Adolescence,* 21(3), 277–303.

Brown, J. E., Bennett, J. M., & Hanna, G. (1981). *The Nelson–Denny Reading Test, Form E.* Chicago, IL: Riverside Publishing.

Chandler, M. (1987). The Othello effect: Essay on the emergence and eclipse of skeptical doubt. *Human Development,* 30, 137–159.

Chandler, M., Boyes, M. & Ball, L. (1990). Relativism and stations of epistemic doubt. *Journal of Experimental Child Psychology,* 50, 370–395.

Glaser, B. & Strauss, A. (1967). *The discovery of grounded theory.* Chicago: Aldine.

Hofer, B. K. & Pintrich, P. R. (1997). The development of epistemic theories: Beliefs about knowledge and knowing and their relation to learning. *Review of Educational Research,* 67, 88–140.

King, P. M. & Kitchener, K. S. (1994). *Developing reflective judgment: Understanding and promoting intellectual growth and critical thinking in adolescents and adults.* San Francisco: Jossey-Bass.

Kitchener, K. S. (1983). Cognition, metacognition, and epistemic cognition. *Human Development,* 26, 222–232.

Kramer, D. A. (1983). Postformal operations? A need for further conceptualization. *Human Development,* 26 (2), 91–105.

Kuhn, D. (1991). *The skills of argument.* New York: Cambridge University Press.

Lerner, R. M. (1982). Children and adolescents as producers of their own development. *Developmental Review,* 2, 342–370.

Miles, M. B. & Huberman, A. M. (1984). *Qualitative data analysis: A sourcebook of new methods.* Beverly Hills, CA: Sage.

Moshman, D. (1998). Cognitive development beyond childhood. In W. Damon, D. Kuhn, & R. Siegler (Eds.), *Handbook of child psychology: Vol. 2. Cognition, perception, and language* (5th ed., pp. 947–978). New York: Wiley.

Moustakas, C. (1994). *Phenomenological research methods.* Thousand Oaks, CA: Sage.

Perry, W. G., Jr. (1970). *Forms of intellectual and ethical development in the college years.* New York: Academic Press.

Piaget, J. (1985). *The equilibration of cognitive structures.* Chicago: University of Chicago Press.

Pintrich, P. R., Marx, R. W., & Boyle, R. A. (1993). Beyond cold conceptual change: The role of motivational beliefs and classroom contextual factors in the process of conceptual change. *Review of Educational Research,* 63, 167–199.

Ryan, M. P. (1984). Monitoring text comprehension: Individual differences in epistemological standards. *Journal of Educational Psychology,* 76 (2), 249–258.

Schoenfeld, A. H. (1985). *Mathematical problem solving.* San Diego, CA: Academic Press.

Schommer, M. (1994). An emerging conceptualization of epistemological beliefs and their role in learning. In R. Garner & P. A. Alexander (Eds.), *Beliefs about text and instruction with text* (pp. 25–40). Hillsdale, NJ: Erlbaum.

Strauss, A., & Corbin, J. (1990). *Basics of qualitative research: Grounded theory procedures and techniques.* Newbury Park, CA: Sage.

Vygotsky, L. S. (1978). *Mind in society: The development of higher psychological processes.* Cambridge, MA: Harvard University Press.

APPENDIX A

Interview Questions

Introductions (probe and ask for examples where necessary.)

1. Refer to the "truth is unchanging" essay. Tell me about your responses to that statement (remind them if they can't remember). How do you feel about the statements you made? Explain and give examples.
2. What beliefs do you have, along these lines, that will never change? What are they? Why won't they change? If they will change, why? How certain are you about this? Explain.
3. How are you different now than when you were younger in terms of your beliefs? Explain and give examples.
4. What kinds of experiences have shaped your beliefs? How did they influence you? Give specific examples.
5. What terms would you use to describe your feelings about your beliefs?
6. Can you tell me about experiences when you doubted your beliefs? What was it like? How did you resolve your doubts? Give examples.
7. What kinds of doubts do you think other people have experienced? Give examples.
8. How has the experience of doubting your beliefs affected your interpersonal relationships? Self-perceptions? Explain.

APPENDIX B

Eight Steps of Phenomenological Data Reduction (Moustakas, 1994)

Step 1: *Listing and preliminary grouping*—From individual transcripts every expression relevant to the experience is listed and labeled the "horizons."

Step 2: *Reduction and elimination*—Each expression is tested for two requirements:
1. Does it contain a moment of the experience and essential aspects of the experience that are necessary for understanding it?; and
2. Is it possible to abstract and label it?
    a. Eliminate expressions not meeting requirements, along with overlapping, repetitive, and vague expressions.
    b. Expressions that remain are "core horizons."

Step 3: *Clustering and thematisizing the core horizons*—Core horizons that are related are clustered into a thematic label.

Step 4: *Final identification of the core horizons and themes by application and validation*—Core horizons are checked against each complete transcript. Two questions are asked:
1. Are they expressed explicitly in the complete transcript?; and
2. Are they compatible in the complete transcript? (If not, deleted).

Step 5: *Individual textural description*—Using the relevant, validated core horizons and themes, an individual textural description is constructed for each participant. Included are verbatim examples from transcription.

Step 6: *Textural composite description*—Using the individual textural description and verbatim examples, a textural composite is created to represent the group experience as a whole.

Step 7: *Individual structural description*—using the meanings and essences of the experience and incorporating core horizons and themes, individual structural descriptions are constructed for each participant.

Step 8: *Structural composite description*—rom Steps 1–7, a structural composite is developed to represent the meanings and essences of the experience, representing the group as a whole (i.e., *The process model of epistemic belief change.*)

11

Mapping Basic Issues for Identifying Epistemological Outlooks

Jill Fitzgerald
*University of North Carolina
at Chapel Hill*

James W. Cunningham
*University of North Carolina
at Chapel Hill*

In this chapter, we detail a two-part framework for identifying epistemological stances that can be used by researchers, theorists, and practitioners to examine either personal or theoretical outlooks on knowledge. The framework is a result of a study of central issues in major historical and current epistemological stances (Cunningham & Fitzgerald, 1996).

There are several goals for this chapter. First, in the education, natural sciences, and social sciences fields in recent years, there has been a dramatic increase in attention to epistemological issues in research, teaching, and assessment (e.g., Alvermann, 1993; Fenstermacher, 1994; Gjertsen, 1989; McLaren, 1992; Hofer & Pintrich, 1997; Rosenau, 1992). Philosophical terms with epistemological slants such as constructivism, critical theory, hermeneutics, and postpositivism now abound. Clearly, some familiarity with variant philosophical positions is imperative if one is to richly understand current educational research and practice. Our framework is one representation that might help nurture such familiarity.

A second purpose of the chapter is to encourage educators to consider epistemological stances that are often implicit in educational organizational policies, journals, research methods, and popular educational practices (Myers, 1986). Since education deals with knowledge, epistemology is really education's most fundamental concern (Morris & Pai, 1976; Peterson, 1986). However, many hotly debated issues are contentious at least in part because they focus on "surface" issues rather than deeper underlying epistemologies. Consider for example, current debates about the extent to which phonics should be explicitly taught to young children. If debaters examined the underlying epistemological bases in competing themes on "best practice," they would likely find different outlooks on the degree to which phonics knowledge is a significant part of a theoretical process of reading as well as different outlooks on how the reading process develops in a typically developing reader. That is, an epistemological thrust reveals different stances on what knowledge counts most and how that knowledge is acquired. Recognizing these epistemological bases might facilitate clearer national focus on the significant issues embedded in such disputes.

A third purpose is to help individual educators to clarify their own stances about knowledge and knowing. A deeper understanding of epistemology can lead to a self-awareness often associated with enhanced personal satisfaction (Sire, 1988). It can also enable informed change in personal outlooks on professional issues in education.

A fourth purpose is to suggest that there are specific ways in which our framework for understanding epistemology in particular may be useful to researchers or theorists who are studying personal epistemology, defined as individuals' beliefs and thinking about the nature of knowledge and knowing. For example, the framework might be used to help researchers codify or describe individual's perspectives. Researchers could use the framework to guide design of questionnaires, interviews, or other methodological means for ascertaining participants' perspectives. After data collection, the framework could again serve as a guide for assessing respondents' outlooks.

Another example of the usefulness of our framework for investigators and theorists in the area of personal epistemology is the possibility that it might aid in providing clearer definitions of what is being studied. Numerous conceptual and methodological problems have previously been identified in research on individuals' thinking and beliefs about the nature of knowledge and knowing (Hofer & Pintrich, 1997). Among all of the problems, clear delineation of the construct of personal epistemology stands out as one of the most crucial issues deserving immediate attention (Hofer & Pintrich, 1997). The framework might help in this regard, for example, if it seems feasible that the seven issues identified in our framework might function as central dimensions, setting boundaries for what is meant by personal epistemology.

THE EPISTEMOLOGICAL FRAMEWORK

Seven Main Issues in Epistemology

The first part of our framework consists of seven main issues in epistemology, each of which is a continuum along which some epistemologies differ. We began with three overriding concerns in the theory of knowledge: what constitutes or counts as knowledge, where knowledge is located, and how knowledge increases. For each global concern, one or more specific issues (totaling seven) permit a relatively fine-grained analysis of epistemological positions. The seven issues in the map are posed as questions that can be asked of any theory, research, or practice to determine its position relative to these central issues. The seven issues are shown in Table 11.1 and comprise the columns of Figure 11.1 In the following section, each issue is explained.

Issue 1: Can We Have Knowledge of a Single Reality Independent of the Knower?

Although this question always has either a yes or a no answer, the explanations vary considerably for how an answer is justified. Some no answers are categorical while others seem to fall somewhere toward the middle between yes and no by granting practical, aesthetic, or metaphorical benefits to the pretense of a single reality. Categorical negatives vary in that some deny the existence of a single reality while others merely deny the possibility of knowing such a reality.

Issue 2: Is There Such a Thing as Truth?

While this question originally goes back to the Sophists in ancient Greece, and in modern form to David Hume in the middle 1700s, it and Issue 3 are the questions that place us most squarely in current epistemological discussions. Most epistemologists have agreed there is such a thing as truth, but have varied on what constitutes truth. A few epistemologists have denied the existence of truth.

TABLE 11.1
Seven Main Issues and Three Overriding Concerns in Epistemology

What constitutes or counts as knowledge?

Issue 1: Can we have knowledge of a single reality independent of the knower?

Issue 2: Is there such a thing as truth?

Issue 3: What primary test must proposed knowledge pass in order to be true?

Issue 4: Is knowledge primarily universal or particular?

Where is knowledge located?

Issue 5: Where is knowledge located relative to the knower?

How is knowledge attained?

Issue 6: What are the relative contributions of sense data and mental activity to knowing?

Issue 7: To what degree is knowledge discovered versus created?

Note: This table is from: Cunningham and Fitzgerald (1996), p. 41.

FIG. 11.1 Positions of Five Clusters of Epistemology on Seven Epistemological Issues. *This figure is from Cunningham and Fitzgerald (1996), p. 40.*

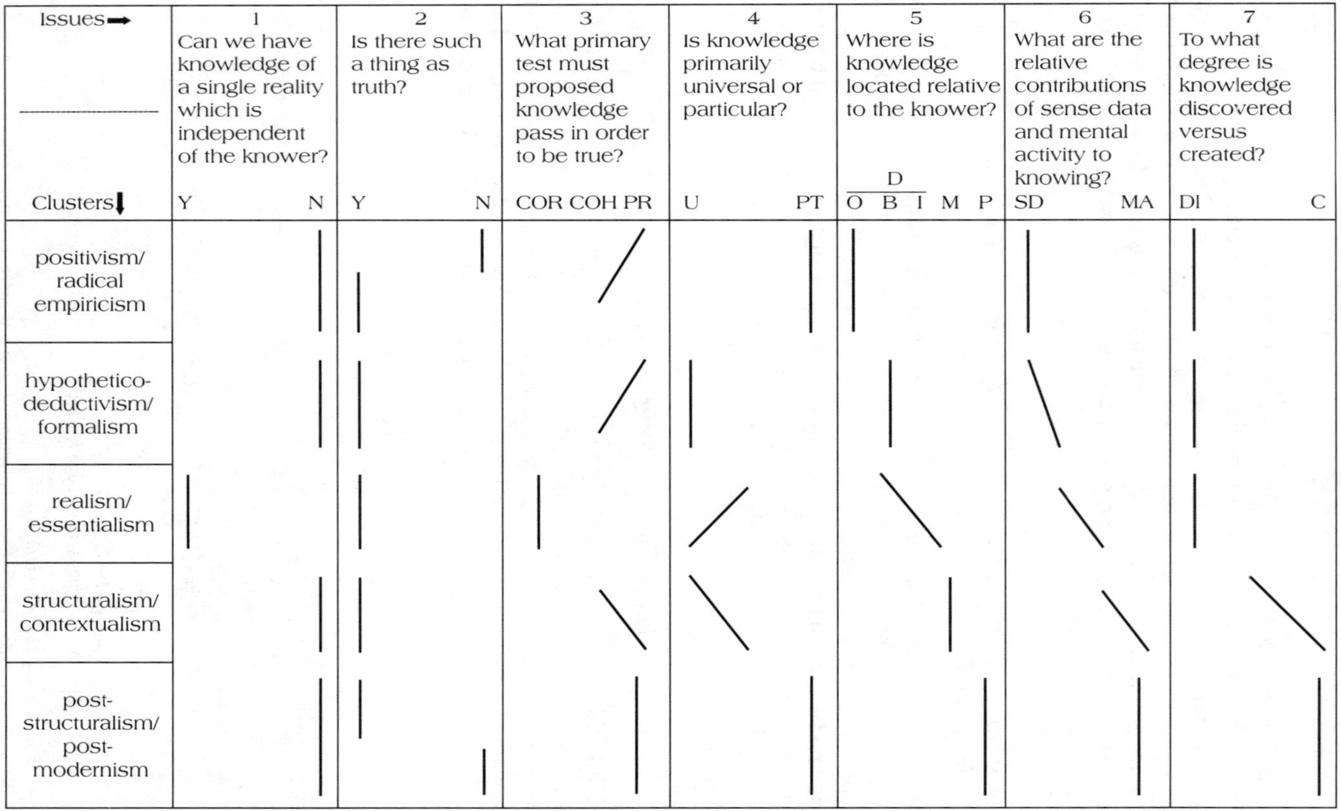

Note. Y=Yes, N=No; COR=Correspondence, COH=Coherence, PR=Pragmatic; U=Universal, PT=Particular; D=Dualism, O=Outside, B=Between, I=Inside, M=Monism, P=Pluralism; SD=Sense Data, MA=Mental Activity; DI=Discovered, C=Created.

Issue 3: What Primary Test Must Proposed Knowledge Pass in Order to be True?

Epistemologists have disagreed on the criterion for truth. Some have held a correspondence theory of truth: The true is what corresponds to the real, i.e., the truth fits the facts. Others have held a coherence theory of truth—if a proposition or belief is coherent with a system of ideas assumed to be true, that proposition or belief is also assumed to be true. Still others have held a pragmatic theory of truth, where they consider the value of believing certain propositions.

Issue 4: Is Knowledge Primarily Universal or Particular?

From William of Ockham [1285–1349] to the present, some epistemologists have contended that all knowledge is knowledge of particulars, of instances. These thinkers have argued that all definitions, abstract terms, generalizations, models, and theories are just names and systems of naming that humans arbitrarily attach to particular objects and events. On the other hand, from ancient times until recently, most philosophers have sought universal knowledge. All definitions, abstract terms, generalizations, models, and theories that purport to be true are universals.

Issue 5: Where Is Knowledge Located Relative to the Knower?

There are three views of where knowledge is located relative to the knower: (a) Dualism has incorporated three positions: knowledge resides outside the knower; knowledge resides inside the knower; knowledge resides between knower and knowledge in their interaction. (b) Monism is the notion that knowledge resides not in the knower, or in the known, or even between them, but in the process of knowing itself. Monists have often elevated a single unifying idea or principle to resolve dualisms. For example, the proletariat, the Aryan race, linguistic determinism, feminism, and social justice have each been used by different monists as the lens through which to interpret all ideas and events. These monisms (also called totalisms) each dismiss, override, or integrate all other knowledge concerns and distinctions with their single ideal or criticism. Some monists stress that knowledge is socially constructed. Monistic social constructionism must be consonant, i.e., it must aim to achieve consensus, agreement, or community. (c) Pluralism, the view that knowledge is located in multiple places, fragments the knower into several contradictory knowers, and the known into several different knowns, depending on the perspective taken. In contrast to the social constructionism of consonance in monism, pluralists often hold to a social constructionism of dissonance. That is, knowledge is seen as located in many places, and one cannot say it is located more in one place than another. When knowledge appears different at two or more sites, pluralists see no need to resolve the differences.

Issue 6: What Are the Relative Contributions of Sense Data and Mental Activity to Knowing?

For the last 100 years or so, answers to this question have varied from one extreme to the other. On one pole has been the view that only propositions verified by observed phenomena should be called knowledge. On the other pole has been the view that the world is always interpreted through different lenses of concepts and beliefs, and that there exists no independent criterion for deciding if one lens is more valid than another. Between the poles, a range of answers captures the various attempts to explain knowledge acquisition or construction as the sum, interaction, or transaction of sense data and mental activity, whether personal or sociocultural.

Issue 7: To What Degree Is Knowledge Discovered Versus Created?

If knowledge is discovered through collecting data or apprehending reality, subjectivity and cultural bias are threats to its discovery, and objectivity is necessary. On the other hand, if knowledge is created, either individually or culturally, objectivity is a ruse by the powerful to exclude other views, and taking a perspective is unavoidable. Middle positions on this issue often deny the possibility of objectivity while advocating other criteria for evaluating knowledge claims.

Five Epistemological Clusters

This section describes the second part of our framework—thumbnail sketches of five epistemological clusters, each concluding with a summary of the cluster's stance on the seven issues. The sketches emphasize each cluster's most important distinguishing characteristics. Controversies within a cluster are only noted when they add to a better understanding of what unifies the cluster.

Each cluster is labeled with two of its most important epistemologies. Two and only two epistemologies were chosen to name each cluster to achieve parsimony while preventing the identification of a cluster with any single epistemology. The clusters of epistemology have an order, but it is not chronological. They lie along a multivariate continuum, comprised of the seven issues.

Positivism/Radical Empiricism

All empiricists, whether positivists or not, whether radical or not, hold the view that immediate sense experience is the primary source and sanction for knowledge. However, it was probably David Hume [1711–1776] who first formulated an empiricism so pure it merits the label radical (Hume, 1739–1740/1978). Unlike earlier empiricists like John Locke [1632–1704] (Locke, 1690/1975), Hume rejected the possibility of knowledge beyond immediate sensations. He opposed all religion and argued against the possibility of knowing causation in science. Later, Auguste Comte [1798–1857] coined the term positivism to describe his pure empiricism that removed all metaphysical thinking from pursuits of knowledge (Comte, 1830/1988).

In the twentieth century, the epistemological stance of this cluster was carried forward in philosophy by the logical positivists (especially Rudolf Carnap [1891–1970] and A. J. Ayer [1910–1989]), and in psychology by the behaviorists (especially John Watson [1878–1958] and B. F. Skinner [1904–1990]) (q.v., Ayer, 1946; Carnap, 1934; Skinner, 1953; Watson, 1925). The unique contribution of the logical positivists was that they incorporated language analysis into their philosophy of science. In their hands, the positivism/radical empiricism cluster became as concerned with the language used to express or discuss knowledge as it had always been with objective sense data. Logical positivism and behaviorism reigned in American education and educational research until the 1980s. Its influence can still be felt whenever behavioral objectives or operational definitions are used.

Summary.   Epistemologists in this cluster hold that statements about a single, independent reality behind sensations are meaningless (Issue 1). Some positivists/radical empiricists (the skeptics) have denied all truth claims, while others (the reductionists) have agreed that truth exists, but only in the form of operational statements verified by data (Issue 2). Skeptics refute all tests of truth, but reductionists either test the truth of a proposition by its consistency with the body of related propositions (coherence theory) or, more commonly, by its results (pragmatic theory of truth) (Issue 3). Positivists/radical empiricists emphasize particulars, namely sense data and atomic propositions. Each instance has to be investigated since generalizations are always inductive (Issue 4). Dualism of subject and object is stressed and knowledge is seen as located outside the subject, in the sensations that comprise the objects of perception (Issue 5). Epistemologists in this cluster rely as much as possible on data gathered by the senses or scientific instruments (Issue 6). Great efforts are made to eliminate subjectivity. Whatever generalizations, correlations, or predictions are induced from data are supposedly discovered rather than created because they are implicit in the data (Issue 7).

Hypothetico-Deductivism/Formalism

Many empiricists moved away from positivism/radical empiricism after the middle 1800s. The uniquely American epistemology, pragmatism, was born in the 1870s as an empiricism that refused to limit knowledge to sensations. Over the next five or six decades, the pragmatists C. S. Peirce [1839–1914], William James [1842–1910], and John Dewey [1859–1952] moved American science and epistemology somewhat away from an empiricism of sources to an empiricism of context and effects (Dewey, 1929; James, 1907/1982; Peirce, 1923). For them, knowledge was not what was certain, but what related to important areas of life and helped improve things for people.

In Europe, in the 1920s and 1930s, another group of empiricists (led by C. G. Hempel [1905]) determined that positivism had been a failure because it could not account for scientific theories. Hempel's covering laws opposed all radical empiricisms generally, and logical positivism specifically, by deducing laws from theories and then testing them rather than inducing them from data as all positivists claimed to do (Hempel, 1965). Hempel's work began the most influential philosophy of science of the twentieth century: hypothetico-deductivism.

The most influential hypothetico-deductivist of recent times was probably Karl Popper [1902–1994] who rejected all positivists' attempts to verify operational statements. For many empiricists, Popper effectively destroyed the skepticism of radical empiricism by contending that, however they may originate, scientific theories and hypotheses can never be verified, only falsified, by data (Popper, 1934/1959).

The pragmatists and hypothetico-deductivists tended to be formalists, emphasizing the form over the content of theories. They employed new studies of language, signs, and mathematics to develop principles for scientific theorizing. This formalism is still seen whenever there is an emphasis on the scientific method or criticism of theories as theories, such as that they lack elegance or make too many assumptions.

The distinguishing characteristics of this cluster lie in the overlap among pragmatism, hypothetico-deductivism, and formalism. That intersection is an empiricism that (a) deduces hypotheses and knowledge statements from theories, (b) uses the form and consequences of theories to evaluate their claims to truth, and (c) collects objective data with the potential to falsify theories. The entire edifice of inferential statistics and experimental design across a number of fields stands as a product of this cluster.

Summary.   Epistemologists in this cluster are antirealists who sometimes sound like realists. Theories and statements referring to a reality underlying the objectively observable can be meaningful, but only as useful fictions—temporary knowledge to be abandoned when more useful fictions come along (Issue 1). Those in this cluster answer the second question "yes" (Issue 2) as long as the answer to the third question is that truth is determined by coherence or pragmatism rather than correspondence (Issue 3). Because one inexplicable, replicable exception supposedly falsifies the grandest theory, the only truths worthy of the name are universal (Issue 4). As for the location of knowledge, this cluster is always dualistic and knowledge is located between the subject and the object (Issue 5). Sense data provide the ultimate sanction for knowledge, but the mind also contributes to knowledge through theory building and deducing testable hypotheses from theories. There is a role for cognitive or social constructivism, but it is not allowed to deviate far from objectively gathered sense data or canons such as internal consistency and parsimony (Issue 6). This limited constructivism is not ordinarily viewed as creating knowledge. Instead, the discovery of knowledge is seen as requiring active participation in established methods of inquiry (Issue 7).

Realism/Essentialism

All realists hold that objects of knowledge exist independently of the knower, and that the world is capable of being known, at least in part, as it is in itself. Knowledge is seen as correspondence between belief or acceptance and reality. In a naive form, realism is probably the epistemology of animals, assuming they uncritically believe whatever their senses tell them. In a commonsense form, realism has probably always been the epistemology of the ordinary person. Naive realism is refuted by the existence of dreams and hallucinations, but commonsense and other types of realism are harder to refute because their advocates claim to discriminate between fact and illusion most of the time.

Realism was not considered an epistemology at all until the empiricists Locke [1632–1704], Berkeley [1685–1753], and Hume [1711–1776] cast doubt on the assumptions ordinary people live by. In doing so, they drew a reaction that led to a considered epistemology of realism. Thomas Reid [1710–1796] based his realism on the consensus of sensible and perceptive people untutored in philosophy (Reid, 1764/1970). The same reasoning was refined and used with considerable power by later realists such as George Moore [1873–1958] and George Santayana [1863–1952]. The argument is simply that those who deny the existence of a single independent reality, while lecturing or writing, make liars of themselves in their daily lives as they consistently manifest animal faith in the independent existence of other objects and minds (Moore, 1959; Santayana,1923/1955). Should we not follow their example rather than their words?

Many realists have also been empiricists. They are usually referred to as scientific realists. Scientific realists pursue a clear and full understanding of cause-and-effect relationships. They are model builders who want to be able to represent every level and facet of reality, however hidden that aspect may be from ordinary view.

Prior to the rise of empiricism, the dominant philosophy of the West was essentialism, formulated by Aristotle [384–322 B.C.] and reformulated by Thomas Aquinas [1225–1274]. Essentialism holds that every particular object has real properties that define it (its essence), and that, for every class of objects, a set of properties defines the possibilities of that class (its essence) (Aquinas, trans. 1970; Aristotle, trans. 1975).

Summary.   For this cluster, there is a single reality independent of the knower by definition (Issue 1). Realists/essentialists believe that truth exists (Issue 2) and that truth is what corresponds to reality (Issue 3). Most realists/essentialists have believed in the real existence of both particulars (facts and essences) and universals (laws) (Issue 4). Realists/essentialists are either dualists or monists, depending on whether knowing is seen as occurring in the knower, in the interaction between knower and object, or is itself a process separate from either knower or object (Issue 5). To most realists/essentialists, the senses by themselves are gullible and the mind by itself is blind, but together the senses and the mind can overcome the limits of either alone (Issue 6). Realists/essentialists have disagreed about the amount of discovery versus creation involved in knowing. Scientific realists have generally thought they were discovering independent facts and truths. Critical realists have generally considered knowledge a creative achievement, needing reason and imagination to develop ideas and semblances that do the real world justice (Issue 7).

Structuralism/Contextualism

The epistemologies in this cluster oppose both empiricism and realism with the contention that the world is completely or partially created (constructed) by the mind, language, and/or sociocultural influences. This cluster is heir to epistemological idealism, which, in turn, was heir to rationalism, including rational skepticism. Rational skepticism developed when the Sophists [5th century B.C.] perfected the art of being publicly doubtful about any proposition, however apparent to common sense or supported by systematic observation (e.g., Protagoras as represented by Plato {trans. 1992a, 1992b}). Rationalism developed as Socrates [470–399 B.C.], Plato [428–347 B.C.], and Aristotle [384–322 B.C.) established the use of rigorous thinking and argument to go beyond the information given by the senses (Aristotle, trans. 1966; Plato, trans. 1928). As empiricism and science developed and became more influential after the Renaissance, René Descartes [1596–1650], Benedict Spinoza [1632–1677], and G. W. Leibniz [1646–1716] used reason, logic, mathematics, and rational skepticism as alternatives and supplements to the more dominant data-gathering methods of science (q.v., Descartes, trans. 1984–1985; Leibniz, trans. 1934; Spinoza, 1677/1985).

The great revolution of epistemological idealism occurred when Kant attempted to resolve the conflict between Leibniz' rationalism and Hume's empiricism. His solution was to pose the prior existence of categories that structure all perceptions (Kant, 1787/1966), making him the father of subjective idealism and all other top-down views. Kant's followers in the arts (romanticists) and in philosophy (German metaphysical idealists), however, refused to accept his human subjectivism. Their solution was to make the universe or nature the expression of a single mind or spirit. This solution received its most articulate and influential formulation in the philosophy of Hegel (q.v., 1807/1977).

Hegel's epistemology was a totalism. To totalists, the world is monolithic and can be known through understanding its universal principle. In a totalism, every particular is only understood in terms of its relations to the whole system. There is no content or substance in the system other than the relations themselves. The wholeness of the totalism is what gives meaning to each aspect or element of the system.

The influence of Kant's subjectivism and Hegel's totalism has been enduring in economics (Karl Marx [1818–1883] and his followers) and psychoanalysis (Sigmund Freud [1856–1939] and his followers) (q.v., Freud, 1900/1976; Marx, trans. 1986).

The contextualist wing of this cluster was dominant in American social science from the 1890s until the 1970s. Contextualism filtered the epistemologies of Kant and Hegel through American rugged individualism and the pragmatisms of Peirce, James, and Dewey. These influences muted Hegel's totalism, making the effect of the whole on the parts in any system of ideas contextual rather than total.

The structuralist wing of this cluster developed in French social science and philosophy through much of the twentieth century. Its development and influence has been manifest in linguistics (Ferdinand de Saussure [1857–1913]; Noam Chomsky [1928]), anthropology (Claude Lévi-Strauss [1908]), and literary criticism (Roman Jakobson [1896–1982]; Jonathan Culler [1944]) (q.v., Chomsky, 1968; Culler, 1975; Jakobson, 1961/1981; Lévi-Strauss, 1958/1963; Saussure, 1915/1983).

The work of decentering the subject was begun by the structuralists. The term subject in epistemology historically implied autonomy and agency of the individual person. Before structuralism, the individual was generally seen as knowing whatever is knowable via the senses and/or the mind, either by common sense or through the scientific method, reason, or intuition. Because structuralists see every unit as part of a whole that gives it meaning, including each individual in society, they have tended to decenter the subject. In other words, they removed the individual from the center of the act of knowing and situated that person as one element in a knowledge system.

Contextualism is probably best seen as a middle position between essentialism and structuralism. To contextualists, each particular is somewhat dependent on its relation to the whole for its meaning, yet contextualism preserves the individual existence of particulars. Wholes and particulars are both seen to contribute to the nature of the knowledge system. Contextualism permits individualism and subjectivism, while structuralism stresses collectivism and social interaction.

The structuralism/contextualism cluster stresses relations (as either structures or context), transactions of knower and known, and the role of the mind (operating either individually or socially through language) in the creation of knowledge. All structuralists and contextualists stress wholes and systems to some extent, and all oppose dualism. Their overall notions of meaning and truth emphasize coherence and consonance.

Summary. Epistemologists in this cluster deny independent reality, or at least the possibility of knowing it (Issue 1). Epistemological idealists have always held a high view of truth (Issue 2) as long as truth is seen as a coherent system rather than a set of discrete facts (Issue 3). As the heirs of idealism, structuralists/contextualists usually follow this tradition (Issues 2 & 3). There is, however, a strong current of pragmatism among some epistemologists of this cluster, particularly contextualists. So the test of truth is either coherence or pragmatism (Issue 3). Knowledge is considered to be universal in that it is a system with an overriding principle (e.g., social justice) or process (e.g., inquiry) that accounts for and unifies all parts. Structuralists usually deny or ignore particularities. Contextualists emphasize the universality of the process or principle while also maintaining the uniqueness of particulars (Issue 4). Those in this cluster are epistemological monists. Knowledge is located in the dynamic of knowing, within inquiry itself. It is more of a process than a product (Issue 5). Structuralists/contextualists stress the role of the mind (or community of minds) as interpreter of data. Sense data is held to reveal nothing unless it is interpreted (Issue 6). Creation is emphasized over discovery, but discovery is not entirely precluded, at least in contextualism. Knowledge is a constructive process of transacting with ideas, either individually or in a social context. Knowers construct knowledge and are constructed by knowledge (Issue 7).

Poststructuralism/Postmodernism

This newest cluster of epistemologies has dominated most discussions of knowledge in western Europe and North America since the 1970s. Disenchantment with modernism in general and structuralism in specific increased until it reached a crescendo, as writers from various fields moved beyond modernist and structuralist theories. Among the more influential of these writers were Jacques Lacan [1901–1981], Louis Althusser [1918–1990], Jacques Derrida [1930], Michel Foucault [1926–1984], Thomas Kuhn [1922], Jean Baudrillard [1929], and Roland Barthes [1915–1980] (q.v., Althusser, 1965/1969; Barthes, 1970/1974; Baudrillard, 1973/1975; Derrida, 1967/1976; Foucault, 1984; Kuhn, 1970; Lacan, 1966, 1971/1977). When they and their followers were not being original, they often based their considerations of knowledge on the work of Friedrich Nietzsche [1844–1900] and Martin Heidegger [1889–1976] (q.v., Heidegger, 1927/1962; Nietzsche, 1911/1968).

Poststructuralists also based their ideas on the work of structuralists in various fields, including in some cases their own earlier works. For example, poststructuralism has typically completed the work of decentering the subject begun by the structuralists to the point that every individual is seen as merely the site of cultural influences. All subjective idealism and contextualism are rejected.

Postmodernism is a reaction against the claims to universality and the metanarratives that dominated rationalism from Descartes [1596–1650] through the structuralists. To postmodernists, modernism gave the world science, reason, western civilization, Marxism, Freudianism, and other totalisms. Each of these totalisms tells a grand story that relates everything to everything else by using the system's universal principle as a theme. By making everything subordinate to a master narrative, each of these systems places some ideas, persons, and groups at the center and others at the periphery of the story being told. In short, power—not truth—drives all modernisms.

Because poststructuralism is a structuralism without a unifying principle, the key concept of poststructuralism is dissonance. Every metanarrative that attempts to establish a unifying principle for a system can be deconstructed, i.e., shown to be dissonant (incoherent) rather than consonant. Each person is intersubjective, a mass of contradictory impulses, drives, and memories, and influenced by experiences. Each piece of language is intertextual, internally inconsistent, and externally related to a host of texts that contradict each other in many ways.

Summary.   Epistemologists in this cluster insist that there are as many different realities as there are knowers (Issue 1). Those in this cluster deny what they call Truth with a capital T, but allow what they refer to as many truths with a small t. All claims to Truth are seen as arbitrary acts of power that include and exclude (Issue 2). For nihilists, all tests of truth are refuted. For cultural relativists, the test of truth is pragmatism (Issue 3). All knowledge is considered particular and local (Issue 4). As for the location of knowledge, poststructuralists/postmodernists hold a pluralist view: knowledge is located at many different sites. Knowledge does not exist outside the individuals and communities who know it (Issue 5). Mind is given near-total veto power over the senses in that every sensation or pattern of sensations is held to be a perspective rather than a fact. Moreover, how one learns to see, hear, and so forth is held to be entirely sociocultural. Perspectives themselves can be deconstructed—shown to be comprised of conflicting perspectives (Issue 6). All knowledge is created and all claims to discovery of knowledge are refuted. The knowledge that is constructed, however, lacks coherence, revealing that it is the result of power struggles (Issue 7).

HOW THE EPISTEMOLOGICAL ISSUES AND CLUSTERS CAN HELP RESEARCHERS AND PRACTITIONERS: AN EXAMPLE FROM THE FIELD OF READING EDUCATION

In this section, we provide one example from our previous study (Cunningham & Fitzgerald, 1996) of how our two-part framework can be applied. In particular, we apply the two-part framework to understand the epistemological underpinnings of Rosenblatt's (1938, 1969, 1978, 1985a, 1985b, 1993, 1994) theory of the reading process. In a sense, the epistemological stance we uncover may also be considered its author's personal epistemological outlook that is embedded in the theory. We want to emphasize that we are not trying to pigeonhole the theory. Instead, we attempt to coarsely analyze the theory as a means of enriching our view of the knowledge embodied in the theory.

Rosenblatt's Transactional View of the Reading Process: A Contextualist Position in the Structuralism/Contextualism Cluster

Summary of Rosenblatt's Transactional View of Reading

In Rosenblatt's transactional view, reading occurs through a transaction between a specific individual and a specific text. A key feature of Rosenblatt's view is that she shuns the word interaction because it implies a dualism in which the reader and the text are two separate entities that act on one another. Rather, she uses the

word transaction to refer to the reader and text as aspects of the totality of reading, "each conditioned by and conditioning the other" (1978, p. 16). Each forms
an environment for the other.

There are several critical features of the transaction. First, the mind is active.
Second, the reader is attentive "to the images, feelings, attitudes, and associations
that the words evoke in him" (1969, p. 34). Rosenblatt does not spell out the
mechanisms of this attentiveness, but she explicitly says that it is not done by reasoning alone. Third, the reader's past experiences and current preoccupations
make "possible not only a recognition of shapes of letters and words but also
their linkage with sound, which are further linked to what these sounds point to
as verbal symbols" (1969, p. 37).

Fourth, one basic reading process is used in a continuum of situations that are
different according to the reader's stance or where the reader holds his or her attention. The continuum is a mix of public (lexical, analytic, abstracting) and private (experiential, affective, associational) elements (Rosenblatt, 1994). It is
called the efferent-aesthetic continuum, efferent meaning scientific and aesthetic
meaning artistic. In the efferent stance, a reader "pays more attention to the cognitive, the referential, the factual, the analytic, the logical, the quantitative aspects
of meaning (1994, p. 1068). In the aesthetic stance, the reader "pays more attention to the sensuous, the affective, the emotive, the qualitative" (Rosenblatt,
1994, p. 1068). Every reading entails both stances, but across readings, the two
stances happen in different proportions.

Fifth, in her earlier writings, Rosenblatt underscored the importance of the social and cultural context saying that responses are "the organic expression not only
of a particular individual, but also of a particular cultural setting" (1938, p. 139).

Finally, Rosenblatt specifically declines to try to diagram or model the reading
process, eschewing information-processing views. She describes the theory using
language that helps to create a feeling of what reading is in her view. For instance,
she calls the meaning evoked during a mainly aesthetic reading transaction a
poem. A poem is what the reader "makes of his responses to the particular set of
verbal symbols" (1978, p. 12). The sequenced text symbols have magnetisim.

Applying the Seven Epistemological Issues
to Locate Rosenblatt's Theory on the Terrain

Where is knowledge located relative to the knower?   Dualism of text and
reader is rejected. Reader and text exist in reciprocity, and boundaries of each are
blurred. So the poem happens as the transaction occurs through the reader, the
symbols evoked, and the reader's responses to the evoked symbols. This appears
to be a monist outlook because Rosenblatt suggests a sense of unity and/or resolution during the transaction. For this issue (column 5 of Fig. 11.1), Rosenblatt's
view of reading is most closely aligned with the structuralist/contextualist cluster.

*What are the relative contributions of sense data and mental activity to know-
ing?*   Sense data and mental activity are inextricably involved. They are contrib-

utors to meaning. Meaning may be somewhat gleaned from the page, but the mind's knowledge and processes cannot be separated. Even so, Rosenblatt stresses interpretation more than print contributions. In this way, her thinking is in keeping with Kant and Hegel who denied dualism but continued to emphasize the rational and aesthetic over the empirical. On this issue then (column 6 of Fig. 11.1), the transactional view is most aligned with the structuralism/contextualism cluster.

To what degree is knowledge discovered versus created? Rosenblatt emphasizes creation and re-creation most. "The text . . . offers guidance and constraint, yet it is also open, requiring the creative contributions of the reader" (Rosenblatt, 1985a, p. 36). On this issue (column 7 of Fig. 11.1), Rosenblatt's view is most aligned with the bottom-most clusters.

Can we have knowledge of a single reality independent of the knower? In our exploration here of a reading theory, we rephrase this question to: In the reading process, is there an external existence of meaning? Or does meaning exist independently of the reader? In the transactional view of reading, the answer is "No." Meaning has no external reality. Rosenblatt said:

> If he cannot feel on his own pulses the impact of Keats' words, and if he cannot out of his own past experiences with life and language, no matter how paltry they may seem to him, find the substance for responding to the great structures of Shakespeare's tests and what they point to, there will be for him no ode, no Othello. If a literary work of art is to ensue, the reader must turn his attention as fully as possible toward the transaction between himself and the text (1978, p. 28).

So on this issue (column 1 of Fig. 11.1), taken collectively along with the preceding issues just discussed, Rosenblatt's position is more clearly located toward the bottom clusters. The need to take a collective look also holds true for each of the remaining issues.

Is there such a thing as truth? Rosenblatt (1994, p. 1078) believes that "absolutely determinate meaning is impossible," but she adheres to Dewey's notion of warranted assertibility. Although permanent, absolute truth is not possible, but agreeing on certain criteria of evaluation of interpretation, warranted assertions, or alternative truths, are possible. Consequently, on this issue (column 2 of Fig. 11.1), Rosenblatt avoids the skepticisms of the radical empiricists at the very top and nihilists at the very bottom of the clusters.

What primary test must proposed knowledge pass in order to be true? Coherence is the main test of the truth of evoked meaning. When more of an aesthetic stance is taken, the test considers the internal consistency among the symbols prompted by print and the reader's response. When more of an efferent stance is taken, the test considers the coherence of evoked meaning with its logic and references and the response of a knowledgeable public. On this issue (column 3 of Fig. 11.1), Rosenblatt's position seems consistent with the structuralism/contextualism cluster.

Is knowledge primarily universal or particular? The particular is clearly emphasized over universals. "There is no such thing as a generic reader or a generic literary work . . . The novel or poem or play exists, after all, only in the interactions with specific minds. The reading of any work of literature is, of necessity, an individual and unique occurrence involving the mind and emotions of some particular reader" (Rosenblatt, 1938, p. 23). Still, there is some sense of universality in the transactional view. For instance, aesthetic and efferent stances lie on a continuum. The two do not involve distinctly different process (Rosenblatt, 1994). On this issue (column 4 of Fig. 11.1), the transactional theory of reading seems anchored near the cusp between the structuralism/contextualism and poststructuralism/postmodernism clusters.

Summary. Rosenblatt's transactional view of the reading process reflects a view of knowledge that might be described as mainly contextualist. At the very least, there are many elements of her outlook that are shared by the contextualist epistemology. Rosenblatt (1994) herself distinguishes her outlook from structuralist and poststructuralist positions, most particularly in the area of language. In structuralist and poststructuralist philosophies, language is viewed as an autonomous, self-contained system, and words and concepts form dyadic relationships (e.g., de Saussure, 1915/1983). From a contextualist perspective, language has three faces conjointly linked as sign, object, and interpretant (e.g., Peirce, 1933, 1935).

What has been gained by applying the framework to understand the transactionalist perspective of the reading process? First, we have a richer understanding of what is meant by transaction. By gleaning its approximate alignment in relation to contextualism within the structuralist/contextualist cluster, knowledge about that cluster has been brought to bear on the transactional perspective. Second, a base has been laid for a way to evaluate the internal consistency or coherence of the theory. Having been located in the epistemological terrain, we can use the epistemological questions to ask whether the transactional theory is consistent with the general outlook of that cluster. Third, the exploration helps to reveal a better understanding of why Rosenblatt emphasizes what she does within the transactional view.

DISCUSSION

We now turn to additional thoughts about how and why epistemological analysis, and in particular, applying the framework we have presented, might be useful. Many of the ideas that follow remain to be investigated as possibilities in future studies. First, the understandings emanating from application of the epistemological framework we presented here might be related to understanding the links between theory and practice. For instance, many would argue that ideally, classroom instruction is driven by an underlying epistemological outlook. If you have a particular theory of knowledge, you are likely to teach and assess in ways that are consistent with that outlook. Different epistemological outlooks result in different forms of instruction and assessment. Consequently, teachers who use the framework provided here to clarify their own or others' epistemological stances in relation to current views of a particular learning process (such as the reading process) can then extend their analyses by linking stances with their potential for instructional implications.

Next, as we said earlier, the epistemological framework presented here might be a useful tool for individuals interested in discovering their own epistemological premises on a wide array of professional concerns. For instance, a researcher might ask the seven epistemological questions with his or her own view of a particular theory or construct in mind, such as his or her view of the reading process or of beliefs about a particular issue or topic. By locating the answers to the questions, the professional can assess the extent to which his or her stance is aligned with a particular epistemological cluster. The researcher might then wish to consult second or first sources for more information about that cluster.

Similarly, a researcher might use the framework provided here to discern epistemological stances on various issues, constructs, or topics for a wide variety of research participants. One example of this utility might be that the framework could be used to codify individuals' perspectives. That is, individuals could be asked questions and/or observed as they are carrying out an activity (such as leading a reading group in a classroom) that reveal their epistemological outlooks. These outlooks could be located on the continuum of clusters laid out in our framework. Such a research activity would likely involve a great deal of conceptualization and pilot work, as it might be difficult to create "good" questions or decide on focal behaviors that actually would enable clear inferences about individuals' epistemological stances. But it is highly likely that individuals' personal epistemologies could be located on the continuum, at least relatively if not specifically within a particular cluster. A research activity such as this might be enlightening.

Researchers assessing personal epistemologies of research participants might find the framework useful for identifying those epistemologies and also for then assessing participants' actions and/or practices in relation to identified views of knowledge and knowing.

Also, the framework can be used to better understand various aspects of research. Research is driven by researchers' underlying stances on knowledge and knowing. A researcher's epistemological outlook strongly influences what counts as important research questions. For instance, expanding from the transactional reading process theory we explicated earlier, it is easy to see that researchers who share such a perspective would likely include the kinds of knowledge that count most: individual readers' purposes, stances, and responses, and generally knowledge that is situation specific. Consequently, focal research topics for these researchers are likely to revolve around these sorts of knowledge as well as, for instance, how individuals in various social settings come to understand and form purpose, take stances, and make responses. Such researchers would not be interested at all in studying, for example, the internal mental mechanisms often described by information-processing flowcharts.

A researcher studying personal epistemologies who holds a positivist perspective on knowledge and knowing is not likely to be interested in studying how individuals' participation in a particular cultural group functions to shape beliefs about knowledge and knowing. On the other hand, an investigator whose own epistemological outlook is more aligned with structuralism/contextualism might find such a research issue to be fascinating.

Finally, research method is generally inextricably linked to the kind of knowledge being studied. Different epistemological outlooks are associated with distinct research methodologies. For instance—here we draw a rough depiction—investigators who have a radical empiricist outlook are more likely to choose more "objective" methods that enable "discovery" of "true answers." To the contrary, investigators more inclined toward a postmodern perspective are more likely to use methods that allow internal stances to become public with minimal researcher intrusion and that may be more discursive in nature, such as case studies.

REFERENCES

Althusser, L. (1969). *For Marx* (B. Brewster, Trans.). London: Allen Lane/The Penguin Press. (Original work published 1965)

Alvermann, D. E. (1993). Researching the literal: Of muted voices, second texts, and cultural representations. In D. J. Leu & C. K. Kinzer (Eds.), *Examining central issues in literacy research, theory, and practice*. Forty-second Yearbook of the National Reading Conference (pp. 1–10). Chicago: National Reading Conference.

Aquinas, T. (1970). *Commentary on the posterior analytics of Aristotle* (F. R. Larcher, Trans.). Albany, NY: Magi Books.

Aristotle (1966). *Metaphysics* (H. G. Apostle, Trans.). Bloomington: Indiana University Press.

Aristotle (1975). *Posterior analytics* (J. Barnes, Trans.). Oxford: Clarendon Press.

Ayer, A. J. (1946). *Language, truth, and logic* (2nd ed.). London: V. Gollancz.

Barthes, R. (1974). *S/Z* (R. Miller, Trans.). New York: Hill & Wang. (Original work published 1970)

Baudrillard, J. (1975). *The mirror of production* (M. Poster, Trans.). St. Louis, MO: Telos Press. (Original work published 1973)

Carnap, R. (1934). *The unity of science* (M. Black, Trans.). London: Kegan Paul, Trench, Trubner & Co.

Chomsky, N. (1968). *Language and mind*. New York: Harcourt, Brace & World.

Comte, A. (1988). *Introduction to positive philosophy* (P. Descours, H. G. Jones, & F. Ferré, Trans., F. Ferré, Ed.). Indianapolis, IN: Hackett. (Original work published 1830)

Culler, J. D. (1975). *Structuralist poetics: Structuralism, linguistics and the study of literature*. Ithaca, NY: Cornell University Press.

Cunningham, J. W., & Fitzgerald, J. (1996). Epistemology and reading. *Reading Research Quarterly, 31*, 36–60.

Derrida, J. (1976). *Of grammatology* (G. C. Spivak, Trans.). Baltimore, MD: Johns Hopkins University Press. (Original work published 1967)

Descartes, R. (1984–1985). *The philosophical writings of Descartes* (Vols. 1–2, J. Cottingham, R. Stoothoff, & D. Murdoch, Trans.). New York: Cambridge University Press.

Dewey, J. (1929). *Experience and nature* (2nd ed.). LaSalle, IL: Open Court.

Fenstermacher, G. D. (1994). The knower and the known: The nature of knowledge in research on teaching. In L. Darling-Hammond (Ed.), *Review of research in education* (Vol. 20, pp. 3–56). Washington, DC: American Educational Research Association.

Foucault, M. (1984). *The Foucault reader* (P. Rabinow, Ed.). New York: Random House.

Freud, S. (1976). *The interpretation of dreams* (J. Strachey, Trans. & Ed.). New York: Penguin Books. (Original work published 1900)

Gjertsen, D. (1989). *Science and philosophy: Past and present*. New York: Penguin Books.

Hegel, G. W. F. (1977). *The phenomenology of spirit* (A. V. Miller, Trans.). Oxford: Clarendon Press. (Original work published 1807)

Heidegger, M. (1962). *Being and time* (J. Macquarrie & E. Robinson, Trans.). New York: Harper & Row. (Original work published 1927)

Hempel, C. G. (1965). *Aspects of scientific explanation and other essays in the philosophy of science*. New York: The Free Press.

Hofer, B. K., & Pintrich, P. R. (1997). The development of epistemological theories: Beliefs about knowledge and knowing and their relation to learning. *Review of Educational Research, 67,* 88–140.

Hume, D. (1978). *A treatise of human nature* (L. A. Selby-Bigge, Ed., P. H. Nidditch, Ed. of Rev. ed.). Oxford: Oxford University Press. (Original work published 1739–1740)

Jakobson, R. (1981). *Selected writings (Vol. 3): Poetry of grammar and grammar of poetry* (S. Rudy, Ed.). New York: Mouton (Original work published 1961)

James, W. (1982). *Pragmatism: A new name for some old ways of thinking*. Franklin Center, PA: Franklin Library. (Original work published 1907)

Kant, I. (1966). *Critique of pure reason* (F. M. Müller, Trans.). Garden City, NY: Anchor Books. (Original work published 1787)

Kuhn, T. S. (1970). *The structure of scientific revolutions* (2nd ed.). Chicago: University of Chicago Press.

Lacan, J. (1977). *Écrits: A selection* (A. Sheridan, Trans.). New York: W. W. Norton. (Original work published 1966, 1971)

Leibniz, G. W. (1934). *Philosophical writings* (M. Morris, Trans.). New York: E. P. Dutton.

Lévi-Strauss, C. (1963). *Structural anthropology* (C. Jacobson & B. G. Schoepfe, Trans.). New York: Basic Books. (Original work published 1958)

Locke, J. (1975). *An essay concerning human understanding* (P. H. Nidditch, Ed.). Oxford: Clarendon Press. (Original work published 1690)

Marx, K. (1986). *The essential writings* (2nd ed.). (F. L. Bender, Ed.). Boulder, CO: Westview Press.

McLaren, P. (1992). Literacy research and the postmodern turn: Cautions from the margins. In R. Beach, J. Green, M. Kamil, & T. Shanahan (Eds.), *Multidisciplinary perspectives on literacy research* (pp. 319–339). Urbana, IL: National Conference on Research in English.

Moore, G. E. (1959). *Philosophical papers*. New York: Macmillan.

Morris, V. C., & Pai, Y. (1976). *Philosophy and the American school: An introduction to the philosophy of education* (2nd ed.). Boston: Houghton Mifflin.

Myers, G. (1986). Writing research and the sociology of scientific knowledge: A review of three new books. *College English, 48,* 595–610.

Nietzsche, F. (1968). *The will to power* (W. Kaufmann & R. J. Hollingdale, Trans., W. Kaufmann, Ed.). New York: Random House. (Original work published 1911)

Peirce, C. S. (1923). *Chance, love, and logic: Philosophical essays* (M. R. Cohen, Ed.). New York: Harcourt Brace.

Peirce, C. S. (1933). *Collected papers* (vol. 3). (P. Weiss & C. Hartshorne, Eds.). Cambridge, MA: Harvard University Press.

Peirce, C. S. (1935). *Collected papers* (vol. 6). (P. Weiss & C. Hartshorne, Eds.) Cambridge, MA: Harvard University Press.

Peterson, M. L. (1986). *Philosophy of education: Issues and options*. Downers Grove, IL: InterVarsity Press.

Plato (1928). *The works of Plato* (B. Jowett, Trans., I. Edman, Ed.). New York: Modern Library.

Plato (1992a). *Protagoras* (S. Lombardo & K. Bell, Trans.). Indianapolis: Hackett.

Plato (1992b). *Theaetetus* (M. J. Levett, Trans.). Indianapolis: Hackett.

Popper, K. R. (1959). *The logic of scientific discovery* (K. Popper, J. Freed, & L. Freed, Trans.). London: Hutchinson. (Original work published 1934)

Reid, T. (1970). *An inquiry into the human mind* (T. Duggan, Ed.). Chicago: University of Chicago Press. (Original work published 1764)

Rosenau, P. M. (1992). *Postmodernism and the social sciences: Insights, inroads, and intrusions*. Princeton, NJ: Princeton University Press.

Rosenblatt, L. M. (1938). *Literature as exploration*. New York: D. Appleton-Century.

Rosenblatt, L. M. (1969). Towards a transactional theory of reading. *Journal of Reading Behavior, 1*, 31–49.

Rosenblatt, L. M. (1978). *The reader the text the poem: The transactional theory of the literary work*. Carbondale and Edwardsville: Southern Illinois University Press.

Rosenblatt, L. M. (1985a). The transactional theory of the literary work: Implications for research. In C. Cooper (Ed.), *Researching response to literature and the teaching of literature* (pp. 33–53). Norwood, NJ: Ablex.

Rosenblatt, L. M. (1985b). Viewpoints: Transaction versus interaction—A terminological rescue operation. *Research in the Teaching of English, 19*, 96–107.

Rosenblatt, L. M. (1993). The transactional theory: Against dualisms. *College English, 55 , 377–386.*

Rosenblatt, L. M. (1994). The transactional theory of reading and writing. In R. B. Ruddell, M. R. Ruddell, & H. Singer (Eds.), *Theoretical models and processes of reading* (4th ed., pp. 1057–1092). Newark, DE: International Reading Association.

Santayana, G. (1955). *Scepticism and animal faith*. New York: Dover. (Original work published 1923)

Saussure, F. de (1983). *Course in general linguistics* (R. Harris, Trans.). London: Duckworth. (Original work published 1915)

Sire, J. W. (1988). *The universe next door* (2nd ed.). Downers Grove, IL: InterVarsity Press.

Skinner, B. F. (1953). *Science and human behavior*. New York: Free Press.

Spinoza, B. (1985). *Ethics*. In E. Curley (Ed. & Trans.), *The collected works of Spinoza* (Vol. 1, pp. 408–617). Princeton, NJ: Princeton University Press. (Original work published 1677)

Watson, J. B. (1925). *Behaviorism*. New York: W. W. Norton.

III

Methodological Issues in the Study of Personal Epistemology

12

Critical Elements in the Design and Analysis of Studies of Epistemology

Phillip Wood
University of Missouri at Columbia

CarolAnne Kardash
University of Missouri at Columbia

Research in students' epistemic cognition is typified by much good faith effort designed to reveal the role of epistemic cognitions in classroom performance and the increasing sophistication of students' reasoning about ill-structured problems. Despite this effort, it is often difficult to assess the quality of such research and to integrate this area of research with other perspectives. Part of the difficulty, we believe, is due to the fact that researchers often fail to attend to significant issues in the design of studies and appropriate use of standard statistical techniques, such as analysis of variance and factor analysis. A second problem results from the use of research designs that do not anticipate the alternative explanations that a reasonable skeptic could raise regarding proposed effects. The aim of this chapter is to promote better practices in the design and analysis of epistemology research by outlining some of these considerations.

Studies of Epistemology
Are Often Underpowered

Increasingly, researchers in student epistemology are attracted to the use of interview or other free response assessment formats. It is often hoped that these techniques will capture the rich, complex detail of such reasoning. Use of such techniques is both labor and cost intensive and therefore often limited to rather small sample sizes. In spite of the limitations imposed by such small samples, several studies have successfully found rather substantial differences across educational level. Generally, however, these studies have been less successful in identifying particularly effective educational interventions, or, in longitudinal assessments, in detecting patterns of differential growth over the college years.

This pattern of results is not surprising from the standpoint of experimental design and occurs because such studies frequently lack statistical power. "Power" in statistical parlance refers to the odds that a researcher will conclude that a relationship or difference will be statistically significant, given that such a difference in fact exists. Fortunately for researchers in higher education, our best estimates of the amount of improvement in performance on critical thinking and reflective judgment measures is roughly one standard deviation (Pascarella & Terenzini, 1991), an amount that Cohen (1988) would describe as a "large" effect size for psychological research. In the presence of such a large difference, standard statistical tests are quite likely to detect differences between groups. As an example of this, consider Fig. 12.1 (taken from Conner & Wood, 1999), which shows two power curves as a function of sample size based on norming information for freshmen and senior performance on the Reasoning About Current Issues Test (RCI), a measure based on the Reflective Judgment Model (see King & Kitchener, chap. 3, this volume, for details on the Reflective Judgment Model and Wood, Kitchener & Jensen, chap. 14, this volume, for discussion of the rationale and development of the RCI).

This figure shows, for example, the odds of correctly concluding that seniors do, in fact, score higher than freshmen on the RCI. Two curves are shown here to reflect the choice of whether the researcher chooses to employ the freshman standard deviation (of 0.230) or the senior standard deviation (of 0.199) as the base measure of variability in the two populations and, as such, bracket the variability one is likely to encounter in subsequent research. It can be seen that a relatively modest sample size of only 42 (21 freshmen and 21 seniors) yields odds of a statistically significant result that are well over 80%. Obviously, research designs that investigate shorter education intervals require larger sample sizes but such a question requires the use of a much larger sample size. For example, Conner and Wood (1999) describe how a two year follow-up requires roughly 126 participants, while detection of the very small change from the freshman to the sophomore year found for such data requires sampling a projected 3,770 participants! (Some caution is appropriate for such an estimate, given that the sophomores on which this estimate is based are largely those who enrolled in introductory psy-

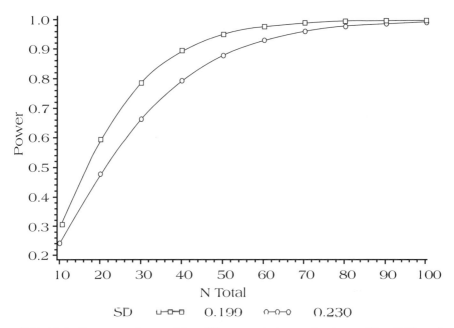

FIG. 12.1   Power analyses of the differences between freshmen (M = .542) and seniors (M = .749) based on standard deviations of freshmen (.230) and seniors (.199).

chology during their sophomore year, suggesting perhaps that this group of sophomores may not be typical of the larger population of sophomores in college.) It should be evident from these remarks that when extensive written or oral performance assessments of freshmen and seniors are done, or when samples are taken from small institutions or departments with few students, that the researcher is unlikely to detect even substantial changes in epistemology.

Tests of Statistical Interaction Require Much Larger Sample Sizes

Although the "good news" of this line of research is that statistically significant differences between freshmen and seniors can be found, researchers and other stakeholders in assessment are rarely interested in stopping there. Many interesting questions for such research involve assessing differential patterns of performance. Unfortunately, the sample sizes required to detect differential patterns are much larger than those necessary to detect simple main effects. As an example of this, consider a rather extreme scenario in which one group of seniors shows the usual pattern of performance found in the RCI while the other shows no gain at all. Conner and Wood (1999) present analyses that show that roughly 160 participants are necessary to detect such a pattern of differential effect with at least 80% odds of success. Again, it is very unlikely that a population of seniors would show no change during the college years (some change is likely due to general maturation, for example). Therefore, even the estimate of estimated 160 participants is a lower bound on the likely size of the required sample. For shorter term studies, such as two-year investigations involving one group that did not change, Conner and Wood found that 496 participants would be necessary for a power of .80.

This point merits discussion in light of the interest on the part of some researchers in assessing whether short-term interventions, such as critical thinking courses, service learning exercises, or experiential learning exercises have an effect on epistemology. In practice, some researchers (e.g., King & Kitchener, 1994) caution that short-term interventions are unlikely to have an effect on epistemology because epistemology develops slowly over a long period of time. We believe that there may be interventions that are effective in promoting epistemology, but that the effect size associated with such interventions is likely small, given that the gains across the two years from the freshman to junior years are modest. Additionally, of course, it would be necessary to include a comparable control group in the study and the interaction test for demonstrating the effectiveness of the intervention, which requires the use of large samples. Thus, although we also share some skepticism that short-term intervention studies will find significant effects, we feel that this is probably due to statistical power considerations rather than any special characteristics of the construct of student epistemology.

Research Hypotheses and Design

Even given that a particular study may be sufficiently powered to detect significant differences in a population of students, it is necessary to embed these results in the context of other rival explanations for a proposed effect. Given the relatively new status of epistemological questions in educational research, researchers often have as their goal establishing that differences exist on such measures as a function of educational level or are interested in showing that epistemological beliefs have a nonzero correlation with academic performance. Research hypotheses in the area often take the form of relatively simple hypotheses, such as "Do students' epistemology scores increase over time?" or "Do college seniors score higher than college freshmen?" or "Is student epistemology correlated with academic performance and/or discipline?" Although this step is a useful first step in justifying the relevance of epistemological beliefs, it seems reasonable for researchers in epistemology to take a more critical approach to the claims they make in their studies.

Specifically, researchers should consider plausible alternative explanations that a reasonable skeptic might raise regarding a proposed effect. As such, the design of a research study in epistemology must take care to anticipate such alternatives. Alternate explanations can be addressed in ancillary analyses or, failing that, addressed in the discussion section by outlining what new studies could be done. All too often, discussions of study limitations seem limited to only one or two relatively standard experimental limitations, with little comment as to future directions that research could now take in light of the concluded research. To paraphrase Brutus in *Julius Caesar*, it often seems that epistemology researchers come to "praise Caesar and not to bury him." If it is our mission to increase awareness of student epistemology in the broader research community, we must be willing to defend the position that the proposed effects we wish to claim are not an artifact of some other confounding variable or deficiency in research design.

Third Variable Explanations

In the design of research, we often neglect rather obvious third variable explanations for proposed effects. For example, any correlation between epistemology and academic performance could be due to the fact that both constructs are related to general verbal ability. If one were to adjust epistemology and performance variables for the effects of verbal ability, the correlation between the two measures would be negligible. Given that general personality variables such as need for cognition have been related to individuals' willingness to attend to and process information (Caccioppo, Petty, Feinstein, & Jarvis, 1996), it seems reasonable to include such variables in studies in order to determine whether it is the epistemology per se that is related to performance, or whether individuals who are disposed to think about information excel academically in addition to holding more sophisticated epistemological beliefs. Given that general academic aptitude and prior academic achievement are frequently available on undergraduate populations, it also seems reasonable to gather such information as well. These issues are especially important to consider when differences between men and women or between ethnic groups are to be considered. Given that performance differences exist on verbal reasoning measures and personality, and given that performance across these groups will differ as a function of the intact educational population under consideration, it seems important to gather this information when attempting to document such differences.

Sampling Considerations for Cross-Sectional Research

As mentioned before, some "first step" designs in epistemological studies are cross-sectional in nature and involve comparisons of individuals at varying levels of education. As pointed out by many researchers in higher education, there are a number of reasons why such a design is not equivalent to a prospective study. To name just two issues, academic attrition in college is substantial and the academic majors of seniors are quite different than for beginning students. Given these issues, however, it is important that researchers take care to measure as many of these relevant variables as they can (such as, again, academic aptitude and prior academic achievement variables) that are often related to collegiate attrition as well as personality variables that may be related to selection of some academic majors. In this way, researchers can then address these issues by matching or selecting on these variables to eliminate gross differences between the two populations. Although it seems clear that matching or controlling for academic attrition variables is reasonable, the question of whether personality or dispositional variables should be partialed out of disciplinary effects or educational level effects is far less clear-cut. At least we should explore the extent to which these variables overlap with the effects we find.

Design Considerations for Prospective Research

Given that cross-sectional research can be criticized based on confounds associated with the use of intact groups, researchers often believe that longitudinal studies will provide a stronger basis for conclusions. In this area as well, though, care must be taken to guard against alternate explanations for proposed effects. For example, Kronholm (1996) conducted a prospective study of 80 students designed to test whether a one-semester instructional intervention could improve reasoning on the Reflective Judgment Interview. In spite of the comments regarding power raised earlier, she found a significant interaction between time and experimental condition and concluded that the instruction promoted reasoning on the Reflective Judgment Interview. Inspection of the patterns of means for the study, however, showed that the intervention group was significantly lower than the control group at the baseline assessment and that the means for the two groups were roughly equivalent on retesting. Thus, it is unclear whether the intervention group was merely catching up to the control group during this time, and whether a control group with more comparable levels of performance would also show increases in performance as well. I should stress that we don't disbelieve that the proposed intervention promotes reasoning, but we just don't know whether it does yet due to the nonequivalence of the two groups used.

Choice and Interpretation of Statistical Methods

More broadly, a general caution in the use of statistical techniques in epistemological research deals with the uncritical use of statistical techniques to test hypotheses. This problem is not unique to this area, and one of the authors has discussed these issues at length within the context of general methodological techniques in psychology (Sher & Wood, 1997). Although the limitations of technique are spelled out in more detail in that work, it is helpful to remember that statistical techniques may not be robust to violations of assumptions. Specifically, researchers should investigate whether outliers exist in the data, whether a proposed effect is due to the presence of a relatively small number of influential observations, and whether a research finding may be an artifact of the measurement instrument employed.

Increasingly, hierarchical linear models, growth curves, and other structural equation models are employed in large research designs. The relative strengths and weaknesses of these advanced techniques cannot be discussed at length here but are covered in more detail in Sher and Wood (1997). Two techniques were not reviewed there and have been extensively employed in the development of epistemological scales: reliability theory (especially in reporting of internal consistency estimates) and exploratory factor analysis. Exploratory factor analysis, for example, is often used to determine subscales of an instrument and to determine the underlying structure of epistemological beliefs. It is particularly important to discuss the relationship between the theoretical assumptions of the factor model in epistemological research, especially given that the standard defaults for many statistical programs may not be reasonable in this context.

Internal Consistency

Although it is agreed that internal consistency estimates are essential in the evaluation of a scale, it is also important to use them intelligently. To that end, it is helpful to discuss what reliability theory does and does not tell a researcher about a scale. The reliability of a scale may be thought of as that proportion of variability in scores due to "true score" variability. As such, it can be thought of as a type of "R-Square" in predicting observed scores on a measure if individuals' true scores were known. It should be kept in mind (as we will discuss in the example to follow) that low internal consistency may prevent a researcher from uncovering differences between groups that may, in fact, be present. As a result, researchers who find that a measure is not internally consistent can, rather than discounting a measure, choose to increase the items representing the construct in order to obtain a more reliable measure. This seems particularly reasonable in epistemology research given that such reasoning and the vocabulary used to express such reasoning may be complex. More items may be necessary to triangulate on a participant's score.

Second, when calculating internal consistency, it is important to remember that the design of the study may affect the values that are obtained. Studies that sample a wide range of performance (such as those that compare freshman to senior performance) will demonstrate higher internal consistency than studies based on only a restricted range of performance (as might occur in a study of an educational intervention targeted to entering college students). All too often, it seems, reviewers of this literature uncritically report internal consistency estimates, noting the mix of values, and concluding that "estimates vary." In addition, researchers who are designing studies should be careful to evaluate whether internal consistency estimates from prior research are appropriate for their research design. For example, King and Kitchener (1994) report that the Reflective Judgment Instrument yielded a coefficient alpha of .96 in their study of high school students, college juniors, and graduate students. Although this is useful information for other researchers planning to investigate performance on a similar range of ability, it is not a particularly useful estimate for a researcher who wishes to investigate the internal consistency in a study of students who are all at one level of educational attainment. Wood (1997), for example, in a secondary analysis of available Reflective Judgment Interview data, found that the internal consistency of the Reflective Judgment Interview ranges between .73 to .85 within educational level.

Exploratory Factor Analysis

As a final point, it should be kept in mind that it is not necessarily the case that internal consistency, by itself, is a measure of the dimensionality of a construct. It assumes that one construct underlies the pattern of response, but does not test this assumption. Exploratory factor analysis has been used as a tool to this end. However, as with all techniques, conceptual considerations also affect choices in statistical analysis options and the default options are not necessarily the most appropriate here.

Determining the Number of Factors. Often, researchers examine the eigenvalues obtained in an exploratory factor analysis as indicating the number of underlying dimensions. Frequently, the Kaiser–Guttman criterion is used and all factors with eigenvalues greater than 1 are retained. Although this approach has the advantage that several factors will likely be retained, such an approach has several limitations. First, as Loehlin (1992) has demonstrated, even randomly generated data with no underlying structure will generate some factors with eigenvalues greater than 1. Loehlin also mentions that chance fluctuations can cause factors to exceed or fail the cutoff. Third, the number of eigenvalues that are greater than 1 depends also on the number of variables under consideration for the factor analysis. Factor analysis of relatively few items will result in fewer factors with eigenvalues greater than 1, those with several items will generate several greater than 1. A more obscure point relates to the issue of communality estimates. Factor analyses that employ squared multiple correlations on the diagonal will yield fewer factors exceeding unity than other estimates that assume a higher value for communality, as frequently occurs when iterative techniques are used to improve the communality estimates.

To this end the scree test (Cattell, 1966) is usually used, in which those factors are retained that depart from the general slope of eigenvalues associated with the higher factors. Even this approach, however, has its limitations. Most problematically, the scree test is applied to factors that are uncorrelated. If it is the case, however, that the underlying factor structure involves factors that are correlated (as discussed next), uncritical use of the scree test will result in retaining fewer factors than in fact underlie the data. As a result, choice of dimensionality that corresponds to that assumed by the researcher seems a useful beginning for considerations of dimensionality. If the recovered pattern of factor loadings conforms to this conceptual framework, then the researcher has at least established that the expert judgment involved in the construction of the instrument has some empirical support. It may still be the case, however, that reasonable skeptics may wish to construct alternative plausible models for the data that fit the data reasonably well. Hopefully, the choice of models may be made based on replication of findings and an appeal to the predictive utility of the models in predicting other behaviors.

Use of Orthogonal Factor Models. Although some researchers such as Schommer (chap. 6, this volume and 1990) and Jehng, Johnson, and Anderson (1993) have assumed that epistemological beliefs constitute discrete sets of orthogonal beliefs in development of their instruments, this assumption seems somewhat counterintuitive given the assumption by other researchers (such as King & Kitchener, 1994) who assume that such epistemic cognitions are closely related. It would seem that it is a testable hypothesis to investigate whether such factors are, in fact, orthogonal, given that a number of oblique rotation solutions such as promax (Hendrickson & White, 1964) and KD (Kaiser & Madow, 1974) rotations have been developed and are commonly available in statistical packages.

Practically speaking, choice of an orthogonal model for the factor structure will likely result in the research failing to find "simple structure," meaning that if an orthogonal structure is imposed on data that are actually taken from a correlated factor model, individual items are likely to load on more than one factor. Oblique factor models, by their design, minimize cross-loadings on multiple factors by estimating a correlation between factors.

The issue of rotation is also often overlooked in exploratory factor analysis models. The Varimax rotation (Kaiser, 1958) is almost always employed in reported factor solutions due in part, perhaps, to the fact that it is the default option in many statistical packages and partly due to the fact that it often does yield interpretable solutions. The researcher, however, should keep in mind that other orthogonal rotations for the data do exist and that methodologists have often discussed the relative merits of such rotations. Varimax, for example, has been known to spread the explained variability across several factors while other techniques, such as Quartimax (Neuhaus & Wrigley, 1954) have been found to recover a single general factor more often (Loehlin, 1992). The point here, as related to studies of epistemological development, is that if a single underlying dimension of epistemological development exists within a survey, rotational procedures such as Varimax are designed not to recover such latent variables. Instead, use of such rotations may result in an overcompartmentalization of components of epistemology that may reflect common method variability or some pattern of hierarchical organization of components of epistemology.

Third, the stability of a given pattern of rotated results is closely related to the number of factors assumed in the analysis. Traditional factor analysts refer to "factor fission" and "factor fusion," terms originally coined by R. G. Cattell to denote the phenomenon that factors rotated to simple structure often group differently depending on the number of factors assumed in the model. Thus, while one factor analysis may show a pattern of mixed loadings across several content areas, another solution may reveal a distinct and clean solution. This phenomenon is further accented in research settings where individual items that do not perform well are dropped from subsequent analyses.

As a final point, considerations of rotation and factor fusion/fission do not exhaust the possible relationships between factors. It may be, for example, that observed factors may themselves be facets of a general superfactor underlying the data (Schmid & Leiman, 1957). Estimation of such superfactor models involves the use of confirmatory factor analysis and the reader is referred to Loehlin (1992) for a general description and to Sher & Wood (1997) for an application to prospective research models. The upshot of these comments, however, is designed to highlight the point that the convergence of a exploratory factor models should be examined under a number of possible models. Some of these model assumptions, such as the model of correlated factors, may seem quite reasonable to all reasonable researchers, while others may be more open to debate. To the extent that different approaches all yield the same general pattern, however, stronger evidence regarding a study's conclusions can be made.

Use of Parcels.   Frequently, researchers have composed small subsets of conceptually homogenous items in an effort to reduce the number of variables in the model and to refine the patterns of loadings in a more general factor model. Although this practice reflects, to an extent, traditionally recommended practice (see, for example, Anderson & Gerbing, 1984), Marsh, Hau, Balla, and Grayson (1998) report that better factor solutions result from inclusion of as many indicators per factor as possible. An additional caution raised by Hofer and Pintrich (1997) is that use of item parcels in factor analysis does not test whether the a priori groups, in fact, cleanly and clearly represent the underlying assumed factor.

Exploratory Factor Analysis Example

As an example of how these methodological concerns can influence the analysis and interpretation of factor analysis, we would now like to present an exploratory factor analysis of items from two epistemological measures.

DIMENSIONS OF PERSONAL EPISTEMOLOGY AS ASSESSED BY TWO OBJECTIVE SURVEYS OF BELIEFS

Schommer (1990) originally hypothesized that personal epistemology comprised five related but independent dimensions that addressed beliefs about the structure, certainty, and source of knowledge, and control and speed of knowledge acquisition. She wrote 63 items to address these dimensions, and three educational psychologists reviewed the items and categorized them into 12 subsets. The subsets associated with each of the five, hypothesized epistemological dimensions (all stated from a naive perspective) were: Seek Single Answers and Avoid Integration ("Simple Knowledge"); Avoid Ambiguity and Knowledge is Certain ("Certain Knowledge"); Don't Criticize Authority and Depend on Authority ("Omniscient Authority"); Can't Learn How to Learn, Success is Unrelated to Hard Work, and Ability to Learn is Innate ("Innate Ability"); and Learning is Quick, Learn the First Time, and Concentrated Effort is a Waste of Time ("Quick Learning"). Undergraduates rated each item using a Likert scale. Responses were factor analyzed using the 12 subsets rather than the 63 items as variables. Principal axis factoring with Varimax rotation yielded four factors that corresponded fairly closely to Schommer's original hypotheses regarding which subsets should load on which factors. However, the two "authority" subsets failed to load on a separate factor as originally hypothesized, one of the subsets written to assess Quick Learning loaded instead on the Innate Ability factor, and a second subset also written to assess Quick Learning did load on that factor but had a substantial loading (.34) on the Innate Ability factor as well. Finally, the subset Avoid Ambiguity loaded on the Simple Knowledge rather than the Certain Knowledge factor.

Additional factor analyses of the 12 subsets of items using the same procedures as in the 1990 study have been reported in several subsequent studies conducted by Schommer and her colleagues (Schommer, 1993; Schommer, Calvert, Gariglietti, & Bajaj, 1997; Schommer, Crouse, & Rhodes, 1992). Schommer's Simple Knowledge factor has been remarkably stable across all these studies. Three of the subsets—Avoid Ambiguity, Seek Single Answers, and Avoid Integration—have loaded on this factor in each of the four studies. In two of the studies, the subset Depend on Authority has loaded on this factor as well. Similarly, her Knowledge is Certain subset has loaded consistently on the Certain Knowledge factor, although in two of the studies the Don't Criticize Authority subset has loaded on this factor as well. The Learning is Quick subset has loaded consistently on the Quick Learning factor, although the subset Ability to Learn is Innate has loaded (using a criterion of .30 or greater) on the Quick Learning factor as well in two of the studies. Finally, the Innate Ability factor has consistently been composed of three subsets: Learn the First Time, Can't Learn How to Learn, and Success is Unrelated to Hard Work. Thus, the structure yielded from empirical investigations appears to be generally stable, although the factor structure does not yield a one-to-one correspondence with the pattern of loadings Schommer originally hypothesized.

Like Schommer, Jehng (1991) took the position that people's beliefs about the nature of knowledge and learning comprise a set of relatively independent dimensions. He developed 51 items that were targeted toward assessing the following dimensions (all stated from the naive perspective): beliefs that knowledge is unchanging and thus can be known with certainty (Certainty of Knowledge); beliefs that knowledge is handed down by experts rather than self-constructed

(Omniscient Authority); beliefs that the learning process is regular, orderly, pre-scribed, and consists of passively accepting already formulated truths (Rigid Learning in Jehng's, 1991, dissertation and Orderly Process in the Jehng, Johnson, & Anderson, 1993, article); beliefs that the ability to learn is innate and fixed, rather than acquired (Innate Ability); and beliefs that learning is an immediate, quick process (Quick Learning). As in the Schommer 1990 study, the accuracy of Jehng's a priori assignment of each individual item to one of the five dimensions was judged by asking three faculty members in educational psychology to verify his item assignments. Based on their assessment, 86% of the items were judged to fit logically with the dimension to which they had been assigned.

In a later article based on his dissertation, Jehng et al. (1993) conducted a confirmatory factor analysis (CFA) of the survey of epistemological beliefs. Their work produced a 34-item, five-factor model of epistemological beliefs that they confirmed using LISREL (Joreskog & Sorbom, 1988). Again, what is important to note here is that Jehng et al. never attempted to verify their assignment of individual items to the five hypothesized dimensions by factor analyzing the individual items and verifying that they actually loaded on the factors to which they had been assigned a priori.

Purpose of the Present Study

Schommer's (1990) survey of epistemological beliefs has received considerable attention and use by researchers. Its appeal is no doubt due to a variety of different factors. First, its objective format allows for easy administration and scoring within a reasonable amount of time. Second, the idea of distinct dimensions of epistemological beliefs makes sense and is intuitively appealing. Third, several researchers have been able to demonstrate a relationship between scores on at least some of its factors and performance on various learning tasks. Much of this research utilizing Schommer's 63-item epistemological beliefs questionnaire has involved replication of her methodology, namely factoring of 12 subsets of the 63 items as variables, rather than factoring of the individual variables. Although such analyses have produced results that are fairly similar to hers (cf., Kardash & Scholes, 1996), factoring of the subsets has also revealed that many of the subsets fail to load cleanly on just one of her four factors.

During the past 10 years, one of the present authors has attempted to individually factor the items from both Schommer's and Jehng et al.'s (1993) surveys. Regardless of whose survey was used, the individual items consistently failed to load onto the factors to which they had been assigned a priori by either Schommer (1990) or by Jehng et al. (1993). Such empirical findings underscore Hofer and Pintrich's (1997) concern that "there are conceptual and measurement issues that remain unresolved" (p. 108) with respect to the Schommer survey. The primary measurement issue that they raise is that Schommer has factored only her 12 subsets of items—no individual factoring of the 63 items has ever been reported. In their view, "the absence of confirmatory factor analysis on the full slate of 63 items, not just the subsets of items, also raises doubts about the evidence presented for the substantive validity of the questionnaire. It is not clear from the factor analyses whether the full set of 63 items would actually load onto the four or five proposed factors because no item analysis has been reported, only factor analyses of the a priori subsets of items" (p. 110). This same criticism can be raised as well regarding Jehng's survey of epistemological beliefs (Jehng, 1991; Jehng et al., 1993).

The primary purpose of the present study was to assess the dimensions of personal epistemology as revealed by a factor analysis of the individual items of an 80-item self-report survey that included 58 of Schommer's 63 original items as well as the additional items developed by Jehng and his colleagues (Jehng, 1991; Jehng et al., 1993). Of particular interest was the question of whether the individual items would load onto the factors that they had been assigned a priori by Schommer and by Jehng. Additional research questions dealt with the investigation of correlations among the factors that emerged, and with the psychometric properties of scales formed on the basis of the factors. The factors were also used as a framework for investigation of the effects of gender and educational level on epistemological beliefs, since both of these variables have been reported to influence epistemological beliefs in previous studies (Jehng et al., 1993; Schommer, 1993; Schommer et al., 1997).

Method

Sample. A convenience sample of 793 students was comprised of 259 males (32.7%) and 519 females (65.4%) (15 participants declined to indicate their gender), ranging in age from 17 to 52, with a mean age of 22.35 ($SD = 4.68$). Regarding ethnicity, 636 respondents were Caucasian (80.2%), 40 were African American (5.0%), 26 were Asian (3.3%), 6 were Hispanic (0.8%), 3 were Native American (0.4%), and 15 listed their ethnicity as "other" (1.9%), and 67 declined to note their ethnicity. Educational levels represented were: 12 freshmen (1.5%), 205 sophomores (25.9%), 182 juniors (23.0%), 167 seniors (21.1%), 2 postbaccalaureate students (0.3%), 171 first-year medical students (21.6%), 16 master's students (2.0%), and 20 doctoral students (2.51%). (Sixteen students did not list an educational level.) Four-hundred and fifteen students (52.3%) were enrolled in the College of Education. The remaining divisions in which students were enrolled were: 200 (25.2%) in Arts and Sciences, 79 in Business (10.0%), 9 in Engineering (1.1%), 2 in the School of Human Environmental Sciences (0.3%), 6 (0.8%) in the School of Health-Related Professions, 1 (1.1%) in the School of Natural Resources, and 8 (1.0%) in the School of Nursing. Taken together, students represented 41 separate academic majors.

Scale Development. The 80-item questionnaire comprised 58 of Schommer's (1990) original 63-item epistemological beliefs questionnaire. Previous administrations of Schommer's 63-item questionnaire to samples of undergraduates by the second author of this chapter had revealed that the undergraduates consistently experienced difficulty answering two of the items from her subset "Avoid Integration," two items from the "Knowledge is Certain" subset, and one item from the "Seek Single Answers" subset. Student comments about these items indicated that they "didn't understand what the item meant" or found the items "unclear" or "ambiguous." Based on student comments, these five items were not included on the 80-item version of the questionnaire.

Twenty-nine of the items from Schommer's scale appeared in Jehng's (1991) survey as well. The 80-item questionnaire used in the present study thus contained 29 items that were common to both Schommer's and Jehng's scales, 29 items that appeared only on Schommer's scale, and 22 items that were unique to Jehng's scale. In addition, two faculty from education, who were instructed to be conservative with respect to making wording changes, were asked to review the items for clarity. As a result, slight changes were made to the wording of nine items. In one case, a substantial change was made to an item; We changed the item that asked how often a student consulted their parents to read: "Whenever I encounter difficulties in life, I consult someone with expertise in the area."

Similarly, of the 22 items that were unique to Jehng's questionnaire, we retained his exact wording for 19 items, and made slight wording changes to three items. Six of the 29 items common to both questionnaires were worded identically on both scales, and we retained this wording. For the remaining 23 items, the wording that was judged as "clearer" by both faculty members doing the rating was retained. Using this criterion, we chose Jehng's wording for 15 of the 23 items, Schommer's wording for 5 of the items, and wrote our own versions of three of the common items. As an example, Schommer's version of one of these three latter items was: "Students who are 'average' in school will remain 'average' for the rest of their lives." Jehng's version of the same item was: "Students who are mediocre in high school will remain mediocre in college." The rewritten version that we used in the present study was: "Students who are average scholastically in high school will likely remain average scholastically in college."

Procedures. Following procedures similar to those used by both Schommer (1990) and Jehng (1991), our participants were told that the 80 items were intended to discern their "opinions about learning and the nature of knowledge in your academic major (i.e., if you are a science major, your opinions about learning in science)" and that they should indicate the degree to which they agreed or disagreed with each statement using a 5-point Likert-type scale (1 = "strongly disagree," 3 = "unsure," 5 = "strongly agree"). Participants were given as much time as they needed to complete the survey. Consistent with Jehng et al. (1993), we later recoded the data so that high scores (agreement) would indicate more sophisticated (advanced) beliefs about learning.

Results

Factor Analysis of the 80-Item Instrument. Prior to factor-analyzing the data, we computed the internal consistency of the 80-item scale. Coefficient alpha was .83, with item-total correlations ranging from –.08 to .50. Six items had negative item-total correlations, and 10 had item-total correlations less than .10. These 16 items were eliminated from further analyses. We then re-ran the reliability for the 64-item scale, which yielded an alpha of .86.

Data were analyzed using the SPSS/PC statistical computing package (SPSS Inc., 1997). Principal axis factoring extraction was performed on the 64 items to estimate the factorability of the correlation matrix and to determine the maximum number of factors. The Kaiser-Meyer-Olkin measure of sampling adequacy was .85, indicating that factor analysis was appropriate for analysis of the data.

Although eighteen factors met the Kaiser–Guttman retention criteria of eigenvalues greater than unity, inspection of the scree plot indicated one large factor with an eigenvalue of 7.54, two factors with eigenvalues of 3.89 and 2.73, and two smaller factors with eigenvalues of 1.91 and 1.83, respectively. The remaining 13 factors had eigenvalues ranging from 1.46 to 1.02. Both the size of the eigenvalues and the scree plot appeared consonant with a five-factor solution, and we used principal axis factoring to examine the factor structure of this solution.

Five-Factor Solution. The five-factor solution accounted for a total of 22.05% of the variance after extraction, and appeared to reproduce the correlation matrix well (201 [9%] of the nonredundant residuals had an absolute value greater than .05). Factor analyses under maximum likelihood, principal components, and generalized least squares extractions with Promax rotation for the five-factor solution yielded a roughly similar pattern of rotated factor patterns. Thirty-eight of the 64 items met our criteria of loading at least .35 with minimal overlap (< .25) on any other factor. Thirty-one of these items were identical to those items that loaded in the three-factor solution described earlier. When the maximum likelihood five-factor solution was subjected to varimax, oblimin, and quartimax rotations, the same general pattern of loadings was found as under the Promax rotation. The only difference (as mentioned previously) was that the factor structure appeared to be somewhat simpler under the oblique rotations than under the orthogonal extractions. Based on this, we concluded that the five-factor solution was stable across both various extraction and rotation techniques. Factor loadings after Promax rotation, communalities, eigenvalues, and percentage of variance accounted for by each factor after extraction appear in Table 12.1. One observation of the number of items in each factor is that the items in the instrument appear to sample the first three factors well, with a relatively smaller number of items reflected in the last two factors. Our description and interpretation for each factor follows.

TABLE 12.1

Eigenvalues, Percent Variance Explained, Factor Loadings and Communalities for Items from Schommer and Jehng et al.'s Epistemological Beliefs Surveys: Promax Rotation of Principal Factors[a].

Items	Factor 1 Speed of Knowledge Acquisition	Factor 2 Structure of Knowledge	Factor 3 Knowledge Construction and Modification	Factor 4 Characteristics of Successful Students	Factor 5 Attainability of Objective Truth	h^2 Communality
Factor 1: Speed of Knowledge Acquisition						
Usually, if you are ever going to understand something, it will make sense to you the first time. (R)	.70	—	-.14	—	.12	.44
If something can be learned, it will be learned immediately. (R)	.65	—	—	—	.15	.39
You will just get confused if you try to integrate new ideas in a textbook with knowledge you already have about a topic. (R)	.50	.11	—	—	—	.30
Almost all the information you can understand from a textbook you will get during the first reading. (R)	.49	—	—	—	—	.18
Working on a difficult problem for an extended period of time only pays off for really smart students. (R)	.49	—	—	.15	—	.36
The information we learn in school is certain and unchanging. (R)	.40	—	.14	—	.17	.23
If I can't understand something quickly, it usually means I will never understand it. (R)	.37	—	—	.23	-.12	.34
Most words have one clear meaning. (R)	.37	—	.14	—	.19	.21
Eigenvalue 7.54						
Variance Explained 10.63%						

Factor 2: Structure of Knowledge

Item					
I like information to be presented in a straightforward fashion; I don't like having to read between the lines. (R)	−.32	.64	—	.14	—	.41
If professors would stick more to the facts and do less theorizing, one could get more out of college. (R)	.14	.53	.13	—	—	.39
It is annoying to listen to lecturers who cannot seem to make their mind up as to what they really believe. (R)	—	.48	—	−.16	—	.23
I really appreciate instructors who organize their lectures carefully and then stick to their plan. (R)	−.18	.44	—	—	—	.20
When I study, I look for the specific facts. (R)	−.12	.41	—	—	.12	.20
It's a waste of time to work on problems that have no possibility of coming out with a clear-cut answer. (R)	.20	.41	.15	—	—	.30
When I learn, I prefer to make things, as simple as possible. (R)	−.12	.41	—	.12	—	.16
The best thing about science courses is that most problems have only one right answer. (R)	—	.39	—	—	.11	.21
It is difficult to learn from a textbook unless you start at the beginning and master one section at a time. (R)	.33	.38	−.12	−.12	—	.25
I don't like movies that don't have a clear-cut ending	—	.37	—	—	—	.16
A good teacher's job is to keep students from wandering from the right track. (R)	—	.35	−.12	—	.16	.20

Eigenvalue 3.89
Variance Explained 4.87%

TABLE 12.1
(Continued)

Items	Factor 1 Speed of Knowledge Acquisition	Factor 2 Structure of Knowledge	Factor 3 Knowledge Construction and Modification	Factor 4 Characteristics of Successful Students	Factor 5 Attainability of Objective Truth	h^2 Communality
Factor 3: Knowledge Construction and Modification						
Today's facts may be tomorrow's fiction.	—	—	.47	−.21	.17	.24
Wisdom is not knowing the answers, but knowing how to find the answers.	—	−.15	.46	—	—	.24
Even advice from experts should be questioned.	.17	—	.46	−.22	.15	.27
A sentence has little meaning unless you know the situation in which it was spoken.	—	—	.43	−.11	.11	.18
Forming your own ideas is more important than learning what the textbooks say.	−.29	.11	.43	.13	.16	.19
I try my best to combine information across chapters or even across classes.	—	—	.43	—	−.13	.27
I find it refreshing to think about issues that experts can't agree on.	−.13	.42	.42	—	—	.34
A really good way to understand a text-book is to reorganize the information according to your own personal scheme.	—	—	.41	—	—	.17
The most important part of scientific work is original thinking.	−.16	—	.41	—	—	.16
The only thing that is certain is uncertainty itself.	−.17	—	.38	—	.15	.12
You should evaluate the accuracy of information in textbooks if you are familiar with the topic.	.15	—	.32	−.12	—	.17
Eigenvalue			2.73			
Variance Explained			3.11%			

Factor 4: Characteristics of Successful Students

Being a good student generally involves memorizing a lot of facts. (R)	-.16	.12	—	.49	.19	.24
Successful students understand things quickly. (R)	.15	—	-.22	.47	—	.30
The really smart students don't have to work hard to do well in school. (R)	—	—	—	.44	—	.22
Understanding main ideas is easy for good students. (R)	—	.11	-.13	.42	.11	.23
Some people are born good learners; others are just stuck with a limited ability.	—	—	—	.39	—	.18
Eigenvalue				1.91		
Variance Explained				1.78%		

Factor 5: Attainability of Objective Truth

Scientists can ultimately get to the truth. (R)	—	—	—	.16	.56	.34
If scientists try hard enough, they can find the answer to almost every question. (R)	—	—	—	.16	.46	.29
You can believe most things you read. (R)	—	—	.13	—	.36	.19
Eigenvalue					1.83	
Variance Explained					1.66%	

[a] Factor loadings with absolute values < .10 are indicated by —.

Inspection of the rotated solution in Table 12.1 reveals that the eight items assigned to Factor 1 generally tap beliefs about the process of learning, with an emphasis on the time it takes for learning to occur. We chose to label this factor "Speed of Knowledge Acquisition." Four items are from Schommer's (1990) Learning is Quick subset, and a fifth item is from her Learn the First Time subset. The other three items comprising this factor came from Schommer's Avoid Integration, Knowledge is Certain, and Seek Single Answers subsets. Low scores on this factor represent the view that learning is a quick, "all or nothing," fairly straightforward process, while high scores represent the idea that learning is a complex, gradual process requiring both time and effort.

Factor 2 deals with participants' perceived "Structure of Knowledge" and contains 11 items. Low scores on this factor represent a view that knowledge is composed of discrete, unambiguous pieces of information, while high scores represent the view that knowledge is often complex, interrelated, and ambiguous, with the implication that sometimes there is no "one right answer."

Factor 3 was labeled "Knowledge Construction and Modification" (10 items). This factor reflected participants' awareness that knowledge can be acquired and modified through strategies such as integrating information from various sources, reorganizing information according to a personal scheme, questioning information, and recognizing the tentativeness of information. High scores on this factor reflect the idea that knowledge is constantly evolving, is actively and personally constructed, and should be subjected to questioning. By contrast, low scores on this factor reflect a view that knowledge is certain, passively received, and accepted at face value.

Factor 4 consisted of only five items dealing with "Characteristics of Successful Students." This factor included items from the following Schommer (1990) subsets: Avoid Integration, Learning is Quick, Success is Unrelated to Hard Work, and Ability to Learn is Innate. (Four of the five items appeared on both the Schommer and Jehng et al., 1993, scales, although those researchers assigned the items to their Orderly Process, Quick Learning, and Innate Ability scales.) Although some of the items comprising this factor are similar to those that loaded on Schommer's (1990) Innate Ability factor, Factor 4 also included beliefs about the speed of acquisition of learning and the structure of knowledge. Low scores on this factor represent the view that successful students are "born that way," that they can understand main ideas and memorize facts easily, and that they accomplish learning tasks quickly and with little effort. By contrast, high scores on this factor reflect a rejection of the view that the ability to learn is innate; rather, successful students are characterized by their recognition that learning takes time and effort.

Factor 5, labeled "Attainability of Truth," comprises three items from two of Schommer's subsets: Knowledge is Certain and Don't Criticize Authority. (Again, two of these items appeared as well on the Jehng et al., 1993, survey and were assigned to the Certainty of Knowledge and Omniscient Authority scales.) Low scores on this factor represent the view that there is an objective truth that can be known if scientists try hard enough to find it. High scores on this represent a rejection of the notions of objective truth and "single right answers," and a skepticism concerning the veridicality of information that one reads. Interestingly, this factor emerged in a recent similar factor analysis of epistemological beliefs (Hofer, 2000). Factor correlations for the Promax rotation are given in Table 12.2. Of interest in this pattern of correlations is the finding that the Speed of Knowledge Acquisition, Knowledge Construction and Modification, and Characteristics of Successful Students factors were substantially related. Correlations with the Attainability of Objective Truth factor were somewhat lower.

Correlations of Scale Scores and Academic Indices.   Table 12.2 also displays the observed correlations among factor scores on the five epistemological belief factors and their relationships to participants' self-reported ACT scores and college GPAs. In general, the pattern of observed correlations between factor scores is similar to the estimated correlations between factors in the Promax rotation. the only exception to this is the correlation between the Speed of Knowledge Acquisition factor and Characteristics of Successful Students, where the observed correlation (.60) is higher than the Promax rotation (.49). This discrepancy is probably due to the presence of more factorially complex items for the Characteristics of Successful Students factor. Interestingly, all factors with the exception of Attainability of Objective Truth are positively and significantly associated with academic aptitude, as measured by self-reported ACT scores. By contrast, only the Speed of Knowledge Acquisition and Structure of Knowledge factors are associated positively with general academic achievement, as measured by college GPAs.

To determine whether epistemological beliefs predicted academic performance over and above that accounted for by ACT scores, we regressed students' GPAs on ACT and epistemological beliefs using sequential regression and entering ACT scores into the equation first. The squared multiple correlation coefficient for the entire model was .46, $F (6, 412) = 18.53, p < .001$. After Step 1, with ACT scores in the equation, $R^2 = .17$, $F_{inc} (1, 417) = 87.02, p < .001$. After Step 2, with the five epistemological belief factor scores added to the model, $R^2 = .21$(adjusted $R^2 = .20$), $F_{inc} (5, 412) = 4.17, p < .001$. ACT scores and participants' factor scores on Speed of Knowledge Acquisition, Characteristics of Successful Students, Attainability of Objective Truth, and Knowledge Construction and Modification accounted for statistically significant variance percentages of 12%, 4%, 1%, 1%, and 1% respectively, as indicated by the squared, semipartial correlations. Based on this, the strongest individual contribution to the prediction of academic performance appears to be the Speed of Knowledge acquisition scale.

TABLE 12.2

Correlations Between Five Epistemological Belief Factors, Self-Reported ACT Scores, and College GPA[a]

Variables	Speed of Knowledge Acquisition	Structure of Knowledge	Knowledge Construction and Modification	Characteristics of Successful Students	Attainability of Objective Truth	Self-Reported ACT scores
Speed of Knowledge Acquisition	—					
Structure of Knowledge	.29**[b] .25[c]	—				
Knowledge Construction and Modification	.49** .42	.13** .10	—			
Characteristics of Successful Students	.60** .49	.16** .11	.34** .26	—		
Attainability of Objective Truth	.04 .00	.28** .22	-.22** -.18	-.07 -.10	—	
Self-Reported ACT scores	.26**	.32**	.28**	.10*[d]	-.06	—
College GPA	.25**	.14**	.08	.07	-.05	.42**

[a] Correlations among the five-scale scores are based on $N = 793$. Correlations between five-scale-scores and ACT scores and GPA are based on $n = 423$ and $n = 436$, respectively.
[b] $** p < .001$, two-tailed.
[c] Second entry denotes correlation between factors from Promax rotation.
[d] $* p < .05$, two-tailed.

Summary Statistics for the Five Scales. We computed scale scores for each of the five factors by summing and taking the mean of only those items that loaded clearly on each factor. We next calculated the internal consistency for each scale. Alpha coefficients for the Speed of Knowledge Acquisition, Structure of Knowledge, Knowledge Construction and Modification, Characteristics of Successful Students, and Attainability of Objective Truth scales were .74, .72, .66, .58, and .54, respectively. Item-total correlations were also fairly high, however, it should be noted that internal consistency is lower for the two factors composed of only five and three items.

Differences in Epistemological Beliefs as a Function of Sex and Educational Level. We next examined whether men and women differed on the five epistemological beliefs scales and whether differences existed as a function of educational level (see Table 12.3). Twenty of the participants declined to indicate either their gender or educational level on the survey, and these individuals were eliminated from these analyses. We also elected to collapse the educational level variable in order to secure a more balanced general linear models design. For the remaining 258 male and 515 female participants, we elected to group freshmen and sophomores together as "underclassmen;" and to combine seniors, postbaccalaureate students, and first-year medical students as "seniors" after separate analyses with seniors and medical students revealed no significant differences between the two groups on any of the scales. Masters and doctoral students were combined as "graduate students." Thus, "educational level" had four levels: underclassmen ($n = 216$), juniors ($n = 182$), seniors ($n = 339$), and graduate students ($n = 36$).

These data were entered into a 2 (Gender) $\times$ 4 (Educational Level) $\times$ 5 (Scale) repeated measures general linear model. A significant main effect was found for Educational Level, $F(3, 765) = 3.83$, $p < .01$ (eta squared = .02), as well as interactions involving Gender $\times$ Scale, $F(3.54, 2708.06) = 6.65$, $p < .001$ (eta squared = .01), Educational Level $\times$ Scales, $(10.62, 2708.06) = 2.68$, $p < .01$ (eta squared = .01), Gender $\times$ Educational Level $\times$ Scales interactions, and Educational Level $\times$ Scales, $(10.62, 2708.06) = 2.39$, $p < .01$ (eta squared = .01). A significant but conceptually uninteresting main effect was also found for Scale. (Degrees of freedom were adjusted using the Greenhouse–Geisser correction.)

Posthoc analyses of simple effects on the three-way interaction was conducted looking at the effects of gender on the five factors for each separate educational level. All posthoc analyses were conducted using the Bonferroni adjustment for multiple comparisons. Separate variance t-tests are reported for any comparisons for which the equality of variances assumption was violated.

For underclassmen, males scored significantly higher than did females on the Structure of Knowledge ($t(214) = 2.67$, $p < .01$), and Knowledge Construction and Modification scales ($t(214) = 2.37$, $p < .05$). By contrast, females scored

TABLE 12.3

Means and Standard Deviations for the Five Epistemological Beliefs Scales as a Function of Sex and Educational Level.

Educational Level / Sex	Factor 1 Speed of Knowledge Acquisition		Factor 2 Structure of Knowledge		Factor 3 Knowledge Construction and Modification		Factor 4 Characteristics of Successful Students		Factor 5 Attainability of Objective Truth	
	Mean	Standard Deviation	Mean	Standard Deviation	Mean	Standard Deviation	Mean	Standard Deviation	Mean	Standard Deviation
Underclassmen (Freshmen & Sophomores) (N = 216)										
Males (N = 43)	3.97	0.68	2.71	0.55	3.89	0.42	3.05	0.79	3.41	0.64
Females (N = 173)	4.22	0.46	2.47	0.52	3.71	0.43	3.36	0.71	3.61	0.75
Juniors (N = 182)										
Males (N = 43)	4.12	0.48	2.64	0.59	3.94	0.40	3.17	0.75	3.32	0.95
Females (N = 139)	4.29	0.54	2.65	0.54	3.71	0.45	3.30	0.76	3.54	0.81
Seniors (Seniors, Postbac, Beg. Medical) (N = 339)										
Males (N = 163)	4.18	0.52	2.71	0.55	3.79	0.46	2.98	0.72	3.51	0.80
Females (N = 176)	4.44	0.41	2.77	0.55	3.91	0.47	3.35	0.73	3.54	0.69
Graduate Students (Masters & Ph.D.) (N = 36)										
Males (N = 9)	4.36	0.38	3.27	0.79	4.18	0.43	3.24	0.47	3.33	0.69
Females (N = 27)	4.14	0.79	3.01	0.75	4.12	0.48	3.47	0.59	3.65	0.83

significantly higher than males on the Speed of Knowledge Acquisition (t (52.13) = −2.21, p < .05), and Characteristics of Successful Students scales (t (214) = −2.51, p < .05). Generally, the magnitude of these differences is similar, ranging from roughly .4–.5 of a standard deviation.

For juniors, males again scored significantly higher than did females on the Knowledge Construction and Modification scale (t (180) = 3.04, p < .01), performing, on average .55 of a standard deviation higher than females. Females continued to score higher than did males on the Speed of Knowledge Acquisition scale, although the effect size for this comparison was lower (.34 of a standard deviation) and was only marginally significant (p = .06).

For seniors, females scored significantly higher than did males on the Speed of Knowledge Acquisition (t (307.78) = −5.12, p < .001), Characteristics of Successful Students scales (t (337) = −4.71, p < .001), and Knowledge Construction and Modification (t (337) = −2.26, p < .05). The magnitude of this difference was .54 and .51 of a standard deviation for the first two scales, and .26 for the third.

In sum, the sex differences associated with Speed of Knowledge Acquisition appeared to consistently favor women across all educational levels, while the Structure of Knowledge and Knowledge Construction and Modification scales favored men, but only during the early college years.

Male and female graduate students did not differ as a function of gender on any of the five scales, although, in light of the discussion of statistical power earlier in this chapter, this could be due to the smaller sample size associated with this group.

Additionally, we also wished to explore the degree to which the observed educational level differences and gender differences could be attributed to differences in general academic aptitude as measured by self-reported ACT composite. To this end, we conducted an analysis of covariance for the data mentioned earlier. We chose to exclude graduate student data because several graduate students did not report their ACT composite scores. When this covariate was included, however, the main effect for educational level was no longer significant (F = 1.58; p > .2), meaning that no significant differences in educational level were found after adjusting scores for general verbal ability. Although a reasonable skeptic of epistemological beliefs could reasonably argue that this analysis showed that observed differences in epistemological beliefs are due to general academic aptitude differences, we also note that the interaction of educational level and scale remained significant. Posthoc follow-up tests for such an interaction revealed that the Speed of Knowledge Acquisition, Structure of Knowledge, and Knowledge Construction and Modification scales means were different across educational levels, while performance on the Characteristics of Successful Students and Attainability of Objective Truth was no longer significantly different across the groups. The sex main effect, interaction of gender and scale, as well as the gender by educational level by scale interaction all remained significant. Generally, the effect of the covariate on adjusted scores was to reduce, but not eliminate the differences between freshmen men and women while accentuating sex differences between men and women for the junior and senior groups.

Discussion

Our factoring of the individual items from Schommer's (1990) and Jehng et al.'s surveys of epistemological beliefs support these investigator's contention that epistemological beliefs are multidimensional. This conclusion is further supported by the observed education level by sex by scale interaction, meaning that the pattern of means is significantly different for men and women across the educational levels examined. The finding that some of the factors are poorly sampled in existing instruments points to the need for the development of additional items in these areas in order to successfully replicate the factor structure proposed here and to yield more internally consistent scales reflecting these constructs. Furthermore, there appears to be support for the notion that epistemological beliefs are related to student success, as measured by undergraduate GPA above and beyond student academic aptitude.

On the other hand, these analyses raise several questions as well. First, the magnitude of observed differences in epistemological belief is somewhat smaller than has been found for other measures of epistemological reasoning such as the Reflective Judgment Interview (King & Kitchener, chap. 3, this volume). Generally, such research has found a one standard deviation improvement in critical thinking ability, if one adopts the standard deviation of the freshman sample as a reference group (Pascarella & Terenzini, 1991). The magnitude of differences between underclassmen and seniors for the epistemic beliefs measured here is somewhat lower: The Structure of Knowledge Factor yielded a .40 standard deviation improvement, while the Speed of Knowledge Acquisition, Knowledge Construction and Modification, and Characteristics of Successful Students factors yielded .29, .23 and .17 standard deviation differences, respectively. The Attainability of Objective Truth factor had only a .06 standard deviation difference between freshmen and undergraduates.

Given the rather limited scope of this study, some consideration of third-variable explanations for these educational level differences is appropriate. Given that academic attrition is significant and high over the course of undergraduate study, it may be that such cross-sectional findings of educational level differences merely reflect motivational and intellectual characteristics of individuals who persist in college, or who differentially elect to participate in research across educational levels. It could be that these differences reflect some personality construct that develops during college. For example, a separate study of the development of need for cognition in undergraduate students reveals an approximately one-half standard deviation difference between freshmen and seniors (Wood,

Pearson, & Conner, 1999). Alternatively, this finding could mean that sophistication in epistemological beliefs are merely a part of the general increase in general intelligence resulting from collegiate study. Some caution is also obviously appropriate for the claim that general increase in epistemological beliefs given that educational level differences were not found after adjusting scores for general academic aptitude. As a result, it seems appropriate to conclude that the five scales described here are not facets of one underlying continuum of epistemic sophistication and that therefore a MANOVA approach is inappropriate. Another approach, of course, is to abandon the factors that do not yield educational level differences.

Similarly, although it is heartening to find that the two scales that yielded the highest freshman/senior difference, Speed of Knowledge Acquisition and Structure of Knowledge, also correlate with a measure of academic performance, some caution seems in order given possible third-variable explanations for the association. It seems reasonable to believe that all three variables are likely related to general personality characteristics (such as conscientiousness, perseverance, or need for cognition). This seems especially true for the Structure of Knowledge factor, which, although reflecting an epistemological position, also asks the student to indicate what they "like," "appreciate," "prefer," or "find annoying." It would seem reasonable to infer that this scale also includes some component of motivational or personality constructs in addition to epistemic beliefs. Future researchers wishing to use instruments such as these will want to include motivational and personality variables in addition to general academic aptitude to address these alternative interpretations.

Other Issues in Evaluation of Factor Analytic Models

Space does not permit an extensive discussion of other issues in the design and evaluation of factor analytic models of epistemic cognition, but these issues are critical to a full evaluation. First, many items in such scales may share common method variance or may otherwise demonstrate a pattern of "correlated measurement error." For example, items that ask the student to rate the expertise of a classroom instructor may obviously be correlated due to factors related to the evaluation of the instructor and may not reflect the epistemic cognition of the student per se. It is possible to specify such correlated errors in subsequent confirmatory factor models to test the degree to which correlated measurement errors lead to an overestimate of the factor loadings associated with such items.

Given that the items from this survey ask the student to rate various aspects of the educational experience, caution must be exercised in making the inference that observed differences between students at different educational levels or in different curricular contexts actually reflect different levels of complexity in epistemic cognition. For example, if an item that asks students whether "memorizing facts" is a good way to succeed in college demonstrates differences between students from different academic disciplines, we cannot be sure that this reflects on the actual complexity of students' reasoning, given that the classroom experiences of students are quite different, and memorizing may be more closely linked to success in, say, mathematics than it is in curriculum design. Although this is acknowledged by many researchers in their discussion of individual items, the point is somewhat neglected in general conclusions regarding disciplinary effects. The "problem" may well be in our curriculum and grading policies and not reflect students' reasoning ability.

Finally, structural models, both confirmatory and exploratory, make the assumption that we know that the directionality of causation between manifest variables and factors. This may not be the case and statistical models that consider alternative causal structures may, in fact, improve model fit. Although space does not permit an extensive discussion of this point, several new tools are being developed that allow researchers to generate plausible alternative models for their data. Given the size and scope of many studies of epistemology and the several alternative models that can be generated, one is often left with the feeling that there may be another reasonable alternative model out there that hasn't been considered. The Tetrad project has been a particularly promising statistical model and computer program for exploring such possibilities (see Wood, 1995; 1998, for a more extended discussion and application to structural equation models).

Although research in epistemic cognition has been the object of much theoretical interest and research, the fact still remains that this area remains largely underreported to the broader psychological and educational community. This situation can be improved, we feel, through improved design of research to detect the differences of interest. We also believe that some of this situation may be improved by demonstrating that epistemic cognition is distinct from other, more familiar constructs. Finally, some of the proof of the conceptual pudding may lie in demonstrating the distinct component that epistemic cognitions play in performance. The statistical tools to accomplish this are far from "single correct approaches" to the research hypotheses at hand. Given that researchers in this area wish to promote a more nuanced complex reasoning ability in our students that anticipates and integrates the multiple perspectives, it seems reasonable to expect no less from our own research designs.

REFERENCES

Anderson, J. C. & Gerbing, D. W. (1984). The effect of sampling error on convergence, improper solutions, and goodness-of-fit indices for maximum likelihood confirmatory factor analysis. *Psychometrika, 49,* 155–173.

Cacioppo, J. T., Petty, R. E., Feinstein, J. A., & Jarvis, W. B. G. (1996). Dispositional differences in cognitive motivation: The life and times of individuals varying in need for cognition. *Psychological Bulletin, 119,* 197–253.

Cattell, R. B. (1966). The scree test for the number of factors. *Multivariate Behavioral Research, 1,* 245–276.

Cohen, J. (1988). *Statistical power analysis for the behavioral sciences. 2nd ed.* Hillsdale, NJ: Erlbaum.

Conner, J. & Wood, P. K. (1999). Power considerations in the design of assessment research. Available on the World Wide Web at: http://www.missouri.edu/~wood.

Hendrickson, A. E., & White, P. O. (1964). Promax: A quick method for rotation to oblique simple structure. *British Journal of Mathematical and Statistical Psychology, 17,* 65–70.

Hofer, B. K. (2000). Dimensionality and disciplinary differences in personal epistemology. *Contemporary Educational Psychology, 25,* 378–405.

Hofer, B. K., & Pintrich, P. R. (1997). The development of epistemological theories: Beliefs about knowledge and knowing and their relation to learning. *Review of Educational Research, 67,* 88–140.

Jehng, J. J. (1991). *The nature of epistemological beliefs about learning.* Unpublished doctoral dissertation, University of Illinois, Urbana-Champaign.

Jehng, J. J., Johnson, S. D., & Anderson, R. C. (1993). Schooling and students' epistemological beliefs. *Contemporary Educational Psychology, 18,* 23–35.

Joreskog K. G., & Sorbom O. (1988). *LISREL 7: A guide to the program and applications,* Chicago: SPSS.

Kaiser, H. F. (1958). The varimax criterion for analytic rotation in factor analysis. *Psychometrika, 23,* 187–200.

Kaiser, H. F. & Madow, W. G. (1974, March). The KD method for the transformation problem in exploratory factor analysis. Paper presented at the meeting of the Psychometric Society, Palo Alto, CA.

Kardash, C. A. M. & Scholes, R. J. (1996). Effects of preexisting beliefs, epistemological beliefs, and need for cognition on interpretation of controversial issues. *Journal of Educational Psychology, 88,* 260–271.

King, P. M. & Kitchener, K. S. (1994). *Developing Reflective Judgment: Understanding and promoting intellectual growth and critical thinking in adolescents and adults.* San Francisco: Jossey-Bass.

Kronholm, M. (1996). The impact of developmental instruction on reflective judgment. *Review of Higher Education, 19,* 199–225.

Loehlin (1992). *Latent variable models. 2nd. ed.* Hillsdale, NJ: Erlbaum.

Marsh, H. W., Hau, K. T., Balla, J. R., & Grayson, D. (1998). Is more ever too much? The number of indicators per factor in confirmatory factor analysis. *Multivariate Behavioral Research, 33,* 181–220.

Neuhaus, J. O. & Wrigley, C. (1954). The quartimax method: An analytic approach to orthogonal simple structure. *British Journal of Statistical Psychology, 7,* 81–91.

Pascarella, E. & Terenzini, P. (1991). *How college affects students: Findings and insights from twenty years of research.* San Francisco: Jossey-Bass.

Schmid, J. & Leiman, J. M. (1957). The development of hierarchical factor solutions. *Psychometrika, 22,* 53–61.

Schommer, M. (1990). Effects of beliefs about the nature of knowledge on comprehension. *Journal of Educational Psychology, 82,* 498–504.

Schommer, M. (1993). Epistemological development and academic performance among secondary students. *Journal of Educational Psychology, 85,* 406–411.

Schommer, M., Calvert, C., Gariglietti, G., & Bajaj, A. (1997). The development of epistemological beliefs among secondary students: A longitudinal study. *Journal of Educational Psychology, 89,* 37–40.

Schommer, M., Crouse, A., & Rhodes, N. (1992). Epistemological beliefs and mathematical text comprehension: Believing it is simple does not make it so. *Journal of Educational Psychology, 84,* 435–443.

Sher, K. J. & Wood, P. K. (1997). Methodological issues in conducting prospective research on alcohol-related behavior: A report from the field. In K. Bryant, M. Windle, & S. G. West (Eds.) *New methodological approaches to alcoholism prevention research.* (pp. 3–41). Washington DC: APA.

SPSS (1997). *SPSS Version 7 Users' Manual.* Chicago: SPSS.

Wood, P. K. (1995). Toward a more critical examination of structural models: A review of Tetrad II. *Structural Equation Modeling, 2,* 277–287.

Wood, P. K. (1997). A secondary analysis of claims regarding the Reflective Judgment interview: Internal consistency, sequentiality and intraindividual differences in ill-structured problem solving. *Higher Education: Handbook of theory and research.* (pp. 245–314) Edison, NJ: Agathon.

Wood, P. K. (1998). Response to "The TETRAD project: Constraint based aids to causal model specification." *Multivariate Behavioral Research, 33,* 149–156.

Wood, P. K., Pearson, M., & Conner, J. (1999). Need for cognition as an affective outcome measure of higher education: Differences by ethnicity, sex, and academic achievement, manuscript in preparation.

13

Development and Validation of the Epistemic Belief Inventory (EBI)

Gregory Schraw
University of Nebraska at Lincoln

Lisa D. Bendixen
University of Nevada, Las Vegas

Michael E. Dunkle
The Gallup Organization

Introduction

This chapter examines adults' beliefs about the nature and acquisition of knowledge, or epistemic beliefs. Our main goal is to describe the development of an epistemic beliefs scale modeled after Schommer's (1990) four-factor instrument. Previous research has linked epistemic beliefs to a variety of cognitive tasks, including moral and argumentative reasoning (Bendixen, Schraw, & Dunkle, 1998; Kuhn, 1991; Walker, Rowland, & Boyes, 1991), reflective judgment (Kitchener & King, 1981), cognitive development (Benack & Basseches, 1989; Chandler, Boyes, & Ball, 1990), and reading comprehension (Cunningham & Fitzgerald, 1996). These studies suggest two general outcomes. One is that it is possible to measure different epistemic beliefs. A second is that these beliefs are related to thinking, problem solving, and reasoning in important ways.

This chapter reports on the ongoing validation of the Epistemic Beliefs Inventory (EBI). We first summarize two core issues in recent research and provide a theoretical and methodological overview of our research, then describe the development of the EBI. We also compare the EBI to the Epistemological

Questionnaire (EQ) developed by Schommer (1990). We discuss our findings with respect to implications for future instrument development. Last, we discuss several limitations of the present research.

Theoretical and Methodological Issues

Researchers investigating epistemic beliefs have encountered two main problems thus far. The first is identifying an exhaustive yet concise set of epistemic beliefs. The second is developing a reliable and valid measure of these beliefs. The present research focuses primarily on the latter problem; however, it is important to say a little about the former. Interest in epistemic beliefs has been strong since William Perry's initial work in the 1970s (Perry, 1970). Since then a number of epistemic beliefs have been proposed and a number of conceptual frameworks have been developed to investigate and explain these beliefs. Many of these conceptual frameworks are reviewed by Hofer and Pintrich (1997). However, one framework has been especially important in recent research. Schommer described five beliefs pertaining to Certain Knowledge (i.e., absolute knowledge exists and will eventually be known), Simple Knowledge (i.e., knowledge consists of discrete facts), Omniscient Authority (i.e., authorities have access to otherwise inaccessible knowledge), Quick Learning (i.e., learning occurs in a quick or not-at-all fashion), and Innate Ability (i.e., the ability to acquire knowledge is endowed at birth). Currently, there is debate as to whether Schommer's five beliefs constitute genuine epistemological dimensions (Hofer & Pintrich, 1997), but especially the omniscient authority and innate ability dimensions.

Regarding the second problem, Schommer (1990, 1993) conducted a number of studies over the last decade measuring a variety of epistemic beliefs using a 63-item paper-and-pencil instrument. Schommer (1990) found factor-analytic evidence for four of the five beliefs, but failed to identify an omniscient authority factor. This exclusion is important given that researchers have postulated a relationship between beliefs about authority and skilled reasoning (cf. Curtis, Billingslea, & Wilson, 1988; Damon, 1988; Jehng, Johnson, & Anderson, 1993; Perry, 1970; Presley, 1985). In more recent studies, Schommer (1990) and Kardash and Scholes (1996) found that epistemic beliefs (e.g., Certain Knowledge and Quick Learning) were related to text understanding. Schommer, Crouse, and Rhodes (1992) reported that beliefs in simple knowledge negatively affected complex problem solving. As beliefs in complex, incremental knowledge increased, problem solving improved.

Rationale for the Present Research

The present research was intended to expand and refine previous work on epistemic beliefs. We did so in two ways. One way was to construct an instrument that measures the five epistemic beliefs described by Schommer (1990). Our goal was to develop an instrument that was shorter, measured all five hypothesized beliefs, and was more reliable than other instruments. A second way was to examine the relationship among epistemic beliefs and previously unmeasured outcome variables such as moral reasoning (Bendixen, Schraw, & Dunkle, 1998) and well-defined and ill-defined problem solving (Schraw, Dunkle, & Bendixen, 1995).

We constructed the Epistemic Beliefs Inventory (EBI) to measure adults' beliefs about Certain Knowledge, Simple Knowledge, Quick Learning, Omniscient Authority, and Innate Ability. Previous studies have failed to report an omniscient authority factor using the EQ. In addition, several pilot studies comparing the EQ and EBI yielded a variety of factors on the EQ. One possible explanation is that Schommer (1990) and Schommer et al. (1992) analyzed the EQ after first creating 12 parcels (i.e., theoretically based subsets of items). Parcelling items prior to analysis may have a dramatic impact on observed factor solutions (Hall, Snell, & Foust, 1999).

Construction of the EBI was guided by several objectives. One was to construct an instrument in which all of the items fit unambiguously into one of five categories that corresponded to the five hypothesized epistemic dimensions. This should lead to relatively high item-to-factor loadings for each item in the ensuing factor analysis. We did so by creating a large pool of items, reducing and revising that pool, and revising items further using empirical feedback. A second objective was to yield an omniscient authority factor as part of our solution and to relate this factor to cognitive outcome measures. Several previous studies have reported that beliefs about authority are related to comprehension and decision making (Curtis et al., 1988; Presley, 1985), although Schommer (1990, 1993) failed to report this factor. For this reason, we included the EQ in the present validation study to determine whether the EQ and EBI differed in their ability to yield an omniscient authority factor. A third objective was to produce an instrument that was more efficient than the EQ. Specifically, by creating more homogeneous factors, it should be possible to explain a greater proportion of sample variation with half the items of the EQ, as well as demonstrate a higher level of criterion validity (Hofer & Pintrich, 1997).

Empirical Predictions

We made several predictions regarding the EQ and EBI. First, we predicted the EBI would yield the five factors hypothesized previously. Each of these factors was expected to include four or five items that had item-to-factor loadings in excess of .40. We expected the EQ to yield more than five factors with eigenvalues greater than 1 (i.e., the traditional minimal cutpoint for interpreting a factor) when all 63 items were entered into the analysis individually rather than as parcels. It is important to note that this procedure does not replicate Schommer's strategy, but reflects common factor-analytic practice.

Our second prediction was that the EBI would explain more of the total sample variation in the data space than the EQ, and at least 50% of the total sample variation. The primary reason for this prediction is that all items on the EBI were expected to load on the five specified factors. In contrast, a number of items on the EQ were expected to load on factors other than the five epistemic factors proposed by Schommer (1990).

Our third prediction was that the EBI would demonstrate better predictive validity than the EQ when composite scale scores were used to predict a measure of reading comprehension. Specifically, we expected each of the five hypothesized factors on the EBI to explain unique variation in reading comprehension.

Our fourth prediction is that the EBI would have equal or better reliability compared to the EQ during initial testing and at retest. We expected the EBI to replicate its factor structure using retest data at a one-month interval. We expected poorer fitting replication data from the EQ, in part due to the larger number of factors it would yield.

Validation of the Epistemic Belief Inventory

Participants. One hundred sixty undergraduates (104 females, 56 males) enrolled in an introductory educational psychology class at a large midwestern university participated as part of their course requirement. Ages ranged from 18 to 46 (M = 21.36, SD = 4.73). Approximately 12% of participants were older than 22. Four percent were freshmen, 42% sophomores, 43% juniors, and 11% seniors. This sample was similar to those reported by Schommer.

Materials. The materials consisted of Schommer's (1990) 63-item Epistemological Questionnaire, the 28-item Epistemic Beliefs Inventory (see Appendix A) and a reading comprehension test. A description of the EQ is available in Schommer (1990). Items used in the EBI were constructed based on the criteria for each of the five epistemic factors described by Schommer (1990). A pool of approximately 25 items was written for each of the five hypothesized factors. Twelve items were selected from these categories. A content analysis of items and several pilot studies led to the development of a 32-item version of the EBI used by Bendixen et al. (1998). Revision of the 32-item version into a 28-item version produced the current version of the EBI.

Some of these items were paraphrased from statements used by Schommer (1990). For example, we changed "The really smart students don't have to work hard to do well in school" to "Really smart students don't have to work as hard to do well in school." Approximately 75% of items were new; seven items were paraphrases of items appearing on the EQ. These items are noted in Appendix A.

We especially were interested in writing statements that eliminated multiple factor loadings and bore a clear relationship to the relevant construct (see Hofer & Pintrich, 1997, for a further discussion). We also included seven items that explicitly made reference to the legitimacy of omniscient authority (e.g., People should always obey the law). Each of the 28 items was written as a grammatically simple statement that individuals responded to using a five-point Likert scale in which 1 corresponded to "strongly disagree" and 5 corresponded to "strongly agree." Individuals made their ratings by circling the number that most closely reflected their agreement with the statement.

Individuals also completed a reading comprehension test. The target text consisted of a 800-word passage entitled "The Burning of Kuwait" containing both expository and narrative elements adapted from *Time* magazine (Elmer-DeWitt, 1991). This story described the environmental after-effects of the Persian Gulf War. The test consisted of 18 four-item multiple-choice questions that required readers to make across-text inferences about the material included in the story. Correct answers on the test were summed to create a single composite score.

Procedure.   Individuals were tested in groups of 15 to 35 students and received identical instructions. All sessions were conducted by the authors. There were no time limits on any of the experimental tasks. Individuals first completed the two questionnaires. The Epistemological Questionnaire was administered first, followed immediately by the Epistemic Beliefs inventory. During the next stage, participants were given a five-page booklet that included simple cover instructions and "The Burning of Kuwait" text. The instructions specified that students should read the story as carefully as possible. Rereading and marking the text were allowed, although students were not allowed to take notes. Individuals were asked to wait quietly for everyone to finish if they completed the story before others. After reading, study booklets were collected, and all participants were given a copy of the 18 multiple-choice tests with cover instructions.

Retest data was collected one month later. Individuals received a packet during their regularly scheduled class period that included the EQ, EBI, and written instructions. Participants were asked to complete the two questionnaires and return their packets to their instructors during the next class session (i.e., two days later). Of the 160 packets distributed, 124 were returned with completed questionnaires within the designated time period.

Findings

The EQ and EBI were analyzed in two ways. The first was a principal factor analysis with oblique rotation (i.e., correlated factors). The second was a principal factor analysis with varimax rotation (i.e., uncorrelated factors). Since both analyses led to highly similar solutions in which none of the factors were correlated above the traditional .30 level, only the principal factor analysis with varimax rotation solutions are reported.

It is important to note that Schommer's EQ has not been subjected to an exploratory factor analysis previously. Schommer (1990) asked experts to sort the 63 items on the EQ into 12 subsets (i.e., parcelled items). An analysis of these subsets generally yielded four factors. In the present analysis, we conducted identical exploratory analyses on both the EQ and EBI without prior parcelling of items.

Analysis of the EQ. The principal factor analysis yielded 19 factors with eigenvalues greater than 1 that explained 72% of the total sample variation. We selected the first five observed factors for closer inspection to determine whether they corresponded to the five hypothesized factors. These factors explained 35% of the total sample variation. Items with loadings greater than .30 were used to construct composite scores for each factor. Many of the remaining 14 factors included one or two items and did not suggest clearly interpreted factors in the context of Schommer's hypothesized five-factor model. Factor labels, item-to-factor loadings, eigenvalues, and values of coefficient α for each of the five factors are shown in Table 13.1.

The five factors were labeled Innate Ability, Certain Knowledge 1, Incremental Learning, Certain Knowledge 2, and Integrative Thinking. Two of these factors (Innate Ability, Certain Knowledge 1) corresponded to factors reported by Schommer (1990, 1993). Two other factors (Incremental Learning, Integrative Thinking) differed from results. A fifth factor (Certain Knowledge 2) was consistent with Schommer's prediction, but represented a separate construct than Certain Knowledge 1. An inspection of items in Table 13.1 indicates that Certain Knowledge 1 pertains to the likelihood that scientists will ultimately discover universal truths; hence, it represents an Accessibility to Certain Knowledge factor. In contrast, Certain Knowledge 2 pertained to the degree to which certain knowledge exists; thus, it represented a Likelihood of Certain Knowledge factor. One point worth noting about the two Certain Knowledge factors is that without

TABLE 13.1
Factor Structure of the Epistemological Questionnaire (EQ).

Factor 1: Innate Ability (Eigenvalue = 2.02; α = .74)
  Successful students understand things quickly. (.79)
  The really smart students don't have to work as hard to do well in school. (.71)

Factor 2: Certain Knowledge 1 (Eigenvalue = 1.75; α = .74)
  Scientists can ultimately get to the truth. (.80)
  If scientists try hard enough, they can find the truth to almost anything. (.80)

Factor 3: Incremental Learning (Eigenvalue = 1.52; α = .64)
  The most successful people have discovered how to improve their ability to learn. (.87)
  I try my best to combine information across chapters or even across classes. (.51)

Factor 4: Certain Knowledge 2 (Eigenvalue = 1.40; α = .53)
  The only thing that is certain is uncertainty itself. (.90)
  Nothing is certain but death and taxes. (.45)

Factor 5: Integrative Thinking (Eigenvalue = 1.38: α = .61)
  If a person forgot details, and yet was able to come up with new ideas from a text,
    I would think they were bright. (.83)
  The most important part of scientific work is original thinking. (.47)
  To me studying means getting the big ideas from the text, rather than details. (.31)

a strong endorsement of Certain Knowledge 2, which presumes that certain knowledge exists, Certain Knowledge 1, which presumes that certain knowledge will be identified, becomes logically irrelevant.

These findings indicated that the EQ does not yield the five hypothesized factors when items are entered into the factor analysis without a priori groupings. Using a priori groupings presumably reduces within-instrument variability because it relies on 12 composite scores rather than 63 individual items. Whether a priori groupings are justified remains a question for confirmatory factor analysis (Hofer & Pintrich, 1997). Based on our exploratory analysis, however, the use of a priori groupings may lead to substantially different interpretations of the EQ compared to Schommer's (1990, 1993) reported findings.

Analysis of the EBI. The EBI was analyzed using the same factor-analytic procedures used to analyze the EQ. Two items (6, 19) were reverse keyed prior to the analysis. This analysis yielded five factors with eigenvalues greater than one that explained 60% of the total sample variation. Factor labels, item-to-factor loadings, eigenvalues, and values of coefficient α for each of the five factors are shown in Table 13.2.

TABLE 13.2
Factor Structure of the Epistemic Beliefs Inventory (EBI).

Factor 1: Omniscient Authority (Eigenvalue = 1.63: α = .68)
  People shouldn't question authority. (.73)
  Children should be allowed to question their parent's authority. (.66) *
  When someone in authority tells me what to do, I usually do it. (.62)

Factor 2: Certain Knowledge (Eigenvalue = 1.63; α = .62)
  The moral rules I live by apply to everyone. (.72)
  What is true today will be true tomorrow. (.63)
  Parents should teach their children all there is to know about life. (.50)

Factor 3: Quick Learning (Eigenvalue = 1.47; α = .58)
  Working on a problem with no quick solution is a waste of time. (.71)
  If you don't understand a chapter the first time through, going back over
    it won't help. (.53)
  If you don't learn something quickly, you won't ever learn it. (.49)

Factor 4: Simple Knowledge (Eigenvalue = 1.43; α = .62)
  Instructors should focus on facts instead of theories. (.78)
  Too many theories just complicate things. (.57)
  Most things worth knowing are easy to understand. (.44)

Factor 5: Innate Ability (Eigenvalue = 1.36; α = .62)
  How well you do in school depends on how smart you are. (.76)
  Smart people are born that way. (.56)
  Really smart students don't have to work as hard to do well in school. (.30) **

Note: * = reversed keyed; ** = paraphrased from Schommer (1990).

The five factors were labeled Omniscient Authority, Certain Knowledge, Quick Learning, Simple Knowledge, and Innate Ability. These factors were identical to the five epistemic dimensions hypothesized by Schommer (1990). Each factor included at least three items with loadings in excess of .30. None of the items with loadings in excess of .30 on one factor loaded on another factor. Each factor also was characterized by a marker variable loading in excess of .70 that was indicative of the presumed underlying construct (see Table 13.3).

These findings indicated that the EBI yielded the five hypothesized factors described earlier. Compared to the exploratory analysis of the EQ, the EBI explained substantially more sample variation than the five primary factors on the EQ. In addition, the EBI did not yield additional, difficult to interpret factors as did the EQ. A comparison of internal consistency coefficients using Cronbach's α indicated that the two instruments were quite similar on this dimension, although neither instrument produced factors that were highly reliable.

Relationship to Reading Comprehension.   Two stepwise multiple regression analyses were conducted using five composite scale scores from the EQ or EBI. Scores for each item on a scale were summed to create a single composite score. The purpose of these analyses was to examine the relationship between each instrument and inferential reading comprehension. The main rationale for using reading comprehension in the present study is that a belief in Certain Knowledge, Simple Knowledge, and Omniscient Authority may limit the degree to which a reader constructs inferences about the text's meaning (Cunningham & Fitzgerald, 1996; Kardash & Scholes, 1996). The Burning of Kuwait text was used because it presented a view of the Gulf War that questioned the authority of the United States military presence. Epistemic beliefs were expected to affect the kind of inferences made about this text that would not occur with more objective cognitive tests such as solving analogies or series completion problems. Overall performance on the reading comprehension test ($M = 10.51$, $SD = 3.34$) was the dependent variable. Cronbach's alpha was .83.

TABLE 13.3
Means and Standard Deviations for Factor Scores Using Items Reported in Tables 13.1 and 13.2.

	EQ		EBI	
	Mean	SD	Mean	SD
Factor 1	4.76	1.73	9.03	2.12
Factor 2	5.19	1.52	6.61	2.32
Factor 3	7.78	1.32	4.62	1.47
Factor 4	6.48	1.80	8.57	2.16
Factor 5	6.84	1.21	8.22	1.75

We also examined zero-correlations among the 10 EQ and EBI factors and their correlations with the reading comprehension score. All composite scores for the five EQ factors were uncorrelated. This was expected given that factors were extracted in a manner that guarantees they will be significantly uncorrelated. All composite scores for the EBI were uncorrelated with one exception. In this case, the Certain and Simple Knowledge factors were correlated positively, r = .25. Table 13.4 also shows the correlations between the EQ and EBI. In general, EQ factors were uncorrelated with EBI factors with two exceptions. One was that the Certain Knowledge factor on the EQ was correlated positively with the Certain and Simple Knowledge factors on the EBI. This suggests that both instruments may tap the same Certain Knowledge dimension, even though the magnitude of these correlations is quite low (i.e., r > .50). A second exception was that the Integrative Learning factor on the EQ was correlated negatively to the Quick Learning factor on the EBI scale. This correlation suggests that quick learning may impede deeper learning. Last, Table 13.4 reveals that the EQ factors were uncorrelated with the reading comprehension tests, while the EBI factors showed modest though significant correlations with it.

Standardized regression coefficients (i.e., β), and unique variance explained by each factor are shown in Table 13.5. None of the factors from the EQ explained a significant proportion of variation on the reading test. In contrast, four of the five factors from the EBI had significant loadings. These results indicated that four of the EBI's five factors explained a modest, though statistically significant, proportion of variance in the reading test. Using a simultaneous regression solution, the five factors included in the EBI explained 10.8% of total sample

TABLE 13.4
Zero-Order Correlations Among Variables

	1	2	3	4	5	6	7	8	9	10	11
EQ FACTORS											
Innate Ability	—										
Certain Knowledge 1	−.11	—									
Incremental Learning	−.13	.03	—								
Certain Knowledge 2	.09	.13	.12	—							
Integrative Thinking	.06	.03	−.06	−.12	—						
EBI FACTORS											
Omniscient Authority	−.06	−.03	.04	.00	.10	—					
Certain Knowledge	−.01	.36	.03	−.07	−.12	.16	—				
Quick Learning	−.09	−.12	.04	−.13	−.22	.08	.03	—			
Simple Knowledge	.04	.19	−.13	.08	−.15	.25	.09	−.16	—		
Innate Ability	.09	.03	−.01	.00	−.04	.18	.15	.30	−.13	—	
Reading Comprehension	.09	.04	.07	.14	.11	.11	.23	.31	−.36	−.29	—

Note: Correlations greater than .16 and .21 were significant at the $p < .05$ and .01 levels respectively.

TABLE 13.5
Standardized Regression Coefficients and Proportion of Unique Variance
Explained by each of the EQ and EBI Factors.

	EQ		EBI	
	β	r^2_c	β	r^2_c
Factor 1	DNL	—	DNL	—
Factor 2	DNL	—	.19*	.026
Factor 3	DNL	—	.17*	.020
Factor 4	DNL	—	−.22*	.033
Factor 5	DNL	—	−.17*	.026

Note: β = final standardized regression coefficient; r^2_c = change in r^2;
DNL = did not load; * = $p < .05$.

variation in the reading test. A test of R^2 was significant, F (5, 154) = 3.73, $p < .01$. While this is a relatively small proportion of variance explained, it is consistent with previously observed effect sizes (Benack & Besseches, 1989; Chandler et al., 1990; Curtis et al., 1988; Jehng et al., 1993; Presley, 1985; Schommer, 1990). The five factors used from the EQ explained .029% of total sample variation. This value did not differ significantly from zero, $p > .25$.

Retest Data

The EQ and EBI were completed a second time one month later. A principal factor analysis with varimax solution was performed on each instrument. These analyses yielded 17 factors for the EQ that explained 39% of sample variation and five factors for the EBI that explained 64% of sample variation. Two of the five EQ factors (i.e., Certain Knowledge 1 and Certain Knowledge 2) were identical to the initial analysis. Coefficient α for each replicated factor was .71 and .49. The test–retest correlation between factors was .51 for Certain Knowledge 1 and .67 for Certain Knowledge 2. The Incremental Learning factor was partially replicated. Coefficient alpha was .51; the test–retest correlation was .41. The two remaining factors did not yield clear interpretations. One two-item factor included "You should evaluate the accuracy of information in a textbook, if you are familiar with the topic" and "Often, even advice from experts should be questioned." A second two-item factor included "Working on a difficult problem for an extended period of time only pays off for really smart students" and "Educators should know by now which is the best method, lectures or small group discussions."

Three of the EBI factors (i.e., Omniscient Authority, Certain Knowledge, and Quick Learning) were identical to the initial factor analysis. The Innate Ability factor included one additional item (i.e., People's intellectual ability is fixed at birth) that was not included in the original analysis. The Simple Knowledge factor was replicated with one exception; the statement "Most things worth knowing are easy to understand" (item-to-factor loading = .44) was replaced by "Things are simpler than most professors would have you believe" (item-to-factor loading = .32). Coefficient a for the Omniscient Authority, Certain Knowledge, Quick Learning, Simple Knowledge, and Innate Ability factors reached .65, .63, .60, .66, and .63, respectively. Test–retest correlations for these factors were .66, .81, .66, .64, and .62, respectively. These values were equivalent to the values of coefficient a reported in the time-1 analyses reported earlier, as well as previous research using a slightly modified version of the EBI (Bendixen et al., 1998).

CONCLUSIONS

These findings suggest four conclusions: (a) the two instruments differ with respect to the number of factors they yield and the degree to which these factors match theoretical predictions, (b) differences exist with respect to the proportion of sample variance explained by the two instruments, (c) the EBI had better predictive validity than the EQ when correlated with a test of reading comprehension, and (d) the EBI had considerably better test–retest reliability than the EQ.

One problem we have experienced with Schommer's EQ in previous exploratory uses is that it consistently yields a large number of potentially interpretable factors, each accounting for a relatively small share of total sample variation. The present results were typical of these earlier findings. Another problem is that factors emerged that were not predicted. In the present case, the Incremental Learning and Integrative Thinking factors did not fit into the hypothesized five-factor model proposed by Schommer (1990). In comparison, the five factors identified by the EBI provided a close fit with the five epistemic dimensions hypothesized by Schommer (1990).

The two instruments also differed with respect to the proportion of sample variation they explained. The first five factors on the EQ explained 35.5% of total variation, while the EBI explained 60% of total sample variation. A one-month replication led to values of 39% and 64% respectively. Generally, the EBI explained 20% more sample variance with one-half the items of the EQ. There are at least two reasons for these differences. One was that the EBI contained a smaller number of items that were more homogeneous. A second reason was that more items loaded highly on one of the five observed factors on the EBI. These two properties of the EBI resulted in a substantial increase in variance explained.

A third difference concerned construct validity, or the degree to which the two instruments, and their individual factors, measured the hypothesized constructs. One interpretative problem of the EQ in the present study is that it generated two Certain Knowledge factors. Certain Knowledge 1 reflected assumptions about scientific discovery. Why this dimension was independent of Certain Knowledge

2, which reflected beliefs about the certainty of knowledge itself, remains unclear. Presumably, the latter provided a more realistic measure of certain knowledge as described by Schommer (1990). In comparison, the EBI did not have any obvious interpretive problems in that each of the factors was conceptually distinct and all of the items that loaded on individual factors were related logically to the relevant construct.

The EBI also had better predictive validity than the EQ. Four of the five factors from the EBI were modestly, though significantly, related to the test of reading comprehension. In contrast, none of the EQ factors was significantly correlated with total reading comprehension scores. One explanation of these differences is that composite scores from the EBI were more variable (see Table 13.3) and therefore more likely to increase the observed magnitude of r (Crocker & Algina, 1986).

A final difference was that the EBI yielded a close replication of factors between the initial and replication analyses, while the EQ did not. This indicated the EBI is more reliable over time than the EQ. The replication analysis revealed the same number of factors, the same item-to-factor loadings for each test item, the same amount of sample variation explained, and an acceptable test–retest correlation among the five factors.

The results of this study suggest that the EBI adequately measures the five epistemic dimensions hypothesized by Schommer (1990), including the Omniscient Authority factor. The EBI also had several advantages over an exploratory analysis of the EQ. These differences pertained to the amount of sample variation explained and stability over time. We believe the EBI provides a useful complement to the EQ for measuring epistemic beliefs during a single occasion or across time. This represents an important addition to the epistemic belief literature. We recommend that researchers use both the EBI and EQ until further validation research is conducted. Future studies should address two issues: (a) establishing the convergent and discriminant validity of these instruments using a wider range of criterion variables, and (b) providing a confirmatory test of the measurement model implied by the hypothesized five-factor solution.

Limitations and Future Research

Several caveats are in order. One is that it is unclear how well any paper-and-pencil instrument will measure epistemic beliefs. One advantage of self-report instruments such as the EQ and EBI are their ease and efficiency. Nevertheless, serious questions remain regarding their construct validity that can only be answered through continued research. Second, in an absolute sense, the EBI showed relatively poor criterion validity (i.e., predicting performance on conceptually related outcomes) with measures of reading comprehension even though it outperformed the EQ. This finding raises questions about the utility of epistemic beliefs as predictors of traditional learning outcomes such as reading comprehension. One possibility is that reading comprehension is unaffected by the reader's epistemic beliefs. An alternative explanation is that the EBI may be too insensitive to detect differences in reading comprehension. Again, continued research is needed to compare the EBI and EQ to a variety of outcome measures to triangulate them. Third, the present study used relatively few participants and utilized an exploratory rather than confirmatory analysis strategy. Replication is needed using new participants and a broader set of outcome measures.

Our findings also suggest two broad directions for future research. One direction is to provide additional construct validation data for the EQ and EBI. Presently, it is unclear what these two instruments measure and the extent to which they measure the same or unrelated constructs. An inspection of the correlations in Table 13.4 suggests they measure unrelated constructs. We urge researchers to examine the construct validity of these instruments as carefully as possible.

A second direction is to examine in much greater detail the relationship among self-reported epistemic beliefs, epistemic beliefs measured through in-depth verbal interviews (Kuhn, 1991), and a variety of relevant outcome measures. Three salient cognitive outcome measures seem especially important to us, including moral reasoning, critical thinking and argumentation, and identity formation. Bendixen et al. (1998) found that self-reported epistemic beliefs explained roughly 30% of variation in moral reasoning scores. Nevertheless, researchers do not understand fully how beliefs affect the reasoning process. Kuhn (1991, 1999) found that epistemic world views are related to the use of critical thinking and argumentation skills. Studies are needed that examine what beliefs affect these processes, and how changing epistemic beliefs affect critical thinking and argumentation. At present, there are no studies that examine how epistemic beliefs are related to identity formation or how individuals resolve identity crises.

We close by reemphasizing the need for future research. The study of epistemic beliefs is in its infancy. Researchers need better instrumentation and methodology to construct a better theoretical and applied understanding of epistemic beliefs. Even at this stage, it is clear that epistemic beliefs are related in important ways to basic cognitive skills such as reading and problem solving. More research is needed to investigate the relationships among epistemic beliefs and complex cognitive skills such as moral reasoning and identity formation. Another pressing need is to investigate the role of epistemic beliefs in life-span development.

REFERENCES

Benack, S., & Basseches, M. A. (1989). Dialectical thinking and relativistic epistemology: Their relation in adult development. In M. L. Commons, J. D. Sinott, F. A. Richards, & C. Armon (Eds.), *Adult development. Volume I: Comparisons and applications of developmental models*, (pp. 95–110). New York: Praeger.

Bendixen, L. D., Schraw, G., & Dunkle, M. E. (1998). Epistemic beliefs and moral reasoning. *The Journal of Psychology, 13,* 187–200.

Chandler, M., Boyes, M., & Ball, L. (1990). Relativism and stations of epistemic doubt. *Journal of Experimental Child Psychology, 50,* 370–395.

Crocker, L., & Algina, J. (1986). *Introduction to classical and modern test theory.* Chicago, IL: Holt, Rinehart & Winston.

Cunningham, J. W., & Fitzgerald, J. (1996). Epistemology and reading. *Reading Research Quarterly, 31,* 36–61.

Curtis, J., Billingslea, R., & Wilson, J. P. (1988). Personality correlates of moral reasoning and attitudes toward authority. *Psychological Reports, 63,* 947–954.

Damon, W. (1988). *The moral child.* New York: The Free Press.

Elmer-DeWitt, P. (1991, March 31). The burning of Kuwait. *Time, 137,* 36–37. New York: Time Magazine.

Hall, R. J., Snell, A. F., & Foust, M. S. (1999). Item parcelling strategies in SEM: Investigating the subtle effects of unmodeled secondary constructs. *Organizational Research Methods, 2,* 233–256.

Hofer, B. K., & Pintrich, P. R. (1997). The development of epistemological theories: Beliefs about knowledge and knowing and their relation to learning. *Review of Educational Research, 67,* 88–140.

Jehng, J. J., Johnson, S. D., & Anderson, R. C. (1993). Schooling and student's epistemological beliefs about learning. *Contemporary Educational Psychology, 18,* 23–35.

Kardash, C. M., & Scholes, R. J. (1996). Effects of preexisting beliefs, epistemological beliefs, and need for cognition on interpretation of controversial issues. *Journal of Educational Psychology, 88,* 260–271.

Kitchener, K. S., & King, P. A. (1981). Reflective judgment: Concepts of justification and their relationship to age and education. *Journal of Applied Developmental Psychology, 2,* 89–116.

Kuhn, D. (1991). *The skills of argument.* New York: Cambridge University Press.

Kuhn, D. (1999). A developmental model of critical thinking. *Educational Researcher, 28,* 16–26.

Perry, W. G., Jr. (1970). *Forms of intellectual and ethical development in the college years.* New York: Academic Press.

Presley, S. L. (1985). Moral judgment and attitudes toward authority of political resisters. *Journal of Research in Personality, 19,* 135–151.

Schommer, M. (1990). Effects of beliefs about the nature of knowledge on comprehension. *Journal of Educational Psychology, 82,* 498–504.

Schommer, M. (1993). Epistemological development and academic performance among secondary students. *Journal of Educational Psychology, 85,* 406–411.

Schommer, M., Crouse, A., & Rhodes, N. (1992). Epistemological beliefs and mathematical text comprehension: Believing it is simple does not make it so. *Journal of Educational Psychology, 84,* 435–443.

Schraw, G., Dunkle, M. E., & Bendixen, L. D. (1995). Cognitive processes in well-defined and ill-defined problem solving. *Applied Cognitive Psychology, 9,* 523–528.

Walker, H. A., Rowland, G. L., & Boyes, M. C. (1991). Personality, personal epistemology, and moral judgment. *Psychological Reports, 68,* 767–772.

APPENDIX A

Items included in the Epistemic Beliefs Inventory (EBI)

1. Most things worth knowing are easy to understand.
2. What is true is a matter of opinion.
3. Students who learn things quickly are the most successful.
4. People should always obey the law.
5. People's intellectual potential is fixed at birth.
6. Absolute moral truth does not exist.
7. Parents should teach their children all there is to know about life.
8. Really smart students don't have to work as hard to do well in school.
9. If a person tries too hard to understand a problem, they will most likely end up being confused.
10. Too many theories just complicate things.
11. The best ideas are often the most simple.
12. Instructors should focus on facts instead of theories.
13. Some people are born with special gifts and talents.
14. How well you do in school depends on how smart you are.
15. If you don't learn something quickly, you won't ever learn it.
16. Some people just have a knack for learning and others don't.
17. Things are simpler than most professors would have you believe.
18. If two people are arguing about something, at least one of them must be wrong.
19. Children should be allowed to question their parents' authority.
20. If you haven't understood a chapter the first time through, going back over it won't help.
21. Science is easy to understand because it contains so many facts.
22. The more you know about a topic, the more there is to know.
23. What is true today will be true tomorrow.
24. Smart people are born that way.
25. When someone in authority tells me what to do, I usually do it.
26. People shouldn't question authority.
27. Working on a problem with no quick solution is a waste of time.
28. Sometimes there are no right answers to life's big problems.

Note: Items 3, 8, 9, 12, 17, 20, and 21 were adapted from items used by Schommer (1990).

14

Considerations in the Design and Evaluation of a Paper-and-Pencil Measure of Epistemic Cognition

Phillip Wood
University of Missouri at Columbia

Karen Kitchener and Laura Jensen
University of Denver

Since the work of Perry (1970), increased attention has been paid to the development of epistemological assumptions, particularly among adolescents and adults. Generally, it seems clear that assumptions, about the nature of knowledge and the process of knowing develop over time and that education plays an important role in this development (Hofer & Pintrich, 1997; King & Kitchener, 1994). However, as Hofer and Pintrich (1997) point out, multiple questions remain to be answered from the conceptual and empirical relationship between the models to their generalizability to non-Euro-Americans to the mechanisms for the acquisition and change of epistemological assumptions.

Part of the difficulty in addressing these questions has been methodological. As others (Hofer & Pintrich, 1997) have noted, individuals' "epistemological theories do not yield themselves readily" (p. 130). Because the development of personal epistemologies has been seen as a kind of meaning-making for the most part, methodologies such as interviews or essays have been chosen to allow individuals to construct written verbal responses either in relationship to standardized problems or in a more open-ended format (Baxter Magolda, 1992; Belenky, Bond, & Weinstock, 1997; Kitchener & King, 1981; Kuhn, 1992; Moore, 1991; Wood & Lynch, 1998). These methodologies in and of themselves are to some extent to blame for many of the existing holes in the database since they are often cumbersome to use and time-consuming and expensive to score. On the other hand, the questionnaires that are currently available (Schommer, 1990; Moore, 1989) have both empirical and conceptual problems (Hofer & Pintrich, 1997; Wood & Kardash, chap. 12, this volume).

In this chapter, we consider some of the trade-offs involved in moving from a production measure of epistemic cognition designed to ascertain the epistemology that participants use in justifying their position to recognition measures that give participants a limited number of choices between which they must choose. In doing so, we draw from our own research experience on the Reflective Judgment Model.

As described in more detail elsewhere in this volume (King & Kitchener, chap. 3, this volume), the Reflective Judgment Model describes the development of seven different forms of epistemic cognition. These forms are descriptively distinct from each other and develop sequentially. They can be summarized into three general categories: the prereflective, the quasireflective, and the reflective. Generally, those in the prereflective period (Stages 1–3) assume that knowledge is gained from an authority figure or through direct, personal observation. In other words, "to see is to know." Knowledge gained in these ways is assumed to be absolutely correct. Individuals holding these assumptions often do not perceive the ambiguity in a situation even when clear uncertainty is presented to them. During the quasireflective period (Stages 4 and 5), individuals recognize that real uncertainty exists about some issues. They argue that knowledge cannot be had with certainty. They do not understand, however, how to justify knowing anything in the face of ambiguity and often conclude many points of view are equally correct. By contrast, at the reflective level, an individual's assumptions represent the epistemological position that although knowledge is not a "given," probabilistic knowledge can be constructed by evaluating existing evidence and expert opinion (King & Kitchener, 1994).

EPISTEMIC COGNITION AND ILL-STRUCTURED PROBLEM SOLVING

Epistemic cognition is particularly critical when the individuals' reasoning about real-world problems is considered, although as Hofer and Pintrich (1997) argued, it may also be called for in other situations. The real-world problems considered in the Reflective Judgment Model are those which are the object of ongoing controversy, even among qualified experts. Examples of such problems include the safety of food additives, determination of the genetic component of behavior, and the evaluation of the economic impact of social policy.

In addition to establishing the sequentiality of the levels and age and educational level differences, one of the major goals of research conducted on the Reflective Judgment Model has been to establish that such reasoning is different from that seen in the deduction and inference problems, which are usually the object of psychological and educational research on problem solving or critical thinking. In traditional research in these areas, the problems under consideration contain all information necessary for a successful solution in their presentation. Procedures for organizing the information and arriving at the correct answer are agreed on as being sound. Simon (1973; 1978) has characterized such problems as "well-structured" and contrasts them with "ill-structured problems" in which the individual must actively organize and structure information which is incomplete and at times conflicting in order to arrive at a solution. In other settings, this distinction has been one of contrasting "academic" versus "real-life" intelligence or as "puzzle solving" versus "problem solving" (Neisser, 1976; Kitchener, 1983).

The use of ill-structured problems to elicit epistemic assumptions in Reflective Judgment research was somewhat of a serendipidous occurrence, however. Initially Kitchener & King, (1981) developed intellectual dilemmas that pesented opposing points of view about controversial issues. They found, however, that the problems written were particularly useful in eliciting epistemological assumptions. Because they were ill-structured and provided respondents with conflicting perspectives on an issue, they set up a controversy that required respondents to consider the certainty of knowledge, the source of knowledge, and their justification for claiming to have knowledge. Because repeated use of the term "ill-structured problem" becomes cumbersome to read, in the following section we will at times use the terms "dilemma" or "controversy" to designate an ill-structured problem.

There is considerable rationale for conducting research on ill-structured problem solving. First, as Simon (1973, p. 187) noted, much problem-solving effort is actually directed to structuring problems and only a fraction of it at solving problems once they are structured. Understanding how individuals' epistemological assumptions affect how they structure problems in Reflective Judgment assessments can provide links to other cognitive theories, such as those involving expertise. Second, as noted by King and Kitchener (1994) and the Association of American Colleges (1991), the abilities of individuals to draw reasonable conclusions in the presence of incomplete and even conflicting data is a fundamental goal of higher education and the basis for the design and justification of much of liberal and general education at the undergraduate level. To the extent that psychometrically sound instruments can be developed that are conceptually and empirically distinct from other cognitive abilities, researchers will not only gain new insights about the relationships between the development of personal epistemology and other aspects of human cognition, but will be clearer on the contribution of higher education to such reasoning ability.

OTHER TYPES OF REAL-WORLD PROBLEM SOLVING THAT ARE NOT NECESSARILY ILL-STRUCTURED PROBLEM SOLVING

Ill-Defined Problems

It is important to point out, however, that not all research in real-world problem solving necessarily deals with the solution of ill-structured problems nor allows researchers to study the role of epistemic assumptions in problem solving. Sternberg (1982), for example, outlined examples of research in which individuals were asked to solve "ill-defined problems." These consisted of asking participants to construct a hat rack from an unlikely set of components (for example, Maier, 1933; Hoffman, Burke, & Maier, 1963), asking participants to tie two strings together in a room when the strings are arranged far enough apart so that it is difficult to grasp both simultaneously (Maier, 1933; Raaheim, 1974), or asking students to think of a novel way to deliver radiation to a tumor without destroying surrounding tissue (Duncker, 1926; Gick & Holyoak, 1980). Ill-defined problems are quite distinct from ill-structured problems in three key respects. First, answers to ill-defined problems can be unambiguously evaluated in terms of their correctness (for example, the two strings either are or are not tied together by the participant). One would not expect individuals (much less "experts" about such problems) to disagree as to whether a proposed solution was satisfactory. Second, participants are not asked to weigh conflicting truth claims of disciplines or approaches to the problem in these situations. Finally, generation of successful solutions to such problems usually involves insight and establishing novel connections between stimuli or novel uses for stimuli. Thus, they do not require individuals to consider the certainty of knowledge, the source of knowledge, nor how they can justify claims that they have knowledge. As Sternberg (1982) notes, once one sees the solution for a given ill-defined problem, one can successfully solve the problem. This observation stands in contrast to problem solving in Reflective Judgment, where such test–retest effects seem minimal (Kitchener, King, Wood, & Davison, 1989). Even when participants are shown examples of more sophisticated solutions, they frequently fail to comprehend such answers (as evidenced by their failure to successfully paraphrase such statements) (Kitchener, Lynch, Fischer, & Wood, (1993).

Ecologically Valid Problems

A second type of real-world problem solving has been used in approaches described as "ecologically valid." These types of assessment have regained attention by researchers because of their promise to detect specific types of cognitive deficits, such as those commonly associated with problematic alcohol consumption and to describe problem solving as it actually occurs. However, just because problems are ecologically valid does not mean that they can be or are used by researchers to tap epistemological assumptions. For example, Nixon and Parsons (1991) administered Kuhn and Brannock's (1977) plant test measure of formal operations as their ecologically valid measure. This instrument, although "real-world," requires a single answer or set of answers by following combinatorial and deductive rules to arrive at a satisfactory solution. By contrast, another study of ecologically valid problem solving (Nixon, Tivis, & Parsons, 1995) is potentially closer to ill-structured problem solving. In this study, researchers asked participants to list and evaluate plans of action in various interpersonal settings. For example, they were asked to list possible reactions to an adolescent's violation of curfew. Although it is certainly the case that alternative and internally coherent solutions for such problems exist, there are two respects in which these problems differ from those considered in the Reflective Judgment Model. First, participants' attention was not directed to the issue of how reasonable people or experts could disagree about such answer. Second, operational scoring of the solutions to these issues consisted of counting the number of alternative solutions, without specific evaluation of the adequacy of the proposed answers. As a result, respondents did not have to grapple with epistemological questions or how to justify their beliefs in the face of uncertainty of knowledge. In other words, it appears that ill-structured problems were used to measure ideational fluency about real-world problems, and the role of epistemological assumptions in such problem solving was not tapped.

ASSESSING EPISTEMIC COGNITION USING ILL-STRUCTURED PROBLEMS

The Reflective Judgment Interview

The Reflective Judgment Interview (RJI) was designed to elicit data on respondent's basic assumptions about the nature of knowledge and how it is gained (King & Kitchener, 1994). The standard version consists of four ill-structured problems and a standard set of interview questions. The interview questions were chosen to elicit assumptions about the nature of knowledge and how respondents justify their beliefs in the face of uncertainty. Each question corresponds to an aspect of the Reflective Judgment scoring rules. For example, nature of knowledge has three subcomponents about which respondents are questioned: What can we know and how uncertain can we be?; How concretely can we know?; and How can different knowledge claims be understood? (See King & Kitchener, 1994, or Wood, 1997, for summary of the standard problems, a list of the interview questions, and a detailed rationale for the choice of the questions.)

A standardized set of interview questions was chosen to increase the probability that the same construct was being measured with different individuals. Similarly, a procedure was identified for rating the data and individuals who wished to use the interview were asked to become trained in its use. Once trained, individuals were required to reach a certain level of competency to improve the probability that there would be comparability in the way the instrument was used and scored across studies in different settings.

While Perry's model and method of assessment had elicited assumptions about morality, epistemology, and identity development, Kitchener & King (1981) chose to focus on ill-structured problems in the intellectual domain. They chose problems about which, we believed, the general public would have some information and that covered a range of domains from history (the building of the pyramids) to social science (the objectivity of news reporting) to science (chemical additives to foods) to religion (creationism versus evolution). An example follows:

> People often have to make decisions that may affect their health such as deciding whether to eat foods or drink beverages that contain artificial sweeteners. There have been conflicting reports about the safety of these additives. For example, some studies have indicated that even in small amounts, artificial sweeteners (such as NutraSweet) can cause health problems, making foods containing them unsafe to eat. Other studies, however, have indicated that even in large amounts, artificial sweeteners do not cause health problems, and that the foods containing them are safe to eat.

Choosing general dilemmas that are not tied specifically to college settings has allowed the measure to be used with both high school students (Brabeck & Wood, 1990; Kitchener & King, 1981; McKinney, 1985; Van Tine, 1990) as well as older adults with and without college education (Glenn, 1992).

The problem stimuli used in the Reflective Judgment Interview share several characteristics in addition to their ill-structured nature in order to keep a parallel format across dilemma topics. (See King & Kitchener (1984) for a list of these characteristics.) This increases confidence that any obtained differences in performance across the topics are due to the topic area and not some other characteristic of the problem stimulus.

First, as already noted, Reflective Judgment topics are chosen to have general current interest. This level of generality entails not only that the topic be written at a reading level appropriate for all participants, but that the major issues dealt with in the problem can be easily communicated. In some cases, particular dilemmas have been written for specific target populations. For example, in Kitchener and Wood's (1987) study of German college students, it was decided to substitute a dilemma topic dealing with nuclear power generation in place of the creation/evolution dilemma because pilot discussions with German students revealed they were unfamiliar with debates about creation versus evolution. More recently, we have found that our own university students appear unfamiliar with issues surrounding the building of the pyramids, which were more widely discussed in the late 1970s, and there is some evidence that the chemical additives problem is less engaging for some students than it once was (Friedman, 1995; Samson, 1999).

Because the emphasis of the instrument is to document general assumptions about knowledge and concepts of justification, introduction of highly specialized knowledge into the stimulus materials confounds knowledge of such information with complexity of justification. This point is not made to rule out the possibility of Reflective Judgment assessments on topics (perhaps within an academic major) that draw on specialized knowledge from a curriculum. New problems have evolved on the causes of alcoholism and the origins of gay, lesbian, and transsexual lifestyles among others. The point here though is that care has been taken to assure some degree of uniform generality in terms of topical interest and information and, in many situations, this facet of design should be included when writing other ill-structured problem topics.

Second, the text of a dilemma topic specifically refers to the fact that disagreements exist about the solution to this issue and, in many cases, indicates that experts from different perspectives endorse opposing positions on the issue. Although it may be the case that the disagreement among experts may be unknown to the participant, interviewers are instructed to either pose the disagreement as a hypothetical question or to give a short example of such disagreement. Probing for participants' beliefs about why experts may disagree gives raters information about the participants' understanding of the role of authorities in creating knowledge, and this is important in clarifying epistemological beliefs.

Data on the RJI

If Reflective Judgment level is an outcome of higher education, it seems natural to investigate whether increases in this ability are particularly associated with the curricular contexts of students' academic major. Although increases in Reflective Judgment as a function of years of educational experience have been frequently replicated and are substantial, specific dilemma effects for the Reflective Judgment Interview have been found for only graduate student populations, with little evidence for such problem specificity to undergraduate majors. In fact, there has been remarkable consistency in undergraduates' responses across the standard problems (King & Kitchener, 1994; Wood, 1997).

In graduate populations, however, distinct differences have been found in overall level of Reflective Judgment, with doctoral students from the social sciences (such as psychology and sociology) demonstrating more sophisticated reasoning than doctoral students in mathematics and related disciplines (such as statistics and computer science) (King, Wood, & Mines, 1990). The search for specific differences as a function of dilemma topic has been less frequently investigated, but some initial findings are available. DeBord (1993) found rather pronounced disciplinary differences in his study of beginning graduate students but found no effects at the undergraduate level. Specifically, hc found that beginning doctoral students reasoned more complexly about dilemmas with psychological content (such as the relative merits of medications to resolve depression) than those without such content.

For undergraduate populations, performance on particular dilemma topics has not been found to vary as a function of academic major. Although these explorations have been statistically underpowered due to assessment of seniors from several academic majors (see Wood & Kardash, chap. 12, this volume, for a discussion of this issue), it seems that such disciplinary differences, in present, are rather small in magnitude at the undergraduate level. Whether such differences are found in the consistency of epistemic assumptions when using measures other than the Reflective Judgment Interview or whether such effects exist in subgroups of individuals (such as academically gifted or honors students) remains, of course, to be seen. Clearly, the preponderance of evidence from the Reflective Judgment Interview appears, at this point, to argue for more similarity than divergence in ill-structured problem solving across curricular topics.

Other Ill-Structured
Problem-Solving Research

It should be noted that other research in ill-structured problem solving has been done that has not examined epistemological assumptions, for example, explorations of expertise. Although research in the development of expertise in such areas as chess is well-developed, research on expertise about ill-structured problems has received less attention. This research has shown that some real-world ill-structured problems are not closely tied to traditional ideas of intelligence as, for example, Ceci and Liker's (1986, 1987) research on gambling expertise among professional gamblers. Other research has attempted to document how individuals organize and interpret large amounts of data into decision frameworks, as in Johnson's (1988) study of how members of an admitting committee of physicians evaluated medical school applications. Lawrence (1988) and Voss and Post (1988) looked at the evaluation of conflicting explanations in studies of the behavior of magistrates in deciding court cases and evaluating the advantages and disadvantages of economic policies in the Soviet Union.

These latter two examples more closely resemble the problems involved in Reflective Judgment research in that they call on the individual to consider multiple representations for the problem at hand, to isolate the elements of the problem within these perspectives and to consider, at least in theory, how and when additional evidence might be gathered to arrive at a decision. In other ways, they did not. Participants in the Lawrence (1988) and Voss and Post (1988) studies were not, for example, informed about the disagreement of qualified experts for the problem. Furthermore, in Reflective Judgment research, the goal is not only to identify expert cognition about the problem, but also to describe the less sophisticated approaches of novices and the specific interim structures that emerge over the course of development from adolescence to adulthood.

The means by which problem adequacy was evaluated in Reflective Judgment assessments is also quite different. The Reflective Judgment Model does not focus on the cognitive elaboration of stated evidence or on decisions to apply stop rules in the decision process. Instead, several aspects of the interview focus directly on questions of epistemic cognition. Specifically, participants are asked to give reasons for differences of opinion at both the expert and nonexpert levels. At other points in the interview they are asked to comment on whether a definite answer can be found or known with certainty.

These questions are asked in order to ascertain what one believes is knowable about the problem at hand and how evidence is used to construct and evaluate a position on the topic. As such, the Reflective Judgment Model differs from other research applications to such ill-structured problems in its focus on the degree to which sophisticated epistemic cognitions are used to justify the individual's opinion in the face of uncertain knowledge, to resolve contradictory evidence or authority, and to organize the information available to the individual. These epistemic cognitions appear to be used consistently by individuals across a number of domains. Thus, they are one aspect of the perceptual filter that individuals use in evaluating available evidence and opinion. Because the focus of the assessment is also on evidence and opinion related to epistemological position, the Reflective Judgment Model is not merely a model of semantics of epistemological terms. Individuals may (and at times do) define "truth," "facts," and "experts" differently across the different problem topics. In other words, the use of ill-structured problems does not guarantee that epistemological assumptions are examined. Researchers must design measures to elicit assumptions about what can be known and how it is known. Although the dilemma topics and semistructured format of the Reflective Judgment Interview served the purpose of generating rich yet ratable data for research purposes, the considerable expense involved in training, administering, and scoring the interview led us to investigate whether more traditional means of assessment could provide such information on participants' epistemic cognitions.

Consequently, we have used the Reflective Judgment Model as a basis for the construction of aspects of an objective measure of epistemic cognition. We based our subsequent measurement approaches on the belief that individuals who possess a given level of epistemic cognition when structuring their responses to ill-structured problems will also demonstrate collateral behaviors that are amenable to an objectively scorable format. Our latest efforts focus on two skills that were conceptually grounded in the Reflective Judgment Model: the ability to discriminate between statements that represent more and less sophisticated epistemic assumptions about a given issue, and the ability to endorse more sophisticated statements as being similar to one's own from among several alternatives. Before explaining these skills in greater detail, it is helpful to consider some of the approaches we explored en route to the present instruments.

The Reflective Judgment Essay

One simple strategy for obviating the expense of training interviewers, scheduling interviews, and avoiding transcription costs is to administer the Reflective Judgment Interview questions, along with appropriate follow-up questions, in an essay format. This approach is described in Wood and Lynch (1998), accompanied by an extended discussion of how such an approach can inform aspects of classroom instruction. Unfortunately, the method does not seem to be a promising assessment approach because it does not result in generation of ratable data, even if one adopts the strategy of allowing revisions of essays in response to queries designed to clarify comments. Several difficulties appear responsible for this.

First, some individuals attempt to dismiss the entire essay exercise by saying that they do not have sufficient information about the issue, cannot have an opinion on the matter, and/or are not interested in the topic. If these things occur during the Reflective Judgment Interview, interviewers are trained to respond with questions as to why an opinion cannot be had or to ask the participant to consider, hypothetically, what would be needed in order to form an opinion. If participants report that they have no interest, interviewers respond by asking what the individual would do if they did consider the topic relevant and wanted to form an opinion on the topic. In a comparable essay, students become frustrated when asked to rewrite their essays after such feedback.

Second, it is possible in the semistructured interview to distinguish between public behaviors and private belief. Some participants, for example, will report in the interview setting that they would consider some opinions to be better than others, but would not think of actually telling anyone that their opinion is better than someone else's. Even when feedback stresses the confidential nature of the essay, it appears that the act of writing about one's opinion as "better" is off-putting to many and results in cloudy statements about how one cannot judge opinions with little information as to why this is the case.

Third, and perhaps most importantly, it is much easier to avoid the controversy that each problem poses in an essay format, and thus fails to disclose underlying epistemic assumptions. In the case of the Reflective Judgment Interview, participants or interviewers may consider specific examples as a way of communicating that a real controversy exists. This almost never occurred in essay material despite instructions that encouraged students to discuss examples and elaborate on their assumptions. In addition, individual terms that would be defined within the interview are left unclear in the essay format. For example, when a participant mentions "having a perspective" on the issue, interviewers are trained to ask for a short definition of the term or an explanation to determine how the term is being used, which is important for accurate scoring. In a classroom essay exercise, use of such words is much more frequent than in the interview and participants become frustrated and easily fatigued when asked to be more specific about the meaning of such terms when writing.

In summary, although the use of an essay format can be a useful classroom exercise to both inform the instructor about the level of sophistication of students and as a way to stimulate classroom discussion and integration of key concepts in the course, the essay simply does not yield ratable data for research purposes.

The Computerized Reflective Judgment Assessment

Because the essay format yielded data that were simply too difficult to manage, the next assessment approach involved attempts to present participants with the standard probe questions of the Reflective Judgment Interview. Participants were then asked to select between several paragraph summaries that most closely approximated their views on the question. These summaries were written to reflect stage-typical responses to the question. We felt this approach would be promising because the structure of the argument would now be controlled and all terms would be explicitly defined where necessary. Although we were aware (as we mention next) that making this change moved the assessment from one requiring the individual to produce an argument to one in which the individual merely needed to recognize and endorse an argument, it was hoped that the benefits would outweigh the disadvantages.

Unfortunately, after a large "think-aloud" protocol pilot of this format, it too was abandoned. Participants found the task of having to read the summary statements time-consuming and fatiguing. They found answering all probe questions about a topic to be boring. Some expressed frustration at the summary statements they were asked to endorse, maintaining that their own opinions were not well-captured by the available alternatives. Others held they would have an opinion only in special cases and that it wasn't possible to answer such a general question. Most problematically, many freshmen selected summary statements for idiosyncratic reasons. Even though they often could not even paraphrase a particular statement, some selected statements far above what one would expect under the Reflective Judgment Interview. Some students freely confessed they had no idea what some of the summary statements meant, but they explained their choices with statements such as: "This one sounds like how my teachers talk in class and I really like the words they use," "I like the word 'perspective' better than 'opinion' because it's a longer word," or "These things all make the same conclusion, so I just picked one out." Although these problems occurred less frequently in senior data, the internal consistency of the data was poor. Coefficient alpha ranged from .3 to .4, despite attempts to revise the stimulus materials.

The Reasoning About Current Issues Test, Recognition Component

After the disappointing performance of the computerized format, an attempt was made to develop a paper-and-pencil measure that asked participants to read over a set of short summary statements that corresponded to different levels of epistemic complexity. Three interim instruments were developed and tested over the period of the next three years and were used, on a pilot basis, by researchers interested in having some measure dealing with epistemic cognition. In brief, revisions to these instruments abandoned the lockstep progression through major interview questions for each dilemma topic, and employed a format similar to Rest's Defining Issues Test (Rest, 1979) by presenting individuals with five different problems. One of the problems, chemical additives, came from the interview. The other four were created about more contemporary issues such as the causes of alcoholism, using the same criteria that were used to develop the dilemmas for the RJI (see previous section). Participants were asked to write a short response to a question on the given topic in their own words and asked to rate, on a Likert scale, the extent to which each of 10 short written responses were similar to their own written response. Each of the statements represented the epistemic assumptions of one level of the Reflective Judgment Model. These statements are shorter than those used in the earlier summary statements and do not cover all ratable aspects of the level.

After rating the statements, participants are asked to rank three statements as most similar to their own views. In order to control for endorsements of merely impressive vocabulary, statements were included that contained grammatically correct but nonsensical statements. In a similar fashion to Rest's Defining Issues Test, scoring techniques involved estimation of the level of reasoning most often ranked as similar to the participant's own views. Given the small number of statements for each dilemma topic, this estimate is calculated across all dilemma topics. After minor revisions, this instrument appeared to demonstrate an internal consistency that, while not as impressive as that found for the Reflective Judgment Interview, was acceptable for large-scale assessment (ranging from the low to mid .70's, depending on the sample). Participants appear to be able to complete the instrument in a reasonable amount of time, taking anywhere from 30 to 45 minutes to complete it. Correlations with the RJI are in the high .30's.

The Reasoning About Current Issues Test, Discrimination Component

A second component of the RCI was developed based on insights from Kitchener et al. (1993) and the aforementioned think-aloud protocols. Individuals with relatively unsophisticated views toward a problem failed to discriminate between more and less sophisticated arguments. Kitchener et al. (1993) reported data suggesting that this failure to discriminate occurred more often between statements that reflected the individual's modal RJ level and statements written at higher levels. In this part of the RCI, the participant is asked to be the instructor for a hypothetical undergraduate class in which an assignment has been given to write a short essay. Seven pairs of essays are then presented to the participant, and the participant is asked to compare the two essays in each of these pairs by means of three or four Likert items that ask them to evaluate the complexity of the arguments. Care was taken to ensure that the vocabulary was roughly similar across all essays and that the length of response was roughly similar. For example, one essay pair consists of essays reflecting Reflective Judgment levels 2 and 4. Participants are asked, "Which of these individuals is reasoning more complexly about this issue?" or "Which of these individuals better understands how scientists make conclusions about this issue?" As before, think-aloud protocols were used in the initial stages of development and, as before, substantial changes were made in response to this feedback. For example, asking the direct question, "Which of these students is thinking more critically about the issue?" was dropped because participants understood this question to be asking them to identify which student essay was more adversarial or abrasive. Students, particularly freshmen, appear to enjoy the role of "instructor" and the instrument appears to be relatively quick to administer, with individuals completing the seven essay comparisons in approximately 15 minutes. This instrument has also been found to produce reasonably internally consistent response. Coefficient alpha between Likert items within a given essay comparison ranges from the high .70's to low .80's, depending on the sample. Consonant with Kitchener et al.'s report, however, ability to successfully discriminate between some levels of the Reflective Judgment Model does not appear to be closely tied with ability to discriminate between other levels. For that reason, overall scores from this section of the instrument are based on the total number of occasions that the more sophisticated essay was judged superior. It should be noted that the section of the measures does not ask about epistemic cognitions directly. Rather it is based on the observation that more advanced epistemic cognitions are also more cognitively complex, a notion supported by Fischer's skill theory (Kitchener & Fischer, 1990). Correlations with the RJI have been in the low .40's, suggesting it is measuring a construct that is related to but not identical to the RJI.

FURTHER INSTRUMENT EVALUATION

We no longer feel we can produce an "objectively scorable" version of the Reflective Judgment Interview. Rather, we have instead focused on developing other assessment instruments that tap into related skills that are based on the Reflective Judgment Model. Consequently, the question arises as to how one may judge whether these new attempts have been successful and reflect some aspect of the development of epistemic cognition. Given the fact that these instruments may also be used in large-scale assessment settings, it is also critical that the psychometric properties of the instruments be assessed to determine if they are equally appropriate for men and women, and for students from various ethnic backgrounds. Although this work is currently under way, we can provide a report of initial findings and the research currently under way.

Educational Level Differences

One criterion for judging the utility of these instruments is to ask whether they appear to uncover differences between students that are similar in magnitude to those found for the Reflective Judgment Interview. As King and Kitchener (1994) and Wood (1997) report, the effect size for freshman/senior differences associated with the Reflective Judgment Interview is roughly one standard deviation. In fact, based on data from about 5,000 undergraduate and graduate students, educational level differences in the stage most often endorsed in the Recognition component of the RCI appear to also recover a one standard deviation difference. The number of correct discriminations between essays on the Discrimination measure, however, appears to yield a much smaller difference between freshmen and seniors. One of the luxuries of a larger sample is the ability to estimate whether these differences are attributable to other third variable explanations. Happily, the effect size associated with both measures remains roughly the same after adjusting the scores for the effects of academic aptitude (as measured by actual, estimated, or self-reported ACT composite scores), for example. Additionally, despite the large sample size associated with the study, we find no evidence of differences between men and women or as a function of ethnicity. This conclusion is based on a sample that included African Americans, Asian Americans, Euro-Americans, and Latino Americans.

DIRECTIONS FOR FUTURE RESEARCH

Based on our data gathered to date, we are aware that much of the most interesting work remains to be done in order to understand relationship of how constructs of epistemic cognition are related to aspects of personality and problem solving. One very important, yet underresearched, topic deals with the question of whether differences in epistemic cognition represent a distinct aspect of problem-solving ability or merely reflect individuals' motivation to deal with the problem or some other aspect of personality. Some initial work based on the Reflective Judgment Interview has explored the relationship between Reflective Judgment Interview performance and Need for Cognition (Cacioppo, Petty, Feinstein, Jarvis, & Blair, 1996), while other work has sought to elucidate the relationship between performance on the Reflective Judgment dilemma dealing with homosexuality as it relates to the construct of tolerance toward homosexuals (Guthrie, 1996). Other possible research questions concern the relationship of the

Reflective Judgment Instrument to measures of the Big Five personality dimensions (Costa & McCrae, 1992, 1995).

A second set of research questions centers around better understanding of the "distinct yet related" abilities measured by the discrimination and recognition portions of the RCI. Why, for example, does only a one-half standard deviation difference in the discrimination portion of the RCI occur? Does this measure tap the ability to evaluate the complexity of a given argument, or does this difference merely represent an increased attention to reading? In other words, do the two parts of the RCI tape different skills and are there different educational interventions that might be designed to improve those skills? Could students, for example, be taught to read more carefully for the epistemic assumptions in argument?

Third, the question of whether dilemma topic effects exist for specific populations needs to be further investigated as does the effect of including more or less information in the problems. As mentioned before, preliminary evidence suggests that some dilemmas such as food additives are not perceived as relevant for contemporary student populations. Additionally, the possibility of disciplinary effects for particular topics as a function of academic major is an additional arena of inquiry. Another dimension of the stimulus materials in studies of epistemic cognition concerns the amount of information and problem structure to be revealed to the participant at the outset. Kardash and Scholes (1996), for example, provided participants with extensive background on conflicting experts' opinion concerning whether HIV was a cause of AIDS in order to evaluate the effect of that information on epistemic cognition. Additional studies investigating the effects of stimulus materials on forms of epistemic cognition need to be examined. As such, participants in the study who did not believe that experts could disagree about this topic were faced with the task of denying that part of the stimulus materials are true.

CONCLUSION

At this point in our search for objectively scorable measures, we are very aware that such measures are not a "paper-and-pencil interview" but rather assess aspects of epistemic cognition that are related but distinct from the behaviors assessed by the Reflective Judgment Interview. While we think that the benefits of being able to conduct large-scale assessments with these measures will enable us to answer other questions related to their validity as well as the importance of epistemic cognition in problem solving and other aspects of life, it is important to recognize the limits of objective measures. They do not allow individuals to make their own meaning. On the other hand, by focusing on epistemic cognition and its relationship to ill-structured problem solving and by providing a more economical way to assess them, we hope a greater focus can be placed on ill-structured problem solving as an outcome of higher education. In addition, by paying attention to subskills such as recognition and discrimination, educators will also have information that can stimulate new classroom interventions. Much to instructors' surprise, for example, students sometimes fail to recognize a more sophisticated view of a problem even when it is handed to them in its entirety. This failure to discriminate between less and more sophisticated arguments or to perceive the structure of a justification may underlie the frustration that some instructors feel when they wonder if some students would recognize a sound argument "if it bit them on the nose." These instruments direct us concretely back to points raised by Kitchener and Fischer (1990) that instruction designed to promote cognitive development must provide explicit supports and appropriate challenges to students. An approach, which assumes that students will be instantly able to reason in an epistemologically sophisticated way about ill-structured controversies if they are presented with such topics, is not an effective instructional strategy.

ACKNOWLEDGMENTS

This research was supported in part by Department of Education Grant #R309F70060 to Dr. Karen Kitchener, Principal Investigator and Phillip Wood, Co-Principal Investigator.
Address correspondence to the first author at: 210 McAlester Hall, University of Missouri-Columbia, Columbia, MO 65211.

REFERENCES

Association of American Colleges (1991). *The challenge of connecting learning: Liberal learning and the arts and sciences major. Volume 1.* Author: Washington, DC.
Baxter Magolda, M. (1992). Cocurricular influences on college students' intellectual development. *Journal of College Student Development, 33,* 203–213.
Belenky, M. F., Bond, L. A., & Weinstock, J. S. (1997). *A tradition that has no name: Nurturing the development of people, families, and communities.* New York: Basic Books.
Brabeck, M. M., & Wood, P. K. (1990). Cross-sectional and longitudinal evidence for differences between well-structured and ill-structured problem-solving abilities. In M. L. Commons, C. Armon, L. Kohlberg, F. A. Richards, T. A Grotzer, & J. D. Sinnott (Eds.), *Adult development 2: Models and methods in the study of adolescent and adult thought,* (pp. 133–146). New York: Praeger.
Cacioppo, J. T., Petty, R. E., Feinstein, J. A., Jarvis, W., & Blair, G. (1996), Dispositional differences in cognitive motivation: The life and times of individuals varying in need for cognition. *Psychological Bulletin, 119,* 197–253.
Ceci, J. J. & Liker, J. K. (1987). A day at the races: A study of IQ, expertise, and cognitive complexity. *Journal of Experimental Psychology, 116,* 90.
Churchman, C. W. (1971). *The design of inquiring systems: Basic concepts of systems and organization.* Basic Books: New York.
Costa, P. T., Jr., & McCrae, R. R. (1992). *Revised Neo Personality Inventory (NEO-PI-R) and NEO Five-Factor Inventory (NEO-FFI) professional manual.* Odessa, FL: Psychological Assessment Resources.

Costa, P. T., Jr., & McCrae, R. R. (1995). Primary traits of Eysenck's P-E-N system: Three- and five-factor solutions. *Journal of Personality and Social Psychology, 69*, 308–317.

DeBord, K. (1993). Promoting Reflective Judgment in counseling psychology graduate education. Unpublished masters thesis, University of Missouri-Columbia.

Duncker, K. (1926). A qualitative (experimental and theoretical) study of productive thinking (solving of comprehensible problems). *Journal of Genetic Psychology, 33*, 642–708.

Friedman, A. (1995). The relationship between intellectual disposition and Reflective Judgment in college women. (Doctoral dissertation, Boston College, 1995). *Dissertation Abstracts International, 56*(09), 3468A, (University Microfilms No. AAI96-02073).

Gick, M. L. & Holyoak, K. J. (1980). Analogical problem solving. *Cognitive Psychology, 12*, 306–355.

Glenn, D. D. (1992). The relationship of graduate education and Reflective Judgment in older adults (Doctoral dissertation, Indiana University, 1992). *Dissertation Abstracts International, 53*(12), 4253A, (University Microfilms No. AAI93-10330).

Guthrie, V. L. (1996). *The relationship of levels of intellectual development and levels of tolerance for diversity among college students.* Unpublished doctoral dissertation, Bowling Green State University, Bowling Green, Ohio.

Hofer, B. K. & Pintrich, P. R. (1997). The development of epistemological theories: Beliefs about knowledge and knowing and their relationship to learning. *Review of Educational Research, 67*, 88–140.

Hoffman, L. R., Burke, R. J., & Maier, N. R. F. (1963). Does training with differential reinforcement on similar problems help in solving a new problem? *Psychological Reports, 13*, 147–154.

Johnson, E. J. (1988). Expertise and decision under uncertainty: Performance and process. In M.T. Chi, R. Glaser, & M. J. Farr (Eds.) *The nature of expertise* (pp. 209–228). Erlbaum: Hillsdale, NJ

Kardash, C. M. & Scholes, R. J. (1996). Effects of preexisting beliefs, epistemological beliefs, and need for cognition on interpretation of controversial issues. *Journal of Educational Psychology, 88*, 260–271.

King, P. M., & Kitchener, K. S., (1994). *Developing Reflective Judgment: Understanding and promoting intellectual growth and critical thinking in adolescents and adults.* Jossey-Bass: San Francisco.

King, P. M., Wood, P. K., & Mines, R. A. (1990). Critical thinking among college and graduate students. *The Review of Higher Education, 13*, 167–186.

Kitchener, K. S. (1983). Cognition, metacognition, and epistemic cognition: A three-level model of cognitive processing. *Human Development, 26*, 222–232.

Kitchener, K. S. & Fischer, K. W. (1990). A skill approach to the development of reflective thinking. In D. Kuhn (Ed.), Developmental perspectives on teaching and learning thinking skills. *Contributions to Human Development, Vol. 23* (pp. 48–62). Basel, Switzerland: S. Karger.

Kitchener, K. S., & King, P. M. (1981). Reflective Judgment: Concepts of justification and their relationship to age and education. *Journal of Applied Developmental Psychology, 2,* 89–116.

Kitchener, K. S., Lynch, C., Fischer, K., & Wood, P. K. (1993). Developmental range in Reflective Judgment: The effect of contextual support and practice on developmental stage. *Developmental Psychology, 29*, 893–906.

Kitchener, K. S., King, P. M., Wood, P. K. & Davison, M. L. (1989). Sequentiality and consistency in the development of Reflective Judgment: A six-year longitudinal study. *Journal of Applied Developmental Psychology, 10*, 73–95.

Kitchener, K. S. & Wood, P. K. (1987). Development of concepts of justification in German university students. *International Journal of Behavioral Development, 10*, 171–185.

Kuhn (1992). Thinking as argument. *Harvard Educational Review, 62*, 155–178.

Kuhn, D. & Brannock, J. (1977). Development of the isolation of variables scheme in experimental and "natural experiment" contexts. *Developmental Psychology, 13*, 9–14.

Lawrence, J. A. (1988). Expertise on the bench: Modeling magistrates' judicial decision making. In M. T. Chi, R. Glaser, & M. J. Farr (Eds.) *The nature of expertise* (pp. 229–259). Erlbaum: Hillsdale, NJ.

Maier, N. R. F. (1933). An aspect of human reasoning. *British Journal of Psychology, 35*, 144–155.

McKinney (1985). Reflective Judgment: An aspect of adolescent cognitive development (Doctoral dissertation, University of Denver). *Dissertation Abstracts International, 47*, 402B.

Moore, W. S. (1989). The Learning Environment Preferences: Exploring the construct validity of an objective measure of the Perry scheme of intellectual development. *Journal of College Student Development, 30*, 504–514.

Moore, W. S. (1991). *Tuning in to student voices: Assessment and the Perry scheme of intellectual and ethical development.* (ERIC document, Reproduction Service No. ED 322 868).

Neisser, U. (1976). General, academic, and artificial intelligence. In Resnick, L. (Ed.) *The nature of intelligence.* Hillsdale, NJ: Erlbaum.

Nixon, S. J. & Parsons, O. A. (1991). Alcohol-related efficiency deficits using an ecologically valid test. *Alcoholism: Clinical and Experimental Research, 15*, 601–606.

Nixon, S. J., Tivis, R., & Parsons, O. A. (1995). Behavioral dysfunction and cognitive efficiency in male and female alcoholics. *Alcoholism: Clinical and Experimental Research, 19*, 577–581.

Perry, W. G. (1970). *Forms of intellectual and ethical development during the college years.* New York: Holt, Rinehart & Winston.

Raaheim, K. (1974). *Problem solving and intelligence.* Universitetsforlaget: Oslo.

Rest, J. R. (1979). *Development in judging moral issues.* University of Minnesota Press: Minneapolis, MN.

Samson, A. W. (1999). Latino college students and reflective judgement. Unpublished doctoral dissertation, University of Denver.

Schommer, M. (1990). Effects of beliefs about the nature of knowledge on comprehension. *Journal of Educational Psychology, 82*, 498–504.

Simon, H. A. (1973). The structure of ill-structured problems. *Artificial Intelligence, 4*, 181–201.

Simon, H. A. (1978). Information-processing theory of human problem solving. In W. Estes (Ed.), *Handbook of learning and cognitive processes. Vol. 5.* Erlbaum: Hillsdale, NJ.

Sternberg, R. J. (1982). Reasoning, problem solving, and intelligence. In R. J. Sternberg (Ed.) *Handbook of human intelligence.* (pp. 227–307). Cambridge University Press: New York.

Van Tine, N.B. (1990). The development of Reflective Judgment in adolescents. *Dissertation Abstracts International, 51*, 2659.

Voss, J. F. & Post, T. A. (1988). On the solving of ill-structured problems. In M. R. Chi, R. Glaser, & M. J. Farr (Eds.) *The nature of expertise* (pp. 261–285). Erlbaum: Hillsdale, NJ.

Wood, P. K. (1983). Inquiring systems and problem structure: Implications for cognitive development. *Human Development, 26*, 245–314.

Wood, P. K. (1997). A secondary analysis of claims regarding the Reflective Judgment Interview: Internal consistency, sequentiality and intraindividual differences in ill-structured problem solving. *Higher education: Handbook of theory and research.* (pp. 245–314) Edison, NJ: Agathon.

Wood, P. K. & Lynch, C. (1998). Using guided essays to assess and encourage reflective thinking. *Assessment Update, 10*, 14–15.

IV

Perspectives on
Discipline-Specific
Epistemology

15

"Knowing What to Believe": The Relevance of Students' Mathematical Beliefs for Mathematics Education

Erik De Corte
University of Leuven, Belgium

Peter Op 't Eynde
University of Leuven, Belgium

Lieven Verschaffel
University of Leuven, Belgium

INTRODUCTION

In the 1960s, research on affect typically focused on the relationship between students' attitudes toward mathematics and their achievement in mathematics (for a review see Aiken, 1970, 1976). Most of these studies were carried out separately from research on mathematics learning by researchers in differential and social psychology; they used a psychometric approach and the main data-collection technique consisted of administering questionnaires to large groups of students (McLeod, 1994). Only small effects were found (correlations ranging from .20 to .40), and meta-analyses, including also more recent studies in this tradition, emphasize that a more differentiated perspective on the relation between attitudes and achievement in mathematics is necessary, taking into account such variables as, for example, gender, grade level, and ethnic background (e.g., Ma & Kishor, 1997). A major criticism of these older studies was also that they lacked a strong theoretical foundation (McLeod, 1992).

Alternatively, since the 1970s, scholars working from a more cognitive perspective aimed at understanding the processes that characterize students' mathematical learning and problem solving by using, for example, thinking-aloud

297

protocols. In general, this shift in perspective was accompanied by a separation of attitudes, as an affective construct, from beliefs, as a cognitive construct (Richardson, 1996). As research in educational psychology became more and more cognitively oriented, the typical studies of attitudes toward mathematics moved out of the limelight, while teachers' and students' beliefs about mathematics moved to the foreground as an important research topic (e.g., Schoenfeld, 1983; Thompson, 1984; Underhill, 1988). Meanwhile, over a decade of research has contributed to a better understanding of the relevance of beliefs for mathematical learning and problem solving. For instance, Schoenfeld (1992) concludes from his and others' research (e.g., Lampert, 1990) that "Students' beliefs shape their behavior in ways that have extraordinary powerful (and often negative) consequences" (p. 359).

Students' beliefs as well as misbeliefs (i.e., their naive and incorrect beliefs) determine the way they engage in mathematical learning and problem solving, and the kind of strategies they use. For instance, students who think mathematics are useful, interesting, and important are more likely to work hard. Pokay and Blumenfeld (1990) found that these value beliefs indirectly predicted high school grades in geometry through effort and the use of effective learning strategies (see also, Seegers & Boekaerts, 1993). More troublesome is the fact that research also shows that a lot of students hold the misbelief that almost all mathematical problems can be solved by direct application of the facts, rules, formulas, and procedures shown by the teacher (see Frank, 1988; Garofalo, 1989; Schoenfeld, 1985a). When learning mathematics, they will put their energy in memorizing rules and procedures, but they will never come to a full understanding of mathematics.

Notwithstanding the general agreement among researchers nowadays that students' beliefs have important influence on mathematical learning and problem solving, from a conceptual viewpoint there is still a lack of clarity on the specific nature of beliefs and even more with respect to the different beliefs that are studied in relation to mathematical learning and problem solving. Some define a belief about mathematics as an affective construct (e.g., McLeod, 1992), while others see it as a (meta)cognitive one (e.g., Garofalo & Lester, 1985).

In studying the role of students' beliefs scholars discuss topics as different as:

- Beliefs about the nature of mathematics and mathematical learning and problem solving (e.g., Carter & Yackel, 1989; Frank, 1988; Garofalo & Lester, 1985 ; Schoenfeld, 1985a, 1985b; Spangler, 1992).
- Beliefs about the self in the context of mathematics learning and problem solving, i.e., motivational beliefs (e.g., Carter & Norwood, 1997; Kloosterman, Raymond, & Emenaker, 1996; Pajares & Miller, 1994; Seegers & Boekaerts, 1993; Stipek & Gralinski 1991; Vanayan, White, Yuen, & Teper, 1997).

- Beliefs about mathematics teaching and the social context of mathematics learning and problem solving (e.g., Cobb, Yackel, & Wood, 1989; de Abreu, Bishop, & Pompeu, 1997).
- Epistemological beliefs (e.g., Schommer, Crouse, & Rhodes, 1992).

In this chapter we first explore how mathematics-related beliefs are conceived and differentiated in the most representative literature; attention will also be paid to the relationship among beliefs and knowledge. Against this background and on the basis of the available empirical research, we then attempt to develop a more comprehensive framework in which students' distinct mathematics-related beliefs are defined, and their relationship to mathematical learning and problem solving is analyzed. Next we focus on the impact of instruction on the development in students of certain well-known naive and/or incorrect beliefs about mathematics. Taking seriously that many students develop such misbeliefs, a brief review follows of studies in which instructional environments have been designed and implemented that seem to be supportive of the development of more adequate beliefs in relation to mathematics and mathematics learning. Some final comments focusing on directions for future research conclude the chapter.

MATHEMATICS–RELATED BELIEFS: A PRELIMINARY VIEW

In his pioneering work on mathematical beliefs, Schoenfeld (1985a), starting from a cognitive perspective, has introduced the following definition:

> Belief systems are one's mathematical world view, the perspective with which one approaches mathematics and mathematical tasks. One's beliefs about mathematics can determine how one chooses to approach a problem, which techniques will be used or avoided, how long and how hard one will work on it, and so on. Beliefs establish the context within which resources, heuristics, and control operate (p. 45).

This definition focuses on beliefs about mathematics, involving also beliefs about mathematics learning and problem solving. Schoenfeld stresses the relevance of beliefs for learning and problem solving by clarifying the relationship between beliefs and other components of mathematical competence, namely the knowledge base (resources), problem-solving strategies (heuristics), and metacognitive skills (control) (see also Schoenfeld, 1992). However, he limits his discussion to students' beliefs about mathematics, and does not distinguish other kinds of beliefs that students have and how they influence mathematical learning and problem solving.

Other authors have taken a more comprehensive and more differentiated approach to students' beliefs. For example, McLeod (1992), who stresses the affective aspect of beliefs, distinguishes between beliefs about mathematics, beliefs about self, beliefs about mathematics teaching, and beliefs about the social context of mathematics education. Taking a motivational perspective, Kloosterman (1996) has developed a model of the beliefs/motivation/achievement process in mathematics in which he relates beliefs to, for instance, the notion of expectancy of success in Atkinson's (1957) expectancy-value theory of achievement motivation. In his model he tries to critically integrate McLeod's four kinds of beliefs into two basic types: beliefs about mathematics as a discipline, and beliefs about learning mathematics. The latter type involves three subcategories: beliefs about oneself as a learner of mathematics, beliefs about the role of the teacher, and beliefs about learning mathematics. However, Kloosterman (1996) adds that his model "should not be viewed as a model of 'the' key beliefs that lead to motivation in mathematics. Rather, it is a model of a number of potentially important factors. I have tried to justify these factors, but justification for alternative factors is also possible. Note that there is considerable overlap among the factors in the model" (p. 143).

What still seems to be lacking is a research-based theoretical framework—an overall structure in the terminology of McLeod (1992)—for the study of beliefs in mathematics education. Students' beliefs about mathematics clearly are situated at the intersection of the cognitive and the motivational, or better affective, domain. This dual nature, and more importantly the separated cognitive and motivational research traditions that correspond with it, makes it difficult to come to the intended overall structure. However, the fact that a variety of mathematics-related beliefs are studied from different research perspectives does not necessarily have to be a disadvantage; to the contrary. It only asks for a more general synthesizing model in which the different results can be placed and understood in relation to each other. So far, such a comprehensive theoretical model is lacking, and looks like what this research field needs.

In view of elaborating such a model, it is important to first clarify further what we mean by beliefs, i.e., what is the nature of beliefs. A proposition is believed when the proposition's meaning is represented in a mental system and is treated as if it was true (Gilbert, 1991). Students believe that 'mathematics is computation' the moment they perceive mathematics to be that way. After all, comprehending a concept or proposition is believing it. The moment we comprehend a concept we implicitly accept it as true. Only in a second phase in confrontation with other concepts and propositions or new situations will we question it and maybe consciously change our mind (Spinoza, 1982). Young children's uncritical acceptance of everything they see and are told is a prototypical example, "We begin by believing everything; whatever is, is true" (Bain, 1859, p. 511).

From an epistemological perspective a belief is an individual construct, while knowledge is essentially a social construct. Beliefs refer to what 'I' believe to be true, regardless of the fact that others agree with me or not. Knowledge, on the other hand, requires a truth condition. This condition entails an agreement in a community that a certain proposition is agreed on as being true (Green, 1971). This consensus gives it its higher epistemic standing (Fenstermacher, 1994). Knowledge goes beyond the individual and is situated in communities of practice. It is distributed in the world among individuals, the tools, and the books they use (Greeno, Collins, & Resnick, 1996; Salomon & Perkins, 1998). Of course, this is not to say that individuals cannot possess knowledge. However, the ultimate epistemological criteria to discriminate between belief and knowledge are not situated in the individual, but in the social context.

From a psychological perspective, beliefs and knowledge are closely related constructs. Students' problem-solving behavior will always be directed by what they believe to be true, implying knowledge as well as beliefs. Both constructs determine in close interaction students' understanding of specific mathematical problems and situations. Moreover, students' beliefs and knowledge are both fundamentally determined by the sociocultural environment they live and work in. After all, the ways in which humans view the world and interact with it reflect their understanding of the basic beliefs and fundamental knowledge shared with members of their family, intellectual discipline, and other groups in which they function (Alexander, Schallert, & Hare, 1991).

Since the end of the 1980s, the importance of contextual factors for knowledge and learning has been highlighted by the situated cognition and learning paradigm that emerged in reaction to the mentalistic/computational view of learning and thinking (Brown, Collins, & Duguid, 1989). Situativity theory has quite rightly stressed that learning is enacted essentially in interaction with the social and cultural contexts resulting in clusters of situated knowledge. Several researchers have pointed out that, as knowledge, beliefs are also organized in clusters around specific situations and contexts (Bogdan, 1986; Green, 1971). As constituting elements of a person's entire belief system these clusters are framed in a person's subjective rationality. People always strive for a coherent belief system; only then they are able to function in an intelligible way. Beliefs that are perceived as incompatible will be changed, and consequently also the clusters they are part of. Depending on the centrality of these changing beliefs in a person's entire belief system, this will also affect other clusters. Carter and Yackel (1989) compare the process that characterizes a change in a person's central and fundamental beliefs with a paradigm shift. The equilibrium a belief system is trying to hold, or, for that matter, the driving force behind a change in beliefs is, however, not primarily logical in nature, but rather psychological. Snow, Corno, and Jackson (1996) rightfully acknowledge that:

> Human beings in general show tendencies to form and hold beliefs that serve their own needs, desires and goals; these beliefs serve ego-enhancement, self-protective, and personal and social control purposes and cause biases in perception and judgment in social situations as a result (p. 292).

Consequently, beliefs do not only carry denotative, but also connotative, evaluative meaning (Snow et al., 1996). Students' networks of beliefs provide not only the context within which they perceive and understand the world, but also play an emotional and motivational role in their learning and problem solving (McLeod, 1992; Power & Dalgleish, 1997).

The subjective rationality underlying the organization of a belief system rarely is consciously known by the student. Rather it reveals itself in students' different mathematics-related beliefs, the way they actually perceive specific mathematical problems, and how they solve them. In recognizing and interpreting the different beliefs students hold and the relations between these respective beliefs, one always has to be aware of the previously-mentioned structural characteristics of a belief system, i.e., the principle of situational clustering and the principle of a subjective coherence (rationality). This implies that what to an outsider might look like contradictory beliefs, probably will not be perceived as such by the individual itself. For example, Schoenfeld (1985b) reports data on students' beliefs where he concludes that "On the one hand, there was a tendency to regard mathematics learning largely as a matter of memorization. On the other hand, the students expressed significant support for the idea that mathematics is interesting and challenging, allowing a great deal of room for discovery" (p.14).

It might well be that, in the former case, they were expressing their beliefs about school mathematics, while in the latter they were giving their view on the use of mathematics in society. As long as students are convinced that what they learn in school has little or no resemblance with or relevance for what happens in the real world, they can smoothly live with these two beliefs about mathematics without perceiving any contradiction (Verschaffel, Greer, & De Corte, 2000).

Starting from these reflections on the nature of beliefs and the functioning of belief systems we will attempt to develop in the next section a comprehensive framework of students' mathematics-related beliefs.

A CATEGORIZATION OF
MATHEMATICAL BELIEFS

It is generally assumed that students' mathematics-related beliefs determine in important ways their learning and problem-solving behavior through cognitive as well as motivational and affective processes (see Kloosterman, 1996; Schoenfeld, 1985a). However, an in-depth analysis of the role beliefs play in mathematics learning and problem solving should start from a further specification of the different kinds of beliefs and their respective influence. As mentioned earlier, Kloosterman (1996) and McLeod (1992) already presented categorizations of students' mathematics-related beliefs. They discussed the role of different beliefs taking, respectively, theories on motivation and affect as a starting point. Their categories of beliefs are colored by the perspective taken, leading to overlapping but not identical categories with sometimes different names.

Although those pioneering contributions deserve credit for putting beliefs on the research agenda and certainly extended our understanding on the role of beliefs in mathematical learning and problem solving, there is nevertheless—as both authors themselves argue—a need for a more comprehensive framework of students' mathematics-related beliefs. In our opinion, such an overall structure should be grounded in a theory of beliefs, rather than in a motivational or affective theory. As Thompson (1992) points out:

> Researchers interested in studying (teachers') beliefs should give careful consideration to the concept, both from a philosophical as well as a psychological perspective. Philosophical works can be helpful in clarifying the nature of beliefs. Psychological studies may prove useful in interpreting the nature of the relationship between beliefs and behavior as well as in understanding the function and structure of beliefs (p. 129; our parentheses).

This should not necessarily lead to completely different categories of beliefs than those presented by McLeod (1992) and Kloosterman (1996), but different interpretations of and overlap between categories should be resolved and relations between categories should be clarified.

Our categorization of mathematics-related beliefs represents a first step in the direction of such a more comprehensive approach. Taking into account the fundamental insights in the nature of beliefs and believing discussed in the previous section (see e.g., Bogdan, 1986; Gilbert, 1991; Green, 1971), it tries to integrate major components of the models of McLeod and Kloosterman, as well as the results of the research already done on the role of students' beliefs in mathematical learning and problem solving. However, at present our beliefs categories are not grounded in a specific psychological theory of mind. Generally speaking, the present level of psychological understanding does not permit too many statements about how exactly the content of mental representations is organized (Power & Dalgleish, 1997). Since a comprehensive theory of mind is lacking, a more heuristic approach is indicated. Inspired by the heuristic model on the domains of mind content developed by Power and Dalgleish (1997), we distinguish:

1. Beliefs about mathematics education.
2. Beliefs about the self in relation to mathematics.
3. Beliefs about the social context, i.e., the context of mathematical learning and problem solving.

BELIEFS ABOUT MATHEMATICS EDUCATION

Students' general beliefs about mathematics education are located in this category. We differentiate between the following subcategories:

- Beliefs about mathematics, such as formal mathematics have little or nothing to do with real thinking or problem solving.
- Beliefs about mathematical learning and problem solving; for instance, mathematics learning is memorizing.
- Beliefs about mathematics teaching; for example, a good teacher first explains the theory and gives an example of an exercise before he or she asks us to solve mathematical problems.

In line with Schoenfeld's (1985a) definition quoted earlier, students' beliefs about mathematics education reflect their view on what mathematics is like: the perspective with which they approach mathematics and mathematical problems and tasks. 'What is mathematics' is a question often asked throughout history and the answers given differed with the time (De Corte, Greer, & Verschaffel, 1996). Recently, the view of mathematics as a body of absolute facts and procedures, dealing with quantities and forms, with certain knowledge, is under attack. Several authors (e.g., Ernest, 1991; Schoenfeld, 1992; Tymoczko, 1986) advocate a conceptualization of mathematics as an activity grounded in human practices, a science of patterns with problem solving at the heart of it. Such fundamental issues are captured by students' beliefs about mathematics. Furthermore, what we fundamentally think about mathematics and mathematical knowledge is closely related to what we think mathematics learning, on the one hand, and mathematics teaching, on the other, are like (Hofer & Pintrich, 1997). Therefore, we consider these three kinds of beliefs to be closely related, clustered so to say; they seem to constitute three interrelated subsets of beliefs about mathematics.

Based on empirical research, several scholars stressed the importance of beliefs about mathematics and about mathematical learning and problem solving (e.g., Garofalo, 1989, Greeno, 1991; Kloosterman, 1996; McLeod, 1992). In these studies mainly two kinds of data-collection techniques were used, namely questionnaires (e.g., Kouba & McDonald, 1986; Schoenfeld, 1985b; Yackel, 1984), and interviews (e.g., Kloosterman, 1996; Spangler, 1992). In addition, more anecdotal data have been collected inferring students' beliefs from their problem-solving behavior (e.g., Lester, Garofalo, & Kroll, 1989). Descriptive in nature, most of these studies reveal the kind of beliefs about mathematics and mathematics learning students hold at different ages. Scholars usually also make interpretative inferences on the impact of these respective beliefs on learning and problem solving. But, rarely the influence of specific beliefs about mathematics and/or beliefs about mathematical learning and problem solving on students' performance is studied through carefully designed and well-controlled experiments or using advanced statistical analyses techniques, e.g., path analyses (for an exception, see Schommer et al., 1992). Whatever research methods scholars use, they all deliver converging evidence concerning the prevailing beliefs students hold about the nature of mathematics and about mathematical learning and problem solving. Lampert (1990) characterizes this common view about mathematics as follows: Mathematics is associated with certainty, and with being able to give quickly the correct answer; doing mathematics corresponds to following rules prescribed by the teacher; knowing math means being able to recall and use the correct rule when asked by the teacher; and an answer to a mathematical question or problem becomes true when it is approved by the authority of the teacher. A more extended list of typical student beliefs derived from the literature is given by Schoenfeld (1992; see also Mtetwa & Garofalo, 1989; Stodolsky, Salk, & Glaessner, 1991):

Mathematics problems have one and only one right answer.

There is only one correct way to solve any mathematics problem—usually the rule the teacher has most recently demonstrated to the class.

Ordinary students cannot expect to understand mathematics; they expect simply to memorize it and apply what they have learned mechanically and without understanding.

Mathematics is a solitary activity, done by individuals in isolation.

Students who have understood the mathematics they have studied will be able to solve any assigned problem in five minutes or less.

The mathematics learned in school has little or nothing to do with the real world.

Formal proof is irrelevant to processes of discovery or invention (p. 359).

An important question from a theoretical perspective is whether and how these mathematics-related beliefs are linked to more general epistemological categories as proposed, for instance, by Hofer and Pintrich (1997) and by Schommer et al. (1992). In this respect, Schommer et al. (1992) point out that some of students' beliefs about mathematics are very closely related to their epistemological beliefs. For example, the belief mentioned at the outset of this section that 'Formal mathematics has little or nothing to do with real thinking and problem solving' can, according to these authors, be rephrased as a general epistemological view: 'Knowledge is best characterized as isolated facts rather than interrelated facts,' and, thus, be subsumed under the general epistemological category 'simplicity of knowledge,' one of the major dimensions distinguished by both Hofer and Pintrich (1997) and Schommer (1992). In a similar way a number of other beliefs identified by Lampert (1990) and Schoenfeld (1992) can be linked to Hofer and Pintrich's (1997) four basic categories of epistemological beliefs, namely certainty of knowledge, simplicity of knowledge, sources of knowledge, and justification for knowing:

Certainty: mathematics is associated with certainty (Lampert);

Simplicity: knowing math means being able to recall and use the correct rule when asked by the teacher (Lampert); the mathematics learned in school has little or nothing to do with the real world (Schoenfeld); mathematics problems have one and only one right answer (Schoenfeld);

Sources: doing math corresponds to following rules prescribed by the teacher (Lampert); formal proof is irrelevant to processes of discovery and invention (Schoenfeld);

Justification: an answer to a mathematical question becomes true when it is approved by the authority of the teacher (Lampert); there is only one correct way to solve any mathematics problem—usually the rule the teacher has demonstrated (Schoenfeld).

However, much more research is needed to unravel the relationships between domain-specific beliefs in a variety of subject-matter fields, on the one hand, and the basic dimensions of epistemological theories, on the other. Indeed, if episte-mological beliefs, i.e., beliefs about the nature of knowledge and the processes of knowing, are essentially very fundamental and general in nature (Hofer & Pin-trich, 1997), then mathematics-related beliefs may not be considered as episte-mological beliefs as such, but rather be perceived as domain-specific manifesta-tions of the general epistemological dimensions.

Students' beliefs about how mathematics should be taught in class and what the teacher should do, have been studied much less. Frank (1988) pointed out that junior high students traditionally believe that the role of the mathematics teacher is to transmit mathematical knowledge and to verify that students have received this knowledge. This view is confirmed in an interview study by Kloosterman (1996) with 44 third to sixth graders: almost all of them perceived the teacher as the transmitter of knowledge and the source of answers. Using data of 29 of those pupils, Kloosterman et al. (1996) investigated their beliefs about groupwork as a method for studying mathematics in class. Interestingly, they found a substantial variation among pupils' beliefs, but also significant fluctuations from positive to negative beliefs about groupwork and vice versa over the three years of the lon-gitudinal study. The authors attribute this at least in part to the wide variety of teacher beliefs about the effectiveness of groupwork as well as to the kind of group activities students actually experienced in class (see also Carter & Nor-wood, 1997). While we basically agree with this perspective, one needs to also be aware of the fact that teachers do not always teach as they preach (see e.g., Thompson, 1992). Teachers may regularly stress the importance of groupwork, but only occasionally allow their students to actually work in groups during the mathematics lessons. Some students will buy what their teachers say and believe them but only at a rhetorical level (Schoenfeld, 1985b). They will in general be-lieve that groupwork is an effective way to work and learn in the mathematics class, but at a practical level, as far as their behavior in this specific class is con-cerned, they will believe the opposite and act accordingly. As already mentioned previously referring to Schoenfeld (1985b), students can perfectly hold such seemingly contradictory beliefs.

The preceding discussion shows that over the past 10 years efforts have been made to map out students' beliefs about mathematics and mathematics learning and teaching. The underlying idea of those endeavors is that those beliefs have a significant impact on students' motivation for and strategic approach to learning tasks and problems, and consequently on their school performance (see e.g., Kloosterman, 1996). However, today convincing empirical evidence for this hypothesis is still largely lacking.

BELIEFS ABOUT THE SELF

Students' beliefs about the self in relation to mathematics refer to what in the motivational research literature is labeled as motivational beliefs (e.g., Pintrich & Schrauben, 1992). We differentiate between:

- Goal orientation beliefs, such as the most satisfying thing for me in this mathematics course is trying to understand the content as thoroughly as possible.
- Task value beliefs; for instance, it is important for me to learn the course material in this mathematics class.
- Control beliefs; for example, if I study in appropriate ways, then I will be able to learn the material in the course.
- Self-efficacy beliefs; for instance, I'm confident that I can understand the most difficult material presented in the readings for this mathematical course.

The differentiation in beliefs about the self is based on a general sociocognitive model of motivation that proposes three basic motivational constructs (Pintrich, 1989): expectancy, value, and affect. Expectancy components refer to students' beliefs that they can accomplish a task, i.e., self-efficacy beliefs and control beliefs. Value components focus on the reasons why students engage in learning and problem solving and become manifest in their goal orientation beliefs and task value beliefs (Pintrich, Smith, Garcia, & McKeachie, 1993). The affective component includes students' emotional reactions to tasks and to their performance (Pintrich & Schrauben, 1992). Although important, these reactions are rather a consequence of beliefs than beliefs as such. Emotions and emotional acts are perceived as expressions of beliefs (Carter & Yackel, 1989). McLeod (1992) points out that "students hold certain beliefs about mathematics and about themselves that play an important role in the development of their affective responses to mathematical situations" (p. 578). Especially beliefs about the self strongly determine students' emotions during problem solving (Op 't Eynde, De Corte, & Verschaffel, 1999). After all, "the processing of social information important to the person is intrinsically affect-laden so that such cognitions as beliefs about the self and one's personal future are themselves 'hot' and emotional"

(Mischel & Shoda, 1995, p. 252). Therefore, we do not perceive affect as a separate category of beliefs about the self.

Several researchers (e.g., Ames & Archer, 1988; Fennema, 1989; Stipek & Gralinski, 1991; Vermeer, 1997) have addressed the influence of self-beliefs about mathematical problem solving, often reporting gender differences in relation to differences in performance. For instance, Fennema (1989) found that "males have more confidence in their ability to do mathematics, report higher perceived usefulness, and attribute success and failure in a way that has been hypothesized to have a more positive influence on achievement" (p. 211).

Questionnaires or interviews were also used in most studies to describe the self-beliefs students hold in relation to mathematical learning and problem solving (e.g., Kloosterman & Cougan, 1994; Vanayan et al., 1997). Yet, several scholars have made rather fine-grained analyses of the influence of students' beliefs about the self on mathematical learning and problem solving using path analysis and covariance analysis (e.g., Pajares & Miller, 1994; Seegers & Boekaerts, 1993). Seegers and Boekaerts (1993), for instance, investigated in a group of eight graders the influence of more general motivational beliefs (goal orientation, attributional style, self-efficacy) on task-specific appraisals (subjective competence, task attraction, personal relevance), as well as the way in which these general and task-specific variables determine performance on mathematics tasks. They found that motivational beliefs only had an indirect influence on performance through the task-specific appraisals, and more specifically, through the perceived competence in the task. The advancement of our understanding of the relevance of beliefs about the self in relation to mathematics can greatly benefit from such continued in-depth analyses. In stressing the role of variables at the task level they clarify the exact ways in which these beliefs influence mathematical learning and problem solving. More studies investigating students' self-beliefs at the subject level together with their task-specific appraisals are needed to unravel the mechanisms through which students' self-beliefs determine mathematics learning and problem solving.

BELIEFS ABOUT THE SOCIAL CONTEXT, I.E., THE CLASS CONTEXT

This category of beliefs about the social context of mathematics education refers to students' views and perceptions of the classroom norms, including the social and the sociomathematical norms, that direct teachers' and students' behavior in their specific classroom (Cobb & Yackel, 1998). It includes their perceptions about the role of the teacher as well as their own and their fellow students' role in their mathematics classroom, but also students' beliefs about aspects of the class culture that are specific to mathematical activity. The latter refers, for example, to students' view on what counts as a different solution or as an acceptable explanation in their class.

Already in 1983 Schoenfeld pointed out that cognitive actions are:

often the result of consciously or unconsciously held beliefs about (a) the task at hand, (b) the social environment within which the task takes place, and (c) the individual problem solver's perception of self and his or her relation to the task and the environment (p. 330).

Since then researchers on mathematics learning and teaching have shown an increasing interest in studying the so-called culture of the mathematics classroom (Nickson, 1992; Cobb & Yackel, 1998), and the influence of the social environment in which learning tasks and problem solving take place (see also e.g., de Abreu et al., 1997; McLeod, 1992). As argued and shown by Cobb and his coworkers, teacher's and students' individual beliefs about their own role, and the role of the others in the class are the psychological correlates of the classroom social norms relating to, for instance, how whole-class discussion takes place (Cobb et al., 1989). Furthermore, sociomathematical norms, i.e., norms that are specific to mathematics (e.g., what counts as a good solution?), have an impact on specifically mathematical beliefs (Yackel & Cobb, 1996; see also Cobb & Yackel, 1998). Both classroom social norms and sociomathematical norms determine the interaction patterns that teacher and students mutually establish, in which implicit definitions are embedded about what mathematics is like, about how a problem should be solved, about the criteria for being a good student, etc. Students develop their sense of what it means to do mathematics and what they and the others are expected to do in mathematics lessons from their actual experiences and interactions during the classroom activities in which they engage (Henningsen & Stein, 1997). Thus, as argued by de Abreu et al. (1997), beliefs and attitudes are the product of social life rather than being located in an autonomous individual. Beliefs about the nature of mathematics education, about oneself, and about the class context are constructed in an attempt to make sense of classroom life during mathematics instruction.

However, the different messages on what mathematics is like embedded in the social context of the class are not always easy to grasp. It is even more difficult to understand how exactly these social processes influence the development of student beliefs. Schoenfeld (1985b) reports of a questionnaire study in ninth to twelfth grades on students' beliefs about mathematics education. One of the most surprising but interesting results was that a large number of students gave a very strong 'agree' rating for the statement: 'Good mathematics teachers show students lots of different ways to look at the same question.' The reason for the researcher's surprise was that very little of such teacher behavior was observed in the classroom studies conducted in parallel with this investigation. Schoenfeld (1985b) concludes: "Their response suggests either a strong acceptance of part of the mythology about teaching, or some degree of wishful thinking" (p.13). Furthermore, he points out that these beliefs may reflect the beliefs of their teachers or a more general social view rather than that they emerge from their own experience.

As noted in a previous section, students can live comfortably with such contradictions, sometimes even without noticing them. Often contradictions between students' general beliefs (like the one about 'good mathematics teachers' mentioned earlier), on the one hand, and their actual problem-solving behavior, on the other, are explained by referring to the fact that they hold conflicting beliefs at an unconscious level (Schoenfeld, 1985b). However, this is not necessarily the case. Indeed, students' behavior might be directed by a context-specific belief based on their classroom experiences, that from the students' perspective is not at all in contradiction with the more general belief, because the two beliefs are referring to different contexts, respectively the specific class context and a more general context.

An illustration that students actually are sensitive to this distinction between the general level and the specific class context can be found in a study of Vanayan et al. (1997) with third and fifth grade students. They observed clearly different patterns in students' answers on the question 'if they liked mathematics' as compared to 'if they liked mathematics in class.' The proportion of boys who reported liking the mathematics in class was similar in both grades and was about the same as in third grade girls (52%). A smaller percentage of girls in fifth grade reported that they like mathematics in class. Interestingly this pattern was not observed when students were asked whether they liked mathematics.

Until now there is little research that addresses these beliefs about the specific social context of the class, and how they relate to the more general beliefs. These general beliefs are abstracted from one's experiences and from the classroom culture in which one is embedded (Schoenfeld, 1992); but, this culture is such a complex phenomenon of rules and interactions that there is clearly no linear relation between 'a class context' and more general beliefs about mathematics and the self. Therefore, in order to fully understand the influence of mathematics-related beliefs on students' learning and problem solving, it is necessary to focus in future inquiry not only on their general beliefs about mathematics education and the self, but also on their beliefs about the mathematics class context in which they have to perform.

DEVELOPMENT OF NAIVE AND INCORRECT BELIEFS IN STUDENTS THROUGH INSTRUCTION

Early in this chapter it was mentioned that a lot of students hold naive or incorrect mathematics-related beliefs. A list of typical beliefs falling in this category compiled by Schoenfeld (1992) was already given in a previous section. Also, Lampert's description of the (incorrect) common view about mathematics that students are affected with has been mentioned before.

It is obvious that such misbeliefs, for example, mathematics is associated with certainty and with being able to give quickly the correct answer, can have detrimental and/or inhibitory effects, motivationally as well as cognitively, on students' learning activities and on their approach to mathematics problems. This raises an important question, namely how do such incorrect views of mathematics and mathematics learning and teaching develop in youngsters? The previous section already showed that beliefs about the class context are strongly determined by the activities, experiences, and interactions in the classroom. Taking this into account, and without excluding the impact of other factors such as the home and the general cultural environment, the plausible hypothesis is then, that formal mathematics education has a major influence on the development of the different categories of students' mathematics-related beliefs. Indeed, it looks self-evident that the mathematical practices students are subjected to in class, the formal and informal interactions in the classroom, as well as the implicit rules that regulate classsroom practices and interactions substantially influence and shape those beliefs (Schoenfeld, 1992).

In line with this hypothesis, researchers largely agree that many of students' naive and incorrect beliefs are the consequence of the traditional educational practices that still prevail in mathematics classroom today. For instance, Lampert (1990) claims that the common incorrect view of mathematics she describes is acquired through years of watching, listening, and practicing in the mathematics classroom. This standpoint is echoed and extended in the following striking quote from Greeno (1991):

> In most school instruction, what students mostly do is listen, watch, and mimic things that the teacher and textbook tell them and show them. If students' epistemologies are influenced at all by the experiences they have, then most students probably learn that mathematical knowledge is a form of received knowledge, not something that is constructed either personally or socially. Another probable outcome for many students is a belief that they were endowed with a low level of mathematical ability and that there is little or nothing they can do to become mathematically able. The links between classroom experiences and students' personal epistemologies undoubtedly are subtle and complex, and classroom experience undoubtedly is just one factor in determining what students believe about mathematical knowledge and about themselves as mathematical knowers and learners. Even so, it seems likely that the influence of current classroom practices on the epistemological beliefs and understandings of most students is largely negative (p. 81–82).

Schoenfeld (1988) has reported empirical support for these claims in an article with the strange title, "When Good Teaching Leads to Bad Results: The Disasters of 'Well-Taught' Mathematics Courses." Schoenfeld made a year-long intensive study of one tenth grade geometry class with 20 pupils, along with periodic data collections in 11 other classes (210 pupils) involving observations, interviews with teachers and students, and questionnaires relating to students' perceptions about the nature of mathematics. The students in those classrooms scored well on typical achievement measures, and the mathematics was taught in a way that would generally be considered good teaching. Nevertheless, it was found that students acquired debilitating beliefs about mathematics and about themselves as mathematics learners, such as 'all mathematics problems can be solved in just a few minutes,' and 'students are passive consumers of others' mathematics.' It is obvious that such misbeliefs are not conducive to a mindful and persistent approach to new and challenging learning tasks and problems. Therefore, it is most crucial to understand how classroom environments can be organized to promote the development of more positive and appropriate mathematics-related beliefs.

FOSTERING APPROPRIATE BELIEFS IN NOVEL AND POWERFUL LEARNING ENVIRONMENTS

If mathematical classroom practices can have detrimental effects on students' beliefs, it is plausible to hypothesize that alternative learning environments can be designed that foster positive mathematics-related views in children. However, until now research in which the impact of specific educational interventions has been systematically studied is scarce. Of course, there have been developed and implemented over the past years—especially at the primary school level—novel, so-called powerful learning environments based on new theoretical insights about mathematics learning and teaching. Major principles underlying those environments in different combination and to distinct degrees are: the constructivist view of learning, the conception of mathematics as human activity, the crucial role of students' prior formal and informal knowledge, the orientation toward understanding and problem solving, the importance of interaction and collaboration in doing and learning mathematics, and the need to embed mathematics learning in authentic and meaningful contexts. Well-known examples of this new approach to mathematics education are: the Jasper Project of the Cognition and Technology Group at Vanderbilt (1997), the Freudenthal Institute's Realistic Mathematics Education (Gravemeijer, 1994), Cobb et al.'s (1989, Cobb & Yackel, 1998) constructivist approach to mathematics, and Lampert's (1990) mathematical discourse approach. It is quite likely that the classroom practices in each of those novel learning environments have a positive impact on students' beliefs about mathematics, and, moreover, the reports about several of these projects contain some—often anecdotal—data on changes in student beliefs.

In two recent studies—one by Higgins (1997) and one carried out in our own Center (Verschaffel, De Corte, Lasure, Van Vaerenbergh, Bogaerts, & Ratinckx, 1999)—the question concerning the effects of instructional interventions on students' mathematics-related beliefs was addressed more directly.

Higgins (1997) studied the effect of one year-long instruction in mathematical problem solving on middle school students' attitudes and beliefs about problem solving and mathematics, as well as on their problem-solving ability. Two sixth grade teachers, four seventh grade teachers, and their students (137) participated in the study. One sixth grade teacher and two seventh grade teachers were trained in mathematical problem solving and received coaching in problem-solving instruction. These three teachers of the experimental classes taught their students five heuristic problem-solving skills at the beginning of the school year: guess and check, look for a pattern, make a systematic list, make a drawing or model, and eliminate possibilities. They used direct instruction, first demonstrating the skill and then giving students exercises to practice the skill during the following five days. After the five weeks needed to complete this initial phase, students were presented in the following lessons challenging open problems for which there was no immediately obvious way to determine a solution. Students could work on these problems for a week. In addition to these weekly challenge problems, approximately 80 lessons focusing on problem solving were taught over the school year; these lessons covered the normal topics of the curriculum, but using powerful instruction techniques as, for example, small-group discussions and guided discovery.

The teachers of the control classes had not received any specific training in mathematical problem solving, and did not use an instructional approach that involved the integration of problem-solving activities in their lessons.

To assess students' beliefs Higgins administered near the end of the school year in the experimental and the control classes a beliefs questionnaire based on an instrument developed by Schoenfeld (1989) and consisting of 39 questions in a Likert-type format; in the beginning of the next school year semistructured interviews were held with 27 experimental and 27 control students (divided over three ability groups).

Higgins found significant positive effects on students' beliefs in the group that received problem-solving instruction in comparison with the students who got traditional instruction. Major observations derived from the questionnaire data were the following: experimental students generally perceived mathematics as more than facts and procedures to be memorized; they claimed that they could solve real problems with common sense, and that they had to think hard to answer teacher questions. Furthermore, the experimental students had more positive beliefs about the usefulness of mathematics and more sophisticated definitions of mathematical understanding; they also displayed more perseverance when solving problems. However, the problem-solving instruction also had an unexpected side effect. Indeed, the experimental students tended to equate problem solving with using the heuristic skills they had learned, believing that these rules could solve all problems. This shows at the same time the complexity of tracing how exactly instructional interactions influence the development of mathematics-related beliefs. Overall Higgins' instructional problem-solving environment can certainly be called successful, but it is not at all clear which aspects of her approach to teaching problem solving are responsible for the positive effects and which for the creation of the observed misbelief about problem solving.

In our Center we recently carried out a design experiment in which a learning environment for teaching and learning how to model and solve mathematical application problems was developed and implemented in four fifth grade classes (Verschaffel et al., 1999). The basic design principles of this new classroom environment relate to: 1) using a varied set of carefully designed complex, realistic, and challenging word problems, 2) applying a variety of highly interactive instructional techniques, especially small-group problem solving and whole-class discussion, and 3) creating a new classroom climate and culture based on novel social and sociomathematical norms. In this environment the pupils of the experimental classes learned to master a series of heuristics embedded in an overall metacognitive strategy for solving mathematical application problems; meanwhile the children of comparable control classes followed the regular mathematics lessons. The implementation (by the classroom teachers) and the effectiveness of the experimental learning environment were tested in a study with a pretest-posttest-retention test design with an experimental and a control group.

Among a wide variety of instruments administered before and after the intervention to the four experimental and seven comparable control classes to measure the effects of this powerful learning environment, there was also a self-made Likert-type questionnaire aimed at assessing pupils' beliefs and attitudes about (teaching and learning) mathematical word problem solving. Based on factor analysis this questionnaire consists of two reliable subscales: a first subscale containing seven items dealing with pupils' 'Pleasure and persistence in solving word problems' (for instance: 'I like to solve word problems,' 'Difficult problems are my favorites' . . .), and a second subscale with 14 items expressing a 'Problem- and process-oriented view on word problem solving' (for instance: 'There is always only one solution to a word problem'; 'Listening to explanations of alternative solution paths by other pupils, is a waste of time' . . .). Analysis of the questionnaire data showed that, as predicted, the experimental group scored significantly higher than the control group on both scales after the intervention, while the scores of both groups did not differ significantly on the pretest. But these effects, though significant, were small in terms of effect size; however, one should take into account that the intervention consisted of only 20 lessons spread over a three-month period.

Together with the results of Higgins' study, these findings are promising in the sense that they provide initial support for the hypothesis that it is possible to enhance in students positive mathematics-related beliefs through appropriate instructional interventions. Due to the complexity of the intervention and the quasiexperimental design of the study, it is also here—like for Higgins' investigation—impossible to draw conclusions about the relative contribution of the three main characteristics of the new classroom environment to the observed positive effects. Interesting in this respect, however, is that there are some remarkable similarities between Higgins' and our intervention. Indeed, both learning environments focused on the teaching of a heuristic approach to mathematics problem solving using nontraditional open and challenging problems, on the one hand, and stimulating a lot of discussion about those problems and the different strategies applied to solve them, on the other.

FINAL COMMENTS

There is today rather general agreement in the mathematics education community that students' mathematics-related beliefs have substantial impact on their learning and performance in mathematics. This standpoint is, for instance, expressed in the following way in the well-known *Curriculum and Evaluation Standards for School Mathematics* (National Council of Teachers of Mathematics, 1989): "These beliefs exert a powerful influence on students' evaluation of their own ability, on their willingness to engage in mathematical tasks, and on their ultimate mathematical disposition" (p. 233).

The preceding review of the research relating to these beliefs shows, however, that this field of inquiry is still rather in its infancy. Of course, there is no doubt that—since the pioneering contribution of Schoenfeld in 1983—sufficient evidence has been accumulated suggesting that students' beliefs about mathematics education, about themselves as learners of mathematics, and about the specific context of their mathematics class are critical to their learning processes. However, at present from a theoretical, methodological, and empirical perspective the major output of the past investigations provide us only with a good baseline for the needed continued research.

From a theoretical point of view the field of mathematics-related beliefs is still conceptually rather ill-structured. Different categories of relevant beliefs have been identified and described, but our attempt to develop an overarching research-based conceptual framework has not brought us much further than differentiating and juxtaposing the major beliefs categories. What is especially lacking is a better understanding of the relationships and interactions between the different categories of beliefs. A related issue that has to be addressed more thoroughly is the relationship between mathematics-related beliefs and more general epistemological beliefs (Hofer & Pintrich, 1997).

In view of further inquiry that aims at unraveling the relationships between the distinct kinds of beliefs, there is also a strong need for instrumental research focusing on the design of assessment techniques that constitute a better validated operationalization of students' mathematics-related beliefs. So far the majority of the studies has used questionnaires or interviews. Questionnaires are usually based on or adapted from Schoenfeld's (1985b) measure. However, hardly any data are available concerning the psychometric qualities of those instruments. Starting from the available theoretical and methodological baseline referred to earlier, more comprehensive instruments have to be designed and validated. This also holds true for interview schemas, which until now also lacked a solid theoretical basis.

As mentioned previously when discussing students' beliefs about mathematics education, a major gap in the existing body of research is that—while it is often claimed that beliefs have an important impact, directly or indirectly, on student performance—strong empirical evidence supporting this claim is still scarce. What is especially lacking is a good understanding of the processes by which beliefs influence learning and problem solving. However, in this respect the now available research results are suggestive of some hypotheses according to which students' mathematics-related beliefs affect their learning and problem-solving behavior through cognitive and metacognitive as well as motivational and affective processes (see Kloosterman, 1996; Schoenfeld, 1985a). For instance, Schoenfeld's (1985a) work suggests how students' beliefs about mathematics and mathematics learning and problem solving influence the way in which they approach a problem and the kind of problem-solving strategies they use. Studies from a motivational perspective indicate how students' beliefs about the self have a significant impact on their task-specific appraisals and effort investment, and, through these mediating processes, on their mathematics performance (e.g., Kloosterman, 1996; Pokay & Blumenfeld, 1990; Seegers & Boekaerts, 1993). McLeod (1992) points to the important way in which students' beliefs about mathematics education and the self determine their affective responses in mathematical situations. Not so much the kind of emotions students experience seems to be of importance, but the way they deal with them. In a recent exploratory study (Op 't Eynde et al., 1999) we found that especially differences in students' self-efficacy and task-value beliefs explain the way students' deal with emotions during problem solving and their influence on the problem-solving process (see also, McLeod, Metzger, & Craviotto, 1989).

Thus, scholars are only beginning to discover the processes by which mathematics-related beliefs influence learning and problem solving, and starting from the available work more specific hypotheses need to be generated in view of continued inquiry. Both qualitative approaches and advanced quantitative methods using techniques such as path analyses are appropriate for the kind of in-depth and more fine-grained analyses needed to unravel the relationships between different kinds of beliefs, as well as the mechanisms by which beliefs affect students' learning, motivation, and achievement.

One issue that deserves to be especially mentioned here is gender, since it has often been shown that mathematics is a gender-sensitive domain. As the preceding review shows, gender has until now not been studied systematically in relation to mathematics beliefs (see also Kloosterman, 1996). As argued by Hofer and Pintrich (1997) with respect to research on epistemological theories in general, there is a need for more investigations that explore gender-related differences and patterns in mathematics-related beliefs.

Finally, we have until now only little knowledge and understanding of how positive beliefs about mathematics can be stimulated in students, and how misbeliefs that many children seem to hold can be remedied. Therefore, a major challenge for continued future inquiry is the systematic study of the interplay among students' beliefs and instructional interventions through design experiments (De Corte, 2000) aiming at unraveling the impact on mathematics-related beliefs of novel learning environments based on our present knowledge of effective learning processes.

REFERENCES

Aiken, L. R. (1970). Attitudes toward mathematics. *Review of Educational Research, 40*, 551–596.

Aiken, L. R. (1976). Update on attitudes and other affective variables in learning mathematics. *Review of Educational Research, 46,* 293–311.

Alexander, P. A., Schallert, D. L., & Hare, V. C. (1991). Coming to terms: How researchers in learning and literacy talk about knowledge. *Review of Educational Research, 61,* 315–343.

Ames, C., & Archer, J. (1988). Achievement goals in the classroom: Students' learning strategies and motivation processes. *Journal of Educational Psychology, 80,* 260–267.

Atkinson, J. W. (1957). Motivational determinants of risk-taking behavior. *Psychological Review, 64,* 359–372.

Bain, A. (1859). *The emotions and the will.* London: Longmans, Green.

Bogdan, R. J. (1986). The importance of belief. In R. J. Bogdan (Ed.), *Belief: Form, content, and function* (pp. 1–16). New York: Oxford University Press.

Brown, J. S., Collins, A., & Duguid, P. (1989). Situated cognition and the culture of learning. *Educational Researcher, 18*(1), 32–42.

Carter, C. S., & Yackel, E. (1989, April). *A constructivist perspective on the relationship between mathematical beliefs and emotional acts.* Paper presented at the Annual Meeting of the AERA, San Francisco.

Carter, G., & Norwood, K. S. (1997). The relationship between teacher and student beliefs about mathematics. *School Science and Mathematics, 97*(2), 62–67.

Cobb, P., & Yackel, E. (1998). A constructivist perspective on the culture of the mathematics classroom. In F. Seeger, J. Voigt, & U. Waschescio (Eds.), *The culture of the mathematics classroom* (pp. 158–190). Cambridge: Cambridge University Press.

Cobb, P., Yackel, E., & Wood, T. (1989). Young children's emotional acts while engaged in mathematical problem solving. In D. B. McLeod & V. M. Adams (Eds.), *Affect and mathematical problem solving: A new perspective.* New York: Springer.

Cognition and Technology Group at Vanderbilt. (1997). *The Jasper Project. Lessons in curriculum, instruction, assessment, and professional development.* Mahwah, NJ: Erlbaum.

de Abreu, G., Bishop, A. J., & Pompeu, G., Jr. (1997). What children and teachers count as mathematics. In T. Nunes & P. Bryant (Eds.), *Learning and teaching mathematics: An international perspective* (pp. 233–264). Hove, UK: Psychology Press.

De Corte, E. (2000). Marrying theory building and the improvement of school practice: A permanent challenge for instructional psychology. *Learning and Instruction, 10,* 249–266.

De Corte, E., Greer, B., & Verschaffel, L. (1996). Mathematics teaching and learning. In D. C. Berliner & R. C. Calfee (Eds.), *Handbook of educational psychology* (pp. 491–549). New York: Macmillan.

Ernest, P. (1991). *The philosophy of mathematics education.* London: Falmer.

Fennema, E. (1989). The study of affect and mathematics: A proposed generic model for research. In D. B. McLeod & V. M. Adams (Eds.), *Affect and mathematical problem solving: A new perspective* (pp. 205–219). New York: Springer.

Fenstermacher, G. (1994). The knower and the known: The nature of knowledge in research on teaching. In L. Darling-Hammond (Ed.), *Review of research in education* (Vol. 20, pp. 1–54). Itasca, IL: Peacock.

Frank, M. L. (1988). Problem solving and mathematical beliefs. *Arithmetic Teacher, 35,* 32–35.

Garofalo, J. (1989). Beliefs and their influence on mathematical performance. *Mathematics Teacher, 82*, 502–505.

Garofalo, J., & Lester, F. K. (1985). Metacognition, cognitive monitoring, and mathematical performance. *Journal for Research in Mathematics Education, 16*, 163–176.

Gilbert, D. T. (1991). How mental systems believe. *American Psychologist, 46*, 107–119.

Gravemeijer, K. (1994). *Developing realistic mathematics education.* Utrecht, The Netherlands: Freudenthal Institute, University of Utrecht.

Green, T. (1971). *The activities of teaching.* New York: McGraw-Hill.

Greeno, J. G. (1991). A view of mathematical problem solving in school. In M. U. Smith (Ed.), *Toward a unified theory of problem solving. Views from the content domains* (pp. 69–98). Hillsdale, NJ: Erlbaum.

Greeno, J. G., Collins, A. M., & Resnick, L. B. (1996). Cognition and learning. In D. C. Berliner & R. C. Calfee (Eds.), *Handbook of educational psychology* (pp. 15–46). New York: Macmillan.

Henningsen, M., & Stein, M. K. (1997). Mathematical tasks and student cognition: Classroom-based factors that support and inhibit high-level mathematical thinking and reasoning. *Journal for Research in Mathematics Education, 28*, 524–549.

Higgins, K. M. (1997). The effect of year-long instruction in mathematical problem solving on middle school students' attitudes, beliefs, and abilities. *Journal of Experimental Education, 66*, 5–28.

Hofer, B. K., & Pintrich, P. R. (1997). The development of epistemological theories: Beliefs about knowledge and knowing and their relation to learning. *Review of Educational Research, 67*, 88–140.

Kloosterman, P. (1996). Students' beliefs about knowing and learning mathematics: Implications for motivation. In M. Carr (Ed.), *Motivation in mathematics* (pp. 131–156). Cresskill, NJ: Hampton Press.

Kloosterman, P., & Coughan, M. C. (1994). Students' beliefs about learning school mathematics. *Elementary School Journal, 94*, 375–388

Kloosterman, P., Raymond, A. M., & Emenaker, C. (1996). Students' beliefs about mathematics: A three-year study. *Elementary School Journal, 97*, 39–56.

Kouba, V. L., & McDonald, J. L. (1986). Children's and teachers' perceptions and beliefs about the domain of elementary mathematics. In D. Lappan & R. Even (Eds.), *Proceedings of the eighth annual meeting of the North American chapter of the International Group for the Psychology of Mathematics Education* (pp. 250–255). East Lansing, MI: Michigan State University.

Lampert, M. (1990). When the problem is not the question and the solution is not the answer: Mathematical knowing and teaching. *American Educational Research Journal, 27*, 29–63.

Lester, F. K., Garofalo, J., & Kroll, D. L. (1989). Self-confidence, interest, beliefs, and metacognition: Key influences on problem-solving behavior. In D. B. McLeod & V. M. Adams (Eds.), *Affect and mathematical problem solving: A new perspective* (pp. 75–88). New York: Springer.

Ma, X., & Kishor, N. (1997). Assessing the relationship between attitude toward mathematics and achievement in mathematics: A meta-analysis. *Journal for Research in Mathematics Education, 28*, 26–47.

McLeod, D. B. (1992). Research on affect in mathematics education: A reconceptualization. In D. A. Grouws (Ed.), *Handbook of research on mathematics teaching and learning* (pp. 575–596). New York: Macmillan.

McLeod, D. B. (1994). Research on affect and mathematics learning in the JRME: 1970 to the present. *Journal for Research in Mathematics Education, 25*, 637–647.

McLeod, D. B., Metzger, W., & Craviotto, C. (1989). Comparing experts' and novices' affective reactions to mathematical problem solving: An exploratory study. In G. Vergnaud (Ed.), *Proceedings of the Thirteenth International Conference for the Psychology of Mathematics Education* (Vol. 2, pp. 296–303). Paris: Laboratoire de Psychologie du Développement et de l'Education de l'Enfant.

Mischel, W., & Shoda, Y. (1995). A cognitive-affective system theory of personality: Reconceptualizing situations, dispositions, dynamics, and invariance in personality structure. *Psychological Review, 102*, 246–268.

Mtetwa, D., & Garofalo, J. (1989). Beliefs about mathematics: An overlooked aspect of student diffi-culties. *Academic Therapy, 24,* 611–618.

National Council of Teachers of Mathematics. (1989). *Curriculum and evaluation standards for school mathematics.* Reston, VA: National Council of Teachers of Mathematics.

Nickson, M. (1992). The culture of the mathematics classroom: An unknown quantity? In D. A. Grouws (Ed.), *Handbook of research on mathematics teaching and learning* (pp. 101–114). New York: Macmillan.

Op 't Eynde, P., De Corte, E., & Verschaffel, L. (1999, August). *A socioconstructivist perspective on the role of emotions in mathematical problem solving.* Paper presented at the Eighth. EARLI Conference in Göteborg, Sweden.

Pajares, F., & Miller, M. D. (1994). Role of self-efficacy and self-concept beliefs in mathematical problem solving: A path analysis. *Journal of Educational Psychology, 86,* 193–203.

Pintrich, P. (1989). The dynamic interplay of student motivation and cognition in the college class-room. In C. Ames & M. Maehr (Eds.), *Advances in motivation and achievement: Motivation-enhancing environments* (Vol. 6, pp. 117–160). Greenwich, CT: JAI Press.

Pintrich, P. R., & Schrauben, B. (1992). Students' motivational beliefs and their cognitive engage-ment in academic tasks. In D. Schunk, & J. Meece (Eds.), *Students' perceptions in the classroom: Causes and consequences* (pp. 149–183). Hillsdale, NJ: Erlbaum.

Pintrich, P. R., Smith, D. A. F., Garcia, T., & McKeachie, W. J. (1993). Reliability and predictive va-lidity of the Motivated Strategies for Learning Questionnaire (MSLQ). *Educational and Psycho-logical Measurement, 53,* 801–813.

Pokay, P., & Blumenfeld, P. C. (1990). Predicting achievement early and late in the semester: The role of motivation and use of learning strategies. *Journal of Educational Psychology, 82,* 41–50.

Power, M., & Dalgleish, T. (1997). *Cognition and emotion: Form order to disorder.* Sussex, UK: Erl-baum Taylor & Francis Ltd.

Richardson, V. (1996). The role of attitudes and beliefs in learning to teach. In J. Sikula (Ed.), *Hand-book of research on teacher education* (2nd ed., pp. 102–119). New York: Macmillan.

Salomon, G., & Perkins, D. N. (1998). Individual and social aspects of learning. In P. D. Pearson & A. Iran-Nejad (Eds.), *Review of research in education* (Vol. 23, pp. 1–25). Washington, DC: AERA.

Schoenfeld, A. H. (1983). Beyond the purely cognitive: Belief systems, social cognitions, and metacognitions as driving forces in intellectual performance. *Cognitive Science, 7,* 329–363.

Schoenfeld, A. H. (1985a). *Mathematical problem solving.* Orlando, Florida: Academic Press.

Schoenfeld, A. H. (1985b, April). *Students' beliefs about mathematics and their effects on mathemati-cal performance: A questionnaire analysis.* Paper presented at the Annual Meeting of the Ameri-can Educational Research Association, Chicago, IL.

Schoenfeld, A. H. (1988). When good teaching leads to bad results: The disasters of "well-taught" mathematics courses. *Educational Psychologist, 23,* 145–166.

Schoenfeld, A.H. (1989). Explorations of students' mathematical beliefs and behavior. *Journal for Research in Mathematics Education, 20,* 338–355.

Schoenfeld, A. H. (1990). On mathematics as sense-making: An informal attack on the unfortunate divorce of formal and informal mathematics. In D. N. Perkins, J. Segal, & J. Voss (Eds.), *Informal reasoning and education* (pp. 281–300). Hillsdale, NJ: Erlbaum.

Schoenfeld, A. H. (1992). Learning to think mathematically: Problem solving, metacognition, and sense making in mathematics. in D. A. Grouws (Ed.), *Handbook of research on mathematics teaching and learning* (pp. 334–370). New York: Macmillan.

Schommer, M., Crouse, A., & Rhodes, N. (1992). Epistemological beliefs and mathematical text comprehension: Believing it is simple does not make it so. *Journal of Educational Psychology, 84,* 435–443.

Seegers, G., & Boekaerts, M. (1993). Task motivation and mathematics in actual task situations. *Learning and Instruction, 3,* 133–150.

Snow, R. E., Corno, L., & Jackson III, D. (1996). Individual differences in affective and conative functions. In D. C. Berliner & R. C. Calfee (Eds.), *Handbook of educational psychology* (pp. 243–310). New York: Macmillan.

Spangler, D. A. (1992). Assessing students' beliefs about mathematics. *Arithmetic Teacher, 40*, 148–152.

Spinoza, B. (1982). *The ethics and selected letters* (S. Feldman, Ed., and S. Shirley, Trans.). Indianapolis, IN: Hackett.

Stipek, D. J., & Gralinski, H. (1991). Gender differences in children's achievement-related beliefs and emotional responses to success and failure in mathematics. *Journal of Educational Psychology, 83*, 361–371.

Stodolsky, S. S., Salk, S., & Glaessner, B. (1991). Student views about learning math and social studies. *American Educational Research Journal, 28*, 89–116.

Thompson, A. G. (1984). The relationship of teachers' conceptions of mathematics and mathematics teaching to instructional practice. *Educational Studies of Mathematics, 15*, 105–127.

Thompson, A. G. (1992). Teachers' beliefs and conceptions: A synthesis of the research. In D. A. Grouws (Ed.), *Handbook of research on mathematics teaching and learning* (pp. 127–146). New York: Macmillan.

Tymoczko, T. (1986). Introduction. In T. Tymoczko (Ed.), *New directions in the philosophy of mathematics* (pp. xiii–xvii). Boston: Birkhauser.

Underhill, R. (1988). Mathematics learners' beliefs: A review. *Focus on Learning Problems in Mathematics, 10*, 55–69.

Vanayan, M., White, N., Yuen, P., & Teper, M. (1997). Beliefs and attitudes toward mathematics among third and fifth grade students: A descriptive study. *School Science and Mathematics, 97*, 345–351.

Vermeer, H. J. (1997). *Sixth grade students' mathematical problem-solving behavior: Motivational variables and gender differences*. Leiden, The Netherlands: UFB, Leiden University.

Verschaffel, L., De Corte, E., Lasure, S., Van Vaerenbergh, G., Bogaerts, H., & Ratinckx, E. (1999). Learning to solve mathematical application problems. A design experiment with fifth graders. *Mathematical Thinking and Learning, 1,* 195–229.

Verschaffel, L., Greer, B., & De Corte, E. (2000). *Making sense of word problems*. Lisse, The Netherlands: Swets & Zeitlinger.

Yackel, E. (1984). *Mathematical belief systems survey*. West Lafayette, IN: Purdue University.

Yackel, E., & Cobb, P. (1996). Sociomathematical norms, argumentation, and autonomy in mathematics. *Journal for Research in Mathematics Education, 27*, 458–477.

16

Beliefs About Science: How Does Science Instruction Contribute?

Philip Bell
University of Washington

Marcia C. Linn
University of California, Berkeley

INTRODUCTION

Beliefs about science inquiry are shaped by news accounts, consumer reports, historical summaries, journal articles, textbook descriptions, and, recently, Internet materials. We define beliefs about scientific inquiry broadly to include images of the nature of science, the purposes and activities of scientists, the goals of science courses, and the learning strategies appropriate for understanding scientific material. This chapter explores how students interpret, process, combine, distinguish, and critique these images of science as well as how innovative, inquiry-based science instruction can help shape the images of science held by students.

Specifically, we arc interested in students' understanding of the following questions: What convinces people to accept a scientific idea? How is knowledge created in a science field? What are good science experiments? Why do scientists sometimes disagree? What can be concluded from experiments? Why do scientific ideas change? How do scientists design experiments? How do scientific methods vary by discipline? What are the best ways to learn science? How do scientists critique experiments? And how should citizens interpret science experiments?

Our research on student science learning suggests that students develop a repertoire of ideas about science rather than a cohesive view (Linn & Hsi, 2000). This perspective resonates with the idea that students have complex cognitive ecologies about science based on varied sources and experiences (e.g., Strike & Posner, 1992). It stands in contrast to developmental accounts that view epistemological sophistication as domain-general and uniform. In this chapter we explore the origins of student ideas about inquiry, the development of views of inquiry, and the impact of science courses on student ideas. We illustrate our views with longitudinal studies of student views of science and with instructional studies using Science Controversy Online: Partnerships in Education (SCOPE) collaborative debate projects.

The Repertoire of Ideas and Knowledge Integration

Student ideas of inquiry are often connected to specific contexts or problems. For example, student views of various disciplines within science and even courses about science vary (cf. Driver et al., 1996). Furthermore, during science inquiry students may assert that everything in the science text is true while at the same time repeating that science is always changing. They may say that scientists disagree because they dislike each other, because they have done different experiments, or because they have different opinions. Yet in the same response students may also assert that scientists can resolve disputes with experiments. Often student answers vary depending on the question, science topic, or characteristics of the interviewer.

For students to develop a cohesive and coherent perspective on scientific inquiry they need to integrate, connect, sort out, and combine their repertoire of ideas as well as incorporate the different images of science they encounter. From this perspective, effective science instruction adds new ideas to the mix held by students and encourages them to compare, prioritize, link, and evaluate their ideas as well as to seek a cohesive view of science inquiry. We call this process knowledge integration and have developed instruction to promote the development of more cohesive ideas by students. Our assessments, designed concurrently with instruction, are created to document progress in gaining a coherent perspective.

We contrast the repertoire of ideas perspective on student beliefs about the nature of scientific inquiry with a developmental perspective. Piaget's early writings, (e.g., Piaget, 1969) for example, took a structuralist perspective, arguing for stages of development that were "in equilibrium" and therefore coherent albeit composed of non-normative ideas. Piaget (Inhelder & Piaget, 1958) illustrated the point by showing that children need a consistent view of nonconservation of continuous and discontinous quantity when young. Piaget's later writing elaborated the structuralist view but also added features such as "horizontal décalage" to account for variations across contexts and tasks (Piaget, 1968; Inhelder & Piaget, 1958). Researchers inspired by the Piagetian view look for common patterns of domain-general reasoning at each age, rather than focusing on domain-specific repertoires of ideas.

Some of these accounts reflect an essentialist view in the sense that they assume that the specific stage of reasoning is essential to interpreting the behavior of the individual. These essentialist views confer status on the developmental unfolding of understanding. They resonate with an oft-repeated quote from Piaget dismissing the role of education in development as, "the American question." In a later section we show how our research and especially our case studies raise questions about this view. For example, this view neglects important uncertainties and legitimate conflicts that seem, to us, powerful forces in development. This view also has difficulty explaining large cultural differences in development and significant contextual influences on behavior. Many researchers have documented contextual factors in reasoning that seem to threaten the validity of essentialist claims (e.g., A recent example serves to illustrate the problem. A child being tested for admission to a competitive elementary school was asked to count backwards from 10 to 1 and responded, "I don't know how." The worried parent, listening to the child said, "But what do you say when you are igniting a model rocket?" To which the child responded, "10, 9, 8 . . . . .").

Images of Science in Society

The repertoire of views perspective resonates with the disparate images of science students encounter in their lives. For example, controversy and debate are central features associated with the advance of scientific knowledge that provide complex images for students (Bell, 1998). In this section, we analyze the images of science that students might encounter and characterize common responses to these images.

Popular news accounts of science frequently emphasize controversy, highlight the personalities of the investigators, discredit previous research, promote polarized depictions of different theoretical camps, and either ignore or simplify the limitations of the methodologies and technologies of the field to account for why a controversy might be a rational aspect of the scientific endeavor. For example, reports of research on cholesterol in the diet, cancer cures, or energy conservation often emphasize conflicting perspectives, quick fixes, and personal attacks. Summaries of scientific investigations often personalize the findings with anecdotal evidence rather than reporting compelling research findings and depict science as perverse.

Advertisements often base claims on flimsy evidence. Students can frequently critique weak arguments (e.g., Linn, de Benedictis, & Delucchi, 1982). However, students who can critique an advertisement or persuasive message may use it later to buttress their own argument while "forgetting" the source of the information. This phenomenon referred to as "cite-amnesia" in the psychological literature means that students may rely on invalid or inaccurate information gleaned from persuasive messages (see Davis, 1998, for recent research on students' scientific critiquing of advertisements).

Consumer publications such as *Consumer Reports,* various health or wellness letters, and hobbyist guides attempt to synthesize science research and conduct additional tests in order to provide a public service to product users. Consumer publications typically compare alternatives using some set of criteria. They often profile the individuals involved in the preparation or the creation of the products. These publications may provide insight into scientific inquiry by emphasizing controversy and exploring the complexity of decisions. Consumer publications often make clear the methodologies used for comparing products and point out the limitations or weaknesses of the approaches. Many publications provide critiques of popular accounts of products, raising awareness among readers of the potential threats to the validity of claims encountered in the popular press. Thus consumer publications may enrich and expand images of scientific inquiry. At the same time, however, these reports often provide relatively definitive ratings and readers may lose track of the nuances and accept the ratings without question.

Historical summaries of scientific inquiry (e.g., Watson & Crick, 1968; Darwin, 1975; Keller, 1983), often emphasize the excitement of science, argue for considering personal characteristics of scientific inquiry, and provide idiosyncratic perspectives on scientific advance. Contrasting alternative accounts of historical advance provides readers with insights into the process and interpretive nature associated with scientific controversies as well as the personalities of the individuals involved in the discoveries. For example, Watson and Crick's account of the discovery of the double helix structure for DNA has been questioned by others (Sayre, 1975).

When textbooks attempt to synthesize historical accounts of a discovery, they often omit controversy and personality. They frequently tell a compelling story of one advance followed by another. These textbook accounts of scientific advance may confuse students because they, at best, emphasize the logical progression of straightforward discovery and the coherence of scientific knowledge rather than the serendipitous, personality-filled, conjectural, and controversial nature of most scientific breakthroughs.

Journal articles provide a particular picture of scientific results that differs from the active intellectual atmosphere found in the laboratory (Latour & Woolgar, 1986). Scientific journal articles often erase controversy from the record, leaving the disputes and discussions behind the closed doors of the scientific laboratory. Individuals attending scientific meetings may be surprised at the contrast between the active debate that goes on when people present their results and the seemingly logical progression laid out in a journal article. Journal editors are rarely willing to devote space to blind alleys or wrong paths even if research teams wished to provide this information. Furthermore, individuals relying largely on journal articles as a source of scientific information and as an insight into the inquiry process may not understand that these successes stand in contrast to failures, faulty methodologies, and misguided decisions typical of complex investigations. Taken as a group, journal articles on a similar topic can capture the contrasting perspectives on a research topic—often characterized by alternative networking as used by different research programs. Thus journal articles and historical or sociological accounts of discovery often take dramatically different perspectives on the same set of events.

Science textbooks devote limited space to any evidence of scientific controversy—typically less than 1 in 100 pages makes any mention of controversy (Champagne, 1998). Textbooks provide support for the accounts of scientific advance found in journal articles. Often textbooks are written by committees and not only fail to emphasize controversy but also provide incoherent accounts of different fields because authors use terminology differently or fail to build on and make connections across topics (Roth, 1989). Textbook science experiments, frequently described by students as "cookbook" labs, reinforce this view of straightforward discovery. When students follow a set protocol in order to replicate a well-established finding, they may come to believe that science consists of the simple, unproblematic unfolding of new information or "truths." These views are quite distant from the actual controversy that pervades much of leading edge scientific research. Textbook accounts also often ignore the interpretive and conjectural dimensions associated with the development of new scientific knowledge.

The Internet currently offers a substantially different perspective on scientific inquiry. Searching on any topic in science is likely to yield a vast array of information that varies in reliability, validity, replicability, and connection to normative scientific ideas. As an opportunity for students to develop the ability to critically evaluate scientific information, the Internet is unparalleled (Bell, 1998; Linn, 1999). Reviewing Internet materials will require students to carefully reflect on the connections between diverse sources of information. They need to learn to identify established scientific sources in order to validate conclusions and to apply appropriate disciplinary criteria to the arguments and evidence represented (Bell, Davis, & Linn, 1995; Clark & Slotta, 2000). Given the increasing reliance on the Internet reported by consumers, science courses need more than ever before to prepare students to evaluate sources with a critical eye. Students who have come to rely on textbooks may lack skills necessary for analyzing Internet materials.

Promoting Knowledge Integration

Given the varied images of science that learners encounter, it makes sense that they hold a repertoire of diverse ideas. While successful science learners link and connect their ideas, selectively explore and incorporate competing perspectives, and build a more coherent and robust understanding, most students find this process of knowledge integration challenging. Even mature scientists often report holding multiple views of science inquiry linked to distinct disciplines (e.g., Mayr, 1997).

Creating instruction to foster the knowledge integration process involves knowing where students start and providing opportunities for students to make

links and connections among ideas, to sort out their perspectives, to critique accounts of inquiry, and to reprioritize their views. We refer to instruction that
achieves this goal as scaffolded knowledge integration (Linn & Hsi, 2000; see
also Bell, 1998; Davis, 1998).

This type of instruction promotes a lifelong quest for pragmatic, coherent, and
useful understanding of science. By pragmatic we mean an understanding of science that connects to the kinds of personal experiences students are likely to encounter throughout their lives. By coherent we mean a view of scientific inquiry
that is connected across investigations and reflects the diverse sources of information about inquiry available in society. By useful, we mean a view of inquiry
that helps students make personal decisions in areas of scientific importance.

To explore inquiry perspectives we address the following questions: How do
students view science?, Do views of science inquiry influence science learning?,
and How do science courses influence images of inquiry? We conclude by synthesizing the answers to these questions and identifying areas for further research.

HOW DO STUDENTS VIEW SCIENCE?

The varied research studies in this volume and elsewhere show that students hold
a repertoire of diverse, incoherent ideas about inquiry and may see each discipline
as distinct. Some research programs seek to demonstrate that understanding of inquiry proceeds similarly across disciplines or to reveal core ideas by attempting to
study understanding of inquiry using decontextualized materials or by asking students to ignore information beyond that in the problem. Others view inquiry as a
topic that is best understood within a particular discipline and study inquiry in one
context. From the perspective of science, it may even be useful to distinguish disciplines since views of inquiry vary depending on the methodological techniques
and questions in each field (cf. Driver et al., 1996). Thus, views of inquiry concerning the fossil record may differ significantly from views of inquiry about the
mechanics of motion. Views of inquiry may also vary depending on the context of
the activity. Students may apply a different image of inquiry to a classroom experiment, an experiment reported in a popular magazine, or a decision about a personally relevant problem. Images of science may also depend on prior experience
with the science topic as well as perceptions about the availability of information.
Students often puzzle about ways that one might gain insight into events that occurred in the past (e.g., the extinction of dinosaurs), or about places that are difficult to observe firsthand (e.g., has there ever been life on Mars?).

Even asking students about science can elicit multiple views. For example,
when we question middle school students about whether they want to work as a
scientist when they are older, many respond in the negative but then go on to describe a future, desired career as a doctor or veterinarian. These multiple views of
science may lead to odd responses to decontextualized questions about "science"
in the abstract.

Many research studies have explored views about science by asking students to design scientific tests, critique experiments, and describe the nature of science in fairly general ways. This might be viewed as the study of students' enacted beliefs about the nature of science. Initially this work was popularized by Piaget who studied students' reasoning about scientific phenomenon such as the behavior of pendulums, the factors governing sinking and floating, and the behavior of balance beams. Piaget concluded that student's ability to understand and explain scientific inquiry followed a set of stages leading eventually, in adolescence, to the understanding of hypothetical experimentation (Inhelder & Piaget, 1970).

Subsequently, researchers replicated and extended these findings identifying situations where students reasoned in a more sophisticated manner than Piaget would predict as well as situations where reasoning was less sophisticated (e.g., Eylon & Linn, 1988). Additional factors were found to influence students' ability to design and interpret scientific experiments. For example, Case (1978) showed that students as young as 7 or 8 could control variables in scientific experiments when the situation was relatively straightforward. Siegler and Richards (1979) showed that students reduced complex situations such as balance beams to more simple rules such as "heavier goes down" or "longer goes down." Linn and Pulos (1983) extended this rule-based reasoning to problems having to do with displacement and showed that students who receive relatively straightforward experience made gains in understanding displacement by sorting out the rules they used (also Burbules & Linn, 1991). Tschirgi (1980) demonstrated that students interpret experiments in the context of their own understanding of the phenomena; thus when students design experiments to determine what will make a cake taste good, they are uninterested in leaving out sugar since they are sure sugar is necessary to make a cake taste good. Others asked students to reason about familiar situations that included counterintuitive results such as "cheese causes colds" (Kuhn, Amsel et al., 1988). They found that adolescent students had considerable difficulty taking a hypothetical stance toward these investigations, contrary to Piaget's theoretical perspective. Strauss (1977) and Inhelder and Piaget (1970) both demonstrated that under some circumstances students reason in a seemingly sophisticated way when young and become more confused as they gain experience with inquiry. Linn, Clement, Pulos, and Sullivan (1989) contrasted everyday problems with problems involving apparatus from mechanics and found that students were more successful in solving everyday problems than in dealing with physics problems commonly used in Piagetian research. Recently, Clark and Slotta (2000) demonstrated that students' critiques of scientific materials varied depending on the authority associated with the source and the amount of advance organization available in the situation. All these studies demonstrate that students hold a vast array of perceptions of scientific inquiry and draw on (or enact) them depending on the context of the problem.

Longitudinal studies of student's views of inquiry suggest that students add more diverse ideas to their perspectives of inquiry over time, perhaps reflecting experience with more of the images of scientific inquiry available in society. For example, Linn and Hsi (2000) asked students to interpret the rats problem (Fig. 16.1) and the rods problem (Fig. 16.2) at eighth, tenth, and twelfth grade. These problems were selected because the students in the longitudinal investigation had different information about them. For the rods problem shown in Fig. 16.2, students studied heat and temperature in eighth grade and therefore gained disciplinary knowledge relevant to the question. For the rats problem shown in Fig. 16.1, many students had no previous experience considering the implications of the studies of animals for human behavior. The longitudinal trajectory on these two problems gives insight into how students develop an understanding of scientific inquiry with and without regard to instruction about the disciplinary subject matter.

Linn and Hsi (2000) describe four case studies. One student, Lee, expected scientists to all have different ideas and therefore wasn't surprised that the scientists and other individuals depicted in these two problems disagreed with each other.

FIG. 16.1   Rats question used in tests and interviews for longitudinal study.

A university researcher believed that interesting, educational experiences in early life lead to larger brains. She took one litter of rats and placed each rat in its own, empty cage at birth. She took another litter of rats and placed all of them in a single large cage filled with toys, mazes, and exercise wheels.

When all the rats were adults, she measured the brain size of each rat. The rats raised alone in the empty cages had smaller brains than the rats raised together in the interesting environment. Based on this experiment, she concluded that children who have interesting, educational experiences in preschools will grow up to be more intelligent adults than children who do not attend preschool.

a. Do you think the conclusions will be accepted by other scientists?
   (circle one)   yes   no   Cannot predict
b. Why or why not?

A preschool teacher disagreed with the researcher. She said that the rat experiment could not be used to explain the advantages of preschool.

c. How could the researcher convince the teacher that she was right?
d. How could the teacher convince the researcher that she was right?

FIG. 16.2   Rods question used in tests and interviews for longitudinal study.

Erin, a scientist, compared three rods, one made of plastic, one made of diamond, and the other made of copper. All of the rods were the same length and thickness. Erin placed the end of each rod into a beaker of boiling water (100°C).

After 10 minutes, she measured the temperature at the other end of each rod. The diamond rod was the hottest, the copper rod was second, and the plastic rod was the coolest. Erin concluded that diamond was the best conductor of heat and that copper is a better conductor than plastic.

a. Do you think the conclusions will be accepted by other scientists?
    (circle one)   yes   no   cannot predict

b. Why or why not?

Max, another scientist, disagreed because he knew that copper is an excellent conductor of electricity and he said no one uses diamonds in their electrical equipment.

c. How could Max convince Erin that he was right? (Circle one.)
    A. Tell her the right answer.
    B. Describe an experience to support his conclusion.
    C. Design an experiment to show that his answer
        was correct.
    D. Other _____

d. What is the **main reason** for your choice?
e. How could Erin convince Max that she was right? (Circle one.)
    A. Tell him the right answer.
    B. Describe an experience to support her conclusion.
    C. Design an experiment to show that her answer
        was correct.
    D. Other _____
    F . What is the **main reason** for your choice?

Lee did not expect scientists to buttress their arguments with valid findings and instead remarked that scientists could have changed their minds or could "have written the wrong thing and found out that it was wrong." For the rats and rods problems, Lee generally responded, "I don't know" to questions about scientific inquiry. In one area, however, Lee drew on out-of-school experience with animals to reason in a more sophisticated way. Lee asserted that the experiment might not be valid because the mice might not have come from the same litter. In twelfth grade, Lee pointed out that the experimenters should do a study comparing children who went to preschool with those who did not. These two answers incorporate disciplinary knowledge that allows Lee to recognize threats to the validity of generalizing from animal studies to human studies. Thus on the one hand, Lee could make a valid claim about an experiment but on the other hand Lee did not expect scientists to reconcile valid claims.

Another case study student, Sasha, also asserted that scientists disagree but critiqued the conclusions from the two experiments based on relatively superficial factors. For the rods problem, Sasha said that diamonds would be too expensive and, for the rats problem, that it might have to do with attention at home. By twelfth grade Sasha had a more sophisticated view of rats but not rods. Thus in twelfth grade, Sasha said that brain size doesn't always mean more or less intelligence, that the rats' brains are different from the brains of children, and that children may react differently to preschool opportunities. Sasha's ideas about the rods experiment remained superficial, perhaps reflecting little opportunity to learn more about the topic between eighth and twelfth grade. Sasha could explain that scientists disagreed for varied reasons, giving different responses depending on the question.

Case study student, Pat, in contrast to Lee and Sasha, at every opportunity connected a large number of disciplinary ideas to the questions about rods and rats. Pat saw these questions as very incomplete and used them to reveal a wide range of disconnected ideas about science. In eighth grade, Pat requested more evidence for both rats and rods. Pat asserted that the rats experiment would need to be replicated with humans and the rods experiment would need to be replicated many times with different pieces of glass. After eighth grade science, Pat distinguished between these situations. Pat criticized the rats conclusion complaining that the experiment addressed a question about rats not humans. For the rods experiment, Pat concluded that multiple texts were not necessary but wondered about different experimental conditions such as alternative temperatures. Thus Pat was able to distinguish experiments where the conclusions are directly connected to the investigation from those where there is a conceptual leap between the investigation and the conclusions but did not expect to generalize to all conditions in either case.

The fourth case study student, Chris, become more skeptical of experimental findings over time. In eighth grade, Chris accepted experimental conclusions, essentially reiterating the views of the researchers. Chris said, for example, that in the rats experiment when individuals have more experience their knowledge keeps growing. This statement is similar to the findings of Tschirgi (1980) where students responded to experimental findings by describing consistent observations in nature. At the same time Chris did distinguish between rats and rods, remarking that rats are different because you can use the metal rods over and over again but you can't use the same rat more than once. In high school, Chris was more cautious. Chris remarked that it would be difficult to test the conclusions from the rat experiment with children because it would not be good for the children to be alone. For the rods, Chris asserted that the findings were consistent with results from other experiments about insulation and conduction. Chris used knowledge from science classes to interpret both of these experiments and showed a propensity to evaluate in terms of coherence with related observations. Chris also, at times, questioned the validity of experiments but did not connect validity with inference consistently.

These four case studies illustrate how specific science information and insights into the generalization of scientific results lead to more sophisticated responses to questions asked in this longitudinal study but also show how these students have many views of the same situation that are not linked or connected. The four case study students vary in their ability to recognize that the rat experiment requires extrapolation beyond the rats while the rod experiment only requires drawing conclusions about pieces of the same material. Over time, all four of the case study students raise some issues about generalizability of the rats findings and two of the students become more confident in generalizing the rods findings. These changes in interpretations appear to reflect increased knowledge of the disciplines of science as well as about the methods used in different fields. These students all reorganize their repertoire of ideas to combine a broader range of ideas over time.

These longitudinal cases buttress the conclusion that students are likely to develop a repertoire of views of inquiry and to have some difficulty linking and connecting those ideas into a coherent perspective. The cases show the impact and importance of disciplinary knowledge as crucial to the development of understanding of inquiry.

These findings have implications for the choice of experimental investigations and the topics covered under scientific inquiry in science courses. Often students study science at one level of analysis and are asked to generalize to another level of analysis. For example, students might study how viruses enter cells and then be asked to generalize to select drugs for treatments. Students might understand how a virus infects a cell but not have enough understanding of the whole human system to know how a drug could prevent a virus from infecting a given cell or how a virus might lead to disease. Similarly, in studying physics topics such as heat and temperature, students might have a molecular kinetic model of heat transfer and find it difficult to apply this model to questions about, for example, home insulation. Designing courses that allow students to exercise their abilities to extrapolate from experiments and reflect on how extrapolation works may help them develop coherent images of scientific inquiry. This approach could also help students connect their everyday and school science experiences with an understanding of inquiry.

Issues such as designing experiments that control variables become more complex in this account because students may lack understanding of the variables. Thus in the rats experiment, students seemed at times to recognize that extrapolating results from rats to humans was troublesome and at other times to accept that extrapolation uncritically. Similarly students at times failed to appreciate how variables were controlled in the rods experiment and at other times questioned the variables chosen by the experimenter. These reactions suggest that students have, in their repertoire, a basis for developing the rich understanding that they will need to interpret the complex popular messages of science they will encounter in their lives. In a later section we briefly describe and explore instruction that builds on these fledgling ideas to help middle and high school students understand current scientific controversies through debate, argumentation, and critique.

These results also raise questions about the trajectory of inquiry understanding. Students' ability to look at experiments from the standpoint of internal validity, generalizability, relevance, usefulness, and methodological soundness, may depend on disciplinary knowledge and problem context. Rather than implying that there is a single (or solitary) understanding that students need concerning inquiry, it seems useful to try to characterize some of the rich complexity of disciplinary inquiry and investigate understanding of this complexity. Problems involving artificial situations such as whether blue squares lead to the production of green triangles provide but one perspective on the complex views of inquiry held by students. Design of instruction that prepares students for a future filled with naturally occurring inquiry problems such as selecting among partially successful medical treatments or determining a nutritious diet requires studying a broader range of problems and considering additional factors.

DO STUDENT VIEWS OF SCIENCE INQUIRY INFLUENCE SCIENCE LEARNING?

Researchers have hypothesized that student's views of the nature of science inquiry and the nature of knowledge itself might influence their ability to learn science (Bell, 1998; Burbules & Linn, 1991; Driver et al., 1996; Carey & Smith, 1993; Carey & Smith, 1995; Hofer, chap. 1, this volume; Baxter Magolda, chap. 5, this volume; Schommer, chap. 6, this volume). Students appear to hold a diverse set of views rather than a coherent perspective at any stage in their development. Questions that focus on different disciplines or require varied experimental methods elicit alternative perspectives on science knowledge and inquiry from students. As a result, finding relationships between the nature of scientific knowing and the learning of science depends on what aspects of knowing one taps.

A variety of research studies have examined this relationship between student's views of the nature of science and their propensity to learn science. These studies sometimes look for predictive relationships and sometimes look for parallels in the development of understanding. Research to date tends to support the view that in both understanding of the nature of scientific inquiry and understanding of specific science disciplinary topics, students develop a diverse set of views and slowly sort them out and organize them more coherently in response to instruction and opportunities to reflect.

Songer (1989) researched students' views of science inquiry and distinguished static and dynamic perspectives. Students with a static perspective viewed science knowledge as established and unlikely to change. These students often asserted that everything in the science textbook is true. Students with a dynamic perspective recognized that science was constantly in a state of controversy and that different perspectives were held by different individuals or groups on leading edge topics. Students taking the dynamic view held relatively diverse perspectives on why scientists disagreed and how scientists worked out differences of opinion. They often viewed scientists as making conjectures that might be true but also suspected that scientists were "perverse." Songer found that about 15% of the students in eighth grade science held static views and 15% held dynamic views. Most students, therefore, held a mixed perspective on science inquiry including both dynamic and static views. This is consistent with the findings reported in the longitudinal cases suggesting that most students hold a multitude of perspectives on science inquiry. Songer found that there was a moderate relationship between students' perspectives on science inquiry and their understanding of science subject matter consistent with the perspective that in both these areas students were sorting out their ideas. Schoenfeld (1985) has also looked at static and dynamic perspectives on mathematics learning. He reports similar, moderate correlations between students' views of the nature of mathematics and their ability to learn mathematics.

Linn and Eylon (in press) studied students learning displaced volume. They found a moderate relationship between performance and beliefs about the complexity of inquiry. Students who gained understanding of displaced volume also were students who had a more dynamic, complex image of inquiry. They also found that on a delayed posttest the students who continued to make progress on understanding displaced volume were also students who had a more dynamic perspective on the nature of inquiry. Many students who independently seek robust understanding of inquiry also seek robust understanding of displaced volume.

Davis (1998) investigated students' propensities toward making sense of complex scientific information, referring to this as autonomous learning. She found that individuals who reported a tendency toward learning autonomously, were also more successful in making sense of complex information. These findings are consistent with those of Songer (1989) and Schoenfeld (1985), showing that as students develop their understanding of a discipline they also develop their understanding of inquiry.

A variety of researchers have interviewed students who studied the Computer as Learning Partner curriculum (Songer, 1989; Madhok, 1992) about their perspectives on the nature of science. These investigations demonstrate, in general, that students vary with regard to their perceptions of the relevance of scientific courses for their personal lives; that students often report that memorizing is more successful than understanding in traditional science courses; and that many students believe that science is too difficult for the average student to understand. These perspectives on the nature of science and science learning are moderately related to student's progress in science courses. As we will see in the next section, courses that emphasize these learning opportunities introduce students to new views of the nature of science inquiry and science learning.

All of these studies support the perspective that students' ability to understand scientific inquiry develops by a process of adding new ideas and sorting out a repertoire of views. Most students hold relatively mixed views of scientific inquiry, at times believing that science is static, at times reporting it as dynamic, and at times taking a relativistic view of science. Typically, the same student can express all three of these perspectives. Students whose ideas are more coherent with regard to science inquiry, also tend to have more coherent ideas about other aspects of science. The more students learn about science the more likely they are to have an opportunity to sort out their views of inquiry as well as their understanding of the discipline. However, relationships between understanding inquiry and understanding the discipline are not straightforward.

Today, science inquiry is often taught separately from science disciplinary knowledge. To the extent that science instruction minimizes or neglects the connections between inquiry and research in a discipline, students may have difficulty developing coherent connections among these topics. If experimental results are not critiqued from the standpoint of their validity, reliability, generalizability, methodological limitations, and connections to related scientific findings, then it would be surprising if students developed an appropriately nuanced understanding of inquiry methods. We know from analysis of science textbooks that students are rarely called on to critique experiments and that controversy is frequently neglected in the curriculum. In the next section we turn to examine the impact of science courses on images of inquiry.

HOW DO SCIENCE COURSES INFLUENCE IMAGES OF INQUIRY?

Several researchers have examined the impact of courses that emphasize critique, inquiry, ways of knowing, valid and invalid argumentation, and generalizability to see whether these instructional opportunities can change student's perspectives on the nature of science inquiry (Carey & Smith, 1993; Davis, 1998; Chen & Klahr, 1999). A series of investigations of science, technology, and society examine this question (e.g., Kumar & Chubin, 1999).

One line of research takes an abstract perspective emphasizing "critical thinking skills," using problems that are often less complex and sometimes topics other than science to alert students from the general, logical character of scientific reasoning. These instructional perspectives have had limited success in changing students' understanding of science inquiry. For example, Linn and Hsi (2000) report a study where Derek Newell developed a relatively comprehensive course on inquiry and incorporated it into instruction on heat and temperature. Newell did not make connections between the inquiry portion of the instruction and the heat and temperature portion of the actual instruction. As a result, students' understanding of inquiry developed to some extent but it was not connected to their understanding of heat and temperature so they could not design better experiments in this discipline. In a study of predicting displaced volume, Burbules and Linn (1991) asked students about their disciplinary understanding, provided students with results from various types of inquiry as well as textbook accounts of scientific findings, and then tested student progress in understanding the discipline. The information about inquiry did not influence students' ability to make sense of the science discipline.

Similarly, programs such as the critical thinking program (Covington, 1984) and other approaches to teaching reasoning improve students' ability to reason about problems emphasized in the curriculum but do not help students reason about problems in the science disciplines more generally. Research suggests that experts also have difficulty interpreting experimental findings in unfamiliar fields because of their lack of understanding of the methods and conventions in those different fields (Nersessian, 1989; Jasanoff, 1995). Research with expert scientists reveals similar difficulties in generalizing scientific procedures to complex everyday problems (Lewis & Linn, 1994; Linn & Hsi, 2000). When the development of understanding of science inquiry proceeds somewhat independently from the development of science disciplinary knowledge, connections between inquiry and disciplinary understanding may remain weak.

Teaching Personally Relevant Understanding Through Inquiry

When instruction does examine the relationship between inquiry and disciplinary knowledge, can courses impact understanding of the discipline as well as the understanding of inquiry? Researchers studying the Computer as Learning Partner curriculum (Linn & Hsi, 2000) have examined whether views of the relevance of science, the difficulty of science, and the value of memorizing to learn science change as a result of participating in the curriculum. Songer (1989) reported that students viewed science as more relevant to their lives after studying this curriculum. This is not surprising since the curriculum specifically emphasizes personally relevant problems. Prior to studying this curriculum, most students indicated that science was not relevant to their lives and that nothing that they learned in science classes could be useful. Songer also reported that student's perception of memorizing and understanding as learning strategies for science changed. Basically, prior to studying the curriculum, students relied more on memorization in studying science than they did after studying the curriculum. Many students reported that in this course understanding was essential for success, while in previous courses, memorizing was useful because the tests required memorized information.

Madhok (in preparation) replicated the Songer results for five semesters of the Computer as Learning Partner instruction. She found that for each semester studied, students viewed science as more relevant to their lives after studying the curriculum. She also found that students thought science was more useful and preferred understanding over memorizing as a result of studying the curriculum. In addition, Madhok found that when students were asked whether science was too difficult for ordinary students to understand they were more likely to say yes prior to studying the curriculum than after studying the curriculum. Taken together these results suggest that asking students to understand scientific topics and apply them to personally relevant problems helps them see the value of developing a connected understanding of science.

Teaching Through Argumentation and Collaborative Debate

To understand the relationship between science learning and science inquiry, Bell (1998) engaged over 25 classes of eighth grade students in argument construction and collaborative debate about a controversial topic in science for approximately a three-week period (see example in Fig. 16.3). The project is currently

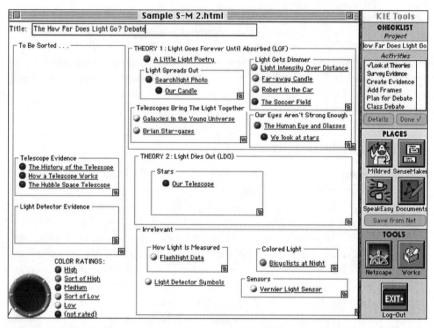

FIG. 16.3 Student argument map created during a classroom science controversy project about the nature of light.

available as part of the "Science Controversies Online: Partnerships and Education" (SCOPE) project[1] that focuses students' classroom inquiry around scientific evidence found on the Internet (see Bell, Davis, & Linn, 1995, for a description of the origins of this approach). Working in pairs, students critiqued a set of
evidence relevant to a debate topic and constructed an argument as they made
sense of the evidence. Student groups then presented their arguments during a
two-day collaborative debate activity in the classroom; each group also responded to questions about their argument from their peers and the classroom
teacher. We distinguish a collaborative debate from other forms of debate in that
students are encouraged to collectively explore the topic through their discussions rather than just engage in polarized debating for the sake of winning the argument. Before and after the SCOPE debate project, students were asked to reflect and describe the role of debate in science. The data was analyzed and
individual responses were coded into emergent categories. Since students frequently included multiple epistemological ideas in their responses, categories
were not coded to be mutually exclusive. Of the eight emergent categories representing students' epistemological thinking, there were significant gains in three
categories as a result of the debate instruction (see Table 16.1).

_____

[1]More information about SCOPE is available on the Web at http://www.scope.educ.
washington.edu.

TABLE 16.1
Student views of usefulness of debate in science and typical types of responses
(adds to over 100% because some students gave several answers).

Epistemological Categories –Typical types of responses	Pretest Percent (N = 166)	Posttest Percent (N = 170)
Social expansion of the repertoire • Debate brings about new perspectives • Debate can help everybody see all sides of a problem • Debate allows you to understand what people are thinking	40%	37%
Social discrimination of the repertoire • In debate scientists can compare and revise their ideas • In debate someone can show you a better idea (one that makes more sense)	17%	36%[a]
Enhances evidentiary support for arguments • Debate helps them explain their evidence more thoroughly • In debate others can help you identify evidence to support your theory	6%	26%[b]
Helps test arguments • Debate can assure a scientist that they are correct by "disproving" another scientist's ideas • Debate helps scientists see when they are wrong • In debate you can see who has better answers to questions	18%	24%
Promotes individual learning • In debate others might help expand your ideas • In debate you can learn more about your own ideas	7%	18%[c]
Allows synthesis of a topic • Debate helps scientists realize "the truth" about things • In debate you can come to conclusions about problems	22%	18%
Supports compromise • In debate scientists can come up with a compromise that is better than single ideas alone	5%	8%
Other • Debating is different than arguing	18%	21%

[a] $t = 3.81$; $p = .0002$
[b] $t = 5.21$; $p < .0001$
[c] $t = 2.91$; $p < .01$

First, students developed an understanding that a scientific debate can enhance the evidentiary support for arguments. Prior to instruction only 6% of the students made any mention of how scientists report and support arguments with evidence while following instruction a quarter of the students talked about this as being a characteristic of scientific debate. Students talked about how a debate can "encourage scientists to produce the evidence they need to support their theory" and "help them explain their evidence more thoroughly." They also described how other individuals in the debate can help you identify evidence to support your theory. These gains suggest that students are developing an epistemological understanding of scientific evidence.

Second, students demonstrated a significant gain in understanding of how a social group can help scientists discriminate between their ideas. Before the debate only 17% of the students described the social influence on one's thinking, and after instruction 36% of the students identified this as a feature of debate. Thus, students reported that during a debate "scientists can compare and refine their ideas," "someone can show you a better idea," and scientists can "together come up with something better" than they would on their own. More students believed that scientists compare and revise their ideas and as a result of this process might come up with a more accurate or complete view of a scientific phenomena after the debate. Engaging in a collaborative classroom debate helps students view science as a social endeavor (Driver et al., 1996).

The final category that showed a significant gain focused on how scientific debates can promote learning among the individuals participating. Only 7% of the students mention this prior to instruction while 18% mention it following instruction. Students report for example that when they participate in debate with other students they "learn new stuff" and that others might "help expand your idea." Several students mention that you can "learn more about your own ideas" as a result of participating in science debates. Interestingly, students, as a result of participating in a debate activity, also recognize that a debate helps them understand their own ideas about science. This connection helps us understand how students with a more dynamic view of knowledge construction in science might develop a more sophisticated understanding of the science.

Taken together, these results also suggest that participating in a scientific debate helps students gain insight into the inquiry process. Participating in a collaborative debate as opposed to conducting a scientific experiment following a cookbook approach is ideally suited to illustrating how science inquiry works. Scaffolded debate instruction can provide students with individual and social mechanisms for exploring a controversial topic and enhancing their understanding of the nature of science in the process.

A second study of collaborative debate, conducted with three classes of seventh grade students in an urban middle school demonstrates the cultural influence on students' epistemological understanding (Linn, Shear, Bell, & Slotta, 1999; Shear, 1998). One of the classes, composed of Russian-bilingual students, engaged in a debate project focused on a current scientific controversy—an apparent increase in the number of physical deformities in frog populations from across North America (Fig. 16.4 shows a screenshot from the Deformed Frogs debate project). Many of the students in this class had only been living in the United States for one or two years, having recently emigrated from countries in the former Soviet Union. Their classroom teacher—who taught them throughout the day in all subject areas—did not have a science background and sporadically taught the subject. Before using the debate project, she relied on activities in the available science textbook.

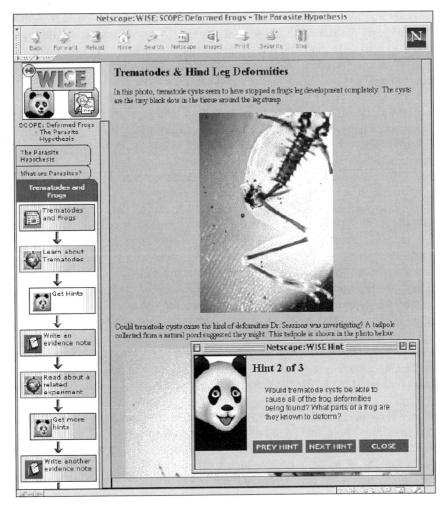

FIG. 16.4   Web-based curriculum project including scientific evidence and hints about the Deformed Frog controversy.

The Russian-bilingual students responded to a written test assessing their understanding of the nature of science before and after the instruction. At the beginning of the year, 87% of the students indicated that science consisted of a static collection of factual knowledge about the natural world—only 13% had any questions about this view. After students had learned about the frog controversy, developed their own arguments about the topic, and engaged in a classroom debate about the various hypotheses, 60% of the students indicated that scientific understanding was not static but that it evolved over time, representing a gain of more than 400%.

The teacher reported that instruction in Russian republics presents science subject matter as a set of truths that have been firmly established. These students had obviously developed an image of science that was consonant with this approach to science instruction. Interestingly, many of these students were able to refine their understanding of the nature of science when science instruction was focused on understanding and debating scientific evidence and theory related to a current controversy. Although this study does not report on the long-term influence of argumentation and debate on student epistemologies, it does substantiate the strong cultural influences on students' images of science.

Introducing collaborative debate into science class requires careful design. Debate activities can elicit stereotypes about who succeeds in science. Historically science has been the discipline of well-educated males. Many hold the belief that science is a male domain. Students sometimes disparage the comments of females in science class and males typically dominate class discussion (e.g., Wellesley, 1992; Hsi, 1997; Linn & Hsi, 2000). Collaborative debate activities have the potential, if carefully designed, of countering these images by showcasing the thoughtful contribution of students from diverse backgrounds. In our research we have explored ways to design debates that promote equity. Our longitudinal results show that students who participate in our Computer as Learning Partner curriculum generally view opportunities for males and females as equal in science (Linn & Hsi, 2000). In contrast, although more women now follow careers in science, many feel thwarted by obstacles and barriers when they enter graduate programs or take jobs in male-dominated workplaces (e.g., Linn, 1998). Introducing controversy and debate into science class might prepare male and female students to work collaboratively together on leading edge science research or it might reinforce stereotypes and discourage diversity. Advancing equity in science requires research on how to make debate and controversy an opportunity to promote the intellectual contributions of diverse students.

To make a debate successful in science class, careful design is necessary (see Bell, 1998). Students need a debate topic that is accessible and researchable. The Deformed Frogs! controversy proved ideal. It was originally popularized by students in Minnesota, making it interesting to other students. Our scientist and teacher partners helped us pick a level of analysis for the debate that made sense to students and could help them learn about important concepts and relationships in biology without sacrificing the nature of the controversy itself (Linn, 1999; Linn et al., 1999).

Introducing debate into science class also provides considerable challenges. Teachers have rarely dealt with controversies in science since textbooks obliterate this information from the curriculum, so the idea of having a classroom debate is frequently surprising to teachers. To help teachers develop the pedagogical content knowledge appropriate for running a debate, we created a video of classroom debate sequences (see Caribiner International, 1999). This example illustrates ways to structure a debate such that all students can participate. Often shouting matches lead to inequitable participation with the loudest and most aggressive students predominating. Working with teachers interested in teaching about controversy, we have identified mechanisms for instituting debates that are more successful (Bell 1998; Bell & Linn, 2000; Linn & Clark, 1997; Linn & Hsi, 2000). For example, in the debate every student is asked to come to class prepared to participate and then groups are selected randomly to present their arguments and evidence. During the debate, all students write at least one question about each presentation. All students are expected to ask a question during the debate at some point. All students turn in their questions. Students receive grades on the debate based on their class participation, their presented arguments, their lists of questions, and their performance on a test comprised of short essays about the controversy.

The coordination of evidence and claim also present a challenge to students (Bell, 1998; Bell & Linn, 2000). In part, we introduce these dimensions of argumentation using a courtroom metaphor. Students can quickly understand the idea of supporting, contradicting, and irrelevant evidence with respect to particular claims when presented in the context of courtroom proceedings. We use the metaphor to get them started in their argumentation process since it draws on relevant prior epistemological knowledge students bring to the endeavor. Students then proceed to make sense of this coordination process within the context of the controversy topic at hand.

To measure students' understanding of science inquiry we asked students what might be learned from debate and how scientists participate in debates. We also conducted semistructured interviews about the responses with some students. We found some connections between student inquiry experiences in science class and their beliefs about science inquiry, and continue to explore these connections (Bell & Linn, 2000).

These results suggest that science instruction shapes student ability to understand scientific inquiry. Traditional courses taken prior to eighth grade appear to reinforce a view of science as static and a view of science learning as best accomplished through memorization. Courses designed to engage students in knowledge integration using collaborative debate help students modify these perspectives. Further research will improve the impact of programs like these on understanding of inquiry in science.

CONCLUSIONS

Students come to science class with a broad range of different images of science inquiry—some acquired in school, others acquired out of school. Frequently, these images are disconnected from each other and tied to the context of the question asked. Thus if students are asked to explain everyday or personally relevant problems, they are likely to build on images of inquiry from the popular press or personal experience. In contrast, if students are asked to comment on topics learned in the science textbook, they are likely to draw on images of inquiry emphasized in the kinds of experiments they have done in science class. Often these experiments lack some of the features of experimentation characteristic of ongoing scientific research. For example, experiments conducted in class may follow a relatively straightforward protocol and have few uncertainties. Students may conclude that in science class understanding and resolving controversies is discouraged. Research shows that when students explore controversial topics in science and connect these topics to personally relevant issues, they gain both understanding of inquiry and understanding of a complex science topic.

Research also shows that when students participate in science courses that offer a broad array of inquiry practices combined with opportunities for synthesis, their understanding of science inquiry is enhanced. Students develop a more coherent set of images of science when specifically supported in connecting diverse examples such as the rods and rats described earlier. These findings suggest that courses with a more robust perspective on science inquiry can help students add new perspectives on inquiry to their repertoire of ideas. Courses that help students sort out, prioritize, and organize these ideas can enhance understanding of inquiry and promote a disposition to make sense of inquiry. This research suggests that the propensity to analyze controversy stems from instruction. These results call for a research program that contrasts the essentialist perspective on the development of understanding of inquiry and the repertoire of models perspective on this type of understanding

Research on collaborative debate in science class suggests that activities such as debate, when buttressed by opportunities to gather and understand evidentiary information, can substantially influence students' images of the nature of science inquiry and help students connect ideas from diverse experiences to their view of the nature of science. The collaborative debate instruction that we have described focuses on supporting students in the process of developing and debating scientific arguments related to controversial topics in science.

The Science Controversies Online: Partnerships and Education (SCOPE) project is currently researching a variety of activities that introduce controversy into science class and engage students in researching contemporary scientific controversies (Linn, in press; Linn et al., 1999; Bell, 1998). Currently, the SCOPE project offers schools the opportunity to engage students in contemporary controversies including the Deformed Frogs! controversy, the Malaria controversy, and the Genetically Modified Food controversy. In several classroom contexts, we have demonstrated how controversy-focused curricula can foster students' epistemological sophistication with respect to the dynamic nature of science and the role of debate for such deliberations. Many additional epistemological dimensions of controversy merit investigation, including: the relationship between policy decisions (which are often quite blunt) and scientific understanding (which is often quite nuanced), how scientists go about planning subsequent investigations, how argumentation and debate vary across disciplines or subdisciplines (Cetina, 1999), how controversies evolve over long periods of time, among others. We invite researchers to use SCOPE units and investigate their impact on students' learning in diverse settings.

The repertoire of views perspective summarized here raise interesting questions concerning the development of general understanding of inquiry. Does epistemological sophistication have a general, essentialist trajectory or is it better understood as situational, contextual, and disciplinary-specific? Clearly students express more sophisticated ideas after studying a science discipline, but the causes of this epistemological sophistication appear closely aligned with instruction.

From the perspective of instructional design, the repertoire of views perspective on science inquiry has proven fruitful. We have provided evidence that classroom debate can improve students' images of science over the course of instruction, leading us to believe that particular instructional experiences are a crucial component of epistemological sophistication. Further research could explore variations in the design of these instructional experiences. The studies conducted to date reinforce two design principles described by Linn and Hsi (2000): Instruction should leverage student's previous experiences and epistemic knowledge, and instruction should enable students to revisit their ideas in naturally occurring learning situations.

Introducing critique and collaborative debate activities from the very earliest science courses would help students develop a more robust understanding of the nature of science and the nature of science controversy. If carefully designed, collaborative debate activities can also shed light on current scientific controversies and ameliorate stereotyped views of who succeeds in science. Too often critique and controversy are neglected in the science curriculum. As the results discussed here suggest, we can bring to life the nature of scientific inquiry through opportunities for students to explore controversial science issues. When students critique and debate experimental findings they gain insight into the process of science and are poised to become lifelong science learners.

ACKNOWLEDGMENTS

This material is based on research supported by the National Science Foundation under grant REC 98-73160 and REC 98-05420. Any opinions, findings, and conclusions or recommendations expressed in this publication are those of the authors and do not necessarily reflect the views of the National Science Foundation.

The authors appreciate the help and encouragement of the Science Controversies Online: Partnerships in Education and WISE project research groups. Special thanks are due Jim Slotta, Linda Shear, Sherry Seethaler, Jacquie Madhok, Chris Hoadley, Doug Clark, Elizabeth A. Davis, Sherry Hsi, and Britte Cheng for helpful interpretation of data and thoughtful discussion. Preparation of this manuscript was made possible with help from Christina Kinnison, Rosie Chae, Carole Strickland, and Lisa Safley.

REFERENCES

Bell, P. (1998). *Designing for students' science learning using argumentation and classroom debate.* Unpublished doctoral dissertation, University of California, Berkeley, CA.

Bell, P., Davis, E. A., & Linn, M. C. (1995). The Knowledge Integration Environment: Theory and design. In J. L. Schnase & E. L. Cunnius (Ed.), *Proceedings of the Computer Supported Collaborative Learning Conference, CSCL '95, Bloomington, IN* (pp. 14–21). Mahwah, NJ: Erlbaum.

Bell, P., & Linn, M. C. (2000). Scientific arguments as learning artifacts: Designing for learning on the Web in KIE. *International Journal of Science Education, Special Issue, 22(8),* 797–817.

Burbules, N. C. & Linn, M. C. (1991). Science education and the philosophy of science: Congruence or contradiction? *International Journal of Science Education, 13*(3), 227–241.

Carey, S. & Smith, C. (1993). On understanding the nature of scientific knowledge. *Educational Psychologist, 28*(3), 235–251.

Carey, S. & Smith, C. (1995). On understanding the nature of scientific knowledge. In D. N. Perkins, J. L. Schwartz, M. M. West, & M. S. Wiske (Eds.), *Software goes to school: Teaching for understanding with new technologies* (pp. 39–55). New York, NY: Oxford University Press.

Caribiner International. (1999). [Film]. Computers, Teachers, Peers: Science Learning Partners. (Available from Lawrence Earlbaum Associates, Mahwah, NJ.)

Case, R., Ed. (1978). *Implications of developmental psychology for the design of effective instruction.* Cognitive Psychology and Instruction. New York: Plenum.

Cetina, K. N. (1999). *Epistemic cultures: How the sciences make knowledge.* Cambridge, MA: Harvard University Press.

Champagne, A. (1998). *Kill all the mosquitoes or cure malaria?* American Association for the Advancement of Science [AAAS]; Philadelphia, PA.

Chen, Z. and D. Klahr (1999). All other things being equal: Children's acquisition and transfer of the Control of Variables Strategy. *Child Development 70:* 1098–1120.

Clark, D. & Slotta, J. D. (in press). Interpreting evidence on the Internet: Sex, lies, and multimedia. *International Journal of Science Education, Special issue 22*(8), 859–871.

Covington, M. V. (1984). The motive for self-worth. In R. Ames & C. Ames (Ed.) (pp. 78–114). New York: Academic Press.

Darwin, C. (1975). *The origin of species* (6th ed.). Franklin Center, PA: Franklin Library.

Davis, E. A. (1998). *Scaffolding students' reflection for science learning.* Unpublished doctoral dissertation, University of California, Berkeley, CA.

Driver, R., Leach, J., Millar, R., & Scott, P. (1996). *Young people's images of science.* Buckingham, UK, Open University Press.

Eylon, B. S. & Linn, M. C. (1988). Learning and instruction: An examination of four research perspectives in science education. *Review of Educational Research 58*(3): 251–301.

Hsi, S. (1997). *Facilitating knowledge integration in science through electronic discussion: The Multimedia Forum Kiosk.* Unpublished doctoral dissertation, University of California, Berkeley, CA.

Inhelder, B. & Piaget, J. (1958). *The growth of logical thinking from childhood to adolescence: An essay on the construction of formal operational structures.* London, Routledge & Kegan Paul.

Inhelder, B. & Piaget, J. (1970). *The early growth of logic in the child; Classification and seriation.* New York, Humanities Press.

Jasanoff, S. & [et al.] (Ed.). (1995). *Handbook of science and technology studies.* Thousand Oaks, CA: Sage Publications.

Keller, E. F. (1983). *A feeling for the organism: The life and work of Barbara McClintock.* San Francisco, CA: W. H. Freeman.

Kuhn, D., Amsel, E., O'Loughlin, M., & with the assistance of L. Schauble (1988). *The development of scientific thinking skills,* (Developmental Psychology Series). Orlando, FL: Academic Press.

Kumar, D. & Chubin, D. (Eds.) (1999). *Science, technology, and society education: A resource book on research and practice.* Kluwer Academic Press.

Latour, B. & Woolgar, S. (1986). *Laboratory life: The construction of scientific facts.* Princeton, NJ: Princeton University Press.

Lewis, E. L. & Linn, M. C. (1994). Heat energy and temperature concepts of adolescents, adults, and experts: Implications for curricular improvements. *Journal of Research in Science Teaching* 31(6): 657–677.

Linn, M. C. (1998). When good intentions and subtle stereotypes clash: The complexity of selection decisions. *Educational Researcher, 27*(9), 15–17.

Linn, M. C. (in press). How can new media improve university research and instruction? *Proceedings of the New Media Workshop, Leopold Franz University, March 4, 1999, Innsbruck, Austria.* Germany, Gabler.

Linn, M. C. (April 25, 1999). Controversy, the Internet, and deformed frogs: Making science accessible. *Proceedings of National Academy of Sciences annual meeting symposium (NAS '99: Washington, DC).*

Linn, M. C., de Benedictis, T., & Delucchi, K. (1982) Adolescent reasoning about advertisements: Preliminary investigations. *Child Development, 53,* 1599–1613.

Linn, M.C. & Clark, H. (November, 1997). When are science projects learning opportunities? *Research Matters—To the Science Teacher, National Association for Research in Science Teaching.*

Linn, M. C., Clement, C., Pulos, S., & Sullivan, T. (1989). Scientific reasoning during adolescence: The influence of instruction in science knowledge and reasoning strategies. *Journal of Research in Science Teaching, 26*(2), 171–187.

Linn, M. C. & Eylon, B. S. (in press). Knowledge integration and displaced volume. *Journal of Science, Education, and Technology.*

Linn, M. C. & Hsi, S. (2000). *Computers, Teachers, Peers: Science Learning Partners.* Mahwah, NJ: Erlbaum.

Linn, M. C. & Pulos, S. (1983). Male-female differences in predicting displaced volume: Strategy usage, aptitude relationships, and experience influences. *Journal of Educational Psychology, 75,* 86–96.

Linn, M. C., Shear, L., Bell, P., & Slotta, J. D. (1999). Organizing principles for science education partnerships: Case studies of students' learning about 'rats in space' and 'deformed frogs.' *Educational Technology Research and Development, 47*(2), 61–85.

Madhok, J. J. (1992). Effect of gender composition on group interaction. In K. Hall, M. Bucholtz, & B. Moonwomon (Eds.), *Locating power: Proceedings of the second Berkeley Women and Language Conference* (pp. 371–385). Berkeley, CA: Berkeley Women and Language Group, University of California at Berkeley.

Madhok, J. (in preparation). *Longitudinal impact of a technology enhanced inquiry curriculum on views of science learning and science career choice.* Unpublished doctoral dissertation, University of California, Berkeley, CA.

Mayr, E. (1997). *This is biology: The science of the living world.* Cambridge, MA: Belknap Press of Harvard University Press.

Nersessian, N. J. (1989). Conceptual change in science and in science education. *Synthese, 80,* 163–183.

Piaget, J. (1968). *Le Structuralisme.* Paris, Presses universitaires de France.

Piaget, J. (1969). *The child's conception of the world*. Totowa, NJ, Littlefield, Adams & Co.

Roth, K. J. (1989). Science education: It's not enough to 'do' or 'relate.' *American Educator*, 16–22, 46–48.

Sayre, A. (1975). *Rosalind Franklin and DNA*. New York: W. W. Norton & Co., Inc.

Schoenfeld, A. H. (1985). *Mathematical problem solving*. Orlando, FL: Academic Press.

Shear, L. (1998). When science learners are language learners: Designing linguistically aware instruction to teach science 'the knew way' Unpublished master's thesis. Berkeley, CA: University of California at Berkeley.

Siegler, R. S. & Richards, D. D. (1979). The development of time, speed, and distance concepts. *Developmental Psychology 15:* 288–298.

Songer, N. B. (1989). Promoting integration of instructed and natural world knowledge in thermodynamics. Unpublished doctoral dissertation, University of California, Berkeley, CA.

Strauss, S. (1977). *Educational implications of U-shaped behavioural growth*. [A position paper for the Ford Foundation], Tel-Aviv, Israel: Tel-Aviv University.

Strike, K. A., & Posner, G. J. (1992). A revisionist theory of conceptual change. In R. A. Duschl & R. J. Hamilton (Eds.), *Philosophy of science, cognitive psychology, and educational theory and practice*. Albany, NY: SUNY Press.

Tschirgi, J. E. (1980). Sensible reasoning: A hypothesis about hypotheses. *Child Development, 51,* 1–10.

Watson, J. D. & Crick, F. (1968). *The Double helix*. New York: New American Library.

Wellesley College Center for Research on Women (1992). *How schools shortchange girls* (Executive Summary). Washington, DC: American Association of University Women Educational Foundation, AAUW.

17

Characterizing Fifth Grade Students' Epistemological Beliefs in Science

Anastasia D. Elder
Mississippi State University

Students' beliefs about the nature of science and scientific knowledge are considered an important and vital part of their science education (Duschl, 1994; Lederman, 1992; National Research Council, 1996). Although the role of these beliefs are viewed as fundamental for learning and understanding science, little attention has been paid to young students' views of the nature of knowledge in science. Elementary school is a time during which children are exposed to formal instruction in science and acquire an understanding of the world around them (Bruer, 1993), and thus may develop some comprehension of the nature of scientific knowledge. The goal of this study is to describe fifth grade students' beliefs about the nature of scientific knowledge.

In an effort to address what young students think about the nature of knowledge in science, this study explores and characterizes the epistemological beliefs of fifth grade students who studied hands-on, inquiry-based science. Although current research on students' scientific epistemological beliefs does not share a common conceptualization of these beliefs, five constructs figure prominently in studies of older students: the purpose of science, the changing nature of science, role of experiments in developing scientific theories, coherence of science, and source of science knowledge (Elder, 1999). This chapter evaluates young students'

347

epistemological beliefs by describing each of the five constructs and in doing so helps to complete a developmental portrayal of students' epistemological understanding. Thus, the major question addressed in this chapter is: What do fifth grade students think and believe about the nature of knowledge in science (i.e., the purpose of science, changeability of science, role of experiments in developing scientific theories, coherence of science, and source of science knowledge)?

EXTENDING RESEARCH ON EPISTEMOLOGICAL BELIEFS TO ELEMENTARY STUDENTS

Existing literature on students' epistemological understanding in science has highlighted older students' beliefs, partly stemming from assumptions regarding limits on children's thinking (e.g., Chandler, Boyes, & Ball, 1990; Inhelder & Piaget, 1958). The majority of studies investigating students' epistemological beliefs in science have focused on adolescent or postadolescent students including middle school (e.g., Carey, Evans, Honda, Jay, & Unger, 1989; Songer & Linn, 1991), high school (e.g., Roth & Roychoudhury, 1994; Ryan & Aikenhead, 1992), and college students (e.g., Hammer, 1994). Two lines of research support extending research on epistemology to elementary students. Evidence from cognitive developmental literature (e.g., Montgomery, 1992; Wellman, 1990) advocates the idea that a developing epistemology likely exists at a young age. In addition, effects of instructional practices point to the positive influence of an inquiry-based instructional context that stresses a supportive, questioning environment combined with authentic scientific activities for students' epistemological understanding (Carey et al., 1989; Lederman & Druger, 1985; Solomon, Duveen, Scott, & McCarthy, 1992). Curricular reform efforts in elementary education have been directed at establishing inquiry science instruction for all students (Collins, 1997; National Research Council, 1996). Thus, young students who are taught science in an inquiry-based program may be sensitive to epistemological issues and may develop sophisticated conceptions about the nature of knowledge in science. This study explores the epistemological beliefs of fifth grade students in a supportive, instructional context studying hands-on, inquiry-based science.

CONCEPTUALIZING BELIEFS

Existing literature on epistemological beliefs has attempted to characterize the nature of students' beliefs about knowledge in science. Although no standard conceptualization for examining epistemological beliefs in science has been utilized, a number of issues common in the literature have emerged. Five constructs have been central in efforts to investigate students' beliefs about the nature of knowledge in science: (1) the purpose of science, (2) changeability of science, (3) role of experiments in developing scientific theories, (4) coherence of science, and (5) source of science knowledge. These constructs reflect others' work on personal epistemology (Hofer & Pintrich, 1997).

Purposes and Changing Nature of Science

Epistemological understanding of science includes comprehending the purposes of science activity and the changing nature of the field. Some students in middle school with a specialized curriculum exhibited a sophisticated understanding that science aimed to explain phenomena (Carey et al., 1989), that scientific experiments tested out ideas and explanations for how things work (Solomon, Scott, & Duveen, 1996), and that science knowledge changed over time (Songer & Linn, 1991). Less sophisticated students considered the goal of science as discovering and inventing things (Carey et al., 1989; Solomon et al., 1996) and believed that science knowledge remained stable (Songer & Linn, 1991). Minimal research has been conducted with elementary-aged students regarding their beliefs about the purposes of science or their beliefs about the changing nature of science (cf., Driver, Leach, Millar, & Scott, 1996; Smith, Houghton, Maclin, & Hennessey, 1997; Vekiri, Baxter, & Pintrich, 1998). Given that inquiry curricula positively affected middle school students' epistemological beliefs, it is expected that to some extent students in an inquiry-based, hands-on elementary science program will hold sophisticated beliefs about the purposes of science and changing nature of science.

Role of Experiments in Science

The role of experiments has been investigated in terms of students' understanding of the interplay between theory and evidence. Students' understanding of this topic has been differentiated into students' ability to distinguish between ideas and evidence, and students' ability to coordinate the two (Duveen, Scott, & Solomon, 1993). In addition, students' ideas about the role of experiments in science have been investigated in relation to students' demonstrated understanding of a specialized science curriculum (Carey et al., 1989), and conjointly with reasoning about scientific topics (Driver et al., 1996) and reasoning in experiment situations (Kuhn, Amsel, & O'Loughlin, 1988). For the most part, evidence of students' understanding of the role of experiments for the progress of science remained mixed: Few students understood how science coordinated evidence from experiments to create or verify scientific theories (Carey et al., 1989; Kuhn et al., 1988). However, some research with young children indicated that they were beginning to display an understanding of the differences between theory and evidence (Samarapungavan, 1992; Sodian, Zaitchik, & Carey, 1991). The quality of understanding about the role of experiments in science endorsed by elementary students in special inquiry-based curriculum remains to be documented. Given their exposure and experience with performing experiments and conducting scientific activities, elementary students in a hands-on science program are expected to hold relatively sophisticated beliefs about how experiments are different than, and contribute to, developing scientific knowledge.

Coherence of Scientific Knowledge

Students' beliefs about the coherence and sources of science knowledge have been researched with high school and college students. A majority of high school students in one physics class endorsed the idea that scientific knowledge is based on facts and comes from textbooks and lectures (Roth & Roychoudhury, 1994). Also, some college students expressed beliefs that science was a collection of separate pieces of knowledge (i.e., formulas and symbols) that only experts were able to understand in terms of a coherent system rather than an integrated body of knowledge made up of concepts in which one could construct their own understanding (Hammer, 1994). Such evidence may indicate that the relatively sophisticated ideas of coherence and sources (i.e., that science knowledge is a coherent system of concepts that is derived from thinking and reasoning) develop later than other constructs that make up epistemological beliefs in science (e.g., knowledge as changing). Given that high school and college students often hold naive views regarding these constructs and that little evidence points to these views being altered by instruction (e.g., Roth & Roychoudhury, 1994), it seems likely that elementary students even in an inquiry environment would likely possess a naive understanding as well.

Sources of Scientific Knowledge

Research on beliefs about the sources of scientific knowledge has relied on a limited representation of that construct. In most studies, issues concerning the sources of science knowledge were represented as a dichotomy between knowledge being constructed by oneself or knowledge being handed down by authority figures (e.g., teachers or experts). Such a dichotomy is problematic in two respects. First, it confounds issues regarding the activity and independent nature of how science ideas arise. Constructing one's own knowledge involves taking an active role and engaging in an independent endeavor while receiving knowledge from authority involves a passive role that is dependent on others. It is not clear what is the valued aspect of constructing one's knowledge—being active, being independent, or being both active and independent. In addition, characterizing sources of knowledge as either from authority or from thoughtful reflection overlooks other kinds of sources students may attribute to science knowledge, for example, passive and independent sources such as an idea just popping into one's mind or active and dependent ones, such as interacting with places or things for developing one's ideas. Thus, this study differentiates between active and independent dimensions when examining sources of scientific knowledge. I expect that young students in hands-on, inquiry-based classrooms in which they conduct scientific experiments will view scientific knowledge as being derived from active and dependent endeavors, consistent with their experiences in the science classroom.

Second, the dichotomy between constructing ones' own understanding versus receiving knowledge from another ignores differences between students' own sources and what students think scientists use as sources. Distinguishing between the sources of a student's ideas and the sources students attribute to scientists is potentially an important feature for investigating students' beliefs about knowledge in science (Hogan, 2000). Students' views regarding science may differ depending on whether they are considering the kinds of activities and thinking they do in school science versus the kinds of activities and thinking in which they believe expert scientists engage (Driver et al., 1996).

Although Driver et al. (1996) considered this an important distinction, they did not explicitly investigate it. This chapter will attempt to directly address this issue. Asking students about their own ideas may in part reflect their understanding of science as a part of school and may miss what they believe to be the authentic nature of science or at least an idealized version they attribute to scientists. To some extent, during school, science knowledge does come from teachers and books. Yet if asked about scientists, students may endorse a more sophisticated epistemological understanding that science knowledge originates and develops from scientists' active thinking, testing, and refining of ideas and theories.

CONTEXT OF STUDY

Participants included 211 students from nine fifth grade classrooms in a large, urban school district in Southern California. Students were of a diverse background: 42% Latino, 37% African American, 17% Caucasian or Asian, and 4% unknown or other. Fifty-seven percent were male and two-thirds qualified for free or reduced lunch.

Science instruction at the elementary grades in this school district was based on an inquiry model of learning in which students learn science through participation in a guided set of hands-on activities and investigations. At each grade level, kindergarten through grade five, students studied four units encompassing a range of science areas (i.e., life, earth, physical), each for approximately nine weeks. Fifth grade topics included the nature of electricity, physical and chemical properties of common substances, astronomy of the sun and earth, and behavior of crayfish. During the course of each unit, students worked in groups to manipulate equipment and materials, conduct experiments, and generate questions for further inquiry. For example, when studying electricity, students connected wires, batteries, and bulbs to create a circuit, determined the path of electricity, and learned about resistance and polarity. For this study, fifth grade students investigated either a unit on electricity (Circuits, $n = 113$) or chemical properties (Powders, $n = 98$) during the third or fourth quarters of their school year.

MEASURING EPISTEMOLOGICAL BELIEFS

A written questionnaire assessing epistemological beliefs consisted of two parts. Part I asked students to respond to three open-ended items in writing. These questions served to elicit some of the students' initial epistemological beliefs and were directed at capturing their understanding of the purpose of science by asking about their definitions of science (What do you think science is?) and the sources for their own and scientists' ideas for doing science (Where do your ideas to do science experiments come from? Where do you think scientists get their ideas for doing science experiments?).

Part II asked students to indicate how much they agreed or disagreed with 25 Likert-scaled items (e.g., scientific beliefs change over time) aimed at pinpointing specific epistemological beliefs and evaluating dimensions of students' beliefs. Students were asked to respond to each item using a 5-point scale (1 = strongly disagree; 3 = somewhat disagree/somewhat agree; 5 = strongly agree). Items were adapted from other work (e.g., Rubba & Andersen, 1978; Schommer, 1990) or created to address issues of the changing nature of science, role of experiments for doing science, coherence of scientific knowledge, and authority figures and materials as sources of scientific ideas (see Table 17.1).

The questionnaire was completed during the third week of a nine-week, hands-on science unit. A researcher visited each classroom and read all questions aloud. For the open-ended items students wrote responses in spaces provided on the questionnaire. For the Likert-scaled items, students marked how much they agreed or disagreed with each statement.

TABLE 17.1
Sample Likert-Scaled Items from Epistemological Beliefs Questionnaire

Construct	Example Item
Changing Nature of Science	After scientists find the answer to a problem, the answer could change.
Role of Experiments	Good ideas are based on evidence from many different experiments.
Coherence of Knowledge	In science, there is always a simple answer to a question.
Source of Knowledge	Sometimes you just have to believe what the teacher says in science, even if you don't understand it.

STUDENTS' VIEWS OF THE PURPOSES
OF SCIENCE

When asked, "What do you think science is?" students generated a variety of definitions of science that revealed their thinking about the purpose of science. Because of the exploratory nature of this study, coding categories for students' responses were empirically derived. Student responses were categorized through an iterative process of reading students' responses, noting patterns and similarities, reviewing categories and revising the categories as necessary. Category development was guided by the kinds of purposes for science students conveyed in their definitions. Two raters individually coded 25% of student responses. The author was one rater; a research assistant was the other rater. The author coded the remaining 75% of the responses. Interrater agreement, calculated by computing a ratio of agreements to all codes (i.e., agreements plus disagreements), was 82%. Discrepancies were resolved through discussion. Three groupings of students were formed based on the relative sophistication of their understanding of the purpose of science: those with poor, fair, and good definitions of science.

Grouped together as having poor understanding were students who believed science to be a task to be learned or were vague. These students either expressed an idea of science as an end product (e.g., a task) or were unable to convey a sense of the purposes of science nor supply a description of science. Instead they offered unrelated ideas pertaining to their value for science (e.g., "it is fun") or were vague ("it is research"). Thirty percent of students expressed poor understanding of the purpose of science.

Students who defined science in terms of explaining phenomena and/or as a process of learning were considered as providing good definitions with a relatively sophisticated understanding of the purpose of science. Recognizing that science aims to explain the workings of the world was considered the best quality purpose of science based on previous research with seventh grade students (Carey et al., 1989). Expressing an understanding that the purpose of science is to explain phenomena or a process of learning captured the most sophisticated thinking of the fifth grade students in this study. These students viewed science as more than performing activities and/or completing a school-related task; they regarded science as making a contribution to understanding phenomena (e.g., "to learn how things work"; "to discover new things never thought of before"). Twenty-three percent of students were categorized in this way.

Students classified as having a fair definition of science either emphasized activities or endorsed a combination of good and poor definitions. These students often stressed the activity of doing science but without relating much purpose to those activities (e.g., "to do all kinds of different things . . . to work with live animals"). In addition, this classification included students with unclear understanding of the purposes of science. They generated relatively unsophisticated and sophisticated purposes simultaneously (e.g., "Science is an important thing to learn . . . science helps you understand things"). Forty-seven percent of students were classified as having fair definitions of science.

Most fifth grade students did not hold sophisticated beliefs about the purposes of scientific work. Approximately 75% of the students exhibited fair or poor understanding of the purpose of science as seen in their definitions: For example, they believed science involved engaging in activities (e.g., completing projects, making observations) or completing school-related tasks. To some extent such understandings reflected students' participation in a hands-on science curriculum (i.e., they do perform experiments and participate in activities). For the most part, these students did not acquire a larger sense of the goals of science as a way to explain and learn about the world around them.

SOURCES OF STUDENTS' IDEAS AND SCIENTISTS' IDEAS IN SCIENCE

In answering the questions, "Where do your ideas to do science experiments come from?" and "Where do you think scientists get their ideas for doing science experiments?", students' responses were grouped according to two dimensions: (1) whether their sources stemmed from an active versus passive agent, and (2) whether their sources stemmed from independent versus dependent endeavors. Active agency was judged if the agent (i.e., student or scientist) was actively seeking or doing science. A passive agency referred to receiving ideas without much work; the ideas appeared without active effort or were given to the agent. Determination of an active or passive agent was based on how the idea came about. For example, responding that ideas in science came from thinking and wondering about the world was judged as active while responding that the ideas came from one's head was judged as passive. Merely relating that ideas originated in one's mind was not considered indicative of an active role. Students of this age are capable of comprehending that ideas arise from mental activity; beginning in their preschool years, children come to understand thinking as an internal, mental activity (Flavell, Green, & Flavell, 1995). In addition, the type of endeavors the agent engaged in was judged according to whether others (either people or things) were involved. Sources were judged as independent if the generation of ideas was accomplished by the agent alone; they were judged as dependent when the generation of ideas relied on others' input or relied on interaction with materials. This categorization scheme is summarized in Table 17.2.

Note that students' responses were classified according to each of the two dimensions separately. Hence, a student's response included classification according to role of agent (active or passive or both) and the type of endeavor (independent or dependent or both). For example, naming the teacher as the source of one's ideas was coded as passive and dependent. When more than one source was mentioned, each response was considered. For example, a student might write that her

TABLE 17.2

Coding Scheme for Categorizing Students' Responses of the Sources of Their Ideas and Scientists' Ideas for Science: Descriptions and Examples for Role of Agent and Type of Endeavor

Role of Agent	Description	Example
Active	Ideas originate from active ventures: thinking, wondering, being curious, performing activities, interacting with things, exploring places, or studying materials.	• I think my ideas come from anything. I may look at something and say that looks like something I can make an experiment out of. • Maybe they just want to find out something never found so they think of an experiment to find out.
Passive	Ideas arise in a passive manner: from one's mind, brain, head. Also, from teachers, books, television, computers, or family members.	• My mind, books, and TV. • Other scientists and books.
Both	Ideas originate from both active ventures and in a passive manner.	• TV shows, my brain. I just think about stuff and then try it. • They get it from books and by thinking hard and studying.

Type of Endeavor	Description	Example
Independent	Ideas come from independent ventures: from ones' mind, brain, head or thinking, wondering, and being curious.	• It comes from my brain and I think hard so I know what to do. • If they have a question they try to figure it out, not ask their mom.
Dependent	Ideas come from dependent ventures: from teachers, books, television, computers, or family members or from performing activities, interacting with things, exploring places, or studying materials.	• From my class, home, or science stores. • They watch other people and learn. Museums and stuff.
Both	Ideas come from both independent and dependent ventures.	• From my head and brain and teachers. From friends. • They probably get their ideas from books and they make them up.

Note: Two examples are listed: the first from students' responses about the sources of their own ideas, the second about the sources of scientists' ideas.

ideas come from thinking and from a science book. For the role of agent, this student was classified as expressing both active (for thinking) and passive (for the science book) sources. For the type of endeavor, the student was classified as expressing both independent (for thinking) and dependent (for the science book) sources for his or her ideas. The three categories within each dimension were mutually exclusive; that is, a student was classified according to one and only one category within a dimension (i.e., active, passive, or both; and independent, dependent, or both).

Two raters individually coded 25% of student responses. The author was one rater; a research assistant was the other rater. The author coded the remaining 75% of the responses. Interrater agreement was computed as the ratio of agreements to all codes (i.e., agreements plus disagreements). Discrepancies were resolved through discussion. For the sources of their own ideas, interrater agreement was 83% on active/passive role of agent and 91% on independent/dependent type of endeavor. For sources of scientists' ideas, agreement between raters was 85% on active/passive role of agent and 92% on independent/dependent type of endeavor.

For descriptive purposes, proportions of students reporting various kinds of sources for their own ideas and scientists' ideas are displayed in Table 17.3. Regarding their own ideas, 66% of students generated passive types of sources, such as books, teachers, family members, or their mind or brain. When asked about scientists' ideas, the largest proportion of students named active endeavors (e.g., wondering, performing activities). Passive sources for scientists' ideas (e.g., brain, other people, and books) were named by 42% of the students. Although students frequently named passive sources for both themselves and scientists, the nature of these passive sources varied. Almost twice as many students responded that "my brain" was the source of their own ideas than "their brain" was the source of scientists' ideas. After "their brain," the single largest passive source named for scientists were books followed by other people, other scientists, school, and computers. For their own ideas, students' named "my brain" followed by their teacher, books, classmates, and television. Students named both independent and dependent sources equally for their own ideas and scientists' ideas. Students named dependent kinds of sources (e.g., a book, a teacher) most often, regardless of whether they were generating sources for their own or scientists' ideas.

TABLE 17.3
Proportions of Students Who Generated Various Kinds of Sources for Their Own and Scientists' Ideas for Science

	Active	Passive	Both	Independent	Dependent	Both
Own Ideas	.21	.66	.13	.38	.42	.20
Scientists' Ideas	.48	.42	.10	.42	.45	.13

Next, it was investigated if students differentiated how they conceived of their own ideas from how they believed scientists conceived ideas. Students' responses about the active nature of the sources of their own ideas were related to students' responses about the active nature of the sources for scientists' ideas[1] by Fisher's Exact, $p < .001$. In general, students who named active endeavors for their own ideas also attributed active endeavors for scientists' ideas. Students who relied on passive sources for their ideas attributed scientists' ideas equally to active and passive sources. Students appeared to attribute active sources for scientists even though for themselves they mostly endorsed passive sources. Students' endorsement of passive sources for their own ideas in science is reflective of their science-learning experiences in school—relying on books or teachers, for example. They hold an alternate view, which includes more active ventures for scientists performing authentic work in the field.

Students' responses about the independent nature of the sources for their own ideas were also related to students' responses about the independent nature of the sources of scientists' ideas, $X^2(4) = 40.93$, $p < .001$. Unlike the pattern for the active nature of their sources, students responded similarly when prompted about their ideas and scientists' ideas: Approximately two-thirds of the students were consistent in their responses regarding independence of their sources. In general, students who gave independent sources for their own ideas also named independent sources for scientists' ideas, and students who named dependent ventures as sources for their own ideas also named dependent ventures for scientists' ideas. Students who named both independent and dependent sources for their own ideas named independent sources, dependent, or both independent and dependent sources for scientists in almost equal proportions.

LIKERT-SCALED RESPONSES

Creating the Epistemological Belief Scales

Recall that students were asked to indicate on a five-point scale how much they agreed or disagreed with statements concerning their beliefs about (1) the changing nature of science, (2) the role of experiments in science, (3) the coherence of science knowledge, and (4) the sources of science knowledge. Items (see Table 17.1) were first grouped into four scales according to theoretical criteria (i.e., construct they intended to represent when created). Items with a negative valence

---

[1]When attempting to perform chi-square analyses, some of the cells contained small expected values (i.e., less than 5). In such cases, the chi-square is not reliably calculated. To correct for these instances, it is suggested that categories be combined (see Shavelson, 1996). Thus, students from the category of both (active and passive) were collapsed into the active category. In the following analyses, the active category includes students who mention any active sources (and may or may not list passive ones, too) while the passive category includes students who only name passive sources. This was not true for the independent dimension. All three categories (independent, dependent, and both) are utilized in analyses considering students' sources for how ideas in science are generated.

were reverse coded such that high means on the scales represented strong endorsement of the epistemological belief in the direction as stated by the name of the scale. For example, the item "Scientific knowledge is always true" was reversed coded so that strong endorsement of the item as written was translated into a low endorsement for a scale about the changing nature of science.

Next, in an effort to check on the reliability of the scales, specifically the internal consistency of the items that made up these scales, Cronbach alpha coefficients were calculated. Based on these results, some items were dropped or moved to other scales such that three scales were created—Change, Reason, and Authority (see Table 17.4). In addition, multidimensional scaling (MDS) analyses were conducted to confirm the scales. MDS is a technique for exploring and understanding the underlying structure of data that uses similarity information among items to create a descriptive model for representing the data (Kruskal & Wish, 1978). It was conducted as a follow-up to the reliability analyses because of the relatively low alpha coefficients on some of the scales.

First, nine items about the changing nature of science were found to be reliable (i.e., alpha = .67) and were grouped together in a scale termed Change. Second, items about the coherence of knowledge dropped out of the analyses. The fifth grade students did not endorse these items in any consistent way as indicated by a low Cronbach alpha level (less than .40). One reason could have been that the items were ambiguous or misleading and/or the wording was problematic for fifth grade students. Another reason could have been that students at this age are unclear in their beliefs and understanding of knowledge in science being a coherent system of interrelated concepts as opposed to a mere collection of facts. Prior research on this construct has documented naive beliefs for high school and college students (Hammer, 1994; Roth & Roychoudhury, 1994). Third, not all items originally intended to express ideas about the source of knowledge were found to be consistent with one another. Specifically, items about science being a con-

TABLE 17.4
Epistemological Beliefs Scales: Descriptions and Examples

Construct (Scale)	α	Description	Example Item (Number of items)
Changing Nature of Science (Change)	.67	Knowledge in science changes and develops over time	"Scientific beliefs change over time." (9 items)
Role of Experiments and Source of Knowledge (Reason)	.52	Scientific knowledge derives from testing and experimenting and from reasoning and thinking	"Part of doing science is asking questions about other people's ideas." (6 items)
Source of Knowledge (Authority)	.64	Scientific knowledge comes from authority figures, including teachers and books	"Whatever the teacher says in science class is true." (4 items)

structivist endeavor did not fit with items about scientific knowledge originating from authority figures and materials. Instead, beliefs about constructivist sources had a better fit with items regarding the role of experiments. Because of these results, items about constructing ones' own ideas in science and those items aimed at understanding the role of experiments in developing scientific theory were grouped together in a scale called Reason, and items referring to authority sources in science were grouped together in a scale termed Authority.

The grouping of these items together to create the Reason scale was confirmed with multidimensional scaling (MDS). MDS results confirmed that items about constructing knowledge in science (e.g., "I should be able to do the experiments I read about in science books"). were close to those items regarding experiments in science (e.g., "Experiments are used to test different predictions") and far from those about authority as source of knowledge (e.g., "In science, I have to believe what the science books say about stuff, even if they may be wrong"). Hence, a composite scale termed Reason included items about constructing ones' own ideas in science and those items aimed at understanding the role of experiments in developing scientific theory. Apparently, elementary-aged students are not likely to view scientific knowledge coming from authority and knowledge being constructed as opposite ends of a single continuum as suggested in other research (e.g., Roth & Roychoudhury, 1994). Instead, their beliefs about knowledge being constructed are related to their beliefs about the role of experiments in contributing to scientific theory.

In sum, three separate scales emerged from the data; a scale representing students' beliefs about the coherence of knowledge did not materialize from this data. A scale for students' beliefs about the changing nature of knowledge and one for their beliefs about authority as a source of knowledge were created, named Change and Authority, respectively. Items about the role of experiments and items about constructing scientific knowledge were combined into a single scale, named Reason.

DESCRIPTIVE STATISTICS OF THE EPISTEMOLOGICAL BELIEF SCALES

Mean endorsement and variability of the three epistemological belief scales for fifth grade students were calculated. Students highly endorsed items regarding knowledge arising from testing and thinking ($M = 4.0$ out of 5 points on the Reason scale). There was little variation in students' responses to this scale ($SD = .55$). To a lesser extent students endorsed ideas that scientific knowledge develops over time ($M = 3.5$ on the Change scale). This scale showed a slightly larger amount of variability ($SD = .62$). On average, students disagreed that scientific knowledge comes from authority ($M = 2.6$ on the Authority scale). This scale showed the greatest variability ($SD = .88$); some students endorsed beliefs that scientific knowledge comes from authority while others strongly rejected that idea.

CONCLUSIONS

Describing Fifth Grade Students' Epistemological Beliefs in Science

In general, elementary students' individual epistemological beliefs in science reflected a mixture of naive and sophisticated understanding. On the one hand, students displayed little understanding that science involves the effort to explain phenomena. Rather, students' definitions of science mainly conveyed the idea that the purpose of science was to engage in activities (e.g., completing projects, making observations), reflecting to some extent students' participation in a hands-on science program. Only about one-quarter of the students viewed science as a learning endeavor. On the other hand, fifth grade students tended to regard scientific knowledge as a developing, changing construct that is created by reasoning and testing. Students' strong endorsement of the Reason scale suggests that they may have some implicit sense of a distinction (and interplay) of theory and evidence and some understanding of the role of testing and thinking in developing scientific ideas. This idea is counter to other research conclusions (Kuhn, 1991).

Furthermore, students differentiated between their scientific endeavors and what scientists do. When considering sources of ideas in science, students tended to attribute passive endeavors to themselves (from books, television, or other people) and active endeavors to scientists (thinking and wondering or actively interacting with materials). As suggested by Driver et al. (1996), students apparently do differentiate between "school science" and "real science" to some extent, as evidenced by their different responses regarding the sources of ideas in science for themselves and scientists.

This study considered such a distinction in reference to how students perceived of the sources of scientific ideas, but did not extend the analysis to the other constructs. For example, in asking about their beliefs about the purpose of science, they were not asked for their definitions of science both in school and out of school, or if they perceived a difference between how they might define science and how they think a scientist might define science. It is not clear how students interpreted the question, "What do you think science is?" Many children may have limited themselves to thinking about school science in particular (given that is how they are most likely to experience science).

Future Directions

Exploring students' beliefs helped to identify several areas for future research. One area in need of further understanding involves how students' epistemological understanding actually influences their scientific reasoning. Additional work on students' reasoning during experimentation (e.g., Samarapungavan, 1992; Schauble, 1990) could help to further characterize students' beliefs about constructing knowledge in science and do so in an authentic context. Moreover, such research can go beyond mere characterizations of students' epistemological understanding, pointing to ways in which their beliefs affect their decisions or thinking during a science activity.

In addition, future research on students' epistemological beliefs should pay attention to potential differences in how students regard the nature of scientific knowledge they study in school versus the nature of knowledge they attribute to "real" science. Such an effort may enable us to better comprehend the actual ways students are conceiving of science and thinking about the nature of knowledge in science. Studies could also address the effects behind these distinctions. What are the ramifications for students' science understanding if they believe that science in school is not genuine or, at least, not relevant to the kind of work they believe science to be?

Finally, additional questions regarding characterizing students' epistemological conceptions remain to be researched: For example, are different epistemological issues, such as considering science to be a changing and evolving endeavor, particularly important for development of sophisticated beliefs of other constructs? Examining interrelations among the epistemological constructs may help answer this question as well as give insight into how students integrate their epistemological understanding.

Summary and Implications for Instruction

Examining epistemological beliefs individually revealed that students hold some sophisticated notions (e.g., highly endorsed ideas that scientific knowledge changes over time and results from reasoned, constructive efforts) and some naive notions (e.g., science as an activity rather than directed by aims to explain phenomena in the world). In general, this study found that fifth grade students in hands-on science classrooms do hold beliefs about the nature of science knowledge; that is, from a developmental perspective, it is appropriate to begin asking elementary-aged students about their epistemological beliefs. Moreover, it may be worthy to consider that young students may be receptive to instruction that focuses on advancing their epistemological understanding. Given that many students possess an inaccurate, naive sense of the purposes of science, it seems useful for instruction to begin by addressing students' understanding of the goals of science activity. Furthermore, because students' epistemological views become aligned with teachers' epistemological conceptions (Lederman & Druger, 1985) and because sophisticated epistemological views are fostered by inquiry-based instructional environments (e.g., Carey et al., 1989; Solomon et al., 1992), it is worthwhile to nurture sophisticated beliefs in teachers while simultaneously cultivating appropriate, instructional environments that enable students to develop sophisticated epistemological beliefs. Overall, elementary students' blooming epistemological understanding should not be ignored.

REFERENCES

Bruer, J. T. (1993). *Schools for thought: A science of learning in the classroom.* Cambridge, MA: MIT Press.

Carey, S., Evans, R., Honda, M., Jay, E., & Unger, C. (1989). 'An experiment is when you try it and see if it works': A study of grade 7 students' understanding of the construction of scientific knowledge. *International Journal of Science Education, 11*, 514–529.

Chandler, M. J., Boyes, M., & Ball, L. (1990). Relativism and stations of epistemic doubt. *Journal of Experimental Child Psychology, 50*, 370–395.

Collins, A. (1997). National science education standards: Looking backward and forward. *Elementary School Journal, 97*, 299–313.

Driver, R., Leach, J., Millar, R., & Scott, P. (1996). *Young people's images of science.* Philadelphia: Open University Press.

Duschl, R. (1994). Research on the history and philosophy of science. In Gabel, D. (Ed.), *Handbook of research on science teaching and learning* (pp. 443–465). New York: Macmillan.

Duveen, J., Scott, L., & Solomon, J. (1993). Pupils' understanding of science: Description of experiments or 'a passion to explain'? *School Science Review, 75*, 19–27.

Elder, A. D. (1999). *An exploration of fifth grade students' epistemological beliefs in science and an investigation of their relation to science learning.* Unpublished doctoral dissertation, University of Michigan.

Flavell, J. H., Green, F. L., & Flavell, E. R. (1995). Young children's knowledge about thinking. *Monographs of the Society for Research in Child Development, 60* (1, Serial No. 243).

Hammer, D. (1994). Epistemological beliefs in introductory physics. *Cognition and Instruction, 12*, 151–183.

Hofer, B. K. & Pintrich, P. R. (1997). The development of epistemological theories: Beliefs about knowledge and knowing and their relation to learning. *Review of Educational Research, 67*, 88–140.

Hogan, K. (2000). Exploring a process view of students' knowledge about the nature of science. *Science Education, 84*, 51–70.

Inhelder, B. & Piaget, J. (1958). *The growth of logical thinking from childhood to adolescence.* New York: Basic.

Kruskal, J. B. & Wish, M. (1978). *Multidimensional scaling.* Beverly Hills, CA: Sage.

Kuhn, D. (1991). *The skills of argument.* Cambridge: Cambridge University Press.

Kuhn, D., Amsel, E., & O'Loughlin, M. (1988). *The development of scientific thinking skills.* San Diego: Academic Press.

Lederman, N. & Druger, M. (1985). Classroom factors related to changes in students' conceptions of the nature of science. *Journal of Research in Science Teaching, 22*, 649–662.

Lederman, N. (1992). Students' and teachers' conceptions of the nature of science: A review of the research. *Journal of Research in Science Teaching, 29*, 331–359.

Montgomery, D. E. (1992). Young children's theory of knowing: The development of a folk epistemology. *Developmental Review, 12*, 410–430.

National Research Council. (1996). *National science education standards.* Washington, DC: National Academy Press.

Roth, W. & Roychoudhury, A. (1994). Physics students' epistemologies and views about knowing and learning. *Journal of Research in Science Teaching, 31*, 5–30.

Rubba, P. A., & Andersen, H. (1978). Development of an instrument to assess secondary school students' understanding of the nature of scientific knowledge. *Science Education, 62*, 449–458.

Ryan, A. G., & Aikenhead, G. S. (1992). Students' preconceptions about the epistemology of science. *Science Education, 76*, 559–580.

Samarapungavan, A. (1992). Children's judgments in theory choice tasks: Scientific rationality in childhood. *Cognition, 45*, 1–32.

Schauble, L. (1990). Belief revision in children: The role of prior knowledge and strategies for generating evidence. *Journal of Experimental Child Psychology, 49*, 31–57.

Schommer, M. (1990). Effects of beliefs about the nature of knowledge on comprehension. *Journal of Educational Psychology, 82,* 498–504.

Shavelson, R. J. (1996). *Statistical reasoning for the behavioral sciences* (3rd ed.). Boston: Allyn and Bacon.

Smith, C., Houghton, C., Maclin, D., & Hennessey, M. G. (1997). *Understanding 6th graders' epistemologies of science: Teasing apart the effects of schooling and development.* Paper presented at the annual meeting of the American Educational Research Association, Chicago, IL.

Sodian, B., Zaitchik, D., & Carey, S. (1991). Young children's differentiation of hypothetical beliefs from evidence. *Child Development, 62*, 753–766.

Solomon, J., Duveen, J., Scott, L., & McCarthy, S. (1992). Teaching about the nature of science through history: Action research in the classroom. *Journal of Research in Science Teaching, 29*, 409–421.

Solomon, J., Scott, L., & Duveen, J. (1996). Large-scale exploration of pupils' understanding of the nature of science. *Science Education, 80*, 493–508.

Songer, N. B., & Linn, M. C. (1991). How do students' views of science influence knowledge integration? *Journal of Research in Science Teaching, 28*, 761–784.

Vekiri, I., Baxter, G. P., & Pintrich, P. (1998). *Scientists invent, discover, and explain; Images of science in elementary hands-on science classrooms.* Paper presented at the annual meeting of the American Educational Research Association, San Diego, CA.

Wellman. H. M. (1990). *The child's theory of mind.* Cambridge, MA: MIT Press.

18

A Comparison of Epistemological Beliefs and Learning from Science Text Between American and Chinese High School Students

Gaoyin Qian
Lehman College
The City University of New York

Junlin Pan
Northern Illinois University

Since the late 1980s, there has been an increasing interest among educational re-searchers (Carey, Evans, Honda, Jay, & Unger, 1989; Driver, Leach, Millar, & Scott, 1996; Hammer, 1994, 1995; Larochelle & Desautels, 1991; Qian & Alver-mann, 1995; Schommer, 1997; Solomon, Duveen, & Sott, 1994; Songer & Linn, 1991, also see Hofer & Pintrich, 1997 for review) in studying students' epistemo-logical development and epistemological beliefs. According to Hofer and Pin-trich (1997), epistemological beliefs refer to individuals' conceptions "about the nature of knowledge and the nature or process of knowing" (p. 117). Researchers have examined how students know, how the nature of knowledge and knowing is related to students' learning, and how students' epistemological beliefs inform classroom instruction in different content areas (Carey et al., 1989; Driver et al., 1996; Hammer, 1995; Larochelle & Desautels, 1991; Qian & Alvermann, 1995; Schommer, 1997; Solomon et al., 1994; Songer & Linn, 1991).

In this chapter, we focus on how students' epistemological beliefs are related to conceptual change learning in science and how students with different cultural and educational backgrounds may differ in their epistemological beliefs. Concep-tual change learning is a learning process that involves students in conceiving of the inconsistency between their existing knowledge structure and knowledge to be learned. In conceptual change learning, students may need to modify or restructure their prior knowledge, depending on the kinds of knowledge structure they have.

First, we will discuss how conceptual change learning relates to students' epistemological beliefs about science, use of refutational text, and motivational goals. Second, we delineate findings from a comparison between American and Chinese students in their epistemological beliefs and conceptual change learning.

Researchers and theorists (Driver, Asoko, Leach, Mortimer, & Scott, 1994; Pintrich, Marx, & Boyle, 1993; Posner, Strike, Hewson, & Gertzog, 1982; Strike & Posner, 1992) have developed different theoretical models to explain conceptual change learning. The earlier theoretical model was based on Piaget's cognitive model and schema theory. Posner and his colleagues (Posner et al., 1982) theorized that students must reorganize or replace their incomplete knowledge structure in order to move from their commonsense conceptions to new and scientific conceptions.

Researchers (Alvermann, Smith, & Readence, 1985; Anderson, 1977; Maria & MacGinitie, 1981) also acknowledged that conceptual change learning depends not only on the amount of prior knowledge students possess, but also the kinds of knowledge they possess. For example, the concept of classifying students' incomplete knowledge structure into accretion, tuning, and restructuring has gained recognition in research on conceptual change learning (Qian & Alvermann, 1995; Rumelhart & Norman, 1978). Students who need to tune or restructure their prior knowledge are more likely to experience difficulties in conceptual change learning than are those who need only to accrete their existing knowledge. This is because tuning or restructuring requires students to go through a learning process that involves substantial changes in or even replacement of existing knowledge, while accretion only assumes moderate modification or addition to the existing valid, but incomplete, knowledge structure.

With the development of sociocultural and motivational theories, an increasing number of researchers have examined the role of students' motivational goals, their epistemological beliefs, and various social factors in conceptual change learning (Driver et al., 1994; Pintrich et al., 1993; Strike & Posner, 1992). Strike and Posner (1992), in their newly revised theoretical model for conceptual change learning, postulated that students' motivational goals and social factors in conceptual change learning should be considered as "dynamic and in constant interaction and development" (p. 160). Pintrich et al. (1993) specified the nature of students' motivational goals. They pointed out that beliefs and motivational goals are related to students' levels of cognitive engagement and persistence in academic settings and the depth of text processing. From a Vygotskian perspective, Driver et al. (1994) stressed that conceptual change learning is socially constructed. Conceptual change learning in science involves both personal and social processes rather than a purely cognitive process that can be stimulated simply by challenging students' commonsense conceptions through discrepant events. As a result, there has been a body of research that has examined conceptual change learning through a multidimensional lens, that is, cognitive, epistemological, motivational, and sociocultural (Dole & Sinatra, in press; Guzzetti, Williams, Skeels, & Wu, 1997; Maria, 1997, 1998; Qian & Alvermann, 2000; Ridgeway & Dunston, 2000).

Secondary School Students' Epistemological Beliefs About Science

Increased interest in the study of students' epistemological beliefs in education owes much to the development of Perry's theory of college students' beliefs about the nature of knowledge (Schommer, 1989). Based on the findings of previous research (Coulson, Feltovich, & Spiro, 1986; Dweck & Leggett, 1988; Schoenfeld, 1985; Spiro, Vispoel, Schmitz, Samarapungavan, & Boerger, 1987), Schommer (1989) postulated that students' personal epistemological beliefs function as a system with independent multiple dimensions. She included dimensions of students' beliefs about knowledge and learning from studies involving elementary school students. Dweck's (Dweck & Leggett, 1988) research added further insights into dimensions of epistemological belief systems. She and her colleagues (Diener & Dweck, 1978, 1980; Licht & Dweck, 1984) demonstrated the influence of students' beliefs about the nature of intelligence on achievement motivation. Students who believe that intelligence is a fixed entity are more likely to endorse performance goals and have maladaptive cognitive functioning than those who believe it is incremental.

In the study of students' epistemological beliefs, researchers (Diener & Dweck, 1978, 1980; Schommer, 1993) have identified beliefs about simple knowledge, certain knowledge, quick learning, and innate ability as being strong predictors of students' cognitive performances and affective responses. The Qian and Alvermann study (1995) investigated the relation between two variable sets: (a) the subtests of epistemological beliefs and performance goals, and (b) Conceptual Understanding and Application Reasoning posttests in conceptual change learning. The results obtained from this study demonstrated that beliefs about simple/certain knowledge and quick learning predict students' learning a science concept from refutational text. More specifically, students' immature beliefs about learning and knowledge related to difficulties in their conceptual understanding of Newton's law of motion and their ability to apply the newly learned concept. These results parallel the recent finding that students' epistemological maturity predicts their conceptual change learning about photosynthesis through the use of computer simulation (Windschitl, 1997).

In the study of students' beliefs about the nature of science, Driver et al. (1996) have found that students tended to believe that (a) the purpose of science is to re-describe an event or phenomenon; (b) an authority figure warrants scientific knowledge, and (c) scientific knowledge is acquired through an empirical process. Their findings are in line with previous research (Carey et al., 1989; Larochelle & Desautels, 1991; Solomon et al., 1994) and have implications for conceptual change learning. For example, the finding that students believe that the purpose of science is intended to describe an event may help explain why students would experience difficulties in conceptual change learning. Conceptual change learning, like learning other science concepts, requires students to see beyond their daily observations and their intuitive understanding of a natural phenomenon. Students who view science as simply seeking to invent cures or devices to help people would be less likely to understand that scientific knowledge does not emerge solely from observation or the description of a natural phenomenon.

The fact that students saw an authority figure as a warrant for truth or knowledge and viewed theories as fixed entities would seem to have implications for conceptual change learning. Students who hold such beliefs may be less likely to be dissatisfied with their intuitive understanding of a natural phenomenon, and therefore, will be unsuccessful in conceptual change learning. These findings suggest that students who have commonsense conceptions and naive epistemological belief systems will be less likely to meet the challenges and achieve conceptual change than students who have similar commonsense conceptions but more complex and mature belief systems. Most of the findings about students' epistemological beliefs, however, are from studies that involved college-age students in learning social studies or mathematics (Ryan, 1984; Schommer, 1990; Schommer & Dunnell, 1994; Schommer et al., 1992). Only a few studies (e.g., Carey et al., 1989; Driver et al., 1996; Hammer, 1995; Larochelle & Desautels, 1991; Qian & Alvermann, 1995; Schommer, 1997; Solomon et al., 1994; Songer & Linn, 1991) have involved secondary school students' beliefs about science.

Despite a large body of research on epistemological beliefs, crosscultural studies were almost nonexistent. Most studies predominantly involved students who grew up in Western-styled school cultures that posit "formal abstract reasoning," "a movement toward individualism of thought," and "a freedom from the dictates of authority" (Hofer & Pintrich, 1997, p. 130).

Role of Refutational Text in Conceptual Change Learning

Research on refutational text (Maria & MacGinitie, 1987; Alvermann & Hynd, 1989; Guzzetti et al., 1997; Qian & Alvermann, 1995; also see Guzzetti, Snyder, Glass, & Gamas, 1993 for review) has established that such a text has a positive effect on eradicating students' misconceptions. Refutational text is a text that explicitly contrasts or challenges intuitive understandings of natural phenomena with scientifically accepted theories. Researchers also examined a variation of refutational text: soft expository text. Soft expository text is "a coherent text that combines narrative with expository structures" (Guzzetti et al., 1993, p. 128). Both refutational expository text and considerate soft expository text have also been found to be effective in facilitating students' conceptual change learning. The effectiveness of refutational expository text and its variations has been basically found with elementary school students.

Mixed results, however, were found from studies of types of text used with secondary students to promote conceptual change (Alvermann & Hynd, 1989; Guzzetti, 1990; Guzzetti & Hynd, 1995). Alvermann and her colleagues (Alvermann & Hynd, 1989; Alvermann, Hynd, & Qian, 1990) found that refutational expository text is more effective in facilitating conceptual changes than is narrative text. Their results show that the use of storylike structure in eradicating misconceptions is not effective with secondary students. One possible explanation of this finding is that the narrative version of the refutational text contained extraneous information that may have distracted students from focusing on the core concept of the text. Other researchers (Garner, Alexander, Gillingham, Kulikowich, & Brown, 1991; Garner, Gillingham, & White, 1989; Graves, Prenn, Earle, Thompson, Johnson, & Slater, 1991; Hidi & Baird, 1988) have documented that including interesting but extraneous information disrupts learning important ideas from text.

In conclusion, researchers (Alvermann & Hynd, 1989; Guzzetti et al., 1993; Qian & Alvermann, 1995) have found that students' misconceived notions about natural phenomena need to be challenged in some way in order for conceptual change learning to be successful. Instructional strategies such as designing refutational text, teaching through demonstrations, or using refutational text with monitored discussion were found to be effective in the classroom situations.

Relationship Between Goal Orientations and Conceptual Change Learning

In the study of goal orientations, previous research has demonstrated that students who endorse learning goals tend to use high-level cognitive strategies, resort to metacognitive and self-regulatory strategies, seek challenging learning tasks, and have positive affect (Nolen, 1988; Pintrich & Garcia, 1991). According to Dweck and Leggett (1988), goal orientations are linked with and explained by belief systems. Goal orientations (performance goals versus learning goals) are believed to mediate between individuals' beliefs about intelligence and learning patterns. Students who endorse performance goals may resort to low-level strategies, avoid challenges and difficulties, and give up easily while reading about a counterintuitive science concept because of challenges they face and obstacles and difficulties they experience in learning the science concept from expository text. Challenges students face come from the tenacity of their existing misconceptions as well as from direct confrontation of those misconceptions in classroom instruction. Research (Alvermann et al., 1990; Hynd, McNish, Lay, &

Fowler, 1995; Hynd, McWhorter, Phares, & Suttles, 1994) established that one of the most effective and common strategies in conceptual change instruction is to directly challenge students' existing misconceptions. Achieving conceptual change depends on the students' willingness to face these challenges.

Learning counterintuitive scientific concepts and obtaining information from expository text may evoke students' maladaptive behaviors because of the difficulties they encounter. First, the difficulties may be due to students' lack of relevant past learning experiences in science (Licht & Dweck, 1984). A shift in content or concepts may cause some problems in science learning. Licht and Dweck observed that students will:

> show decrements in learning and performance when a subject area undergoes a major shift that requires the mastery of new concepts and skills (i.e., a shift in content or concepts that requires a great deal of persistence in the face of difficulty). Such shifts occur in all subject areas but are more frequent in some (e.g., mathematics and science) (p. 629).

Second, difficulties lie in students' naive understanding of a concept. Their misconceived notion will impede conceptual change learning. Alvermann et al. (1990) documented that students with misconceptions will find science learning extremely difficult if the concepts they are expected to learn are counterintuitive to their everyday real-world experiences.

Researchers (Brunson & Matthews, 1981; Diener & Dweck, 1978, 1980; Licht & Dweck, 1984) have documented that students who endorse performance goals tend to avoid obstacles or use ineffective strategies in the face of difficulty, and consequently limits an individual's attainments. In contrast, students with learning goals show a tendency to pursue challenging tasks, to generate effective strategies in the face of obstacles and difficulties, and eventually to succeed in progressing toward their valued goals (Dweck & Leggett, 1988). In summary, performance goal-oriented and learning goal-oriented students exhibit striking differences in: (a) attribution for failure, (b) affective responses, (c) academic performances, and (d) self-efficacy.

Research on motivation suggests that students who endorse performance goals will be more likely to develop maladaptive behaviors. These maladaptive behaviors will impede the students' ability to deal with challenging academic tasks and to overcome difficulties in learning counterintuitive scientific concepts from text.

Differences Between American and Chinese Students in Epistemological Beliefs

Research on epistemological beliefs, motivational goals, and refutational text forms the theoretical rationale for the comparison of epistemological beliefs and conceptual change learning between American and Chinese students. We are particularly interested in (a) investigating the differences in beliefs about learning and knowledge between American and Chinese high school students, (b) examining the effectiveness of refutational text in facilitating Chinese students' conceptual change learning, and (c) assessing the contribution of epistemological beliefs and motivational goals to conceptual change learning among American and Chinese students.

The comparison is based on the results of two separate studies that involved high school students in the United States and China. These studies were based on Dweck and Leggett's (1988) theoretical model of learning, which implies that students who hold naive epistemological beliefs and who are performance goal-oriented are less likely to relinquish their misconceptions about a scientific notion and make conceptual changes than those who hold mature epistemological beliefs and who are learning goal-oriented.

The comparison also responds to a call for crosscultural research on epistemological beliefs (Hofer & Pintrich, 1997). The study of Chinese students' epistemological beliefs will open a new avenue to examine the relation between Chinese school cultures and the development of students' beliefs about knowledge and knowing. Unlike American students, Chinese students grew up in school cultures that emphasize collectivism, acceptance of consensus, and respect for authority (Pai, 1997).

Based on the previous discussion, the questions listed next guided the investigation.

1. What are the differences or commonalities between American and Chinese students in their beliefs about knowledge and ability to learn?
2. Can refutational text facilitate Chinese students' conceptual change learning as effectively as it did among American counterparts? Is there an interaction effect between the knowledge group (i.e., accretion, tuning, and restructuring) and the cultural group (i.e., American and Chinese) in conceptual change learning?
3. How do epistemological beliefs and motivational goals contribute to conceptual change learning among American and Chinese students?

The first study involved 95 American students who were eleventh and twelfth grade students from science classes of an Honors Program at a public high school in New York City. The Honors Program offered advanced placement courses in all subject areas. More than 90% of the students in the Honors Program attended college, while about 90% of the students were qualified for either free or reduced price lunch. The original sample included 190 students, but there were 95 students who were absent on the days when either pretests or posttests were administered. The data obtained from these 95 students were eliminated from the analyses; therefore, the final sample size was 95. Of the 95 students, 35 were male (37%) and 60 were female (63%). The mean age of the students was 17 years and 5 months. There were 51 eleventh grade and 44 twelfth grade students. Of the 95

372 QIAN AND PAN

students, there were 37 African Americans (39%), 13 Asian Americans (13%), 31 Hispanic Americans (33%), 6 students from other ethnic groups (7%), and 8 students (8%) who did not indicate their ethnicity.

The second study involved 184 Chinese students who were eleventh and twelfth grade students from a "key" public high school in Shanghai, China. The "key elementary and secondary schools" in China are funded with more government resources, equipped with better teaching facilities, and staffed with more qualified and experienced faculty than the ordinary public schools. Of the 184 students, 99 were male (54%) and 85 were female (46%). The mean age of the students was 16 years and 9 months. There were 95 (52%) eleventh grade and 89 (48%) twelfth grade students. About 88% of the students had the opportunity to attend college. In both studies, the same text materials, measures, questionnaires, and procedures were used.

Refutational Text.   A refutational expository text titled "Newton's Theory of Motion" was used in the study (Alvermann & Hynd, 1989; Alvermann et al., 1990). According to Fry's (1977) readability formula, the text was suitable for ninth grade students to read. The 606-word expository passage was adapted from an article written for *Scientific American* (McCloskey, 1983). According to Alvermann and Hynd (1989), the accuracy of the information presented in the passage was verified by a University of Georgia research professor of physics. The passage directly confronted alternative conceptions about Newton's first law of motion. In particular, it contradicted the notion of impetus theory, which was an incorrect pre-Newtonian conception of projectile motion.

Epistemological Belief Questionnaire.   For the purpose of these two studies, a 32-item Epistemological Belief Questionnaire was used (Qian & Alvermann, 1995). The questionnaire was reduced and adapted from Schommer's 53-item revised epistemological belief questionnaire for high school students (Schommer & Dunnell, 1994). The Qian and Alvermann (1995) study documented three factors that underlie the 32-item Epistemological Belief Questionnaire: (a) Quick Learning with 15 items (e.g., Learning is a slow process of building up knowledge), (b) Simple-Certain knowledge with 11 items (e.g., If scientists try hard enough, they can find the truth to almost everything), and (c) Innate Ability with 6 items (e.g., The really smart students don't have to work hard to do well in school). The analysis of the data with the Chinese sample indicated that alpha (internal consistency) was equal to .65 for Quick Learning, .27 for Simple-Certain Knowledge, and .53 for Innate Ability. The overall alpha for the revised Epistemological Belief Questionnaire was equal to .54.

Goal Orientation Questionnaire.   A Goal Orientation Questionnaire has been adapted from a four-item subscale Extrinsic Goal Orientation and a seven-item subscale Intrinsic Goal Orientation in the Motivated Strategies for Learning Questionnaire (MSLQ) developed by Pintrich, Smith, Garcia, and McKeachie

(1991). The Goal Orientation Questionnaire consists of a total of 11 items. Pintrich et al. (1991) reported that the subscales Intrinsic Goal Orientation and Extrinsic Goal Orientation had reliability coefficients of .74 and .62 respectively.

Prior Knowledge Pretest and Achievement Posttest.   The Prior Knowledge Test was administered in an effort to screen and classify students' existing knowledge about Newton's law of motion. The Prior Knowledge Test consisted of two subtests: the True/False Test, and the Application Problem.

The 10-item True/False subtest was used in previous studies (Alvermann & Hynd, 1989; Alvermann et al., 1990). It was constructed to evaluate commonly held alternative conceptions about projectile motion. The two-item Application Problem subtest required students to study diagrams of a moving object and then indicate the path a projectile shot from a cannon would take. In addition, the subtest required students to provide the reasoning behind their choice. The format and content of the items on the True/False Test and Application Problem differed from the Achievement Posttest to prevent knowledge retention.

The Achievement Posttest consisted of two subtests: Conceptual Understanding and Application Reasoning. The 20-item Conceptual Understanding subtest was transformed from Alvermann and Hynd's (1989) 20-item True/False Test into a four-alternative multiple-choice format (Qian & Alvermann, 1995). The test was designed to assess students' understanding of Newton's theory related to the path of a projectile. Alvermann et al. (1990) reported that the 20-item True/False Test had a reliability coefficient in the low .70s. The four-item Application Reasoning subtest required students to study diagrams of a moving object and then indicate the path the moving object would take. The test also required students to select a statement that best explains the reasoning behind their choices.

Procedures.   The Epistemological Belief Questionnaire, Motivational Goal Questionnaire, and Prior Knowledge Pretest were administered together prior to the start of the experiment. Students were required to learn Newton's theory of motion by reading a refutational text. Students were told that they were going to investigate the concept of motion. Then they were asked to read and study the text as though they were studying for a test, using any method they wished to study the text. Students were given up to 15 minutes to read and study the passage. Then, they were required to work for three minutes on a word scramble. Finally, students had 30 minutes to finish the Achievement Posttest.

The first author translated refutational text, the Epistemological Beliefs Questionnaire, Goal Orientation Questionnaire, and prior knowledge pretest, and achievement posttest into Chinese. The translation of the Epistemological Beliefs Questionnaire and Goal Orientation Questionnaire was verified by a Chinese scholar who earned a Ph.D. in Second Language Acquisition and Teaching. The translated prior knowledge pretest, achievement posttest, and refutational text were verified by a Chinese professor of physics who teaches physics at a college in the U.S.

The data on the Application Problem pretest were examined to classify students into three groups: (a) accretion, (b) tuning, and (c) restructuring. The accretion group consisted of students whose answers to the application questions were incomplete but correct (that is, they displayed no alternative conceptions). The tuning group consisted of students whose answers to the application questions showed some alternative conceptions. Finally, the restructuring group consisted of students who had misconceived knowledge of the concept on the Application Problem.

Differences in Beliefs Between American and Chinese Students

Simple independent t-tests were used to assess the differences between American and Chinese students in their beliefs about learning and ability. The results indicated that Chinese students as a group tended to believe more strongly than American students that knowledge is simple, $t(242) = 8.14$, $p = .001$, and ability to learn is innate, $t(230) = 3.70$, $p = .001$, although American students had a stronger performance goal orientation than did Chinese students, $t(188) = 2.06$, $p = .04$. American students believed more strongly than their counterparts that learning is quick, but the difference was not statistically significant (see Table 18.1 for descriptive statistics).

The Chinese students in the present study had stronger beliefs about simple and certain knowledge and innate ability to learn than the American students. The finding is worth exploring because the results are not consistent with the literature on epistemological beliefs (Schommer & Dunnell, 1994). Research on epistemological beliefs documented that students with better academic achievements (gifted) tend to have more mature beliefs than less successful students (nongifted). However, this does not appear to be the case with those Chinese students who were admitted into the "key" school through highly competitive entrance exams. One explanation for their stronger beliefs about certain and simple knowledge is that their beliefs may have been heavily influenced by the school cultures that encourage docility and respect for authority, foster building consensus over controversial issues, but discourage assertiveness and raising "why" questions regardless of their academic performance (Pai, 1997). The Chinese students' less mature beliefs may also be related to the lack of exposure to multiple sources of information and knowledge. Most of the students during the interview responded that they rely on authority figures such as parents or well-known scientists for the information.

Chinese students were found to have stronger beliefs about innate ability to learn. Students' beliefs may be related to the highly selective process of China's educational system (Qian & Huang, 1997). Due to limited resources, only a small proportion of students have an opportunity to pursue undergraduate study. The selection of the best among students as early as children entering kindergarten has caused a chain of reaction in elementary and secondary schools. Schools have to

TABLE 18.1

Means, Standard Deviations, and Correlation Matrix for the Measures on Both American and Chinese Students.

Variables	Max Score	Chinese n = 184		American n = 95		QL	SK	IA	PG	TF	AP	CU	AR
		M	SD	M	SD								
Quick Learning (QL)	75	29.34	7.23	29.66	5.31	1.00	-.03	.21	.08	-.06	.08	-.15	-.16
Simple-Certain Knowledge (SK)	55	35.06	7.72	28.07	5.47	.01	1.00	.31	.26	-.12	-.04	-.03	-.09
Innate Ability (IA)	30	14.65	4.26	13.03	3.44	.12	.42	1.00	.15	-.06	-.02	-.04	-.06
Performance Goals (PG)	55	31.22	5.63	32.52	5.46	.06	.33	.24	1.00	-.11	-.13	-.08	-.09
True/False (TF)	10	7.60	1.62	4.30	1.57	.07	-.18	.02	.24	1.00	.23	.42	.16
Application Problem (AP)	4	2.80	.88	1.94	.99	.01	-.10	-.15	-.18	.22	1.00	.29	.11
Conceptual Understanding (CU)	20	14.78	3.48	12.76	3.31	.00	-.24	-.14	-.18	.65	.38	1.00	.56
Application Reasoning (AR)	4	3.06	1.19	2.26	1.17	-.04	-.23	-.13	-.09	.51	.33	.72	1.00

Note: The correlation coefficients on the lower left side of the diagonal were obtained from the American sample, while those on the upper right side of the diagonal were obtained from the Chinese sample.

compete with each other to send their best students to "key elementary and secondary schools." Elementary school teachers are judged by the number of their students who can succeed in going to the key secondary schools, while secondary school teachers are evaluated based on their students' success in going to college. School administrators' high expectation has led teachers to assign extra amounts of homework to their students. As a result, children have to do a lot of worksheets and are expected to learn more than what the curriculum requires. Despite their hard work and efforts, many students will be kept out of the key schools due to the cut-off score. Going through the highly selective process may help students develop the belief that they cannot succeed unless they are born smart.

Relationship Between Beliefs and Motivational Goals

Multiple regression analyses were used to examine the relationship between students' epistemological beliefs and motivational goals among American and Chinese students separately. The three factors (Quick Learning, Simple-Certain Knowledge, and Innate Ability) derived from the 32-item Epistemological Belief Questionnaire were used as predictors, and the score from the 11-item Goal Orientation Questionnaire was used as an outcome measure.

The results indicated that there was a statistically significant relationship between epistemological beliefs and motivational goals among American and Chinese students. The regression model used to process the data on Chinese students explained about 8% of the variance, $R = .28$, $F(3, 180) = 5.16$, $p = .0019$, $MS_e = 29.67$, while the regression model for American students explained about 12% of the variance, $R = .35$, $F(3, 91) = 4.25$, $p = .007$, $MS_e = 29.58$. Therefore, a moderate relationship was found to exist between students' epistemological beliefs and motivational goals.

The moderate relationship between the epistemological beliefs (Quick Learning, Simple-Certain Knowledge, and Innate Ability) and Performance Goals adds support for the relationship theorized by Dweck and Leggett (1988). According to Dweck and Leggett, goal orientations are directly linked with and explained by belief systems. Goal orientations (performance goals versus learning goals) are believed to mediate between individuals' beliefs about intelligence and learning patterns. The moderate association between belief systems and goals appears to support Dweck and Leggett's proposed theory about the relationship between naive belief systems and performance goals.

Predictability of Beliefs and Motivational Goals

Canonical correlation analyses were conducted to examine whether students who had immature beliefs about learning, knowledge, and ability, and who endorsed performance goals, would fail to overcome their naive theories about

Newton's law of motion. One set of variables consisted of Quick Learning, Simple-Certain knowledge, Innate Ability, and Performance Goals, and the other set of variables consisted of Conceptual Understanding and Application Reasoning. Means, standard deviations, and correlation coefficients for all variables are reported in Table 18.1.

The analysis of the data on American students indicated that only the first dimension was considered meaningful in terms of the amount of variance explained ($R_c^2 = .12$), based on both the magnitude of the canonical correlation ($R_c = 34$) and statistical tests of them, Wilk's Lambda = .79247, $F(16, 355) = 1.76, p = .036$.

The structure coefficients associated with the four predictor variables for this meaningful dimension were as follows: Quick Learning, −.25; Simple-Certain Knowledge, −.65; Innate Ability, −.58; and Performance Goals, .35. The first canonical factor loaded heavily on Simple-Certain Knowledge and to a lesser extent on Innate Ability and Performance Goals. According to Huberty and Weisenbaker (1992), the importance of each predictor could be assessed by conducting four separate canonical correlation analyses, each with one predictor removed. In this study, four separate canonical correlation R_c^2s were obtained so that comparisons could be made. The results indicated that R_c^2 dropped from an initial value of .12 to .9 (25% decrease) when Innate Ability was removed and to .10 (16% decrease) when Simple-Certain Knowledge or Performance Goals was removed. In contrast, R_c^2 did not drop substantially from .12 to .11 (8% decrease) when Quick Learning was removed. Evidently, in predicting conceptual change learning among high school students, Innate Ability, Simple-Certain Knowledge, and Performance Goals were more important predictors than was Quick Learning. In contrast, the analysis of Chinese students' data indicated that none of the dimensions was considered meaningful in terms of the amount of variance explained.

One of the purposes of the present study is to examine the contribution of epistemological beliefs and motivational goals to conceptual change learning by assessing the strength of the relationship between (a) epistemological beliefs and motivational goals and (b) conceptual understanding and application reasoning among American and Chinese students.

With the American students, the significant association between the two variable sets indicates that students who have immature beliefs about knowledge are less likely to relinquish their naive theories in conceptual change learning. This finding is consistent with previous literature on epistemological beliefs. Students' naive epistemological beliefs are strongly associated with ineffective strategies, negative affects, passivity, and lack of cognitive flexibility (Dweck & Leggett, 1988; Schommer & Dunnell, 1994; Schommer et al., 1992). Studies of epistemological beliefs have demonstrated that in the face of difficulty and challenging tasks, students' academic performance is affected by their beliefs about intelligence (Dweck & Leggett, 1988), about knowledge, and about learning (Ryan, 1984; Schommer & Dunnell, 1994; Schommer et al., 1992).

The assessment of the relative importance of the predictors addresses the issue about which variables contribute substantially to high school students' conceptual change learning. Results obtained from structure coefficients in canonical correlation analyses with the American sample indicate that beliefs about Innate Ability, Simple-Certain Knowledge and Performance Goals contribute more to conceptual change learning than does Quick Learning.

The relatively greater contribution made by beliefs about Innate Ability to conceptual change learning suggests that among American students, beliefs about ability to learn appear to be more strongly associated with conceptual change learning than their beliefs about Simple-Certain Knowledge and Performance Goals. This finding, however, does not parallel the results of other studies of epistemological beliefs (Qian & Alvermann, 1995; Schommer & Dunnell, 1994; Schommer et al., 1992). Studies in the literature have not documented that beliefs about Innate Ability predict students' academic performance, although some have provided evidence of the association of innate ability with goal orientations, levels of cognitive functioning, and choice of challenging tasks (e.g., Dweck & Bempechat, 1983). Further research is needed to investigate high school students' belief systems in general and the contribution of each factor to their conceptual change learning in particular.

The finding that beliefs about Simple-Certain Knowledge is a more important predictor is consistent with previous research that shows students who believe knowledge is certain tend to draw absolute conclusions for an unfinished passage (Schommer, 1993). The relative importance of Simple-Certain Knowledge in conceptual change learning also provides support for findings in a series of studies (Qian & Alvermann, 1995; Ryan, 1984; Schommer et al., 1992). In these studies, researchers found that students' beliefs about simple knowledge contribute substantially to their overall performance on an achievement test, their overestimation of what they understood, their tendency to resort to relatively superficial text processing strategies, and their failure to relinquish alternative conceptions about the projectile motion.

The contribution of Performance Goals to conceptual change learning is also important. The positive correlation between the Performance Goals and conceptual change learning has demonstrated that students who endorse performance goals are more likely to overcome naive theories about the projectile motion. This finding appears to support Nicholls' (1984) description about ego-involvement and task-involvement. He argues that learning will be facilitated even if students are ego-involved. The worse case is that students are neither ego- nor task-involved. In the present studies, American high students appear to thrive in coceptual change learning with strong performance goals. This finding is consistent with results from studies of students' motivation in conceptual change learning (Hynd, Holschuh, & Nist, 2000; Lee & Brophy, 1996). Hynd et al. (2000) have acknowledged the important role that performance goals (e.g., making good grades) play in conceptual change learning among both high school and college students.

In contrast, among predominantly European-American students, a negative correlation between students' goal orientations and conceptual change learning was documented (Qian, 1993). The significantly negative correlations between performance goals and overall achievement, and between performance goals and application reasoning indicate that students who endorse performance goals are less likely to overcome naive theories on overall achievement and application reasoning than those who endorse learning goals. A sizable body of literature has documented a very strong association of goal orientations with engagement of high level cognitive strategies and probability of using the strategies in accomplishing complex learning tasks (Nolen, 1988; Pintrich & De Groot, 1990; Pintrich & Garcia, 1991; Wolters, Yu, & Pintrich, 1996).

With the Chinese students, however, there is no significant relationship found between epistemological beliefs and conceptual change learning, although students demonstrated significant conceptual change learning. One explanation to this nonsignificant result may be that the epistemological beliefs are not strong predictors of Chinese students' achievements in learning. This speculation parallels the results in a study of scientific epistemological beliefs among Chinese students in Taiwan (Tsai, 1998). Tsai reported that students' science achievement was not related significantly to their scientific epistemological beliefs, although the kinds of beliefs predict students' ways of viewing science, their metacognitive ability, cognitive structures, and strategies used in learning science.

Another speculation is that the epistemological belief questionnaire may need to be adapted to take into account Chinese culture and students' school experiences because the questionnaire used in the present study was originally developed for white middle-class adults in the U.S. (Schommer, 1998). Evidence obtained from an item analysis with the Chinese sample indicates there are some problematic items that do not fit the factor structures. The internal consistency is low with the overall 32-item questionnaire (alpha = .54) in general and with Quick Learning (alpha = .27) in particular.

Chinese students were still able to accomplish conceptual change learning despite the fact they demonstrated stronger immature beliefs about learning and knowledge than American students. Their success in conceptual change learning may be explained by their strong performance goals like their American counterparts. This explanation is supported by recent studies of students' motivation in conceptual change (Hynd et al., 2000; Lee & Brophy, 1996). Hynd et al. (2000) reported that both high school and college students consider making good grades as strong motivation to persist in conceptual change learning. They argued that students must be more motivated than usual in order to succeed in the change. Lee and Brophy (1996) observed that students tended to be cognitively engaged, recognize conceptual conflicts, and make efforts to understand the scientific notions even if their strong motivation stemmed from "a sense of duty to fulfill the student role" (p. 315).

Effects of Refutational Text

This research question was concerned with the effect of refutational text on conceptual change learning. Students were classified into three groups (accretion, tuning, and restructuring) based on their prior knowledge pretest score.

Chinese students.   Three simple t-tests were used to compare the percentage correct scores between the pretest and posttest. The results indicated that students who need to tune showed significant conceptual change learning ($t = -2.75$, $df = 28$, $p = .01$), although those who need to restructure made substantial but not statistically significant gains in conceptual change learning ($t = -1.57$, $df = 13$, $p = .14$). In contrast, students who need to accrete their knowledge did not show significant gains after they read the refutational text (see Table 18.2 for the descriptive statistics).

American students.   The same procedures were used to analyze the data on American students. Students in all three groups (e.g., accretion, tuning, and restructuring) demonstrated that the refutational text facilitated their conceptual change learning.

A post hoc research question was concerned with the interaction effect between knowledge group (i.e., accretion, tuning, and restructuring) and cultural group (i.e., American and Chinese) on the Achievement Test. Two separate ANCOVAs were used to analyze the data. One ANCOVA used Conceptual Understanding as the outcome measure and True/False pretest as covariate, while the other ANCOVA used Application Reasoning as the outcome measure and Application Problem as Covariate. However, there was no significant interaction effect found between knowledge group and cultural group.

The finding that refutational text is effective is consistent with literature on refutational text (Alvermann & Hynd, 1989; Guzzetti, 1990). The finding has added to the literature that the effectiveness of refutational text is replicated by involving not only high school American students but also their counterparts in China. The nonsignificant results of the interaction effect suggest that the effect

TABLE 18.2
Means and Standard Deviations for the Accretion, Tuning,
and Restructuring Groups.

	N	*Pretest (Percentage scores)*		*Posttest*	
		M	*SD*	*M*	*SD*
Accretion	141	78.21	12.26	76.38	16.84
Tuning	29	64.53	11.21	72.84	14.84
Restructuring	14	53.06	15.77	60.41	23.72

of refutational text on conceptual change has similar patterns regardless of kinds of prior knowledge students possess and the cultural backgrounds they are from.

However, there are several limitations of the comparison between American and Chinese high school students in their epistemological beliefs and conceptual change learning. First, students in the American sample obviously have more socially, economically, and ethnically diverse backgrounds than those in the Chinese sample. The difference has limited the generalizability of the findings in the present studies. Second, the unequitable measures were used as pretests and posttests. Future studies need to address this concern by using equitable measures so that conceptual change can be directly evaluated.

Despite the limitations, the findings in the present study have several theoretical implications. First, the finding that the use of refutational text is effective implies that this particular kind of text facilitates conceptual change learning not only among American students but also students in China despite their immature beliefs about learning and knowledge. Second, the implication relates to the contribution of epistemological beliefs to conceptual change learning among American students. Although researchers acknowledge the importance of Simple-Certain Knowledge and Quick Learning, the finding that Innate Ability contributes more than other factors implies a different theoretical model of epistemological beliefs for non-white American high school students in conceptual change learning.

Finally, the present comparison of epistemological beliefs and conceptual change learning between American and Chinese students also suggests several directions for future research. First, the nonsignificant relation between the two variable sets: (a) epistemological beliefs and motivational goals and (b) conceptual change learning with the Chinese sample, has an implication for research on epistemological research from a crosscultural perspective. Future research is needed to identify dimensions that underlie Chinese students' epistemological beliefs by taking into account their unique cultural, educational, and social backgrounds. Focus should also be on finding ways that will be able to characterize Chinese students' epistemological beliefs. Second, results of separate factor analyses with both American and Chinese samples indicated that some items of the 32-item epistemological belief questionnaire did not load heavily or consistently on the factors identified in a previous study (Qian & Alvermann, 1995). The inconsistent and low loadings of items suggest a need for further research to identify dimensions that underlie non-white American and Chinese students' epistemological beliefs. Third, efforts are needed to gain insight into students' conceptions about the nature of knowing and knowledge in specific contexts and situations. Earlier studies used survey-type questionnaires to obtain students' conceptions about the nature of knowing and knowledge in general. Recent studies (Driver et al., 1996; Hammer, 1995; Leach, Millar, Ryder, & Sere, 1999) have been conducted to explore ways to provide intended contexts for students so that researchers are able to find out what specific instances students have in mind in their responses. Future research is needed to present students in the contexts and situations that are directly linked to conceptual change learning.

ACKNOWLEDGMENTS

The authors wish to acknowledge that the two studies were in part supported by grants from PSC-CUNY Research Award Program and Lehman College Foundation Faculty Advancement Award, The City University of New York.

REFERENCES

Alvermann, D. E., & Hynd, C. R. (1989, December). *The influence of discussion and text on the learning of counterintuitive science concepts.* Paper presented at the annual meeting of the National Reading Conference, Austin, TX.

Alvermann, D. E., Hynd, C. R., & Qian, G. (1990, November). *Preservice teachers' comprehension and teaching of a physics principle: An experimental intervention.* Paper presented at the annual meeting of the National Reading Conference, Miami, FL.

Alvermann, D. E., Smith, L. C., & Readence, J. E. (1985). Prior knowledge and comprehension of compatible and incompatible text. *Reading Research Quarterly, 20,* 420–436.

Anderson, R. C. (1977). The notion of schemata and the educational enterprise: General discussion of the conference. In R. C. Anderson, R. J. Spiro, & W. E. Montague (Eds.), *Schooling and the acquisition of knowledge* (pp. 415–432). Hillsdale, NJ: Erlbaum.

Brunson, B. I., & Matthews, K. A. (1981). The type A coronary prone behavior pattern and reactions to uncontrollable stress: An analysis of performance strategies, affect, and attributions during failure. *Journal of Personality and Social Psychology, 40,* 906–918.

Carey, S., Evans, R., Honda, M., Jay, E., & Unger, C. (1989). 'An experiment is when you try it and see if it works': A study of grade 7 students' understanding of the construction of scientific knowledge. *International Journal of Science Education, 11,* 514–529.

Coulson, R. L., Feltovich, P. J., & Spiro, R. J. (1986). *Foundations of a misunderstanding of the ultrastructural basis of myocardial failure: A reciprocating network of oversimplifications.* Unpublished manuscript, Southern Illinois University, School of Medicine, Illinois.

Diener, C. I., & Dweck, C. S. (1978). An analysis of learned helplessness: Continuous changes in performance, strategy, and achievement cognition following failure. *Journal of Personality and Social Psychology, 36,* 451–462.

Diener, C. I., & Dweck, C. S. (1980). An analysis of learned helplessness: The processing of success. *Journal of Personality and Social Psychology, 39,* 940–952.

Dole, J. A., & Sinatra, G. M. (1998). Reconceptualizing change in the cognitive construction of knowledge. *Educational Psychologist, 33* (2–3), 109–128.

Driver, R., Asoko, H., Leach, J., Mortimer, E., & Scott, P. (1994). Constructing scientific knowledge in the classroom. *Educational Researcher, 23,* 5–12.

Driver, R., Leach, J., Millar, R., & Scott, P. (1996). *Young people's images of science.* Bristol, PA: Open University Press.

Dweck, C. S., & Bempechat, J. (1983). Children's theories of intelligence. In S. Paris, G. Olsen, & H. Stevenson (Eds.), *Learning and motivation in the classroom* (pp. 239–256). Hillsdale, NJ: Erlbaum.

Dweck, C. S., & Leggett, E. L. (1988). A social-cognitive approach to motivation and personality. *Psychological Review, 95,* 256–273.

Fry, E. B. (1977). Fry's readability graph: Clarifications, validity, and extension to level 17. *Journal of Reading, 21,* 242–252.

Garner, R., Alexander, P. A., Gillingham, M. G., Kulikowich, J. M., & Brown, M. (1991). Interest and learning from text. *American Educational Research Journal, 28(3),* 643–659.

Garner, R., Gillingham, M. G., & White, C. S. (1989). Effects of "seductive details" on macroprocessing and microprocessing in adults and children. *Cognition and Instruction, 6,* 41–57.

Graves, M. F., Prenn, M. C., Earle, J., Thompson, M., Johnson, V., & Slater, W. H. (1991). Improving instructional text: Some lessons learned. *Reading Research Quarterly, 26,* 110–122.

Guzzetti, B. (1990). Effects of textual and instructional manipulations on report acquisition. *Reading Psychology, 11,* 49–62.

Guzzetti, B., & Hynd, C. R. (1995, April). *Students' reactions to refutational science text.* Paper presented at the annual meeting of the American Educational Research Association, San Francisco, CA.

Guzzetti, B. J., Snyder, T. E., Glass, G. V., & Gamas, W. S. (1993). Promoting conceptual change in science: A comparative meta-analysis of instructional interventions from reading education and science education. *Reading Research Quarterly, 28,* 116–161.

Guzzetti, B. J., Williams, W. O., Skeels, S. A., & Wu, S. M. (1997). Influence of text structure on learning counterintuitive physics concepts. *Journal of Research in Science Teaching, 34,* 700–719.

Hammer, D. (1994). Epistemological beliefs in introductory physics. *Cognition and Instruction, 12,* 151–183.

Hammer, D. (1995). Epistemological considerations in teaching introductory physics. *Science Education, 79,* 393–413.

Hidi, S., & Baird, W. (1988). Strategies for increasing text-based interest and students' recall of expository texts. *Reading Research Quarterly, 23,* 465–483.

Hofer, B. K., & Pintrich, P. R. (1997). The development of epistemological theories: Beliefs about knowledge and knowing and their relation to learning. *Review of Educational Research, 67,* 88–140.

Hynd, C. R., McNish, M., Lay, K., & Fowler, P. (1995). *High school physics: The role of text in learning counterintuitive information.* (Reading Research Report). Athens, GA: The University of Georgia, National Reading Research Center.

Hynd, C. R., McWhorter, Y., Phares, V., & Suttles, W. (1994). The role of instructional variables in conceptual change in high school physics topics. *Journal of Research in Science Teaching, 31,* 933–946.

Hynd, C. R., Holschuh, J., & Nist, S. (2000). Learning complex scientific information: Motivation theory and its relation in students' perceptions. *Reading & Writing Quarterly, 16,* 23–57.

Larochelle, M., & Desautels, J. (1991). 'Of course, it's just obvious': Adolescents' ideas of scientific knowledge. *International Journal of Science Education, 13,* 373–389.

Leach, J., Millar, R., Ryder, J., & Sere, M. G. (1999, April). *An investigation of high school and university science majors' epistemological reasoning in the context of empirical investigations.* Paper presented at the annual meeting of the American Educational Research Association, Montreal, Canada.

Lee, O., & Brophy, J. (1996). Motivational patterns observed in sixth grade science classroom. *Journal of Research in Science Teaching, 33(3),* 303–318.

Licht, B. G., & Dweck, C. S. (1984). Determinants of academic achievement: The interaction of children's achievement orientations with skill area. *Developmental Psychology, 20,* 628–636.

Maria, K. (1997). A case study of conceptual change in a young child. *Elementary School Journal, 98,* 67–88.

Maria, K. (1998). My analysis of the Jennifer Vignette. In B. Guzzetti & C. Hynd (Eds.), *Theoretical perspective on conceptual change* (pp. 209–223). Mahwah, NJ: Erlbaum.

Maria, K., & MacGinitie, W. R. (1981, December). *Prior knowledge as a handicapping condition.* Paper presented at the meeting of the National Reading Conference, Dallas, TX.

Maria, K., & MacGinitie, W. R. (1987). Learning from texts that refute the reader's prior knowledge. *Reading Research and Instruction, 26,* 222–238.

McCloskey, M. (1983). Intuitive physics. *Scientific American, 248,* 122–130.

Nicholls, J. (1984). Conceptions of ability and achievement motivation. In R. Ames and C. Ames (Eds.), *Research on motivation in education: Vol. I. Student motivation* (pp. 39–73). New York: Academic Press, Inc.

Nolen, S. (1988). Reasons for studying: Motivational orientations and study strategies. *Cognition and Instruction, 5,* 269–287.

Pai, Y. (1997). *Cultural foundations of education.* Columbus, OH: Merrill.

Pintrich, P. R., & De Groot, E. (1990). Motivational and self regulated learning components of classroom academic performance. *Journal of Educational Psychology, 82,* 33–40.

Pintrich, P. R., & Garcia, T. (1991). Student goal orientation and self-regulation in the college classroom. In M. Maehr & P. R. Pintrich (Eds.), *Advances in motivation and achievement: Goals and self-regulatory processes* (Vol. 7, pp. 371–402). Greenwich, CT: JAI Press.

Pintrich, P. R., Marx, R. W., & Boyle, R. A. (1993). Beyond cold conceptual change: The role of motivational beliefs and classroom contextual factors in the process of conceptual change. *Review of Educational Research, 63,* 167–199.

Pintrich, P. R., Smith, D. A. F., Garcia, T., & McKeachie, W. J. (1991). *A manual for the use of the motivated strategies for learning questionnaire (MSLQ).* Ann Arbor, MI: The University of Michigan Press.

Posner, G. J., Strike, K., Hewson, P., & Gertzog, W. A. (1982). Accommodation of a scientific conception: Toward a theory of conceptual change. *Science Education, 66,* 211–227.

Qian, G. (1993, April). *Relations between secondary school students' epistemological beliefs, motivational patterns, and conceptual change: A review of research literature.* Paper presented at the meeting of the National Association of Research in Science Teaching, Atlanta, GA.

Qian, G., & Alvermann, D. E. (1995). The role of epistemological beliefs and learned helplessness in secondary school students' learning from science text. *Journal of Educational Psychology, 87,* 282–292.

Qian, G., & Alvermann, D. E. (in press). The relationship between epistemological beliefs and conceptual change learning. *Reading & Writing Quarterly, 16,* 59–74.

Qian, G., & Huang, T. (1997). Happiest but least cheerful: The paradox of population and education policies in China. In P. J. Thompson (Ed.), *Environmental education for 21st century: International and interdisciplinary perspectives* (pp.59–66). New York: Peter Lang.

Ridgeway, V. G., & Dunston, P. J. (in press). Content determines process: Seeing the familiar in new ways. *Reading & Writing Quarterly, 16,* 119–138.

Rumelhart, D. E., & Norman, D. A. (1978). Accretion, tuning, and restructuring: Three modes of learning. In J. W. Cotton & R. L. Klatzky (Eds.), *Semantic factors in cognition* (pp. 37–53). Hillsdale, NJ: Erlbaum.

Ryan, M. P. (1984). Monitoring text comprehension: Individual differences in epistemological standards. *Journal of Educational Psychology, 16,* 248–258.

Schoenfeld, A. H. (1985). *Mathematical problem solving.* New York: Academic Press.

Schommer, M. (1989). *Effects of beliefs about the nature of knowledge on comprehension.* Unpublished doctoral dissertation, University of Illinois, Illinois.

Schommer, M. (1990). Effects of beliefs about the nature of knowledge on comprehension. *Journal of Educational Psychology, 82,* 498–504.

Schommer, M. (1993). Epistemological development and academic performance among secondary students. *Journal of Educational Psychology, 85,* 406–411.

Schommer, M. (April, 1997). *The development of epistemological tutoring: Case studies.* Paper presented at the annual meeting of the American Educational Research Association, Chicago, IL.

Schommer, M. (1998). The influence of age and education on epistemological beliefs. *British Journal of Educational Psychology, 68,* 551–562.

Schommer, M., & Dunnell, P. A. (1994). A comparison of epistemological beliefs between gifted and nongifted high school students. *Roeper Review, 16(3),* 207–210.

Schommer, M., Rhodes, N., & Crouse, A. (1992). Epistemological beliefs and mathematical text comprehension: Believing it is simple does not make it so. *Journal of Educational Psychology, 84,* 435–443.

Solomon, J., Duveen, J., & Sott, L. (1994). Pupils' images of scientific epistemology. *International Journal of Science Education, 16 (3),* 361–373.

Songer, N. B., & Linn, M. C. (1991). How do students' views of science influence knowledge integration? *Journal of Research in Science Teaching, 28,* 761–784.

Spiro, R. J., Vispoel, W. P., Schmitz, J. G., Samarapungavan, A., & Boerger, A. E. (1987). Knowledge acquisition for application: Cognitive flexibility and transfer in complex content domains. In B. K. Britton & S. M. Glynn (Eds.), *Executive control processes in reading* (pp. 177–199). Hillsdale, NJ: Erlbaum.

Strike, K. A., & Posner, G. J. (1992). A revisionist theory of conceptual change. In R. Duschl & R. Hamilton (Eds.), *Philosophy of science, cognitive science, and educational theory and practice.* Albany, NY: SUNY Press.

Tsai, Chin-Chung. (1998). An analysis of Taiwanese eighth graders' science achievement, scientific epistemological beliefs, and cognitive structure outcomes after learning basic atomic theory. *International Journal of Science Education, 20,* 413–425.

Windschitl, M. (1997). Student epistemological beliefs and conceptual change activities: How do pair members affect each other? *Journal of Science Education and Technology, 6,* 37–47.

Wolters, C. A., Yu, S. L., & Pintrich, P. R. (1996). The relation between goal orientation and students' motivational beliefs and self regulated learning. *Learning & Individual Differences, 8(3),* 211–238.

Conclusion

19

Future Challenges and Directions for Theory and Research on Personal Epistemology

Paul R. Pintrich
Combined Program in Education and Psychology
The University of Michigan

The chapters in this volume reflect recent theory and research on the nature and role of personal epistemology. The authors have outlined the current status of their own thinking and discussed some of the results from their own research programs on epistemological beliefs and thinking. As in any field, there are diverse views about the nature of personal epistemologies and what role they may play in learning and development. Nevertheless, if the field is to advance, it seems important to try to develop consensus about some of the theoretical, conceptual, and methodological challenges in research on personal epistemology. In addition, it is useful for both experienced researchers as well as novices in this area to have a map of future avenues for research on personal epistemology.

This chapter will address both these goals by reviewing and highlighting the contributions from all the other chapters in this volume. My colleague and coeditor, Barbara Hofer, in her introductory chapter, outlined a number of questions for theory and research on personal epistemology. I will discuss these questions in this concluding chapter based on the other chapters in the book. I have organized the questions around eight general issues that seem to be salient for research on personal epistemology (Hofer & Pintrich, 1997). My general strategy will be to attempt to develop a consensus position for each of these questions based on the ideas and results presented throughout this book. In other words, given the chapters in this book, what do we currently know, or at least seem to agree on, in terms of the nature and role of personal epistemologies. I will present this position as a proposition to guide future theory and research. At the same time, it is clear that there are dissenting voices and that these perspectives need to be heard. Accordingly, for each proposition, I also will present conflicting views that challenge the consensual position. Finally, I will suggest some possible avenues for future research that may help us resolve some of these disagreements. I hope that this direct representation of a thesis and antithesis will lead to some dialectical thinking and propel all of us to develop new theories, models, and research to clarify these issues.

1. Nature of the Construct of Personal Epistemology

All of the chapters in this volume, in one way or another, raise theoretical issues regarding the nature of epistemological thinking. As Hofer notes in her introduction, one of the key questions concerns the definition of the construct of personal epistemology. All of the chapters in this book use somewhat different labels including epistemological thinking, epistemic cognition, epistemological beliefs, epistemological theories, ways of knowing, epistemological reflection, and epistemological resources or repertoires. The diversity of these labels suggests that all the different models might not be concerned with the same construct or, at a minimum, might not define the boundaries of the construct in the same manner (Hofer & Pintrich, 1997). The key issue concerns what should be considered as the core or essence of personal epistemology and what should be left out of the definition or considered as related but distinct constructs.

   Proposition 1—Personal epistemology concerns an individual's cognitions about the nature of knowledge and the nature of knowing.   Given this proposition, personal epistemology would include cognitions and beliefs about the certainty of knowledge (objectivist versus relativist versus multiplist views), the simplicity of knowledge (simple, concrete versus complex, contingent, context-dependent), the source of knowledge (external authorities versus personal voice), and justifications for knowing (criteria for making knowledge claims, use of evidence, use of reasoning). All of the models in this volume reflect some of these aspects and there is little disagreement that an individual's cognition about knowledge and knowing should be central in a personal epistemology (Hofer & Pintrich, 1997).

   There is, of course, disagreement about whether all these aspects are essential components of a personal epistemology and some models tend to stress one aspect or another such as the role of certainty or the nature of authority and source of knowledge (cf. Clinchy; King & Kitchener; Kuhn & Weinstock; Moore). In addition, there is not consensus on whether a personal epistemology is best represented as cognitions, beliefs, attitudes, ways of thinking, or reasoning skills to name a few possible modes of representation that are reflected in this volume. Nevertheless, even with these disagreements, there is consensus that a personal epistemology includes some aspects of an individual's cognition or personal stance toward the nature of knowledge and knowing.

Dissenting Voices to Proposition 1—Personal epistemologies also include an individual's cognitions and beliefs about the nature of learning, intelligence, instruction, classrooms, domain-specific beliefs about disciplines, and beliefs about the self.   Although there is consensus that cognitions about knowledge and knowing are part of a personal epistemology, there are many models represented in this volume that include other aspects as an important component of a personal epistemology. In some ways, it is not surprising that beliefs about the nature or learning (e.g., quick versus slow), the use of different learning strategies or activities to acquire knowledge, and how people learn, study, and comprehend (e.g., Hammer & Elby; Qian & Pan; Schommer; Schraw, Bendixen & Dunkle; Wood & Kardash) are considered as part and parcel of a personal epistemology. It is logical that as individuals grapple with the nature of knowledge and knowing, their cognitions and beliefs about how knowledge is acquired and how people learn or come to understand ideas are also activated or evoked. In the same manner, their perceptions about the nature of instruction and classrooms (e.g., Baxter Magolda; De Corte, Op't Eynde, & Verschaffel; Moore) may be intimately bound up with their beliefs about learning. That is, as individuals think about how people learn, they also may think about the best ways for teaching people ideas or their own personal preferences for different types of classroom contexts.

Somewhat farther removed, but still potentially related are beliefs about intelligence or innate ability and the self such as motivational beliefs (e.g., De Corte et al; Schommer; Schraw, et al; Wood & Kardash). For example, it may be that the underlying substrate for beliefs about learning is beliefs about intelligence and innate ability. If one believes that intelligence or ability to learn is fixed and immutable, then beliefs about how easy or difficult or quick or slow learning is may be different than if one believes that intelligence is inherently changeable. In this way, beliefs about intelligence may constrain the range of beliefs about learning. In a similar manner, motivational beliefs about the self in terms of self-efficacy for learning or interest and value for a subject area may facilitate or constrain beliefs about learning or even how knowledge is conceived (De Corte et al.). Clinchy's description of some of her noncollege individuals clearly show how their low perceptions of self-efficacy or confidence are intertwined with the nature and quality of their epistemological thinking.

Finally, as the chapters on domain-specific beliefs (Bell & Linn; De Corte et al; Elder; Qian & Pan) show, individuals have different beliefs about the nature of mathematics and science, the process of knowledge generation and evaluation, the role of experts, and the certainty of knowledge in these domains. In some ways, these chapters focus on the core aspects of knowledge and knowing, but they highlight the fact that there may be specific domain differences in the nature of knowledge and knowing that need to be considered in our models of personal epistemology. For example, within the general domain of science, there are generally accepted and defined ways of "scientific" knowing (e.g., use of the scientific method) that may differ from other ways of knowing in other domains (i.e., art, music, English literature, history, social work, clinical psychology, education) as well as general epistemological thinking (cf., Baxter Magolda; Clinchy; Moore).

Accordingly, these domain-specific models are concerned not just with how an individual constructs a general personal epistemology, but how individuals construct their "scientific" epistemology or their "mathematical" epistemology. In these domain-specific models the dimensions of epistemology are basically isomorphic with the dimensions noted in Proposition 1, but the actual positions along the dimensions might vary as a function of the domain. For example, general models of personal epistemology might include a position on the continuum for "personal experience" as an important aspect of the nature of knowing, while a scientific epistemology might discount this position on the continuum in favor of the use of scientific data and reasoning. In this case, individuals could have different personal "epistemologies" depending on whether a scientific domain was activated or a more general epistemological perspective was evoked in the context.

In any event, the key issue is whether these other beliefs about learning, intelligence, instruction, domains, and the self should be included as part of a personal epistemology. At one level, it may be a personal choice or preference of the researchers in terms of how they conceive of their theory or model. In this case, there may be no particularly good way to adjudicate among the differing models. On the other hand, this personal choice method can lead to problems in conceptual clarity and difficulties in developing a coherent and cumulative body of knowledge about the development of epistemological thinking. For example, if there are multiple and varying definitions of the construct, then it makes it difficult to summarize developmental trends and develop generalizations across research studies (Hofer & Pintrich, 1997).

Of course, one way to proceed on this definitional problem is to propose theoretical models that explicitly develop the logical and conceptual links between cognitions about knowledge and knowing and all the other potential constructs such as beliefs about learning, intelligence, and instruction. In this case, there should be some discussion about how these different constructs are cognitively represented by the individual. For example, in more classic developmental models that assume a more unitary (or stage-like) central conceptual structure, then all these different cognitions and beliefs should be closely related and show similar change over time (even allowing for the perpetual problem of horizontal decalage). In contrast, other cognitive models might propose that cognitions about knowledge and learning are both relatively independent dimensions, or separable knowledge structures or "schemas," or distinct "nodes" in a network of cognitions and beliefs. However, these models might suggest that they are closely related so that activation of one schema (or nodes) for knowledge beliefs also tends to activate schemas (or nodes) for beliefs about learning and intelligence. In any event, there has been little theoretical work on the nature of representation of these beliefs and there is a need for the application of more recent cognitive psychological models (e.g., connectionist models) to the area of epistemological thinking. For example, if epistemological thinking is best represented by different resources as suggested by Hammer and Elby, then these different types of resources may be connected in some type of node-network model as suggested by connectionist models.

Beyond this theoretical work, there are of course empirical avenues to pursue in addressing the problem. As noted in several chapters in this volume (Elder; Qian & Pan; Schommer; Schraw et al; Wood & Kardash), there is factor analytic work that demonstrates that beliefs about the nature of knowledge and knowing (certainty of knowledge, attainability of truth, simplicity of knowledge, source/authority, stability/changing nature of knowledge, reasoning/justification, etc.) are separable dimensions from beliefs about learning (quick learning) or intelligence (innate ability). At the same time, other research that relies more on interviewing methodology (e.g., Baxter Magolda; Clinchy; Moore) suggests that beliefs about knowledge and other aspects such as learning, instruction, and intelligence are related to each other and in some cases intimately bound together.

This divergence in the findings from different methodologies does not help us in resolving the issue of construct definition. At some level, the empirical work is constrained by the theoretical assumptions of the different models, so models that assume a more unitary central structure of beliefs and use interviewing methods, find it hard to separate out the different dimensions. In contrast, it is not surprising that models that start with an assumption of different dimensions, and then use self-report questionnaires with separate items reflecting the different dimensions, ultimately find factor structures with three, four, or five or more separable dimensions. Future research that uses a multitrait multimethod (MTMM) approach (see Pintrich, Wolters, & Baxter, 2000; Winne & Perry, 2000) would help in this respect. These types of studies would have individuals respond to an array of questionnaires, interviews, and other tasks, and then examine the convergence and divergence of constructs across the different methods. The MTMM approach allows one to separate out method variance and make inferences about constructs across the different methodologies.

In addition, following a more connectionist model, there may be useful applications of experimental and reaction time methodologies that would provide some traction on the problem of construct definition. For example, data from experimental and reaction time methods could be used to model how epistemological thinking may resemble a "state" rather than a specific schema or cognitive structure. As Smith (1998) has pointed out, connectionist or PDP models make very different assumptions about the nature of representations than more classic structural or schema models. There is a need for the use of more experimental methodologies to try to model how epistemological thinking may be represented cognitively as a state or network rather than schemas or theories. Although there is much to be done in terms of working out the details of these experimental and reaction time methods, this type of data would provide us with more evidence about the relations between the dimensions, than can be gathered in simple factor analytic studies based on questionnaire methods.

2. Components of a Personal Epistemology

Beyond the issue of what should be considered as core aspects of a personal epistemology, a key question concerns the number and independence of the components of a personal epistemology. There are three general positions on this issue represented in the chapters in this volume and these three positions reflect three classic perspectives on the nature of development—developmental, cognitive, and contextual (Overton, 1984). The more classic cognitive developmental models propose a more unitary structure that changes over time (e.g., Moore; King & Kitchener; Kuhn & Weinstock), but most of the other chapters in this volume reflect cognitive or contextualist models that include a number of different inde pendent dimensions or components of personal epistemology. The key question is how many independent dimensions or components are necessary to define a personal epistemology.

Proposition 2—There are more than one and less than ten independent dimensions that are necessary to define an individual's personal epistemology. This proposition is a little less definitive than the previous proposition, but it reflects the general lack of consensus in the chapters in this volume. This proposition is based on a general cognitive approach to epistemological thinking that allows for the possibility of multiple dimensions or components that are somewhat independent of each other. The chapters that use more quantitative and questionnaire instruments seem to converge around three (Qian & Pan) or four (Elder) or five (Schommer; Schraw et al.; Wood & Kardash) dimensions of a personal epistemology. However, for all of these chapters except Elder, the dimensions include quick learning and innate ability as factors, although they may have different labels in some of the studies. For example, the factor characteristics of successful students in Wood and Kardash overlaps with both the quick learning and innate ability dimensions. If these two factors were excluded based on Proposition 1, then the range would be from one (Qian & Pan) to three (Schommer; Schraw et al.; Wood & Kardash) to four (Elder). Hofer and Pintrich (1997) have suggested four knowledge-specific independent dimensions in their review of the work in this area. Hofer (2000) also has found some preliminary empirical support for the existence of four dimensions.

However, Fitzgerald and Cunningham suggest that there are seven key questions that can provide a map of an individual's epistemological outlook. The answers to these seven questions provide a description of how an individual approaches and thinks about epistemological issues. The seven issues in their framework parallel many of the dimensions discussed in other chapters in this volume as well as the four main dimensions proposed by Hofer and Pintrich (1997). At the same time, there may be other knowledge-specific dimensions (e.g., the simplicity of knowledge, the purpose of knowledge) that are not quite represented in the Fitzgerald and Cunningham framework of seven dimensions. Moreover, if the other factors such as quick learning and innate ability are included, then there are clearly more than seven independent factors. Given this lack of consensus and the possibility of more than seven dimensions, in the interest of parsimony, ten seems a reasonable number to suggest as the upper limit to the number of independent dimensions.

Dissenting Voices to Proposition 2—The Unitary Voices.   The models and research based in more classic cognitive developmental models (Baxter Magolda; Chandler, Hallett, & Sokol; Clinchy; Moore; King & Kitchener; Kuhn & Weinstock) tend to reject the more general cognitive perspective that there are multiple independent dimensions or components. These developmental models do not necessarily reject the idea that there are different aspects (i.e., source and justification of knowledge) that comprise epistemological thinking, but rather they tend to reject a strong version of the independence assumption. For these models, an individual's beliefs and thinking about the different aspects tend to cohere into a "position" or "level" or "phase" or "stage" that reflects an organized and qualitatively different manner of thinking than other positions or phases. In this manner, the difference between these cognitive developmental models and the more cognitive perspective reflected in Proposition 2 reflects the traditional organismic and mechanistic metatheories that underlie the models (Overton, 1984; Pepper, 1942). That is, the cognitive developmental models assume that epistemological thinking is more qualitative, organic, or holistic (the whole is greater than the parts) and can't be broken down into independent components, at least not coherently. In contrast, the more mechanistic cognitive models do assume that there can be a quantitative analysis of the components and that these somewhat independent components can be described and summarized in some manner to represent the nature of epistemological thinking.

Besides the general organismic assumption of qualitatively different phases, some of the developmental models assume a unitary position because they propose only one basic or overarching dimension. For example, Kuhn and Weinstock suggest that the main dimension or essence of epistemological thinking is the coordination of the subjective and objective dimensions of knowing. On the basis of parsimony and accessibility, they propose that the main developmental task in epistemological development is the coordination of the subjective and objective with the objective perspective dominating initially, followed by a reliance on subjectivity, culminating in a more balanced objective-subjective perspective on knowing. Chandler et al. also focus on a more limited conception of epistemic development that involves judgments regarding the subjective and objective dimensions of knowing.

In summary, the cognitive developmental models tend toward a more unitary conception of epistemological development. Some of the models reject the multiple independent dimensions idea because of organismic assumptions about how different dimensions cohere into qualitatively different levels or phases of development. Other models offer a dissenting voice because they basically limit their discussion of epistemological development to a single dimension.

Dissenting Voices to Proposition 2—The Resources and Situated Voices. Beyond the developmental-organismic rejection of multiple dimensions due to a focus on more unitary structural positions, there are models that would not accept Proposition 2 because it limits the number of dimensions to some number under ten. The best exemplar of this position in this volume are the chapters that adopt a resources view of epistemological development. For example, Hammer and Elby propose that there are many different epistemological resources that students draw on as they think and reason about everyday life as well as life in schools. By creatively mapping the construct of *p*-prims from the conceptual change literature to epistemological thinking, they suggest that there are four general categories of resources that are similar to the four dimensions noted earlier in some respects. More important, within these four general categories they list over 25 different resources that children (and adults) may use in their epistemological thinking. In a similar manner, Bell and Linn suggest that students may have a repertoire of ideas about science that involves a number of different aspects of knowledge about science.

Moreover, in both these chapters, the key assumption is that the resources are situated in different contexts and that different contexts may activate or invoke different resources. Of course, many of the other chapters also assume that epistemological beliefs are situated, but the difference in these two chapters is that the underlying assumption owes more to a contextualist metatheory (Overton, 1984; Pepper, 1942) than a cognitive organismic or mechanistic metatheory. That is, a more situated, contextualist perspective would suggest that the number and type of epistemological resources that are used in any situation can vary from context to context, depending on the features of the context. Accordingly, in Hammer and Elby's model, students may use the resource of knowledge as propagated stuff (from the general category of sources of knowledge) in one context with few of the other resources activated, while in a different context resources from all four of the general categories may be used. In this case, the number and nature of epistemological resources varies from context to context.

In contrast, a more cognitive perspective in line with Proposition 2 would suggest that there are four dimensions of epistemological thinking that are activated in all contexts, but the individual's position on any of the four dimensions could vary as a function of situational and contextual features. For example, the same student might think differently about the source of knowledge (experts versus personal experience) in a natural science context (chemistry) in contrast to a social science (psychology) context (Hofer, 2000). Accordingly, the cognitive perspective would assume that there are four dimensions that are "stable" across contexts, although an individual's position on any of the four dimensions could vary by context. In this way, the cognitive position allows for and even predicts horizontal decalage, that is, differences in positions as a function of context, while the more unitary developmental-organismic position has difficulties explaining why a general central conceptual structure (level, phase) would produce such differences in thinking as a function of context.

In summary, there are dissenting voices to Proposition 2. On the one hand, the more developmental models represent the side of the continuum that favors a more unitary or holistic view of epistemological thinking as stages, levels, or phases. On the other side, the resources perspective reflects a more contextualist and situated view that argues for a diversity and multiplicity of epistemological resources. In the middle of this continuum, the various cognitive models propose some diversity by suggesting a number of relatively independent dimensions of epistemological thinking. At the same time, while these models allow for some situatedness of thinking, they do not assume that there is an unlimited number of contextually dependent resources or dimensions of epistemological thinking.

Future directions for empirical research on this issue are problematic in some ways. That is, if one accepts the general characterization of the metatheories that underlie the developmental, cognitive, and contextualist models, then there is an incommensurability in some of the key assumptions of the theories (Overton, 1984; Pepper, 1942). The organismic and mechanistic metatheories are basically at odds over the best way to characterize development and there are few empirical routes to address this issue that will be accepted by followers of the different metatheories. In addition, a strong contextualist position makes assumptions about the situated and historical nature of development that both organismic and mechanistic theories do not accept, again making it difficult to generate empirical evidence that will be accepted in the different camps. Accordingly, it may be difficult to develop empirical research that would provide unequivocal evidence to different researchers to adjudicate among the different claims for the nature and number of components.

Nevertheless, a continued commitment to empirical research on this issue would be helpful. It is not clear to me that more descriptive factor analytic work on self-report instruments will provide much new evidence that is relevant to the issue concerning the number of dimensions, as this work will always be circumscribed by the items used and the underlying theory that generates the items. In terms of research from the various cognitive and developmental perspectives, it seems that more detailed experimental work that is similar in some ways to the theory of mind research (cf., Chandler et al.; Wellman & Gelman, 1998) could provide evidence regarding the theory-like nature of individuals' epistemological beliefs. In other words, research that attempts to describe the underlying representations or cognitive structures is needed. For the more contextualist models, there is a clear need for research that moves beyond simple descriptions of potential epistemological resources in context to longitudinal and microgenetic research that tracks the use of resources over multiple contexts within the same individuals. This type of data would provide important information regarding the intraindividual stability of resource use as well as the contextual sensitivity of the resources. These studies should provide more evidence about this issue, although given some basic incommensurability in the underlying metatheories, there will always be some theoretical choices to be made by individual researchers.

3. Domain Generality Versus Domain Specificity in Epistemological Thinking

The issue of domain generality versus specificity in epistemological thinking is very clearly related to the three general perspectives of developmental, cognitive, and contextual approaches. Given their assumption of qualitative differences and unitary structures, developmental models usually propose that epistemological thinking is domain general. In fact, in much of the developmental research, very general questions are used to elicit epistemological thinking (e.g., Baxter Magolda; Clinchy; Moore) or tasks are used that are knowledge-lean or do not require much disciplinary knowledge (King & Kitchener). In contrast, both cognitive and contextualist models do allow for domain-specificity in epistemological thinking, although the extent of domain-specificity varies, with contextualist models assuming not only domain-specificity, but high levels of contextual variation.

Proposition 3—Epistemological thinking is domain-specific.   At some level, this proposition is probably not controversial at all. Almost all the chapters in this volume either explicitly or implicitly endorse this proposition. This may not have been the case earlier in the research on epistemological thinking as developmental stage models certainly dominated the field. However, with the rise of general cognitive models, almost all psychological theory and research has become more focused on tracing the domain-specificity of cognition, motivation, and behavior. Accordingly, even stage models began to accept the general premise that thinking and beliefs could be domain-specific or tied to specific contexts. So, for example, even current proponents of the Perry developmental model of epistemological thinking (e.g., Moore) note that the model and the positions refer to thinking in the context of structured academic environments in Western cultures (cf., Qian & Pan).

Accordingly, there is no real need to present formal dissenting voices to this third proposition. The more important issue concerns the refinement of our definitions of domains and contexts. For example, for many of the models in this volume, particularly the more developmental ones, domains refer to larger areas of our lives, from academic to work to the personal and social arenas of our lives. For other more cognitive models, domains have been synonymous with school subject areas (i.e., mathematics, science, reading, social studies) or disciplines (e.g., mathematics, chemistry, psychology, statistics). Finally, for strong contextualist models, domains may be too broad a category and these models often propose a focus on epistemological thinking within a domain (mathematics or science), but also how the classroom context represents and shapes the nature of knowledge and knowing within that domain (Bell & Linn; Hammer & Elby). Accordingly, there is a need for clear statements about domain boundaries in our models.

A second related issue for future research regarding the domain specificity of epistemological thinking concerns the range of applicability of thinking. In other words, given a particular model and a definition of domain, how does epistemological thinking vary by domain? If there is an expectation that epistemological thinking will vary by academic, work, personal, and social domains, what is the evidence for such variations? Moreover, if there is evidence that epistemological thinking varies within the academic domain by discipline as suggested by some of the models in this volume, how does this evidence fit a more general model that suggests that epistemological thinking should be similar within the broader category of the academic domain? If there is a general structure or position or level for the academic domain, how can our models explain more specific discipline differences?

In the same fashion, Schommer has suggested that there is moderate consistency in epistemological beliefs across disciplines, but it is not clear how this consistency is best represented in our models. It may be that there is some hierarchical multilevel structure of beliefs, with more classroom/context-specific beliefs at the bottom, which are then organized into more discipline or school subject beliefs, followed by more general domains (academic, work, personal) and finally, some superordinate higher level structure. This suggestion is similar to Chandler et al.'s idea that epistemological thinking moves from a "retail" level (more specific) to a "wholesale" level (more general) over the course of development. In addition, it suggests that the nature of the hierarchy or structure of relations could change with development. This type of hierarchical model also parallels some of the research on self-concept and identity, which suggests that individuals organize their beliefs about themselves into a hierarchical model with different levels reflecting different contexts and domains of expertise (Pintrich & Schunk, 1996). In any event, there is a need for formal testing of these ideas that will help to clarify the nature and the range of the domain specificity of epistemological thinking.

4. Nature of Developmental Change

Related to the development of domain specificity, the next issue concerns the nature of the general developmental change in epistemological thinking. Although there is clearly disagreement about the core of epistemological thinking, and hence not consensus on the endpoint of development, there is fairly high agreement on the nature of developmental change.

Proposition 4—Epistemological thinking becomes more "sophisticated" over the course of development. Again, at some level, all the models represented in this volume are in line with the proposition that an individual's thinking about epistemological issues not only changes over time, but that it develops towards a more sophisticated perspective or stance toward knowledge and knowing. The developmental models are the most explicit in their endorsement of this proposition by postulating some final position, level, phase, or stage as the endpoint of epistemological development. The endpoint is defined in many ways, depending on how the model conceptualizes epistemological thinking in relation to Proposition 1, but the fairly well-established trend is that individuals move from some more objectivist perspective through a relativistic one, to a more balanced and reasoned perspective on the objectivist–relativistic continuum, with this latter position reflecting a more sophisticated manner of thinking. Moreover, many of these models include the additional general developmental principle that not only is thinking more sophisticated at the higher levels, but that higher levels represent an integration and reorganization of the lower levels of thinking.

The cognitive models would endorse the developmental trend toward more sophisticated beliefs and thinking, although they generally would not accept the idea that higher levels represent an integration of lower levels. As noted earlier, cognitive models do not represent epistemological thinking in terms of integrated, holistic levels or stages or positions, opting for more independence among a number of different dimensions. Accordingly, given this type of model, individuals could vary in their sophistication on any of the multiple dimensions, independent of their thinking or beliefs on other dimensions. For example, they could show a fairly high level of sophistication about the certainty of knowledge, but have a less sophisticated view of the source of knowledge. In this type of model, the assumption of independent dimensions with individual variation on any of the dimensions precludes the possibility of there being an integration of beliefs within positions or levels as in the developmental models.

The contextual models might be expected to reject the fourth proposition or at least dissent from a strong version of it. However, it seems more likely that they would propose a similar developmental progression given the changing nature of contexts with development. That is, if epistemological resources are tied to contexts, then as contexts change and become more sophisticated, then the resources used also would be expected to become more sophisticated. For example, as students move through K–12 settings and then into college contexts, it could be assumed at some global level that these classroom contexts would allow for the presentation of more sophisticated views of knowledge and resources. Individuals in these contexts could then be socialized into using more sophisticated epistemological resources. In this case, development or use of resources would not be constrained be some age-linked cognitive developmental mechanisms, but would be a function of the nature of the contexts that individuals encounter over the course of development.

Of course, this type of argument begs the classic question of the differences between development and learning. For the developmental models, the key phrases in Proposition 4 are "sophisticated" and "over the course of development." Developmentalists would argue that developmental change from less sophisticated to more sophisticated thinking is more than just learning how to use different resources in different contexts. It is more than just the acquisition or flexible use of different resources in different contexts. In the cognitive or contextualist perspectives, students could just learn or acquire different beliefs or use different resources without major conceptual or developmental change. In contrast, developmental change involves a qualitative reorganization of the underlying cognitive structures that transcends contexts. In other words, development and learning cannot be equated; development is more than just the acquisition of different or new beliefs and resources.

As with Proposition 3, there is not disagreement in principle with Proposition 4, but rather, there are subtle differences among the models in terms of how they would describe the change from unsophisticated to sophisticated beliefs over the course of development. Accordingly, one direction for future theory and research is to clarify these differences. The developmental models specify endpoints in their models and assume that moving toward those endpoints constitutes the development of sophisticated epistemological thinking. Chandler et al. propose an interesting recursion model where epistemological thinking is "sophisticated" at a more local or domain-specific level and then with development eventually becomes more sophisticated at a global or more domain-general level. There is a clear need for research on this type of developmental change over time.

The cognitive models follow the general developmental pattern of becoming more sophisticated over time to some extent, but they have not completely specified how variations in the sophistication of thinking for different dimensions should be treated developmentally. For example, what does it mean developmentally if an individual progresses toward a more sophisticated view of the certainty of knowledge but still has rather divergent views regarding the source of knowledge or other dimensions of epistemological thinking? In the same fashion, it is not clear in some contextualist models what the endpoints of development might be (e.g., Hammer & Elby). For other models, it may be defined contextually or in terms of the accepted disciplinary epistemology. For example, in the discipline-based models the desired endpoint of development is that students should come to understand and adopt the general scientific epistemology or the mathematical epistemology. These is a need for more research on how the different dimensions or domains are coordinated in development.

In addition, in contextualist models, it may not be warranted to assume that contexts become more sophisticated over time. If one thinks of the general progression of the nature of teaching and the curriculum in elementary, high school, and college classrooms, this assumption may be borne out by experience. However, it is possible that given the rise of constructivist teaching in many science and math classrooms (Bell & Linn; De Corte et al.) in the earlier grades, then some college classrooms, particularly in the natural sciences, may not be as constructivist and may be more objectivist. In this case, the contexts would not reflect a general trend that moves from objectivist to relativistic to some balance between objectivist-relativistic perspectives. Moreover, in a contextualist model, it is not clear how development should be conceptualized in terms of both intraindividual and interindividual variations in the nature of contexts over time. That is, if individuals move into and out of different types of contexts that vary in their epistemological perspectives over time, how can development be characterized in terms of developing more sophistication over time? In any event, it is clear that there is a need for more longitudinal research on these issues, not just cross-sectional studies, in order to trace the nature of developmental change.

5. Mechanisms of Change

Along with describing the nature of developmental change, there is a need for more research on the mechanisms that drive development. This is an age-old question in general cognitive developmental research, but it has not been addressed in as much detail or specificity in the research on epistemological thinking. In fact, given the vagueness of the research on this issue, it is possible to state a proposition that is general enough that all models can be covered by it.

Proposition 5—Epistemological development is a function of both internal psychological mechanisms as well as contextual facilitators and constraints. Basically, this proposition is a restatement of the general developmental and psychological principle that development is a function of both the person and the context, which is hard to reject at a global level. On the other hand, it does mean that strong cognitive developmental claims about internal cognitive processes (e.g., equilibration) or strong contextualist claims about socialization processes (e.g., scaffolding) as the sole or main mechanisms of change are not warranted. In other words, our theories have to be more sensible with developmental models needing to attend more to contextual factors and contextualist models not being allowed to banish internal cognitions as potential mechanisms for change.

Of course, where there is more disagreement among the different models is in terms of how necessary or sufficient are the different mechanisms for change. For example, all cognitive developmental models would accept that contextual factors can play a role. Even Piaget, the prototypical developmentalist, had external factors in his theory, although he emphasized the internal cognitive process of equilibration as essential to developmental change. In epistemological research, all the developmental models (Baxter Magolda; Chandler et al.; Clinchy; King & Kitchener; Kuhn & Weinstock; Moore) also would accept the proposition that external factors can play an important role in development. In fact, in the research on college students, it was the transition to college and the exposure to new and different ways of thinking from professors and other students that often sparked epistemological development. At the same time, most of the cognitive developmental models would reserve a special role for cognitive equilibration (assimilation and accommodation) processes and most would suggest that cognitive disequilibrium, if not necessary for development, would be sufficient to drive change.

In the same manner, both the developmental and cognitive models would propose that various cognitive mechanisms related to belief revision or conceptual change (Dole & Sinatra, 1998; Pintrich, Marx, & Boyle, 1993) would play an important role in development. For example, in these models some cognitive mechanism like metacognitive awareness of differences between one's own beliefs or knowledge and other external representations of beliefs or knowledge (i.e., in texts, in lectures, in teachers' and peer's comments) may not be sufficient for change, but is often considered necessary. Moreover, some of these models also suggest that personal motivational or affective factors can play an important role (cf., Dole & Sinatra, 1998; Pintrich et al., 1993). For example, in this volume, Bendixen proposes that epistemic doubt plays a crucial role in epistemological development. Her conceptualization of epistemic doubt includes both cognitive dissatisfaction or disequilibrium, which would involve some confusion cognitively as well as emotions such as fear or anxiety. In her model, it appears that epistemic doubt is necessary for epistemological development, although she notes the importance of contextual factors (e.g., confrontation with opposing views as presented by other students) as an important generator of epistemic doubt.

In contrast, contextualist models might not disagree that cognitive factors like equilibration or metacognitive awareness can play a role; they just would not see any need to propose that they are necessary or sufficient for development. Obviously, for these models, the nature of the context is much more important than personal cognitive, motivational, or affective mechanisms. Models that stress contextual factors as essential in epistemological development place much more emphasis on the contextual features that can drive development. These features can include the nature of the materials (texts, activities, software, Internet sites, etc.) that present opposing views and different ways of reasoning and thinking (e.g., Bell & Linn). In addition, the nature of the discourse and the quality of the interactions between peers and teachers (or other adults) can present different models of epistemology as well as different ways of knowing and thinking. Almost all the models represented in this volume note that peer interactions in formal classroom settings or outside the classroom in other settings like dormitories or cafeterias can facilitate epistemological development. In these interactions, students are often challenged to think differently due to opposing perspectives being presented and argued about in the discussions or debates (e.g., Bell & Linn; Bendixen; Moore). Beyond the interactions, both Bell and Linn and De Corte et al. stress how more constructivist teaching that involves creating a classroom climate that supports and sustains inquiry and problem solving, that develops norms for discussion of knowledge claims and evidence, and actively involves the students in open-ended activities and tasks will help to facilitate epistemological development.

At the same time, it is not clear that any of these contextual factors are necessary for epistemological development. Many of these developments in constructivist teaching were not implemented until recently, but clearly the developmental work, particularly the earlier research by Perry and others in the 1970s, shows that students still develop more sophisticated thinking without the benefit of the "new" constructivist teaching. This suggests that development can take place without some of these contextual features being present. However, the developmental research does suggest that students who attend college are more likely to show more sophisticated epistemological thinking than those who do not attend college (Hofer & Pintrich, 1997). Although self-selection threats to internal validity can't be ruled out completely in the developmental studies, it does seem likely that something about the college context does facilitate epistemological development. Accordingly, some of the contextual factors may be sufficient to promote development, but what is key is determining what the contextual features are and how they operate to promote development.

In summary, there is no need for research that pits internal psychological mechanisms against contextual features as facilitators of epistemological development. It will be more productive and make Proposition 5 less vague to have research that addresses how the internal and contextual factors work together to promote or constrain epistemological development. This will involve research in naturalistic settings that describes not just the contextual features that are operating, but also the internal cognitive, as well as motivational and affective, factors that contribute to development. In addition, as we have some models that have begun to sketch out potential relations between contextual and internal factors (see Dole & Sinatra, 1998; Pintrich et al., 1993), more experimental research may be warranted in order to examine more specifically how the different factors interact. Of course, some of this more experimental research should be microgenetic, allowing for development to occur over time, not just learning within a circumscribed hour or less experimental session. This type of research will provide us with much better evidence and allow us to specify in greater detail how the internal and contextual factors operate together to facilitate or constrain epistemological development.

6. Relations of Personal Epistemologies to Cognition, Motivation, and Learning

For the most part, research on personal epistemologies has studied epistemological beliefs and thinking as an important aspect of cognitive development. In many ways, this research has rightly focused on the development of epistemological thinking with little consideration of how it might be related to other aspects of academic cognition, motivation, and learning in classrooms. More recently, there have been efforts to understand how personal epistemologies are linked to other relevant academic outcomes. There is high consensus that personal epistemologies should be linked to cognition, motivation, and learning with any disagreements due to differences about the specific nature of the relations.

Proposition 6—Personal epistemologies can facilitate and constrain academic cognition, motivation, and learning. Although the developmental research on epistemological thinking suggests some linkages between epistemological positions and college learning (Baxter Magolda; Moore), more recent quantitative research has explicitly examined these relations. In her research program on epistemological beliefs, Schommer was one of the first to tease out the specific relations between personal epistemologies and academic cognition and learning. She has shown that more sophisticated epistemological beliefs are correlated with better cognitive strategy use, reading comprehension, and academic performance. In this volume, similar relations have been obtained across different types of subjects, tasks, and contexts (see Schraw et al.; Qian & Pan; Wood & Kardash). In addition, some of this research has shown that more sophisticated epistemological beliefs are positively related to adaptive motivational beliefs (Hofer & Pintrich, 1997; Qian & Pan).

At the same time, almost all of this research has been correlational in design, precluding more explicit tests of the nature of the relations between personal epistemologies and other academic outcomes. In addition, there is a need for better theoretical specification of how and why sophisticated epistemological beliefs seem to facilitate cognition, motivation, and learning and less sophisticated beliefs seem to constrain these same academic outcomes. Hofer and Pintrich (1997) suggested that epistemological beliefs may function as implicit theories that can give rise to certain types of goals for learning (e.g., mastery, performance, completion goals). These goals then function as the specific personal goals and guides for self-regulatory cognition and behavior (including the use of learning and metacognitive strategies), which then influence academic performance and achievement. It is these personal goals and self-regulatory strategies that mediate the relations between personal epistemologies and academic achievement. This is one proposal for how personal epistemologies may be linked to cognition, motivation, and learning, but it has not been tested empirically. Moreover, the type of experimental, microgenetic, longitudinal, and dynamic process-oriented research designs necessary to test these causal relations have not been used in the extant research. There is a clear need to move beyond one-time point correlational designs and the use of self-report measures in order to begin to specify more fully the relations between personal epistemologies and cognition, motivation, and learning.

The explicit or implicit assumption in much of this research is that personal epistemological theories are precursors to various academic outcomes. At one level, the postulation of this causal direction makes sense theoretically. If personal epistemologies are deeply embedded, implicit theories or stances or positions or beliefs, then they can play an important causal role in the dynamics of classroom learning. At the same time, it seems likely that these relations should be reciprocal, with academic success and learning outcomes feeding back into individuals' theories about knowledge and knowing. Accordingly, our research needs to investigate this possibility.

However, from a more holistic perspective on personal epistemologies, it is difficult to separate out beliefs and theories about knowing from other aspects of cognition and motivation, including the self and identity. From this dissenting perspective, it would not make sense to try to specify the causal relations between personal epistemologies and other academic outcomes such as cognition, motivation, and learning because they are not independent from one another. Finally, from a contextual standpoint, it also would be difficult, if not foolhardy, to try to specify the relations between various internal psychological constructs such as personal epistemologies, cognition, motivation, and learning. Contextual models would expect that not only would the nature of these constructs change in different contexts, but the relations among them would be highly context-sensitive. Accordingly, it would be difficult to make generalizations about how personal epistemologies might facilitate or constrain cognition, motivation, and learning that would hold across different contexts.

In summary, there is consensus that personal epistemologies should be related to academic cognition, motivation, and learning. The disagreements center on the nature of the relations and the possibility that we can develop useful generalizations about the nature of these relations. There is a clear need for research that examines this issue that reflects the different theoretical and dissenting perspectives on personal epistemologies. The research might generate different findings and different relations, but if we are clear on our assumptions and models, then progress can still be made on understanding how and why personal epistemologies are related to cognition, motivation, and learning in academic contexts.

7. Gender and Group Differences in Personal Epistemologies

There is quite a long history of research on gender differences in epistemological thinking (Clinchy). On the one hand, there is a fair amount of research that suggests that there are important gender differences in personal epistemologies and ways of knowing (Baxter Magolda; Clinchy). On the other hand, other research finds few gender differences (e.g., King & Kitchener; Schommer). Accordingly, there is not consensus about the role of gender in epistemological thinking. Nevertheless, there may be utility in making a fairly controversial proposition in order to spur future research.

Proposition 7—There are no important gender differences in epistemological thinking and the development of personal epistemologies.   This proposition may be one of the most controversial of the eight listed in this chapter and there clearly are dissenting voices. Although there are some empirical studies showing few, if any, gender differences in epistemological thinking, this proposition is made more on the basis of a theoretical perspective on the nature of group differences, not just by gender but also by ethnicity, class, and culture. The argument is based on the idea that gender, at least in terms of a simple dichotomy between males and females, is an insufficient construct to explain group differences. Beyond the fact of the overlap in the distributions or nature of thinking between males and females, the more important issue is that gender is more likely a proxy for other constructs that are correlated with male-female status. These other constructs are the ones that need to be considered and examined in our models.

For example, Harter, Waters, and Whitesell (1997) have shown that it is not gender per se that explains the loss of voice in young females over the course of development as suggested by Gilligan and her colleagues (Gilligan, 1982; Gilligan, Lyons, & Hanmer, 1989). The research by Harter et al. (1997) shows that it is gender orientation in terms of a masculinity-femininity dimension that better explains the loss of confidence in school settings. In their work, it was only a subset of females who endorsed a more feminine gender orientation that showed the typical pattern of a loss of voice or confidence. Females who were more androgynous did not show the same debilitating pattern. In addition, there was some evidence to suggest that males that endorsed more traditional feminine values (sensitive, warm, gentleness, empathic), making them more androgynous in their gender orientation, were lower in voice than their more masculine male counterparts. Of course, gender orientation was correlated with male-female status, but empirically gender orientation did differentiate among subsets of females who showed different patterns in terms of their loss of voice. The more important theoretical point is that gender is not an explanatory construct in and of itself. There are other constructs such as gender orientation that may provide a better explanation of both average male-female group differences as well as interindividual variation within groups.

A similar argument can be made for group differences by ethnicity, class, or culture, although these group differences rarely have been investigated, and certainly not to the same extent as gender in research on epistemological thinking. Gian and Pan in this volume found that Chinese students did seem to have somewhat different beliefs than American students, more strongly endorsing claims that knowledge is simple and certain as well as the belief that the ability to learn is innate. In addition, they showed that the relations among the epistemological beliefs and other constructs like learning and motivation did seem to vary between the two groups. Nevertheless, there was clearly overlap in the distributions of these two groups and it will be important in future research to examine the potential psychological and cultural constructs that underlie these crosscultural differences.

For example, Hong, Morris, Chiu, and Benet-Martinez (2000) have argued that some crosscultural differences in cognition may not be best explained by very general constructs such as individualistic-collectivist value orientations, but rather by the differential activation of specific knowledge structures or implicit theories that are relevant to the task at hand but are related to cultural background. In this case, these knowledge structures or implicit theories could be activated by different tasks or different contexts and then serve to guide cognition, including beliefs, thinking, and reasoning. In this manner, it is the content and functioning of the knowledge structures and theories that are important, not cultural group membership per se. In addition, this type of cognitive model allows for contextual sensitivity across individuals as well as interindividual variation within different cultural groups.

The same argument could be made for explaining potential ethnic differences in epistemological thinking, although there has been almost no empirical evidence on this issue. In any event, it would be important to investigate the underlying knowledge structures or implicit theories that different ethnic minority groups have in different contexts and how these structures might guide their epistemological thinking. One avenue for this research would be to examine how ethnic identification (similar in some ways to gender orientation, involving the endorsement of particular values associated with different ethnic groups) might moderate the relations between ethnic group membership and epistemological thinking.

In summary, the key element underlying the seventh proposition is that simple group membership in different genders, ethnic groups, socioeconomic classes, or cultures is not sufficient to explain potential group differences. There is a need to move beyond surface-level characteristics such as biological sex or ethnicity or income/education level or culture to examine the underlying psychological and cultural constructs that might generate differences in personal epistemologies. There are a number of important leads to pursue and we do have some theoretical models that should prove particularly useful in this research.

Dissenting Voices—There are important and salient gender, ethnic, class, and crosscultural qualitative differences in epistemological thinking.   The dissenting voices are many and they make a number of different arguments for the importance of these categorical distinctions. First, the research on women's ways of knowing (Baxter Magolda; Clinchy) has shown that there are gender-related patterns in epistemological thinking. Some of this work also suggests that socioeconomic status may be implicated in epistemological development as well. This more developmental work that uses interviews has been more likely to find gender differences, while the more quantitative research (e.g., King & Kitchener; Schommer) has found few gender differences. However, beyond the empirical findings that may be due to methodological differences, there are more important theoretical differences that would give rise to the dissenting voices. There are many theoretical issues, but two general theoretical arguments can be made against Proposition 7.

First, many of the dissenting voices would reject Proposition 7 on the basis of a more holistic perspective on gender and other group or cultural differences. As noted in the earlier section regarding Proposition 2, the developmental models tend to assume a more holistic and interdependent model about the components of epistemological thinking, rejecting attempts to atomize a general pattern of thinking into various semi-independent dimensions. Following a similar logic, there are models that would reject any attempts to separate gender from potential underlying gender-related orientations, knowledge structures, or implicit theories. These models would assume that gender is such an all-encompassing and salient category of social life that it is difficult if not impossible to separate gender from how individuals think and reason. Accordingly, suggestions like Proposition 7 are ill-conceived and misleading because of their reductionistic approach to gender and their attempts to explain away gender differences by an appeal to underlying psychological constructs.

A similar argument can be made for potential ethnic, class, or crosscultural differences. Again, there are other models outside research on epistemological thinking that stress the salience and importance of ethnicity or class or culture and these models would tend to reject the idea that any differences can be explained in terms of underlying psychological knowledge structures or implicit theories. For these models, an individual's cognition, motivation, identity, self, and ways of being in the world are so intimately tied to their ethnicity, class, or cultural background that it is not possible to separate them in any coherent manner. In fact, for many of these other models, attempts to develop psychological models to explain gender, ethnic, class, or cultural differences by the use of constructs and generalizations that cut across group differences reflects a faith in and reliance on a reductionistic scientific epistemology that is outmoded in our postmodern world.

The second general argument against building more general models that can explain gender, ethnic, class, or cultural differences reflects a more functionalist approach to the problem. This approach would accept the possibility that there are underlying orientations, knowledge structures, implicit theories, or ways of thinking that might be related to gender, ethnic, class, or cultural group membership. However, this approach would suggest that the content of these knowledge structures or theories or ways of thinking could be so different for different groups that it is difficult to develop generalizations that cut across group membership. For example, for gender it is not just that males and females might vary on their gender orientations in terms of masculinity and femininity values, but that the meaning of the values are quite different for males and females (e.g., being empathic means something quite different to males and females). In terms of epistemological thinking, connected knowing may be more associated with females, but even if males endorse some aspect of connected knowing, it may mean something quite different for them than for females.

The same argument applies to ethnic, class, and cultural differences. Ethnic, class, and cultural groups might think about epistemology in terms of similar structures or theories, but the content of these theories are quite different. In addition, this more functionalist approach allows for the possibility that there are aspects or dimensions of the theories that are quite different from other groups. For example, in motivational research, there are some models that suggest that the content of African Americans' implicit theories about motivation and academic success in America are quite different from normative models. These content differences are crucial to understanding their motivation and achievement and would not have been revealed unless research explicitly addressed the ethnic differences (Pintrich & Schunk, 1996). In a similar fashion, there may be epistemological theories and ways of thinking that have not been discovered because we have not fully investigated ethnic, class, or crosscultural patterns or perspectives.

Finally, a functionalist approach also would be in line with more contextualist models that would suggest that group membership differences could emerge from the nature of interactions with people and institutions (schools, families) in different contexts. In this case, as different cultures (e.g., American versus Chinese, see Gian & Pan), or subcultures based on gender or ethnicity or class, can develop different ways of representing knowledge and ways of thinking, these differences would create group differences in epistemological thinking. Moreover, these group differences would be tied to the different nature of the contexts, and making generalizations about individuals, without considering the contextual and cultural variations, would not be very meaningful, if not impossible.

In summary, there are dissenting voices to Proposition 7 and its implication that we can develop general models of epistemological thinking that can transcend potential group membership differences. There is a clear need for more research on these issues, especially the potential ethnic, class, and cultural differences. Although there may be some basic incommensurability between more scientific and postmodern models, this does not mean that there is no role for empirical research on these issues. It just means that we have to be clear about our theoretical models, our metatheoretical assumptions, and the limits and warrants of our empirical evidence.

8. Methods and Measurement in the Study of Personal Epistemologies

There is considerable variability in how personal epistemologies are measured as one can see from the diversity of research designs and assessment procedures used in the chapters in this volume. Historically, researchers who used qualitative interviews in descriptive studies tended to rely on these methods. Researchers who presented more structured tasks or problems to individuals continued to use these methods over time. Researchers who used correlational designs and self-report questionnaires also have tended to use this methodology repeatedly. However, as is clear from the chapters in this volume, we are witnessing a change in these monomethod tendencies and seeing much more willingness on the part of researchers to use a diversity of methods.

Proposition 8—Personal epistemologies can and should be assessed using a diversity of methodologies. Stated in this manner, there is probably little controversy in this proposition. However, if this proposition is taken to mean that multiple methods should be used within the same study or research program, there may be some disagreement with it. Traditionally, research programs seem to rely on using the same methods over time. This can lead to problems such as consistent method variance being confounded with the substantive results. For example, if questionnaire measures are continually afflicted with problems of accuracy in self-reports, and only questionnaire measures are used over time, then these accuracy problems can't be easily detected in the research. In the same manner, interview methods may be susceptible to social desirability or interviewer bias effects. All methods have some limitations and these limitations are always a threat to the internal validity of the research.

Studies that use several different methods to assess similar constructs can provide data on the validity and reliability of the measures. More important, as noted

earlier, MTMM studies can be used to distinguish method variance from important substantive differences between different constructs and the relations among
the constructs. Given the status of the field and all the substantive and methodological differences, these types of studies and the data yielded from them would
be very useful in addressing many of the issues raised in this chapter. This is not
meant to suggest that every study should use multiple methods, but rather that
some diversity of methods be represented within programs of research.

Of course, the developmentalists might disagree with the simple inclusion of
more quantitative measures to supplement their general qualitative interviews,
while they might accept the inclusion of production-type tasks used in the research on the Reflective Judgment model (King & Kitchener; Wood & Kardash;
Wood et al.). This rejection of questionnaires would reflect their commitment to
a more holistic perspective (as noted earlier), which is compatible with the Reflective Judgment developmental framework and less compatible with the cognitive perspectives that underlie much of the questionnaire work. It is not the case
that diversity of methods should be used just to encourage diversity among research programs. Diversity should be used when there are specific research questions that need to be addressed in order for progress to be made within the research program or in the area of epistemological research more generally (see
Wood et al.; Wood & Kardash).

The contextualists also might disagree with the inclusion of standardized
questionnaire measures in their studies. They would reject the use of these general questionnaires because they assume that it is not possible to assess personal
epistemologies out of context. Questionnaire items are usually not contextualized
and ask for responses to fairly general statements about epistemological issues.
Of course, there are questionnaires that are more contextualized for different disciplines (e.g., Elder), but for some contextualists such as Hammer and Elby, even
discipline-specific measures are still too general to accurately assess personal
epistemologies in context. In this case, it may be that the inclusion of interviews
or production tasks along with the more contextualized observations of language
use and discourse patterns in context would provide important evidence regarding the contextual nature of personal epistemologies.

In summary, there is a need for different methods to be used across different
research programs. Moreover, within research programs there is a serious need to
address problems of internal and external validity (see Wood & Kardash). It
seems clear that interview methods and production tasks can produce important
information regarding personal epistemologies. In addition, questionnaire methods also can be used, although there may be more disagreement about their validity from developmental and contextual researchers. It is important that there is
more psychometric research on the validity and reliability of the various questionnaires available. Some of the chapters in this volume (Elder; Qian & Pan;
Schommer; Schraw et al.; Wood & Kardash; Wood et al.) not only offer questionnaire instruments that can be used to assess personal epistemologies, but also

demonstrate the kind of psychometric validity research that is needed if we are to make progress in the development of valid questionnaire instruments. At this point in the development of the field, this is an area that represents one of the biggest methodological challenges.

CONCLUSION

The research on personal epistemologies is moving from an area of research of interest to a fairly small group of dedicated researchers to a position of salience in the general research efforts on development and learning in context. The chapters in this volume represent the state of the art in the field. It is clear that there is some consensus in the field around the eight issues discussed in this chapter, but it is also apparent that we have many theoretical, conceptual, and methodological challenges to face in future research. The eight propositions outlined here are offered in the hope of spurring more debate and empirical research about the nature of development of personal epistemologies. It is through this type of intellectual discussion and scientific approach to the problems in the field that we will be able to make progress in understanding personal epistemologies. As we come to better understand how individuals think and reason about knowledge and knowing, we should not only be able to improve learning and instruction, but also come to better understand ourselves.

REFERENCES

Dole, J., & Sinatra, G. (1998). Reconceptualizing change in the cognitive construction of knowledge. *Educational Psychologist, 33,* 109–128.
Gilligan, C. (1982). *In a different voice.* Cambridge, MA: Harvard University Press.
Gilligan, C., Lyons, N., & Hanmer, T. (1989). *Making connections.* Cambridge, MA: Harvard University Press.
Harter, S., Waters, P., & Whitesell, N. (1997). Lack of voice as a manifestation of false self-behavior among adolescents: The school setting as a stage upon which the drama of authenticity is enacted. *Educational Psychologist, 32,* 153–173.
Hofer, B. (2000). Dimensionality and disciplinary differences in personal epistemology. *Contemporary Educational Psychology, 25,* 378–405.
Hofer, B. & Pintrich, P. R. (1997). The development of epistemological theories: Beliefs about knowledge and knowing and their relation to learning. *Review of Educational Research, 67,* 88–140.
Hong, Y., Morris, M., Chiu, C., & Benet-Martinez, V. (2000). Multicultural minds: A dynamic constructivist approach to culture and cognition. *American Psychologist, 55,* 709–720.
Overton, W. F. (1984). World views and their influence on psychological theory and research: Kuhn-Lakatos-Laudan. In H. W. Reese (Ed.), *Advances in child development and behavior* (Vol. 18, pp. 191–226). Orlando, FL: Academic Press.
Pepper, S. (1942). *World hypotheses: A study in evidence.* Berkeley, CA: University of California Press.

Pintrich. P. R., Marx, R., & Boyle, R. (1993). Beyond cold conceptual change: The role of motivational beliefs and classroom contextual factors in the process of conceptual change. *Review of Educational Research, 63,* 167–199.

Pintrich, P. R., & Schunk, D. (1996). *Motivation in education: Theory, research, and applications.* Englewood Cliffs, NJ: Merrill Prentice Hall.

Pintrich, P. R., Wolters, C., & Baxter, G. (2000). Assessing metacognition and self-regulated learning. In G. Schraw & J. Impara (Eds.), *Issues in the Measurement of Metacognition.* (pp.43–97). Lincoln, NE: Buros Institute of Mental Measurements.

Smith, E. (1998). Mental representation and memory. In D. Gilbert, S. Fiske, & G. Lindzey (Eds.), *The handbook of social psychology: Vol. 1* (4th ed., pp. 391–445). New York: McGraw-Hill.

Wellman, H. & Gelman, S. (1998). Knowledge acquisition in foundational domains. In W. Damon (Series Ed.) & D. Kuhn & R. Siegler (Vol. Eds.), *Handbook of child psychology: Vol. 2. Cognition, perception, and language* (5th ed., pp. 523–573). New York: Wiley.

Winne, P., & Perry, N. (2000). Measuring self-regulated learning. In M. Boekaerts, P. R. Pintrich, & M. Zeidner (Eds.), *Handbook of self-regulation* (pp. 531–566). San Diego, CA: Academic Press.

Author Index

Subject Index